AMERICAN CASE FURNITURE AT YALE UNIVERSITY

This publication has been made possible

by generous grants from

THE ANDREW W. MELLON FOUNDATION

and

THE HENRY LUCE FOUNDATION

AMERICAN CASE FURNITURE

in the Mabel Brady Garvan
and Other Collections at Yale University

GERALD W. R. WARD

PHOTOGRAPHS BY CHARLES UHT

YALE UNIVERSITY ART GALLERY
NEW HAVEN · CONNECTICUT

Copyright © 1988 Yale University Art Gallery

ALL RIGHTS RESERVED

Library of Congress Catalogue Card Number 86–51323

ISBN 0-300-03357-5

DISTRIBUTED FOR YALE UNIVERSITY ART GALLERY
BY YALE UNIVERSITY PRESS · NEW HAVEN AND LONDON

Printed in the United States of America

To my parents

CONTENTS

Foreword BY MARY GARDNER NEILL	PAGE ix
Preface BY PATRICIA E. KANE	xi
Acknowledgments	xiii
Matter in Place: Some Thoughts on Case Furniture	3
Short Titles and Abbreviations	19
Notes to the Catalogue	27

THE CATALOGUE

Color Plates	33
Boxes, Table Chests, and Other Small Objects (CATS. 1–19)	57
Chests and Chests with Drawers (CATS. 20–50)	81
Chests of Drawers (CATS. 51–77)	123
Chest-on-Chests (CATS. 78–92)	163
Dressing and Bureau Tables (CATS. 93–121)	195
High Chests of Drawers (CATS. 122–149)	235
Desks (CATS. 150–171)	289
Desk and Bookcases, Library Bookcases, and Secretaries (CATS. 172–193)	327
Cupboards and Presses (CATS. 194–203)	375
Buffets (CATS. 204–213)	397
Sideboards, Cabinets, and Cellarettes (CATS. 214–230)	413
Pianos and Radio (CATS. 231–233)	447
Appendix	455
Concordance	471
Index	473
Photograph Credits	485

FOREWORD

The core of Yale University's renowned collection of American furniture is the gift, begun in 1930, of Francis P. Garvan, class of 1897, in honor of his wife, Mabel Brady Garvan. The presence of the Garvan Collection at Yale has encouraged other alumni and benefactors to make gifts of fine furniture to the university. Significant among these are the donations of C. Sanford Bull, Olive Louise Dann, Charles Stetson, Gifford Phillips, and Doris M. Brixey. Although early American furniture forms the major part of the collection, in the last fifteen years the Art Gallery's holdings have expanded to include works from the nineteenth and twentieth centuries. The collection has broad appeal; it is used extensively by students and is enjoyed by numerous gallery visitors.

The publication of catalogues of permanent collections is an important mission of an art museum. Essential support for this current undertaking, the third volume in a series on the Art Gallery's collection of American furniture, was provided by two foundations to whom we are profoundly grateful. The Andrew W. Mellon Foundation's munificent grant to the gallery for catalogues of the permanent collection funded the preparation of the manuscript, including the costs of salaries, photography, and wood identification. The Henry Luce Foundation awarded the gallery a generous grant to cover the production expenses for this volume. In addition, it should be noted that without the ongoing support of the Friends of American Arts at Yale, the Art Gallery would not be able to undertake projects such as this.

The often unacknowledged benefactors of art museums are those individuals and foundations who provide funds for the conservation of our treasures. The pieces of furniture illustrated herein have been cared for over the course of the last fifteen years through funds provided by the Dobson Foundation. Many of them were conserved especially for presentation in this volume with the cabinet- and finishwork being carried out expertly by Peter Arkell.

Gerald W. R. Ward has prepared this volume with his usual care, thoroughness, and skill. The contributions of those individuals who helped in this task are acknowledged here. Thomas Michie and Gordon Sands, graduate students in the History of Art and American Studies

respectively and Marcia Brady Tucker Fellows in the American Arts Office, provided research assistance. E. Irving Blomstrann, Joseph Szaszfai, and especially Charles Uht exercised infinite patience in making the photographs with which these pages are illustrated. Patricia R. Lisk meticulously edited the manuscript. Howard I. Gralla designed a volume as distinguished as his previous efforts for the Art Gallery. We are also grateful to Judith Metro of Yale University Press for her work in arranging for the distribution of the volume.

MARY GARDNER NEILL
The Henry J. Heinz II Director

PREFACE

SINCE 1965 when the Art Gallery published *American Pewter: Garvan and Other Collections at Yale* by Graham Hood, there has been a continuous series of works that records the American decorative arts collections in a comprehensive way. A two-volume catalogue on the silver collection, *American Silver: Garvan and Other Collections in the Yale University Art Gallery* by Kathryn Buhler and Graham Hood, appeared in 1970. At about that time a decision was made to publish the American furniture collection in a series of separate volumes divided by form. The first of the furniture catalogues, *The American Clock, 1725–1865: The Mabel Brady Garvan and Other Collections at Yale University* by Edwin A. Battison and myself was published in 1973. Three years later the seating furniture and beds at Yale were recorded in my book *300 Years of American Seating Furniture: Chairs and Beds from the Mabel Brady Garvan and Other Collections at Yale University*. The present volume, *American Case Furniture in the Mabel Brady Garvan and Other Collections at Yale University* by Gerald W. R. Ward, is the third in this series. It will be followed by a fourth and final volume on tables and looking glasses being prepared by David L. Barquist.

Yale's catalogues of its American decorative arts collections have always cut new ground. Graham Hood's *American Pewter* was the first checklist of a major collection of American pewter as was the Buhler and Hood catalogue in the field of American silver; *The American Clock* was the first clock catalogue in which the movement of each clock was described and illustrated; and *300 Years of American Seating Furniture* was the first American furniture catalogue to describe structural elements in detail and to give a thorough appraisal of the objects' state of preservation. The second checklist of the pewter collection, *American and English Pewter at the Yale University Art Gallery: A Supplementary Checklist* by David L. Barquist, records pewter acquired for the collection since the Hood checklist of 1965.

American Case Furniture, which nearly completes the task of having the American furniture collection at Yale published in its entirety, continues a long tradition. Like its forebears, it provides a comprehensive assessment of each object including a description of its physical

properties, a complete publication and exhibition record, an account of its history of ownership, meticulous analyses of its visual and structural features, an accurate appraisal of its state of preservation, and an evaluation of its relationship to other known examples. In addition, *American Case Furniture* advances the standards of furniture scholarship in a number of ways. Gerald Ward devised a particularly careful and conscientious method for carrying out the microscopic identification of the woods used in each piece. Guided by expert wood anatomist R. Bruce Hoadley, the usual routine of sampling was refined and carefully supervised, leaving much less to chance and inflicting less lasting damage on each piece. Gerald Ward has also introduced the device of an appendix with shortened entries for those objects that were judged to have been conceived as forgeries or that have been extensively restored or altered; hence, the book provides scholars and students with a comprehensive record of the case furniture in Yale's study collection.

Case pieces are the most difficult of all furniture forms to catalogue. Because of their size, they require more time to be examined, to be photographed, and to be described. Organizing the help needed to move the larger pieces for photography and physical examination can be a daunting task. Gerald Ward has responded to the challenge well. Not only has his assessment of each piece been scrupulous, it has also yielded several notable discoveries. Gerald Ward was the one who raised the shelf paper and read John Townsend's name on the drawer bottom of the Newport high chest in the Brixey bequest. His keen eye also discerned "Samuel Dunlap" painted on the backboards of a New Hampshire chest of drawers. For the scholar, student, and collector, Gerald Ward has produced a volume that records faithfully and in detail a wealth of information about Yale's American case furniture.

PATRICIA E. KANE
Curator of American Decorative Arts

ACKNOWLEDGMENTS

The process of cataloging American furniture at Yale has been a lengthy one, beginning in earnest when the Yale Furniture Study was established in 1960 at 149 York Street. Many of the people involved in the early stages of the process are mentioned in the preliminaries to the first two volumes in the series of published catalogues, the works on clocks and seating furniture. Their work in laying the foundation for this volume was equally important, and, although I have not repeated their names here, I am grateful to them all. John T. Kirk's extensive work on the collection during the 1960s, including his detailed work sheets on most of the objects at Yale, has formed the backbone of the published volumes, including this one. I first developed an interest in furniture as a graduate student in John's class in the American and New England Studies Program at Boston University in 1972, and I have been grateful to him for advice and counsel ever since.

The opportunity to work at Yale was given to me by the late Charles F. Montgomery, with whom I had the privilege to work from 1974 to 1978. I miss his presence and leadership in the field of American decorative arts and material culture more with every passing day.

Mr. Montgomery's successor, Patricia E. Kane, made the completion of the furniture catalogues a priority, and I am grateful for her guidance and patience. As coauthor and author of the clock and seating furniture catalogues, she established the format and style for this volume and set a high standard that I have endeavored to emulate. Patricia has read the manuscript, and many of the insights offered, especially those concerning construction and condition, are indebted to her keen eye and precise analytical abilities.

Alan Shestack secured funding for this project and allowed me to bring it to completion after my family and I moved to Delaware in 1983. Alan's support and encouragement have been essential to this project.

I would like to extend my personal thanks to the Mellon and Luce foundations for their financial support of the research for and production of this volume.

Many staff members and students at Yale have contributed to this publication during its preparation, and I acknowledge their help with gratitude. In particular, Kevin L. Stayton, Thomas S. Michie, and Gordon Sands offered much help during their stints as graduate fellows; they shared their research unstintingly, and their work is reflected in many of the entries in this catalogue. Peter Arkell taught me a great deal while he was on the Art Gallery staff as our furniture conservator and later when he worked for the museum on a free-lance basis. His understanding of and sympathy for old furniture was of great assistance in evaluating the objects in this catalogue; their fine condition and appearance when photographed are a tribute to his skill. David Barquist, Janine Skerry, Robert M. Soule, Robert C. Soule, Richard Moore, Fred D'Amico, Nan Ross, Rosalie Reed, Diane Hoose, Louisa Cunningham, Lisa Jandorf, Mary Ann Nelson, Bill Cuffe, Bill Goodman, Marian Vaillant, Elizabeth Pratt Fox, and many others provided assistance along the way. The project could not have been undertaken without the careful assistance of the movers employed by the firm of Cohen and Powell, particularly the late Joe Naski. Greer Allen and John Gambell of Yale University Printing Service and Judy Metro of Yale University Press helped with production and distribution of the volume. Some of the information in this book was derived through workshops and other sessions held by the Friends of American Arts at Yale, and I am grateful to many members of the Friends for sharing their considerable expertise.

A special word of thanks is reserved for Marion Sandquist, my colleague in the Yale Furniture Study for six years and a good friend then and now. Marion has been involved in this project since its inception and has held things together while it has moved forward in its halting manner. On many occasions since I moved to Delaware, Marion, her husband, Stan, and her daughter Laura have provided me with a place to stay while on research trips back to New Haven. Their friendship has meant a great deal.

Many curators, collectors, and scholars have given freely of their time and advice as this manuscript was in preparation, and it is not possible to thank them all individually. I am particularly grateful to Barbara Adams, C. Douglass Alves, Jr., Dorothy Armistead, Michael Brown, Mrs. Beekman Cannon, Charles and Mary Carpenter, Cecie Clement, Edward S. Cooke, Jr., and Carol Warner, Wendy A. Cooper, Abbott L. Cummings, Bert Denker, Rob Egleston, Deborah Federhen, Don Fennimore, Betty Guinan, Ruth Hagy, Morrison H. Heckscher, John and Judy Herdeg, Benjamin A. Hewitt, William N. Hosley, Jr., Katherine S. Howe, Elizabeth Jarvis, Brock Jobe, Mrs. Norman Dudley Johnson, Myrna Kaye, Sylvia Lahvis, Art Leibundguth, Marlene A. Lobsiger, Florence S. Mayer, Ed McBain, Roderick A. McLean and Suzanne G. McLean, Michael Moses, Roger Mower, Steve Parks, Charles Parsons, Douglas M. Preston, Francis J. Puig, Ellie Reichlin, Nancy Richards, Julie A. Riesenweber, Mrs. Andrew Ritchie, Frances Gruber Safford, Robert Blair St. George, Shelly A. Schaenen, John J. Snyder,

ACKNOWLEDGMENTS

The process of cataloging American furniture at Yale has been a lengthy one, beginning in earnest when the Yale Furniture Study was established in 1960 at 149 York Street. Many of the people involved in the early stages of the process are mentioned in the preliminaries to the first two volumes in the series of published catalogues, the works on clocks and seating furniture. Their work in laying the foundation for this volume was equally important, and, although I have not repeated their names here, I am grateful to them all. John T. Kirk's extensive work on the collection during the 1960s, including his detailed work sheets on most of the objects at Yale, has formed the backbone of the published volumes, including this one. I first developed an interest in furniture as a graduate student in John's class in the American and New England Studies Program at Boston University in 1972, and I have been grateful to him for advice and counsel ever since.

The opportunity to work at Yale was given to me by the late Charles F. Montgomery, with whom I had the privilege to work from 1974 to 1978. I miss his presence and leadership in the field of American decorative arts and material culture more with every passing day.

Mr. Montgomery's successor, Patricia E. Kane, made the completion of the furniture catalogues a priority, and I am grateful for her guidance and patience. As coauthor and author of the clock and seating furniture catalogues, she established the format and style for this volume and set a high standard that I have endeavored to emulate. Patricia has read the manuscript, and many of the insights offered, especially those concerning construction and condition, are indebted to her keen eye and precise analytical abilities.

Alan Shestack secured funding for this project and allowed me to bring it to completion after my family and I moved to Delaware in 1983. Alan's support and encouragement have been essential to this project.

I would like to extend my personal thanks to the Mellon and Luce foundations for their financial support of the research for and production of this volume.

Many staff members and students at Yale have contributed to this publication during its preparation, and I acknowledge their help with gratitude. In particular, Kevin L. Stayton, Thomas S. Michie, and Gordon Sands offered much help during their stints as graduate fellows; they shared their research unstintingly, and their work is reflected in many of the entries in this catalogue. Peter Arkell taught me a great deal while he was on the Art Gallery staff as our furniture conservator and later when he worked for the museum on a free-lance basis. His understanding of and sympathy for old furniture was of great assistance in evaluating the objects in this catalogue; their fine condition and appearance when photographed are a tribute to his skill. David Barquist, Janine Skerry, Robert M. Soule, Robert C. Soule, Richard Moore, Fred D'Amico, Nan Ross, Rosalie Reed, Diane Hoose, Louisa Cunningham, Lisa Jandorf, Mary Ann Nelson, Bill Cuffe, Bill Goodman, Marian Vaillant, Elizabeth Pratt Fox, and many others provided assistance along the way. The project could not have been undertaken without the careful assistance of the movers employed by the firm of Cohen and Powell, particularly the late Joe Naski. Greer Allen and John Gambell of Yale University Printing Service and Judy Metro of Yale University Press helped with production and distribution of the volume. Some of the information in this book was derived through workshops and other sessions held by the Friends of American Arts at Yale, and I am grateful to many members of the Friends for sharing their considerable expertise.

A special word of thanks is reserved for Marion Sandquist, my colleague in the Yale Furniture Study for six years and a good friend then and now. Marion has been involved in this project since its inception and has held things together while it has moved forward in its halting manner. On many occasions since I moved to Delaware, Marion, her husband, Stan, and her daughter Laura have provided me with a place to stay while on research trips back to New Haven. Their friendship has meant a great deal.

Many curators, collectors, and scholars have given freely of their time and advice as this manuscript was in preparation, and it is not possible to thank them all individually. I am particularly grateful to Barbara Adams, C. Douglass Alves, Jr., Dorothy Armistead, Michael Brown, Mrs. Beekman Cannon, Charles and Mary Carpenter, Cecie Clement, Edward S. Cooke, Jr., and Carol Warner, Wendy A. Cooper, Abbott L. Cummings, Bert Denker, Rob Egleston, Deborah Federhen, Don Fennimore, Betty Guinan, Ruth Hagy, Morrison H. Heckscher, John and Judy Herdeg, Benjamin A. Hewitt, William N. Hosley, Jr., Katherine S. Howe, Elizabeth Jarvis, Brock Jobe, Mrs. Norman Dudley Johnson, Myrna Kaye, Sylvia Lahvis, Art Leibundguth, Marlene A. Lobsiger, Florence S. Mayer, Ed McBain, Roderick A. McLean and Suzanne G. McLean, Michael Moses, Roger Mower, Steve Parks, Charles Parsons, Douglas M. Preston, Francis J. Puig, Ellie Reichlin, Nancy Richards, Julie A. Riesenweber, Mrs. Andrew Ritchie, Frances Gruber Safford, Robert Blair St. George, Shelly A. Schaenen, John J. Snyder,

Allen Stokes, Scott T. Swank, Kevin Sweeney, Beatrice Taylor, Neville Thompson, Robert F. Trent, David Warren, Richard Woodward, Bruce Young, and Philip Zea. My colleagues in the Publications Office at Winterthur—Ian M. G. Quimby, Catherine E. Hutchins, Patricia R. Lisk, and Alma Sorber—have provided a rational and supportive atmosphere during the final stages of this project. Their tolerance has been much appreciated.

Several people have been most closely involved in the preparation of this book. Most of the photography for the volume was done by Charles Uht. His clear and eloquent pictures will render this book useful long after the text has been updated by new research. The only objects not rephotographed especially for this book were those that had been taken already by E. Irving Blomstrann. It has been a pleasure to work with Chuck and Irving, not only on this project but on several earlier ones as well. Each is a consummate professional and a pleasure to work with closely and for long hours. The same is true of Professor R. Bruce Hoadley, who performed the majority of the wood analyses offered here. Widely recognized in the field of wood anatomy and wood technology as one of the nation's leading experts, Bruce was kind enough to bring his considerable skills to bear on this project, thus enriching the final results tremendously. Subsequently, his expertise has been called upon by several other museums, and his annual seminars at the University of Massachusetts have done a great deal to develop wood identification skills in the curatorial ranks.

I am deeply indebted to my colleague Patti Lisk, who has brought her full array of editorial skills to bear on this manuscript. As one who, on occasion, wears the hat of both author and editor, I can fully appreciate how fortunate I was to secure the services of an editor as skilled, fair, thorough, and dedicated as Patti.

This is the sixth book that I have had the privilege of working on with Howard Gralla as either author, editor, or both. The joy of seeing one's work transformed into pages designed by Howard goes a long way toward alleviating the pain and suffering of research and writing. I am grateful to Howard not only for his elegant design and typography but for his expert supervision of this book's production as well.

Much of my work on the last stages of this book was accomplished on weekends, on vacations, and at night, and it would not have been possible to bring it to completion without many sacrifices, both personal and financial, by my wife, Barbara McLean Ward, and our son, Geoffrey W. R. Ward. In addition, as a scholar in the field in her own right, Barbara has contributed many valuable insights along the way and has freely given of her own time to provide assistance.

The dedication of the book to my parents, Arleen Burdick Ward and W. Ralph Ward, Jr., expresses my love and my indebtedness to them for their support of my education and endeavors.

MATTER IN PLACE: *Some Thoughts on Case Furniture*

Wherever we go in the contemporary landscape we run across these signs: boundaries, roads, and places of assembly. We read them at once, and we not only read them, we create them ourselves, almost without realizing that without them we could not function as members of society. To me this universal need— and universal ability—to organize space, to divide it into microspaces, assemble them into macrospaces, is impressive evidence that there is a common, unchanging human nature. But each age, each society develops its own unique kind of spatial organization. There are societies which cannot rest until they have defined every space, natural or man-made, in conveniently human or political categories.
JOHN BRINCKERHOFF JACKSON
Discovering the Vernacular Landscape
(New Haven and London: Yale University Press, 1984), pp. 28–29.

IN INTRODUCTORY ESSAYS to recent catalogues of public and private collections, authors have explored the design, construction, and regional characteristics of early American furniture. Oswaldo Rodriguez Roque, in his *American Furniture at Chipstone*, explored the aesthetic dimension of furniture from the seventeenth century through the neoclassical period, while Morrison H. Heckscher pursued a similar line of investigation, with more emphasis on regional expressions of given styles, in his preface to the catalogue of furniture in the Queen Anne and Chippendale styles in the Metropolitan Museum of Art. The shop practices of urban and rural craftsmen and the nature and evolution of joinery and cabinetmaking were the focuses of essays by Brock Jobe and Philip Zea in *New England Furniture: The Colonial Era*, Jobe and Myrna Kaye's selective catalogue of the collection of the Society for the Preservation of New England Antiquities. Furniture made and owned in Maryland during three centuries was the focus of Gregory Weidman's catalogue of the collection at the Maryland Historical Society.

These essays, appearing within a year or so of each other, provide excellent modern appraisals of the design, construction, and regional characteristics of early American furniture. Although they vary in style and emphasis, they share a common outlook in that they focus on furniture from the point of view of the maker, with the consumer entering the picture primarily as an arbiter of taste or a seeker of status. Yet, while relatively few people *made* furniture in the seventeenth, eighteenth, and early nineteenth centuries, nearly everyone *used* furniture. One could argue that an examination of questions of function—both practical functions and symbolic ones—is of equal importance to our study of furniture and is one that has been relatively little explored in traditional histories of American furniture.

This brief essay will examine some of the varied functions that case furniture has fulfilled in America since the middle of the seventeenth century. Organized like a chest of drawers, the narrative will move forward in a discrete series of sections, each meant to be suggestive rather than exhaustive of a given topic. The vast majority of objects in this catalogue, due to the nature of the Yale collection, date before 1830, so attention will be focused on the earlier period. In the study of furniture, however, elements of continuity are as important as evidence of change, perhaps even more so. Thus the dimensions of case furniture will be considered as a continuum from the middle of the seventeenth century to our own time.

Case furniture is a term that is more easily understood than precisely defined. Its distinguishing characteristic is that it is designed to hold other objects: to store, conceal, protect, and organize them. The box and the drawer (a lidless box) are its building blocks, the rectangle and square its common expression in geometry. Thomas Sheraton, in *The Cabinet Dictionary* (London, 1803), noted, "Box, in its most common acceptation, denotes a small chest or coffer for holding any thing." With allowances for increases in size and complexity, case furniture as a whole is comprised of those articles designed and used "for holding any thing." Whether they provide a large open space for general storage, as in a capacious seventeenth-century chest (cat. 21), or many little spaces in a very specialized form, such as a medicine chest (cat. 16), case objects can best be broadly defined by their storage function.

Such a broad definition, of course, can result in some seemingly strange bedfellows. This catalogue, for example, includes objects as small as a seventeenth-century carved box (cat. 2) and as large as a Charleston library bookcase (cat. 188) standing more than eleven feet high. For the purposes of this catalogue, case furniture was defined to include boxes; chests (including chests with drawers); chests of drawers; chest-on-chests; dressing tables; high chests of drawers; desks; desk and bookcases and their relations; cupboards; buffets, or corner cupboards; sideboards and cabinets; pianos and radios; and a few other minor forms. (Another variation of case furniture, the clock, was treated separately in an earlier volume of the Yale series.)

Having defined case furniture's special role in the world of furniture as a whole as one of storage and containment, it must be said immediately that it shares this role with other types of furniture. Drawers are found on many types of furniture classified as tables and even on some chairs, such as writing-arm Windsors. One type of furniture included in this catalogue— the dressing table—signifies by its very name the overlapping functions that furniture fulfills. If tables are defined as objects to work at, to eat upon, and to display articles on, the lines of demarcation between these categories of furniture can become even more blurred. The slant-front lids of desks and desk and bookcases fall forward to be supported by lopers, and thus form a table for working and writing. The tops of seventeenth-century cupboards, eighteenth-century high chests, and nineteenth-century sideboards and cabinets were often used for the display of articles, such as silver, pewter, glass, ceramics, and sculpture. An inclusive definition of case furniture would encompass such articles as worktables, designed for the storage of sewing equipment and materials, which will be treated in the next volume of this series. Seating furniture, defined as objects to sit, recline, or sleep on, would seem to be a much more distinct category. Yet clothing piled on a chair or draped over its arms can be, in some households, almost a permanent form of storage, and since Gothic times or even earlier, the broad, flat surface of a chest top has offered space for sitting, sleeping, or working. Barbara McLean Ward has called attention to an incident in Cambridge, Massachusetts, in 1676, when a Jonathan Cane entertained a group of young men for an evening of singing, dancing, and drinking. The next morning, young Mr. Cane "was layd on a chest a sleep." She also has indicated that during the seventeenth century, the estates of many individuals included little in the way of seating furniture, although one or more chests might be present, suggesting that chests often were pressed into service as seating, as well as storage, furniture. In Oliver Goldsmith's *Deserted Village* (1770), the English novelist observed that the village chest "contrived a double debt to pay, A bed by night, a chest of drawers by day." This multivalent nature of a single form is a reminder that the use of furniture, especially of long-established forms such as the chest, does not always follow rigid boundaries. Just as we should be wary about being overly dogmatic about questions of terminology for furniture, we should be cautious in accepting strict definitions about how objects were used by people on an individual basis.[1]

AS CONTAINER

Despite these problems of overlap and blurriness, the idea of enclosed containment seems to be the essential feature that distinguishes case furniture in its normative capacity. Almost anything might find its way into a type of case furniture, but in regular practice clothing and textiles were generally stored in chests and chests of drawers; books, business papers, and money in desk and bookcases; dining equipment in sideboards; glass and crockery in corner cupboards; bottles in cellarettes; and so forth. The tradition of storing articles in boxes and drawers is so ingrained in Western society that we often fail to recall or to recognize that it is not necessarily a common aspect of all civilizations. Although the chest and coffer are ancient forms, dating to Egypt, Greece, and Rome, in some cultures case furniture has not developed in the quantities or massive sizes typical of Western society. Large case furniture of the kind represented so well in this volume has not been a significant part of many societies in Africa, the Middle East, India, and Southeast Asia. In Japan, the case objects in use, including book chests and cabinets, are in general low, diminutive, and unobtrusive. While the throne, chair, or stool has had an almost universal role as a symbol of authority and hierarchy, massive case furniture like a Salem gentleman's secretary (cat. 184) or a towering Philadelphia chest-on-chest (cat. 89) is not encountered as frequently in a worldwide context. Cupboards and chests are an important part of the repertoire of Chinese furniture forms, however, suggesting that whatever the impulse that lies behind the formation of these objects might be, it is not an exclusively Western one.[2]

The existence of case furniture, of course, is predicated on the existence within the culture of clothing, textiles, and small consumer goods that can be (or are perceived as *having* to be) put somewhere. Moreover, large examples of case furniture are based on the assumption that they will not be moved frequently, that the society for which they are made is a stable rather than nomadic one. The increasingly specialized and complex forms of case furniture that begin to develop in the eighteenth century all give testimony to the greater number and variety of consumer goods available beginning at that time. The proliferation of desk and bookcases in the eighteenth century, as noted by Edward S. Cooke, Jr., reflects a change in reading habits from an "intensive" experience typical of the seventeenth century to "extensive" reading habits characteristic of the eighteenth. Thus, when Susanna Atkinson of Portsmouth, New Hampshire, died in 1796, her "Large Book case & drawers" held a "Library Containing 300 Vol.," testimony to the greater number of books available to a wide reading public by that time. The existence of a desk and bookcase implies a relatively high level of literacy, the necessity of conducting correspondence, and the importance of keeping records and filing them so

that they can be retrieved, perhaps through a system of pigeonholes marked with the letters of the alphabet, as recommended by Thomas Chippendale. A federal-period sideboard suggests the importance of formal dining with an extensive array of glasses, dishes, tablecloths, utensils, and beverages required. Many sideboards also housed a chamber pot for the use of men after dinner, thus providing essential services for the meal from beginning to end.[3]

All of this is obvious. We take it for granted that order needs to be imposed on our physical surroundings, that a rational system of storage and retrieval is a fact of life. The necessity for a means of containing and confining goods seems to be an ingrained part of Western and some other cultures. As anthropologist Mary Douglas noted, "dirt is matter out of place."[4] Case furniture gives people a place to put their matter, to keep things from becoming "dirt." One can even see the development of case furniture, in America and elsewhere, and the emphasis placed on it as three-dimensional expression of some of the symbolic manifestations of the anal-retentive character, particularly excessive neatness and acquisitiveness. To stretch a point, the presence of chamber pots in sideboards might well underscore this relationship.

AS BARRIER

The small coffer (cat. 18) made in 1816 for a Philadelphia society of German immigrants offers the best example in the Yale collection of the age-old function of case furniture as a secure barrier against the outside world. Presumably made to store the cash and assets of this society, the coffer is opened with the traditional three locks, with the key to each presumably held by a different member of the society and all three necessary to open the chest and obtain access. The facade is opaque, the contents within out of sight and secure. The coffer thus presents a barrier between the outside and the inside, a physical barrier that can stand as an allegory for the distinction between the outside world of Philadelphia and the inner brotherhood of the immigrant society. Its wall set up a barrier or boundary that gives definition to the group's identity. The same can be said of all case furniture: it creates a distinction between the possessions of its owners and those of others. By concealing and protecting articles, it creates an inner world sheltered from the outer world.

Ward has noted the importance a seventeenth-century chest might have had in defining a person's identity: "The chest often contained clothing to cover all the parts of the body, and blankets and textiles to protect it. In many cases, it was the safe resting place for all of a person's worldly belongings, all that gave him or her a sense of separate identity. It was the one space over which an individual could have total control. The one space he or she could protect, survey, and rearrange. In seventeenth-century England a corpse was 'chested' before intern-

ment and the terms chest and coffin were used synonymously. Hence, the chest became the ultimate enclosure for the body itself which was finally wrapped in a linen sheet—like those so often stored in chests—in preparation for burial." Just as the human chest contains the vital organs of the body, the furniture chest contains the vital matter of living, the material goods we need or think we need, and in any event the goods we almost inevitably have.[5] The chest serves as a barrier between individuals, separating and differentiating their material possessions and creating a sense of identity.

The function of concealment is a critical one and is also of interest culturally. Articles stored in a chest of drawers, for example, are hidden out of sight of casual view. They must be revealed drawer by drawer, little by little, as each drawer is pulled out and then replaced. The clothes hanging in a clothespress (cat. 203), however, are revealed all at once as the doors are thrown open. Concealment is important in each form, yet the manner in which the barriers are removed is different. Some Pennsylvania clothespresses (cats. 201, 202) combine a tier or two of drawers below the cupboard doors, thus combining these two approaches to concealing (and in turn revealing) goods. Although it is difficult to be precise, the manner of how furniture is opened and what is revealed in the process may be suggestive of attitudes toward privacy and the individual. Objects that combine doors and drawers provide something of a solution that allows the owners to reveal their possessions (and thus perhaps themselves) in a piecemeal fashion. One cupboard door can remain locked while the other is opened, both doors can remain shut while the drawers below are pulled out, and so forth. The individual's vulnerability is reduced by these solutions, and their degree of privacy heightened. The increasing number of objects dating from the eighteenth century with multiple drawers and storage units suggests that furniture forms were responding to the same type of changes that Henry Glassie in *Folk Housing in Middle Virginia* referred to as Georgianization.[6]

The question of security and privacy also comes into play with many desks and desk and bookcases. There is a good deal of evidence that articles of value were stored in desks, which often had the most complex and secret locking systems and hiding devices. In 1747, for example, "a gold necklace and locket, and a gold locket, and a pair of gold buttons, six silver teaspoons, and two large silver spoons" were stolen from Timothy Scarf's escritoire or desk. (The same object also held "a bed quilt, and some bed linnen, a set of fine hugabug napkin[s], and Sundry other Things," all probably kept in the lower wide drawers.) Similarly, in 1748 George Rogers's desk contained paper money and coinage, silver, gold, and stone buckles, necklaces, buttons, lockets, and other forms of jewelry.[7] Today, many of the secret drawers and other devices that secured Rogers's goods (or that failed to protect Scarf's) seem familiar and easy to find, and it is hard to imagine that they served any true security function. However, in the eighteenth century, a potential thief, from a lower socioeconomic class, might not have

been as familiar with these secret drawers as we are today. In any case, his attempts to unlock a complex device would have slowed him down and allowed time for his discovery. In some cases, these secret drawers are so complex that they still present a challenge, even after one has opened them several times. A Connecticut desk and bookcase (cat. 179) is an excellent example of this. Of all the objects in the Yale collection, it has the most complex and difficult to find hidden compartments. Five steps—the unlocking of the slant-front lid, the removal of the valance drawer, the removal of a partition dividing the pigeonhole, the release of a spring lock (allowing the center section to be brought forward), and the removal of a blind lid—are required to reach the two small drawers squirreled away on the interior. This system is considerably more subtle than those on many urban examples (cat. 174), raising the question of why so much secrecy was necessary. In a recent essay dealing with class consciousness in the Connecticut Valley in the eighteenth century, Robert B. St. George has suggested that the midcentury was a period in which the traditional position of the elite was being challenged.[8] A desk and bookcase like the Yale example reflects the owner's need to protect his private papers and cash from his neighbors and from his servants and thus may provide material evidence of this growing tension between the classes. The Chapin-style desk-on-frame (cat. 155) is another good example of a rural, or at least micropolitan object, with an exceedingly well concealed secret compartment, in this instance a hollowed-out box hidden within the backboard of the frame.

Locks are found on many of the objects in this catalogue. They range from the clever turn-buckle allowing access to the upper drawers and the iron lock enclosing the doors of the seventeenth-century Boston chest of drawers with doors (cat. 51) to the lock on the Alexander Roux cabinet (cat. 224), opened with keys stamped with the maker's name, to the lock on the plate drawer of the Stickley sideboard (cat. 225). The use of locks on case furniture, their placement, their incidence on urban versus rural furniture, and other questions need to be explored in great detail. Barbara Carson and Cary Carson have pointed out that these locks can "conjure up a vanished social system of masters and servants, the work routine of a staff of (usually female) domestics, and even something as intangible as the ambivalent trusting-yet-distrustful relationship between workers and supervisors."[9] Did the master of the house retain the keys to the bottle drawer of the sideboard or to the cellarette, or did he entrust the responsibility to the butler or another servant? Who would be held accountable for the safekeeping of the wine and the silver?

AS ORGANIZER

Case furniture not only contains other articles and protects them from vermin and thieves but also provides in many instances a means of organizing those articles into a rational system. (At least it provides the opportunity to do so, although the contents of many a jumbled desk drawer belie this function.) Although change is very slow, and old forms become unfashionable but are never abandoned, it seems that the number of storage units within a typical object tends to increase as time passes. The large, open cavity of a seventeenth-century joined or board chest, with several cubic feet of undifferentiated open space, is often seen as representative of a traditional, older view of the world. Partitioned only in some instances by a small lidded till, the chest primarily provides a single open space. Things have to be piled on top of each other, and those at the top removed before those on the bottom can be reached.

By the time of settlement in America, or very shortly thereafter, the chest of drawers had come into vogue, with its four or more compartmentalized storage units allowing easier access to categories of objects stored together in the same drawer; however, no example of case furniture in the Yale collection whose date range is entirely encompassed within the seventeenth century contains more than six separate storage compartments. By the end of the century, high chests of drawers would have as many as nine units (cat. 122), and at some time in the eighteenth century the number of storage units within a given, representative object reaches levels that must be considered modern. A Norwich desk (cat. 160), for example, contains twenty-two discrete storage units, including nineteen in its interior alone. A Massachusetts desk and bookcase (cat. 174) could have more than forty separate units. The nineteenth-century Wooten patent desk, a form not represented in the Yale collection, is perhaps the height of the case-furniture-as-organizer syndrome.[10]

An unusual instance where the contents of a seventeenth-century chest of drawers were itemized bears repeating in this context. In 1694, the "old Chest of drawers" of Ursulla Cutt of Portsmouth, New Hampshire, contained an extensive variety of goods in its four drawers. Its upper drawer held sewing equipment, glasses, jewelry, and some silver flatware. The second drawer held more jewelry, including gold rings, a pearl necklace, two small canvas tablecloths, and more textiles. The drawer below contained parcels of linens and other textiles. The fourth and presumably bottom drawer held a more diverse assortment of goods, including sewing materials, clothing, sheets, and blankets as well as a looking glass, four earthenware dishes, and an old pewter pot. Seemingly much larger than the other three drawers, this bottom drawer functioned much as a chest, with a variety of articles kept in long-term storage.

The other three drawers served, after a fashion, as boxes, with more specialized items grouped together and available more readily.[11]

Cutt's chest of drawers represents an early form of the organization of goods into different compartments and categories. This tendency was present at a very early stage in this country, and it has continued, of course, to the present. An early object in the Yale collection, the aforementioned Boston chest of drawers with doors (cat. 51), is matched by the more recent Osborn family chest of drawers with doors (cat. 76) made in the late 1920s. This quirk in the collection is nevertheless a demonstration of this dimension of furniture, the stability of forms over time. No early example of case furniture in the Yale collection would puzzle a person of the late twentieth century (although the 1930s Philco radio [cat. 233] might present the biggest challenge). The forms of case furniture have not changed much since 1700, suggesting, perhaps, that human nature between the eighteenth century and the present has not changed much either.

Historian John Demos, however, working in the other direction, has surmised that people of the seventeenth century would not have known what to do with an object as complex as the Newport desk and bookcase of the 1780s in the Yale collection (cat. 177), although it would present no puzzles to us today.[12] If we can accept Demos' hypothesis, then the complexity of case furniture can be seen as a useful index of modernization. The seventeenth century can be seen as a watershed in human experience, as a time when underlying assumptions about the act of life were different. Yale's Boston chest of drawers with doors, a significant object in so many ways, gathers additional importance by being one of the few exceptions that prove the rule that the seventeenth century was fundamentally different. Its form is a precursor of changes that would not affect the population as a whole for nearly half a century or more. Its early date—perhaps 1650 or even a few years earlier—is a remarkable document of the changes that were going to take place in New England as the seventeenth century drew to a close. The chest is a statement, as eloquent as the written word, that new forms, new ways of ordering experience, and new means of organizing life were present in Boston by midcentury. Life was not necessarily regarded any longer as a unified whole. It became more multidimensional, with different objects required for different activities and different spheres of life. Room use was becoming more function specific, and object storage was responding in the same fashion.[13]

The affection for old forms was lasting, however. Many chests with drawers were made, allowing the user the comfort of the old form with the convenience and organizational capabilities of the new. Often these objects were decorated on their exterior to resemble chests of drawers (cat. 36), thus being what has been called a "compromise solution" by Kenneth L. Ames. Some chests of drawers had their drawer fronts ornamented to appear as if they con-

Matter in Place 11

tained more drawers than they actually did (cat. 52). This habit persisted quite late into the eighteenth century, as represented by the Dunlap-style chest-on-chest-on-frame (cat. 88), which appears to have a total of thirteen drawers, although in reality it houses only eight separate compartments.[14]

AS VEHICLE FOR DISPLAY

While the container aspect of case furniture is its organizing principle, these objects also function as vehicles for display. One might say that while they are based on a system of covert (private) storage, they also provide the opportunity for overt (public) display. There were two basic aspects of this display function, one involving the case object as a stand or prop for the visual display of smaller, often precious objects, and a second wherein the case object itself was primarily, if not exclusively, designed to be displayed as a work of art, as a barometer of taste, or as evidence of wealth and social position. Many case objects, of course, combined both of these dimensions. In some instances, as with the rococo-revival sideboard (cat. 223), the overt dimension is as important, if not more so, than the covert one. With its shelves and deep, wide top, this walnut sideboard offers a stage for the display of the owner's silver, ceramics, glass, and other accoutrements. Its small drawers and lower cupboards are no more important than its function as a display stand, and more than half of its height is given over to its display shelves. Richly carved with figures of game, fish, fruit, and flowers, the sideboard itself was meant as a display object, dominating its surroundings by its sheer physical mass and exuberant ornament, almost becoming what Ames has called "an altar piece of the dining room."[15]

In some cases, as with the Roux cabinet (cat. 224), the overt display aspect of the object itself is even more dominant. This cabinet offers some beautiful but nevertheless cramped storage space in its interior of shallow shelves veneered with bird's-eye maple, but the object itself—with its painted porcelain plaques, marquetry, and bronze moldings and mounts—is what is important. With a sculpture or clock resting on its center shelf, the cabinet would sit like a jewel in a Victorian interior, valued for what it was rather than for what it contained. It was principally a work of art, a symbol of its owner's taste, wealth, desires, and pretensions, with any thought of prosaic function being of secondary or even peripheral interest.

The function of American case furniture as a display stand dates to the seventeenth century, when silver, pewter, ceramics, and glass were arrayed on the tops of cupboards in the homes of the well-to-do. The high chest of drawers, some fitted with special steps (cat. 137), were also used in this fashion when they became popular at the end of the seventeenth century. This aspect of their use was retained into the eighteenth century, although it was lost with the

development of the broken-scroll pediment in the so-called Queen Anne style of the 1730–1760 period. A high chest without the ability to display goods on top was a much different object, culturally, than a flat-top high chest. The arena for display had changed to the mantel or to the buffet, or corner cupboard. With the growing tendency to have specific rooms for specific activities, with one living space no longer sufficing for entertaining and sleeping, as in the seventeenth-century parlor, the high chest moved to more private spaces in chambers and no longer needed to have an overt display function. The architectural buffet offered display space in the public rooms. Often fitted with glazed doors (cat. 206) that intermediated between the goods and the outside world by offering a transparent barrier that nevertheless could still be secured with a lock, buffets began to serve the overt display function that cupboards and high chests had fulfilled earlier.[16]

AS A FURNISHING ANCHOR

By its very size, much case furniture challenges the definition of furniture as movable goods. Once in place, it tends to remain fixed and stable. Almost every example in this catalogue is a frontal object, with the rear left unfinished and meant to be placed against a perimeter wall. With classically derived cornice moldings and pediments that correspond to door and window treatments, large case furniture is especially architectonic in nature and can be seen as an integral part of the woodwork in certain instances where furniture and interior trim were created in a coordinated fashion. Case furniture thus differs significantly from chairs and tables, which in the eighteenth century were meant to be placed against the walls when not in use and moved to the center of the room when needed. Their size and their weight precluded such movement of most case furniture, although there are exceptions, of course, such as portable desks (cats. 169, 170) and small boxes such as a medicine chest (cat. 16).

The significance of weight has been given little attention by historians of American furniture, although it has attracted the attention of anthropologists and others who have found evidence of broad cultural differences in the weight of furniture favored by some cultures. Edward T. Hall, for example, in *The Hidden Dimension*, refers to the importance of the "weight of most German furniture." Hall explains, "To a German, light furniture is anathema, not only because it seems flimsy but because people move it and thereby destroy the order of things, including intrusions on the 'private sphere.'"[17] One wonders if this attitude influenced eighteenth-century Pennsylvania German furniture or objects made in Pennsylvania in the Anglo-American style by German craftsmen. A chest-on-chest such as cat. 90, for example, is so sturdily constructed with full dustboards, heavy wooden pegs, and thick drawer linings as to

be almost immovable. Does its overengineered, redundant construction reflect a world view that could be construed as German in its emphasis on stability and order? It is interesting to speculate that such is the case, especially when these massive Pennsylvania objects are compared with New England ones, where dustboards are frequently absent, where drawer linings are thinner, where case tops, bottoms, and backboards are liable to be thinner and lighter, and where construction on the whole is more expedient and serviceable than that found in Pennsylvania furniture. There are numerous exceptions to such patterns, of course, and overengineered furniture is liable to have been made in rural areas where there was little or no Germanic influence. But it is tempting to speculate on the subject, for as Benno M. Forman pointed out, Germanic construction details such as wedged tenons and wedged dovetails are present both in overtly Pennsylvania German furniture and in Anglo-American–style objects made by craftsmen with Germanic backgrounds.[18] The weight and the massiveness of this furniture suggest with equal strength the presence of a Germanic mentality at work in its creation. The strength with which an object is endowed, the relative abundance of materials with which it is constructed, each must be an indication of the maker's stand or view toward issues of stability versus change, toward obsolescence, toward his view of the future. The weight and mass of furniture, in turn, may have influenced the behavior of the consumer, creating an association between furniture and stability and permanence.

Their frontal nature and placement against walls is a broad indication of their role in Western society, where furniture is placed against outside walls in a formal, fixed arrangement. This system is so commonplace that we take it for granted, although in other cultures, such as in Japan, there is much more emphasis on mobility and shifting shapes that create a sense of flux and impermanency, and objects are gathered in the center of the room rather than lined up around the periphery.[19]

AS A VEHICLE OF STATUS AND STYLE

Like all other types of furniture, case furniture also serves as a vehicle for the use of new styles and designs and as an expression of its owner's status. The importance of case furniture can even be considered crucial in this regard, since by its very size (in most instances) and by its expense (again in most instances) it virtually demands attention. The Badlam/Skillin chest-on-chest (cat. 82), for example, made for the Derby family, represents an extreme form of this aspect of case furniture, one enhanced by the presence of carved allegorical figures infused with symbols (presumably) of the New Republic. Monumental in size, embellished with neoclassical carved ornament and architectural motifs, and rich in iconography, this object was

recognized by its maker as "being of Consequence enough to merit great attention." Presumably given by Elias Hasket Derby of Salem, often called America's first millionaire, to his daughter, this chest-on-chest is a revealing statement about the Derby family's level of stylishness, their interest in symbolism, and their belief that objects could reinforce their position as commercial leaders in federal-period Salem. The carved figures—probably Virtue flanked by Peace and Plenty—may have made a political statement as well.

There are examples in the Yale collection of the almost instantaneous diffusion of styles from abroad to America, as with the Boston chest of drawers with doors (cat. 51), and other examples which indicate that Americans preferred to retain older forms long after they had been outmoded in England. The large number of high chests in the Yale collection reflects Francis P. Garvan's collecting interests, of course, but also the historical fact that Americans maintained a preference for the high chest of drawers for more than a century. Examples in the Yale collection can be dated from the 1690s to the 1780s or 1790s. What significance can be derived from this acknowledged preference for a specific form? One is hard pressed to say, yet the answer to such a question is liable to reveal much about the nature of American life, probably much more than an analysis of any American innovations in design or construction. Forms get at the essence of people; ornament springs from a small world of designers and craftsmen.[20]

As with all other types of furniture and objects, many of the objects in this catalogue perform as nonverbal communication. For example, recent studies have focused on the parlor organ and the sewing machine as working in this manner, and the pianos and radio in this catalogue probably functioned in the same fashion. The large cabinet radio (cat. 233), for example, was the focal point of family entertainment and gatherings in the 1930s, when households would cluster around the new instrument for information and entertainment.[21]

As scholars from such fields as anthropology, folklore, linguistics, ethnography, and sociology have taken an interest in American furniture during the last few decades, there has been much theoretical debate about the "meaning of things." In commentary ranging from the sophisticated to the simplistic, many writers have argued persuasively and convincingly that three-dimensional objects tell us a great deal about the people who made and used them. There is little doubt that such is the case. No one can seriously argue that furniture is not a means of conveying information about the human condition in a silent yet eloquent fashion.[22] This has been understood by people for many years, and undoubtedly was understood intuitively, if not explicitly, by the makers and owners of the furniture included in this catalogue. What is needed now are studies that demonstrate *what* furniture tells us about people. What answers does it provide that other sources of material do not? What can it tell us about art,

about economics, about labor relationships, about religion, or about social relationships that confirms or contradicts what we know from traditional sources?

Those of us with an interest in furniture need to respond to these questions by preparing books and articles that use furniture as evidence. It is with that goal in mind that catalogues such as this can serve a useful function: by presenting a good deal of objective information about the holdings of an institution, thereby reducing a scholar's research time and giving some basic material from which to start. For using objects as evidence is a difficult and time-consuming skill to learn, one quite different from using object-related evidence, such as trade catalogues, prescriptive literature, inventories, and other written and pictorial sources. While objects must be understood in the context of *all* the evidence, they do tell us things that the written sources do not.

It is occasionally stated that studies of the decorative arts and material culture have been too object centered, too inbred, too concerned with the epistemology of the object, or too ahistorical. No doubt much of this is true, yet it begs the question. If studies based on objects are to tell us anything about people that we cannot learn from other sources, they must be based on an even closer and more careful scrutiny of the objects themselves. Only by actually examining the object itself, its construction, ornamentation, form, and evidences of use, can the object lead us into deeper insights. Furniture can help us to recapture the history of those people who lived below the level of historical scrutiny while also illuminating the lives of otherwise well-documented individuals. It can help us to learn more about the neglected history of women. It can shed light on the vernacular and on the high style. But it can only do so if the skills of a connoisseur—"one who understands the details, technique, or principles of an art and is competent to act as a critical judge"—are employed. Connoisseurship has become a much maligned word in some circles, but it is an essential skill that the historian needs to possess in order to deal with objects as evidence. Connoisseurship, like a catalogue such as this, is a means to an end and not an end in itself.

A colleague once mentioned that a catalogue such as this runs the risk of being little more than a footnote in other people's work. Nothing could please me more; it is my hope that people will find the information in this volume useful as raw material in preparing the works of synthesis that this field still sorely needs.

NOTES

1. Douglas Ash, "Gothic," in Hayward, *World Furn.*, p. 27; Barbara McLean Ward, introduction to *A Place for Everything: Chests and Boxes in Early Colonial America* (Winterthur, Del.: Henry Francis du Pont Winterthur Museum, 1986), pp. 5–6; Goldsmith is quoted in Molly Harrison, *People and Furniture: A Social Background to the English Home* (London: Ernest Benn, 1971), p. 99.

2. John R. Harris, "Egypt," Joan Liveridge, "Greece, Rome," Margaret Medley, "China," J. Hillier, "Japan," and Anthony Christie, "The Middle East, India and South East Asia," in Hayward, *World Furn.*, pp. 10–18, 276–288; Roy Sieber, *African Furniture and Household Objects* (New York: American Federation of Arts; Bloomington and London: Indiana University Press, 1980).

3. Cooke, pp. 24–25; Jane C. Giffen, "A Selection of New Hampshire Inventories," *Historical New Hampshire* 34, nos. 1–2 (Spring–Summer 1969): 71; Thomas Chippendale, *The Gentleman & Cabinet-Maker's Director* (3d ed, London, 1762; reprint, New York: Dover Publications, 1966), pl. 74; Lawrence Stone, *The Family, Sex and Marriage in England, 1500–1800* (New York: Harper and Row, 1977), p. 401 pl. 17.

4. Mary C. Douglas, *Purity and Danger: An Analysis of Concepts of Pollution and Taboo* (New York: Praeger Publishers, 1966), p. 35.

5. Ward, *Place for Everything*, p. 7.

6. Henry Glassie, *Folk Housing in Middle Virginia* (Knoxville: University of Tennessee Press, 1975).

7. *Pennsylvania Gazette* (4 June 1747), as reprinted in *Antiques* 99, no. 4 (April 1971): 588. Reference courtesy of Nancy Goyne Evans. Jobe and Kaye, pp. 226–229.

8. Robert Blair St. George, "Artifacts of Regional Consciousness in the Connecticut River Valley, 1700–1780," in *Great River*, pp. 29–39.

9. Barbara G. Carson and Cary Carson, "Things Unspoken: Learning Social History from Artifacts," in *Ordinary People and Everyday Life: Perspectives on the New Social History*, ed. James B. Gardner and George Rollie Adams (Nashville: American Association for State and Local History, 1983), p. 194.

10. For the Wooten desk, see Betty Lawson Walters, *The King of Desks: Wooten's Patent Secretary* (Washington, D.C.: Smithsonian Institution Press, 1969); and *Wooten Patent Desks: A Place for Everything and Everything in Its Place* (Indianapolis: Indiana State Museum; Oakland, Calif.: Oakland Museum, 1983).

11. New Hampshire Provincial Probate Records, 3:33–34, as reprinted in *Antiques* 98, no. 1 (July 1970): 58. Reference courtesy of Richard M. Candee.

12. Response of John Demos in John T. Kirk et al., comps., "Giving an Elephant to Blind Men? The Cross-Disciplinary Role of a Desk and Bookcase," *Arts* 59, no. 2 (October 1984): 99.

13. Benno M. Forman, "The Chest of Drawers in America, 1635–1730: The Origins of the Joined Chest of Drawers," *Winterthur Portfolio* 20, no. 1 (Spring 1985): 1–30; and Trent, "Postscript," discuss the importance of the Yale example in detail and in context.

14. Kenneth L. Ames, *Beyond Necessity: Art in the Folk Tradition* (Winterthur, Del.: Winterthur Museum, 1977), pp. 67–70.

15. Kenneth L. Ames, "The Battle of the Sideboards," in *Winterthur Portfolio* 9, ed. Ian M. G. Quimby (Charlottesville: University Press of Virginia, 1974), p. 5.

16. For additional remarks, see Gerald W. R. Ward, "Some Thoughts on Connecticut Cupboards and Other Case Furniture," *Old-Time New England* (forthcoming).

17. Edward T. Hall, *The Hidden Dimension* (Garden City, N.Y.: Doubleday, 1966), p. 129.

18. See Forman, "German Influences," passim.

19. Hall, *Hidden Dimensions*, pp. 139–143.

20. Montgomery, "Regional Preferences and Characteristics," discusses the American retention of the high chest after it had gone out of fashion in England.

21. Kenneth L. Ames, "Material Culture as Nonverbal Communication: A Historical Case Study," *Journal of American Culture* 3, no. 4 (Winter 1980): 619–641; Diane M. Douglas, "The Machine in the Parlor: A Dialectical Analysis of the Sewing Machine," *Journal of American Culture* 5, no. 1 (Spring 1982): 20–29.

22. For one view of current literature, see Kenneth L. Ames, "The Stuff of Everyday Life: American Decorative Arts and Household Furnishings," in *Material Culture: A Research Guide*, ed. Thomas J. Schlereth (Lawrence: University Press of Kansas, 1985), pp. 79–112. See also Jules David Prown, "Mind in Matter: An Introduction to Material Culture Theory and Method," *Winterthur Portfolio* 17, no. 1 (Spring 1982): 1–19.

SHORT TITLES AND ABBREVIATIONS

Bible Boxes
Bible Boxes: English Oak Table Boxes, Slopes, Desks and Cabinets of the 16th and 17th Centuries. St. Albans, Hertfordshire, England: Crispin, 1978.

Bjerkoe
ETHEL HALL BJERKOE, assisted by John Arthur Bjerkoe. *The Cabinetmakers of America.* Garden City, N. Y.: Doubleday & Co., 1957.

Boston Furn.
Boston Furniture of the Eighteenth Century: A Conference Held by the Colonial Society of Massachusetts, 11 and 12 May 1972. Publications of the Colonial Society of Massachusetts, vol. 48. Edited by Walter Muir Whitehill, Jonathan L. Fairbanks, and Brock W. Jobe. Boston: Colonial Society of Massachusetts, 1974.

Buckley, "Fine Federal Furn."
CHARLES E. BUCKLEY. "Fine Federal Furniture Attributed to Portsmouth." *Antiques* 83, no. 2 (February 1963): 196–200.

Burroughs, *Southern Antiques*
PAUL H. BURROUGHS. *Southern Antiques.* Richmond: Garrett & Massie, 1931.

Burton, *Charleston Furn.*
E. MILBY BURTON. *Charleston Furniture, 1700–1825.* Contributions from the Charleston Museum, XII. Charleston, S.C.: Charleston Museum, 1955.

Butler, *Sleepy Hollow*
JOSEPH T. BUTLER. *Sleepy Hollow Restorations: A Cross Section of the Collections.* Tarrytown, N.Y.: Sleepy Hollow Press, 1983.

Carpenter
RALPH E. CARPENTER, JR. *The Arts and Crafts of Newport, Rhode Island, 1640–1820.* Newport, R.I.: Preservation Society of Newport County, 1954.

Cathers
DAVID M. CATHERS. *Furniture of the American Arts and Crafts Movement: Stickley and Roycroft Mission Oak.* New York: New American Library, 1981.

Chinnery
VICTOR CHINNERY. *Oak Furniture, the British Tradition: A History of Early Furniture in the British Isles and New England.* Woodbridge, Suffolk, England: Antique Collectors' Club, 1979.

Comstock
HELEN COMSTOCK. *American Furniture: Seventeenth, Eighteenth, and Nineteenth Century Styles.* New York: Viking Press, a Studio Book, 1962.

Comstock, "Bull Coll."
HELEN COMSTOCK. "The C. Sanford Bull Collection of New England Furniture." *Antiques* 70, no. 2 (August 1956): 140–141.

Comstock, *Concise Encyclopedia*
HELEN COMSTOCK, ed. *The Concise Encyclopedia of American Antiques.* 2 vols. London: Connoisseur, 1958.

Cooke
EDWARD S. COOKE, JR. *Fiddlebacks and Crooked-backs: Elijah Booth and Other Joiners in Newtown and Woodbury.* Waterbury, Conn.: Mattatuck Historical Society, 1982.

Cooper, *In Praise of America*
WENDY A. COOPER. *In Praise of America: American Decorative Arts, 1650–1830, Fifty Years of Discovery since the 1929 Girl Scouts Loan Exhibition.* New York: Alfred A. Knopf, 1980.

DAPC
DECORATIVE ARTS PHOTOGRAPHIC COLLECTION, HENRY FRANCIS DU PONT WINTERTHUR MUSEUM, Winterthur, Del.

DEF
RALPH EDWARDS and PERCY MACQUOID. *The Dictionary of English Furniture from the Middle Ages to the Late Georgian Period.* 3 vols. 1924–1927. 2d rev. ed. London: Country Life, 1954.

Documented New Hampshire Furn.
Plain & Elegant, Rich & Common: Documented New Hampshire Furniture, 1750–1850. Text by John F. Page and James L. Garvin. Concord: New Hampshire Historical Society, 1979.

Downs
JOSEPH DOWNS. *American Furniture: Queen Anne and Chippendale Periods in the Henry Francis du Pont Winterthur Museum.* New York: Macmillan Company, 1952.

Dyer, "Press Cupboard"
WALTER A. DYER. "The Tulip-and-Sunflower Press Cupboard." *Antiques* 27, no. 4 (April 1935): 140–143.

Elder, *Maryland Queen Anne and Chippendale Furn.*
WILLIAM VOSS ELDER III. *Maryland Queen Anne and Chippendale Furniture of the Eighteenth Century.* Baltimore, Md.: October House for the Baltimore Museum of Art, 1968.

Elder and Bartlett, *John Shaw*
WILLIAM VOSS ELDER III and LU BARTLETT. *John Shaw, Cabinetmaker of Annapolis.* Baltimore, Md.: Baltimore Museum of Art, 1983.

Fabian
MONROE H. FABIAN. *The Pennsylvania German Decorated Chest.* New York: Main Street Press, 1978.

Failey, *Long Island*
DEAN F. FAILEY, with the assistance of Robert J. Hefner and Susan E. Klaffky. *Long Island Is My Nation: The Decorative Arts, 1640–1830.* Setauket, N.Y.: Society for the Preservation of Long Island Antiquities, 1976.

Fales, *Am. Painted Furn.*
DEAN A. FALES, JR. *American Painted Furniture, 1660–1880.* Illustrations and design editor, Robert Bishop; general editor, Cyril I. Nelson. New York: E. P. Dutton, 1972.

Fales, *Deerfield*
DEAN A. FALES, JR. *The Furniture of Historic Deerfield.* New York: E. P. Dutton, 1976.

Fales, *Essex County Furn.*
DEAN A. FALES, JR. *Essex County Furniture: Documented Treasures from Local Collections, 1660–1860.* Salem, Mass.: Essex Institute, 1965.

Fairbanks and Bates
JONATHAN L. FAIRBANKS and ELIZABETH BIDWELL BATES. *American Furniture, 1620 to the Present.* New York: Richard Marek Publishers, 1981.

Fairbanks and Trent, *New England Begins*
JONATHAN L. FAIRBANKS and ROBERT F. TRENT. *New England Begins: The Seventeenth Century.* 3 vols. Boston: Museum of Fine Arts, 1982.

Fitzgerald
OSCAR P. FITZGERALD. *Three Centuries of American Furniture.* Englewood Cliffs, N.J.: Prentice-Hall, 1982.

Flayderman Coll.
Colonial Furniture, Silver & Decorations . . . The Collection of the Late Philip Flayderman. Sale 3804. 2–4 January 1930. New York: American Art Association, Anderson Galleries, 1930.

Forgeries and Restorations
The American Clock, 1725–1865, Forgeries and Restorations in American Furniture: Two Yale Student Exhibitions, May 18–June 28, 1974. Text by Douglass Scott, Joan Ketter, and Michael Boodro. New Haven, Conn.: Garvan Furniture Study, 1974.

Forman, "German Influences"
BENNO M. FORMAN. "German Influences in Pennsylvania Furniture." In Scott T. Swank et al. *Arts of the Pennsylvania Germans,* edited by Catherine E. Hutchins, pp. 102–170. New York: W. W. Norton, 1983.

Forman, "Urban Aspects"
BENNO M. FORMAN. "Urban Aspects of Massachusetts Furniture in the Late Seventeenth Century." In *Country Cabinetwork and Simple City Furniture,* edited by John D. Morse, pp. 1–34. Charlottesville: University Press of Virginia, 1970.

Garvan Coll.
Furniture and Silver by American Master Craftsmen of Colonial and Early Federal Times . . . Sold by Order of Francis P. Garvan. Sale 3878. 8–10 January 1931. New York: American Art Association, Anderson Galleries, 1931.

Garvan, *Pennsylvania German Coll.*
BEATRICE B. GARVAN. *The Pennsylvania German Collection.* Handbook in American Art, no. 2. Philadelphia: Philadelphia Museum of Art, 1982.

Gilbert, *Furn. at Temple Newsam*
CHRISTOPHER GILBERT. *Furniture at Temple Newsam House and Lotherton Hall: A Catalogue of the Leeds Collection.* 2 vols. Leeds, England: National Art-Collections Fund and the Leeds Arts Collection Fund, 1978.

Girl Scouts Exhibition
Loan Exhibition of Eighteenth and Nineteenth Century Furniture and Glass. New York: American Art Galleries, 1929.

Goyne, "Bureau Table"
NANCY A. GOYNE. "The Bureau Table in America." In *Winterthur Portfolio 3*, edited by Milo M. Naeve, pp. 24–36. Winterthur, Del.: Henry Francis du Pont Winterthur Museum, 1967.

Great River
The Great River: Art and Society in the Connecticut Valley, 1635–1820. Hartford, Conn.: Wadsworth Atheneum, 1985.

Greenlaw
BARRY A. GREENLAW. *New England Furniture at Williamsburg.* Williamsburg Decorative Arts Series. Edited by Graham Hood. Williamsburg, Va.: Colonial Williamsburg Foundation, 1974. Distributed by University Press of Virginia.

Hagler, *American Queen Anne Furn.*
KATHARINE BRYANT HAGLER. *American Queen Anne Furniture, 1720–1755.* Dearborn, Mich.: Edison Institute, 1976.

Halsey and Tower, *Homes of Our Ancestors*
R. T. H. HALSEY and ELIZABETH TOWER. *The Homes of Our Ancestors as Shown in the American Wing of the Metropolitan Museum of Art of New York.* New York: Doubleday, Page, 1925.

Handbook
SCHOOL OF THE FINE ARTS, YALE UNIVERSITY. *Handbook: A Description of the Gallery of Fine Arts and the Collections.* New Haven: Associates in Fine Arts at Yale University, 1931.

Hayward, *World Furn.*
HELENA HAYWARD, ed. *World Furniture: An Illustrated History.* London: Hamlyn, 1965.

Heckscher
MORRISON H. HECKSCHER. *American Furniture in the Metropolitan Museum of Art.* Vol. 2, *The Late Colonial Period: The Queen Anne and Chippendale Styles.* Edited by Mary-Alice Rogers; photographs by Richard Cheek. New York: Metropolitan Museum of Art and Random House, 1985.

Hepplewhite
GEORGE HEPPLEWHITE. *The Cabinet-Maker and Upholsterer's Guide.* 3d ed. London, 1794. Reprint. New York: Dover Publications, 1969.

Hewitt
BENJAMIN A. HEWITT, PATRICIA E. KANE, and GERALD W. R. WARD. *The Work of Many Hands: Card Tables in Federal America, 1790–1820.* New Haven: Yale University Art Gallery, 1982.

Hipkiss
EDWIN J. HIPKISS. *Eighteenth-Century American Arts: The M. and M. Karolik Collection.* Cambridge, Mass.: Harvard University Press for the Museum of Fine Arts, Boston, 1941.

Holloway
EDWARD STRATTON HOLLOWAY. *American Furniture and Decoration: Colonial and Federal.* Philadelphia: J. B. Lippincott, 1928.

Hornor
WILLIAM MACPHERSON HORNOR. *Blue Book, Philadelphia Furniture, William Penn to George Washington, with Special Reference to the Philadelphia-Chippendale School.* Philadelphia: By the author, 1935.

Hosley and Zea, "Decorated Board Chests"
WILLIAM N. HOSLEY, JR., and PHILIP ZEA. "Decorated Board Chests of the Connecticut River Valley." *Antiques* 119, no. 5 (May 1981): 1147–1151.

Hummel, *American Chippendale Furn.*
CHARLES F. HUMMEL. *A Winterthur Guide to American Chippendale Furniture: Middle Atlantic and Southern Colonies.* New York: Crown Publishers, a Winterthur Book/Rutledge Books, 1976.

Hummel, *With Hammer in Hand*
CHARLES F. HUMMEL. *With Hammer in Hand: The Dominy Craftsmen of East Hampton, New York.* Charlottesville: University Press of Virginia, 1968.

Jobe and Kaye
BROCK W. JOBE and MYRNA KAYE. *New England Furniture: The Colonial Era.* Boston: Houghton Mifflin Co., 1984.

Kane "American Furn."
PATRICIA E. KANE. "American Furniture in the Yale University Art Gallery." *Antiques* 117, no. 5 (June 1980): 1314–1327.

Kane, *Furn. New Haven Colony*
PATRICIA E. KANE. *Furniture of the New Haven Colony: The Seventeenth-Century Style.* New Haven, Conn.: New Haven Colony Historical Society, 1973.

Kane, "Hadley Chest"
PATRICIA E. KANE. "The Seventeenth-Century Furniture of the Connecticut Valley: The Hadley Chest Reappraised." In *Arts of the Anglo-American Community in the Seventeenth Century*, edited by Ian M. G. Quimby, pp. 79–122. Charlottesville: University Press of Virginia, 1975.

Kane, "Joiners of Hartford County"
PATRICIA E. KANE. "The Joiners of Seventeenth-Century Hartford County." *Connecticut Historical Society Bulletin* 35, no. 3 (July 1970): 65–85.

Kane, "New Haven Colony Furn."
PATRICIA E. KANE. "New Haven Colony Furniture: The Seventeenth-Century Style." *Antiques* 103, no. 4 (May 1973): 950–962.

Kettell
RUSSELL HAWES KETTELL. *The Pine Furniture of New England*. New York: Doubleday, Doran, 1929.

Kettell, *Early American Rooms*
RUSSELL HAWES KETTELL, ed. *Early American Rooms*. Portland, Maine: Southworth-Anthoensen Press, 1936.

Kirk, *Am. Furn. & Brit. Trad.*
JOHN T. KIRK. *American Furniture and the British Tradition to 1830*. New York: Alfred A. Knopf, 1982.

Kirk, *Conn. Furn.*
JOHN T. KIRK. *Connecticut Furniture: Seventeenth and Eighteenth Centuries*. Hartford, Conn.: Wadsworth Atheneum, 1967.

Kirk, *Early Am. Furn.*
JOHN T. KIRK. *Early American Furniture: How to Recognize, Evaluate, and Care for the Most Beautiful Pieces—High-style, Country, Primitive, & Rustic*. New York: Alfred A. Knopf, 1970.

Kirk, *Impecunious Collector's Guide*
JOHN T. KIRK. *The Impecunious Collector's Guide to American Antiques*. New York: Alfred A. Knopf, 1975.

Kirk, "Sources"
JOHN T. KIRK. "Sources of Some American Regional Furniture." *Antiques* 88, no. 6 (December 1965): 790–798.

Lockwood
LUKE VINCENT LOCKWOOD. *Colonial Furniture in America*. 2 vols. 3d ed. New York: Charles Scribner's Sons, 1926.

Lovell, "Boston Blockfront Furn."
MARGARETTA MARKLE LOVELL. "Boston Blockfront Furniture." In *Boston Furniture of the Eighteenth Century: A Conference Held by the Colonial Society of Massachusetts, 11 and 12 May 1972*. Publications of the Colonial Society of Massachusetts, vol. 48, edited by Walter Muir Whitehill, Jonathan L. Fairbanks, and Brock W. Jobe, pp. 77–136. Boston: Colonial Society of Massachusetts, 1974.

Luther
CLAIR FRANKLIN LUTHER. *The Hadley Chest*. Hartford, Conn.: Case, Lockwood, & Brainard Co., 1935.

Lyon
IRVING WHITALL LYON. *The Colonial Furniture of New England: A Study of the Domestic Furniture in Use in the Seventeenth and Eighteenth Centuries*. Boston: Houghton Mifflin Co., 1924.

McClelland
NANCY MCCLELLAND. *Duncan Phyfe and the English Regency, 1795–1830*. New York: William R. Scott, 1935.

McElroy, "Furn. in Philadelphia"
CATHRYN J. MCELROY. "Furniture in Philadelphia: The First Fifty Years." In *American Furniture and Its Makers: Winterthur Portfolio 13*, edited by Ian M. G. Quimby, pp. 61–80. Chicago: University of Chicago Press, 1979.

Mayhew and Myers
EDGAR DEN. MAYHEW and MINOR MYERS, JR. *New London County Furniture, 1640–1840*. New London, Conn.: Lyman Allyn Museum, 1974.

Melchor et al., *Raised-Panel Furn.*
JAMES R. MELCHOR, N. GORDON LUHR, and MARILYN S. MELCHOR. *Eastern Shore, Virginia, Raised-Panel Furniture, 1730–1830*. Norfolk, Va.: Chrysler Museum, 1982.

MESDA
MUSEUM OF EARLY SOUTHERN DECORATIVE ARTS, Winston Salem, N.C.

Miller
EDGAR G. MILLER, JR. *American Antique Furniture: A Book for Amateurs*. 2 vols. Baltimore, Md.: Lord Baltimore Press, 1937.

Miller, *Furn. New York Cabinetmakers*
V. ISABELLE MILLER. *Furniture by New York Cabinetmakers, 1650 to 1860*. New York: Museum of the City of New York, 1957.

MMA, *19-Century America*
BERRY B. TRACY, MARYILYNN JOHNSON, MARVIN D. SCHWARTZ, and SUZANNE BOORSCH. *19th-Century America: Furniture and Other Decorative Arts.* New York: Metropolitan Museum of Art, 1970.

Montgomery
CHARLES F. MONTGOMERY. *American Furniture: The Federal Period in the Henry Francis du Pont Winterthur Museum.* New York: Viking Press, a Winterthur Book, 1966.

Montgomery, "Regional Preferences and Characteristics"
CHARLES F. MONTGOMERY. "Regional Preferences and Characteristics in American Decorative Arts, 1750–1800." *Antiques* 109, no. 6 (June 1976): 1196–1211.

Montgomery, "1776—Furniture"
CHARLES F. MONTGOMERY. "1776—How America Really Looked: Furniture." *American Art Journal* 7, no. 1 (May 1975): 52–67.

Montgomery and Kane, *American Art, 1750–1800*
CHARLES F. MONTGOMERY and PATRICIA E. KANE, eds. *American Art, 1750–1800: Towards Independence.* Boston: New York Graphic Society for the Yale University Art Gallery and the Victoria and Albert Museum, London, 1976.

Moses
MICHAEL MOSES. *Master Craftsmen of Newport: The Townsends and Goddards.* Tenafly, N.J.: Americana Press, 1984.

Nagel
CHARLES NAGEL. *American Furniture, 1650–1850.* New York: Chanticleer Press, 1949.

Neat Pieces
Neat Pieces: The Plain-Style Furniture of 19th-Century Georgia. Atlanta, Ga.: Atlanta Historical Society, 1983.

Nutting, *Furn. Pilgrim Century* (1921)
WALLACE NUTTING. *Furniture of the Pilgrim Century, 1620–1720, including Colonial Utensils and Hardware.* Boston: Marshall Jones Co., 1921.

Nutting, *Furn. Pilgrim Century* (1924)
WALLACE NUTTING. *Furniture of the Pilgrim Century (of American Origin), 1620–1720, with Maple and Pine to 1800, including Colonial Utensils and Wrought-Iron House Hardware into the 19th Century.* 2d rev. ed. Framingham, Mass.: Old America Co., 1924.

Nutting, *Treasury*
WALLACE NUTTING. *Furniture Treasury.* 3 vols. Framingham, Mass.: Old America Co., 1928–1933.

Ormsbee, *Story Am. Furn.*
THOMAS HAMILTON ORMSBEE. *The Story of American Furniture.* New York: Macmillan Co., 1934.

Ott
JOSEPH K. OTT. *The John Brown House Loan Exhibition of Rhode Island Furniture.* Providence: Rhode Island Historical Society, 1965.

Page, *Litchfield County Furn.*
JOHN F. PAGE. *Litchfield County Furniture, 1730–1850.* Litchfield, Conn.: Litchfield Historical Society, 1969.

Parsons, *Dunlaps*
CHARLES S. PARSONS. *The Dunlaps & Their Furniture.* Manchester, N.H.: Currier Gallery of Art, 1970.

Parsons, "More Dunlap"
CHARLES S. PARSONS. "More Dunlap." Manuscript, 1976. Yale Furniture Study, New Haven, Conn.

Parsons and Brooke, "Dunlap Cabinetmakers"
CHARLES S. PARSONS and DAVID S. BROOKE. "The Dunlap Cabinetmakers." *Antiques* 98, no. 2 (August 1970): 224–231.

PMA, *Three Centuries*
PHILADELPHIA MUSEUM OF ART. *Philadelphia: Three Centuries of American Art.* Philadelphia: Philadelphia Museum of Art, 1976.

Paul Revere's Boston
Paul Revere's Boston, 1735–1818. Text by Jonathan L. Fairbanks, Wendy A. Cooper, Anne Farnam, Brock W. Jobe, and Martha B. Katz-Hyman. Boston: Museum of Fine Arts, 1975.

Randall
RICHARD H. RANDALL, JR. *American Furniture in the Museum of Fine Arts, Boston.* Boston: Museum of Fine Arts, 1965.

Reifsnyder Coll.
Colonial Furniture: The Superb Collection of the Late Howard Reifsnyder. American Art Galleries. 24–27 April 1929. New York: American Art Association, 1929.

Rodriguez Roque, *Chipstone*
OSWALDO RODRIGUEZ ROQUE. *American Furniture at Chipstone.* Madison: University of Wisconsin Press, 1984.

Rogers, "Garvan Coll. (1962)"
MEYRIC R. ROGERS. "The Mabel Brady Garvan Collection of Furniture." *Yale Alumni* 25, no. 4 (January 1962): 6–17.

Rogers, "Garvan Furn. (1960)"
MEYRIC R. ROGERS. "Garvan Furniture at Yale." In *Connoisseur Year Book, 1960*, edited by L. G. G. Ramsey, pp. 52–63. London: Connoisseur, 1960.

Sack Coll.
American Antiques from Israel Sack Collection. 7 vols. to date. Washington, D.C.: Highland House Publishers, 1976–.

Sack, *Fine Points*
ALBERT SACK. *Fine Points of Furniture: Early American.* New York: Crown Publishers, 1950.

St. George, *Wrought Covenant*
ROBERT BLAIR ST. GEORGE. *The Wrought Covenant: Source Material for the Study of Craftsmen and Community in Southeastern New England, 1620–1700.* Brockton, Mass.: Brockton Art Center/Fuller Memorial, 1979.

Schiffer, *Furn. Chester County*
MARGARET BERWIND SCHIFFER. *Furniture and Its Makers of Chester County, Pennsylvania.* Philadelphia: University of Pennsylvania Press, 1966.

Schiffer, *Miniature Antique Furn.*
HERBERT F. SCHIFFER and PETER B. SCHIFFER. *Miniature Antique Furniture.* Wynnewood, Pa.: Livingston Publishing Co., 1973.

Schwartz, *Amer. Interiors*
MARVIN D. SCHWARTZ. *American Interiors, 1675–1825: A Guide to the American Period Rooms in the Brooklyn Museum.* New York: Brooklyn Museum, 1968.

Sheraton, *Cabinet Dictionary*
THOMAS SHERATON. *The Cabinet Dictionary.* 2 vols. London, 1803. Reprint. New York: Praeger Publishers, 1970.

Sheraton, *Cabinet-Maker and Upholsterer's Drawing-Book*
THOMAS SHERATON. *The Cabinet-Maker and Upholsterer's Drawing-Book.* London, 1793. Reprint. New York: Praeger Publishers, 1970.

Shestack, *Selections*
ALAN SHESTACK, ed. *Yale University Art Gallery: Selections.* New Haven, Conn.: Yale University Art Gallery, 1983.

Singleton
ESTHER SINGLETON. *The Furniture of Our Forefathers.* 2 vols. New York: Doubleday, Page, 1900–1901.

Southern Furn.
Southern Furniture, 1640–1820: A Loan Exhibition in Richmond at the Virginia Museum of Fine Arts, January 21–March 1, 1952. New York: Antiques, 1952.

Springer
LYNN E. SPRINGER. "American Furniture." *Saint Louis Art Museum Bulletin* 15, no. 3 (Summer 1980): 1–48.

Stoneman, *Seymour*
VERNON C. STONEMAN. *John and Thomas Seymour: Cabinetmakers in Boston, 1794–1816.* Boston: Special Publications, 1959.

Stoneman, *Supplement*
VERNON C. STONEMAN. *A Supplement to John and Thomas Seymour: Cabinetmakers in Boston, 1794–1816.* Boston: Special Publications, 1965.

Symonds and Ormsbee, *Antique Furn.*
R. W. SYMONDS and T. H. ORMSBEE. *Antique Furniture of the Walnut Period.* New York: Robert M. McBride, 1947.

Three Centuries of Conn. Furn.
Three Centuries of Connecticut Furniture, 1635–1935. Introduction by Luke Vincent Lockwood. Hartford, Conn.: Tercentenary Commission of the State of Connecticut, 1935.

Trent, "Postscript"
ROBERT F. TRENT. "The Chest of Drawers in America: A Postscript." *Winterthur Portfolio* 20, no. 1 (Spring 1985): 31–48.

Ward, *Eye of the Beholder*
GERALD W. R. WARD, ed. *The Eye of the Beholder: Fakes, Replicas, and Alterations in American Art.* New Haven, Conn.: Yale University Art Gallery, 1977.

Warren, *Bayou Bend*
DAVID B. WARREN. *Bayou Bend: American Furniture, Paintings, and Silver from the Bayou Bend Collection.* Houston: Museum of Fine Arts, 1975.

Wenham, *Collectors' Guide*
EDWARD WENHAM. *The Collectors' Guide to Furniture Design (English and American) from the Gothic to the Nineteenth Century.* New York: Collectors Press, 1928.

YUAG
YALE UNIVERSITY ART GALLERY, New Haven, Conn.

YUAG Bulletin
Bulletin of the Associates in Fine Arts at Yale University (1926–1957). *Yale University Art Gallery Bulletin* (1958–).

YUAG, "All That Glisters"
"All That Glisters: Brass in Early America." Exhibition. Yale Center for American Art and Material Culture, Yale University Art Gallery. 30 March–17 June 1979. Checklist and pamphlet by Marc Simpson.

YUAG, "A Century of Tradition and Innovation"
"A Century of Tradition and Innovation in American Decorative Arts." Exhibition. Yale University Art Gallery. 8 September 1979–20 January 1980. Checklist by Kevin L. Stayton.

YUAG, "Rhode Island Furn."
"Rhode Island Furniture." Exhibition. Yale University Art Gallery, September 1978–January 1979.

YUAG, "Southern Furn."
"Southern Furniture: Baltimore to Charleston." Exhibition. Yale Center for American Art and Material Culture, Yale University Art Gallery. 15 November 1978–15 February 1979. Checklist by Elizabeth Pratt Fox.

YUAG, "A Wide View for American Art"
"A Wide View for American Art: Francis P. Garvan, Collector." Exhibition. Yale University Art Gallery. 8 May–28 September 1980.

NOTES TO THE CATALOGUE

This catalogue is the third volume in a continuing series of publications devoted to the American furniture collections at Yale University, principally the Mabel Brady Garvan Collection housed in the Yale University Art Gallery. The goal of these catalogues is to make photographs and detailed objective information about each example of American furniture at Yale available to a wide audience.

This volume is devoted to case furniture and is divided into twelve sections containing entries for 233 objects in the collection in 1985. Each of the twelve sections (such as chests of drawers or desks) contains entries for objects that share a related form and function. Within each section, the objects are arranged in groups sharing similar gross stylistic features. Each group is then presented individually from north to south by region, with *region* being broadly defined as either New England, the Middle Colonies, or the South. This results in a roughly chronological presentation, although some exceptions occur. The reader should keep in mind that the order of objects adopted here is an artificial one employed solely for the purposes of this book and is not meant to imply or demonstrate any evolutionary or historical structure.

Readers also should be aware that this catalogue is meant to be inclusive rather than selective. A very high percentage of the American case furniture at Yale is included in the main body of entries and in the Appendix. No object has been excluded from this catalogue solely on the basis of aesthetic quality, and many objects that have been restored or altered to a greater or lesser degree have been included. Reference to replaced, added, or missing elements is made in the Condition section of each entry, to which careful readers are referred. Those objects that are clearly fakes, or whose integrity has been thoroughly compromised, are noted in an abbreviated fashion in the Appendix. The Yale collections also include a relatively small number of examples of English and European case furniture; these non-American objects have been omitted from this volume.

Each entry begins with a heading containing the name, place of manufacture, and date of each object as well as the name of its maker or makers when known or when an attribution seems justified. This heading is followed by a sequence of components that contain basic information about the object. The scope and nature of each component is described below.

Description: A detailed written description is provided for each object, beginning in most cases with a discussion of the object's formal visual appearance and then moving to notes on its construction. One or more photographs of each object are provided. The terms *left* and *right* when used in these descriptions and elsewhere in the catalogue refer to the viewer's left or right when looking at the object.

Inscriptions: With the exceptions noted below, reference is made to each inscription presently found on each object. Chalk signatures, printed labels, carved initials, and pencil shop marks are some but not all of the types of inscriptions noted here; however, the presence of Yale University Art Gallery accession numbers, painted in red in one or more locations on each object, and various other Art Gallery and university identifying numbers or stickers, are not recorded here. Most of the objects in the Mabel Brady Garvan Collection retain Francis P. Garvan's identifying number, usually painted in red (although sometimes in white) on one or more locations on the object. The presence of these Garvan numbers has not been noted here.

Condition: Major replacements, restorations, and other alterations are noted here. It is to be understood by the reader that each object has suffered the usual wear and tear commensurate with its age; for the most part, shrinkage

cracks, minor losses, and other customary signs of age are not mentioned. Most of the objects in the collection have been refinished during their lifetimes. Mention is made here of the object's finish usually only in those cases where the finish appears to be old and possibly original or when the finish is a rather glaring modern one. The objects in this collection had been worked on by many people, of course, before they entered Mr. Garvan's or the university's collections. Some dealers' shops, such as that of Jacob Margolis of New York, from whom Mr. Garvan acquired many objects in the 1920s, seem to have practiced more enthusiastic restoration practices than others. The objects in the Garvan Collection, prior to their gift to Yale, were cared for by Umberto Bongioanni, who worked for Mr. Garvan, and later for Mrs. Garvan, from early in this century until about 1940. From the establishment of the Furniture Study until 1977, the Art Gallery staff included a full-time conservator, first Emile Mazzola (1960 to 1972) and then Peter Arkell (1972 to 1977). Since 1977 Peter Arkell has continued to work on objects in the collection while maintaining an independent practice in Branford, Connecticut. Formal restoration reports, containing much greater detail than is given in this catalogue, are a part of the record preserved in each object's file since 1972. Prior to that time, restorations and repairs were noted on each object's work sheet in a less formal manner. Records of restorations conducted prior to 1960, while occasionally extant, are usually missing or extremely sketchy.

Woods: The woods used in the construction of each object and their location within the object are listed here. When no indication is given, the wood listed first is the primary wood, and the wood listed second, after a semicolon, is the secondary wood. Identification of the woods used in the furniture in this catalogue was undertaken in several different ways. For somewhat less than half of the objects, samples were taken by the curatorial staff of each suspected species and sent to Gordon Saltar or to the United States Forest Products Laboratory in Madison, Wisconsin, for microanalysis. This slow process, conducted by several Art Gallery staff members over the course of many years, was largely satisfactory but also contained some important flaws. For one, its accuracy hinged on the ability of the curator to recognize each species used in the fabrication of an object. The samples taken often had to be relatively large, and in some instances positive identification could not be made based solely on the sample. Feeling the need to have a more complete examination of each object made by a wood specialist and recognizing the benefits to the identification process and to the preservation of the object itself, I was fortunate to secure the services in 1984 of R. Bruce Hoadley, professor of wood science, Department of Forestry and Wildlife Management, University of Massachusetts at Amherst. Bruce and I examined together more than half of the objects included here in detail and reviewed many of the identifications made previously. It was often possible to make identification on the spot through the use of a hand lens or, in the vast majority of cases and in every instance where there was a shadow of a doubt, through microanalysis. This process saved wear and tear on the objects and allowed, we felt, for a more thorough and in some instances more accurate identification of the woods used in each object. More detailed information concerning the analysis of each sample is preserved in the file for each object. Latin names for some of the common names used frequently in this catalogue are as follows:

White ash	*Fraxinus americana*
Aspen	*Populus* spp.
Basswood	*Tilia americana*
Beech	*Fagus grandifolia*
Birch	*Betula* spp.
Butternut	*Juglans cinerea*
Eastern red cedar	*Juniperus virginiana*
Atlantic white cedar	*Chamaecyparis thyoides*
American black cherry	*Prunus serotina*
Chestnut	*Castanea dentata*
Cottonwood	*Populus* spp.
Red gum	*Liquidambar styraciflua*
Eastern hemlock	*Tsuga canadensis*
Hickory	*Carya* spp.
Mahogany	*Swietenia* spp.
Hard maple	*Acer saccharum*
Soft maple	*Acer saccarinum* or *Acer rubrum*
Red oak	*Quercus rubra*
White oak	*Quercus alba*
Eastern white pine	*Pinus strobus*
Red pine	*Pinus resinosa*
Southern yellow pine	*Pinus* spp.
Sycamore	*Plantanus occidentalis*
American black walnut	*Juglans nigra*
Yellow poplar	*Liriodendron tulipifera*

Latin names for other species are given in the individual entries.

Dimensions: Dimensions are given to the nearest tenth of a centimeter (2.54 centimeters equals 1 inch). At least three dimensions are given for each object. These are the maximum, or "outside," height (H), width (W), and depth (D), inclusive of all moldings, finials, tops, and other projecting features regardless of their age or condition. In most instances, other dimensions are also provided. These include the case width (CW) and case depth (CD), exclusive of any excrescences. In most cases, these will be the most useful dimensions for making comparisons with related examples. For objects with an upper and a lower case, dimensions are given for the upper case width and depth (UCW and UCD), and the lower case width and depth (LCW and LCD). For desks and desk and bookcases, depth dimensions are given for both the closed and the open positions. For slant-front desks, the case depth (CD) is taken below the slant front.

Exhibitions: Reference is made here in chronological order to every exhibition in which the object has been included, exclusive of several minor in-house exhibitions held during the years at the Art Gallery. The citation given, whenever possible, is to the exhibition catalogue. Many of the objects at Yale were placed on long-term loan to other institutions in the 1930s, 1940s, and 1950s. Information concerning these loans is contained in the object files and is not repeated here except in rare instances.

Bibliography: Reference is made here, again in chronological order, to each time the object has been published (exclusive of the exhibition catalogues listed in the above component but inclusive of sale and auction catalogues). In nearly every instance, the object is illustrated in the publication cited, and reference is usually made only to the figure number or page of the illustration. Readers should keep in mind, however, that the object may well be discussed in one or more places throughout the publication in question. References to illustrations of the object in newspapers or in antiques trade tabloids have been omitted, except in a handful of cases. Similarly, references to illustrations of the object when it was used solely as a publicity picture have been omitted. For example, at the time of the opening of the Mabel Brady Garvan Galleries in 1973, many periodicals printed views of the Garvan installation which included several of the objects in this catalogue; reference to these has been omitted. Complete records, again, are maintained in the object files.

Provenance: The history of ownership for each object is recounted here in as much detail as is known. When the provenance is traditional rather than documented, this has been noted.

These components are followed by a brief comment that discusses such matters as the evidence for the attribution of the object to a specific maker, shop tradition, or region, the existence of related examples, the manner in which the object was used, and other pertinent material. The commentary is followed by the Art Gallery credit line and the object's accession number. The first four digits of the accession number refer (in almost every case) to the year in which the object was acquired by the university; the digits after the period refer to the object's place within the numerical order of gifts and purchases within that year.

Most of the objects illustrated and described in this book are on view in the Mabel Brady Garvan Galleries of the Art Gallery, where they may be seen during normal Art Gallery hours, or are in storage in the Furniture Study at 149 York Street, where they may be examined by appointment. More information about each object is recorded in the object files located in the Furniture Study, files that are continually updated. Inquiries about the collection should be made to the Curator of American Decorative Arts, Yale University Art Gallery, 2006 Yale Station, New Haven, Connecticut 06520.

THE CATALOGUE

Pl. 1
Chest with drawer,
Connecticut Valley, 1670–1710
(cat. 28).

Pl. 2
Chest with drawer,
New Haven, Connecticut, 1660–1700
(cat. 33).

Color Plates 33

Pl. 3
Chest with drawers, probably South Shaftsbury, Vermont, 1820–1830 (cat. 43).

Pl. 4
Chest with drawers, Berks or Montgomery County, Pennsylvania, 1781 (cat. 45).

Pl. 5 Chest of drawers with doors, Boston, Massachusetts, 1650–1670 (cat. 51).

Pl. 6
Chest of drawers, northeastern Massachusetts or New Hampshire, 1795–1815 (cat. 67).

Pl. 7
Chest-on-chest, cabinetwork by Stephen Badlam, carved figures by John and Simeon Skillin, Jr., Dorchester Lower Mills and Boston, Massachusetts, 1791 (cat. 82).

Pl. 8
Chest-on-chest,
North Stonington, Connecticut,
1760–1780 (cat. 84).

38 *American Case Furniture*

Pl. 9
Chest-on-chest-on-frame,
attributed to the Dunlap family,
southern New Hampshire, 1790–1815
(cat. 88).

Pl. 10
Bureau dressing table, attributed to John Townsend, Newport, Rhode Island, 1785–1790 (cat. 109).

Pl. 11
High chest of drawers, Boston area or New York area, 1700–1720 (cat. 122).

American Case Furniture

Color Plates 41

Pl. 12
High chest of drawers, eastern Connecticut or Rhode Island, 1740–1760 (cat. 132).

42 *American Case Furniture*

Pl. 13
High chest of drawers,
Salem, Massachusetts,
1740–1760 (cat. 134).

Color Plates 43

Pl. 14
High chest of drawers,
Philadelphia, Pennsylvania,
1760–1780 (cat. 147).

44 *American Case Furniture*

Pl. 15
Desk and bookcase, attributed to the Townsend-Goddard families, Newport, Rhode Island, 1760–1790 (cat. 177).

Pl. 16 Desk and bookcase, John and Joseph W. Meeks, New York City, 1836–ca. 1855 (cat. 190).

Pl. 17
Cupboard, possibly by Peter Blin, Wethersfield, Connecticut, 1675–1690 (cat. 195).

Pl. 18
Cupboard, New Hampshire, probably Hampton,
1700–1740 (cat. 199).

48 *American Case Furniture*

Pl. 19
Clothespress, Pennsylvania, probably Chester County, 1750–1770 (cat. 201).

Pl. 20
Buffet, North Branford, Connecticut,
1750–1775 (cat. 205).

Pl. 21
Sideboard, Baltimore, Maryland,
1790–1810 (cat. 220).

Pl. 22 Sideboard, New York City, 1855–1865 (cat. 223).

Pl. 23
Cabinet, Alexander Roux, New York City, 1850–1870 (cat. 224).

Pl. 24
Sideboard, designed by Dan Cooper, New York City, ca. 1950 (cat. 227).

54 *American Case Furniture*

Pl. 25
Cellarette, New York City, 1810–1820 (cat. 229).

Boxes, Table Chests, and Other Small Objects

The box is the basic type of case furniture, made in a wide variety of forms only suggested by the Yale holdings. The collection is particularly rich in seventeenth-century boxes of oak and pine, often known today as "Bible boxes," but originally used to hold an assortment of small personal possessions. Inventory references suggest that these boxes were ordinarily placed on top of chests in the seventeenth-century interior, although there must have been considerable variation in their actual use. The examples in the collection are of New England origin, and all but one are of board construction and decorated with carving (cats. 2–8). The exception is an unusual joined box (cat. 1), a rare survival in American furniture. One box (cat. 3) can be attributed with some degree of confidence to Connecticut joiner William Buel, but most examples remain anonymous. Other early related forms not represented in the collection include the writing slope or table desk, a version of the oak box with a raised backboard and a sloping lid, often fitted with small interior compartments for the storage of writing equipment and papers, and the valuables cabinet, a small vertical box housing several boxes behind a hinged door. Several boxes in the collection are fitted with turned or bracket feet (cats. 10–14), a type of table chest particularly popular in Pennsylvania. The ancient origins of the form are suggested by the unusual Philadelphia coffer of 1816 (cat. 18), and the rich variety of specialized boxes made since the eighteenth century is represented by examples made for pipes and tobacco (cat. 15), medical supplies (cat. 16), tools for a Conestoga wagon (cat. 19), and a handful of other forms.

1

1

Box
New England, 1660–1680

Description: Trapezoidal in form, this box is of framed-panel construction. The overhanging top is cleated at the sides, has a thumbnail molding at the front and sides, and is attached to the back with snipe-bill hinges. The sides of the case have molded rails, embellished with red paint, and stop-chamfered stiles. The front rails are molded and painted, and the edges of the front panel are fitted with applied moldings fastened with wooden pins. There is base molding at the front and sides applied with rosehead nails. The four stiles, which are rabbeted to achieve the trapezoidal shape, extend below the base molding to form the feet. The top rails are double pinned at the stiles, while a single pin is used on the bottom rails. Faint grooves marking the placement of the rails remain visible on the rear stiles. The bottom is nailed in place. The rear rails are molded within the box.

Condition: The front board of the top, the two cleats, and the base molding on the right side have been restored. New red paint has been applied to the molded rails. The front board of the bottom is missing.

Wood: White oak.

Dimensions: H 33.2; W 72.1; CW 66.2; D 45.5; CD 43.3.

Exhibition: *Forgeries and Restorations*, no. 16.

Bibliography: Nutting, *Treasury*, no. 149.

Provenance: According to tradition, from Portland, Maine; Wallace Nutting, Framingham, Mass.; by sale in 1928 to Francis P. Garvan, New York, N. Y.

ALTHOUGH the Boxmakers were allied with the Joyners' Company in London, joined and paneled boxes of this kind are not common in English furniture and are encountered very rarely in American furniture.[1] This example was found in Portland, Maine, in the twentieth century, and its sturdy frame and molded stiles are reminiscent of chests and cupboards made in eastern Massachusetts. It is constructed, however, of white oak, thus leaving open the possibility that it was made in England. Boxes of this half-hexagon form, and related boxes in the shape of half an octagon, generally are referred to as lace boxes, and they may have been used to hold the semicircular lace collars or bands worn in the seventeenth century.[2] An American half-octagon-shaped box of board construction and a closely related English example dated 1673 have been published.[3] A century later, this early form was echoed by simple triangular boxes designed to contain the then-fashionable tricorn hats.[4]

The Mabel Brady Garvan Collection 1930.2145

1. Chinnery, p. 364. Chinnery (fig. 3:383) illustrates a rectangular English joined and paneled box dated 1636.
2. Several seventeenth-century American portraits depicting collars of this kind are illustrated in Fairbanks and Trent, *New England Begins*, vol. 3. Early references to boxes for lace bands and ruffles are quoted in *Bible Boxes*, pp. 5–6.
3. The American box, formerly in the collection of Luke Vincent Lockwood and now owned by the Henry Ford Museum (54.17.1), is illustrated in Nina Fletcher Little, *Neat and Tidy: Boxes and Their Contents Used in Early American Households* (New York: E. P. Dutton, 1980), fig. 6. The inscription and date of 1671 on this box are no longer accepted by the museum. The English box is illustrated in Chinnery, fig. 3:379. Another related English example, again of board construction, is illustrated in *Bible Boxes*, fig. 23. A joined and paneled box of uncertain provenance was illustrated and discussed in "The Editor's Attic: A Rare Box," *Antiques* 38, no. 4 (October 1940): 178–179. Similar in form to the Yale example, yet differing in construction, this box was then in a Massachusetts private collection; its present location is not known to the writer. It may or may not be the related box referred to in Nutting, *Treasury*, no. 149. Another English example of the half-hexagon-shaped form, in this instance mounted on a stand, is illustrated in *DEF*, 1: 89 fig. 11.
4. Little, *Neat and Tidy*, figs. 99, 100.

2

Box
Southeastern Massachusetts or coastal Connecticut, 1660–1690

Description: The top of this rectangular box of board construction overhangs at the front and sides and has thumbnail molding at the front and sides. It is attached with pintle hinges to the back; each end of the rear board is shaped so that a small piece projects to serve as a pin which is inserted through the cleat to secure the hinge. The front and back are simply butted and nailed to the sides. The projecting bottom is beveled at the front and sides and is nailed in place. The front is notched at the sides and carved in low relief with a band of alternating pendant and vertical S-scrolls containing leafage.

Inscription: "H S" is carved on the front in the central leaf and probably represents the initials of the unidentified original owner.

Condition: Traces of old reddish-brown paint remain. Small holes have been made in the center top and bottom of the front. Some of the original nails are missing, and, in the cleats, some have been replaced with modern screws. Small holes were made in the bottom board in 1973 when screws were used to secure the box to a display stand in the Garvan Galleries.

Woods: All four sides, cleats, white oak; top, bottom, southern yellow pine.

Dimensions: H 23.0; W 67.1; CW 61.7; D 41.6; CD 38.9.

Provenance: Israel Sack, Inc., New York, N. Y.; by sale in 1929 to Francis P. Garvan, New York, N. Y.

THE carved ornament on the front of this box represents a variation on the S-scrolls and leafage found on furniture made in southeastern Massachusetts. Here, the leafage is surrounded by scrolls with very straight sides, unlike the more curvilinear designs executed by John Houghton, John Thurston, and others working in Dedham, Medfield, and the surrounding area.[1] Like Houghton and Thurston, the maker of this box seems to have been trained, either abroad or in this country, in a tradition with origins in County Suffolk, England. This Suffolk tradition also was carried to the New Haven area by migrating craftsmen, who varied their designs (it has been suggested) to satisfy a clientele whose tastes had been shaped more strongly by London styles.[2] The particular modification of the basic design evident in this box probably represents the personal hand of a craftsman working in southeastern New England. A closely related box, now in the collection of the Henry Ford Museum (24.111.97), has been published.[3] Somewhat similar straight-sided S-scrolls are present on a box in the Brooklyn Museum (49.227), although the leafage contained within them is more stylized.[4]

The Mabel Brady Garvan Collection 1930.2260

1. Robert Blair St. George, "Style and Structure in the Joinery of Dedham and Medfield, Massachusetts, 1635–1685," in *American Furniture and Its Makers: Winterthur Portfolio 13*, ed. Ian M. G. Quimby (Chicago: University of Chicago Press, 1979), figs. 21, 22.
2. St. George, "Style and Structure," p. 28.
3. Robert Bishop, *Guide to American Antique Furniture* (New York: Galahad Books, 1973), fig. 3.
4. Nutting, *Treasury*, no. 130.

3

Box
Attributed to William Buel (d. 1681)
Windsor, Connecticut, 1640–1680

Description: The overhanging top of this large rectangular box has a bead-molded front edge, notched sides, and strips of chip and circular punch carving on each side of the top running from front to back above the location of the cleats. The cleats are nailed to the top with rosehead nails, and their thick back ends are bored to accept a pintle hinge and are shaped with scalloped and notched decoration. An oak board or slat has been nailed to the back of the box, and the ends of this slat are shaped to pins which fit into the cleats. The front and back of the box are rabbeted to accept the sides and are nailed in place. The sides of the box are carved with three rosettes and interlaced guilloche framed by bands of chip and punchwork carving. The front has rosettes, half circles, and pinwheels and is surrounded by the same chip carving and punchwork as found on the ends. The projecting beveled edges of the bottom are carved with dots and small crescents. The bottom is nailed in place. There is a till on the right side of the interior; its lid has a molded edge.

Inscription: "E D" is carved at the bottom edge of the center of the front and probably represents the initials of the unknown original owner.

2

3

Boxes 61

Condition: A small piece about 3 cm in depth has been added across the back edge of the top, and a 5-cm piece of wood has been added to the back edge of the bottom. The front edge of the bottom has been recarved, and there is a patch to the right of the keyhole. The box apparently was stripped and shellacked and was given a wash of red paint prior to its acquisition by the Art Gallery. Small holes were made in the bottom board in 1973 when screws were used to secure the box to a display stand in the Garvan Galleries.

Woods: All four sides, till, white oak; top, bottom, southern yellow pine.

Dimensions: H 23.3; W 81.3; CW 73.0; D 47.8; CD 40.8.

Exhibition: *Great River*, cat. 69.

Provenance: Possibly acquired by Mr. and Mrs. Morgan G. Bulkeley (1837–1922 and 1860–1938 respectively), early collectors and the parents of Houghton Bulkeley (1896–1966); purchased from Houghton Bulkeley's descendants by Nathan Liverant and Son, Inc., Colchester, Conn.; acquired from that dealer by exchange in 1971.

THIS box is the largest of the three known examples attributed to William Buel (or Buell), a joiner born in England who was located in Windsor by the late 1630s. The attribution is based on the close relationship between the carving on this box and one in the Metropolitan Museum of Art (10.125.2) to that on a box, now in the Oneida Historical Society, Utica, New York (1915.2), which descended in the Buel family and which, according to tradition, was made and owned by William Buel.[1] All three boxes are unusual in that they bear carving on their sides as well as their fronts. The Metropolitan Museum box also shares with the Yale example the distinctive construction feature of an oak slat nailed to the back of the box, the ends of which are shaped to pins which fit into the cleats. William's son Samuel (1641–1720) was also a joiner, active in Killingworth, Connecticut, and the possibility exists that he is the maker of this box.[2] A chest with related carving has been published.[3]

It is thought that William Buel was born just north of London, in Chesterton, County Huntingdon.[4] If such was the case, the boxes attributed to his hand, with their well-carved guilloche bands and individualistic ornament, represent an important link to an English regional tradition.

The Millicent Todd Bingham Fund 1971.45

1. Kane, "Joiners of Hartford County," pp. 78–81, fig. 11. The Metropolitan Museum box is illustrated in Lockwood, fig. 227.
2. Fairbanks and Trent, *New England Begins*, no. 173.
3. Lockwood, fig. 11.
4. Kane, "Joiners of Hartford County," p. 78.

4

Box
Connecticut Valley, possibly Windsor or East Windsor, Connecticut, 1670–1710

Description: The projecting top of this rectangular box is cleated and has thumbnail molding at the front and sides. It is attached to the back with snipe-bill hinges. The front and back of the box are rabbeted to receive the sides and are nailed in place. The front is carved with a symmetrical design of a central large flower flanked by flowing and curving tendrils of tulips, leaves, and vines on a matted background, and the sides of the front are notched. The projecting base is shaped with quarter-round molding at the front and sides and is nailed in place. The box retains old brown paint.

Inscriptions: "S L" is carved on the leaves flanking the central motif and probably represents the initials of the unidentified original owner. On the underside of the bottom is "91" in modern black paint.

Condition: The right cleat is a replacement. The top is badly split. Small holes were made in the bottom board in 1973 when screws were used to secure the box to a display stand in the Garvan Galleries.

Woods: All four sides, left cleat, white oak; top, bottom, southern yellow pine.

Dimensions: H 18.3; W 72.6; CW 67.2; D 42.5; CD 40.4.

Exhibition: Kirk, *Conn. Furn.*, no. 3.

Bibliography: Kirk, "Sources," fig. 5; Chinnery, fig. 3:390.

Provenance: Francis P. Garvan, New York, N. Y.; by descent to Mabel Brady Garvan, New York, N. Y.

THIS box is one of a group of at least eight related examples thought to have been made in the Connecticut Valley.[1] The front of each of these boxes is carved with a similar design, roughly symmetrical, featuring a central device from which a meandering vine with leaves and flowers extends against a matted background. The vine, leaves, and flowers of the Yale example are slightly thinner than those of the other

4

examples, leaving more of the front in reserve, and the tulips are more markedly asymmetrical, with an elongated center petal. John Kirk has linked this style of flat carving with that on other Connecticut Valley case furniture and has suggested that the source of the design was furniture made in the Lancashire area of northern England.[2]

Recently, William N. Hosley, Jr., has suggested that the group of furniture of which this box is a part may have been made in the Windsor or East Windsor, Connecticut, area in the 1680s. Hosley has further suggested that at least some of the objects in the group may be the work of Nathaniel Loomis (1657–1733), one of East Windsor's joiners.[3] (It is tempting to hypothesize that the carved initials on the Yale example may stand for a member of the Loomis family.) In the 1690s, Nathaniel Loomis made a box valued at six shillings for Samuel Rockwell of East Windsor, suggesting a contemporary value for the Yale box.[4]

Citing a lack of evidence that any of the Connecticut Valley's leading joiners emigrated from Lancashire, and observing that exact, line-for-line parallels between this American group and English work are not readily available, Hosley has emphasized the potentially original character of the American group's ornament, indicating, "it remains to be proven that this style was not primarily an American innovation." Although a precise relationship between this style of vine-and-leaf carving and an English regional tradition may not have been established conclusively, the variation found in American work in the handling of motifs cannot be said to be an innovation in any significant sense. The English origin of many American joiners is unknown, and many local traditions in England have yet to be studied thoroughly. Parallels may yet be revealed between this Connecticut Valley group and English furniture from an area other than the northwestern counties of Yorkshire, Lancashire, and Westmorland, although the evidence strongly suggests that the origins of the American group lie in the north of England.

The Mabel Brady Garvan Collection 1950.725

1. Among the related boxes are the following examples: in the Metropolitan Museum of Art (10.125.10); in Winterthur Museum (54.102.2); in the St. Louis Art Museum (illustrated in Springer, p. 6); formerly in the collection of H. W. Erving (illustrated in Nutting, *Treasury*, no. 133); in the private collection of Daniel P. Brown, Jr., West Granby, Conn. (formerly in the Philip L. Spaulding collection and illustrated in *Three Centuries of Conn. Furn.*, no. 22); in Old Sturbridge Village (illustrated

Boxes 63

in Marjorie Filbee, *Dictionary of Country Furniture* [New York: Hearst Books, 1977], p. 36); in the Mattatuck Museum, Waterbury, Conn. Related chests are in a private collection (see *Great River*, cat. 80) and Old Sturbridge Village.
2. Kirk, "Sources," p. 791.
3. *Great River*, cat. 80.
4. Kane, "Joiners of Hartford County," p. 80.

5

Box
Connecticut Valley, ca. 1686

Description: The rectangular box has a slightly overhanging cleated top with a thumbnail molding at the sides and front and is attached to the back with snipe-bill hinges. The front and back are rabbeted to accept the sides, and each joint is secured with three rosehead nails. The center of the front is divided into two panels by incised lines; the lower panel contains a stamped date. Flanking this decoration are two panels, each with a carved horizontal diamond and four carved pinwheels, one in each corner. The outside edge of these panels is formed by a vertical line of punchwork on a line with the nails. The bottom projects at the front, is beveled, and is nailed in place with rosehead nails. Traces of old red paint remain.

Inscriptions: The lower panel in the center of the front is stamped "1686."

Condition: The top, the hinges, and the cleats have been replaced, and there are repairs to the backboard around the area of the left hinge. A hole has been made in the top center of the front. There is a large shrinkage crack in the bottom.

Woods: All four sides, white oak; top, bottom, southern yellow pine; replaced cleats, yellow poplar.

Dimensions: H 18.4; W 74.0; CW 67.5; D 39.5; CD 37.9.

Bibliography: "A Record of Old New England," *Antiques* 41, no. 2 (February 1942): 136–137.

Provenance: In the collection of C. Sanford Bull, Middlebury, Conn., by 1942.

THE decoration on this box is a simplified version of the diamond motif found on much seventeenth-century furniture from the northwest of England, particularly from Lancashire, Yorkshire, and Westmorland. On the English examples, the corners or points of the diamonds are usually embellished with scrolls or flags.[1] Although stamped decoration and a diamond shape can be found on several chests from the Wethersfield area and the pinwheel is encountered frequently in Connecticut furniture, the simplicity and relative crudeness of the carving on this example makes a more precise attribution of origin problematical.[2]

Gift of C. Sanford Bull 1950.70

1. Kirk, *Am. Furn. & Brit. Trad.*, nos. 258, 266, 275–282. Also see Chinnery, figs. 4:113–150; and Anthony Wells-Cole, *Oak Furniture from Lancashire and the Lake District* (Leeds, England: Temple Newsam House, 1973).
2. Kirk, *Conn. Furn.*, nos. 32–34.

6

Box
New England, probably Massachusetts, 1670–1710

Description: The cleated top of this rectangular box projects at the sides and has thumbnail molding at the front and sides. It is attached to the back with snipe-bill hinges. The front and back are rabbeted to receive the sides and are nailed in place. The corners of the front are notched, and the center of the front is embellished with a geometric design in the "classical knot pattern" of carved and stamped semicircles and lines, flanked by vertical lines of stamped decoration, now very faint, including a zigzag line at the outside, a line of diamonds or "stars," a line of half circles, and trefoils.[1] The slightly projecting base is beveled at the front and sides and nailed in place. There is evidence that the front edge of the base was decorated with a stamped design related to that on the sides of the front. Traces of old orange and black paint remain.

Inscriptions: Illegible words and numbers, including "36," appear in chalk on the underside of the top. "I(?)J(?) Ingalls" is written in ink on the reverse side of the newspaper used to line the box.

Condition: The interior is lined with a Salem, Massachusetts, newspaper, probably an issue of the *Salem Gazette*, for August, 1841. Small holes were made in the bottom board in 1973 when screws were used to secure the box to a display stand in the Garvan Galleries.

64 *American Case Furniture*

5

6

Boxes

Woods: All four sides, red oak; top, bottom, cleats, eastern white pine.

Dimensions: H 23.9; W 70.6; CW 67.0; D 38.9; CD 38.1.

Provenance: Jacob Margolis, New York, N. Y., by sale to Francis P. Garvan, New York, N. Y.

ALTHOUGH this box of red oak and white pine almost certainly was made in New England, establishing a more precise place of origin is difficult. The use of an early Salem newspaper as a liner suggests that it was made in eastern Massachusetts, but other factors point toward western Massachusetts and the Connecticut Valley as its place of manufacture. The unusual compass-generated designs on the front of the box are related generically to those executed in paint on chests and cupboards from the Hadley, Massachusetts, area, while the stamped decoration on the corners of the front is reminiscent of similar stamped and punched decoration found on chests from the Connecticut Valley.[2]

The Mabel Brady Garvan Collection 1930.2234

1. See Chinnery, diagram 2:27n.
2. Fales, *Am. Painted Furn.*, figs. 20–23; Kirk, *Conn. Furn.*, no. 32; Hosley and Zea, "Decorated Board Chests," figs. 9–10.

7

Box
Connecticut Valley, 1670–1710

Description: The projecting top of this rectangular box is molded at the front and rear, notched at the sides, and pintle hinged to the back. The cleats are nailed to the top and are drilled to accept the pins, which are integral extensions of the back. The right cleat is drilled through, while the left cleat has a blind hole for the pin. The front and back are rabbeted to accept the sides and are nailed in place. Lines of stamped ovals contained within parallel lines run from front to back on each side of the top, and the front has lines of the same ornament running vertically just to the inside of the notched front corners. The front is also decorated with two horizontal molded lines moving across its middle. There is a central iron hasp lock, notched at each side, and below each corner of the lock is an incised, probably compass-drawn, pinwheel. The projecting bottom is beveled on all four sides and is nailed in place. The lock escutcheon is nailed to the front, and the hasp is hinged to the top.

Condition: The box retains an old coat of red paint. The hinge holding the hasp in place has been broken and nails have been added to hold it in place. The action of the hinged top has caused the back to pull away slightly from the sides.

Woods: All four sides, cleats, white oak; top, bottom, southern yellow pine.

Dimensions: H 19.1; W 60.5; CW 55.5; D 39.5; CD 36.5.

Provenance: Frank W. MacCarthy, Longmeadow, Mass.; by sale to Francis P. Garvan, New York, N. Y.

THE incised shadow moldings in combination with the pinwheels and other decoration of this box suggest that it is related to a group of board chests made in the lower Connecticut Valley, "where chisels, gouges, and punches were more often used in addition to planes to decorate chests."[1] The use of large lock plates on Connecticut boxes has been noted,[2] although this feature is seen on English boxes as well.[3] Here, the edges of the lock plate are notched to echo the notching on the sides of the front and top.[4] Further integration of the design is achieved by the repetition of the shadow molding and stamped decoration on the front and top.

The Mabel Brady Garvan Collection 1930.2239

1. Hosley and Zea, "Decorated Board Chests," p. 1146.
2. Randall, no. 3.

8

3. Chinnery, figs. 3:382, 3:384, 3:387.
4. Chinnery, fig. 3:381, is an English box with a similarly notched lock escutcheon.

8

Box
Massachusetts, probably Essex County, 1680–1710

Description: The projecting top of this rectangular box is cleated and has thumbnail molding at the front and sides. The sides are rabbeted to accept the front and back, which are nailed in place. A broad channel across the middle of the front contains applied vertical strips at the ends and in the center, thus creating rectangular recessed panels. These panels are edged with mitered moldings with reentrant points at each side. In the center of each panel there is a compass point surrounded by two concentric circles, visible in a raking light. The base projects, is beveled at the front and sides, and is nailed in place. There are traces of old black paint on the moldings.

Inscriptions: There appears to be some sort of lightly carved face, not original to the box, on the outside of the back.

Condition: The underside of the top bears a reddish stain or paint. The interior is lined with a nineteenth-century wallpaper featuring a strapwork design in beige, white, and green. A large shrinkage crack in the top has been filled. The top, which is now attached to the back with snipe-bill hinges, was pintle hinged originally. Some remains of the original pins can be seen on the backboard, and each edge of the back has been repaired. The cleats were modified by having their large rear portions, which would have been drilled to accept the pins, cut down. Small holes were made in the bottom board in 1973 when screws were used to secure the box to a display stand in the Garvan Galleries.

Wood: Eastern white pine.

Dimensions: H 23.5; W 71.3; CW 64.9; D 37.9; CD 37.3.

Bibliography: Nutting, *Treasury*, no. 129; Chinnery, fig. 3:392; Kirk, *Am. Furn. & Brit. Trad.*, fig. 466.

Provenance: Jacob Margolis, New York, N. Y.; by private sale, or at auction, to Francis P. Garvan, New York, N. Y., possibly in 1927.

In order to accommodate the channel across the front of this box, the sides have been rabbeted to accept the front and the back, rather than the reverse, as is more usually encountered. Although there is little evidence upon which to base an attribution, the mitered moldings with reentrant sides on this box are related to the designs found on the drawers of case furniture associated with Essex County, Massachusetts.[1] John Kirk has published English objects with drawer fronts decorated in a similar manner and has called attention to a related English box that is embellished with spindles as well.[2]

The Mabel Brady Garvan Collection 1930.2237

1. Fairbanks and Trent, *New England Begins*, no. 484; Fairbanks and Bates, p. 19.
2. Kirk, *Am. Furn. & Brit. Trad.*, fig. 465; the English box is illustrated in *DEF*, 1:89 fig. 12. See also *Bible Boxes*, fig. 19.

9

Box with added drawers
Possibly Massachusetts, ca. 1670 and ca. 1710

Description: This object appears to represent an unusual instance in which a seventeenth-century box was fitted at some time in the late seventeenth or early eighteenth century to a frame with two drawers, becoming in essence a

Boxes 67

9

small chest with drawers. The box was made in a normal manner, with the front and back rabbeted to accept the sides, which were nailed in place. The lid of the box was originally attached with snipe-bill hinges; these were removed when the transformation took place, and the top edge of the back of the box was rounded off to accept the top, which was then attached by means of a pintle hinge doweled to applied and shaped cleats. The bottom of the box, which was probably nailed to the underside of all four sides, was removed during the conversion, and a new bottom consisting of two half-lapped boards was installed with nails driven in through the sides of the box. The box was then supported on a framework with four stiles. These stiles were rabbeted on their upper inside edges to accept the box, which was nailed in place through the stiles. The stiles were then rabbeted in the other plane on their outside edges to accept horizontal boards, decorated with two lines of shadow molding, that were nailed to the rabbet and serve as the sides of the object. The rear stiles were also rabbeted on their inside edges to accept the back, a single horizontal board nailed to the rabbet. The front stiles were then joined with a drawer and bottom rail. The front of the box then became the top section in this new chest with two drawers. It was faced with mitered oak strips to bring its surface flush with the stiles and decorated with applied moldings with reentrant sides and with two initial plaques edged with more applied moldings. Heavy half-round molding was applied to the stiles, and to the front of the box and to the drawer rail, to separate and flank the drawers and box visually. Each drawer is decorated with moldings, both applied and cut from the solid, which form rectangles with reentrant pointed sides, and each has a round brass escutcheon with a drop pull. The drawer fronts are beveled, molded, and channeled on their horizontal plane, with applied vertical strips and moldings at the sides and with the reentrant corners also applied. The base molding is shaped from the bottom rail and overlaps the stiles. The drawers are side hung on runners rabbeted and nailed to the stiles. The drawer fronts are rabbeted to accept the sides, which are nailed in place through the front, with the nails then being covered by the applied moldings. The drawer backs are rabbeted to accept the sides, which are nailed through the back. The drawer bottoms are made of two boards joined with a tongue and groove and nailed to a rabbet in the front and to the underside of the sides and back with rosehead nails.

Inscriptions: "M" and "H" are carved on applied plaques fixed to the front of the box.

Condition: See Description. The object has suffered extensively from insect damage and from rot. The rear edge of the top has been pieced, the cleats are new, and it is very likely that the top is a replacement. The lock is missing. The current bottom boards of the box section are in especially poor condition. The box had been nailed shut at one time. Traces of red paint remain on the drawer divider and bottom rail.

Woods: Top, all four sides of original box, stiles, rails, bottom of box, drawer sides, red oak; side and back panels, drawer fronts, backs, and bottoms, applied moldings, eastern white pine; inlaid initial blocks, side blocks on front of box, aspen.

Dimensions: H 71.7; W 78.5; CW 69.2; D 47.5; CD 45.5.

Provenance: Avis and Rockwell Gardiner, Stamford, Conn. (dealers); by sale to Mr. and Mrs. Edward J. Nusrala, St. Louis, Mo.

AT first glance, this object appears to be a classic instance of the recombination of old materials into an unusual, diminutive, rare, and therefore desirable form designed to fool the unwary collector.[1] Typically, the object is without an early provenance and has no known parallels. However, the

materials used in its construction are old and have aged in a manner consistent with a date of ca. 1700, and it is entirely possible that this is an interesting case of an "adaptive reuse" of a seventeenth-century box. The reasons for building a framework around what was apparently a very plain box, barely a generation old at the time of the modification, remain inexplicable. The box hardly had had time to achieve status as a family heirloom worthy of preservation, and its utterly plain nature does not suggest that the box was saved for any intrinsic value, and, in any event, most of the box itself was covered up during the adaptation. The drawers give every sign of age and do not appear to have been removed from another object. They are a little too small to be the drawers from a chest with drawers or chest of drawers, and they are a little too large to fit comfortably in line in a cupboard. The drawer construction is related most closely to that on objects from southeastern Massachusetts, while the use of applied initial plaques was not uncommon in northeastern Massachusetts.[2]

Gift of Mr. and Mrs. Edward J. Nusrala 1984.56

1. The Art Gallery collection, for example, includes a miniature chest with drawers (Appendix, no. 3) that has been embellished with a paneled front and given three drawers instead of one, with turned feet also added; see Nutting, *Treasury*, no. 49.

2. St. George, *Wrought Covenant*, p. 26. Of the twenty-six objects attributed by Robert F. Trent to the "Emery School" of Essex County, twenty-one bear initials; see Trent, "The Emery Attributions," *Essex Institute Historical Collections* 121, no. 3 (July 1985): 218–219 table 2. A cupboard in this group, at the Ipswich Historical Society, bears the same initials as the Yale box.

10

Miniature chest
Northern New England, 1700–1740

Description: This miniature chest rests on four turned feet that are doweled through the bottom. The front and back are rabbeted to accept the sides and are nailed at the top and bottom. The cleated top has a molded front edge and chamfered sides and is attached to the back with snipe-bill hinges. The interior contains a till on the right side; the lid of the till has a molded edge. The chest retains much of its painted decoration on the front and sides. The front is decorated with a central stylized tree flanked by inward

10

curving branches and vertical bands at the sides, all in black (or possibly green) and white on a reddish ground. The sides are decorated with curved brush strokes in white and a dark color on a reddish ground, and the top retains traces of the reddish color. The projecting bottom is shaped to a quarter round at the front and sides and retains traces of green and white paint. It is nailed to all four sides.

Condition: The painted surface of the top is heavily worn, but the painted decoration of the front and sides, although faded, is largely intact. The rear half of the right side has been cleaned, revealing the original colors more accurately. The right rear foot is a replacement.

Woods: Top, bottom, side and bottom of till, basswood; all four sides, top of till, eastern white pine; feet, beech.

Dimensions: H 29.5; W 60.2; CW 56.2; D 33.3; CD 32.4.

Bibliography: *Antiquarian* 9, no. 4 (November 1927): 4.

Provenance: Henry V. Weil, New York, N.Y., by sale in 1927 to Francis P. Garvan, New York, N.Y.

ALTHOUGH varying in detail, the unsophisticated painted decoration of this miniature chest suggests an affinity with a group of painted furniture from northern Massachusetts and southern New Hampshire, including the "Sarah Rowell" cupboard in the Yale collection (cat. 200).[1] The central tree form flanked by leafy branches and the side decoration of commalike swirls indicate a relationship to this group,

although a precise place of manufacture for this example remains undetermined. The vertical zigzag bands on the sides of the front relate to similar carved lines on a New England box in the collection (cat. 6).

The Mabel Brady Garvan Collection 1930.2235

1. For a discussion of this group, see Esther Stevens Fraser, "Pioneer Furniture from Hampton, New Hampshire," *Antiques* 17, no. 4 (April 1930): 312–316; [Nina Fletcher Little], "Collectors' Notes," *Antiques* 86, no. 1 (July 1964): 85–86; and Fales, *Am. Painted Furn.*, p. 45.

11

Table chest

Pennsylvania, 1730–1770

Description: The cleated top of this small chest is attached to the back with wrought-iron strap hinges. The front and back are through-dovetailed to the sides. There is applied base molding at the front and sides; the bottom is a single board nailed in place. The interior contains an open till on the left, divided by partitions into one large longitudinal compartment and three small transverse ones at the rear. The chest is supported on four turned feet.

Inscription: "G.M." is stamped twice on the outside of the back.

Condition: The present set of hinges is at least the second set the chest has had; filled screw holes in the top edge of the back correspond with patches on the lid and indicate the location of small butt hinges. The underside of the top has been planed at each side to correct warpage, and the front left corner has been repaired. The brass escutcheon is a replacement. The till seems to have been reduced in width, and its bottom is a replacement in mahogany. New nails have been added to the dovetails. The feet are another problematical aspect of this object. The ball of the left front foot is considerably smaller, and the reel correspondingly larger, than those on the other three feet. Although the feet have been reglued, they appear to be old, and the bottom of the chest evidently has been supported on feet of some kind for many years, if not originally. Each foot, however, is of walnut, and has a dowel made of beech running through it from top to bottom; the dowel also extends through the bottom of the chest.

Woods: Sides, top, feet, some partitions in till, American black walnut; bottom, southern yellow pine; replaced bottom of till, mahogany; other partitions in till, probably red gum; dowels in feet, beech.

Dimensions: H 33.5; W 66.6; CW 63.3; D 31.6; CD 30.1.

Provenance: Charles Woolsey Lyon, New York, N. Y.; by sale in 1918 to Francis P. Garvan, New York, N. Y.

WITH its new hinges, reworked till, and possibly new feet, only the four sides and base molding remain by which to determine the date and origin of this chest. The combination of walnut and southern yellow pine in conjunction with through-dovetailing suggests Pennsylvania as its source. Somewhat similar miniature, or table, chests with related squarish, almost box dovetails, are dated 1744 and 1776.[1]

The Mabel Brady Garvan Collection 1930.2231

1. Schiffer, *Furn. Chester County*, nos. 127 (Chester County Historical Society), 143 (private collection). See also Schiffer, *Miniature Antique Furn.*, fig. 21, a miniature chest at Winterthur with restored feet; *Garvan Coll.*, no. 96; and another example at Winterthur (59.3583), illustrated in Scott T. Swank, "Proxemic Patterns," in Scott T. Swank et al., *Arts of the Pennsylvania Germans*, ed. Catherine E. Hutchins (New York: W. W. Norton, 1983), p. 53 fig. 14. The term "table chest" is derived from Garvan, *Pennsylvania German Coll.*

12

12

Table chest
Delaware Valley, 1760–1790

Description: The rectangular top is made of two boards and has recessed half-round molding on the front and sides; the lower half of the molding is applied. The top is attached to the back with butt hinges. The sides and front are lap dovetailed, with the joint exposed on the sides; the sides and back are joined in the same fashion, with the joint exposed on the back. The base molding, bracket feet, and central drop are formed of a single board nailed in place. It is mitered to the side boards which are of the same construction but lack the central drop. The bottom is a single board nailed in place. The bracket feet and central drop are braced with conforming horizontal glue blocks. The chest has a lock and a brass escutcheon.

Inscriptions: "R114" appears in yellow chalk on the inside of the front. There are traces of white chalk marks on the underside of the top, and "M D S" is lightly scratched there as well.

Condition: The present brass escutcheon was added in 1964. It approximates the form but is slightly larger than the original; the outline of the original escutcheon can be seen in early photographs of the chest before it was refinished. The hinges and the lock are replacements; shadow marks, nail holes, and a few surviving fragments indicate the size and location of the original strap hinges. There is a large shrinkage crack in the bottom. The glue block behind the left front foot is a replacement, and that foot has been repaired. The applied molding on the left side of the top has been damaged, and there are many new nails and nail holes in each section of this applied molding. The molding on the top does not slip over the side and front of the case as it should perhaps because of shrinkage, the new hinges, or alterations to the molding.

Woods: American black walnut; Atlantic white cedar.

Dimensions: H 21.5; W 48.8; CW 45.7; D 37.5; CD 35.9.

Bibliography: *Reifsnyder Coll.*, no. 150, illus. p. 82.

Provenance: Howard Reifsnyder, Philadelphia, Pa.; acquired at auction in 1929 by Francis P. Garvan, New York, N. Y.

The combination of walnut and cedar, the original use of strap hinges, the form of the bracket feet, and the decorative dovetailing all suggest a Delaware Valley origin for this small chest. A similar example, attributed to Pennsylvania, probably Chester County, is dated 1759, and a more elaborate version with decorative inlays from Schuylkill County was made ten years later.[1] Here, the exposed dovetails appear on the sides of the chest, rather than on the front as is more often the case.

The Mabel Brady Garvan Collection 1930.2439

1. Schiffer, *Miniature Antique Furn.*, no. 19; Philadelphia Museum of Art (53.125.4), illustrated in Garvan, *Pennsylvania German Coll.*, p. 11 no. 5.

13

Table chest with drawers
Pennsylvania, 1760–1800

Description: The rectangular top has applied molding consisting of an ovolo above a cove, grooved and pinned to a V-shaped rabbet. The top is attached to the back with large wrought-iron strap hinges fastened with rosehead nails. The front and back are secured to the sides with wedged through-dovetails. The front has a brass escutcheon, and

Boxes 71

13

there is half-round molding pinned to the front and sides above the two lipped drawers, each with a central brass pull. The base molding, bracket feet, and central drop of the front are formed of a single board pegged to the front. This board is attached to similar boards lacking the central drop on the sides with wedged through-dovetails. There are triangular rear feet nailed and pinned to the bottom. The interior of the chest section has a lidded till on the left; the lid and lower edge of the side are molded. The bottom of the chest is a single board fitted to grooves in the sides. The drawers are separated by a small vertical block pinned to the front and tenoned through the bottom; behind it is a strip serving as a drawer guide. The drawer sides are dovetailed to the front and back; the drawer bottom is a single board, beveled and fitted to a groove in the front and sides and pinned to the back with four wooden pins. The bottom of the object is again a single board, pinned to the sides.

Inscriptions: There is an old inscription consisting of about three illegible words in red chalk on the underside of one of the drawer bottoms. On the upper side of the bottom of the other drawer in black chalk or crayon is the modern "1987 / 26."

Condition: The bottom of the left front foot has been repaired, and the lip of the upper left corner of one of the drawers has been broken. It is possible that the part of the hinges attached to the top are replacements.

Woods: American black walnut; yellow poplar.

Dimensions: H 39.4; W 65.3; CW 60.8; D 29.9; CD 27.7.

Bibliography: Nutting, *Treasury*, no. 100.

Provenance: Henry V. Weil, New York, N. Y.; by sale to Francis P. Garvan, New York, N. Y.

THE massive quality and ponderous weight of this miniature chest belies its small size. Its construction with wedged through-dovetails, extensive use of wooden pins, and walnut and yellow poplar boards points toward a Pennsylvania origin. The chest conforms in most other particulars to the type of construction found on Pennsylvania German chests of all sizes made in the last half of the eighteenth century and through most of the nineteenth century.[1] Although walnut was not the preferred wood for these chests, which were usually made of a softwood and then painted, when walnut was used it was usually not painted and was often inlaid with sulfur. This chest bears an affinity to some far more elaborate Pennsylvania German walnut furniture, including several wardrobes and chests with drawers inlaid with sulfur.[2] The central drop on the front skirt of this chest is found on several related chests of larger size.[3]

The Mabel Brady Garvan Collection 1930.2464

1. Fabian, pp. 38–49.
2. This furniture is now attributed to Peter Holl III (d. 1825) and Christian Huber (1758–1820); see Beatrice B. Garvan and Charles F. Hummel, *The Pennsylvania Germans: A Celebration of Their Arts, 1683-1850* (Philadelphia: Philadelphia Museum of Art, 1982), pl. 1; Forman, "German Influences," pp. 161–162; and Fabian, fig. 208.
3. Fabian, figs. 103, 126, 231.

14

Table chest with drawers
Pennsylvania, 1800–1820

Description: The rectangular top is of a single board and is attached to the back with brass butt hinges. It has applied molding at the front and sides and a rectangle of inlay near the edges. The front is decorated with a rectangle with hollow corners of inlay above two drawers in line, each with a central brass pull and cock-beaded edges. Each side has a curved line of inlay simulating a carrying handle. The front

14

Dimensions: H 25.4; W 43.1; CW 40.2; D 18.6; CD 17.5.

Provenance: Charles Woolsey Lyon, New York, N. Y.; by sale to Francis P. Garvan, New York, N. Y.

Although they share a common form and Pennsylvania origin, this miniature chest is as light and thin as the preceding example is heavy and sturdy. The use of a dark inlay here on the front, sides, and lid, and the presence of cockbeaded drawers and a simply shaped base suggest that this example was made in the federal or neoclassical period in the early nineteenth century. The use of inlay to form trompe l'oeil carrying handles on the sides is an unusual embellishment.

The Mabel Brady Garvan Collection 1930.2465

and back are dovetailed to the sides with decorative through-dovetails. The drawers are separated by a vertical partition with a drawer runner behind and are flanked by small vertical partitions which are dovetailed to form a continuous line with the dovetails joining the front and sides. The base molding and bracket feet on all four sides are each formed of a single piece, through-dovetailed at the corners, and supported behind by vertical glue blocks. The front board has applied cock beading which is broken at the center and drops to form a decorative accent. The interior contains a till on the left side. In each drawer, the sides are dovetailed to the front and back with a single large dovetail; the bottom is a single board set into grooves in the front and sides and nailed with sprigs to the back.

Condition: The hinges are replacements, and a new strip was added to the top edge of the back to secure them in 1952. The till originally had a lid that is now lost. The glue blocks at the rear corners are replacements. One drawer bottom may be a replacement. Two small holes were made in the front base when the chest was attached with screws to a display stand in the Garvan Galleries in 1973.

Woods: American black walnut; drawer linings, eastern white pine; chest bottom, Atlantic white cedar; lower transverse guide, support in center of case, southern yellow pine; cock beading on drawers, inlay, American black cherry.

15

Pipe box
New England, 1750–1800

Description: The top edge of the back of this pipe box has a central pierced disk flanked by curves and scrolls. The sides are shaped with broken reverse curves that move down to the front. The front is pierced with a heart motif above crossed tobacco pipes and has a curved top edge. The single drawer runs the full depth of the box and is housed below the open vertical compartment formed by the four sides. The sides are butted and nailed together, and there are applied moldings nailed to the front and sides of the base and above the drawer. The sides of the lipped drawer are fastened to the front and back with a large dovetail and stand above the bottom; the drawer bottom is fitted to a groove in the front and is attached to the back with a single nail driven in from underneath.

Condition: About two-thirds of the left scroll of the back was missing and replaced in 1964. Several new nails have been used to secure the drawer side dovetails at the rear. The bottom edges of the drawer sides show considerable wear. There is a hole in the drawer front just above the existing brass button pull, marking the location of the original pull. The finish appears to be old.

Woods: Hard maple; chestnut.

Dimensions: H 47.1; W 15.9; CW 13.2; D 12.4; CD 11.7.

its front. In the eighteenth century, pipes were made in lengths ranging from 9 inches to 2 feet or more in length; the compartment in this box could accommodate easily pipes that were 12 inches or more long. The drawer would have been used for tobacco and for smoking equipment such as brass pipe tampers and small tongs of steel or brass used to grasp embers when lighting a pipe.[1] The combination of hard maple and chestnut suggests that this example was made in New England. The use of chestnut as a secondary wood points toward a Rhode Island or eastern Connecticut origin, and related examples featuring a pierced heart motif have been attributed to Connecticut.[2]

The Mabel Brady Garvan Collection 1930.2655

1. For a discussion of tobacco pipes and smoking equipment, see Ivor Noël Hume, *A Guide to Artifacts of Colonial America* (New York: Alfred A. Knopf, 1970), pp. 296–312.
2. Kirk, *Conn. Furn.*, nos. 7, 8. Pipe boxes are relatively common objects, although few are as gracefully curved as this example; for a variety of other New England examples, see *Sack Coll.*, 1:no. 484, 4:no. P3895, 5:nos. P4055, P4279, 6:no. P4732; Fales, *Deerfield*, nos. 566, 567; Kettell, nos. 6–8.

16

Medicine chest
Pennsylvania, 1775–1795

Description: The lid of this medicine chest is hinged and lifts to reveal a total of thirty-six small compartments for bottles, eighteen in the center section and nine in each swinging section. The front half of the chest is divided into two sections, closed with hook and eye, which swing out and back to be parallel with the rear section. When opened, the interior has an upper level of five niches or sections, the outer two greater in width. These niches are divided into two drawers, the upper drawer embellished with a carved shell (with the exception of the center section, which is one drawer fashioned to simulate two). The bottom section of the interior houses a single drawer running the full depth of the chest and with a double recessed front again shaped to simulate two drawers. The slightly projecting base is shaped to a quarter-round nosing. The domed top of the lid consists of several butted boards nailed to all four sides. The sides of the lid and the case are constructed with through-dovetails. The drawer dividers and vertical partitions on the interior

15

Provenance: Francis P. Garvan, New York, N.Y.

DESIGNED to be hung on the wall or to be freestanding, this pipe box served as a holder for inexpensive long-stemmed clay pipes of the kind depicted by the pierced decoration on

74 *American Case Furniture*

16

are housed in grooves, and there are full dustboards. The lower wide drawer in the interior is housed in a compartment with the top butted and nailed to the sides. The bottom is nailed in place. The drawer sides are dovetailed to the front and back, and the drawer bottoms are nailed into rabbets in the fronts, sides, and backs.

Inscriptions: "#769" is written in modern blue chalk on the underside of the bottom of the wide interior drawer.

Condition: Some interior pulls and the upper half of the lock escutcheons are replacements. One section of the domed top is a replacement, and the underside of the top was reinforced in 1965. Modern red baize has been glued to the bottom, and the front edge of the bottom has been pieced. The rear of the right side and back, and the corresponding drawers, are discolored and abraded and may have been damaged by fire or chemicals.

Woods: Mahogany, including bottom and partitions in bottle compartments; Atlantic white cedar.

Dimensions: H 36.9; W (closed) 35.7; W (open) 69.7; CW (closed) 34.7; D (closed) 35.6; CD (closed) 34.7.

Bibliography: *The Early American Collection of Mr. and Mrs. G. G. Ernst, Norwalk, Conn.,* 20–23 January 1926 (New York: American Art Galleries, American Art Association, 1926), no. 803.

Provenance: Acquired by Mr. and Mrs. G. G. Ernst, collectors, of Norwalk, Conn., between about 1898 and 1925; acquired at auction in 1926 by Francis P. Garvan, New York, N. Y.

Such small, portable objects, known variously as a "physic chest," "Travelling doctor's shop," "Family Medicine Chest," or other related names, were used in early America by both physicians and their patients. They were designed to hold small implements such as scales and weights and a mortar and pestle and contained numerous small compartments for bottles and vials of the many drugs used in treating illnesses.[1] This example is nearly identical to two other medicine chests with histories of ownership in the Philadelphia area. One, now owned by the Chester County Historical Society (61-77, Fbx 10), was by tradition owned by Dr. Joseph Gardner (1752-1794), who was born in Chester County, attended medical lectures at the University of Pennsylvania, and practiced medicine in Philadelphia in the late 1780s and early 1790s.[2] The second box, now owned at Bartram's Garden, near Philadelphia, was owned by Dr. James Howell

16a

Boxes 75

Bartram (1783–1818) and may have been owned by his grandfather John Bartram (1699–1777) the botanist. This chest descended in the Bartram family, with the accompanying tradition that it may have been made by James Bartram (1701–1770), a cabinetmaker of Chester County and brother of the botanist.[3] The use of Atlantic white cedar for the drawer linings of the Yale example (and probably in the other two as well) suggests an attribution to the Delaware Valley, and it may well be that James Bartram was their maker. Other published examples include a southern medicine chest in the collection of the Museum of Early Southern Decorative Arts; a labeled example by John Needles (1786–1878) of Baltimore; and a European chest with a history of ownership in America.[4]

The Mabel Brady Garvan Collection 1930.2121

1. *Medicine in Colonial Massachusetts, 1620–1820* (Boston: Colonial Society of Massachusetts, 1980), pp. 380–383. Contemporary references to the form can be found in the Gillows Estimate Book, nos. 1–464 (1787–1788), p. 150 (1787).
2. For Gardner, see James Grant Wilson and John Fiske, eds., *Appletons' Cyclopedia of American Biography*, vol. 2 (New York: D. Appleton, 1888), p. 598.
3. The chest was recently given by Dr. John Bartram to Bartram's Garden. The writer would like to thank D. Roger Mower for sharing information about the family history of this chest. For information on James Bartram, see Schiffer, *Furn. Chester County*, p. 282.
4. Marshall B. Davidson, *The Bantam Illustrated Guide to Early American Furniture* (New York: Bantam Books, 1980), p. 183; Fales, *Deerfield*, p. 284; *Medicine in Colonial Massachusetts*, fig. 77. See also Butler, *Sleepy Hollow*, no. 69; Leslie G. Matthews, *Antiques of the Pharmacy* (London: G. Bell & Sons, 1971), pp. 70–72, fig. 63; and Olive R. Jones and E. Ann Smith, *Glass of the British Military, 1755–1820* (Ottawa: National Historic Parks and Sites Branch, Parks Canada, Environment Canada, 1985), pp. 87–88.

17

Miniature sideboard or chest of drawers
American, 1790–1820

Description: The rectangular top is of a single board and overhangs the case at the front and sides. Its front and side edges are veneered and edged with light-wood stringing at top and bottom. The case holds six veneered drawers, three in line over three deeper drawers in line, with the center drawer in each line wider. Each drawer has a central round brass escutcheon with a knob pull, and each is edged with light-wood stringing. The drawers in the upper tier have inlaid ovals formed by lines of light- and dark-wood stringing, and those in the lower tier have similar stringing forming rectangles with hollow corners. The drawers are flanked by rectangles of light-wood stringing on the four front legs. The top and bottom rail and the drawer dividers are veneered, and the lower edge of the bottom rail is inlaid with alternating light- and dark-wood stringing that extends to the sides and the rear legs. The four legs at the corners are straight on their outside edges and tapered on their inner edges; the two middle legs in the front are tapered on both sides; there are no middle legs in the rear. The front face of the four front legs is outlined with light-wood stringing, interrupted by an inlaid cuff at the front and sides. The top is screwed from underneath to the top front rail and pocket screwed from the inside of the back and sides. There are three transverse braces under the top, slot dovetailed to the top front rail and to the back. The back and sides are slightly recessed single boards tenoned to the legs; the top and bottom rails are slot dovetailed to the corner legs, and the middle legs are housed in the bottom rail and tenoned through the top rail. The drawers are separated by vertical partitions housed in a groove in the back and supported at the bottom by the drawer runner that is tenoned to the back; the partitions are also nailed in place through the back and through the drawer runner. The other drawer runners and guides are nailed and glued to the sides and to the vertical partitions; those on the sides at the bottom level are rabbeted at the

front to the rail, and those in the middle level are tenoned to the drawer dividers. Small strips are glued to the back as drawer stops. The drawer sides are dovetailed to the front and back; the bottoms are beveled on their front and side edges and let into grooves in the front and sides, with no nails used. There are no dustboards or a bottom.

Inscriptions: The modern "C.1317" is written in pencil on the outside of the right side of the upper right drawer.

Condition: Many small repairs were made to the inlays and veneer by Edward Hoepfner in 1952. Some of the drawer bottoms have been repaired, and the back of the lower right drawer has been replaced. The escutcheon on the lower center drawer is missing.

Woods: American black walnut and walnut veneer; light- and dark-wood stringing; eastern white pine.

Dimensions: H 29.7; W 54.5; CW 52.1; D 29.2; CD 27.6.

Bibliography: *Illustrated Catalogue of the Rare and Extremely Choice Collection of Early American and English Furniture Formed . . . by . . . Mr. Louis Guerineau Myers*, 24–26 February 1921 (New York: American Art Association, 1921), no. 557; Schiffer, *Miniature Antique Furn.*, no. 222.

Provenance: Louis Guerineau Myers (d. 1932), New York, N. Y.; acquired at auction in 1921 by Francis P. Garvan, New York, N. Y.

This object has been published as a miniature sideboard, although if proportionally enlarged it would resemble no known object. (Miniature sideboards more akin to their larger counterparts are known, including three examples in the Winterthur collection.)[1] Assigning a precise place of origin to this miniature is thus difficult. The combination of walnut and white pine was common in Pennsylvania, where (it is said) large numbers of miniatures were made.[2] A miniature chest of drawers has been published that contains three drawers in line above a single wide drawer decorated to appear as three in line, thus creating the same basic appearance of drawer arrangement as present in the Yale example. Attributed to Rhode Island, this chest of drawers has inlaid decoration, but it is supported on bracket feet and lacks the overhanging top found here.[3]

The Mabel Brady Garvan Collection 1930.2462

1. Schiffer, *Miniature Antique Furn.*, figs. 217, 219; Jane Toller, *Antique Miniature Furniture in Great Britain and America* (London: G. Bell & Sons, 1966), fig. 22.

2. Schiffer, *Miniature Antique Furn.*, p. 29.

3. *Fine American Furniture, Silver, and Decorative Arts*, 23 January 1982 (New York: Christie, Manson, and Woods International, 1982), no. 391. See also a miniature chest with two drawers and related legs, attributed to Connecticut, illustrated in *Sack Coll.*, 5:1382 no. P4310.

18

Coffer
Philadelphia, Pennsylvania, 1816

Description: The stepped oval top of this coffer, or strongbox, has a central engraved oval plaque and is veneered with mahogany outlined with light-wood stringing and with crossbanding. The horizontal surfaces of the top are veneered with mahogany, while the vertical surfaces are veneered with tiger maple and small rectangles of mahogany. The front of the lid is fitted with a central cast-brass pull flanked by brass knobs, and the lid is attached to the back with four sets of brass butt hinges. The oval case is veneered with four panels of mahogany veneer outlined with maple and tiger-maple veneer. The chest is fitted with three locks, each with with a shield-shaped ivory keyhole surround, and there are brass carrying handles at each side. The chest is supported by four turned ivory feet. The lid opens to an interior with lidded compartments in each end, extending nearly the depth of the case. The plaque is a silvered base metal and is attached to the top with two spikes projecting into the top and with a threaded post held in place from below with a washer and nut. The rounded ends of the base are laminated, and the bottom is nailed in place.

Inscriptions: The engraved plaque on the top reads: "Die Hermann Interstutzungs / PHILADA / Incorporit den lsten May / Im JAHR / 1816. / Bruderschafft." Translated literally, this inscription reads: "The Hermann Relief [or Aid] Brotherhood [or Fellowship], incorporated the first of May in the year 1816." Engraved below the letter L in PHILADA is "J. Bower. Sc." Modern printed labels affixed to the underside of the inner compartments read: "ROBERT F. MURRAY. / CABINET MAKER / 55th St., one door below Chester Ave., West Phila."

Condition: The coffer has undergone some restoration, presumably at the hands of Mr. Murray of Philadelphia, and by Emile Mazzola in 1965. New braces have been added to the inside of the case to correct warpage. The lidded com-

Boxes 77

18

partments in the interior are replacements. There have been many minor repairs to the veneer, and there are new strips in the bottom running from front to back between the feet. New screws also have been added to the bottom.

Woods: Mahogany and maple veneer, some with the tiger figure, over a frame of yellow poplar; lowest and outer portion of lid, cherry; lidded compartments on interior, maple; new braces, oak.

Dimensions: H 41.3; W 77.2; D 41.3.

Bibliography: Beatrice B. Garvan, *Federal Philadelphia, 1785–1825: The Athens of the Western World* (Philadelphia: Philadelphia Museum of Art, 1987), p. 45 fig. 30.

18a

Provenance: Mrs. A. K. Hostetter (dealer), Lancaster, Pa.; by sale in 1936 to Francis P. Garvan, New York, N. Y.

THIS unusual coffer probably served as the ceremonial money chest of an immigrant aid society founded in 1816 in Philadelphia for the relief of newly arrived German immigrants. Such societies were common in Pennsylvania, Maryland, and other areas where there was a heavy influx of German settlers.[1] One of their principal functions was lending money, and with its traditional three locks, this coffer would have served the Hermann Society well as its strongbox or money chest. The coffer also may have been made, as Beatrice B. Garvan has suggested recently, for the grand master of the Hermann masonic chapter in Philadelphia, founded in 1810. Although one cannot be certain, the society (or chapter) was probably named after Arminius (the Latinized form of Hermann), the German national folk hero who thwarted the Roman conquest of Germany before his murder in A.D. 21.[2] By the nineteenth century, his name had become identified with German resistance to Napoleon's forces. Such a nationalistic name would have been an appropriate choice for settlers who wished to retain at least some of their ethnic identity in a new land. John Bower, active in Philadelphia from 1809 to 1819, is perhaps best known for his *View of the Bombardment of Fort McHenry*.[3] In 1816, Bower resided at 80 North Fourth Street in Philadelphia.

The Mabel Brady Garvan Collection 1936.312

1. Erna Risch, "Immigrant Aid Societies before 1820," *Pennsylvania Magazine of History and Biography* 60, no. 1 (January 1936): 15–33.
2. N. G. L. Hammond and H. H. Scullard, eds., *The Oxford Classical Dictionary* (2d ed.; Oxford: Clarendon Press, 1970), p. 121. I would like to thank Scott. T. Swank of Winterthur Museum for initially suggesting this interpretation.
3. *Antiques* 92, no. 4 (October 1967): 562.

19

Conestoga wagon toolbox
Pennsylvania, 1800–1850

Description: The sloping top has notched edges, wrought-iron hinges with simple scroll ends, and a wrought-iron hasp lock. It opens to reveal a plain interior. The front is butted and nailed to the sides, and the box is bound with simple

bands of wrought iron that originally were nailed to the side of the wagon. The sides are shaped at the rear to conform to the side of the wagon and slant forward at the front. Originally, the side of the wagon served as the back of the box. Several layers of blue paint remain.

Condition: The top had been nailed to the sides, and a brace had been added across the back in modern times. These alterations were removed in 1981 when the box was stabilized by being mounted on a display stand shaped to simulate the side of a Conestoga wagon. There has been considerable loss of paint, and there are large cracks in the top.

Wood: Yellow poplar.

Dimensions: H 43.7; W 36.4; CW 34.5; D 20.2; CD varies from 15.5 to 20.1.

Provenance: Francis P. Garvan, New York, N.Y.

Boxes such as this example were fastened to the sides of Conestoga wagons and used to hold a variety of tools and other materials needed to repair these vehicles on their trips westward. Although some examples are ornamented with ornate wrought-iron decoration, this toolbox is relatively plain.[1] Most toolboxes are the work of anonymous craftsmen but an example by Henry S. Hersh (1833-1917) of New Danville, Pequea Township, Lancaster County, is in the collection of the Pennsylvania Farm Museum at Landis Valley.[2]

The Mabel Brady Garvan Collection 1930.5051

1. George Shumway, Edward Durell, and Howard C. Frey, *Conestoga Wagon, 1750–1850: Freight Carrier for 100 Years of America's Westward Expansion* (2d ed.; York, Pa.: George Shumway and Early American Industries Assoc., 1966), pp. 189–196 and passim. The contents of a toolbox are illustrated and listed in fig. 75, and boxes in situ can be seen in many of the illustrations in this book.
2. Beatrice B. Garvan and Charles F. Hummel, *The Pennsylvania Germans: A Celebration of Their Arts, 1683–1850* (Philadelphia: Philadelphia Museum of Art, 1982), checklist no. 140.

19

Chests and Chests with Drawers

One of the oldest of furniture forms, the chest consists of a large box with a hinged lid, designed for the storage of textiles, clothing, and other articles. Most examples are fitted with a lock, and many contain a lidded till on the interior, providing a discrete compartment for holding small items that otherwise would be difficult to locate in the large, undifferentiated open space of the carcass. Some examples are fitted with one, two, or occasionally three drawers housed below the chest section. In some instances, the facades of these chests *with* drawers are decorated to simulate more fashionable chests *of* drawers (cats. 36–43). The collection includes thirty examples, ranging in date from the middle of the seventeenth century to the early nineteenth century. A dozen early New England joined chests (cats. 20–32) are included, among them two chests attributed to Peter Blin of Wethersfield (cats. 26, 27) and four Hadley chests from the upper Connecticut Valley (cats. 28–31). Eleven less expensive board chests from New England (cats. 33–43) are also included, representing a common form of case furniture. Five painted chests decorated in the Pennsylvania German manner (cats. 44–48) and two paneled chests from the eastern shore of Maryland (cats. 49, 50) give geographical diversity to the collection. Chests exhibit a rich variety of style-bearing ornament, including carving, paneling, applied spindles, moldings, and bosses, and painted decoration in the form of solid colors, floral and other decorative designs, stenciling, and graining.

- top
- snipe-bill hinges
- cleat
- shadow molding
- pin
- top rail
- applied boss
- applied split spindle
- applied molding
- side panel
- applied boss
- pull
- left stile

20

20

Chest
Connecticut, probably New Haven, 1640–1680

Description: The cleated rectangular top of this chest has thumbnail molding at the front and sides and is attached to the back with snipe-bill hinges. The front is framed to three panels carved with artificial leaves and rosettes forming arches. The stiles, muntins, and top rail have a shallow molding at their panel edges, and the bottom rail is stop chamfered. The top rail is carved with a band of lunettes; the stiles have convex V-shaped molding at their center with alternating diagonal lines and dots; the muntins are carved with an artificial leaf; and the lower rail has carving, probably in imitation of rope carving, on a convex V-shaped molding above a line of gouged notches. The sides are framed to two panels side by side, with the frame edges molded and chamfered as at front. The back is framed to four panels. The mortise-and-tenon joints are double pinned, with the exception of single pins used in the side muntins. The bottom is made of several boards fitted together with a V-shaped tongue and groove; they are nailed to the underside of the back rail and to a rabbet in the front and sides.

Inscriptions: A Connecticut Tercentenary label is pasted to the inside of the left top rail; a "Connecticut Furniture" (1967) exhibition label is pasted to the underside of the top.

Condition: The cleats have been replaced, and the areas around the hinges and the lock have been repaired. Traces of new black paint are visible on the top. One of the bottom boards is a replacement, and the till is new.

Woods: Stiles, rails, panels, bottom boards, white oak; top, eastern white pine; replaced till, yellow poplar.

Dimensions: H 68.6; W 121.3; CW 115.6; D 49.8; CD 48.5.

Exhibitions: *The Hudson-Fulton Celebration*, vol. 2 (New York, 1909), p. 49 no. 67; *Three Centuries of Conn. Furn.*, no. 1; Kirk, *Conn. Furn.*, no. 9; Kane, *Furn. New Haven Colony*, no. V.

Bibliography: Lyon, fig. 1; Nutting, *Treasury*, no. 1; Kettell, *Early American Rooms*, facing p. 57; Nagel, pl. 3a; Kane, "Joiners of Hartford County," fig. 9; Kane, "New Haven Colony Furn.," fig. 3; Chinnery, fig. 4:193; Elizabeth Stillinger, *The Antiquers* (New York: Alfred A. Knopf, 1980), p. 73; Milo M. Naeve, *Identifying American Furniture* (Nashville,

20a

Chests and Chests with Drawers 83

Tenn.: American Association for State and Local History, 1981), fig. 10; Kirk, *Am. Furn. & Brit. Trad.*, fig. 423.

Provenance: This chest was "Bought, about 1880, in Windsor, Conn., from Havens family," by Irving Whitall Lyon (1840–1896), Hartford, Conn.[1] It passed by descent to his son Irving Phillips Lyon; probably by sale to C. Sanford Bull, Middlebury, Conn., who was the owner listed by Nutting in 1928; probably by sale to Charles Woolsey Lyon (Irving W.'s son and Irving P.'s brother), New York, N. Y.; by sale in 1929 to Francis P. Garvan, New York, N. Y.

ALTHOUGH purchased in Windsor in the late nineteenth century, this chest has in recent years been attributed to New Haven.[2] In common with many examples of carved furniture linked to the New Haven area, the motifs used here in such profusion can be found on many examples of English furniture from the West Country, especially Gloucestershire and Somerset.[3] Patricia E. Kane has called attention to two related chests in the collection of the Metropolitan Museum of Art (47.133.3 and 1931.30) and one in the New Haven Colony Historical Society (1973.318), which share many construction similarities but which appear to have been carved by a different hand.[4] A chest in the collection of the Baltimore Museum of Art has related carving, and similar carved panels are also found on a chest at Historic Deerfield.[5]

The Mabel Brady Garvan Collection 1930.2262

1. Lyon Notebook, 1:92, Irving P. Lyon Papers, Winterthur Library, 78 x 314.596, 602, 602a.
2. Kane, *Furn. New Haven Colony*, no. V.
3. Anthony Wells-Cole, *Oak Furniture from Gloucestershire and Somerset* (Leeds, England: Temple Newsam House, 1979), passim; Kirk, *Am. Furn. & Brit. Trad.*, figs. 424, 425; Chinnery, fig. 4:193a; Kirk, *Conn. Furn.*, no. 274 (a chair identified by Anthony Wells-Cole as "of West Country type . . . said to have come from Exeter").
4. Kane, *Furn. New Haven Colony*, nos. II-IV.
5. Craig Gilborn, *American Furniture, 1660–1725* (London: Country Life Collectors' Guides, 1970), figs. 44, 45; Fales, *Deerfield*, fig. 351.

21

21

Chest
New Haven Colony, possibly Guilford, 1650–1680

Description: The rectangular cleated top is framed to four panels, with the rails stop chamfered and the stiles and muntins molded on their panel edges. The rail at the back of the top is tenoned to the stiles, while the stiles are tenoned to the front rail, which has a molded front edge. The top is attached to the back with snipe-bill hinges. The front is framed with three panels, each carved with the double-heart motif against a matted ground. The top rail and stiles are molded on their panel edges; the muntins have a shadow molding on their panel edges and a central faceted channeling; the bottom rail is stop chamfered at the panel edges and has a shadow molding at the lower edge. The front is fitted with an iron lock and escutcheon. The sides are framed to two panels, with molding and chamfering on the framing elements as on the front. The back is framed to three panels with beveled edges; the back rails, stiles, and muntins are not molded or chamfered, and the panels are riven. The interior contains a lidded till on the right side; the lid is pintle hinged at the stiles and shaped to fit around them. The framing elements of the back are molded and chamfered on the inside to conform with the front. The bottom of the chest is made of five narrow transverse boards, fitted together with a V-shaped joint, and let into grooves in the front and side rails and nailed to the back rail. The chest retains an old coat of reddish-brown paint.

84 *American Case Furniture*

Condition: Two of the bottom boards are replacements, and the side and bottom of the till are new. Modern screws have been added to reinforce the nails joining the bottom to the back rail, and a line of small modern nails appears on the bottom edge of the front and side rails.

Wood: White oak.

Dimensions: H 72.9; W 128.5; CW 122.8; D 61.8; CD 55.9.

Exhibitions: Kirk, *Conn. Furn.*, no. 12; Kane, *Furn. New Haven Colony*, no. XIX.

Bibliography: *Antiques* 16, no. 6 (December 1929): 453; *Flayderman Coll.*, no. 498; Kane, "New Haven Colony Furn.," p. 954; Chinnery, fig. 4:57; Kirk, *Am. Furn. & Brit. Trad.*, fig. 417.

Provenance: From the estate of William B. Goodwin (1866–1950), East Hartford, Conn.; Philip Flayderman, Boston, Mass.; acquired at auction in 1930 by Francis P. Garvan, New York, N. Y.

THE double-heart motif carved on the panels of this chest and the following example can be traced to the West Country of England, probably Gloucestershire, where it was a common feature on pulpits and furniture of the seventeenth century.[1] The use of white oak and the paneled top, unusual in American furniture, raise the nagging thought that this chest may be of English rather than American origin. However, its close relationship to the following example, which has a history of ownership in Guilford, and to other related chests found in America points toward an American origin. A variant of the double-heart motif is found on a chest attributed to Plymouth, Massachusetts; this chest also has a paneled top.[2]

The Mabel Brady Garvan Collection 1930.2265

1. Anthony Wells-Cole, *Oak Furniture from Gloucestershire and Somerset* (Leeds, England: Temple Newsam House, 1976), p. xiv fig. 15, nos. 3, 8, 25. See also Chinnery, fig. 4:57 (top). An English example dated 1655 is in the Philadelphia Museum of Art.

2. St. George, *Wrought Covenant*, no. 41. See also *Sack Coll.*, 6:1630 no. P4741.

22

Chest
Guilford, Connecticut, 1675–1700

Description: The top of this chest is made of four boards butted together horizontally and secured with cleats. The top projects at the sides, has thumbnail molding at the front and sides, and is attached to the back with iron hinges. The chest is of framed-panel construction with riven boards. Each mortise-and-tenon joint is secured with two pins. The front contains three panels, each carved with a double-heart motif against a matted background. The upper rail and stiles have edge molding at the panel edge, and the lower rail is chamfered at the panel edge and has channel molding at the lower edge. The muntins have edge molding and central molding. Each side is framed to a single large panel, and the rails and stiles are decorated with the same motifs as appear on the front. The back contains a large panel consisting of two boards butted together horizontally. The bottom is made of several small boards fitted together with a V-shaped joint, placed in a groove in the front and sides and nailed to the rear rail. The stiles continue below the rails to form the feet. On the interior, the lower inside edge of the rear top rail is

21a

22

23

molded, and the top inside edge of the rear bottom rail is beveled.

Condition: The till, originally located on the right side of the interior, is missing. The present pair of hinges is the third set to be used on the chest; evidence of another set of strap hinges can be seen on the underside of the top, and part of the original snipe-bill hinges remain in the top rail of the back. The cleats are old but not original.

Woods: Top, rails, stiles, front and side panels, white oak; bottom boards, back panel, chestnut.

Dimensions: H 72.5; W 128.2; CW 120.4; D 55.7; CD 54.4.

Exhibition: Kane, *Furn. New Haven Colony*, no. XX.

Provenance: Bequeathed to the university in 1887 by Charles Wyllys Betts (1845–1887), New York, N. Y. An entry in a notebook kept by early furniture historian Irving Lyon refers to this chest and states that Betts "Obtained it from the home of Cornelia Eliot, of Guilford, a descendant of Reverend Joseph Eliot (Mrs. Eva B. Leete, Guilford)."[1] No estate inventory for the Reverend Joseph Eliot has survived.

THE traditional history of this chest in the Eliot family helps to substantiate its attribution to Guilford. Although closely related to the previous example (cat. 21), Patricia E. Kane has suggested that this chest and at least two related examples may be of slightly later date because they are made of thinner pieces of wood and contain fewer and larger panels.[2] A chest with drawer recently acquired by the Museum of Fine Arts, Boston (1982.218), contains both the double-heart motif found on this example and the S-scroll carving found on other Guilford-area objects (cat. 23).

Bequest of Charles Wyllys Betts, B.A. 1867 1887.5

1. Lyon Notebook, 1:19, Irving P. Lyon Papers, Winterthur Library, 78 x 314.565, 569.
2. Kane, *Furn. New Haven Colony*, no. XX, which illustrates related chests in the Metropolitan Museum of Art (10.125.25) and the Art Institute of Chicago (43.1062).

23

Chest
Guilford, Connecticut, 1650–1700

Description: The cleated top of this chest has a thumbnail molding at the front and sides. It consists of three boards butted together and secured by cleats. The chest is of framed-panel construction, and each mortise-and-tenon joint is double pinned, with the exception of the side muntins which are secured with a single pin. The front contains three panels carved with foliated S-scrolls. The muntins are edge molded, and the top rail of the front has edge molding above the panels. The bottom rail is chamfered below the panels and has channel molding on its lower edge. The front stiles have

86 *American Case Furniture*

faint edge molding and continue below the rails to form the feet. The sides have two panels and the rails and muntins are decorated in the same manner as the front. The back is shaped with three panels, and its inner face has edge molding and chamfering echoing the design of the front. Several boards are butted together to form the bottom. They are beveled and fitted into grooves in the front and sides and nailed to the back rail.

Condition: The top and bottom are replacements. The till, originally on the right side of the interior, is missing. The rear legs have been repaired and pieced. Two holes have been drilled through the upper rail of each side to accommodate a rope handle, now missing, which appears in early photographs. The original snipe-bill hinges have been replaced with newer ones installed about 6 cm toward the center.

Woods: Red oak; bottom boards, chestnut.

Dimensions: H 66.0; W 129.5; CW 120.2; D 55.6; CD 55.1.

Exhibition: Kane, *Furn. New Haven Colony*, no. XVI.

Bibliography: Comstock, "Bull Coll.," p. 141; Kirk, *Conn. Furn.*, no. 11 (included in catalogue but not in exhibition).

Provenance: Early history unknown; acquired in 1936 by dealer C. E. H. Whitlock, New Haven, Conn., from the estate of Reuben Tucker, Ansonia, Conn.; by sale in 1937 to C. Sanford Bull, Middlebury, Conn.[1]

THE carved front panels of this chest, with their quarter circles in each corner and half circles at the top and bottom center of each panel, are related to the S-scrolls found on objects now associated most closely with Guilford, Connecticut (see cats. 21, 22). Although it has been suggested that the top, constructed of three narrow oak boards in an English manner, points toward a date early in the seventeenth century for this object, Patricia E. Kane has argued convincingly that the top is new and that the reduced vocabulary of carved ornament present here is an indication of a late seventeenth-century date. In all likelihood, as Kane also suggests, the amount of carving is a better reflection of the depth of the patron's pocketbook than it is a sign of age.

Gift of C. Sanford Bull 1950.68

1. Lyon Notebook, 1:67, Irving P. Lyon Papers, Winterthur Library, 78 x 315.551, 551a, 544.

24

24

Chest with drawer
New England, possibly Boston area, 1660–1700

Description: The cleated top consists of three boards butted together, and it has thumbnail molding at the front and sides. It is attached to the back with snipe-bill hinges. The chest is joined, and the inside edges of the front stiles are chamfered with a stop at the chest bottom. The front is framed with two squared, raised, crossetted panels above a single drawer made to simulate a pair of drawers in line with applied moldings and wooden pulls. The panels are flanked by applied split spindles on the stiles; the muntin has a central groove, and the top rail a central molding. Moldings are applied to the top and bottom drawer rails, and the drawer is flanked by pairs of split spindles on the stiles. Each side of the chest has a square panel at the level of the chest above a rectangular panel at the drawer level; the rails and stiles have applied moldings at their panel edges. The bottom of the chest consists of two half-lapped riven boards nailed to the rails. The back has three horizontal butted boards, one wide

board above two narrow ones, nailed to the case. The drawer is side hung. Its sides are attached to the front with a large dovetail, penetrated by the channel for the runner. The back has beveled edges and is butted and nailed to the sides. The drawer bottom consists of two half-lapped riven boards with beveled front edges let into a groove in the front and nailed to the sides and back. There is no bottom beneath the drawer. The four stiles continue to form the feet; the rear stiles are plain, while the front ones are turned with four rings above a ball foot. The chest retains an old finish and an old coat of red paint.

Inscriptions: "I G" is carved on the back; "G G / B" is painted in black on the underside of the top.

Condition: The cleats have been replaced, and a brace (now missing) once was nailed to the underside of the top. The top contains many nail holes, some of which can be explained as relating to the original cleats or to later braces, but many of them seem inexplicable and suggest that the top may be made up from boards originally used for another purpose. An extra board has been nailed as a patch over the joint of the two boards in the chest bottom. The drawer runners and the right pull on the drawer are replacements. The applied molding on the top and left panel edges of the upper panel on the left side and the moldings on the top and both sides of the upper panel on the right side have been replaced. The right board in the drawer bottom has eight holes, arranged in pairs as if they were the corners of a square, suggesting that the board is a replacement, although it appears to have some age. The chest is probably missing some of its applied ornament on the front. The drawer had a pair of split spindles applied to its center panel (their outline can still be seen); there probably were corbels or other ornaments above the large split spindles on the stiles; and the corners of the front panels may have contained small circular bosses. When illustrated by Nutting in 1928, the pair of small split spindles to the left of the drawer was missing. Old photographs of the chest in Francis P. Garvan's files show them in place; they appear to be old and simply may have fallen off at some time, been saved, and been subsequently restored.

Woods: Top, stiles, rails, drawer sides, applied moldings on drawer, red oak; front and side panels, southern yellow pine; back boards, bottom of chest, drawer bottom, eastern hemlock; base molding, eastern white pine; split spindles, left drawer pull, possibly a maple.

Dimensions: H 86.2; W 86.4; CW 81.6; D 55.3; CD 53.1.

Bibliography: Nutting, *Treasury*, no. 50; Kirk, *Am. Furn. & Brit. Trad.*, fig. 318.

Provenance: Henry V. Weil, New York, N. Y.; by sale to Francis P. Garvan, New York, N. Y.

THIS chest is one of at least four very similar examples that are probably from the same shop. Each of the other three chests known today, one in a private collection and two in the Metropolitan Museum of Art, has two drawers and straight front stiles, but they share the same relatively small size and squarish proportions, and each is ornamented with a common vocabulary of decorative devices. For example, each has front panels like those on the Yale example; the top rail and muntin of each example is molded like the Yale chest; each has split spindles of virtually the same profile applied in the same pattern; each has one drawer shaped like the Yale example; and so forth.[1] The chests in the Metropolitan Museum share many construction characteristics, as well.[2] The somewhat unusual use of hemlock in the Yale chest has not been found in the other chests to date, although their woods have not been microanalyzed. Although the Yale chest has been published recently as being of Connecticut origin, it is suggested here that it was possibly made in or near Boston.[3] The basis of the Connecticut attribution is the relationship between the turned front legs of this example to those on a New Haven–area cupboard in the collection of the Metropolitan Museum.[4] The cupboard's turnings, however, have an oval ball between the reel turnings that is not present on the Yale example. The reel turnings on this chest are more akin to those found on furniture associated with Salem, such as a dressing or chamber table at Winterthur.[5] The profile of the split spindles on these chests also points to a possible origin in the Boston-Salem area. Although spindles of this general shape are commonly found on English furniture, as John T. Kirk has pointed out, they are not encountered as frequently in American objects. Their profile bears at least an affinity to the spindles found on the surviving iron backs or cast backs produced at Hammersmith, the Saugus, Massachusetts, ironworks, and dated between 1655 and 1662. Robert F. Trent has suggested that the wooden patterns for the ornaments on the iron backs were made by Boston craftsmen, including turner Thomas Edsall (1588–1676). One of the known firebacks was owned in Salem, and two other examples were found there.[6] It is possible that the spindles on the iron backs and those on this group of chests stem from the same craftsmen, although they merely may be related expressions of a common form.

88 *American Case Furniture*

One other bit of circumstantial evidence also points toward a Boston-area origin. Although the Yale and Metropolitan Museum chests do not have an early history, the privately owned example was "found in the vicinity of Boston."[7]

The Mabel Brady Garvan Collection 1930.2132

1. The privately owned example in the Erving collection is illustrated in Lockwood, fig. 25; one of the Metropolitan Museum's chests (10.125.32) is illustrated in Nutting, *Treasury*, no. 52; the other example (10.125.33) has not been published.
2. The writer would like to thank Frances Gruber Safford for sharing information on the Metropolitan Museum's chests.
3. Kirk, *Am. Furn. & Brit. Trad.*, fig. 318.
4. Illustrated in Kirk, *Am. Furn. & Brit. Trad.*, fig. 321.
5. Fairbanks and Bates, p. 24.
6. Fairbanks and Trent, *New England Begins*, figs. 32–35, no. 381.
7. Lockwood, p. 37.

25

Chest with drawers

New England, possibly coastal Plymouth Colony, 1650–1700

Description: The cleated top of this chest has thumbnail molding on all four sides and is attached to the back with snipe-bill hinges. The interior of the chest contains a lidded till on the left side. The sides of the lid are notched, and the front edge is molded; the lower edge of the side also has shadow molding and is nailed to the bottom of the till. The front of the chest is framed to three panels below applied serrated molding. The side panels of the front are each divided into four smaller panels with applied moldings and strips. The central panel contains a vertically oriented octagon created by molding, with the outer corners filled with triangular strips. This center panel has an applied split spindle in the center; the stiles have paired split spindles, and each muntin a conforming split spindle. The bottom front rail of the chest section is shaped to heavy molding which overlaps the stiles. Each drawer is decorated to simulate a pair of drawers in line, with applied moldings and wooden pulls. The upper drawer has a split spindle on a center strip and is flanked by split spindles on the stiles. The drawers are separated by lighter molding nailed to a drawer divider tenoned to the stiles. The bottom rail is again shaped to heavy projecting molding that overlaps the stiles, echoing in reverse the upper drawer rail. There is no bottom beneath the lower drawer. The sides of the chest are framed to four panels. The rails, stiles, and muntins have shadow molding down the center, and their panel edges are stop chamfered. The back is framed to three vertical panels behind the chest section; the rails and stiles are chamfered on their panel edges, and the edges of the muntins are beveled. Behind the drawers there is a single horizontal panel running the width of the chest; again, the stiles are chamfered, but the panel edges of the rails are beveled. Inside the chest, the stiles are broadly beveled on their inside edges. The rails have shadow molding at the center and are chamfered on their panel edges; the muntins have beveled edges and shadow molding at center. The bottom of the chest is nailed to the rails. The drawers are side hung. In the top drawer, the sides are nailed to a rabbet in the front with rosehead nails above and below the channel. The back is rabbeted to accept the sides, which are nailed in place through the back, again with two rosehead nails. The drawer bottom consists of two boards half lapped together, with their grain running parallel to the front. The

front board has a beveled edge and is set into a V-shaped groove in the front and nailed to the back.

Inscriptions: "GML" is branded on the top in the center near the front edge. "P E" is scratch-carved on the lid of the till.

Condition: This chest is in poor condition and has been heavily restored. It has been refinished, and much of the applied ornament is new. An iron brace has been screwed to the underside of the top as a reinforcement. The area around the right hinge has been repaired. All four stiles have been pieced below the bottom rails; a small block has been added to the left rear stile to strengthen the addition. New boards have been added to the right side of the chest bottom; originally it probably consisted of two boards half lapped together. The wooden pulls on the drawers, the bottom of the lower drawer, and the drawer runners are replacements. All the applied moldings and strips in the chest section appear to be replacements. All the split spindles, with the possible exception of the small spindle in the center of the upper drawer, also appear to be replacements. The applied moldings on the upper drawer (with the exception of the vertical strip on the far left side) appear to be old, while those on the lower drawer do not show as much wear as the drawer front below and thus are probably new. There is a mortise chiseled in the lower edge of the bottom rail on the right side, as if it were to receive a muntin.

Woods: Stiles, rails, panels, drawer fronts, red oak; top, bottom of chest, drawer bottoms and backs, eastern white pine; sides of upper drawer, bottom of till, chestnut; sides of lower drawer, white oak; side of till, Atlantic white cedar; applied moldings on drawers (with the exception of one new section), split spindle in center of upper drawer, beech; other split spindles, probably beech or maple; other replaced moldings and strips, walnut and beech.

Dimensions: H 94.6; W 95.9; CW 90.9; D 49.6; CD 47.7.

Bibliography: "Accessions," *Connecticut Antiquarian* 5, no. 1 (June 1953): 30; Barbara Snow, "History in Houses, Seventeenth-Century: New England and Pennsylvania," *Antiques* 71, no. 1 (January 1957): 62.

Provenance: Henry V. Weil, New York, N. Y.; by sale to Francis P. Garvan, New York, N. Y.

THIS chest is in such poor condition that assigning it a place of origin is a risky business. Although much, if not all, of the applied ornament is not original, the essential frame of the chest appears to be old and offers some clues as to its place of manufacture. It is an elaborately framed and paneled chest, ornamented on the inside and on the back as well as on the customary front and side. This suggests an affinity with the furniture made in the coastal towns of Plymouth Colony where, as Robert B. St. George has noted, local joiners paid careful attention to the backs of their products, more attention than was customary in the rest of New England.[1] The serrated molding on this chest also evokes thoughts of Plymouth Colony, as does the drawer rails' being secured to the stiles with a lipped tenon, giving the impression of applied molding, as was "invariably" the practice in coastal Plymouth. The use of Atlantic white cedar in the till also points toward the same area, where cedar was used consistently for drawer bottoms. The split spindles on this chest have been restored, with one possible exception, but it is interesting (although not conclusive) that they appear to be simplified versions of the kind seen on many examples of Plymouth furniture. But the drawers of this chest are not made in the usual Plymouth manner (in which the sides are attached to the front by nails driven through the drawer front, and then the nails covered by applied strips), and other differences with furniture from that area exist, preventing as yet a firm attribution.

The Mabel Brady Garvan Collection 1930.2112

1. The information given here concerning the furniture of coastal Plymouth is derived from St. George, *Wrought Covenant*, pp. 25-55.

26

Chest with drawers
Possibly by Peter Blin (d. 1725)
Wethersfield, Connecticut, 1675-1710

Description: The cleated top is of a single board with thumbnail molding at the front and sides, and it is attached to the back with snipe-bill hinges. The front is framed to three panels above two superimposed drawers. The side panels are carved in low relief with a central stem rising to a large tulip at the top, embellished with rows of gouges or notches, and with two tulips flowing out to either side, and are edged with applied moldings. The center panel is carved with three floral ornaments (generally called sunflowers)

and four tulips against a matted ground and within an octagon created by applied moldings; the corners of the panel are filled with triangular pieces. The upper rail has shadow molding at the center and an oval escutcheon in the middle. The stiles have an applied split spindle, and the muntins bear pairs of applied split spindles. There is applied molding on the upper, middle, and lower drawer rails. The drawers are each decorated to appear as a pair in line; each side has applied moldings forming octagons surrounding a central wooden pull flanked by applied oval bosses. The center of each drawer has a pair of applied split spindles on an applied panel, and each drawer is flanked by pairs of matching split spindles on the stiles. The sides are framed to a single panel at the chest level above two vertical panels at the level of the drawers. The upper side rail is molded as on the front, and the upper panel has applied moldings again in the form of an octagon, with an applied oval boss surrounded by small round bosses in the center. The stile separating the two lower panels has central molding, and the panels are edged with applied moldings. The back contains a single panel with beveled edges at the chest level, and another panel is fitted behind the drawers, although there is no bottom rail at the back. The inside of the chest contains a lidded till on the right side; the lid of the till is molded on its front edge, and the bottom is chamfered at the front edge. The edges of the stiles are beveled on the inside. The bottom of the chest consists of three transverse boards fitted together with a V-shaped joint; their front edge is beveled and fitted to a groove in the front rail and nailed to the underside of the back rail. The drawers are side hung on runners nailed to grooves in the stiles. In each drawer, the drawer sides are fitted to a rabbet in the front and nailed above and below the groove for the drawer runner. The bottom is a single board with grain parallel to the front and beveled at the front and sides, fitted to a groove in the drawer front, and nailed to the sides and back with rosehead nails. The applied split spindles, bosses, moldings between the drawers, triangular corners, and moldings on the top rails are painted black; the applied moldings on the panel edges and drawers are painted red with pairs of black squiggly lines at intervals.

26a

26b

Condition: This chest was owned in the nineteenth century by the Yale School of the Fine Arts (see Provenance), and its condition deteriorated. It was restored in 1928 by Anton Mislovits, a cabinetmaker at 78 Elm Street in Hartford, Connecticut, for a fee of $290. A photograph of the chest before restoration (cat. 26c) provides a guide to the repairs Mislovits undertook. The front of the chest section had been modified and hinged so that it would fall forward. This alteration was restored, the hinges removed, and the holes made in the molding on the upper drawer rail patched. Some of the applied ornaments were also replaced. The chest was refinished and given new coats of black and red paint on the appropriate locations. The lock is missing, and the top has been patched in the location of the hasp. A board has been added beneath the lower right drawer runner as a reinforcement.

Woods: Stiles, rails, front and side panels, drawer fronts, sides, and runners, cleats, till, white oak; top, back panels, bottom of chest, drawer bottoms and backs, southern yellow pine; applied spindles and moldings, possibly maple; applied triangular corners, possibly cedar.

Dimensions: H 101.6; W 121.0; CW 113.0; D 54.3; CD 50.5

26

26c Before restoration, ca. 1928

Bibliography: Arthur W. Leibundguth, "An Extreme Example of Artistic License," *Connecticut Antiquarian* 28, no. 2 (December 1976): 12.

Provenance: This chest was acquired by Yale at an unknown date sometime before 1883; it was assigned the accession number 1800.4 to indicate its early presence at the university rather than a specific year. Notes made by George Dudley Seymour (1859–1945) in 1930 and first brought to light by Arthur W. Leibundguth give the following early history for the chest: "The Sunflower Conn chest presented to the Yale School of the Fine Arts in 'ages past' to be used in still life painting by Frank Wayland Fellowes [1833–1900], of New Haven, an amateur painter & sometime a student at the Art School under Prof Weir who having no idea of the value of the chest had the front cut off and hinged so that the chest might be used as a 'property' receptacle without disturbing the objects set on top of the lid for practice in still life painting. I first saw the chest so mutilated and marvelled at the unconscious act of vandalism when I first came to New Haven in 1883. I had then been indoctrinated in the cult of 17th. Cent. N.E. oak peices [sic] by Dr. Lyon of Hartford. The redemption of the chest was too delicate a subject to take up with Prof. Weir but I tried to interest his successor Sargent Kendall in it but failed. Then I endeavored to interest Dean Meeks but failed until under the promptings of Prof. Theo-

dore Sizer he consented to have the chest put in order after I had engaged Mr. Henry Wood Erving to *personally* superintend its restoration by Anton Mitlovitz [*sic*]. Thus at length and after some forty odd years of effort the chest was trucked up to Hartford two or three years ago and put in order. During this process a dealer came in & saw Anton working on it & supposing that it was Anton's own job offered him $6000 cash for it. Then Yale woke up. To-day it is easily worth $10,000. Long before it was sent up to Hartford, it had been relegated to an attic room in the Art School and was a sorry object." After restoration, the chest was placed in the care of the Art Gallery.

THIS chest, the succeeding example (cat. 27), and two cupboards in the Yale collection (cats. 195, 196) are part of a large group of approximately sixty-five objects with related carving and turned decoration.[1] The distinctive nature of this so-called tulip and sunflower furniture has been recognized for many years, and the objects usually have been assigned to the Hartford area, particularly to Wethersfield on the basis of several examples with strong family histories in that town. In 1958, Houghton Bulkeley suggested that the maker of the objects may have been joiner Peter Blin, who arrived in Wethersfield about 1675.[2] Bulkeley cited as evidence for this attribution Blin's exclusive ownership of the necessary carving, joining, and turning tools in Wethersfield during the period ca. 1675–ca. 1725, as well as several other circumstantial factors, but the cornerstone of his argument was the discovery of an account book entry indicating that Blin made a chest worth ten shillings for Gershom Bulkeley (1635–1713) of Wethersfield in 1681. Bulkeley suggested that this document referred to a "tulip and sunflower" chest in his possession that had a traditional history of ownership by Gershom Bulkeley. Despite the tenuous nature of the evidence, which is strongly suggestive but far from conclusive, the attribution of this group to Blin is generally accepted today, with the understanding that some of the objects in the group were produced in shops manned by Blin's former journeymen or apprentices.[3] Of the group, forty-one examples, including the two in the Yale collection, are chests with two drawers, with the drawers invariably decorated with applied spindles, bosses, and moldings to simulate a total of four drawers. The carved tulips on the side panels and the stylized floral ornaments, possibly marigolds, in the center panel of this example are typical of the carving found on many objects in this Wethersfield group, although there is some variation between even the most closely related chests.[4]

Yale University Art Gallery 1800.4

27

1. This figure, based on a file maintained by the writer, should be regarded only as an approximation, as new objects continually come to light and as published examples, upon examination, prove to be modern or otherwise not of the period. Published estimates of the size of the group have ranged from the high 30s to more than 100, although most writers estimate that there are between 60 and 70 surviving examples of the "school," including cupboards, chests, chests with one or two drawers, and boxes.
2. Houghton Bulkeley, "A Discovery on a Connecticut Chest," *Connecticut Historical Society Bulletin* 23, no. 1 (January 1958): 17–19.
3. Fairbanks and Trent, *New England Begins*, no. 257; Randall, no. 9; Fales, *Deerfield*, p. 167.
4. The identification of the "sunflowers" as marigolds is based on evidence contained in the Benno M. Forman Papers, Winterthur Museum.

27

Chest with drawers
Possibly by Peter Blin (d. 1725)
Wethersfield, Connecticut, 1675–1710

Description: The form and construction of this chest are virtually the same as that on the previous example (cat. 26). The major difference between the two lies in the execution of the carved designs on the front panels. Here the lower

flowers on the center panel have leaves underneath, and the long pointed sections of the tulips flanking the upper flower point in toward the center rather than curve away. The tulips on the side panels are smaller and more delicate, and the tulip at the top center lacks the rows of gouges found on the other example. At an early date a strip was nailed to the inside lower edge of the bottom backboard of this chest.

Inscription: A "Connecticut Furniture" (1967) exhibition label is pasted to the underside of the top.

Condition: At one time, the entire chest seems to have been painted green; when this paint was removed prior to the acquisition of the chest by Yale, traces of the original red and black paint remained. New screws have been added to the cleats, and the lid of the till is missing. The wooden pulls on the upper drawer are replacements, as are the small circular bosses encircling the oval bosses on the upper side panels. The small split spindles in the center of the drawers have been replaced; fragments of two original spindles which were broken have been preserved.

Woods: See cat. 26.

Dimensions: H 101.0; W 121.4; CW 113.9; D 54.5; CD 50.1.

Exhibitions: *Girl Scouts Exhibition*, no. 501; Kirk, *Conn. Furn.*, no. 16.

Bibliography: Ormsbee, *Story Am. Furn.*, fig. 19A; Miller, 1: fig. 598; Rogers, "Garvan Furn. (1960)," fig. 2; Kirk, "Sources," fig. 1; Louis B. Wright et al., *The Arts in America: The Colonial Period* (New York: Charles Scribner's Sons, 1966), pl. 181; Daniel M. Mendelowitz, *A History of American Art* (2d ed.; New York: Rinehart and Winston, 1973), p. 62; Chinnery, fig. 4:210.

Provenance: Dr. George Coopernail, Bedford, N.Y.; by sale to Francis P. Garvan, New York, N.Y.

THE tulips carved on the side panels of this example, with their small flower at the top of the stem, are less commonly found on these Wethersfield chests than the broader tulips present on the previous example. Related small tulips are found on only one of the cupboards, four of the two-drawer chests, a single chest with one drawer, and one chest, the example thought to have been made by Blin in 1681 for

27a

27b

94 *American Case Furniture*

Gershom Bulkeley.[1] It usually is thought that the applied split spindles and bosses on these chests, generally of maple, were painted black in imitation of ebony and that the applied moldings on the panel edges were painted or stained red and decorated with black squiggles in imitation of another exotic, imported wood.[2] Perhaps these moldings were meant to simulate snakewood, a tropical wood used on the Boston chest of drawers with doors in the Yale collection (cat. 51), which has a distinctive reddish-brown appearance with black irregular markings.

The Mabel Brady Garvan Collection 1930.2191

1. For illustrations of these objects, see *Garvan Coll.*, no. 398; Nutting, *Treasury*, nos. 59, 61; Lyon, fig. 9; *Antiques* 65, no. 1 (January 1954): 53; Comstock, no. 53 (the age of this example has been questioned); and Kirk, *Conn. Furn.*, no. 15. Another example is in the collection of the Henry Ford Museum.
2. Fairbanks and Trent, *New England Begins*, no. 257.

28

Chest with drawer
Connecticut Valley, 1670–1710
(see pl. 1)

Description: The cleated rectangular top is a single board and has thumbnail molding at the front and sides. It is attached to the back with snipe-bill hinges. The front is framed to three panels over a single drawer with wooden pulls. The stiles and rails are joined with a haunched mitered tenon to permit through-chamfering. The front of the chest is carved with the "Hadley" motif of the type designated "Group 3: Leaf with Scrolls; Subgroup B, Hadley motif with dependent scroll."[1] The rails and stiles and drawer front retain a good deal of original black paint, and the panels have original red paint. The inside edges of the stiles are beveled; there is no till. The back is framed to two panels side by side at the level of the chest section; a board is nailed to the stiles and upper drawer rail behind the drawer. The bottom of the chest consists of three boards fitted together with a half lap and let into a groove in the front and nailed to the upper drawer rail at the back. The sides are framed to two vertical panels side by side at the level of the chest above a single horizontal panel at the drawer level; the rails have shadow molding; the top and middle rail are chamfered on their

28a

28b

Chests and Chests with Drawers

28

panel edges; the stiles are stop chamfered at their panel edges; and the bottom rail is beveled on its panel edge. The top and upper drawer rails are double pinned to the stiles; the front muntins are also double pinned, while those on the side are held with a single pin, as is the bottom rail at the front and sides. The drawer is side hung on runners nailed to the stiles. The sides are dovetailed to the front with a single dovetail above the groove for the drawer runner. The drawer sides are butted to the back and nailed above and below the groove. The drawer bottom is two longitudinal boards, one wide board half lapped to a narrow one at the rear; these are nailed with rosehead nails to a rabbet in the front and to the undersides of the sides and back. There is no bottom below the drawer.

Inscriptions: "M R" is carved on the center panel of the front; a modern inscription in black paint on the outside of the back reads "Boulder Col[?]" above "8931/9."

Condition: The right cleat is missing; the left, and possibly the right, pull on the drawer is new. The escutcheon is a replacement.

Woods: Stiles, rails, muntins, front and side panels, drawer front, drawer sides, drawer runners, white oak; top, bottom of chest, drawer bottom and back, back panels, southern yellow pine.

Dimensions: H 84.5; W 114.3; CW 106.0; D 47.3; CD 45.4.

Exhibitions: *Girl Scouts Exhibition*, no. 501; YUAG, "A Wide View for American Art."

Bibliography: Ormsbee, *Story Am. Furn.*, fig. 19B; Luther, no. 67; Rogers, "Garvan Furn. (1960)," fig. 1; Rogers, "Garvan Coll. (1962)," p. 6; Kirk, *Early Am. Furn.*, fig. 29; Kane, "Hadley Chest," figs. 9, 10, 21, p. 113 no. 45; Chinnery, fig. 4:204; Kane, "American Furn.," fig. 1; Victoria Kloss Ball, *Architecture and Interior Design: Europe and America from the Colonial Era to Today* (New York: John Wiley & Sons, 1980), fig. 1.21; Kirk, *Am. Furn. & Brit. Trad.*, fig. 399.

Provenance: According to Luther (who offers only circumstantial evidence), the carved initials are for Mary (Russell) Root (1686–1738) of Sunderland, Mass. The chest was "discovered" in West Virginia by Luther and subsequently acquired by dealer Frank W. MacCarthy, Longmeadow, Mass., who sold it to Francis P. Garvan, New York, N. Y.

THE Yale collection includes 4 so-called Hadley chests, of which this example is the best preserved in that it retains much of its original painted decoration. More than 125 Hadley chests have survived, distinguished by their characteristic carved scroll, tulip, and leaf motif and sharing a common origin in the upper Connecticut Valley between Hartford and Deerfield. These chests have been divided into eight groups by Patricia E. Kane, primarily on the basis of visual similarities, and this example is part of the largest group, incorporating nearly half (56) of the surviving chests. This group, designated "Group 3: Leaf with Scrolls Type," is characterized by a repetition of the Hadley motif over the entire front of the chest. The "M R" chest is also part of a subgroup of 16 chests, on which the Hadley motif has a dependent scroll.[2] This chest is further embellished by the presence of carved hearts, stars, and other ornaments on the three panels, on the three front rails, and between the pulls on the drawer. Richard Lawrence Greene has suggested that this type of ornament represents in stylized form various fertility symbols derived from the traditional maypole festivities and other folk rituals of provincial England. Hadley chests have been thought to be dower chests for many years, and the presence of these fertility symbols ensured "the fertility of their owners."[3] In light of this interpretation, one might read the pair of carved birds, probably cocks, located in the center of the bottom front rail of this chest, as a symbol considerably more overt than many of those in which Greene has detected sexual meanings. While Greene's argument remains speculative, it is intriguing and represents an important attempt to understand the role of these chests in

late seventeenth- and early eighteenth-century culture. Through-chamfered construction and related motifs have been found on objects from the north of England, and it seems likely that the Hadley chests were made by craftsmen with a background in Lancashire, Yorkshire, or other parts of the North Country.[4]

The Mabel Brady Garvan Collection 1930.2190

1. Kane, "Hadley Chest," pp. 96–98.
2. Luther's pioneering work remains an essential introduction to the Hadley chest group. The modern system of classification was set forward in Kane, "Hadley Chest."
3. "Fertility Symbols on the Hadley Chests," *Antiques* 112, no. 2 (August 1977): 250–257. A dim view of Greene's interpretation is expressed by Robert F. Trent in "Style, Technology, and the Craftsmen: Assessing Regionalism in Seventeenth-Century New England Joinery," in *The Bay and the River, 1600–1900*, ed. Peter Benes and Jane M. Benes (Boston: Boston University Scholarly Publications, 1982), pp. 11–12 n. 4.
4. The best discussion of the English background of the Hadley chest is in Kirk, *Am. Furn. & Brit. Trad.*, chap. 6; see also Kane, "Hadley Chest," p. 92.

29

Chest with drawer
Connecticut Valley, 1670–1710

Description: This chest is very similar in form and construction to the preceding chest (cat. 28), although here very little of the original paint has survived. Some minor variations here include shadow molding on the left side top rail on the inside; shadow molding on the rear faces of the rear stiles; and a single horizontal panel with beveled edges behind the chest section. The front of the chest is carved with the Hadley motif in a variation of the type now designated "Group 3: Leaf with Scrolls" arrangement.

Inscriptions: "IP" is carved in the center panel of the front; "I" is carved in the center of the bottom rail, probably as a decorative device.

Condition: The chest has been refinished; traces of old red paint remain on the panels and of old black paint on the rails and stiles. The applied back-board behind the drawer has been lost.

Woods: Stiles, rails, front and side panels, cleats, drawer runners, front, and sides, white oak; top, back panel, chest bottom, drawer back and bottom, southern yellow pine.

Dimensions: H 87.9; W 116.0; CW 107.7; D 52.4; CD 50.6.

Bibliography: Luther, no. 65; "Living with Antiques: The Connecticut Home of Mr. and Mrs. C. Sanford Bull," *Antiques* 45, no. 4 (April 1944): 191 (carved initials stated as "I D"); Comstock, "Bull Coll.," p. 141; Comstock, *Concise Encyclopedia*, fig. 3b; Comstock, no. 56; Kirk, "Sources," fig. 3; *The Britannica Encyclopedia of American Art* (Chicago: Encyclopaedia Britannica Educational Corp., 1973), p. 195; Ian Cameron and Elizabeth Kingsley-Rowe, eds., *The Random House Encyclopedia of Antiques* (New York: Random House, 1973), p. 170; Kane, "Hadley Chest," p. 114 no. 59.

Provenance: Although this chest was believed to have come from the Parmley family, Luther believed on the basis of the carved initials that it was owned originally by Joanna (Porter) Marsh (1687–ca. 1714) of Hadley. Although the 1725 inventory of her husband's estate included a carved chest with a drawer valued at ten shillings, it simply cannot be assumed that this reference relates to the chest now at Yale. The chest was owned in modern times by a Miss Merwin of Durham, Conn., who was the source of the Parmley family tradition; it was acquired by 1928 by C. Sanford Bull, Middlebury, Conn.

This chest is one of seventeen Hadley chests classified "Subgroup D: Miscellaneous variants of group 3 interpretations of the Hadley motif."[1] Here, for example, one variation is that the carving on the top and middle front rails extends onto the stiles, rather than being terminated abruptly as on the preceding chest. There are also variations in the configuration and placement of the purported fertility symbols. What appears to be the letter *I* carved in the center of the bottom front rail is in all likelihood only such a symbol. Luther called attention to the deep drawer on this chest, which allows for a superimposed repetition of the Hadley motif.

Gift of C. Sanford Bull 1950.67

1. Kane, "Hadley Chest," pp. 114–115.

30

30

Chest with drawer
Connecticut Valley, 1670–1710

Description: This smaller chest is of the same form and construction as the preceding examples, with some minor variations. Here the upper edges of the stiles are chamfered off on the inside of the chest, and there is no shadow molding within the chest. This chest does not have a lock, and the rear stiles are not molded on the back face. A board has been nailed in place, covering the drawer section at the back. The channel for the drawer runner has been cut high on the drawer sides here, with the dovetail coming below. The carved Hadley motifs are in the style now designated "Group 3, Subgroup B: Hadley motif with dependent scroll" (see below).

Inscription: "EE" is carved on the front center panel, probably initials of the unidentified original owner.

Condition: The left cleat and wooden pulls on the drawer are replacements. The surface has remains of old red paint.

Woods: Stiles, rails, front and back panels, cleats, drawer front, sides, and runners, white oak; top, chest bottom, back panels, drawer bottom and back, eastern white pine; one board in bottom of chest section, southern yellow pine.

Dimensions: H 83.3; W 112.3; CW 104.3; D 45.8; CD 43.8.

Bibliography: Luther, no. 29; Kirk, *Early Am. Furn.*, fig. 28; Kane, "Hadley Chest," fig. 17, see also p. 113 no. 58; Chinnery, fig. 4:203.

Provenance: The early history of this chest is unknown; Luther apparently could not find a candidate for original ownership with the appropriate initials prior to the birth of an Elizabeth Eastman in 1733. Owned in the twentieth century by James Davidson, New London, Conn.; by sale to Francis P. Garvan, New York, N. Y.

This Hadley chest forms part of the same Group 3, Subgroup B, as the "M R" chest (cat. 28), but again minor variations can be noted.[1] The orientation of the Hadley motif on the stiles is reversed here, for example, and once again there are differences in the form and disposition of the various fertility symbols. Were one to accept Greene's hypothesis concerning the meaning of these carved ornaments, the device carved in the center of the drawer of this chest could be seen as a somewhat blatant phallic symbol.

The Mabel Brady Garvan Collection 1930.2653

1. Kane, "Hadley Chest," pp. 112–113.

31

Chest with two drawers
Hampshire County, Massachusetts, 1690–1720

Description: The form and construction of this chest with two drawers is closely related to that of the preceding three examples of Hadley chests (cats. 28, 29, 30), again with some minor variations in addition to its greater height and the presence of a second drawer. Here, the sides are framed with two panels, one over the other, and the side rails are not chamfered. The four stiles are turned to ring and vase-shaped legs terminating in ball feet. The greatest variation comes in the structure of the drawers. Both are side hung as in the other three Hadley chests, but here the drawer sides are nailed to a wide rabbet in the front with rosehead nails above and below the channel for the drawer runner. Each drawer bottom is a single board with a beveled front edge let into a groove in the front and nailed to the sides and back. In the upper drawer, the sides are butted to the back and nailed through the back with rosehead nails; in the lower drawer, the back is rabbeted to accept the sides and then nailed. This chest again has an applied board nailed to the back behind the drawers. The carved decoration on the front is classified "Group 2: Hatfield Type" (see below).

Inscriptions: "M" and "D" are carved on the left and right front panels respectively. A Connecticut Tercentenary label is pasted to the inside of the right side of the upper drawer; a "Connecticut Furniture" (1967) exhibition label is pasted to the underside of the top.

Condition: The top, front, and sides have old but not original black paint; traces of red paint can be seen on the panels where they have shrunk away from the grooves in the stiles and rails. The inside of the chest section, back, and underside of the top have been painted black more recently. Modern brass pulls on the drawers are visible in early photographs of the chest; these have been replaced with wooden pulls. A small strip of molding has been added to the inside bottom of the upper drawer at its juncture with the front, to cover a gap caused by shrinkage of the bottom.

Woods: Stiles, rails, front and side panels, drawer fronts, left side of lower drawer, soft maple, probably red maple; top, drawer bottoms, back panels, bottom of chest, southern yellow pine; drawer runners, back and sides of upper drawer, right side of bottom drawer, red oak; back of bottom drawer, sycamore.

31

Dimensions: H 114.1; W 118.1; CW 110.9; D 49.8; CD 47.2.

Exhibitions: *Three Centuries of Conn. Furn.*, no. 17; Kirk, *Conn. Furn.*, no. 21.

Bibliography: Charles Messer Stow, "The Theme of Luxury in the Garvan Collection," *Antiquarian* 15, no. 3 (September 1930): 35; Walter A. Dyer, "The American Chest: Eighteenth Century," *Antiquarian* 17, no. 5 (November 1931): 45; Luther, no. 80; Kirk, "Sources," fig. 2; Kane, "Joiners of Hartford County," fig. 1; Kane, "Hadley Chest," fig. 14 (detail of drawer construction), see also p. 111 no. 10; Chinnery, fig. 4:206; Kirk, *Am. Furn. & Brit. Trad.*, fig. 231.

Provenance: The early history of this chest is unknown. It is said to have been found in Syracuse, N. Y., by dealer Charles R. Morson, New York, N. Y.; by sale in 1929 to Francis P. Garvan, New York, N. Y.

THIS Hadley chest is one of at least eleven examples classified "Group 2: Hatfield Type" by Patricia E. Kane.[1] On most of these Hatfield chests, the use of the Hadley motif is confined to the central panel, and on seven examples, including

Chests and Chests with Drawers 99

this one, the stiles, rails, and muntins are carved with a meandering vine. Although Kane and Robert F. Trent have suggested that these Hatfield chests are so similar as to probably be the work of a single craftsman, John T. Kirk has found enough variation within the group to conclude, probably correctly, that they were produced by more than one shop. Similarities in drawer construction between "Group 2" chests and the so-called tulip and sunflower chests (see cats. 26, 27) suggest that there may be a connection between the two groups of furniture. Like the preceding three examples, the "M D" chest is fashioned with through-chamfered construction. Two other "Group 2" chests also have turned legs.[2]

The Mabel Brady Garvan Collection 1930.2196

1. Kane, "Hadley Chest," pp. 110–111; see also pp. 89–92. Other discussions of Group 2 chests can be found in Marius B. Peladeau, "A Hadley Chest Reconsidered," *Antiques* 117, no. 5 (May 1980): 1084–1086; Fairbanks and Trent, *New England Begins*, no. 301; and Kirk, *Am. Furn. & Brit. Trad.*, p. 97. A table with drawer also may be part of this group; see Fairbanks and Trent, *New England Begins*, no. 311.

2. Luther, nos. 44, 76.

32

Fragment of chest with drawer(s)
Connecticut, probably Guilford–Saybrook area, 1700–1740

Description: This object is all that remains of what originally was a chest with one or more drawers; only the chest section has survived. The cleated top is of two boards butted together and has thumbnail molding at the front and sides. It is attached to the back with snipe-bill hinges. The front is framed with a single fielded panel with canted corners. The sides are framed with a panel containing a raised rectangle. The back contains a single panel with beveled edges. The inside corners of the stiles are chamfered, and the mortise-and-tenon joints are double pinned. There is applied base molding at the front. The front and sides of the chest are decorated with painted designs in red, white, light yellow, and black (possibly originally green and now oxidized to black) on a deep-yellow ground. The raised section of the front panel contains a central two-handled vase holding three roses and vines that flow to each side and terminate in

32

leaves and flowers. The corners of the panel are painted with fleurs-de-lis, and above the raised section is a meandering vine with alternating black and white leaves. Below are leaves and scrolls. The stiles are decorated with painted columns, and the rails with paired waterleafs. The raised rectangles on the side panels have tendriled leaves echoing the decoration of the front. The bottom of the chest consists of three boards held together with V-shaped grooves. Their front edges are beveled and let in a groove in the front lower rail and nailed to the back lower rail.

Inscriptions: There is a faint illegible chalk inscription on the back that may be original. Modern notations include "44.40" painted in white on the outside of the back panel and other numbers in red on the outside of the top back rail.

Condition: The stiles and side panels have been cut just below the bottom front and rear rails. Boards have been nailed to the underside of the chest to serve as skids. The applied molding on the panel edge of the front stile is missing. There are remains of two red leather straps nailed to the underside of the top, and a black leather strap has been nailed over the lock on the inside. The painted decoration has faded and is worn considerably on the sides. There are no traces of paint on the top.

Woods: Top, front panel, front rails, yellow poplar; stiles, side and back rails, cleats, white oak; side panels, back panel, bottom, southern yellow pine; new cleats, eastern white pine.

Dimensions: H 57.5; W 112.1; CW 104.6; D 49.1; CD 46.4.

Bibliography: Kirk, "Sources," fig. 10; Kirk, *Conn. Furn.*, no. 41 (included in catalogue but not in exhibition).

Provenance: Francis P. Garvan, New York, N. Y.

This fragment of a chest with one or more drawers is related by its construction and painted decoration to a group of painted chests and chests of drawers made in towns along the Connecticut shore roughly from Guilford east to Saybrook. These so-called Guilford-Saybrook objects have been associated with the name Charles Gillam (d. 1727) of Saybrook, but there is enough variety in their decoration to suggest the work of more than one craftsman.[1] This chest shares many characteristics with other members of the group, including the large fielded panels with flat rabbets on the sides, the front fielded panels (here the raised section has cut corners), again with flat rabbets, and the oak frame with yellow poplar panels favored for painted surfaces. The two-handled cup, flowers, vines, and fleurs-de-lis on this chest are motifs found on other objects in the group and are derived from a variety of sources.[2] Before this chest was cut down, it probably resembled a chest with drawer in the collection of the Henry Whitfield Museum in Guilford (916029).[3] The bottom of this chest is also made of three boards fitted together with V-shaped grooves, suggesting a further affinity of the Yale chest to the Guilford-Saybrook group. Although these Guilford-Saybrook chests are usually dated to the first quarter of the eighteenth century, it has been suggested that the painted waterleafs and architectural columns on the Yale chest are more representative of motifs popular in the late eighteenth century.[4] The construction of the chest seems more in keeping, however, with the first half of the century, and there is no reason to suspect that the painted decoration is not original. Waterleafs and columns were not unknown in the early eighteenth century, and it is likely that they were adopted by the painter of this chest from an as yet unknown source.

The Mabel Brady Garvan Collection 1930.2765

1. The best reference to these chests is William L. Warren, "Were the Guilford Painted Chests Made in Saybrook?" *Connecticut Historical Society Bulletin* 23, no. 1 (January 1958): 1–10.
2. The sources for these motifs are discussed in Fales, *Am. Painted Furn.*, pp. 24–29; and in Kirk, *Am. Furn. & Brit. Trad.*, pp. 72–74.
3. Illustrated in Warren, "Were the Guilford Painted Chests Made in Saybrook?" fig. 3; and in Nutting, *Treasury*, no. 107. Other related chests include figs. 1 and 2 in Warren's article and figs. 22 and 28 in Fales, *Am. Painted Furn.*
4. Kirk, *Conn. Furn.*, no. 41.

33

33

Chest with drawer
New Haven, Connecticut, 1660–1700
(see pl. 2)

Description: The cleated top has thumbnail molding at the front and sides and is attached to the back with snipe-bill hinges. The front and back are rabbeted to receive the sides and are nailed in place. The back is a single board extending only behind the chest section. The front of the chest is decorated with applied ornament to appear as if it is joined. This effect was achieved by nailing strips of wood to the front to simulate the stiles, rails, and central muntin forming two panels. Within these panels, moldings have been applied in a cruciform pattern, with a large, flat, round boss in each corner, and an oval projecting boss in the center. The panels are surrounded by applied split spindles, the ones on the rails varying in configuration from those on the stiles and the pair on the muntins, and small, round, flat bosses above and below the muntin and at the junctions of the rails and stiles. The drawer front also is divided visually into two panels, simulating a pair of drawers in line, with central applied molding. Each panel of the drawer contains a central wooden pull flanked by split spindles at the sides. The base molding is applied to the lower edge of the drawer front and to the sides of the chest. The sides are shaped with a triangular

notch to form feet. The bottom of the chest section is made of several narrow boards, probably butted with a rabbet over a feathered edge, fitted to a groove in the back, and nailed from underneath to a rabbet in the front. The sides of the drawer are half lapped to the drawer front and nailed through the sides; the wide rabbet in the front extends to overlap the sides of the case. The drawer sides are rabbeted to accept the back and nailed through the sides. The drawer bottom is nailed to the back and to a rabbet in the front. It is again made of several narrow boards butted with a rabbet over a feathered edge. The drawer is supported on runners nailed to the sides; there is no bottom beneath the drawer. The chest retains much of its early paint. The applied moldings, split spindles, and bosses are picked out in black against a red ground. The thumbnail molding of the top is painted black, and thin black strips are barely visible on the top, running from front to back about 29–30 cm from the sides, thus visually dividing the top into three panels.

Inscription: The modern "247 / 1–18" in white chalk appears on the back.

Condition: The cleats are replacements. The top edge of the back has been repaired in the area of the hinge. A large shrinkage crack in the top has been pieced. The backboard behind the drawer is missing; nail holes appear in the sides where it was attached originally. The left side of the drawer front has been pieced, the upper right side has been repaired, and the wooden pulls are replacements. The drawer runners have been replaced, and new oak strips added to the drawer bottom to serve as running strips. Some of the applied moldings and ornaments are new. The original paint has been retouched several times.

Woods: Top, all four sides, back, drawer front, sides, back, applied moldings, yellow poplar; chest bottom, drawer bottom, white oak; applied split spindles, bosses, possibly a maple.

Dimensions: H 76.8; W 115.5; CW 111.3; D 46.9; CD 44.7.

Exhibitions: Kirk, *Conn. Furn.*, no. 26; Kane, *Furn. New Haven Colony*, no. XXIV; Fairbanks and Trent, *New England Begins*, no. 483.

Bibliography: Kirk, *Early Am. Furn.*, fig. 78; Kane, "New Haven Colony Furn.," fig. 10; Joseph T. Butler, *American Furniture from the First Colonies to World War I* (London: Triune Books, 1973), p. 13; Chinnery, fig. 4:226; Kirk, *Am. Furn. & Brit. Trad.*, fig. 164; Trent, "Postscript," fig. 10.

Provenance: Francis P. Garvan, New York, N. Y.

THIS chest for many years has been attributed to central coastal Connecticut, and Robert F. Trent recently has suggested that it is part of a group of furniture made in New Haven in a tradition of London-style joinery that originated there in the shops of William Russell (1612–1664/65) and William Gibbons (here by 1640–d. 1689).[1] Citing as evidence its economical means of construction as well as its pseudo-joined facade, Trent has linked this chest with "an entire class of inexpensive furniture regularly produced in urban shops in England."[2] To date, unfortunately, London furniture of this type has not been studied in detail or published extensively. Presumably this tradition was brought to the New Haven Colony by Russell, Gibbons, and other known and unknown craftsmen who emigrated from London to America. It does seem clear that this group of furniture, which includes the Starr family cupboard in the Yale collection (cat. 194), was produced by the same set of craftsmen. However, this chest and the other related objects might well have been made after the death of Russell in 1664/65 and of Gibbons in 1689. No evidence that Russell and Gibbons worked together has been discovered, nor do any of the objects in the group have a history of descent in either the Russell or the Gibbons family. Thus an attribution of this furniture to "the Russell-Gibbons shops" is something of a misnomer and is worrisome on several accounts. It implies an earlier date for the objects than is necessary; it leads one to think that there was an active partnership where none is known to have existed; and, most important, it suggests a precise attribution to specific people largely on the basis of circumstantial evidence. If the "Russell-Gibbons"–type objects were made in New Haven (in itself hypothesis), and if they are in a style of joinery that could have been used only by a London-trained craftsman (a second supposition), they still might have been made by other New Haven craftsmen known to have been working in the late seventeenth and early eighteenth centuries.[3] Related chests include examples in a private collection, the Wadsworth Atheneum, and the Connecticut Historical Society (45.1133).[4]

The Mabel Brady Garvan Collection 1930.2219

1. Fairbanks and Trent, *New England Begins*, no. 482, contains an excellent analysis of the characteristics of this group of furniture and lists the known examples.
2. Fairbanks and Trent, *New England Begins*, no. 483.
3. Kane, *Furn. New Haven Colony*, app.
4. Nutting, *Treasury*, no. 95; Chinnery, fig. 4:227; *George Dudley Seymour's Furniture Collection in the Connecticut Historical Society* (Hartford: Connecticut Historical Society, 1958), p. 32.

34

34

Chest
Connecticut Valley, 1675–1725

Description: The cleated top has thumbnail molding at the front and sides and shadow molding at the rear edge. It is attached to the back with snipe-bill hinges. The front and back are rabbeted to accept the sides and nailed in place; the bottom is a single mill-sawn board with slightly beveled edges and is nailed to all four sides. The interior of the chest is plain. The sides continue to form the feet and are cut with a triangular notching; the kerf marks on each side of the notch cross slightly above the notch. The front is decorated with five lines of shadow molding and with painted decoration consisting of a red border on all four edges surrounding swirled decoration in the center in brown and yellow. A similar pattern appears on the sides and top; the shadow molding on the sides runs vertically.

Inscription: Roman numerals are incised on the underside of the bottom board.

Condition: The painted decoration appears to be original; it has suffered the most loss on the top. The lock and escutcheon are missing, the cleats have been replaced, and a large shrinkage crack in the top has been repaired. Small blocks were added to the back in 1967 to serve as braces to the hinges, which are replacements.

Wood: Southern yellow pine.

Dimensions: H 60.6; W 139.3; CW 131.5; D 46.8; CD 45.1.

Exhibition: Fairbanks and Trent, *New England Begins*, no. 169.

Bibliography: Walter A. Dyer, "The American Chest: Eighteenth Century," *Antiquarian* 17, no. 5 (November 1931): 48; Fairbanks and Bates, p. 12.

Provenance: Charles Woolsey Lyon, New York, N. Y.; by sale to Francis P. Garvan, New York, N. Y.

SIMPLE board chests of this kind decorated with incised moldings are often associated with the Connecticut Valley between Springfield and Deerfield, Massachusetts, although they undoubtedly were made throughout New England.[1] This example is noteworthy for the fine state of preservation of its painted decoration, which may have been applied in a manner to simulate a more costly joined and paneled chest.[2] The bottom board shows evidence of mill sawing and roman numerals carved at the saw mill to record the number of board feet in the board from which the chest bottom was made.[3]

The Mabel Brady Garvan Collection 1930.2240

1. Hosley and Zea, "Decorated Board Chests," pp. 1146–1151. A related example, dated 1702 and attributed to eastern Massachusetts, is in Randall, no. 13.
2. Fairbanks and Trent, *New England Begins*, no. 169, contains an excellent discussion of this form of painted decoration.
3. Fairbanks and Trent, *New England Begins*, p. 507, fig. 79.

35

Chest with drawer
Central Connecticut, probably East Windsor, 1680–1710

Description: This large chest with drawer is constructed primarily with thick mill-sawn boards. The cleated top projects at the front and sides and has thumbnail molding at the front and sides. It is attached to the back with snipe-bill hinges. The front and back of the chest section are rabbeted to accept the sides and are secured by rosehead nails. The bottom of the chest section is fitted to grooves in the sides and nailed in place through the front, back, and sides. The interior contains a till on the right; the lid of the till is molded. The front of the object is decorated at the sides with square notches and with horizontal shadow molding and two horizontal lines of continuous diamond or lozenge shapes created

35

by grooves cut at an angle. The sides extend below the drawer to form the feet and are shaped with a central triangular cutout. The drawer was fitted originally to receive a wooden bolt descending from the chest section to serve as a lock; part of the bolt and two cleats used to secure the bolt to the inside of the chest survive. Grooves cut in the center of the drawer front and back, and the remains of nails in these grooves and in the drawer bottom, suggest that the drawer was partitioned originally. The drawer sides are channeled and hang on runners nailed to the side of the chest. The drawer sides are let into grooves in the front and back of the drawer and nailed through the front and the back. The drawer bottom is a single board and is nailed to the front and sides. It also is nailed to a thin strip or nailing block running along its rear edge, which in turn is nailed to the drawer back.

Inscriptions: There is a great deal of writing in chalk on the underside of the top, much of it illegible. One inscription, which appears to be early, reads "Stoughton / East Windsor / Hartford [?] Conn." "H T" is incised on the underside of the top as well.

Condition: The cleats on the top are replacements, and the hasp on the top is new. The bottom edge of the drawer front has been pieced at both sides, and the front and sides of the chest have been repainted a reddish color. Modern brackets have been added to strengthen the joint of the drawer sides to the back, and the channels on each drawer side have been repaired at the upper edges. The pulls are missing.

Woods: Top, all four sides, bottom of chest, drawer bottom and back, southern yellow pine; drawer sides, till, white oak.

Dimensions: H 74.1; W 143.3; CW 134.1; D 49.2; CD 45.1.

Exhibition: Kirk, *Conn. Furn.*, no. 28.

Bibliography: Chinnery, fig. 3:400; Hosley and Zea, "Decorated Board Chests," fig. 7.

Provenance: The chalk inscriptions on this chest suggest that it was owned by the Stoughton family of East Windsor. If that was the case, the original owner might have been Thomas Stoughton, who owned "A cubbord A chest & 2 Boxes" valued at a total of £2 at his death in 1684, or his son John (1657–1713).[1] In the twentieth century, the chest was acquired by dealer Henry V. Weil, New York, N. Y.; by sale in 1923 to Francis P. Garvan, New York, N. Y.

THIS object is part of a relatively large group of board chests that share many similarities and that can be traced to the Connecticut Valley.[2] Its early chalk inscription leads one to believe that it was owned originally by one of the numerous members of the Stoughton family in East Windsor and the surrounding area. If that was the case, it may have been made by a member of the Bissell or Loomis families, several of whom were joiners in Windsor and East Windsor in the late seventeenth and early eighteenth centuries. Nathaniel Loomis (d. 1733), for example, made a chest costing eight shillings for Samuel Rockwell of East Windsor in the 1690s, the low price indicating that it was probably made of inexpensive mill-sawn boards, as is the case with this example.[3] The incised "H T" on the underside of the top raises the tantalizing possibility, however, that the chest was made by Henry Treat (1649–1681), a joiner of Wethersfield who is thought to have made and owned a similar board chest dated 1673 and bearing his initials now in the collection of the Wadsworth Atheneum.[4]

The Mabel Brady Garvan Collection 1930.2218

1. Henry R. Stiles, *The History and Genealogies of Ancient Windsor, Connecticut*, vol. 2 (Hartford: Case, Lockwood & Brainard Co., 1891–1892), pp. 725–742.
2. Hosley and Zea, "Decorated Board Chests," p. 1146.
3. Kane, "Joiners of Hartford County," pp. 79–81; the value of board chests is thought to have been less than thirteen shillings in the late seventeenth and early eighteenth centuries; see Hosley and Zea, "Decorated Board Chests," p. 1146.
4. Hosley and Zea, "Decorated Board Chests," fig. 5; see also *Great River*, cat. 80, for more details on Henry Treat.

36

36

Chest with drawers
Eastern Massachusetts, 1700–1735

Description: The rectangular, cleated top is a single board with a half-round molding on the front edge. It is attached with pintle hinges to a strip nailed to the upper edge of the back. The front is decorated to simulate five drawers, two false above three working ones, divided and flanked by half-round moldings. Each drawer has a blind central brass escutcheon and round escutcheons with teardrop pulls and is painted with double foliate scrolls in black against an orange (now faded to red) ground. The same colors are used on the sides in a combwork pattern. The chest interior has a lidded till on the right side; the edge of the till is molded. Of board construction, the front and sides are rabbeted to accept the sides and nailed. The drawer dividers are housed in the side and nailed through the sides; their front edges are shaped to half-round molding. The bottom of the chest is a single board nailed to all four sides, and the back consists of several horizontal butted boards nailed in place. There are no dustboards or a bottom beneath the lower drawer. The sides continue at the rear to form shaped feet, and there is a framework at the front and sides of thick boards. The sides of this framework are tenoned to the front and double pinned. The front is molded to match the applied moldings on the sides. The turned front feet are doweled through this board, and the dowels wedged. The drawers are side hung; the drawer sides are dovetailed to the front with a single large dovetail penetrated by the groove for the drawer runner and reinforced with a nail above the channel. The drawer backs are rabbeted to accept the sides and nailed through the back above and below the runner groove; each bottom is a single board and is nailed to a rabbet in the front and to the sides and back. The drawer dividers all were originally fitted with knobs that could be inserted into a gouge or hole in the drawer bottom above to serve as a locking device.

Inscription: There is an illegible chalk inscription consisting of several words on the underside of the top.

36a

Chests and Chests with Drawers 105

Condition: The painted decoration is in excellent condition, although it has been lost on the top. The drawer runners have been replaced, and small strips have been added to the drawer backs to serve as stops. The left side of the strip for the hinges has been repaired, and two of the backboards are replacements. The locking devices on the drawer dividers have been lost, and the holes patched.

Woods: Sides, top, drawer dividers, back, bottom of chest, applied moldings, drawer fronts, sides, backs, bottoms, eastern white pine; bottom framework, lid of till, cleats, strip for hinges, white oak; front feet, a maple, probably red maple.

Dimensions: H 112.6; W 102.7; CW 98.6; D 51.5; CD 47.6.

Bibliography: Kirk, *Early Am. Furn.*, fig. 69; Kane, "American Furn.," fig. 2; Kirk, *Am. Furn. & Brit. Trad.*, fig. 479.

Provenance: Israel Sack, Inc., New York, N. Y.; by sale to Francis P. Garvan, New York, N. Y.; by descent in 1937 to Mabel Brady Garvan, New York, N. Y.

THE painted scrolls on the front of this chest may have been applied with a stencil, first used to create the scrolls on one side of the drawers and then reversed to outline those on the other side. The drawers in the chest are not graduated in order to permit the repeated use of the same stencil. These scrolls are a less expensive version of the type of scrolls created on English objects with marquetry.[1] A chest with related scrolls and of similar construction is at Winterthur (58.542), and another related chest in a private collection has been published.[2]

The Mabel Brady Garvan Collection 1960.54.2

1. This relationship has been pointed out by Fales, *Am. Painted Furn.*, p. 50; and Kirk, *Am. Furn. & Brit. Trad.*, p. 178. Kirk illustrates an English object (fig. 480) with related marquetry scrolls; an even closer prototype for the Yale chest, in that it has paired scrolls on each side of the drawers, with the center in reserve, is illustrated in Herbert Cescinsky, *English Furniture of the Eighteenth Century*, vol. 1 (London: George Routledge & Sons, 1910), fig. 135.

2. Fales, *Am. Painted Furn.*, fig. 48; Beulah E. Larson, "Living with Antiques: A Salt-box House in Tulsa, Oklahoma," *Antiques* 94, no. 2 (August 1968): 213. A fourth related chest in a private collection is known (DAPC files).

37

37

Chest with drawers
New England, probably eastern Massachusetts, 1733 or 1735

Description: Made to appear as a chest of drawers with five drawers, the front of this object has two simulated drawers over three real ones, divided and flanked by applied double half-round molding. All the real and simulated drawers have stamped brasses and blind escutcheons. The cleated top has double half-round edging at the front and is attached to the back with snipe-bill hinges. The front and back are lapped to the sides and nailed in place; the back consists of two horizontal boards lapped together. The bottom of the chest section is a single board nailed to the sides; the bottom of the entire object consists of a wide pine board at the rear butted to a narrow but thicker oak board at the front, and both boards are nailed in place. The sides extend below the applied base molding to form the rear feet, and the chest is supported by turned front feet. The feet are doweled through the bottom. In each drawer, the drawer sides are dovetailed to the front and back with a single large dovetail

106 *American Case Furniture*

reinforced with a T-head nail. Each drawer bottom consists of two boards butted together and beveled at the front edge. They are fitted into grooves in the front and nailed to the sides and back with T-head nails. There are no dustboards between the drawers.

Inscriptions: Written in red paint on the outside of the back is the faint inscription: "Mad In The Year / Agust 7 day [followed by a slash] 1733 [or 5] / D : Clayton [or Clafton]." The inside of each drawer front is inscribed in chalk, "first," "second," and "third" respectively, moving from top to bottom. "April 16th / 1868" and other illegible notations in green paint appear on the underside of the top. A modern notation in black chalk or crayon reading "H:80" appears on the outside of the back, as does the modern notation in pencil "33.767."

Condition: The drawer runners and the running strips on the drawers have been replaced. The turned feet are considerably worn and rotted. The left rear edge of the top has been repaired. The current brasses are not original to the chest; at one time the working drawers were fitted with wooden pulls, and single holes behind the brasses on the simulated drawers indicate that the object may have been fitted originally with teardrop brasses. Evidence of several layers of red paint remains.

Woods: Eastern white pine; front feet, aspen; front board of bottom, white oak.

Dimensions: H 114.6; W 101.3; CW 97.8; D 46.4; CD 45.1.

Provenance: Francis P. Garvan, New York, N.Y.

THE importance of this chest lies in its early signed and dated inscription. Although the object can be dated to the early 1730s by the inscription, which reads 1733 or possibly 1735, the name of the maker has yet to be deciphered satisfactorily, and his identity remains elusive. The name is probably either D. Clayton or D. Clafton, but to date nothing has been learned about a New England furniture maker active in the 1730s with either of those names or with a variant spelling. The form of this chest is related to another chest with three drawers in the collection (cat. 36) attributed to eastern Massachusetts. In all likelihood, the example under consideration here originally had colorful painted decoration which, unfortunately, has been lost. Perhaps this decoration resembled that on another chest with drawers attributed to Massachusetts and in the collection of Nina Fletcher Little and Bertram K. Little.[1] The Littles' chest, also of pine, has some of the distinctive features found on the Yale chest; for example, its drawers are constructed with a single large dovetail reinforced with nails, its top is molded only along the front edge, and its sides extend to form the rear feet. Double half-round molding is found on a chest with drawers from Taunton, Massachusetts, dated 1742.[2] A related dovetailed chest, with a facade simulating six drawers and with a single half-round molding, has been published.[3]

The Mabel Brady Garvan Collection 1930.2321

1. Fales, *Am. Painted Furn.*, p. 6.
2. Fales, *Am. Painted Furn.*, fig. 46.
3. Jobe and Kaye, no. 8.

38

Chest with drawers
New England, 1700–1750

Description: This chest with two drawers has been fashioned to simulate a chest of drawers with four drawers. Both the two lower drawers, which are real, and the simulated upper two drawers are divided and flanked by double half-round molding. The projecting top has thumbnail molding at the front and sides, and its cleats fall within the chest interior. It is attached to the back with snipe-bill hinges. The sides are half lapped to the front and back and are nailed in place; below the chest section, the rabbet in the front of the sides has been filled with strips of chestnut to receive the molding. The chest bottom is two boards butted together and let into a groove in the sides. The back consists of two horizontal boards butted together and nailed in place. The drawer divider is dovetailed to the sides, there is no dustboard, and the bottom of the object is dovetailed to the sides. There is applied base molding at the front and sides, nailed to blocks above the turned feet and to a strip running behind the front molding. In each drawer, the sides are dovetailed to the front and back, and the drawer bottom is let into a rabbet in the front and nailed to the sides and back.

Inscription: Remnants of a modern paper shipping label remain on the outside of the back.

Condition: The backs of both drawers have been repaired, and modern braces added to reinforce the rear corners of the

38

upper drawer. The bottom of the lower drawer has been repaired, and new running strips have been added to each drawer. The drawer runners within the case have been replaced. The left and right side base moldings have been replaced, and the right corner of the front base molding has been patched. Many new nails have been added at various times to the drawers and to the lower board of the back. A large hole has been gnawed through the right lower corner of the back. The brasses are old but not original, and the iron lock on the top simulated drawer also is not original. The cleats on the top are additions or replacements, and some of the blocks above the feet are also replacements. The chest has been refinished, but traces of old red paint remain.

Woods: Top, sides, front, drawer fronts, moldings, soft maple; top backboards, chest bottom, drawer divider, bottom, eastern white pine; drawer sides, back, and bottoms, bottom backboard, strips applied to front edge of sides, chestnut.

Dimensions: H 89.6; W 97.9; CW 93.5; D 47.4; CD 45.1.

Bibliography: Ormsbee, *Story Am. Furn.*, p. 57; Symonds and Ormsbee, *Antique Furn.*, pl. LVIII.

Provenance: J. Norris, Chestnut Hill, Philadelphia, Pa.; by sale to Francis P. Garvan, New York, N. Y.

ALTHOUGH acquired by Francis P. Garvan as a Pennsylvania object, this chest with drawers more likely was made in New England. The combination of maple, white pine, and chestnut suggests an origin in eastern Connecticut or Rhode Island; the skill and finesse with which the chest is made suggests a trained maker. Perhaps the most unusual feature of the chest, which is in poor condition, is that the real and simulated drawers are not graduated in size from top to bottom as is often the case. Here, the top simulated drawer is higher than its counterpart below. It is almost certain that this chest was originally painted, in a solid color or with graining, as is the case with a Salem high chest of drawers, also of maple, in the Yale collection (cat. 134).

The Mabel Brady Garvan Collection 1930.2054

39

Chest with drawers
New England, 1710–1750

Description: The rectangular top is a single board with a molded edge at the front and sides and with cleats that are nailed in place and fall within the chest interior. It is attached to the back with butt hinges (see Condition). The front of the chest is decorated to appear as a chest of drawers, with two simulated drawers above two working ones, each divided and flanked by half-round molding that is applied (with the exception of the drawer divider, where the molding is run in the stock). Each drawer, real and simulated, has a central blind brass escutcheon flanked by escutcheons with bail pulls. There is base molding applied to the front and sides. The bottom of the case is a single board fitted to grooves in the sides, and the back consists of two horizontal butted boards. There is no dustboard between the drawers. Each drawer side is dovetailed to the front and reinforced with a nail; the drawer back is dovetailed to the sides. The drawer bottoms are each a single board with a beveled front edge fitted to a groove in the front and sides and nailed to the back. The chest bottom consists of two mill-sawn boards nailed in place. The chest is supported on four turned feet doweled through the bottom of the case (see Condition). The front, sides, and top of the chest have been repainted red.

Condition: The top was originally fastened with snipe-bill hinges. Many new nails have been added to the drawers, and

39

new running strips have been added to the drawer sides. Originally, the sides extended to form the feet; they have been cut off below the base molding, and the present turned feet, probably maple, applied. The base molding has been cut to accept the new feet.

Wood: Eastern white pine; new feet, probably maple.

Dimensions: H 93.5; W 94.1; CW 90.2; D 46.7; CD 44.7.

Bibliography: *Fifth Sale of Fine Early American Furniture Gathered by Jacob Margolis*, Sale 1872, 8 November 1924 (New York: Anderson Galleries, 1924), no. 277; Kirk, *Early Am. Furn.*, fig. 176.

Provenance: Jacob Margolis, New York, N. Y.; by sale at auction in 1924 to Francis P. Garvan, New York, N. Y.

THIS chest is basically in good condition, although it has been repainted, and would be a fine example of a broad class of simple eighteenth-century board furniture were it not for the addition of the new turned feet. Originally, the sides would have extended below the base molding and been notched or shaped at the center to form front and rear feet. Here, the sides have been cut off, and as John T. Kirk has pointed out, "the bottoms of the side boards show new sawing and stain; the new bun feet are artificially ovoid in form, the bases are burned, and charcoal comes off the bottom if they are scraped."[1] Despite this alteration, which dramatically alters the visual presence of the object, the remainder of the chest stands as a document of simple New England furniture. An interesting feature is that the drawer sides are dovetailed to the front, while the backs are dovetailed to the sides, a feature that has been noted on some Connecticut furniture.[2]

The Mabel Brady Garvan Collection 1930.2216

1. Kirk, *Early Am. Furn.*, p. 175.
2. Cooke, p. 46.

40

Chest with drawers
New England, 1710–1750

Description: The rectangular top has applied molding at the front and sides that overlaps the case, and it is attached to the back with snipe-bill hinges. The front and back are rabbeted to accept the sides and nailed in place. The front is formed to four graduated drawers, two simulated over two real ones, divided and flanked by applied half-round molding. Each drawer, real and simulated, has a pair of round brass escutcheons with teardrop pulls. The chest bottom is a single longitudinal board fitted to grooves in the sides. The back consists of two horizontal butted boards. The sides continue at the rear to form the feet, and there are turned feet at the front corners (see Condition). The drawer sides are dovetailed to the front (with a single dovetail in the upper drawer and two in the lower drawer) with nails added as a reinforcement. In each drawer, the bottom is a single longitudinal board nailed to a rabbet in the front and to the sides and the back; the drawer back is butted to the sides and nailed through the sides. There is applied molding at the base, and the bottom of the case is again a single board with evidence of mill sawing.

Inscriptions: The modern "G 949" in black appears in the inside bottom of each drawer; "#6 / top," again modern, in white chalk appears on the inside bottom of the chest.

Condition: This chest has been extensively restored and

Chests and Chests with Drawers 109

40

thoroughly refinished. There are traces of reddish-brown paint. The hinges are replacements; at one time the chest was fitted with butt hinges, which were removed when the present staple hinges were attached. The brasses and drawer runners are replacements. The front feet are also replacements. The bottom board has been drilled with holes, now plugged, just to the inside of each existing front foot. The underside of the bottom bears a ring impression around these holes, suggesting that turned feet may have been doweled through them at one time, perhaps marking the original feet or an earlier restoration.

Woods: Eastern white pine; feet, ash.

Dimensions: H 83.9; W 94.3; CW 90.1; D 43.2; CD 41.2.

Bibliography: Nutting, *Treasury*, no. 246.

Provenance: Henry V. Weil, New York, N. Y.; by sale to Francis P. Garvan, New York, N. Y.

THIS chest is another example of a heavily restored object (see also cat. 39). It is possible that here, as with cat. 39, the turned feet are an addition and that the sides of the case originally continued to form both the front as well as the rear feet. Regardless of the age of the feet, the remainder of the chest is in poor condition, having been stripped and refinished, and with other additions and replacements. It retains value today primarily as an example of a plain board chest, undoubtedly painted originally, and characteristic of a large group of common eighteenth-century objects.

The Mabel Brady Garvan Collection 1930.2731

41

Chest with drawers

Connecticut, 1710–1760

Description: The front of this chest with one drawer is divided by applied moldings nailed in place to simulate a division into four drawers. The cleated top has thumbnail molding at the front and sides and shadow molding at its rear edge. It is attached to the top with snipe-bill hinges. The front and back are rabbeted to accept the sides and are nailed in place. The sides continue below applied base molding to form the feet and are shaped with paired reverse curves. The chest bottom is a single board nailed in place. The back consists of a wide board butted against a lower narrow board, with both boards nailed in place. The drawer runners are nailed to the sides, and a strip runs across the front to serve as a support for the drawer. The lipped drawer front is rabbeted to accept the sides, which are held in place with two T-head nails. The drawer bottom consists of three riven boards lapped together; their front and sides are beveled and let into grooves in the drawer front and sides, and they are nailed to the back. The back is rabbeted to accept the sides and is nailed through the back, again with two T-head nails. The interior of the drawer is divided into three units, two small sections flanking a larger center section, with partitions set in grooves in the front and back and nailed in place. Traces of red paint remain on the front of the chest.

Inscriptions: "M H" is written in white paint within a red heart on the second simulated drawer front. Chalk numerals appear on the underside of the top.

Condition: New cleats have been screwed to the outside edges of the top, falling outside the case, and two boards have been nailed to the underside of the top and fall within the case. A metal patch has been nailed to the left side of the front to cover a gnawed hole. The left base molding was replaced

41

in 1968, and new wooden pulls were added to the drawer in 1977.

Wood: Yellow poplar.

Dimensions: H 84.3; W 118.1; CW 112.2; D 50.2; CD 48.5.

Provenance: According to a tradition recorded in the files of Francis P. Garvan, this chest was owned originally by Mary Hale, mother of Nathan Hale (1755–1776), of Coventry, Conn. Unfortunately, Nathan Hale's mother was named Elizabeth (Strong) Hale, and unless one is willing to accept the initials painted on the front as standing for "Mother Hale," this history of ownership in the Hale family cannot be substantiated.[1] Owned in the twentieth century by John Tynan, Middletown, Conn.; by sale to Francis P. Garvan, New York, N. Y.

For many years, this chest was lent by Yale to the Nathan Hale Homestead in Coventry, Connecticut, maintained by the Antiquarian and Landmarks Society, Inc., of Connecticut, on the strength of its unsupported history of ownership in the family of the famous patriot. It is a rather simple chest, in good condition, and it could well have been made by a carpenter working in Connecticut. It represents an interesting stage in the relationship between the chest and the chest of drawers. Here, the tension between these two forms resolved itself in an unusual way. The exterior is fashioned to appear as a chest of drawers, allowing the owner to appear fashionable and modern, while retaining the more traditional interior space of a chest three "drawers" deep. The deception was not carried out even further, however, with either brasses or pulls on the simulated drawers, perhaps for reasons of economy. And yet a desire for more modern, differentiated inner space is indicated by the division of the drawer interior into three compartments.

The Mabel Brady Garvan Collection 1931.1214

1. *Dictionary of American Biography*, s.v. "Hale, Nathan."

42

Chest with drawers
Connecticut Valley, possibly Hatfield, Massachusetts, 1720–1740

Description: The cleated top is made of two boards butted together and has thumbnail molding at the front and sides. It is attached to the back with snipe-bill hinges. The front is visually organized into four graduated drawers, two simulated ones above two real ones, divided horizontally by double half-round molding and flanked by two vertical strips of the same molding applied to the stiles. The working drawers have turned wooden pulls. All four stiles continue below applied base molding and are turned to form baluster-shaped feet. The object is joined, and the sides contain fielded panels. The stiles are beveled on their upper inside edges within the chest section. The bottom of the chest section consists of three boards butted together; their front edges are beveled and fitted to a groove in the front, and they are nailed to the back from underneath. The upper back is framed in behind the chest section, and the lower back consists of two boards lapped together, beveled at their edges, and nailed to the case on all four sides. The drawer runners are nailed to the stiles, and there are no dustboards or a bottom under the lowest drawer. The sides of each drawer are dovetailed to the front and back with four squarish dovetails reinforced with nails in three of the pins; the pins of the rear dovetails extend slightly beyond the back to serve as a stop. The bottom of each drawer is a single board beveled at the front and sides, fitted to a groove in the drawer front and sides and nailed to the back from underneath with

42

T-head nails. The front and sides of the chest are decorated with painted graining in black and brown on an orange or red ground.

Inscriptions: The inside of the back of each drawer bears a joiner's chalk mark. The modern "902 / 249" appears in chalk on the outside of the back. A small piece of modern adhesive tape affixed to the inside of the left top rail bears "G Cole[?] / 16."

Condition: The wooden pulls on the drawers are replacements for the original brasses. Holes on the inside of the chest section indicate that brasses were present originally. The existing painted graining, which probably dates to the first half of the nineteenth century, runs over the location of these holes, which have been filled, on the front of the chest. The graining has worn away on the rear feet, revealing a coat of red paint that may be original.

Woods: Southern yellow pine; stiles, soft maple.

Dimensions: H 122.2; W 104.4; CW 98.2; D 50.5; CD 48.7.

Bibliography: Kirk, *Early Am. Furn.*, fig. 193.

Provenance: Frank W. MacCarthy, Longmeadow, Mass.; by sale to Francis P. Garvan, New York, N. Y.

For many years, this chest and related examples have been attributed to the area of Hatfield, Massachusetts, because several were found there and on the basis of their general relationship to some of the so-called Hatfield type of the so-called Hadley chests (see cats. 29–31). Francis P. Garvan also once owned a related chest with drawers, again purchased from Frank W. MacCarthy, and now in the collection of the Williams College Museum of Art (43.2.11).[1] These two chests share double half-round moldings, fielded panels on the sides, high turned legs, and dovetailed drawers, although the Williams example has a molded cornice below the top and its feet are of a different profile.[2] A relatively late date for this chest is suggested because the drawers are dovetailed and not side hung and the boards used to construct the drawers are slightly thinner than the massive boards used on earlier examples. Here, however, the early feature of an applied board nailed to the lower part of the back has been retained. Simpler versions of this kind of chest, lacking the applied moldings and fielded panels, are thought to have been made in Deerfield and are associated with the name John Hawks. Some of these Deerfield examples also retain traces of old red paint.[3]

The Mabel Brady Garvan Collection 1930.2254

1. *Garvan Coll.*, no. 131. Also illustrated in Karl E. Weston, "American Furniture at Williams College," *Antiques* 45, no. 2 (February 1944): fig. 5.
2. See Leslie B. Keno, *Early American Furniture from the Charles M. Davenport Collection* (Williamstown, Mass.: Williams College Museum of Art, 1978), no. 4.
3. Fales, *Deerfield*, p. 177.

43

Chest with drawers
Probably South Shaftsbury, Vermont, 1820–1830
(see pl. 3)

Description: The rectangular top of a single board is faced with flat applied strips at the front and sides and is attached to the back with iron rectangular hinges. The front is fashioned with two applied simulated drawers above two work-

ing ones, thus appearing to be four graduated and lipped drawers with blind oval lock escutcheons and brass pulls. The front skirt is shaped with a central drop or oval medallion and bracket feet. The sides and back are shaped to simple round arches. In the upper chest section, the front and back are rabbeted to accept the sides and nailed in place. The chest interior contains a lidded till on the right, and the chest bottom is a single board nailed to all four sides. The back of the lower section, behind the drawers, is a single board butted against the top board and nailed in place. Below the chest section on the front, facing strips have been nailed to the edges of the sides, and the skirt is nailed in place. The drawer divider is tenoned to the sides, and the drawer runners are nailed to the sides. There is an additional supporting strip for the bottom drawer nailed to the back. There are no dustboards and no bottom beneath the lowest drawer. The sides of each drawer are dovetailed to the front and back, and the pins project slightly at the rear. Deep kerf marks are visible on the inside of the drawer fronts. Each drawer bottom is a single board let into grooves in the front and sides and nailed to the back. The chest is decorated with paint on the top, front, and sides. The drawer fronts are grained in imitation of a wood veneer, probably mahogany, with stylized crossbanding and stringing. The oval drop in the skirt is grained as a veneered panel surrounded by stringing, and painted stringing is also evident on the sides, top, and edges of the top.

Condition: The painted graining is in good condition and little inpainting is visible under ultraviolet light. The hinges are replacements, and the top edge of the back was repaired when they were installed. The brasses are also replacements. The facing strips on the top have been repaired at several places, and the right front leg and both rear feet have been pieced. Many new nails have been used on the backboards.

Wood: Basswood.

Dimensions: H 94.5; W 98.8; CW 95.7; D 45.8; CD 44.5.

Bibliography: *Antiques* 102, no. 3 (September 1972): 374; "Acquisitions 1972," *YUAG Bulletin* 34, no. 2 (June 1973): 66.

Provenance: This chest was in the hands of at least two dealers, including one named Steckler and another in northwestern Connecticut, before it was acquired by Betty Sterling of Brainstorm Farms Antiques, Randolph, Vt.; by sale in 1972 to the Yale University Art Gallery.

This chest with two drawers is part of a group of more than ten examples of painted furniture thought to have been

43

made in southern Vermont, possibly by Thomas Matteson of South Shaftsbury.[1] The cornerstones of this group are two documented objects: a chest with two drawers bearing the inscription "Thomas Matteson / S. Shaftsbury, Vermont / 1824," and a chest inscribed "Thomas G. Matison / South Shaftsbury / V.t / 1824."[2] However, none of the six men by the name of Thomas Matteson living in South Shaftsbury in the early 1800s has been identified as a woodworker or decorative painter, and it is probable that the inscriptions relate to the owner rather than the maker or painter of the objects. Recently the question of attribution has become even more clouded by the acquisition by Historic Deerfield, Inc., of a chest with two drawers (79.100) inscribed "By J. Matteson" and dated 1803.[3] The Yale chest shares many characteristics with the "Thomas Matteson" group, including the oval panel in the skirt, the painted banding and stringing, the lipped drawers (both simulated and real), the parallel diagonal lines on the legs, the rounded shaping of the side skirts, the hollow corners on the drawers and top, the paired crescents on the top, and the flat strips applied to the front and sides of the lid. Most important, the colorful and exuberant painted interpretation of wood grain here is in keeping with the techniques and skill demonstrated by the as yet unknown painter of these objects.

Millicent Todd Bingham Fund 1972.89

1. This group was first identified by Caroline Hebb in her article "A Distinctive Group of Early Vermont Painted Furniture," *Antiques* 104, no. 3 (September 1973): 458–461. Color illustrations of some of the objects in this article and of other related objects can be found in Fales, *Am. Painted Furn.*, figs. 373, 397; Henry J. Harlow, "Decorated New England Furniture," *Antiques* 116, no. 4 (October 1979): pls. XV, XVI; and Jean Lipman and Alice Winchester, *The Flowering of American Folk Art, 1776–1876* (New York: Viking Press in cooperation with the Whitney Museum of American Art, 1974), fig. 312. See also *Important American Furniture and Folk Art*, Sale 5228, 8 December 1984 (New York: Sotheby's, 1984), lot 105.

2. Hebb, "A Distinctive Group," figs. 2, 2a, 5, 5a.

3. The writer would like to thank Philip Zea for bringing this object to his attention.

44

44

Chest

Lancaster County, Pennsylvania, ca. 1776

Description: The rectangular top is of a single board and has wide, heavy molding fitted with a tongue and groove to its side ends; the front edge of the top has four through-tenons which pierce the molding and are pinned from above.[1] Cyma molding is pinned to the front and sides of the lid beneath the thumbnail molded edges. The top is attached to the back with wrought-iron strap hinges, and there is a crab lock attached with a rivet. The interior holds a lidded till at the left with two drawers below. The lid of the till is molded; the till drawers are lipped, their sides are dovetailed to the front and back, and their bottoms are nailed in place through the sides and are flush with all four sides. The front and back of the chest are joined to the sides with wedged through-dovetails. The front contains boards pegged in place that simulate two roundheaded arches flanking a central pointed arch, each supported by fluted pilasters. The panels are painted white, with flowerpots and flowers in red outlined in black or blue, and the date and initials are in blue. The moldings on the lid and the base molding are painted black; the sides and top of the chest do not appear to have been painted. The bottom consists of two lapped boards, and there are iron carrying handles on the sides. The five turned feet, one in each corner and one at the center of the front, are doweled into a framework of boards at the front and sides. This framework projects slightly, and the base molding is pinned to it, and it in turn is pinned to the bottom.

Inscriptions: "Caspar / Hildebrand" is written in chalk on the underside of the top, where other, illegible chalk inscriptions also appear. The front of the chest has "17 / 76" painted in the side panels and "C·B·H·B·" in the center panel.

Condition: Evidence indicates that this chest originally had a center front foot. The original left rear foot was moved to that location, its upper portion repaired, and a replacement installed at the left rear.

Woods: Chest sides, back, front rails and stiles, lid of till, eastern white pine; applied panels on front, applied moldings on front, side and bottom of till, southern yellow pine; feet, till drawer fronts, American black walnut; applied moldings on sides of top, sides of base framework, white oak.

Dimensions: H 59.8; W 126.6; CW 121.5; D 57.7; CD 55.3.

44a

114 *American Case Furniture*

Bibliography: Montgomery, "1776—Furniture," p. 63; Fabian, fig. 78; Kane, "American Furn.," fig. 7.

Provenance: Originally owned by Caspar Hildebrand whose name appears on the underside of the lid and whose initials (for *CasBar HildeBrand*) are painted on the front. There were people with this name in Lancaster and York counties in the late eighteenth century. Acquired by Francis P. Garvan, New York, N. Y., prior to 1930; by descent in 1937 to Mabel Brady Garvan, New York, N. Y.

ALTHOUGH the painted date of 1776 on this chest might lead one to be suspicious, it is a perfectly plausible date for one of these architectural chests associated with Lancaster County. Dated examples have been found ranging from 1764 to 1795, and the form seems to have declined in popularity after the end of the century.[2] A particularly close example to the Yale chest is in the collection of Winterthur (65.2255).[3] It is dated 1774 and has four initials at the top of the center arch. Like the Yale chest, it was fitted originally with a foot in the center of the front (now missing), and it contains a lidded till with drawers below on the interior. "L W" also is painted on the Winterthur chest, and Monroe Fabian has suggested that the initials may be those of the as yet unknown decorator.[4] Another related chest, in the Philadelphia Museum of Art (25.93.4), is dated 1787, and many other examples have been published.[5]

The Mabel Brady Garvan Collection 1960.54.1

1. This technique is discussed in Forman, "German Influences," p. 139.
2. Fabian, pp. 42–43.
3. Illustrated in Forman, "German Influences," fig. 81; and Fabian, fig. 77.
4. Fabian, p. 124. Fabian was also the first to suggest that the four initials on the Yale chest represent one person's name, rather than the initials of a couple, and to link the initials with the name inscribed on the underside of the lid.
5. Garvan, *Pennsylvania German Coll.*, p. 21 no. 9. See also Fabian, figs. 53, 55, 119, 120, 122, 140, 159.

45

45

Chest with drawers

Berks or Montgomery County, Pennsylvania, ca. 1781
(see pl. 4)

Description: The top consists of two horizontal butted boards with cove molding pegged to the front and heavy molding tongue and grooved in place at the sides to serve as a cleat or batten. The top is secured to the back with wrought-iron strap hinges fastened with nails and rivets. The interior contains a lidded till on the left; the lid and bottom of the till are molded. The front and back are through-dovetailed to the sides with wedged dovetails. The front of the chest is painted with two astragal panels in brown and yellow, containing a name and date in red against a white background. The remainder of the chest is painted with comb- or spongework in green and brown, with fanlike decorations at the corners and top and bottom of the center. The top molding, molding above the drawers, and drawer lips are painted red, and the base molding and bracket feet with brown and yellow combwork matching the ground of the panels. The sides have a single astragal panel at the chest level, and the top was painted with two rounded arches flanking a central astragal panel. The chest bottom and the bottom are pinned in place, and the back is a single board. The rear feet are nailed in place, and the front and sides of the bracket-foot base are dovetailed and supported by shaped vertical blocks nailed with rosehead nails. In each drawer, the sides are dovetailed to the back with wedged dovetails; the bottom is let into a

rabbet in the front and is pinned to the underside of the sides and back. The drawer runners are pegged to the bottom. The center of the front base molding has decorative scrolls and drop.

Inscriptions: Painted on the front of the chest is "Gorg · 1781 · Bossert." On the underside of the lid, strips of paper, including a newspaper printed in English and another paper containing repeated phrases written in ink in German, are pasted to cover a gap created by shrinkage of the top. Some illegible writing in chalk also appears on the underside of the top. The modern "822 / 7–6" is written on the back, and an old shipping tag addressed to Francis P. Garvan is nailed to the underside of the bottom.

Condition: The painted decoration on the top has nearly worn away. The brasses are replacements, and four of the tips of the scrolls on the bracket feet have been replaced. The lock is missing on the lid, and the top edge of the back has split and been repaired with modern screws. New screws have been added to the strap hinges.

Wood: Yellow poplar.

Dimensions: H 66.4; W 121.6; CW 116.6; D 54.5; CD 51.5.

Bibliography: Fabian, fig. 115.

Provenance: Owned originally by a man named George Bossert (or some variant spelling), whose identity is not known. The name and related variants are found in Berks and Montgomery counties, and "Bosserd" in Lancaster County.[1] Acquired before 1930 by Francis P. Garvan, New York, N. Y.

THIS chest has been attributed by Monroe Fabian to an unknown decorator who worked near the Berks–Montgomery county line.[2] This painter made use of stencils in creating the outlines of the panels on this and another related chest, a rare instance of the use of this technique on a Pennsylvania German chest of the eighteenth century.

The Mabel Brady Garvan Collection 1930.2245

1. Fabian, p. 219 no. 21.
2. Fabian, pp. 63, 145.

46

46

Chest with drawers
Lehigh County, Pennsylvania, ca. 1788

Description: The top of this chest has molding pegged to the front and sides and is attached to the back with strap hinges. The chest interior contains a lidded till on the left; the front edge of the lid and the bottom are molded. The front of the chest is painted to three panels, outlined in blue; the side panels contain flowers, possibly tulips and pomegranates, and the center panel contains a large heart-shaped motif with the name and date painted within. There is heavy half-round molding above the two lipped drawers, which are separated by a vertical partition. The flowers, heart outline, letters, and numbers are in red on a white ground, and the moldings on the lid and above the drawers are painted red. The bracket-foot base, dovetailed at the front corners, is painted blue. There are vertical blocks pegged in place behind the front corners of the base and rear triangular feet nailed in the back. The bottom consists of two half-lapped longitudinal boards, and the front and back of the chest are fastened to the sides with wedged through-dovetails. Very squarish, large pegs are used throughout the case construction. The sides of each drawer are dovetailed to the front and back, and the drawer bottoms are of two boards, beveled at the sides and front, let into grooves in the drawer sides and front, and pinned to the underside of the back.

Inscriptions: "MAR GRE DA BO HIN and "1788" are painted in the front center panel. The modern "G1151" appears

116 *American Case Furniture*

twice on the inside of the right drawer. Three small glue outlines are present on the underside of the top; there are chalk numbers and letters there as well.

Condition: The front foot on the left side has been pieced at the bottom. The front of the chest behind the drawers has been repainted. The lock has been replaced, and there has been damage to the front of the chest in the lock area. An extra hinge has been added to the top on the left side, and the area near the hinge repaired.

Woods: Yellow poplar; lid of till, bottom of chest, drawer fronts, eastern white pine.

Dimensions: H 65.8; W 125.1; CW 118.8; D 57.6; CD 55.4.

Bibliography: Nutting, *Treasury*, no. 112.

Provenance: Presumably made for and owned originally by Margreda Bohin, whose identity has not been discovered. Acquired prior to 1928 by Francis P. Garvan, New York, N.Y.

ACCORDING to Monroe Fabian, Pennsylvania German chests embellished with large heart motifs have been found most often in Lehigh County, suggesting a place of origin for this example.[1] The motif was used elsewhere as well, as in another chest, made for Maria Stohlern and also dated 1788, probably made near Lancaster.[2]

The Mabel Brady Garvan Collection 1930.2485

1. Fabian, p. 115.
2. Fabian, fig. 128. For other chests with heart motifs, see Fabian, figs. 165, 180.

47

Chest with drawers
Berks County, Pennsylvania, 1780–1800

Description: The rectangular top consists of two boards with applied molding nailed to the front and sides; the molding overlaps the chest. The top is attached to the back with wrought-iron strap hinges fastened with nails and rivets. The interior contains a till on the left side; the lid of the till and the bottom have a molded front edge. The chest is fitted with an iron crab lock. The front and back are attached to the sides with wedged through-dovetails, and the top dovetail of each corner is reinforced with a wooden peg.[1] The bottom of

47

the chest is a single longitudinal board, and the true bottom consists of two longitudinal boards; they are both pegged in place. Boards with a molded upper edge are pegged to the front and sides at the drawer level; the drawers are separated by a vertical partition tenoned to the front and bottom. The lipped drawers have central brass escutcheons and brass bail pulls. The drawer sides are pinned to a rabbet in the front and attached to the back with wedged through-dovetails. The bottom of each drawer consists of two transverse butted boards pegged to a rabbet in the front and to the sides and the back. The top, front, and sides are painted with white, black, and red designs on a green ground that may have been originally blue. The drawer fronts and surrounding boards on the front and sides are painted a different shade of green. The design on the front features a pair of round arches supported by balusters and enclosing a flowerpot containing tulips and a central "pinwheel" flower. The arches are flanked by columns, and the sides of the front are painted with hearts that overlap the corners and have flowers emanating from their centers. A similar design is painted on the top; the sides feature the heart and flower motif and a pair of columns identical to those on the front. A tulip matching those on the front is painted in black on the outside of the back, perhaps as a practice exercise.

Inscriptions: Glue outlines, probably from two Fraktur, appear on the underside of the top; within one of them is an illegible chalk inscription containing letters and numbers.

Condition: The painted decoration is considerably worn on the top and sides and appears to have been restored on the front. Faint outlines of balusters matching those in the center

Chests and Chests with Drawers 117

of the front appear to the right of each existing column, perhaps indicating an initial error when the lines for the design were first scribed. Although the evidence of wear on the underside of the bottom indicates that this chest has been without feet for a long time (they were missing when the chest was first photographed in 1928), the chest probably was supported originally on a bracket-foot base. A tiny fragment of the original supporting bracket is still attached to the right side. The facing and molding around the drawers on the front has been pieced and replaced, and the drawer guides have been replaced. The locks on the drawers are missing, the central brass escutcheon on the front is a replacement, and at least two of the bail handles are replacements.

Woods: Top, sides, drawers, till, yellow poplar; chest bottom, bottom, eastern white pine.

Dimensions: H 60.2; W 130.3; CW 124.6; D 61.1; CD 58.4.

Bibliography: *Antiques* 14, no. 3 (September 1928): 189; *Catalogue, Early American Furniture . . . to Be Sold . . . by A. J. Pennypacker* (Pennsburg, Pa: A. J. Pennypacker, [ca. 1929]), p. 19.

Provenance: A. J. Pennypacker, Pennsburg, Pa.; by sale in 1928 or 1929 to Francis P. Garvan, New York, N. Y.

ONCE attributed to Lebanon County, Pennsylvania, the large group of chests with this style of painted decoration is now associated with Berks County.[2] The chests in this group vary in detail, but most share the pairs of rounded arches supported by columns and enclosing pots of tulips and "pinwheel" flowers. Hearts overlapping the corners and with flowers stemming from their centers are another motif common to most of this group. Monroe Fabian has suggested that the early examples in this style, including a chest that may be dated as early as 1771, included depictions of human figures that do not appear on chests made as time passed. The Yale chest is a relatively simple example of the style, and it seems very close in feeling and execution to a chest formerly owned by collector Arthur J. Sussel.[3] Another closely related chest is illustrated by Fabian, although in that example the motifs were painted against a bare wood background.[4] Columns similar to those flanking the arches here also appear on a chest owned by the American Museum in Britain, Bath, England.[5]

The Mabel Brady Garvan Collection 1930.2733

1. A diagram of this form of construction can be seen in Helen Cain and Charles F. Hummel, "The Carnation Chests: New Discoveries in Pennsylvania-German Art," *Antiques* 122, no. 3 (September 1982): fig. 2.

2. This group is attributed to Lebanon County in Esther Stevens Fraser, "Pennsylvania Bride Boxes and Dower Chests, II: County Types of Chests," *Antiques* 8, no. 2 (August 1925): 80–81; they are reattributed, to Berks County, in Fabian, figs. 64–72.

3. *Pennsylvania Furniture . . . Part One, from the Estate of the Late Arthur J. Sussel*, 23–25 October 1958 (New York: Parke-Bernet Galleries, 1958), no. 394.

4. Fabian, fig. 71.

5. John G. Shea, *The Pennsylvania Dutch and Their Furniture* (New York: Van Nostrand Reinhold Co., 1980), p. 67.

48

Chest

Centre County, Pennsylvania, 1810–1830

Description: The rectangular top is made of two boards and has molding, consisting of a half-round above a cove, pegged to its front and sides. The molding overlaps the chest, and the top is attached to the back with strap hinges. The front and back are attached to the sides with wedged mitered through-dovetails. The interior contains a lidded till on the left; the edges of the lid and the bottom are molded on their fronts. (An outline for a mortise is scribed and partially cut on the inside of the front on the right side, suggesting an intention to place the till on that side originally.) The bottom of the chest is a single longitudinal board pegged to all four sides. The base molding and bracket feet on the front and sides are each made of a single board, mitered and pegged in

118 *American Case Furniture*

place, and braced with vertical glue blocks. The rear feet are triangular boards similarly attached to the side boards. The front is painted with a design in blue, red, and black against a yellow ground featuring a central flower from which scrolled vines or tendrils flow to each side, terminating in some instances in tulips, incorporating birds, and perhaps suggesting a heart motif. A similar design was painted on the top. The painted designs follow scribed lines. The sides were painted the ground color, the molding on the top and the base molding were painted red, and the feet are painted black.

Inscription: The modern "255 / 7-4" is in white chalk on the outside of the back.

Condition: Although the paint on the top has suffered from abrasion, that on the front and sides remains in excellent condition. The lock is missing, and there is a large shrinkage crack in the bottom. Both feet at the left front corner have been repaired; the rear glue blocks have been replaced.

Wood: Eastern white pine.

Dimensions: H 62.9; W 127.0; CW 121.9; D 55.1; CD 53.2.

Bibliography: Theodore Sizer, "The Mabel Brady Garvan Collection of American Arts and Crafts," *YUAG Bulletin* 4, no. 2 (December 1930): 106; Rogers, "Garvan Furn. (1960)," fig. 20; Kirk, *Am. Furn. & Brit. Trad.*, fig. 171.

Provenance: A. J. Pennypacker, Pennsburg, Pa.; by sale to Francis P. Garvan, New York, N. Y.

CLEARLY of Pennsylvania origin, with its wedged dovetails, sturdy pegs, and painted decoration, this chest recently has been attributed to Centre County, Pennsylvania.[1] It shares a linearity of design and several motifs with chests from that area.[2]

The Mabel Brady Garvan Collection 1930.2222

1. Kirk, *Am. Furn. & Brit. Trad.*, p. 74.
2. Fabian, figs. 189, 243, 256; Fales, *Am. Painted Furn.*, fig. 445.

49

49

Chest
Eastern shore of Virginia, 1790–1800

Description: The rectangular top of this large chest consists of three boards butted together and held with large cleats nailed in place. It has thumbnail molding at the front and sides and is attached to the back with wrought-iron strap hinges. The front of the chest is framed with astral panels flanking a center section containing two small over one large fielded panel. The sides each have a single large fielded panel. The side panel frames are let into a rabbet in the front stiles and nailed through the front stiles. The muntins of the astral panels are formed of a single piece; the central, diamond-shaped panel is secured with additional glue blocks. The muntins, rails, and stiles are molded on their panel edges. Most of the mortise-and-tenon joints are secured with a single pin; the muntins are tenoned through the top rail. The back is a single board rabbeted to accept the sides and nailed in place. The bottom is three boards nailed in place. The stiles continue below the bottom to support the chest, and the decorative base molding and bracket feet are nailed to them on the front and sides.

Condition: The chest originally had a till on the right side; only its supporting strips remain. The strap hinges and the lock have been replaced, and the iron keyhole escutcheon is a replacement or addition. The right rear corner of the top and the upper edge of the back (from the right hinge to the side) have been repaired. A large block has been added to the right

rear corner as a reinforcement. The chest has been stripped and refinished; traces of green and white paint remain.

Wood: Southern yellow pine.

Dimensions: H 79.7; W 157.5; CW 153.0; D 64.5; CD 64.1.

Bibliography: Melchor et al., *Raised-Panel Furn.*, figs. 41–41f.

Provenance: M. L. Watson, Seaford, Del.; by sale to Francis P. Garvan, New York, N. Y.

ALTHOUGH acquired by Francis P. Garvan prior to 1930 as Virginia or Carolinas objects, only recently has research established that this chest and the succeeding example are part of a large group of raised-panel furniture made on the eastern shore of Virginia.[1] This is the largest of several related raised-panel chests that have been published. It is quite closely related to a chest now at Colonial Williamsburg (1930.108), although it appears to be by a different craftsman.[2] The Yale and Williamsburg chests have astral panels, also found on other types of eastern shore furniture, probably derived from plate XXVI of William Salmon's *Palladio Londinensis* (London, 1734), an English architectural book and builder's guide widely used in America. The Yale chest probably was painted originally in a contrasting scheme of green and white similar to that found on the Williamsburg chest, which retains its original paint.[3]

The Mabel Brady Garvan Collection 1930.2486

1. Melchor et al., *Raised-Panel Furn.*, pp. 51–59.
2. Melchor et al., *Raised-Panel Furn.*, p. 53, fig. 40. The entry for the Yale chest states (p. 52), "the side panel frames of this chest are simply butt jointed to the front frame stiles and nailed in place," which is not the case.
3. Melchor et al., *Raised-Panel Furn.*, pl. 3. The Williamsburg chest is also discussed in Wallace B. Gusler, *Furniture of Williamsburg and Eastern Virginia, 1710–1790* (Richmond: Virginia Museum, 1979), pp. 178–179.

50

50

Chest
Eastern shore of Virginia, 1790–1800

Description: This joined chest has a single board top with applied molded edge at the front and sides. It is attached to the back with snipe-bill hinges. The interior contains a till on the right side; the lid of the till is chamfered. The front contains six fielded panels, two arranged vertically on each side of a pair of horizontal panels, and each side has a single fielded panel. The rails, stiles, and muntins are molded on their panel edges. The muntins are mortised and tenoned to the rails but are only pinned in two instances. The stiles of the side panel frames are mortised and tenoned to the top rail and fit into rabbets on the front stiles. The rear stiles are nailed to the back boards. The stiles of the front panel frame also are mortised and tenoned to the top rail, and they are nailed to the front stiles of the sides. The back consists of two horizontal boards fitted together with a tongue and groove and nailed in place. The stiles continue below the case. The front bracket feet and base molding are formed from a single board which is shaped and nailed to the front stiles and the lower rail. The same system is used on the sides; the boards here are shaped with reverse curves rising to a pointed arch. The back feet are rough and are nailed to the lower edge of the backboard and to a rabbet in the rear stiles.

Condition: The chest has been stripped and refinished. Originally the panels and the frame were painted, probably in blue, and the beveled edges of the panels and the moldings probably were picked out in white. The lock is missing.

Wood: Southern yellow pine.

Dimensions: H 66.1; W 131.9; CW 128.6; D 45.0; CD 44.5.

Bibliography: Melchor et al., *Raised-Panel Furn.*, figs. 44–44f.

Provenance: M. L. Watson, Seaford, Del.; by sale to Francis P. Garvan, New York, N. Y.

LIKE the previous example (cat. 49), this chest recently has been attributed to the eastern shore of Virginia. Much smaller than the other Yale chest, this object also has lost its original paint.[1] Similar chests dated 1800 and 1801 are known.[2] These massive chests, like those made well into the nineteenth century by German immigrants and descendants, represent the survival of an old, traditional form in rural areas of the country.[3]

The Mabel Brady Garvan Collection 1930.2995

1. The original color scheme may have resembled that seen in Melchor et al., *Raised-Panel Furn.*, pls. 4, 5.
2. Melchor et al., *Raised-Panel Furn.*, figs. 45, 46.
3. See Appendix, no. 5.

Chests of Drawers

Usually made with four drawers, but sometimes with three or five, the chest of drawers has been a popular and relatively unchanging type of case furniture from the middle of the seventeenth century to the present. With its compartmentalized drawers providing specialized storage space and with a flat fixed top on which articles such as glass and ceramics could be displayed, the chest of drawers (sometimes called a case of drawers in period documents) was a functional and flexible form that has enjoyed a long life. The collection includes a Boston chest of drawers with doors (cat. 51), perhaps the earliest American example of the form to survive. Superbly made by skilled joiners and turners, fashioned of at least six native woods and four exotic tropical species, and in excellent condition, this object stands at the forefront of the development of the form and is probably contemporaneous with English examples. It is joined by six other New England examples dating from the late seventeenth and early eighteenth centuries (cats. 52–57). The mid and late eighteenth-century expressions of the form are represented by five New England blockfront chests of drawers (cats. 58–62), the unusual three-drawer example signed by Bates How and dated 1795 (cat. 63), and two examples made by the Dunlap family of southern New Hampshire (cats. 64, 65), including a five-drawer chest bearing the name Samuel Dunlap. The massive chest of drawers made by Jonathan Gostelowe of Philadelphia in 1789 for his wedding (cat. 66) is the cornerstone for attributing undocumented examples to his shop. The federal period and the early nineteenth century are represented by seven chests of drawers, including a stunning New Hampshire example with brilliant drawer fronts veneered with figured birch (cat. 67) and an example from Charleston, South Carolina (cat. 71). Among the more unusual objects in the collection is the miniature chest of drawers made by Henry Seem of Easton, Pennsylvania, in 1856 while an apprentice (cat. 74). The twentieth century is represented by only three examples, two made in New York City for the Osborn family (cats. 75, 76), including a chest of drawers with doors echoing the Boston example made three centuries earlier, and a large double chest designed by Edward Wormley for Dunbar in the 1950s (cat. 77).

51

Chest of drawers with doors
Boston, Massachusetts, 1650–1670
(see pl. 5)

Description: This chest of drawers with doors is in two cases. The top of the upper case overhangs the case slightly at the front and sides and is edged with applied molding at its front and sides. It is supported at the front and back of each side, and at each side and the center of the front, with corbels decorated with incised lines and dots and with plaques applied below the corbels. There is a dentil course below the top at the front and sides of the case, running between the corbels. The upper case contains two small drawers in line over a single deep drawer. The small drawers are fitted with a central turned wooden pull and contain panels of veneer surrounded by rectangular applied moldings. The small drawers are separated from the deep drawer by applied molding with triple, round, ebonized bosses at the center and each side of the front. The deep drawer is decorated at its center with an upper, small keyhole panel above a larger, vertical panel, each framed with applied moldings. The sides of the drawer hold a horizontal rectangular panel at the center, bordered by applied moldings, bordered in turn by mitered moldings framed by applied moldings, and bordered again by larger mitered moldings again framed by a border of applied moldings. The deep drawer is flanked by pairs of applied spindles on the front stiles in the form of simplified Tuscan columns with urn-shaped tops and rounded, pendant drops. The sides of the upper case are framed with a pair of vertical panels at the height of the deep drawer. The top rail is deep, extending the depth of the small drawers, and holds a central oval ebonized boss and a course of applied molding. The muntin has a central channel molding painted black, and the panels are edged with applied moldings. There is cove base molding at the front and sides of the upper case. The upper case rests on top of the lower case and is slightly restrained by broad torus molding at the top of the lower case. The front of the lower case contains a pair of paneled doors attached to the case with wrought-iron butterfly hinges. The left and right stiles of the lower case hold, from top to bottom, a triglyph, an applied molding, a pair of large applied spindles echoing the profile of those on the upper case, and an oval ebonized boss. The left stile of the right door is exaggerated in width and holds an identical arrangement of elements, appearing to simulate a freestanding center muntin; a wrought-iron lock escutcheon is fitted between its spindles. The top rail of each door holds at center an oval ebonized boss flanked by small, round bosses and a course of applied molding corresponding to that on the stiles; the bottom rails each hold a single ebonized boss. The

Chests of Drawers 125

51b

panels of each door are decorated with applied moldings in a cruciform pattern, with round bosses in each quadrant and strips of decorative veneer in each corner and between the quadrants. The center of each door holds an archway with inlaid keystone and capitals bordered by applied moldings and by raised, beveled moldings of decorative veneer. The sides of the lower case are framed to a pair of vertical panels. The top and bottom rail and the muntin contain central channel molding painted black, and the panels are edged with applied moldings. There is deep cove base molding at the front and sides of the lower case. The chest is supported at the front by large, rather flat turned ball feet with thin necks containing a ring and reel turning and with a scored line encircling the ball at center. The rear feet are formed by extensions of the stiles. The doors of the lower case open to an interior fitted with three wide drawers of nearly equal size, each originally fitted with a pair of leather pulls; an iron staple is fitted to the center of the middle drawer. The top of the upper case is a single longitudinal board pegged to the case; the bottom of the upper case consists of several transverse boards fitted together with a V-shaped joint and nailed to a rabbet in the front and sides and to the undersides of the back. The case is of framed-panel construction. The back is framed to two horizontal panels, with two pegs used to secure the joints of the stiles to the rails and the muntin to the rails; the top rail is of great depth. On the side panels, the muntins are secured with two pegs, while only a single peg is used to secure the joint between the rail and the stile. An ingenious device allows the two small drawers in the upper case to be locked. A small vertical groove is cut on the outside face of the inner side of each drawer, behind the dovetails. A small wooden turnbuckle, nailed to the rear of the center muntin, can be turned and inserted into these grooves, thus holding the drawers fast. This manuever can only be accomplished by reaching up inside the case when the deep drawer is in an open position. The deep drawer could then be closed and locked, effectively sealing the upper case. On the two small drawers in the upper case, the sides are held to the fronts with two dovetails. The back is rabbeted to accept the sides, which are nailed in place through the back with rosehead nails. The bottoms are a single transverse board, beveled on all four sides, let into a groove in the front, and nailed to the underside of the sides and back with rosehead nails. The drawers are side hung on runners applied to the frame. On the deep drawer in the upper case, three dovetails are used to secure the drawer sides to the front, and the drawer is hung on two runners. The back is again rabbeted to accept the sides, which are nailed in place above and below the grooves for the runners. The bottom consists of several transverse boards fitted to a groove in the front, beveled on their front and rear edges, and nailed in place with rosehead nails. The top boards of the lower case are nailed to a rabbet in the front and side rails and to the top of the rear rail. The back of the lower case is framed to three vertical panels in line. The top and bottom front rails are joined to the stiles with a shouldered tenon. On the sides of the lower case, the muntin is secured with two pegs, and the rails and stiles with one. The joints of the door frames are secured with two pegs; the left stile of the right door is, as mentioned, of greater width. The small bosses on the door panels are pegged through the doors. The three drawers in the lower case are fashioned in the same manner as the deep drawer in the upper case, except that only two dovetails are used on the drawer sides and each drawer is hung on only a single runner. The bottom of the lower case consists of several transverse boards nailed in place. The front feet are doweled to slight extensions of the front posts.

Inscriptions: The bottom edge of the drawer fronts in the lower case bear incised marks: "II" on the left side of the top and bottom drawer; "I" and "V" on the right side of the top and bottom drawer; and "X" on each side of the middle drawer. "L.2429" is written in chalk on the outside of the back of the upper case. A small piece of white adhesive tape bearing "802/1–5" in red ink is fixed to the top of the upper case at the right rear corner.

Condition: The chest has survived in superb condition. In the upper case, the outer corbels and the triple bosses on the

left side are replacements. In the lower case, the boss on the lower left side, below the spindles, is a replacement. There have been minor repairs to the midmolding, base molding, and applied moldings on the case. The keyhole panel on the deep drawer in the upper case was probably fitted originally with a lock which has been lost. The right capital of the archway on the raised center section of the right cupboard door is a replacement. The interior drawers in the lower case were originally fitted with leather pulls, of which only fragments remain; scored vertical lines on the drawer fronts mark their location. The turnbuckle for the small right drawer in the upper case has been lost.

Woods: Each case frame, principally white oak and red oak; drawer runners, panels, drawer fronts, most drawer sides and backs, white oak and red oak; top and bottom of upper case, top back rail of upper case, some of drawer linings, chestnut; one board in bottom of middle drawer in lower case, eastern white pine; front feet, soft maple; door frames in lower case, corbels and plaques underneath them, dentils, probably American black walnut; top and bottom of lower case, some drawer linings, light-colored, shaped moldings on doors in lower case, on small drawers in upper case, and most of same type of molding on deep drawer in upper case, cedar; applied bosses, probably maple or cherry; replaced small bosses on upper case, beech; edge molding on top of upper case, flat, beveled moldings on small drawers in upper case, molding separating these drawers from deep drawer below, wide, beveled moldings and some of the thin, shaped moldings on deep drawer, base molding of upper case, torus molding at top of lower case, triglyphs, molding below triglyphs, base molding of lower case, cedrela (*Cedrela odorata*); flat panels of dark, reddish-brown wood with irregular black markings on small drawers in upper case, on deep drawer in upper case, and on doors of lower case, spindles on upper case, snakewood (*Piratinera guianensis*); spindles on lower case, rosewood (*Dalbergia* spp.); pulls on small drawers in upper case, lignum vitae (*Guaiacum* spp.).

Dimensions: H 124.1; W 116.3; UCW 106.3; LCW 106.4; D 60.2; UCD 55.1; LCD 55.6.

Exhibitions: Cooper, *In Praise of America*, fig. 183; Fairbanks and Trent, *New England Begins*, no. 481.

Bibliography: Nutting, *Pilgrim Century* (1924), fig. 218; Halsey and Tower, *Homes of Our Ancestors*, fig. 22; Charles Over Cornelius, *Early American Furniture* (New York: D. Appleton-Century Co., 1926), pl. IX; Nutting, *Treasury*, no. 475; Forman, "Urban Aspects," fig. 3; *The Britannica Encyclopedia of American Art* (Chicago: Encyclopaedia Britannica Educational Corp., 1973), p. 194; Kane, "Hadley Chest," fig. 24; Chinnery, fig. 3:407; John T. Kirk, "The Tradition of English Painted Furniture, Part I: The Experience in Colonial New England," *Antiques* 117, no. 5 (May 1980): 1080; Mahonri Sharp Young, "Of Thee I Sing," *Apollo* 111 (June 1980): 467; Benno M. Forman, "The Origins of the Joined Chest of Drawers," *Nederlands Kunsthistorisch Jaarboek* 31 (1981): 175, fig. 4; Kirk, *Am. Furn. & Brit. Trad.*, fig. 467; Benno M. Forman, "The Chest of Drawers in America, 1635–1670: The Origins of the Joined Chest of Drawers," *Winterthur Portfolio* 20, no. 1 (Spring 1985): fig. 9.

Provenance: The early history of the chest is unknown. In 1924, when it was first published in Nutting's *Pilgrim Century*, it was owned by Mr. J. F. Bernard of Albany, N. Y. Nutting commented that he had been led to believe that the chest had been "found not a very great way from Albany" (p. 235). It was purchased from Bernard by New York dealer

Henry V. Weil, on behalf of Francis P. Garvan, New York, N.Y., probably shortly after the object appeared in Nutting.

GENERALLY recognized as the most important example of American seventeenth-century furniture to survive, this chest of drawers with doors has been the focus of much recent scholarship, particularly by Benno M. Forman and Robert F. Trent. Forman, in a detailed study of the origins of the joined chest of drawers, called attention to the London-style characteristics of the joinery and turnings of this object, deduced that it could only have been made in Boston by London-trained craftsmen, and suggested that early immigrant joiners Ralph Mason (1599–1678/79) and Henry Messenger (d. 1681) and turner Thomas Edsall (1588–1676) were strong potential candidates for the maker of this chest. This attribution was accepted with enthusiasm by Trent, who has pushed the beginning of the date range assigned the chest back to 1635, to coincide with the earliest known date of arrival for a craftsman in the Mason-Messenger-Edsall group. Although the chest might have been made as early as the 1630s or 1640s, most dated English examples were made in the 1650s and 1660s, and it seems most likely that this American chest was made contemporaneously. Forman and Trent, and others, have emphasized several salient features of this object, namely its use of exotic hardwoods (now identified with greater precision), its sophisticated architectural facade with crisp turnings and applied ornaments, and the high quality of its London-style construction, including finished interior surfaces and dovetailed drawer construction.[1] It is unfortunate that we do not know who the owner of this magnificent object was, but surely he was a man of prominence in a community of less than 3,000 people at midcentury.

The Yale chest is part of a group of at least five other objects, including a closely related chest of drawers at the Museum of Fine Arts, Boston (32.219), and several chests with drawers, including an incomplete example in the collection of the Society for the Preservation of New England Antiquities (1940.55).[2]

Part of the aesthetic of these objects and their related English counterparts was the use of exotic woods and precious materials for ornament. Ivory and mother-of-pearl were used on some English examples, and the snakewood found on the Yale chest is also seen occasionally on English examples.[3] The presence of snakewood, lignum vitae, rosewood, and Spanish cedar on the Yale chest indicates the high level of sophistication and the extent of cosmopolitan trade attained in Boston at an early date. These woods are native to Central and South America and may have been obtained directly from their source by Boston merchants, who began trading in the West Indies as early as the 1640s. Snakewood (also called letterwood, specklewood, tortoiseshell wood, and other names) was a highly prized material, exported to England and Europe in the seventeenth century, particularly from Surinam, formerly known as Dutch Guiana. The appearance of the wood was well described by an English Victorian cabinetmaker in the mid nineteenth century: "It is exceedingly hard, and close in the texture; in colour a reddish brown, like red hazel, varied by lighter and darker streaks running with the grain throughout; with numerous black spots, fainter and fewer towards the heart, but increasing towards the outside. The appearance of the wood from these spots, by a little aid of the imagination, may be supposed to resemble letters, or the scales of the reptile whose name it bears. The wood, when fine, is very beautiful." The author noted further: "Its adaptation to cabinet-work being much restricted by the smallness of its size, it is principally used in veneering picture-frames and in turnery, and in the more expensive kind of walking-sticks."[4]

The Mabel Brady Garvan Collection 1930.2109

1. See the works by Forman cited under Bibliography; and the entry by Trent in *New England Begins*, no. 481. Forman examined English examples dated between 1652 and 1667, although he called attention to a chest dated 1647. For English examples, see Forman, "Chest of Drawers in America," figs. 1, 3, 5, 6; Kirk, *Am. Furn. & Brit. Trad.*, figs. 468, 469; *Antiques* 126, no. 6 (December 1984): 1320 (dated 1655); Chinnery, figs. 3:405, 406, 4:46; Gilbert, *Furn. at Temple Newsam*, no. 150; and Percy Macquoid, *A History of English Furniture: The Age of Oak* (London: Lawrence and Bullen, 1904), figs. 207, 210, 211. For objects with similar types of ornament, see Kirk, *Am. Furn. & Brit. Trad.*, figs. 470–472 (cupboard dated 1654), 473 (chest); and Macquoid, *History of English Furniture*, fig. 408 (chest with drawers).

2. For a discussion of the group, see the works by Forman and Trent cited under Bibliography; and Jobe and Kaye, no. 6.

3. Hayward, *World Furn.*, fig. 310; Singleton, facing p. 210.

4. Blackie and Son, *The Victorian Cabinet-Maker's Assistant* (1853; reprint, New York: Dover Publications, 1970), p. 40; see also B. J. Rendle, comp. and ed., *World Timbers*, vol. 2, *North and South America (including Central America and the West Indies)* (Toronto: University of Toronto Press, 1970), pp. 90, 104, 128–129, for notes on the tropical woods used in the Yale chest.

52

52

Chest of drawers
Boston, Massachusetts, 1670–1700

Description: The top consists of two boards with thumbnail molding at the front and sides, and it is pegged to the case. Below the top is complex cyma molding applied to the front and sides. The rails and stiles are joined with mortise-and-tenon joints that are double pegged. The case holds four drawers, including a shallow drawer at the top, a deeper drawer below, and two drawers of the same intermediate size, separated by applied molding that overlaps the stiles. Each drawer is decorated with applied moldings to simulate two drawers in line, separated by a vertical molding with a brass escutcheon. The top drawer has applied moldings forming two rectangular panels, the wide drawer is formed with applied complex moldings to rectangles with reentrant top and bottom, and the bottom two drawers each have pairs of square panels. Each panel has a central round brass escutcheon with a drop pull. There is heavy base molding at the front and sides, the rear feet are formed by extensions of the stiles, and there are turned feet in the front. The sides of the case are framed to two horizontal panels, and the back to two vertical panels. There is a brace under the center of the top housed in the rear rail. The drawers are side hung on runners rabbeted to the stiles. On each drawer, the sides are dovetailed to the front, the dovetail is penetrated by the groove for the drawer runner (except in the deep drawer), and the joint is reinforced with nails. The drawer sides are butted to the back and nailed through the slightly beveled edges of the backboard. Each bottom is a single longitudinal board, beveled on all four sides, let into a groove in the front, and nailed to the underside of the sides and back. The drawer bottoms show evidence of mill sawing. The bottom of the chest is a single longitudinal mill-sawn board nailed in place. The top and the bottom two drawer fronts were grooved for the walnut inlay, with the pine moldings then applied; on the deep drawer, all the moldings are applied to the drawer front. The top drawer was once fitted with a spring lock.

Inscriptions: The top edge of each drawer side is numbered I to IIII from top to bottom.

Condition: The chest has been refinished; when illustrated in *Garvan Coll.* it appears to have had a dark finish, traces of which remain. The applied molding on the lowest drawer divider is a replacement, some of the moldings on the drawers have been replaced, and the front edge of the right side of the base molding has been repaired. The brasses are replacements. The top boards have been reglued, and new blocks added to the inside of the front stiles at the level of the bottom drawer. Cloth, leather, and wooden patches of various dates have been applied over holes in the drawers and bottom. The bottom board has been pieced at the front edge. The grooves on the sides of the deep drawer have been repaired.

Woods: Stiles, front and side rails, cornice and base molding, drawer runners, drawer sides in top and bottom drawer, red oak and white oak; side panels, back panels, back rails and muntin, drawer fronts and bottoms, bottom, eastern white pine; drawer sides in deep drawer and one below, sycamore; applied moldings, eastern white pine; applied strips on drawer fronts, walnut; front feet, soft maple, probably silver maple.

Dimensions: H 94.3; W 98.7; CW 91.7; D 58.4; CD 55.7.

Bibliography: *Garvan Coll.*, no. 402; Walter A. Dyer, "The American Bureau: Primitive to Chippendale," *Fine Arts* 18, no. 2 (January 1932): 38.

Provenance: Henry V. Weil, New York, N. Y.; by sale in 1926 to Francis P. Garvan, New York, N. Y.; by descent in 1937 to Mabel Brady Garvan, New York, N. Y.

THIS chest of drawers is one of a group of more than a dozen surviving related joined chests of drawers made in the Boston area. This group features a shallow top drawer, deep second drawer, and third and fourth drawers of intermediate height; flat horizontal panels on the sides of the cases, without molding or chamfering on the rails and stiles; dovetailed drawer construction; and drawer fronts with applied moldings in a variety of geometrical designs. Some members of the group feature two-part cases and were known to early collectors as "Dedham chests" because one was found in or near that area. They have recently been described as "later productions of the Mason-Messenger shops."[1] The Yale chest is a single-unit example, most closely related to an example now in the Wadsworth Atheneum (1926.318).[2] The Atheneum chest shares the same arrangement of applied moldings as the Yale example on the top two drawers, and the profile of the applied moldings on the drawer dividers is related; it also makes use of sycamore and shares a number of other construction characteristics.[3] An English chest that shares the same arrangement of drawers has been published.[4]

The Mabel Brady Garvan Collection 1942.252

1. See Nutting, *Treasury*, no. 220; a chest of drawers in the collection of George Dudley Seymour, now in the collection of the Connecticut Historical Society (45.1087); and Fairbanks and Trent, *New England Begins*, no. 256. See also Forman, "Urban Aspects," pp. 8–10. A good illustration of how the two-part case was joined can be seen in the Ginsburg & Levy advertisement in *Antiques* 78, no. 2 (August 1960): 99. This chest of drawers was later sold at auction; see *Important American Furniture, Silver, and Decorative Arts*, 2 June 1983 (New York: Christie, Manson, and Woods, International, 1983), no. 357. Other chests with two-part cases are mentioned by Forman, and published examples include one at the Museum of Fine Arts, Boston (40.602), illustrated in Randall, no. 26; one formerly in the collection of Henry W. Erving, illustrated in Lockwood, fig. 46; another in the Goodwin collection at the Wadsworth Atheneum, illustrated in Helen Comstock, "Seventeenth-Century Furniture in the Goodwin Collection," *Antiques* 79, no. 6 (June 1961): fig. 2; and one formerly in the collection of Morris Schwartz pictured in Nutting, *Treasury*, no. 226.

2. Nutting, *Treasury*, no. 230. Other single-unit chests of drawers that are related include one in the collection of the Society for the Preservation of New England Antiquities (1971.66), illustrated in Jobe and Kaye, cat. 11; one advertised by Lillian Blankley Cogan in *Antiques* 125, no. 1 (January 1984): 88; and one illustrated as a line drawing in Singleton, p. 218. A chest with two drawers that is also part of this group is illustrated in Nutting, *Treasury*, no. 23. Jobe and Kaye, pp. 130–133, also provide information on other examples in the group.

3. Phillip Johnston, *Art in Seventeenth-Century New England* (Hartford, Conn.: Wadsworth Atheneum, 1977), no. 24.

4. Kirk, *Am. Furn. & Brit. Trad.*, fig. 458. See also Chinnery, figs. 2:222, 3:412.

53

53

Chest of drawers
Salem, Massachusetts, 1675–1710

Description: The case of this chest of drawers is joined with mortise-and-tenon joints that are double pegged. The case contains a total of five drawers, two narrow ones at the top above three wide drawers below, separated by applied half-round molding. Cove molding is applied at the base at the front and sides; the feet are formed by extensions of the stiles. The sides are framed to a horizontal panel over two vertical ones; the rails and stiles have a central channel molding, the stiles and bottom rail are stop chamfered on their panel edges, and the rails and muntin are chamfered. The back is framed to two horizontal panels with beveled edges. The bottom has butted transverse boards nailed to rabbets in all four sides. The drawers are side hung on runners rabbeted to the stiles. The small drawers in line at the top are separated by a vertical partition housing a runner which serves each drawer; the runner is housed through the back. The sides of the drawers are placed in a rabbet in the front and nailed through the sides, the sides are rabbeted to accept the backs and nailed through the sides, and the bottoms are

American Case Furniture

nailed to a rabbet in the front and to all three sides. The large nails are countersunk. The bottoms of the top small drawers are a single transverse board; the wide drawers have bottoms of a single longitudinal board (pieced in one instance), and one shows evidence of mill sawing.

Condition: This chest of drawers has been refinished and heavily restored. The top is a replacement; it now consists of two boards, one with some age but originally used for another purpose at the front, butted to a new strip about 12 cm wide at the back. The cove molding applied to the front beneath the top is new. The front feet have been pieced below the base molding, and the brasses are new. The most troublesome aspect of the restoration, which probably occurred in the shop of New York dealer Henry V. Weil in the 1920s or earlier, is the almost complete replacement of the applied decoration on the front stiles and drawer fronts. An examination by Patricia E. Kane and John T. Kirk in 1968, when many of these applied ornaments were removed and the pattern of nail holes and other evidence below revealed, indicated that the chest of drawers did have applied ornaments originally. All the applied split spindles, however, are new, although each covers two old nail holes. The walnut veneer or panels on the top small drawers appears to be original, and although the applied moldings have been replaced, old nail holes indicated that some sort of molding had been used originally. The applied elements on the second drawer from the top (the top wide drawer) were restored incorrectly, and the original configuration remains uncertain. The third drawer from the top appears to have been restored correctly, although the moldings above and below the brass drop pulls should have been larger, as they do not cover the old nail holes. The center of the bottom drawer appears to be correct, while the outer panels may have looked like the corresponding sections on a related chest of drawers at the Wadsworth Atheneum (1926.323).

Woods: Rails, stiles, side panels, drawer dividers, drawer runners, drawer fronts and sides, red oak; top, back panel, bottom, drawer bottoms and backs, eastern white pine; applied veneer or panels on top small drawers, probably walnut; moldings and applied strips on drawers, cedar, probably eastern red cedar; new molding beneath the top, probably maple; replaced spindles, cherry or a related fruitwood.

Dimensions: H 95.9; W 112.1; CW 106.2; D 55.0; CD 50.2.

Provenance: Henry V. Weil, New York, N. Y.; by sale in 1925 to Francis P. Garvan, New York, N. Y.

ALTHOUGH this chest of drawers has been heavily restored, it would appear that it is one of a group of at least six related chests of drawers that are thought to have been made in Salem, Massachusetts, possibly by members of the Symonds family of joiners.[1] The other known examples include chests of drawers at the Wadsworth Atheneum (1926.323), the Metropolitan Museum of Art (10.125.686), the Museum of Fine Arts, Boston (32.272), the Massachusetts Historical Society, and the Essex Institute.[2] Although the exact shapes of the original moldings and split spindles on the Yale example are not known, it would appear that the chest of drawers shared the profusion of applied ornament found on the other examples, including the use of multiple pairs of split spindles and the division of the drawer fronts into geometrical panels. The number of panels per drawer level moves in a 2-3-2-3 pattern from top to bottom on each of the other chests of drawers. The other examples have distinctive upper molding cut with diagonal lines above a band of punched decoration and a line of gouged notches, and this feature may have been present on the Yale chest originally. The spindles on the Yale chest, if they were not based on surviving fragments or shadow marks, may have been based on those appearing on the Metropolitan Museum or the Wadsworth Atheneum examples, each of which was published prior to Francis P. Garvan's acquisition of the chest in 1925.[3]

The Mabel Brady Garvan Collection 1930.2215

1. This "geometrical panel" group was discussed by Irving P. Lyon, "The Oak Furniture of Ipswich, Massachusetts: Part VI, Other Affiliates: A Group Characterized by Geometrical Panels," *Antiques* 34, no. 2 (August 1938): 79–81. Modern discussions of the group include Benno M. Forman, "The Seventeenth Century Case Furniture of Essex County, Massachusetts, and Its Makers" (M.A. thesis, University of Delaware, 1968), pl. III and passim; Benno M. Forman, "The Osborne Family Chest Rediscovered," *Historical New Hampshire* 26 (1971): 26–30; and Fairbanks and Trent, *New England Begins*, nos. 274, 285, 484, 485.

2. For illustrations of these chests, see Nutting, *Treasury*, no. 221; Lockwood, fig. 49; Randall, no. 25; Patricia E. Kane, "Furniture Owned by the Massachusetts Historical Society," *Antiques* 109, no. 5 (May 1976): p. II; and Lyon, fig. 26.

3. The Metropolitan Museum's example was published in 1913 by Lockwood, and the Wadsworth Atheneum's example appeared in Nutting, *Pilgrim Century* (1921), p. 59.

54

54

Chest of drawers
Eastern Massachusetts, 1670–1710

Description: The top is pegged to the case and has thumbnail molding at the front and sides, with notch carving at the sides, above cove molding attached to the case at the front and sides. The case holds four drawers—a shallow top drawer above three deeper drawers of nearly equal dimensions. Each drawer has a central brass escutcheon, flanked by simulated rectangular fielded panels. These panels are formed by an applied horizontal strip of walnut with a drop pull at center, edged with applied moldings, and contained within a larger rectangle again formed by applied moldings. The drawers are separated by applied half-round molding attached to the drawer dividers and flanked by vertical panels of walnut strips edged with applied moldings. The mortise-and-tenon joints of the case are double pegged, and the applied moldings are attached in most instances with small, square wooden pins. There is applied cove molding at the front; the rear feet are extensions of the stiles, and there are turned reel and bun feet at the front. The sides are framed to two horizontal panels, as is the back. The bottom consists of three transverse boards, joined with a half lap and nailed to all four sides. The drawers are side hung on runners housed in the stiles. In each drawer, the sides are dovetailed to the front with a single large dovetail penetrated by the groove for the drawer runner and secured with rosehead and T-head nails; the backs are rabbeted to accept the sides and nailed through the back; and the bottom consists of two longitudinal boards half lapped and nailed to a rabbet in the front and to the undersides of the sides and back. The drawer fronts have been painted black to contrast with the applied walnut strips and moldings.

Inscription: A small piece of ruled paper glued to the outside of the back bears the inscription in ink, "Given to / Clara M. Griffin / in 1905."

Condition: The applied half-round molding on the two lower drawer dividers is new, and there have been repairs to the base molding at the center and right corner. Some of the applied moldings on the drawer fronts have been replaced, and the brasses are new. A large shrinkage crack in the top has been filled. The turned feet appear to be old and may be original. There has been extensive insect damage to the lower back panel. The top and middle back rails are in maple and appear to have been glued in modern times; they may be replacements.

Woods: Stiles, side rails, bottom rear rail, sides of bottom two drawers, drawer dividers, drawer runners, top, red oak and white oak; side panels, drawer fronts, sides of top two drawers, chestnut; bottom, drawer bottoms, eastern white pine; back panels, red or Scotch pine; top and middle back rails, soft maple; turned feet, beech; applied strips on drawer fronts and stiles, walnut; applied moldings, cedar, either Atlantic white cedar or northern white cedar; replaced half-round moldings on drawer dividers, yellow poplar.

Dimensions: H 93.0; W 98.4; CW 95.2; D 51.4; CD 50.5.

Bibliography: Walter A. Dyer, "The American Bureau: Primitive to Chippendale," *Fine Arts* 18, no. 2 (January 1932): 39.

Provenance: See Inscription; the identity of Clara M. Griffin has not been discovered. Henry V. Weil, New York, N. Y.; by sale to Francis P. Garvan, New York, N. Y.

THE richly paneled drawer fronts of this chest of drawers, with walnut strips played off against a black background, are given added distinction by the presence of paneled stiles. Other American chests of drawers with paneled stiles are

known, and they probably were an option available to the customer for an extra charge, as were the turned ball feet.[1] The feature is also seen on English chests of drawers of the second half of the seventeenth century.[2] This chest of drawers is related to Boston-area case furniture of the late seventeenth century by its use of walnut and cedar moldings and by its dovetailed drawer construction. Chestnut side panels also are found on a Boston chest of drawers in the Milwaukee Art Museum that has been described as a "late" product of the "Mason-Messenger" shops.[3]

The Mabel Brady Garvan Collection 1930.2391

1. Nutting, *Treasury*, no. 226; Randall, no. 26; Fairbanks and Bates, p. 18 (top).
2. Kirk, *Am. Furn. & Brit. Trad.*, fig. 461.
3. Fairbanks and Trent, *New England Begins*, no. 256.

55

Chest of drawers
New England, 1680–1720

Description: The rectangular top is a single board nailed to the case and has thumbnail molding at the front and sides over cyma reversa molding applied to the case. The case holds three drawers; the top and bottom drawer are the same size, the middle one is deeper, and they are separated by an applied half-round molding that overlaps the stiles. Each drawer is decorated to simulate two in line with a central brass escutcheon flanked by rectangular panels created by applied moldings with a brass with drop pull in the center. The top two drawers were fitted with wooden spring locks, and the bottom drawer with an iron lock (now missing); thus, the escutcheon on the bottom drawer is placed higher on the center strip. There is cove base molding applied to the front and sides. The sides are framed to two horizontal panels. The back contains two butted boards (with a tenon between them at center) flush with the stiles and tenoned to the stiles at the top, middle, and bottom. There is a brace under the center of the top tenoned to the front rail and through the back rail. The bottom consists of two transverse butted mill-sawn boards nailed in place. The rails and stiles are joined with mortise-and-tenon joints that are double pegged. The drawers are side hung on runners housed in grooves in the stiles. In the top and bottom drawer, the sides are dovetailed to the front with a single large dovetail penetrated by the groove for the drawer runners. On the larger center drawer two dovetails are used. On each drawer, the back is butted to the sides and nailed through the sides, and the bottom is a single longitudinal riven board, beveled at the front and sides, let into a groove in the front, and nailed to the underside of the sides and back. The chest has at least two layers of red paint.

Condition: The stiles have been cut at the level of the base molding, and four new feet and a suppporting framework for them added. These new feet are now badly split. The base molding at each side is a replacement, and the left corner of the front base molding has been repaired. The brasses and escutcheons are replacements.

Woods: Stiles, top front rail, soft maple; side and back, bottom front rail, rails, brace under top, drawer dividers, red oak; top, bottom, drawer dividers, side panels, back, drawer fronts, sides, backs, and bottoms, eastern white pine.

Dimensions: H 92.4; W 103.0; CW 101.2; D 53.9; CD 53.0.

Provenance: Francis P. Garvan, New York, N.Y.

Chests of drawers with three drawers are less frequently encountered than those with the more usual complement of

four. An example formerly in the collection of Mr. and Mrs. Herbert B. Newton and similar to the Yale chest of drawers has been published.[1] The middle drawer in this object was deeper than the upper and lower drawers. The drawers were separated by half-round moldings overlapping the stiles, as here, and the sides of the case were paneled in the same manner. The drawer fronts in the Newton chest of drawers had the added embellishment of beveled strips with applied moldings within, creating the paneled appearance. The rear stiles of the Newton chest continued to form the feet, and, based on a photograph, its front feet look questionable. Originally, the four feet on each chest probably were formed by extensions of the stiles. The variety of woods used in the Yale example again suggests that the object was painted originally.

The Mabel Brady Garvan Collection 1930.2229

1. "Made in New England: Furniture from the Collection of Mr. and Mrs. Herbert B. Newton," *Antiques* 46, no. 1 (July 1944): 26 fig. 1.

56

56

Chest of drawers

Boston, Massachusetts, 1690–1710

Description: The slightly projecting top has applied half-round above cove and bead molding that is applied to the case. It is nailed to the case. The chest contains four drawers, the ones at the top and bottom larger than those in the middle. Each has a blind brass escutcheon at center, and each is made to simulate two drawers in line with applied moldings. The top and bottom drawers have mitered beveled strips forming rectangles on each side, with their inner edges faced with applied moldings with reentrant corners. The middle drawers have applied moldings forming rectangles on each side of the drawer, and all drawers are fitted with round brasses with drop pulls. There is applied base molding at the front and sides, pinned in place. The rear stiles continue to form feet in the rear, and there are turned feet in the front. Each side of the case is framed to a fielded panel with a raised and applied center rectangular section edged with applied moldings. The back contains a single panel with beveled edges. The rails and stiles are fastened with double-pinned mortise-and-tenon joints. The drawers are side hung on runners let into grooves in the stiles and are pegged in place. The drawer sides are dovetailed to the front; the backs are butted to the sides and nailed through the sides; and the drawer bottoms consist of two (in one case, three) longitudinal boards joined with a tongue and groove and nailed to a rabbet in the front and to the undersides of the sides and back. The top drawer and the drawer third from the top were fitted with wooden spring locks.

Inscriptions: The modern "115" appears in red on the outside of the back. Three modern printed paper shipping labels are pasted to the back; all are from the American Railway Express Company, Inc., and one is addressed to the Margolis Antique Shop, 1122 Madison Avenue, New York City, and gives an insurance value of $1,000 for the chest of drawers. A pattern of nails on the outside of the back indicates that another label was attached at one time. The insides of the drawers are lined with issues of various newspapers; the top drawer is lined with the *Boston Olive Branch*, 27 March 1852; the second drawer from the top with the *Saturday Evening Post*, Philadelphia, 19 October 1850; the third drawer from the top with an issue of the *American Union*, from Boston and dating to the 1850s; and the bottom drawer is also lined with the *American Union*, Boston, issues dating from January and March 1852. There is an old signature on the newspaper

134 *American Case Furniture*

in the third drawer from the top which appears to read "J. B. Jewitt."

Condition: The chest has been refinished; traces of red and black paint remain. A portion of the molding on the left side panel is replaced, as is the entire base molding. The top has been pieced at the back edge; the underside of the top has a gray, weathered look with what appear to be fresh plane marks around the edges, suggesting that the top has either been replaced or was planed when it was pushed forward and pieced at the back. The brasses are replacements. The front stiles were probably cut off at the level of the base molding and the present feet added; the right stile has lost about half of its thickness at the level of the bottom drawer, and when the new feet were added an irregular board was nailed to the front, side, and back rails as a reinforcement. There is no evidence that this irregular board is the remaining portion of an original full bottom. All four feet have been doweled to a depth of 5–6 cm to accept stem casters; fragments of the stems remain in each foot.

Woods: Rear stiles, rails, drawer dividers, drawer sides, applied moldings, red oak; front stiles, three drawer fronts, beveled strips on top and bottom drawers, replaced turned feet, soft maple; top, side and back panels, drawer bottoms, eastern white pine; front of third drawer from top, beech; backs of top and bottom drawer, eastern hemlock; replaced base molding, probably ash.

Dimensions: H 91.9; W 100.5; CW 95.6; D 58.4; CD 55.6.

Bibliography: *Third Sale of Fine Early American Furniture Gathered during the Last Seven Months by Jacob Margolis, Cabinet Maker of New York City*, Sale 1770, 16–17 November 1923 (New York: Anderson Galleries, 1923), no. 127; Jobe and Kaye, p. 138 fig. 13b.

Provenance: The Garvan files state that the chest of drawers was originally from Ipswich, Mass., according to tradition, but there is no documentation of this tradition. Jacob Margolis, New York, N. Y.; acquired at auction in 1923 by Francis P. Garvan, New York, N. Y.

THIS chest is one of an important group of at least a dozen related Boston-area objects which share the same placement of large drawers at the top and bottom of the case, sandwiching a pair of smaller drawers in between, the use of a large fielded panel on the sides, turned feet, and the additional embellishment of painted decoration on the facade, although the paint on the Yale example and others has been lost.[1]

Several chests in the group, including examples in the Metropolitan Museum of Art, the Brooklyn Museum (49.190.2), and the Chipstone collection, retain much of their elaborate paint scheme.[2] There is a good deal of variation in the configuration of the applied moldings on the drawer fronts within the group.[3] On what appears to be a slightly later, rural, version of this type, done in pine, paint is used exclusively on the drawer fronts to simulate applied moldings.[4]

The Mabel Brady Garvan Collection 1930.2214

1. Fairbanks and Trent, *New England Begins*, no. 256, links this group to a tradition stemming from the Mason-Messenger shops.
2. Comstock, no. 64; Donald C. Peirce, "American Painted Furniture at the Brooklyn Museum, 1675–1875," *Antiques* 110, no. 6 (December 1976): 1292 fig. 1; Rodriguez Roque, *Chipstone*, cat. 3.
3. Other related examples include another chest of drawers in the Metropolitan Museum (10.125.37); Fales, *Deerfield*, no. 374; Kettell, no. 34 (North Andover Historical Society); *Antiques* 94, no. 1 (July 1968): 54 (Los Angeles County Museum of Art); *Antiques* 111, no. 5 (May 1977): 910 (Colonial Williamsburg); Donald F. Frazier, "The General Sylvanus Thayer Birthplace [Braintree, Massachusetts]," *Antiques* 123, no. 5 (May 1983): 1033; *Antiques* 83, no. 2 (February 1963): 165; Nutting, *Treasury*, nos. 224, 228; ex. coll. Sack (photograph in object file, Yale Furniture Study); and Winterthur Museum (56.10.3).
4. Fitzgerald, fig. II–16.

57

Chest of drawers
New England, 1700–1730

Description: There is applied ovolo molding beneath the top. The case contains four graduated drawers, divided by half-round molding applied to the drawer dividers and overlapping the stiles. The rails and stiles are joined with mortise-and-tenon joints that are double pinned. Each drawer is decorated with applied moldings to simulate a pair in line, and each has a central brass escutcheon and two brasses with drop pulls. The bottom rail is shaped to cove molding, and matching molding is pinned to the sides. The sides are framed to two vertical panels; the rails and stiles are edge molded; and the muntin has a central molding, is also molded on its panel edges, and is held in place with two pins. The back is framed to two panels, again side by side, and the muntin is single pegged. There is a diagonal brace under the top that is slot dovetailed to the front and rear rails; there are two braces flanking a diagonal brace on the bottom, all slot

57

dovetailed to the front and rear rails. The drawers are side hung. The sides are dovetailed to the front with a single dovetail penetrated by the groove for the runner, except on the bottom drawer where two dovetails are used. The drawer sides are let into a rabbet in the back and nailed through the back.

Inscriptions: Each side of the bottom edges of the drawer fronts bears a roman numeral, moving in order from I and II on the top drawer to VII and VIII on the bottom drawer. The backs and some bottoms of the drawers have been numbered in pencil in modern times. There is a modern inscription in paint on the outside of the right side of the second drawer from the top that appears to read "No 12 CHS." A Lyman Allyn Museum sticker bearing the number 1932.12 is pasted to the outside of the back.

Condition: This chest of drawers has been refinished and has had more than its share of structural alterations and repairs. The top is made of several narrow and thin boards attached to the case with modern nails, and it is probably a replacement in whole or in part. There is a cloth patch pasted to the underside of the top. Originally the stiles would have continued to form the feet. The four stiles have been cut off at the level of the base molding and four turned feet added; the ball portion of the front feet are round and thick like apples, while those added to the back are shaped more like bagels. The longitudinal brace on the right side of the bottom is missing. The drawer runners are replacements, and the drawers themselves have received considerable repair. They have been renailed throughout; repairs have been made to the drawer bottoms and to the grooves on the sides for the runners; the locks are missing on three drawers, and one has been replaced; and the brasses are new. There are some worrisome inconsistencies in the ways the drawers are fashioned (see below).

Woods: Top, stiles, rails, muntins, side panels, drawer fronts and sides, braces, red oak and white oak; back panels, drawer bottoms and backs, eastern white pine; restored feet, maple.

Dimensions: H 87.7; W 91.4; CW 85.9; D 50.8; CD 48.1.

Bibliography: *Antiquarian* 8, no. 1 (February 1927): 13; *The Jacob Margolis Early American Collection*, 17–19 March 1927 (New York: American Art Association, 1927), no. 350; Wenham, *Collectors' Guide*, no. 183; Ormsbee, *Story Am. Furn.*, fig. 20; Thomas Hamilton Ormsbee, "The Chest of Drawers and Changing Style," *American Collector* 14, no. 3 (April 1945): 8; Nagel, pl. 2c.

Provenance: Jacob Margolis, Inc., New York, N.Y.; acquired at auction in 1927 by Francis P. Garvan, New York, N.Y.

This chest of drawers has undergone extensive restoration, probably in the shop of New York cabinetmaker and antiques dealer Jacob Margolis, and its present condition is such that one can only feel reasonably confident that the case itself and probably the drawer fronts are original to the object. The applied moldings on the drawer fronts, however, are quite crisp; the drawer sides, backs, and bottoms have been extensively renailed and repaired, and there are troublesome inconsistencies in the way they are constructed. For example, small wooden pins were used to fasten the bottom of the top drawer (which once was partitioned and fitted with a spring lock) to the sides and back, but they were not used on the other three drawers; the grain of the wood in the bottoms of the top two drawers runs from front to back, while it runs in the other direction on the bottom two drawers; the front edge of the bottom of three of the drawers is beveled, but it is not beveled on the third drawer from the bottom, and so forth. There are more unexplained nail holes, especially on the drawer bottoms, than one can accept

comfortably. Although the "turnip" feet were admired by Nagel and stated to exhibit "a decided Dutch influence" by Wenham, they are undoubtedly new additions to this object. Based on those features that seem to be old, the most that one can say about this chest of drawers is that it is a relatively simple example of a joined chest made in New England in the early eighteenth century. Among similar examples, one at Winterthur (58.544) is quite similar visually, although it varies in construction.[1] The Winterthur chest has been attributed to Essex County.[2]

The Mabel Brady Garvan Collection 1930.2524

1. Nutting, *Treasury*, no. 231.
2. Benno M. Forman, "The Seventeenth Century Case Furniture of Essex County, Massachusetts, and Its Makers" (M.A. thesis, University of Delaware, 1968), pp. 135–138.

58

Chest of drawers

Newport or Providence, Rhode Island, 1755–1785

Description: The rectangular top has thumbnail molding at the front and sides and is shaped at the front to conform to the blocking of the drawers. The case holds a dressing slide with brass pulls, above four graduated drawers with central brass escutcheons flanked by matching escutcheons with bail pulls. The edges of the slide and the case surrounding the slide and the drawers are outlined with applied cock beading. There is applied base molding at the front and sides above bracket feet. The top is a single board attached to the sides with a blind dovetail. The blocking of the drawers is cut from the solid, and in each drawer the sides are dovetailed to the front and back, the bottom is nailed to a rabbet in the front and sides and to the underside of the back, and there are applied running strips. The top edge of the drawer sides are rounded, and there are partial dustboards. The bottom of the case consists of two butted boards dovetailed to the sides; the base molding at the front is flush with the bottom and has glue blocks within. There are horizontal and vertical blocks attached with glue and rosehead nails at each corner, and the rear triangular feet are blind dovetailed to the side feet, with a vertical block behind.

Inscription: "Bottom" is written in chalk on the underside of the bottom.

Condition: The location of old nail holes on the sides and top does not correspond with those on the back, even when the back (which has been attached with screws in modern times) was removed and rotated, indicating that it is a replacement. New running strips have been added to the drawers, and the drawer runners and some of the drawer stops have been replaced. Small strips have been butted to the rear of each drawer bottom, because of shrinkage. The bottom part of each front foot has been repaired.

Woods: Mahogany; drawer sides, bottoms, backs, yellow poplar; partial dustboards, bottom, blocks, eastern white pine; center portion of slide, eastern red cedar; replaced backboard, chestnut.

Dimensions: H 82.3; W 93.5; CW 89.7; D 53.9; CD 50.3.

Exhibitions: Ott, no. 49; YUAG, "Rhode Island Furn."

Bibliography: *The George S. Palmer Collection . . . with addition of Fine American Pieces Collected by Mr. I Sack*, Sale 2280, 18–20 October 1928 (New York: Anderson Galleries, 1928), no. 268; *The Israel Sack Collections of American Antiques* (Boston, 1928); Nutting, *Treasury*, no. 266; Moses, p. 340 fig. 8.25.

Provenance: Israel Sack, New York, N. Y.; by sale in 1929 to Francis P. Garvan, New York, N. Y.

ALTHOUGH it has been described as a "pull-out writing slide," the "slider" on this chest of drawers more likely was used as a dressing slide for folding clothes. For example, one appears on a "Dressing Drawers" illustrated by Hepplewhite, and the use of cedar on the Yale example reinforces the thought that the slide was used for clothes.[1] Chests of drawers with slides are relatively uncommon; another example attributed to Rhode Island has been published in which the slide is supported by lopers.[2] Although the exposed dovetails and the layered effect of the base construction and the ogee bracket feet are characteristic of Newport furniture, the top of this chest is attached in a manner usually associated with eastern Massachusetts, suggesting that the use of particular construction techniques was not as rigidly circumscribed by place of origin as is sometimes assumed.[3] Recently, Michael Moses has suggested that this chest was made in Newport or Providence.[4]

The Mabel Brady Garvan Collection 1930.2682

1. Hepplewhite, pl. 75. Price books of the late eighteenth century list cedar as an extra option for the shelves of clothespresses and other objects containing textiles and clothing.
2. Ott, no. 50. A slider is also found on chests of drawers attributed to Massachusetts (see, as examples, *Sack Coll.*, 4:978 no. P3740; and *Antiques* 91, no. 5 [May 1967]: inside front cover), and it appears on a Connecticut Valley chest of drawers of 1790–1815 (Fales, *Deerfield*, no. 390). A Portsmouth, N. H., example is illustrated in Jobe and Kaye, cat. 16.
3. Lovell, "Boston Blockfront Furn.," pp. 81–89.
4. Moses, p. 340.

59

Chest of drawers
New England, probably Massachusetts, 1760–1790

Description: The rectangular top has thumbnail molding at the front and sides and is shaped at the front to conform to the blocking of the drawers. The case contains four graduated drawers, outlined by cock beading on the case, each with a central brass escutcheon flanked by matching escutcheons with bail pulls. The blocking of the drawers is cut from the solid; the drawer sides are dovetailed to the front and back, and the top edges of the sides rounded. Each drawer bottom is a single board nailed to a rabbet in the front and to the undersides of the sides and back. The top edge of the back is shaped with beveled edges. There are no partial dustboards. The drawer dividers are through-dovetailed to the sides, and the exposed dovetails are covered on the front by an applied strip; they remain visible on the sides. The top is a single board now nailed to the sides and rests above an undertop that is dovetailed to the sides. The back consists of two horizontal butted boards nailed in place. The chest bottom is a single longitudinal board dovetailed to the sides. The chest is supported by straight bracket feet below a base molding at the front and sides.

Condition: This chest of drawers is another example of the enthusiastic restoration practices used in the shop of Jacob Margolis in the 1920s. Among the many replacements and restorations, the most important is the replacement of the feet. With the possible exception of the upper third of the two front feet, the rest of the feet and the supporting blocking have been replaced. The base molding on the sides is a replacement, as are the brasses. The chest may have been painted at one time, and it has been refinished. The drawers

138 *American Case Furniture*

have been lined with nineteenth-century floral wallpaper, probably of the 1830s, in green and white designs, and with marbleized paper.

Woods: Maple; eastern white pine and southern yellow pine.

Dimensions: H 77.3; W 88.4; CW 83.8; D 51.1; CD 47.5.

Bibliography: Margaretta M. Lovell, "The Blockfront: Its Development in Boston, Newport, and Connecticut," *Fine Woodworking*, no. 23 (July–August 1980): 46.

Provenance: Jacob Margolis, Inc., New York, N. Y.; by sale in 1924 to Francis P. Garvan, New York, N. Y.

THIS chest of drawers is related to Massachusetts work in its use of an applied strip of molding to cover the sliding dovetail that joins the drawer rails to the sides of the case. The joint of the bottom of the chest and the front base molding is in one plane in the Boston manner, but the base molding does not have the "giant dovetail" seen on many Boston objects.[1] Blockfront furniture in maple is not common; another example is in the Winterthur collection (58.1741).[2] Reproductions of the Yale chest of drawers have been made by Harden Furniture Company since 1983.

The Mabel Brady Garvan Collection 1930.2480

1. Lovell, "Boston Blockfront Furn.," pp. 81–89.
2. Downs, fig. 167.

60

Chest of drawers
New England, probably Massachusetts, 1760–1790

Description: The top has thumbnail molding and overhangs the case at the front and sides. The case contains four graduated blockfront drawers outlined by cock beading on the case. Each drawer has a central brass lock escutcheon (blind on the lower two drawers) flanked by matching escutcheons with bail pulls. The bottom tip of the lock escutcheon on the top drawer has been clipped off in order for the brass to fit the drawer. The chest is supported by bracket feet below a base molding at the front and sides. The joint of the drawer dividers to the case sides is covered by an applied facing strip. On each drawer the sides are dovetailed to the front and back, with the exception of the top drawer, where the back is dovetailed to the sides. The drawer bottoms are let into a groove in the front and sides and nailed to the underside of the back. The blocking of the drawer fronts is cut from the solid. There are no dustboards, and the drawer runners within the case are nailed to the sides. The bottom of the chest is set below the base molding, which is dovetailed to two strips applied to the inside of the bottom. The side base moldings and bracket feet are a single piece, butted to the rear feet. These rear feet are shaped to large arched brackets that meet in the center of the back and are nailed in place. The back consists of two horizontal boards joined with a half lap and nailed in place. Sawmill marks appear on the inside of the lower backboard. There are only vertical blocks behind the feet. The projecting top is screwed from underneath to another board that is probably dovetailed to the case sides.

Inscription: A label handwritten in ink pasted to the inside of the bottom of the top drawer reads: "This block front bureau belonged to / Laura M. Wolcott (Mrs. Robert F. Rankin) / daughter of Frederick Wolcott and Betsy Huntington of Litchfield Conn. / granddaughter of Col. Joshua / Huntington of Norwich Con[n] / Sold to Harry Arons of Ansonia [b]y / [M]iss Cornelia W. Rankin May 4 1923."

Condition: The feet have been pieced to the level of the brackets. The projecting top has been pieced at the rear, and its front does not conform to the blocking of the drawers, being too narrow in the center and too wide over the blocking, strongly suggesting that it is a replacement. New strips or moldings have been added to the upper-case sides below the overhang of the top. New screws have been added to the front knee brackets. The back of the top drawer may be a replacement.

Woods: Mahogany; eastern white pine; some glue blocks, yellow poplar.

Dimensions: H 82.1; W 91.9; CW 83.9; D 54.2; CD 47.2.

Bibliography: Nutting, *Treasury*, no. 265; Comstock, "Bull Coll.," p. 140.

Provenance: Owned by Mrs. Laura M. Wolcott Rankin, Litchfield, Conn., and may have descended in her family through her parents, Frederick and Betsy (Huntington) Wolcott of Litchfield, and her maternal grandfather, Col. Joshua Huntington of Norwich, Conn. The chest descended to Mrs. Rankin's daughter, Cornelia W. Rankin, who sold it to dealer Harry Arons, Ansonia, Conn., 4 May 1923. Arons in turn sold the chest to C. Sanford Bull, Middlebury, Conn., prior to 1928.

ALTHOUGH this chest of drawers appears at first glance to be a standard Massachusetts, Boston-area, example, with its use of applied facing strips and Boston-type drawer construction, it has a history of ownership in a Connecticut family, and several factors suggest the possibility that it was made in Connecticut, perhaps in the eastern part of the state. The construction of the bottom here, for example, lacks the "giant dovetail" typical of Boston objects and is recessed below the base molding in a manner similar to the construction of Rhode Island blockfront objects. The clipping of the lock escutcheon on the top drawer and the unusual shaping of the rear feet also suggest a somewhat more provincial origin for this object. Mahogany blockfront furniture was not common in Connecticut, but was by no means unknown. This chest lacks the exuberant character of the best eastern Connecticut blockfront furniture, however, and may represent only a minor variation of the Massachusetts type. Francis P. Garvan once owned a very similar chest of drawers which he acquired from the collection of Fred Wellington Ayer in 1929 but later sold in 1931.[1]

Gift of C. Sanford Bull 1952.50.4

1. *Garvan Coll.*, no. 367.

61

Chest of drawers
Boston, Massachusetts, area, 1760–1790

Description: The top overhangs the case slightly on all four sides, has thumbnail molding on all four sides, and is shaped in conformity with the drawers below. The case holds four graduated blockfront drawers, outlined by cock beading on the case. Each drawer has a central brass lock escutcheon flanked by matching escutcheons with bail pulls. There is base molding at the front and sides, and the case is supported by straight bracket feet with blocked and shaped knee brackets. It has a full dustboard under the top drawer and only partial dustboards beneath the next two lower drawers. On each drawer the sides are dovetailed to the front and back; the bottoms are nailed to a rabbet in the front, let into grooves in the sides, and secured to the underside of the back with wooden pegs, with running strips applied. The top edge of the drawer sides are rounded, and the blocking is cut from the solid. Facing strips are applied over the joint of the drawer dividers and case sides. The drawer runners within the case are nailed to the sides, with small vertical blocks glued to the sides to serve as stops. The base molding is attached flush with the bottom with a "giant dovetail" with square ends; the base molding is formed of two strips to allow for the depth of the central concave blocking. The top consists of two longitudinal butted boards secured to the case with glue blocks on all four sides and nailed through the top front rail. The two horizontal backboards are nailed to rabbets in the sides. The lowest backboard is grooved or notched to accept the triangular rear feet, which project up and are nailed to the case bottom. The feet are reinforced with a framework at the front and sides of the bottom and by vertical- and horizontal-shaped blocks.

Condition: Metal plates were nailed to the bottom of each foot many years ago. The right side of the case has been pieced at the rear.

61

Woods: Mahogany; drawer bottoms and backs, Atlantic white cedar; bottom and back of case, drawer sides, yellow poplar; some blocks, eastern white pine.

Dimensions: H 80.1; W 86.5; CW 80.2; D 50.1; CD 45.5.

Bibliography: Margaretta M. Lovell, "The Blockfront: Its Development in Boston, Newport, and Connecticut," *Fine Woodworking*, no. 23 (July–August 1980): 45 fig. 1.

Provenance: According to a tradition which probably, but not conclusively applies to this object, and which in any event remains unconfirmed, this chest was owned originally by the Reverend Samuel Johnson (1696–1772) of Guilford, Conn. It is said to have passed to his son, William Samuel Johnson (1727–1819); then to his daughter Sarah Elizabeth Johnson Devereaux; to her daughter Georgia Pollak Devereaux Townsend, Albany, N. Y.; and then to her cousin Katherine Devereaux Blake. Blake sold it in 1924 to dealer Willoughby Farr of Edgewater, N. J., who in turn sold it to Francis P. Garvan, New York, N. Y.

In a fine state of preservation, this chest of drawers conforms in most particulars of style and construction to Boston-area blockfront furniture of the last half of the eighteenth century. However, the secondary woods used here are not typical of Boston work. The central drop often located on the front base molding of many examples is missing here.[1] There is some unfortunate confusion in the Garvan files concerning the provenance of this chest; if the Johnson family history could be accepted, it would be an important instance of the diffusion of Boston products into Connecticut.

The Mabel Brady Garvan Collection 1930.2149

1. In addition to the article cited under Bibliography, see Lovell, "Boston Blockfront Furn.," passim.

62

Chest of drawers

Boston, Massachusetts, area, 1760–1790

Description: The top has thumbnail molding at the front and sides, overhangs the case on all four sides, and is shaped in conformity with the blocking of the drawers below. The case holds four graduated blockfront drawers outlined by cock beading on the case. The convex blocking is rounded in profile. There is base molding at the front and sides, and the chest is supported by four short cabriole legs with scrolled and pointed knee brackets, knees with a sharp arris, and claw-and-ball feet. There are partial dustboards beneath the drawers. On each drawer the sides are dovetailed to the front and back and the bottoms are arranged with transverse grain and nailed to rabbets in the front and sides and to the underside of the back. The drawer fronts are cut from the solid, and applied facing strips are used to cover the joint of the drawer dividers and the case sides. The base molding and chest bottom are flush constructed, although no "giant dovetail" is used. The feet are tenoned through the bottom and reinforced with a framework of strips applied to the underside of the bottom at the front and sides and with vertical and horizontal blocks. The top is attached with a sliding dovetail, and the horizontal backboards are nailed to rabbets in the sides.

Inscription: "Bottom" is written in white chalk on the bottom.

Condition: The brasses are replacements. The rear 19.5 cm of the top is probably a replacement, the two rear knee brackets and the right front knee bracket are replacements, and many of the blocks on the base are also replacements.

62

New running strips have been added to the drawers, and the drawer runners within the case have been turned over and reused. Some drawer bottoms have been patched with cloth strips, and there are many new nails in the drawer bottoms. The backboards have been pieced, and new drawer stops added within the case. Many of the minor repairs were undertaken by Edward Hoepfner in 1947.

Woods: Mahogany; eastern white pine; one replaced block on left front foot, spruce (*Picea* spp.).

Dimensions: H 82.3; W 91.3; CW 86.0; D 50.5; CD 46.6.

Bibliography: Nutting, *Treasury*, no. 272; Rogers, "Garvan Furn. (1960)," p. 57; Rogers, "Garvan Coll. (1962)," p. 10; Helen Comstock, "Diversity in Connecticut Block Front," *Antiques* 84, no. 1 (July 1963): 67 fig. 6.

Provenance: Jacob Margolis, Inc., New York, N.Y.; by sale in 1925 to Francis P. Garvan, New York, N.Y.

THE rounded blocking and the fine claw-and-ball feet distinguish this chest of drawers from the preceding examples. The swept-back talons of the carved feet are found commonly on Massachusetts furniture. These blockfront chests of drawers were only one design option available to affluent Boston-area customers, who could choose either bombé or serpentine-front examples of the same form.[1] A related chest of drawers is in the collection of the Museum of Art, Rhode Island School of Design.[2] Similar examples with flattened blocking also have been published.[3]

The Mabel Brady Garvan Collection 1930.2493

1. As representative examples, see Randall, nos. 30, 31; Fales, *Deerfield*, figs. 395, 396, 398; and *Sack Coll.*, 7:2053 no. P5437.
2. Hedy B. Landman, "The Pendleton House at the Museum of Art, Rhode Island School of Design," *Antiques* 107, no. 5 (May 1975): 931.
3. Comstock, no. 297; Fales, *Deerfield*, fig. 393.

63

Chest of drawers
Bates How (b. 1776)
Northwestern Connecticut, 1795

Description: The top overhangs the case only at the front and sides and has thumbnail molding at the front and sides. The front of the top is shaped in conformity with the reverse serpentine drawer fronts below. The case holds three deep graduated drawers outlined with cock beading on the case cut from the solid. Each drawer has a central brass keyhole liner flanked by dual disk escutcheons with bail pulls. The front corners of the case are decorated with rope-carved quarter-round columns terminating at each end with a lamb's-tongue chamfer. The case is supported by a base molding, the lower half of which is carved with gadrooning at the front and sides, and by short cabriole legs terminating in blocky claw-and-ball feet. The chest essentially consists of a dovetailed case to which all applied members are secured with large screws. The visible, projecting top is thus screwed from underneath to another top board that is dovetailed to the sides. The front corner posts are notched, and the quarter columns fastened with screws. The backboard is dovetailed to the sides, with the drawer runners tenoned through the back. The bottom of the case consists of two transverse boards dovetailed to the sides, but neither board extends all the way to the back. The base framework is joined with mortise-and-tenon joints and screwed to the bottom boards. The moldings also are screwed to the base framework. There are small horizontal blocks behind the front skirt and vertical blocks in each corner of the base. On each drawer the

sides are dovetailed to the thick fronts and to the back; the drawer bottoms are rabbeted in their sides and let into grooves in the front and sides and nailed to the underside of the back. There are no dustboards.

Inscriptions: "This Buro was made/In the Year of our Lord/ 1795 / by / Bates How" is written in pencil on the inside of the back. Written in white chalk on the inside bottom of the top drawer is "#3 Bob[?]," and a "Connecticut Furniture" exhibition label is pasted to the inside of the right side of the same drawer.

Condition: The bottom edges of the top drawer have been repaired.

Woods: American black cherry; eastern white pine.

Dimensions: H 98.1; W 100.9; CW 90.8; D 52.9; CD 43.9.

Exhibitions: Kirk, *Conn. Furn.*, no. 69; Page, *Litchfield County Furn.*, no. 22.

Bibliography: Nutting, *Treasury*, no. 267; Kirk, *Early Am. Furn.*, fig. 97.

Provenance: Charles Woolsey Lyon, New York, N. Y.; by sale to Francis P. Garvan, New York, N. Y.

THIS signed chest is the basis for the attribution of at least three other very similar chests with three drawers to Bates How, each made in a sturdy and distinctive manner.[1] The identity of How (or Howe) remains obscure, however. It has been thought that he was one Baits Hait How, born 15 October 1776 in Canaan, Connecticut, making him only eighteen at the time he made the Yale chest.[2] He was the son of Samuel How, Jr. (b. 1732), and his second wife, Lydia (Pain) How, who were married in 1768. Samuel How was born in Stamford but moved with his family to Canaan in Litchfield County at an early age. Virtually nothing else about Bates How has been learned to date. It is possible that his wife died in May 1801, at age twenty-five, and was buried in the Canaan Valley Cemetery; this would suggest that How was still living in the Canaan area when he made the Yale chest. His brother Bowers How (b. 1769) lived for a time in New Marlborough, Massachusetts, and it is possible that Bates also left the northwestern corner of Connecticut for either nearby Massachusetts or New York. On the basis of their relationship to other furniture made or owned in Kent, the Bates How oeuvre has been attributed to Kent.[3] Such a precise attribution must remain tentative, however, until more is known about the elusive Bates How.

The Mabel Brady Garvan Collection 1930.2154

1. The closest parallel is in the Connecticut Historical Society (1967.23.1), illustrated in *Frederick K. and Margaret R. Barbour's Furniture Collection: A Supplement* (Hartford: Connecticut Historical Society,

Chests of Drawers 143

1970), pp. 14–15. Two other chests of drawers that lack the corner columns and gadrooned base molding are in the Mattatuck Museum, Waterbury, Conn. (1983.9), and in a private collection (DAPC, 81.1218). How's name also has been linked to several other objects; see Kirk, *Conn. Furn.*, no. 95; *Antiques* 93, no. 4 (April 1968): 473; and *Antiques* 105, no. 5 (May 1974): 1027.

2. Houghton Bulkeley was the first to research How's genealogy; see Kirk, *Conn. Furn.*, no. 69 n. 2. The genealogical notes here, following his lead, are taken from the records in the Barbour Collection, Connecticut State Library, Hartford, and from Daniel Wait Howe, *Howe Genealogies*, ed. Gilman Bigelow Howe (Boston: New England Historic Genealogical Society, 1929), pp. 419, 431, 450.

3. Kirk, *Conn. Furn.*, no. 69; Downs, no. 181.

64

Chest of drawers
Attributed to the Dunlap family
Southern New Hampshire, 1790–1810

64

Description: The rectangular top is of a single board with beaded top and bottom edges. It overhangs the top and sides and is blind dovetailed to the sides. The case holds four graduated drawers; there is bead molding on the frame surrounding the drawers. There is applied "flowered ogee" molding at the front and sides of the base with four "pearls," above four claw-and-ball feet with S-scroll leg brackets at the front and sides. The back consists of two horizontal half-lapped boards nailed to a rabbet in the top and to the sides. At the bottom there are front and back rails tenoned or dovetailed to the sides above the true bottom, which is a single longitudinal mill-sawn board dovetailed to the sides and pegged to the front and back rails. The feet are square tenoned through the true bottom and the front and back rails; the leg brackets are nailed in place; and there are no glue blocks. In each drawer, the sides are dovetailed to the front and back, and the top edge of the sides is shaped to a bead at center; the bottom is a single longitudinal board rabbeted at its front and sides, let into a groove in the drawer front and sides, beveled at its back edge, and nailed to the underside of the drawer back. One drawer bottom shows signs of having been mill sawn. The drawer runners are nailed to the sides, and there is a thin vertical strip nailed to the sides behind the drawer runners to act as a stop. There are traces of the original red or pink paint remaining.

Inscriptions: "B" appears in white chalk on the inside of each drawer back. The inside of each drawer bottom is numbered from 1 to 4, from top to bottom, although some of these numbers may not be original.

Condition: The chest has been refinished and has lost its original paint. The brasses have been replaced; there was never a lock on the bottom drawer, although two nail holes and the faint outline of an oval escutcheon can be seen. There has been a small repair to the ball of the left rear foot. The drawer runners are replacements, and new running strips have been added to the bottom of the drawer sides.

Woods: Soft maple; eastern white pine.

Dimensions: H 99.4; W 102.9; CW 93.0; D 52.1; CD 47.1.

Bibliography: Marshall B. Davidson, *The American Heritage History of Colonial Antiques* (New York: American Heritage Publishing Co., 1967), fig. 325; Parsons, *Dunlaps*, fig. 53 (included in the catalogue but not in the exhibition); Parsons and Brooke, "Dunlap Cabinetmakers," fig. 10; Marshall B. Davidson, *The Bantam Illustrated Guide to Early American Furniture* (New York: Bantam Books, 1980), p. 181.

Provenance: Charles R. Morson, New York, N. Y.; by sale to Francis P. Garvan, New York, N. Y.

OF all the furniture forms associated with the Dunlap family of joiners and cabinetmakers, chests of drawers are the most common.[1] Of the twenty-six "low chests" (as opposed to high chests and chest-on-chests) known to Charles Parsons in 1976, at least nine, including the Yale example, have four drawers.[2] The overhanging top, beading on the frame, flowered ogee base molding, and characteristic claw-and-ball feet all link this chest to "the Dunlap school."[3] Although this chest was attributed to "W. Dunlap" when it was acquired by Francis P. Garvan, attributions to individual members of the Dunlap family can only rarely be made.[4] Of the related four-drawer chests, those in the Currier Gallery of Art and Winterthur Museum have been published.[5]

The Mabel Brady Garvan Collection 1930.2152

1. Parsons, *Dunlaps*, p. 8.
2. Parsons, "More Dunlap," p. 102.
3. Parsons, *Dunlaps*, pp. 11–15, 73.
4. Parsons, *Dunlaps*, p. 10.
5. Parsons, *Dunlaps*, figs. 52, 54; see also Parsons, "More Dunlap," p. 102 no. 297.

65

Chest of drawers
Samuel Dunlap (1752–1830)
Possibly Salisbury, New Hampshire, 1790–1810

Description: Very similar in construction and design to the previous example, this chest of drawers varies in several important respects. Here the top is of pine and is through-dovetailed to the sides, and there is applied complex molding consisting of ovolo, fillet, cove, and ogee molding fashioned from a single piece and pinned to the front and sides. The drawers are lipped, and the four legs terminate in pad rather than claw-and-ball feet. The two bottom drawers were never fitted with locks. And, again, traces of red paint remain.

Inscriptions: Signed in red paint on the outside of the back: "Samuel / Dunlap." There is a vertical chalk mark on the inside back of each drawer.

Condition: This chest of drawers also has lost its original paint and been refinished. The brasses are replacements; originally they were ovals of a slightly smaller dimension.

Chests of Drawers 145

The left rear foot has been broken and repaired at the ankle, and both leg brackets on the left side have been replaced.

Woods: Soft maple; eastern white pine.

Dimensions: H 126.0; W 103.3; CW 95.2; D 49.5; CD 45.2.

Bibliography: Parsons, *Dunlaps*, fig. 57 (included in catalogue but not in exhibition).

Provenance: Henry Hammond Taylor, Bridgeport, Conn.; by sale to Francis P. Garvan, New York, N. Y.

ALTHOUGH this chest of drawers also was attributed to Whitfield Dunlap when it was acquired by Francis P. Garvan prior to 1930, it recently has been recognized as bearing what appears to be the name of Lieutenant Samuel Dunlap, younger brother of Major John Dunlap (1746–1792). One of at least eight five-drawer "Dunlap school" chests known, it is probably one of the many chests or cases of drawers entered in Samuel Dunlap's account book between 1785 and 1820.[1] In common with other five-drawer Dunlap-school chests, the Yale example has pad feet, a complex cornice molding, and lipped drawers.[2] This is perhaps the only known object bearing Samuel Dunlap's full name; a chest-on-chest in a private collection was found in Henniker and has "S.D." painted twice on the backboards (also see cat. 162).[3]

The Mabel Brady Garvan Collection 1930.2392

1. Parsons, "More Dunlap," p. 102; Parsons, *Dunlaps*, p. 41.
2. Parsons, *Dunlaps*, p. 73, figs. 58–61.
3. Parsons, *Dunlaps*, fig. 8. Other Dunlap-school objects cautiously attributed to Samuel Dunlap include Parsons, *Dunlaps*, figs. 1, 20, 40, 71, 82, 94, 96. See also fig. 100, an interior view of Samuel Dunlap's home in Salisbury.

66

Chest of drawers
Jonathan Gostelowe (1744–1795)
Philadelphia, Pennsylvania, ca. 1789

Description: The serpentine top of this enormous chest of drawers slightly projects on all four sides and has thumbnail molding at the front and sides and canted front corners. The case holds five cock-beaded drawers, two in line over three graduated drawers. Each drawer has a central peacock-

66

shaped lock escutcheon; the two drawers in line are fitted with a central brass and the three wide drawers with a pair of brasses with dual peacock-shaped escutcheons with elaborate bail pulls; the brasses appear to have been gilded originally. The canted front corners of the case are fluted, with five flutes. The sides of the case hold a single large brass backplate with a heavy bail pull. There is base molding at the front and sides of the case, and the case is supported by four bracket feet with canted corners, shaped brackets, and molded bases or platforms. The top of the case is screwed to the front and back rails, and to a middle transverse brace. The front and back rails are dovetailed to the case sides. The back of the case consists of six vertical backboards nailed to the top back rail, to rabbets in the sides, and to the case bottom. There is a full dustboard under each drawer, joined with a tongue-and-groove to the drawer dividers; drawer guides are nailed in place. The drawer dividers are joined to the canted corners and to the case sides. The case sides are made of two vertical boards, and they are secured to the canted front corner boards with multiple glue blocks. The facings of the feet are applied to a three-tier system of blocks. There is one large block with vertical grain at the center of each foot, topped by two horizontal blocks behind the brackets and the base moldings. The rear feet are triangular brackets, and there is a molded platform or base beneath each foot. On the drawers, the sides are dovetailed to the front and back with very fine dovetails. The bottoms are beveled on their front and side edges, let into grooves in the front and sides, and nailed to the underside of the back.

146 *American Case Furniture*

Running strips have been added to the bottoms at the sides, and there are multiple small, square glue blocks secured to the bottoms behind the drawer fronts.

Inscriptions: The drawers have been numbered in chalk in modern times. A paper label taped to the inside of the bottom of the upper right drawer reads: "GERTRUDE H. CAMP / PHONE / WHITEMARSH 1868 / FRANK [torn] / MANAGER / THE HAYLOFT / BETHLEHEM PIKE—WHITEMARSH, PA. / (WEST SIDE OF PIKE—SOUTH OF CHURCH ROAD / #700 WEDDING BUREAU AND DRESSING GLASS / PHILADELPHIA —— 1789 / Made by Jonathan Gostelowe, one of the leading / cabinet makers of Philadelphia, and presented to / his bride, Elizabeth Towers, April 19th, 1789. / these two items [a reference to the dressing glass and stand, 1930.2504] are the best authenticated pieces / of the Philadelphia cabinet makers known. Many / students believe that some of the important pieces / attributed to William Savery are really the work of / Gostelowe, who excelled in workmanship and artistic / expression." Another modern label pasted and thumbtacked to the inside of the left side of the top left drawer reads: "Independence Hall Collection / Accession No. #700 951 / Specimen No. 6 347 / Catalogue No. GERTRUDE H. CAMP LOAN COLLECTION / Object JONATHAN GOSTELOWE'S WEDDING CHEST / AND MIRROR / Remarks / American—Circa 1783. Walnut Wood. See Catalogue / APR-3 1928 / —— 192_ / Wilfred Jordan [signed] / Curator, Independence Hall."

Condition: The chest retains an old, possibly original, finish. Three of the peacock escutcheons are replacements. Some drawer runners have been replaced, and some of the screws securing the top in place appear to be replacements. The left front foot has been repaired, and the platform bases or pads of all four feet appear to be replacements.

Woods: Mahogany; drawer linings, other elements, yellow poplar; backboards, Atlantic white cedar; some blocks, southern yellow pine.

Dimensions: H 104.8; W 145.4; D 68.9.

Exhibitions: William Macpherson Hornor, Jr., *A Loan Exhibition of Authenticated Furniture of the Great Philadelphia Cabinet Makers* (Philadelphia: Pennsylvania Museum of Art, 1935), no. 58; YUAG, "A Wide View for American Art."

Bibliography: Clarence W. Brazer, "Jonathan Gostelowe," *Antiques* 9, no. 6 (June 1926): 388 fig. 3; *Antiques* 10, no. 1 (July 1926): 10; Clarence W. Brazer, "Jonathan Gostelowe," *Antiques* 10, no. 2 (August 1926): 108; *Antiques* 14, no. 4 (October 1928): inside back cover; *Antique American and English Furniture . . . Sold by Order of Mrs. Gertrude H. Camp, "The Hayloft," Whitemarsh, Pa.*, Sale 2310, 18–19 January 1929 (New York: Anderson Galleries, 1929), no. 173; Ormsbee, *Story Am. Furn.*, fig. 26; Thomas Hamilton Ormsbee, "Three Pieces Show Gostelowe's Individuality," *American Collector* 1, no. 13 (14 June 1934): 3; Comstock, *Concise Encyclopedia*, pl. 396; Rogers, "Garvan Coll. (1962)," p. 11; Marshall B. Davidson, *The American Heritage History of Colonial Antiques* (New York: American Heritage Publishing Co., 1967), p. 209 fig. 280; Kane, "American Furn.," p. 1318 fig. 5; Kirk, *Am. Furn. & Brit. Trad.*, fig. 499.

Provenance: According to tradition, this chest of drawers and an accompanying dressing glass and stand (1930.2504), also now at Yale, were made by Philadelphia cabinetmaker Jonathan Gostelowe as a gift to his second wife, Elizabeth Howell (Towers) Gostelowe (d. 1808), on the occasion of their marriage on 19 April 1789 (cat. 66a). (An original pale-blue

66a

Chests of Drawers 147

silk pincushion with "JG" and "ET" formed by cut steel pins is still in place in the center of the top drawer of the dressing-glass stand, lending credence to the tradition.) The objects descended from Gostelowe to his wife, who remarried in 1798, to Mathew Locke; to her sister, Sarah Towers Evans (d. 1815); to her son, Robert Tower Evans (1780–1858) (the chest of drawers is noted as a "bureau" in the second-story back chamber of Evans's house in the 1859 inventory of his estate, and the dressing glass and stand were located in the third-story entry and identified as a "stand"); to Evans's daughter, Martha Postrema Evans (d. 1895); to her niece, Eliza Ferguson Evans Fraser (d. 1920), and her husband John, Brandywine Manor, Pa.; and, finally, to their daughter, Martha Fraser North. In 1920, Mrs. North sold the objects to a dealer in Media, Pa., who in turn sold them to dealer Mrs. Gertrude H. Camp, Whitemarsh, Pa.[1] The chest and dressing glass and stand were acquired at auction in 1929 by Francis P. Garvan, New York, N. Y.

THIS very English-style serpentine chest of drawers with canted corners, undoubtedly by Jonathan Gostelowe, relates very closely to two less massive examples labeled by the master Philadelphia cabinetmaker and is one of a group of at least fourteen (and probably more) chests of drawers associated with Gostelowe's name over the years.[2] The key construction features linking the Yale example and the labeled chests, as identified by Deborah Federhen, include the means of fastening the top to the case, the three-tiered blocking of the feet, and the drawer construction.[3] The feet on these three chests relate closely to the base of the baptismal font made in 1788 by Gostelowe for Christ Church, Philadelphia, where he was married the next year.[4] The design of the brasses on the three key examples relate to several plates in various Birmingham brass founder's catalogues, although a precise source for the peacocks (occasionally referred to as pheasants) on the Yale chest has not been found as yet. The Art Gallery recently received a side chair (1984.32.32, bequest of Doris M. Brixey) labeled by Gostelowe.[5]

The Mabel Brady Garvan Collection 1930.2503

1. This provenance is based primarily on Raymond B. Clark, Jr., "Jonathan Gostelowe (1744–1795), Philadelphia Cabinetmaker" (M.A. thesis, University of Delaware, 1956), pp. 31, 35–40, 121. See also PMA, *Three Centuries*, p. 152, no. 121, for more biographical data on Gostelowe and for a detailed entry on the dressing glass and stand.
2. The labeled examples are at the Philadelphia Museum of Art (Nutting, *Treasury*, no. 322) and Cliveden (Hornor, pls. 107, 108).
3. Deborah Federhen, "Jonathan Gostelowe: Stylish Restraint in Philadelphia" (Seminar paper, University of Delaware, 1984). Other related examples are discussed in this paper, and the traditional attribution of some examples, such as the chest of drawers in the Winterthur collection (Downs, no. 178) are questioned. I would like to thank Federhen and Barbara McLean Ward for sharing this paper with me; a copy is in the Yale Furniture Study object files.
4. *Antiques* 10, no. 2 (August 1926): 126 fig. 8.
5. *Antiques* 18, no. 1 (July 1930): 19 fig. 3.

67

Chest of drawers

Northeastern Massachusetts or New Hampshire, 1795–1815
(see pl. 6)

Description: The top of this serpentine-front chest of drawers is shaped to conform to the drawers and has a line of patterned inlay along its veneered front edge. The case holds four drawers, veneered with feather-grained cuts of birch veneer laid in alternating directions and edged with cock beading. Each drawer has an oval stamped brass escutcheon with a bail pull and a brass keyhole liner. The drawer dividers and front edges of the sides are veneered with crossbanding. The front skirt is shaped to a central drop or tablet of birch veneer outlined with patterned inlay differing from that used on the top. The skirt is also bisected by a line of this same inlay that extends around the sides of the case. The chest is supported on four French bracket feet. The top is screwed from underneath to the upper-case frame, and the case is of dovetailed construction. There are two horizontal backboards nailed in place. The four feet are braced by vertical blocks, and there are horizontal blocks along the sides and behind the front apron. Large triangular braces serve as the rear feet. The drawer fronts are laminated, the sides are dovetailed to the front and back, and the drawer bottoms are let into grooves in the front and sides and nailed to the underside of the back, with applied running strips on the edges.

Inscription: The bottom board bears "Bottom."

Condition: There are three new plywood braces under the top and many small losses and repairs to the veneer and inlay. The left rear foot has been pieced.

Woods: Top, sides, mahogany; drawer dividers, front edge of top and sides, front skirt, front feet, mahogany veneer and

67

light- and dark-wood inlay; drawer fronts, tablet in apron, birch (*Betula* spp.) veneer; eastern white pine.

Dimensions: H 98.4; W 102.6; CW 99.3; D 60.0; CD 53.9.

Exhibitions: *Girl Scouts Exhibition*, no. 699; Donald Blake Webster, *Georgian Canada: Conflict and Culture, 1745–1820* (Toronto: Royal Ontario Museum, 1984), no. 231.

Bibliography: [Homer Eaton Keyes], "Long Text and Brief Sermon," *Antiques* 16, no. 5 (November 1929): 369; Miller, 1: fig. 727; [Homer Eaton Keyes], "American Satinwood Furniture," *Antiques* 44, no. 4 (October 1938): fig. 4; Comstock, no. 467; Rogers, "Garvan Furn. (1960)," fig. 15; Comstock, *Concise Encyclopedia*, pl. 16a; Kirk, *Early Am. Furn.*, fig. 95; Kirk, *Impecunious Collector's Guide*, fig. 161.

Provenance: Israel Sack, New York, N. Y.; by sale in 1929 to Francis P. Garvan, New York, N. Y.

In 1963 Charles Buckley identified a group of furniture which he suggested was made in Portsmouth, New Hampshire.[1] The principal features shared by this group, which includes this chest of drawers, are the use of highly figured birch veneers (usually described as satinwood, and perhaps in some instances the imported West Indian wood was indeed used), and the presence of a dropped panel, or rectangular tablet, in the center of the front skirt, outlined with patterned inlay. High French bracket feet, terminating in a distinctive short, flaring, squared "toe," also are found on many of these objects, as are the large triangular or diagonal braces used as rear feet. Recent research has established that at least some of this furniture, with its strong emphasis on contrasting light and dark materials, was made in Portsmouth and in other parts of New Hampshire.[2] The migration of craftsmen, and hence of designs and practices, was such, however, that cautious students still qualify the attribution of this group of objects by indicating that they may have been made in Massachusetts, north of Boston, where this preference for vivid color contrasts also was prevalent.[3] The Yale chest is most closely related to at least three other examples with serpentine fronts. Two of these chests, one in the Metropolitan Museum of Art and another formerly in the collection of the Metropolitan and now owned by the Art Institute of Chicago (1948.108), differ slightly from the Yale chest in that their drawer fronts are divided by cross-banding into three panels or sections, as is often the case in this kind of "drop-panel" furniture.[4] The birch or satinwood veneer is laid horizontally on the wider side panels and placed vertically on the narrower central panels. A third serpentine-front chest (present whereabouts unknown) is more closely related to the Yale example in that its drawer fronts are veneered with feather-grained mahogany, also laid in alternating directions, leading the eye back and forth across the chest, while the use of birch or satinwood is confined to the drop-panel on its skirt.[5]

The Mabel Brady Garvan Collection 1930.2017

1. Buckley, "Fine Federal Furn.," pp. 196–200.
2. *Documented New Hampshire Furn.*, nos. 6, 23, 56. See also the many examples illustrated in George Michael, "A Study in Identity: Drop-panel Furniture," *National Antiques Review* 3, no. 9 (March 1972): 16–33.
3. Montgomery, nos. 138, 139.
4. Buckley, "Fine Federal Furn.," fig. 1; John W. Keefe et al., *The Antiquarian Society of the Art Institute of Chicago: The First One Hundred Years* (Chicago: Art Institute of Chicago, 1977), no. 143.
5. Buckley, "Fine Federal Furn.," fig. 2.

68

68

Chest of drawers
Massachusetts or New Hampshire, 1800–1820

Description: The top of this bowfront chest of drawers overhangs the case slightly at the front and sides, and its front is shaped in conformity with the drawers below. The case holds four graduated drawers with incised lines simulating cock beading; each drawer has a central bone keyhole liner flanked by oval brass escutcheons with bail pulls. The case is supported by French bracket feet, and the front skirt is shaped to a central round arch flanked by reverse curves. There is a single line of light-wood stringing at the front and sides of the base above the apron. The top is a single board screwed and nailed from below to cleats or strips at the front and back which are in turn dovetailed to the case sides. The horizontal backboards are fitted to a groove in the case sides and nailed in place. The sides are simply arched at their lower ends to form the front and rear side feet; there are no rear feet at the back of the case. The bottom of the chest is a single board only half the depth of the case; the drawer runners are nailed to the sides of the case, and they continue to the rear to form the support for the lowest drawer. On each drawer the fronts are laminated with pine blocks and veneered with tiger maple; the remainder of the front facade is also veneered. The drawer sides are dovetailed to the front and back; the bottoms are beveled on their front and side edges, fitted to a groove in the front and sides, and nailed to the underside of the back, with running strips applied. The front feet are supported by vertical blocks, and there are multiple small glue blocks behind the front apron.

Condition: The brasses are replacements, and the bone keyhole liner on the upper drawer has been damaged. The front apron is also a replacement. The chest was cleaned of an opaque finish by Emile Mazzola in 1963.

Woods: Soft maple and maple veneer; a light-wood inlay; eastern white pine.

Dimensions: H 97.2; W 106.0; CW 102.9; D 59.7; CD 47.3.

Exhibition: *Forgeries and Restorations*, no. 27.

Bibliography: *Flayderman Coll.*, no. 308; Kirk, *Early Am. Furn.*, fig. 96.

Provenance: Philip Flayderman, Boston, Mass.; acquired at auction in 1930 by Francis P. Garvan, New York, N. Y.

This chest of drawers, or round-front bureau, is constructed with an economy of means characteristic of New England furniture. It is marred only by the replacement of its front apron and its new brasses. A serpentine-front Massachusetts bureau at Winterthur (56.532) makes similar effective use of "tiger-striped" maple, and the decorative wood also was frequently used on New Hampshire case pieces.[1]

The Mabel Brady Garvan Collection 1930.2474

1. Montgomery, no. 136.

69

Chest of drawers
Connecticut, 1800–1820

Description: The top of this elliptic-front chest of drawers has a line of light-wood stringing at the front and side edges. The top is flush with the back and has a wide overhang at the

150 *American Case Furniture*

69

front and sides. The case is of dovetailed construction and holds four graduated drawers with cock-beaded edges and central oval brass escutcheons flanked by oval brass escutcheons with bail pulls. There is another line of light-wood stringing on the front edge of the bottom, above the curved apron and French feet. The elliptical drawer fronts are laminated and veneered. The drawer sides are dovetailed to the front and back; the bottoms are of a single board, beveled at the front and sides, and let into grooves in the front and sides and nailed to the underside of the back. There are no dustboards, and the back edge of the drawer dividers have been left rough. The top consists of two butted boards, and it rests on two horizontal strips at the front and rear which are dovetailed to the sides; the top has been screwed from underneath to these strips. The back contains two butted boards nailed in place, and the bottom consists of two butted boards dovetailed to the sides. Each side is made of two butted boards as well. There are triangular feet at the rear; and the feet are supported by vertical and horizontal blocks.

Condition: The backboards have been renailed, although the old nails have been left in place. The brasses are replacements, as are the drawer runners and stops. There is a small patch at the left rear corner of the top. The back of the top drawer has a molded edge and some inexplicable nail holes; it was probably an old board originally used for another purpose. The French bracket feet are the most troublesome aspect of this chest's condition; they have been repaired several times. New vertical blocks have been added behind the front feet.

Woods: American black cherry and cherry veneer; lightwood stringing; drawer fronts, sides, and backs, undertop, bottom, back, eastern white pine; drawer bottoms, chestnut.

Dimensions: H 88.3; W 104.9; CW 96.7; D 60.0; CD 48.2.

Provenance: C. Sanford Bull, Middlebury, Conn.

KNOWN in its own time as a "round front bureau," this cherry chest of drawers with an elliptical front was probably made in Connecticut, where most of the Bull collection was assembled.[1] The use of chestnut points toward an origin in eastern Connecticut, but similar "swelled"-front chests were made in the Litchfield area and throughout the state.[2] The form was common in Anglo-American furniture of the late eighteenth and early nineteenth centuries.[3]

Gift of C. Sanford Bull 1952.50.3

1. Montgomery, p. 179.
2. Page, *Litchfield County Furn.*, no. 26, attributed to Silas E. Cheney (1776–1821).
3. Kirk, *Am. Furn. & Brit. Trad.*, figs. 518–520, 522–524.

70

Chest of drawers
Pennsylvania, 1790–1815

Description: The top has applied molding at the front and sides and surmounts a case holding seven lipped drawers, three in line over four graduated drawers. There is a band of dark veneer bordered at the top and bottom with light-wood stringing above the apron, and the case is supported by French bracket feet. The front apron is shaped to a central drop. The case is of dovetailed board construction, and the back consists of five horizontal half-lapped boards nailed to a rabbet in the sides and top. The rear feet are triangular braces, and there are vertical and horizontal blocks at each foot. A small block is glued behind the drop in the center of the apron. Each drawer is supported by a joined framework, and there are full vertical partitions between the small upper

Chests of Drawers

70

Provenance: A. J. Pennypacker, Pennsburg, Pa.; by sale to Francis P. Garvan, New York, N. Y.

THIS tall walnut chest of drawers is a representative late example of a form made in Pennsylvania from about 1750 into the early nineteenth century. A relatively late date in this series of objects for the Yale chest is indicated by its delicate cornice molding, French bracket feet, band of inlaid decoration, and original use of stamped oval brasses, probably similar in form to those currently on the chest. Earlier examples had bolder moldings, often had an additional row of three drawers in line at the top of the case, and were sometimes supported on a separate, low frame.[1] Related tall chests of drawers also were made in rural parts of northern New England.[2]

The Mabel Brady Garvan Collection 1930.2319

1. For some early examples, see Schiffer, *Furn. Chester County*, figs. 79, 131, 138, 147, 149, 167.
2. As an example, see Fales, *Deerfield*, fig. 400. See also Kirk, *Am. Furn. & Brit. Trad.*, figs. 493, 494.

drawers. The joints of the drawer dividers and the case sides are covered with an applied facing strip. The drawer sides are dovetailed to the front and back; the bottoms are beveled on their front and side edges, let into grooves in the front and sides, and nailed to the underside of the back.

Inscriptions: There are shop marks in white chalk throughout the case.

Condition: The backboards have been renailed; the facing on all the feet has been pieced, and it is completely replaced on the right rear foot. Older press marks beneath the present brasses indicate that they are replacements. The chest was refinished by Emile Mazzola in 1963.

Woods: American black walnut, light- and dark-wood inlay; drawer backs, other elements, yellow poplar; bottom of case, other elements, eastern white pine.

Dimensions: H 137.6; W 106.7; CW 104.0; D 52.0; CD 50.1.

71

Chest of drawers

Charleston, South Carolina, 1795–1815

Description: The top has thumbnail molding at the front and sides, overhangs the case slightly, and is shaped to conform to the serpentine drawer fronts and the canted corners of the case. The case holds four drawers which, unusually, are not graduated; each is 17 cm deep. Each drawer is outlined with light-wood stringing and has a central oval stamped brass lock escutcheon flanked by matching escutcheons with bail pulls. The brasses are decorated with an urn with ram's-head handles. The canted corners of the case have inlaid rectangles with hollow ends of light-wood stringing, enclosing bellflowers at each end. There is a base molding at the front and sides of the case, and the chest is supported by C-shaped bracket feet. The canted corners of the front feet have triglyphs with rounded tops and hollow ends, of light-wood inlay. The inside bracket of each foot is embellished with light-wood stringing conforming to the shape of the foot; the outside faces of the front feet and the rear feet are without stringing. The top of the chest is screwed from underneath to

152 *American Case Furniture*

longitudinal framing boards dovetailed to the case sides at the front and back and additionally secured with the use of multiple transverse glue blocks placed between these boards. The back is framed to two vertical panels; the rails of this assembly are screwed to the top and bottom of the case above and below the muntin, and the stiles are nailed to rabbets in the sides. Pegs are not used in the joints between the rails and stiles. At the base there is a framework of strips at the front, sides, and part of the back which is nailed to the bottom of the case. There are quarter-round vertical blocks in the corners, with horizontal blocks behind the front brackets. The triangular rear feet are dovetailed to the rear side brackets. The base moldings are applied with nails. The drawer runners within the case are housed in grooves, nailed to the sides of the case, and cut off diagonally on their inner ends. There are partial dustboards; the lowest drawer runs on the bottom of the case. The drawer fronts are veneered on a solid board. The drawer sides are dovetailed to the front and back; the bottoms are let into grooves in the front and sides and nailed to the underside of the back; small blocks are glued to the bottom behind the front and at the sides, with runners then applied.

Inscriptions: The drawers are numbered in white chalk on the inside of the back.

Condition: The "dots" of inlay at the base of the triglyph on the right front foot have been repaired with filler. The runner on the right side of the bottom drawer has been replaced, and the partial dustboard under the drawer second from the top is broken on the right corner.

Woods: Mahogany; veneer on the drawer fronts, mahogany; light- and dark-wood inlay; drawer fronts and sides, red cedar; drawer backs and bottoms, back panels and frame, case bottom, other elements, eastern white pine.

Dimensions: H 95.1; W 107.3; D 59.8.

Exhibition: YUAG, "Southern Furn.," no. 14.

Bibliography: Nutting, *Treasury*, no. 255; Kane, "American Furn.," fig. 8; Kirk, *Am. Furn. & Brit. Trad.*, fig. 507.

Provenance: Acquired by C. Sanford Bull, Middlebury, Conn., before 1928.

ALTHOUGH acquired by C. Sanford Bull of Connecticut, whose collection consisted primarily of New England objects, this chest of drawers is part of a group of related objects from the vicinity of Charleston, South Carolina. Among the characteristics of these Charleston chests of drawers, as demonstrated by research undertaken by the Museum of Early Southern Decorative Arts in Winston-Salem, North Carolina, are boldly serpentined facades, canted front corners on the case and feet, stringing on the drawer fronts and C-shaped bracket feet, and red cedar secondary wood.[1] An elaborate example of the form, in the Winterthur collection (57.32.2), is fitted with the additional embellishment of a "dressing drawer" and decorated with fans, cross-banding, and patterned inlay.[2] The Charleston library bookcase (cat. 188) in the Yale collection shares many features with these chests of drawers.

Gift of C. Sanford Bull 1953.50.3

1. Related examples include chests published in Burton, *Charleston Furn.*, figs. 11, 13; *Southern Furn.*, fig. 70; *Antiques* 91, no. 1 (January 1967): 19; and Frank L. Horton, "William Little, Cabinetmaker of North Carolina," *Journal of Early Southern Decorative Arts* 4, no. 2 (November 1978): 8 fig. 3; as well as chests recorded in MESDA research files S-1163, S-8740, S-8743.
2. Montgomery, no. 142. Another related chest with a dressing drawer, thought to be American, is in the collection of the Montreal Museum of Fine Arts (942.Df.11).

72

Chest of drawers
American, possibly Maryland, 1810–1830

Description: This chest of drawers with an elliptic front contains five graduated drawers, the top two in line, with cock-beaded edges and cross-banding on the drawer rails and vertical partition. The drawers have brass knob pulls and brass keyhole liners and are flanked by paneled and reeded stiles. All four stiles terminate in ring and vase-shaped legs with rounded feet. The front edge of the top has triple half-round molding, and the top is shaped to conform with the case. The sides are framed to a single vertical panel, and the back contains two horizontal panels. The veneered top consists of a framework of boards, screwed from underneath and through the back to the carcass. The bottom boards are nailed to the frame. The drawer fronts are laminated and veneered, the drawer sides are finely dovetailed to the front and back, and the drawer bottoms are of two butted longitudinal boards let into grooves in the front and sides and nailed to the underside of the back. There are no dustboards.

Inscriptions: "Bottom" is written in pencil on the underside of the lowest drawer rail. A fragment of a modern shipping tag thumbtacked to the back reads "[BALT]IMORE."

Condition: The lock is missing on the top drawer, and the brasses are replacements. Running strips have been added to the drawers, and the backs pieced to compensate for shrinkage. There have been minor repairs to the veneer, and some of the bottom boards are missing. The inside of the drawer fronts and the back of the case are stained red.

Woods: Stiles, side rails, side panels, mahogany; drawer fronts, drawer dividers and rails, top, mahogany veneer on eastern white pine; other framing elements, including back rails, eastern white pine; drawer backs, bottoms, and sides, back panels, yellow poplar.

Dimensions: H 102.5; W 110.1; CW 107.9; D 61.3; CD 48.2.

Provenance: Purchased by R. T. Haines Halsey (1865–1943) for Francis P. Garvan, New York, N. Y.

OF a form commonly made in many locations along the East Coast during the first decades of the nineteenth century, this chest of drawers probably owes its ultimate source of design to an English pattern book illustration, such as the dressing chest with reeded pilasters and bowed front included in plate 15 of the appendix to Sheraton's *Drawing-Book*. The design as executed here is a later, coarser version, with simply turned feet and paneled sides, although the chest is well made and is probably an urban rather than rural product. It bears an affinity, for example, to a mahogany chest of identical form and similar decoration made by John Needles (1786–1876) of Baltimore about 1815.[1] The Yale chest may have been acquired in Maryland by Halsey when he was teaching at St. John's College in Annapolis between 1928 and 1930.

The Mabel Brady Garvan Collection 1930.2728

1. Charles F. Montgomery, "John Needles—Baltimore Cabinetmaker," *Antiques* 65, no. 4 (April 1954): 293. The drawers on the Yale example lack the mitering on the rear of the drawer runners seen on Needles's work. Another similar chest is illustrated in Miller, 1: no. 749.

73

Chest of drawers

American, possibly New York State, 1820–1840

Description: This tall chest of drawers is of heavy framed-panel construction. There is a raised backboard at the rear of the top, and the top projects slightly at the front and sides. The case holds six drawers; an upper projecting section holds two small drawers in line over a deep drawer, and the lower section contains three graduated drawers. Each drawer has a pair of round brass knob pulls, and each (except for the upper two small drawers) has a brass keyhole liner. The bottom bank of drawers is flanked by applied columns with a rounded upper section above spiral reeding and cross-hatching. The columns have a square base, and the chest is supported at the front by carved paw feet with well-articulated toes and claws. Each side is framed to a single vertical panel, and the back contains two horizontal panels. The front and side edges of the top, the drawer dividers, and the edges of the deep drawer in the upper section are decorated with cross-banding; the drawer fronts, upper stiles, and raised backboard are veneered with carefully selected "flame" mahogany. The raised backboard is screwed to the top and has astragal molding applied to its upper edge. The top of the chest is two butted boards glued to a supporting framework that is in turn screwed to the carcass from inside the case and pocket screwed through the back. It has no dustboards and no bottom. The drawer runners are nailed to the rear stiles and to supporting strips tenoned to the stiles. The projecting section of the front is built up by posts butted to the stiles above the columns, and the drawer divider under the deep drawer is secured to each post. The carved half columns are applied to the stiles; the front feet are probably doweled in place, and the rear feet are formed by extensions of the stiles. In each drawer, the sides are dovetailed to the front and back, and the bottoms consist of two longitudinal boards roughly joined and let into grooves in the front and sides and nailed to the underside of the back. Small blocks are nailed to each side of the drawer dividers to serve as stops.

Inscriptions: There are numerous cabinetmaker's marks in pencil and chalk on the interior.

Condition: The veneer on the top side of the top has been lost, and there are minor repairs to the veneer in many places. The drawer bottoms have been renailed. The left brass on the middle drawer in the lower bank differs from the other brasses and is probably a replacement. Running strips have been added to the bottoms of some drawers.

Woods: Columns and feet, mahogany; drawer fronts, drawer dividers, other surfaces on front exterior, mahogany veneer on eastern white pine; stiles, side panels, back panels, drawer sides, backs, and bottoms, yellow poplar; side rails, bottom front rail, butternut; back rails, other interior elements, eastern white pine.

Dimensions: H 151.6; W 119.4; CW 116.7; D 58.4; CD 48.6.

Provenance: Luella Plummer, Ansonia, Conn.

It is difficult to assign a place of origin to such a common form of empire furniture, although many examples were made in New York City, especially those with elaborate gilt-stencil decoration.[1] This chest of drawers, or dressing bureau,

Chests of Drawers 155

is of the humbler sort, although the quality of carving is good and the flame mahogany veneer attractive. It shares with many other chests of its type the projecting upper section, carved columns, and acanthus and paw carved feet. Many examples of this kind of furniture were made in upstate New York and neighboring Canada, but they were also made in many locations, as witnessed by a fine example made in 1832 in Newport, New Hampshire, by Horace Ellis.[2]

Gift of Luella Plummer 1931.117

1. Fales, *Am. Painted Furn.*, figs. 262, 263; see also figs. 264, 266.
2. Howard Pain, *The Heritage of Upper Canadian Furniture* (Toronto: Van Nostrand Reinhold, 1978), figs. 641, 642; *Documented New Hampshire Furn.*, no. 32.

74

Miniature chest of drawers
Henry Seem
Easton, Pennsylvania, 1856

Description: The top is a single board attached with glue blocks to the frame and is shaped at the front and sides to conform to the case. The case holds four graduated veneered drawers, each with a central heart-shaped keyhole surround inlaid with bone and a pair of round white ceramic pulls. The front corners of the case are rounded, and each side is framed to a single recessed panel. A veneered framework at the base conforms to the shape of the drawers at the front and extends along the sides. The chest is supported by veneered bracket feet, rounded at the front, and without a supporting bracket at the rear. The back is framed to a single panel. In each drawer, the sides are dovetailed to the front and back, and the bottom is a single board let into grooves in the front and sides and nailed to the underside of the back. The drawer bottoms show evidence of circular-saw marks. The drawer dividers are shaped to conform to the drawers and are overlapped by the drawer fronts. The bracket feet are nailed in place to the base framework, and there is a shaped block behind the front feet. It has no dustboards or bottom; the drawer runners and guides are nailed and glued in place.

Inscriptions: Written in pencil on the outside of the back of the top drawer: "Build By Henry Seem when an apprentice at Sam Hogland and Dan Pitenger in Easton / in the year 1856." On the outside of the back panel, also written in pencil, is a similar note: "Build while I / was an Aprentice / In 1856 Easton / Pa / By Dan Pitenger & Sam Hoagland / Henry Seem." There are many shop marks on the interior and the drawers, and there is a column of addition on the inside of the bottom of the top drawer.

Condition: A plugged hole at each side of the rear of the top suggests that the chest was fitted originally with a looking glass, perhaps on a swinging frame. Two screw holes were made in the bottom of the back rail when the object was attached to a display stand in the Garvan Galleries in 1973.

Woods: Walnut; veneered drawer fronts, side panels, base, feet, mahogany; drawer fronts, some framing elements, eastern white pine; drawer sides, bottoms, and backs, other framing elements, yellow poplar; back panel, possibly basswood; drawer dividers, walnut.

Dimensions: H 36.2; W 43.2; CW 41.9; D 22.0; CD 19.4.

156 *American Case Furniture*

Bibliography: Schiffer, *Miniature Antique Furn.*, no. 132.

Provenance: Francis P. Garvan, New York, N. Y.

THIS miniature chest of drawers probably represents an unusual documented instance of an apprentice fashioning such a small object as his "masterpiece," to prove his skills as a cabinetmaker.[1] To date, nothing has been learned about the career of Henry Seem. By 1860, one of his masters, Samuel Hoagland, had died, leaving his widow, Maria, at 188 Northampton Street in Easton, while the other, Daniel Pittenger, was still in business as a cabinetmaker at 189 Northampton Street. Pittinger seems to have been one of the leading furniture makers in Easton and was the only one to advertise in its 1860 directory.[2] His illustrated advertisement contained stock images of furniture in the rococo-revival style and claimed that he operated the "Largest, Cheapest, and most Fashionable Wholesale and retail CABINET WAREROOM" in Easton, where "Sofas, Lounges, Side Boards, Secretaries, Wardrobes, Bureaus, Corner Cupboards, Card, Centre, Side, Dining, Extension, and Breakfast Tables, Wash-Stands, Bedsteads, Looking-glasses, Tea-boards, Chairs, &c., &c." were always on hand. By 1860 Seem is not listed in the Easton directories, and he probably moved elsewhere after the completion of his training.

The Mabel Brady Garvan Collection 1931.1208

1. See Walter Cahn, *Masterpieces: Chapters on the History of an Idea* (Princeton, N. J.: Princeton University Press, 1979), chap. 1, for a discussion of the "artisanal masterpiece."
2. *Boyd's Directory of Reading, Easton, Pottsville, Allentown & Lebanon* (Philadelphia: William H. Boyd, 1860).

75

Chest of drawers

Probably by Harry Eduard Snohr (w. ca. 1926–1935)
for Lord and Taylor
New York, New York, ca. 1929

Description: The rectangular top of this veneered chest of drawers slightly overhangs the front framework to about half the depth of the top drawer front and is slightly recessed at the back and sides. The case contains four drawers, the bottom two of the same depth, and the top two graduated, each with recessed handholds on each side. The front is decorated with a grid pattern formed by double lines of metal (probably aluminum) inlay on the top and bottom drawers and seven vertical lines of metal inlay spaced across the front at regular intervals. The sides are similarly decorated with double horizontal lines of metal inlay at the top and bottom and with three vertical lines. The vertical strips of inlay are continued across the top edge of the top drawer, around the side edges of the top and bottom drawer to intersect with the inlay on the sides, and extend across the recessed portion of the top at the sides. The chest is supported by four square tapered feet doweled at the corners to a base framework screwed in turn to all four sides of the chest bottom. The top consists of two butted veneered boards screwed to the top framework from underneath. The drawer runners are screwed to the sides and held with a tongue and groove to the drawer dividers. The bottom is made of several longitudinal butted boards dovetailed to the sides. The back is a single panel nailed to rabbets in the sides and top framework and to the bottom. On each drawer the sides are stopped slot dovetailed to the front and dovetailed to the back. The drawer bottoms are let into grooves in the front and sides and nailed to the underside of the back. The drawer fronts are veneered on their insides, and they overlap the case at the sides and bottom to give a flush appearance.

Inscriptions: The admonition "keep hands off" appears in pencil on the inside of the back. There are numerous shop marks and numbers in pencil on the inside of the case and drawers. Fragments remain of newspaper printed in English glued to the butted joints of the top and sides on the inside of the case.

Condition: The top was refinished and some of the inlay and veneer glued down in 1978. The bottom of the lowest drawer was water damaged in 1980 and was replaced in plywood of a similar kind. There are traces of gray paint on the base framework and feet.

Woods: Exterior portions veneered in figured maple, probably described as "harewood" when chest was made. Top, sides, drawer dividers, drawer runners, drawer sides and backs, bottom framework, feet, mahogany; core of drawer fronts, bottom boards, case sides, chestnut; back, drawer bottoms, yellow poplar plywood with mahogany facing.

Dimensions: H 98.9; W 106.9; CW 106.9; D 48.2; CD 45.6.

Bibliography: Gordon Eliot Sands, "The Osborn Furniture: Modern Decorative Arts and the Department Store," *Decorative Arts Society Newsletter* 9, no. 3 (September 1983): fig. 8.

75

Gift of J. Marshall and Thomas M. Osborn in memory of Mr. and Mrs. James M. Osborn 1977.40.17

1. Gordon Eliot Sands, "The Osborn Furniture: Modern Decorative Arts and the Department Store," *Decorative Arts Society Newsletter* 9, no. 3 (September 1983): 1–10.
2. Illustrated in Sands, "Osborn Furniture," fig. 9.
3. Sands, "Osborn Furniture," p. 6; the Goodspeeds' chest is illustrated in Jan Juta, "A Modern Apartment in Chicago," *International Studio* 95, no. 393 (February 1930): 53. Recent research by Jennifer C. Toher of David A. Hanks & Associates, Inc., has identified two related objects marked with labels bearing the name "Snohr," probably for the cabinetmaker Harry Eduard Snohr of New York.

76

Chest of drawers with doors
Probably by Harry Eduard Snohr (w. ca. 1926–1935)
for Lord and Taylor
New York, New York, ca. 1929

Provenance: James Marshall Osborn (1906–1976) and Marie-Louise (Montgomery) Osborn (d. 1968), Bronxville, N. Y.; New York, N. Y.; and New Haven, Conn.

THIS chest of drawers is part of a large gift of furniture and other objects originally owned by Mr. and Mrs. James Marshall Osborn given to Yale in 1977 in their memory by their sons (see also cats. 76, 193, 227). Selected by fashion-conscious Marie-Louise Montgomery on the eve of her wedding, this chest and the following chest of drawers with doors were part of a bedroom set probably ordered from the design department of the Lord and Taylor department store in New York City in late 1929 for their apartment in Bronxville, New York. The circumstances surrounding her choice of these objects has been discussed by Gordon Eliot Sands, who also has brought to light the French and American design sources for these objects.[1] Veneered in "harewood," the Osborn chest is a simplified version of a related example exhibited at Lord and Taylor's in 1928.[2] A chest similar to the one exhibited at Lord and Taylor's has survived, and another was published in 1930 in an article on the home of Mr. and Mrs. Charles Goodspeed of Chicago and described as a "Ruhlman cabinet."[3]

Description: A companion piece to the preceding chest of drawers (cat. 75), this object exhibits many of the same construction and decorative features. The object is veneered, and the two doors are decorated with a grid pattern formed by horizontal and vertical lines of metal inlay. The sides are veneered, but without inlaid lines. The doors are attached to the case with brass Soss hinges, with a lock on the right door and a brass spring catch on the upper edge of the left door. The interior contains an open shelf at the top above a bank of four small drawers at the left, flanked by a bank of four wider drawers with shaped sides at the right, all above two wider drawers at the base. Here, the top is flush with the back, recessed at the sides, and stands above and is screwed from underneath to the carcass top. The bottom framework and legs are the same as on the previous chest. The back here is two butted plywood panels, nailed as in the chest, and the bottom is again composed of several longitudinal boards dovetailed to the sides. The drawer construction here varies somewhat. In the bank of small drawers and the two wide drawers below, the vertical wooden pulls are glued to the drawer fronts. The drawer sides are secured to the front and back with grooved and tongued joints and small blocks filled in at the bottom of the joint to strengthen the lap; the bottoms are let into grooves at the front and sides and nailed to the underside of the back. The front of the drawer extends

158 *American Case Furniture*

76

76a

below the base to overlap the drawer runner. On the bank of drawers housed in the upper right section, the sides and back of the drawers are high, and the sides are shaped with a downward curve to the front. The sides are dovetailed to the front and attached to the back with the same tongue-and-groove joint used on the other drawers, and the bottoms are attached in the same manner.

Inscriptions: The brass lock on the drawers is stamped: "RC&S [in a crown] / MADE IN ENGLAND." There are also many shop marks and numbers in pencil on this object.

Condition: The right rear leg was repaired in 1976. There have been minor losses to the veneer.

Woods: Same figured maple veneer as cat. 75; top, sides, doors, drawer runners, partitions in case, drawer fronts, sides, backs, and pulls, bottom framework, legs, mahogany and Spanish cedar; bottom, cores of case sides, chestnut; back panels, bottom of small and wide drawers, yellow poplar plywood with mahogany facing; bottoms of intermediate drawers, Douglas fir plywood.

Dimensions: H 143.6; W 91.5; CW 91.5; D 45.6; CD 43.3.

Bibliography: See cat. 75.

Provenance: See cat. 75.

This chest of drawers with doors, or wardrobe, is also part of the Osborn furnishings that have been discussed by Gordon Eliot Sands (see cat. 75). The inlay, perhaps an "aluminum alloy that will not tarnish" of the kind used by Wolfgang Hoffmann on a cupboard made in 1928, was an alternative, probably a less expensive one, to the wood inlay used on many Continental and English examples.[1] The Osborn wardrobe appears in a ca. 1929–1930 photograph of their Bronxville apartment, along with twin beds made

Chests of Drawers 159

en suite.² Although the Osborns' taste in furnishings has now begun to receive attention,³ James Marshall Osborn is best known as a literary historian and a noted scholar-collector at Yale. The James and Marie-Louise Osborn Collection is a major collection of manuscripts housed at Yale's Beinecke Rare Book and Manuscript Library.

Gift of J. Marshall and Thomas M. Osborn in memory of Mr. and Mrs. James M. Osborn 1977.40.18

1. The Hoffmann cupboard is illustrated in "Seen in the Galleries," *International Studio* 91, no. 377 (October 1928): 12. An English walnut wardrobe with a grid created by light-colored woods, designed by J. Hully of the Bath Cabinet Makers' Co. Ltd., is illustrated in C. Geoffrey Holme and Shirley B. Wainwright, eds., *Decorative Art 1929* (New York: Albert and Charles Boni, 1969), p. 112.
2. Illustrated in Gordon Eliot Sands, "The Osborn Furniture: Modern Decorative Arts and the Department Store," *Decorative Arts Society Newsletter* 9, no. 3 (September 1983): fig. 6.
3. In addition to the Sands article, see also Karen Davies, *At Home in Manhattan: Modern Decorative Arts, 1925 to the Depression* (New Haven: Yale University Art Gallery, 1983), pp. 84–86, no. 66.

77

Long chest

Designed by Edward Wormley (b. 1907) in 1952; manufactured by Dunbar Furniture Company
Berne, Indiana, ca. 1955

Description: The case holds eight drawers, arranged in two tiers of four, and enclosed within a rectangular mitered frame, with rounded edges on the slightly projecting top, sides, and bottom. Each drawer is fitted with a single laminated wood pull covered in brown leather. The case is supported on a recessed leather-covered base. The top, sides, bottom, and back of the case are each a single plywood board; the back projects slightly and is screwed to all four sides. A vertical partition divides the two tiers of drawers, which are supported by a simple framework including a medial runner. There are no dustboards. The base is a rectangular joined frame, with small vertical glue blocks on each inside corner. The leather covering is applied with nails and only partially covers the rear of the frame. The drawer sides are machine dovetailed to the front and back, and the top edges of the sides are rounded. The drawer bottom is a single longitudinal plywood board fitted to grooves in all four sides and reinforced with multiple small glue blocks. A board grooved to accept the medial drawer runner is nailed to the underside of the bottom and reinforced with glue blocks. The upper right drawer is divided into several small compartments by removable transverse partitions fitted to grooves. The chest retains its original coin tray, which is grooved on its bottom to slide on top of these partitions.

Inscriptions: An embossed green metal label with black letters nailed to the inside of the left side of the top left drawer reads: "DUNBAR / BERNE·INDIANA." The underside of the front of the top left drawer is stamped "18 1 N / 1 18"; the drawers beneath it are stamped "18 3 N," "18 5 N," and "18 7 N / 7 18" respectively. The right tier of drawers is similarly stamped, from top to bottom, "18 2 N / 18 2," "18 4N / 18," "18 6 N," and "18 8 N / 18 8."

Woods: Case, grained hardwood plywood, possibly with mahogany facing; back, stained hardwood plywood, with probably a walnut facing on its inside; drawer fronts, bleached walnut veneer over a core wood, with white oak veneer on inside face; drawer sides, backs, partitions in upper right drawer, white oak; drawer bottoms, white oak veneer on top face, over a core wood, with walnut veneer on lower face; coin tray, walnut; drawer supports, blocks, and base, yellow poplar, maple, mahogany, elm, walnut.

Dimensions: H 81.8; W 179.8; D 46.3.

Provenance: Acquired as household furnishings by Mr. and Mrs. Gifford Phillips of Santa Monica, Calif., in the mid 1950s.

77a

77

This chest of drawers and a cabinet (cat. 228) in the Yale collection are part of the "Career Group" of living room, bedroom, and dining room furniture designed by Edward Wormley for the Dunbar Furniture Company and introduced to the market in 1952–1953. Objects in this group remained in Dunbar's line for approximately six to eight years, or longer in some instances. The stated goal of the Career Group was to "provide less costly furniture for the young homemaker with a passion for quality," and therefore the objects were "purposefully designed along simple lines to eliminate expensive details."[1] The Yale chest was no. 664 in the line and was termed a "Long Chest." Options available for the long chest included imported Japanese metal pulls (no. 664A) and 7-inch walnut legs rather than the leather-covered base, with the metal (no. 665) or leather (no. 665A) pulls. A bookcase (no. 677) or a slightly larger "bookcase superstructure" (no. 678) were designed to rest on top of the long chest. Dunbar catalogues illustrated the long chest butted against the cabinet in a bedroom setting.

Gift of Mr. and Mrs. Gifford Phillips, B.A. 1942 1984.14.12

1. Information on the "Career Group" was provided by Marilyn Lobsiger of Dunbar, to whom the writer is most grateful. Photocopies of relevant portions of Dunbar sales catalogues and other material relating to the "Career Group" are in the Yale Furniture Study object files.

Chests of Drawers 161

Chest-on-Chests

The chest-on-chest (sometimes known in period documents as a double chest, and as a tallboy in English usage) simply consists of a chest of drawers standing on another chest of drawers. Derived from two-part seventeenth-century joined examples (cat. 51), the eighteenth-century version is larger, is of dovetailed board construction, and holds from nine to fifteen drawers. Among the fifteen examples in the collection, all dating to the eighteenth or very early nineteenth century, are chest-on-chests from New England and Pennsylvania. The earliest and perhaps most unusual example is the clothespress (cat. 78), in which the upper case is enclosed by a pair of paneled doors. Some chest-on-chests were supported by a third element, a freestanding frame (cats. 87, 88), such as the painted Dunlap-style example in the collection (cat. 88). Another minor variation is seen in a Massachusetts chest-on-chest (cat. 81) where the lower case is fitted with a secretary drawer. The most famous example in the collection is the monumental chest-on-chest made in 1791 for Elias Hasket Derby of Salem by Stephen Badlam, embellished with carved allegorical figures by the Skillin family (cat. 82). The Pennsylvania examples provide a contrast to the New England work and indicate differences in the way the same form was handled by an urban Philadelphia shop (cat. 89) and by one located outside of the city (cat. 90). Two additional Pennsylvania examples, one with and one without a scrolled pediment (cats. 91, 92), complete the holdings.

78

Clothespress
Boston, Massachusetts, area, 1740–1760

Description: This clothespress is in two cases. The upper case is enclosed by paired doors with fielded panels shaped at the top to echo the contour of the pediment. The doors are attached to the case with brass butt hinges, and each door has a brass lock escutcheon, blind on the left. The left door is fitted with a brass bolt at the top and formerly had one on the bottom. The upper case is crowned with a bold scrolled cornice rising to a central arched section enclosing a small drawer with a shaped panel front. The doors open to an interior containing six drawers outlined by cock beading on the case. The top drawer is shaped to conform to the curvature of the cornice, and the five drawers below are graduated. A slider with brass button pulls is housed below the doors. The upper case is virtually the same width and depth as the lower case and fits over pins on top of the lower case. The lower case contains four graduated blockfront drawers, with rounded blocking, and again is outlined by cock beading on the case. There is base molding at the front and sides, and the press is supported by straight bracket feet with shaped knee brackets conforming to the blocking of the drawers. Each drawer (with the exception of the top drawer in the upper case) is fitted with a central brass lock escutcheon (blind in the upper case) flanked by matching escutcheons with bail pulls. The pediment is roofed with transverse slats nailed to the sides, back, and front framing member of the case, with paper strips pasted to the underside. There is a transverse support beneath the small pediment drawer, and a full dustboard beneath the top wide drawer. Screws have been added to secure the cornice molding to the case sides. The drawer dividers are dovetailed to the case sides, with the runners housed in grooves in the sides and drawer guides nailed in place. The horizontal backboards in each case are nailed to rabbets in the sides. The cleated slider is of mahogany. The lower case is of dovetailed board construction; the dovetails joining the drawer dividers to the case sides are exposed. There are full dustboards in the lower case; the base molding is attached to the case bottom with a giant dovetail, although the base molding stands above the bottom slightly, and the bottom drawer runs on strips nailed to the bottom. On each drawer, the sides are dovetailed to the front and back and the bottoms are nailed to rabbets in the front and sides and to the underside of the back, with running strips applied.

78a

Although the base has been extensively reworked, there may have been shaped vertical blocks behind each foot, with smaller shaped horizontal blocks behind the brackets. The top drawer in the upper case is divided by a central vertical transverse partition into two compartments. The door frames in the upper case are constructed with wedged tenons.

Inscriptions: The drawers are numbered in white chalk on the outside of the back. "Top L P" is written in chalk in the underside of the top of the lower case. "T" is written in chalk on the top of the dustboard above the dressing slide. The lowest drawer of the upper case was once lined with newspaper; a remaining fragment bears the date 18 February 1850.

Condition: This object has undergone a good deal of restoration and may well have been taken apart and repaired prior to its acquisition by the Art Gallery. The plinths and finials for center and side finials are missing, there have been repairs to each side of the cornice molding, and two boards in the roof of the bonnet have been replaced. Cracks in the sides of both the upper and lower cases have been filled, and the

78

midmolding applied to the top of the lower case is a replacement. The front of the slider has been replaced, and its right rear side has been repaired. Vertical strips inside the doors of the upper case have been replaced, and the blocks behind them are new. Many of the drawer bottoms have been renailed. The brasses on the top wide drawer in the upper case are replacements. Most of the feet and their blocks have been repaired or replaced; only the vertical block behind the right front foot and the horizontal block behind the front bracket on the left front foot may be old. There have been many other small repairs.

Woods: Mahogany; drawer sides, backs, bottoms, red oak; dustboards, eastern white pine.

Dimensions: H 216.9; W 115.8; UCW 104.4; LCW 104.5; D 55.9; UCD 49.8; LCD 50.1.

Exhibition: Lu Bartlett, ed., *A Bit of Vanity* (Boston: Museum of Fine Arts, 1972), no. 26.

Bibliography: *Boston Furn.*, p. 141 fig. 96.

Provenance: Dr. Michael A. Abrams, Baltimore, Md.; by sale in 1929 to Francis P. Garvan, New York, N.Y.

ALTHOUGH this object might well be called a linen press or a chest-on-chest with doors, Chippendale's use of "Cloaths-Press" is perhaps a better contemporary appellation, and it is the one adopted here. The 1762 edition of the *Director* includes three designs (plates CXXIX–CXXXI) for clothespresses in two cases, each with doors enclosing the upper case and drawers in the lower case. However, Chippendale states that the upper case is meant to contain "sliding Shelves, which should be covered with green Baize, to cover the Cloaths," rather than drawers. There are at least two other clothespresses closely related to the Yale example, each with similar rounded blocking in the lower case, and each with the same distinctive curving pediment and drawer arrangement in the upper case.[1] One of these differs primarily in its use of mirrored doors and appropriate use of red cedar as a secondary wood.[2] The second example, heavily restored, is now in the Yale collection (see Appendix, no. 8). The Green family clothespress has a history in Worcester, Massachusetts, and differs from the other two examples in its lack of doors in the upper case and the absence of a slider. The bold pediments of this group probably are ultimately derived from a Continental source, although English prototypes are known.[3] Other clothespresses of varying style, but with the essential elements of upper and lower cases with drawers and doors covering the upper case, also have Massachusetts connections, suggesting a regional preference for the form.[4] Two Newport presses, each a single case with paired doors enclosing shelves, also are known.[5]

The Mabel Brady Garvan Collection 1930.2726

1. This group was identified and discussed in Lovell, "Boston Blockfront Furn.," pp. 101–108. A fourth example has recently come on the market.
2. Lovell, "Boston Blockfront Furn.," fig. 72.
3. Lovell, "Boston Blockfront Furn.," fig. 73.
4. These include examples with a history in the Payne family of Boston (*Antiques* 78, no. 4 [October 1960]: 302); a history in the Marston family

of Boston (Hagler, *American Queen Anne Furn.* pp. 2–3) and the Robbins family of Milton (*Sack Coll.*, 7: 1872–1873 no. P5166); and a bombé example (*Antiques* 70, no. 2 [August 1956]: 89).

5. Rodriguez Roque, *Chipstone*, no. 1.

79

Chest-on-chest

North Shore, Massachusetts, 1770–1790

Description: The chest-on-chest is in two cases. The upper case contains seven drawers surrounded by cock beading on the case, including three in line over four graduated drawers. The center drawer of the three in line is taller and is carved with a concave shell; the side drawers are curved to conform to the arch of the pediment. The upper case is crowned by a broken-arch pediment closed at the back and is fitted with central and side urn-and-flame finials. The upper case is flanked by fluted pilasters with seven flutes. The upper case rests within restraining molding applied to the top of the lower case. The lower case contains four graduated block-front drawers with rounded blocking, and again the drawers are surrounded by cock beading on the case. The front skirt is shaped to a central drop, and the chest is supported by straight bracket feet with shaped knee brackets. Each wide drawer has a central brass lock escutcheon flanked by matching escutcheons with bail pulls; the two small side drawers in the upper case have a single brass, and the center drawer has a brass ring pull. The brasses retain traces of their original gilding. The roof of the bonnet is formed by transverse slats nailed to the front and back of the case. There are vertical transverse partitions on each side of the central opening in the bonnet, and a transverse board with a beveled front edge is nailed in place above the top middle drawer. Small triangular pieces are glued to the upper inner corner of the two upper side drawers. The dovetails of the vertical partitions flanking the top center drawer are exposed. There is a longitudinal strip running inside the top of the upper case at the front joining the case sides. The horizontal backboards of the upper case are joined with a half lap and nailed to a rabbet in the sides, and the bottom of the upper case is dovetailed to the sides. There are full dustboards below the three drawers in line in the upper case. The lower case is of dovetailed board construction, and there are no dustboards. The

79

drawer runners within the case are applied to the sides of the case. The front base molding is joined to the case bottom with a giant dovetail. There are multiple shaped horizontal and vertical blocks in the corners behind the feet. On each drawer, the sides are dovetailed to the front and back; the bottoms are let into grooves in the front and sides and nailed to the underside of the back. The top edge of the drawer sides are molded to a double half round.

Inscriptions: Both the upper and lower cases are branded numerous times with "TREADWELL." There are illegible

Chest-on-Chests 167

chalk inscriptions on the top of the top of the lower case and on the inside of the second drawer from the top in the lower case. There are other chalk shop marks.

79a

Condition: The side plinths and finials are replacements made in 1963 by Emile Mazzola and Robert M. Soule respectively. The center plinth has been broken and repaired. The left front and rear feet and the right front foot have been broken and repaired. The side bracket on the right rear foot has been burned, and some of the blocks have been replaced.

Woods: Mahogany; eastern white pine.

Dimensions: H 232.9; W 109.4; UCW 99.2; LCW 105.5; D 60.1; UCD 50.2; LCD 57.0.

Exhibition: *Girl Scouts Exhibition*, no. 634.

Bibliography: Lovell, "Boston Blockfront Furn.," figs. 74, 75.

Provenance: This chest-on-chest descended in the family of Miss Flora G. Treadwell, Brooklyn, N.Y., and was purchased from her, probably in 1929, by Ftancis P. Garvan, New York, N.Y. Mr. Garvan's records indicate that Miss Treadwell's family home was in New Market, Mass.; this may well have been a misprint for New Market, N.H., near Portsmouth. The entry for the object in the catalogue for the *Girl Scouts Exhibition* states that the chest "might well have been made in Vermont for it stood in the house of its first owner from the time it was made until a month or so ago," further confusing the issue.

ONE of a large group of chest-on-chests produced by many shops in Boston, Charlestown, Salem, Marblehead, and other parts of Essex County during the last half of the eighteenth century, this Treadwell family example is (potentially) a documented example of great importance.[1] However, interpretation of the chest's documentation remains inconclusive. It seems clear from the branded name and the provenance that the chest descended in a New England family by the name of Treadwell, who lived either in Massachusetts, possibly in New Hampshire, or perhaps even in Vermont. The chest has been attributed, with perhaps more hope than conviction, to one Nathaniel Treadwell, a largely unknown cabinetmaker working in Beverly, Massachusetts, from 1797 to 1799, and possibly active in Ipswich thereafter.[2] The Treadwell name is most closely associated in Essex County with Ipswich, with a vast majority of the people by that name listed in the Essex County probate and deed records up to 1840 being residents of that town. It was a common practice in Portsmouth, New Hampshire, and perhaps elsewhere, for owners of furniture to brand their possessions, so there is no guarantee that the Treadwell brand refers to the maker of the chest.[3] The Yale chest differs in detail from known examples that are documented to specific makers. More than half a dozen related chests with fluted pilasters in the upper case, a blockfront lower case, similar drawer arrangements, and either with bracket or claw-and-ball feet are known, including examples attributed to Benjamin Frothingham of Charlestown, Abraham Watson of Salem, and Nathan Bowen and Ebenezer Martin of Marblehead, and others dated 1767 and 1774.[4] Variations on the form include chests with a serpentine or bombé lower case.[5]

The Mabel Brady Garvan Collection 1930.2195

1. The group is discussed in Lovell, "Boston Blockfront Furn.," pp. 108–112; and Richard H. Randall, Jr., "An Eighteenth-Century Partnership," *Art Quarterly* 23, no. 2 (Summer 1960): 153–161.

2. Lovell, "Boston Blockfront Furn.," p. 109, citing an unpublished list compiled by the Museum of Fine Arts, Boston, which is based on an entry in Henry W. Belknap, *Artists and Craftsmen of Essex County, Massachusetts* (Salem: Essex Institute, 1927), p. 75. A Nathaniel Treadwell, cabinetmaker, was a property owner in Beverly in 1797 and 1799; see Essex County Registry of Deeds, Salem, 161: 254, 165: 233.

3. Myrna Kaye, "Marked Portsmouth Furniture," *Antiques* 113, no. 5 (May 1978): 1098–1104. Even collectors have been known to brand their furniture; see "Collectors' Notes," *Antiques* 110, no. 3 (September 1976): 561.

4. See, as examples, *Boston Furn.*, figs. 1, 76; Randall, no. 40; *Garvan Coll.*, no. 401; Randall, "An Eighteenth-Century Partnership," fig. 2; Springer, p. 13; Fales, *Essex County Furn.*, fig. 75; *Sack Coll.*, 1: 170 no. 450, 4: 980 no. P48.

5. Bombé examples include the stunning chest by John Cogswell of Boston made in 1782 (*Boston Furn.*, fig. 125); the Yale chest is more closely related to the example at Colonial Williamsburg (Greenlaw, no. 81). Chests with serpentine lower cases include an example by Bowen and Martin dated 1780 (Randall, no. 41) and a very provincial-looking example of 1795 by Abner Toppan of Newburyport (Fales, *Essex County Furn.*, no. 41).

80

80

Chest-on-chest

Essex County, Massachusetts, 1760–1790

Description: The object is in two stages. The upper case contains five graduated drawers flanked by fluted pilasters with applied bead molding at the architrave, a plain frieze, and a dentil cornice, and the case is crowned by a triangular broken pediment with complex moldings and dentiling flanking a central finial. The upper case rests within a restraining molding applied to the top of the lower case. The lower case contains four graduated drawers and is supported by ogee bracket feet. Each drawer is fitted with a central brass lock escutcheon flanked by matching escutcheons with bail pulls and is surrounded by cock beading on the case. The upper and lower case are of dovetailed board construction, with facing strips applied over the dovetailed joint of the drawer dividers and the case. The front of the closed pediment consists of a shaped board rabbeted and blocked to the sides that begins above the top drawer. The complex cornice moldings, consisting of six elements, are applied; vertical transverse boards are nailed to a rabbet in the pediment front and to the edges of the backboard; and boards are nailed to the top of each closed triangular section. The top backboard is shaped to serve as the back for each closed section. The drawers in the upper case are supported by a joined framework of strips at the sides and across the back, with drawer guides with scalloped edges on the side runners. The lower case drawers are supported by runners housed and nailed to the sides. There are no dustboards in either case. In each drawer, the sides are dovetailed to the front and back, and the bottoms are nailed to a rabbet in the front and to the undersides of the sides and back, with running strips applied. The bracket feet are supported by horizontal and vertical blocks. The backboards of each case are half lapped and nailed to a rabbet in the sides.

Inscription: "To Bo[x]ford" is written in white chalk across the back.

Condition: The urn support for the finial is new. The drawer bottoms and backboards of the case have been renailed. The blocks for the rear feet have been replaced, the right front foot has been repaired, and about half of the right side front foot is a replacement. Some of the drawer runners are replacements.

Woods: Mahogany; eastern white pine; "flame" section of finial, probably maple; replaced urn support, probably ash.

Dimensions: H 220.6; W 113.9; UCW 101.5; LCW 107.0; D 60.1; UCD 50.1; LCD 55.7.

Bibliography: Nutting, *Treasury*, no. 299; Nagel, pl. 22a; Rogers, "Garvan Coll. (1962)," p. 12.

Provenance: Henry V. Weil, New York, N.Y.; by sale in 1923 to Francis P. Garvan, New York, N.Y.

BOTH this chest and the succeeding example (cat. 81) can be tenuously linked with Boxford, Massachusetts, a small Essex County community north of Boston. If they were not made locally in Boxford, as seems likely, they were probably made in Salem, Marblehead, Charlestown, or perhaps

Chest-on-Chests 169

in Boston itself. The intriguing inscription "To Bo[x]ford" also suggests that they were made elsewhere and shipped to Boxford, just as the Derby family chest-on-chest (cat. 82) was made in Boston and shipped to Salem. These architectural objects share an affinity with known North Shore work in their use of pilasters in the upper case and their fashioning from mahogany and white pine, but the scroll-top pediment seems to have been used more frequently (cat. 79), and the handling of the individual architectural elements here differentiates these two examples from groups assigned to a known maker. One unusual feature shared by these chests is the presence of a cyma-shaped block in the entablature. Other chest-on-chests similar to these examples have been published, including one with an applied drop in the center of the front base molding and another with claw-and-ball feet.[1]

The Mabel Brady Garvan Collection 1930.2079

1. *Antiques* 54, no. 3 (September 1948): 144; undated advertisement of the Antique Galleries, Boston, in the Yale Furniture Study object file; *Important XVIII Century American Furniture . . . From the Collection of Maurice Rubin, Brookline, Mass.*, Sale 1534, 9 October 1954 (New York: Parke-Bernet Galleries, 1954), no. 175. See also a related chest referred to in cat. 81.

81

Chest-on-chest with secretary drawer

Essex County, Massachusetts, 1770–1790

Description: This chest-on-chest is closely related in style and construction to the preceding example (cat. 80), although there are both major and minor differences. The most significant difference is that here the top drawer of the lower case has been fitted with a deep secretary drawer, altering the proportions of the object and necessitating a greater overall height. Although the case drawers are constructed in the same manner, their support systems vary here in that no joined framework is used in the upper case. The dovetailing is of a somewhat finer quality here as well. The construction of the pediment varies slightly; here, the top of the upper case is a single narrow board fitted to the sides, above which there are transverse boards serving as the bottom of the closed section in the center, with the sides remaining open to the slanting tops of the closed pediment. The secretary drawer contains a central paneled prospect door flanked by document drawers with colonnettes with flame finials; the door opens to an interior with a single pigeonhole above a drawer. The central compartment is flanked by four pigeonholes with fixed valances shaped with paired reverse curves over three drawers, two in line with a wider drawer below. The front of the secretary drawer is attached with brass butt hinges to the bottom of the drawer and with a brass quadrant stay to the rounded and shaped sides.

Inscriptions: The right document drawer has a partly illegible pencil inscription including "June," "August," and "November." There is illegible writing on the top of the top of the lower case.

Condition: At one time this chest-on-chest was fitted with an extra fluted plinth supporting a carved eagle as a finial (cat. 81b). It appears here with the flame finial from the preceding example (cat. 80). The chest has been refinished, and the present brasses were added in 1962. The restraining molding on each side of the lower case has been replaced, the right front foot has been repaired, and there has been a patch to the bottom of the lowest drawer in the lower case. There have also been replacements and repairs to the blocking of the feet.

Woods: Mahogany; eastern white pine.

Dimensions: H 222.9; W 108.6; UCW 97.1; LCW 101.9; D 58.6; UCD 49.0; LCD 54.2.

Exhibition: "The Loan Exhibition at the Harrison Gray Otis House," *Old-Time New England* 22, no. 4 (April 1932): 154.

81a

Bibliography: *Flayderman Coll.*, no. 454; Elizabeth Dunn, "American Beautiful," *House Beautiful* 79, no. 10 (October 1937): 56.

Provenance: According to an unsubstantiated tradition, this chest was found in Boxford, Mass. It was in the collection of Philip Flayderman, Boston, Mass., and was acquired at auction in 1930 by Francis P. Garvan, New York, N.Y.

THE unusual feature of a secretary drawer is rarely encountered in American chest-on-chests of this period. Francis P. Garvan at one time owned another example related to this one, and a few others have been published.[1] English examples are also known, and most examples, like this one, have the secretary drawer as the top drawer in the lower case.[2] Although there are minor variances in construction between this example and the preceding chest, it is likely that they are from the same unknown shop. A chest-on-chest like this was probably used in a chamber, or perhaps in a parlor.

The Mabel Brady Garvan Collection 1930.2072

1. *Garvan Coll.*, no. 400.
2. *Antiques* 67, no. 3 (March 1955): inside front cover; Chinnery, fig. 3:437; *DEF*, 1: 129 fig. 24.

81

81b

82

Chest-on-chest
Cabinetwork by Stephen Badlam (1751–1815); carved figures by John (1746–1800) and Simeon (1757–1806) Skillin, Jr.
Dorchester Lower Mills and Boston, Massachusetts, 1791
(see pl. 7)

Description: The chest-on-chest is built in three units. The upper unit forms an architrave with a dentil cornice holding a central drawer carved with swags, leafage, and a bowknot. The broken triangular pediment has a similar cornice molding and holds three carved female figures, with the central figure supported on a plinth with leaf carving. Each figure is clothed in an ankle-length, neoclassical-style dress and wears simple sandals or buskins. The central figure is erect and

Chest-on-Chests 171

82

holds a laurel wreath in her right hand and a liberty pole topped with a Phyrgian cap in her left. Between her breasts is a gilt brooch with a face at its center, probably representing the sun, and her head is encircled with a garland of acanthus. The side figures recline on the broken pediment and gaze at the center figure. The figure on the left holds a large palm frond and is wearing an olive wreath in her hair; that on the right holds a cornucopia filled with wheat sheaves and fruit and wears a wreath of corn in her hair. The upper case holds five graduated cock-beaded drawers, each with a central brass keyhole liner flanked by oval brass pulls. The front corners of the upper case hold three-quarter-round columns with Ionic capitals. The drawers and columns rest on a plinth base shaped in conformity with the lower case. The lower case holds four graduated cock-beaded drawers with serpentine facades, each fitted with brasses as in the upper case. The canted corners of the lower case are carved with a trailing floral vine descending from a bowknot. There is a base molding at the front and sides of the lower case, with a carved floral motif at the front center. The object is supported by four large bracket feet; the canted corners of the front feet and the brackets are carved with acanthus, with the scroll of the inner edge of the front brackets extending into and above the base molding. The sides of the lower case bow out to meet the canted corners. The pediment unit is a dovetailed frame; the plinth for the center carved figure is screwed in place. The upper and lower case are of dovetailed board construction, and there are full dustboards in each case. The horizontal backboards are fitted to a rabbet in the case sides and nailed in place. The front of the pediment drawer extends beyond the drawer sides; it is not fitted with a pull. On the drawers, the sides are dovetailed to the front and back; the bottom is let into a groove in the front and into a rabbet in the sides and is nailed to the underside of the back. The drawers have been lined with a plain white paper. The rear feet are diagonal braces. There are two large vertical blocks supporting each foot, with horizontal blocks behind the brackets.

Inscriptions: Paper shipping labels pasted to the top of both the upper and the lower case read: "For Elias Hasket Derby / Esqr Salem / Keep this side up / & preserve it / from the Sun from wet & from bruises. / It is of Consequence enough / to merit great attention." Because the handwriting on these labels bears a close resemblance to that of Stephen Badlam on other documents, it is believed that these labels were applied when the object was shipped by boat from Badlam's shop in Dorchester Lower Mills to Derby's wharf in Salem.

Condition: There have been repairs to the base and right arm of the central carved figure. The brasses are replacements, and some of the drawer runners have been replaced. The drawer in the architrave has been refinished. In 1974, the other drawer fronts were refinished by Peter Arkell to remove dark stains caused by the application of oil when the object was on loan many years ago. There have been losses and repairs to the veneers and moldings.

82a

Woods: Mahogany; front of drawer in architrave, mahogany; other drawer fronts, mahogany veneer on chestnut; eastern white pine; bottom dustboard in lower case, red pine.

Dimensions: H 256.9; W 130.8; UCW 108.7; LCW 116.8; D 60.3; UCD 50.2; LCD 60.3.

Exhibitions: *Loan Exhibition of Colonial and Revolutionary Relics Under the Auspices of the Gaspee Chapter, Daughters of the American Revolution, April 19 and 20, 1892* (Providence: Rhode Island Historical Society, 1892); YUAG, "A Wide View for American Art."

Bibliography: Fiske Kimball, "Some Carved Figures by Samuel McIntire," *Bulletin of the Metropolitan Museum of Art* 18, no. 9 (August 1923): 195; Felice Davis, "American Furniture: The Second or Revolutionary Period in American Wing of the Metropolitan Museum," *Antiquarian* 5, no. 2 (September 1925): 12; R. T. H. Halsey and Charles O. Cornelius, *A Handbook of the American Wing Opening Exhibition* (2d ed.; New York: Metropolitan Museum of Art, 1925), p. 205; Halsey and Tower, *Homes of Our Ancestors*, fig. 173; Lockwood, fig. 32; William Farquhar Payson, ed., *Mahogany, Antique and Modern* (New York: E. P. Dutton, 1926), pp. 118–119, facing

pp. 56, 118; Holloway, pl. 40; Nutting, *Treasury*, no. 324; Fiske Kimball, "Furniture Carvings by Samuel McIntire," *Antiques* 19, no. 3 (March 1931): 208; Mabel M. Swan, "A Revised Estimate of McIntire," *Antiques* 20, no. 6 (December 1931): 341; *Handbook*, p. 62; Homer Eaton Keyes, "Milton, Beverly, and Salem," *Antiques* 23, no. 4 (April 1933): 142; "Editor's Attic," *Antiques* 31, no. 3 (March 1937): 114; "Outstanding Examples from the Mabel Brady Garvan Collections," *YUAG Bulletin* 8, no. 2 (February 1938): 45; Sherrill Whiton, *Elements of Interior Decoration* (rev. ed.; Chicago: J. B. Lippincott Co., 1944), p. 264; Mabel M. Swan, "Boston's Carvers and Joiners, Part I," *Antiques* 53, no. 3 (March 1948): 198; Nagel, pl. 24; Edwin O. Christensen, *Early American Wood Carving* (Cleveland: World Publishing Co., 1952), p. 132; Mabel M. Swan, "General Stephen Badlam—Cabinet and Looking-glass Maker," *Antiques* 65, no. 5 (May 1954): 380; Larry Freeman, *Antique Furniture Handbooks, Volume 3: Federal–Empire* (Watkins Glen, N.Y.: Century House, 1956), pp. 2, 8; Bjerkoe, pl. 21; Hayward, *World Furn.*, fig. 826; Wayne Craven, *Sculpture in America* (New York: Thomas Y. Crowell, 1968), fig. 1.7; Benjamin A. Hewitt, "The Sources and Inspiration for Simeon Skillin's 'Spirit of America'" (Seminar paper, Yale University, 1972); John Cornforth, "From Mayflower to Monroe: Yale University Furniture," *Country Life* 155, no. 3993 (January 3–10, 1974): 25; Montgomery and Kane, *American Art, 1750–1800*, fig. 70 (included in catalogue but not in exhibition); Tom Armstrong et al., *200 Years of American Sculpture* (Boston: David R. Godine in association with the Whitney Museum of American Art, 1976), figs. 123, 124; Bernard Bailyn et al., *The Great Republic* (Boston: Little, Brown, 1977), p. 228; Marvin D. Schwartz, "The Boston Heritage in Furniture," *Antiques World* 1, no. 10 (October 1979): 91; Carol Olsen, "Stylistic Developments of Ship Figureheads of the United States East Coast," *International Journal of Nautical Archaelogy and Underwater Exploration* 8, no. 4 (November 1979): 323; Charles F. Montgomery, "Francis P. Garvan: He Would Educate the Nation," *Arts in Virginia* 19, no. 3 (Spring 1979): 13; Kane, "American Furn.," p. 1321; Fairbanks and Bates, p. 200; Charles F. Montgomery, "Francis P. Garvan," *Antiques* 121, no. 1 (January 1982): 247; Shestack, *Selections*, p. 56; Sylvia P. Lahvis, "Four Chests with Carved Figures" (Seminar paper, University of Delaware, 1983), pl. 1; John S. Bowan, *American Furniture* (New York: Exeter Books, 1985), p. 80.

Provenance: According to a family tradition, this chest-on-chest was presented by Elias Hasket Derby (1739–1799) and his wife, Elizabeth Crowninshield Derby (1735–1799), of

82b

82c

82d

Salem, Mass., as a wedding present to their daughter Anstis Derby (1769–1836), who married Benjamin Pickman, Jr. (1763–1843), of Salem in 1789. The discrepancy between the date of marriage and the date of 1791 on the bill for the completed chest is usually explained by the theory that the chest was ordered as a wedding present but not completed and delivered until nearly two years later. Elias Hasket Derby's will (docket 7571, Essex County Probate Records, Essex County Courthouse, Salem, Mass.) makes mention of a bequest to Anstis and adds: "And I do in addition to the foregoing give and confirm unto my said daughter Anstis all and what I gave her at the time of her marriage." There are no probate records on file for Anstis Derby Pickman. In the inventory of the estate of Benjamin Pickman, Jr. (docket 50218), which was taken room by room, the only two possibilities that might refer to this object are a "Case Draws" in the "Middle Chamber" valued at $12 and a "Case Draws" in the "Front Western Chamber" valued at $6. No mention of the object is made in Pickman's will of 1843. The next likely owner, however, is Pickman's daughter Martha (1802–1885), who married Samuel Baker Walcott (d. 1854) in 1829. The Walcotts seem to have divided their time between Salem and Hopkinton, N.H. No detailed specification of household goods is given in Samuel Walcott's estate papers (docket 56152), although he did own "Furniture in house in Salem" valued at a total of $900. In his will, dated 1851, Samuel Walcott bequeathed all of his "furniture & household stuff of every kind" to his wife. Martha Pickman Walcott died in Salem in 1885. She left all of her "household furniture and goods, silver and other plate, clothing and books, not enumerated and specified, in a memorandum in writing under [her] hand" to her daughter Elizabeth Packard, wife of Alpheus S. Packard. (The "Schedule of Legacies" bequeathed to her other children does not mention any object that could be the Yale chest.) Martha Walcott's household furniture at 133 Lafayette Street in Salem was valued at only $250 but was not itemized (docket 61881). The chest appears to have been owned by Elizabeth Derby Walcott Packard (1824–1929) and her husband Alpheus from about 1885 to 1919; they lived in Andover, Mass. Elizabeth Packard's will of 1906 (docket 163422) states: "All my household furniture, books, pictures, china, glass, silver, jewelry, and all other articles of household use or ornament, I give to my executor hereinafter named to be distributed by him among my children in accordance with directions which will be found among my papers at my death." This "List of articles to be distributed," however, makes no mention of the Yale chest, for it had already passed to her daughter and out of the family's hands. One of Elizabeth's beneficiaries was to be her daughter Martha W. Packard of Andover. Elizabeth's will specifies that Martha, acting on some misguided advice from her mother, made a bad investment and lost a considerable

Chest-on-Chests 175

amount of money, a sum her mother felt obliged to repay. Elizabeth may have given her daughter the chest about 1919 as one way of repaying her, since the chest was sold in that year to New York dealer Charles Woolsey Lyon. An undated letter from Martha Walcot Packard to Francis P. Garvan gives the following family tradition: "This is the history as it has come to me from my mother: Elias Hasket Derby of Salem (my great-great-grandfather) had the chest made for his daughter Anstiss, when she married Benjamin Pickman, also of Salem, in 1789. It then belonged to their daughter, Martha, who married Samuel Baker Walcott in 1829. My mother inherited it and handed it on to me." Lyon sold the chest to Francis P. Garvan, New York, N.Y., in 1919.

UNTIL 1931, the carving on this chest-on-chest was attributed by most writers to Samuel McIntire (1757–1811), famed architect and carver of Salem, and the cabinetwork was occasionally assigned, somewhat inexplicably, to Joseph True (1785–1873), another Salem carver and woodworker. Upon the publication of Mabel Munson Swan's "Revised Estimate of McIntire" (see Bibliography) in December of that year, however, the attribution to McIntire and True was discredited. Swan discovered several key documents in the Derby family papers at the Essex Institute in Salem which allowed her to attribute the cabinetwork of the Yale chest to General Stephen Badlam of Dorchester Lower Mills and the carving to John and Simeon Skillin, Jr., two members of a well-known Boston family of shipcarvers. The most important of these documents was a bill from Badlam to Elias Hasket Derby dated April 1791, which included, among other charges for furniture, the item "To a case of Draws exclusive of the carving" debited at £19. A comparison of the handwriting on this bill to that on the two unsigned shipping labels on the Yale chest revealed, in Swan's opinion, that the documents were by the same hand. Thus, the chest could be attributed to Badlam with confidence. The bill further specified that Derby was to be credited £1.2.6 for "brasses for the case of Draws purchased by Mr. Derby" in June 1791, suggesting that the cabinetwork was completed by that time. Swan also discovered another bill to Derby from John and Simeon Skillin, in which the Boston carvers charged the wealthy Salem merchant for work performed on his ship the *Grand Turk*. An item appended to this bill charged Derby £6.15.0 for "carv'd work done for a chest of draws pr bill given in." Payment for the bill was rendered by Benjamin Pickman, Jr., acting as agent for his father-in-law, in December 1791. Although it has not been proved conclusively that these bills refer specifically to the Yale chest, the circumstantial evidence is strong, and the Badlam-Skillin attribution has been accepted for the last fifty years.[1]

The significance of the carved figures on the Yale chest has drawn a great deal of attention from many writers, who have interpreted them as symbols of a sometimes bewildering variety of attributes. The most thorough and convincing analysis of their allegorical meaning and iconographic sources has been prepared by Benjamin A. Hewitt in an unpublished paper (see Bibliography). Basing his conclusions on a study of period emblem books and other contemporary documents, Hewitt concluded that the central standing figure represents Virtue, primarily because of the presence of the gilt-sun brooch in addition to the more obvious symbols of her laurel wreath, pike (*hasta*), and Phrygian cap (or *pilleus*), features that have led most writers to identify her as Liberty or Victory. The left figure seems to represent Peace, while the right figure is undoubtedly meant to represent Plenty or Abundance. Pushing the analysis, Hewitt suggests that all three figures when considered as a whole represent America and that they may have other symbolic content as well, including some reference to Derby's three daughters and to the act of marriage. The sources of the Skillins' design have remained elusive, although they were able to draw on a long tradition in Western architecture and art of placing carved busts and figures in the pediments of facades, doorways, and case furniture. They probably derived the general arrangement of their design from an English architectural pattern book, such as James Gibbs, *A Book of Architecture* (1728) or one of several publications by Batty Langley. If Hewitt's understanding of the carved figures as a complex symbol of America is correct, and there is every reason to believe it is plausible, the presence of these symbols elevates an already impressive example of federal-style furniture into an eloquent and emphatic statement of the idealized characteristics of the early Republic.

There is only a small group of American eighteenth-century furniture embellished with carved busts or figures. The Yale chest-on-chest is most closely related in conception and feeling to an even larger and more impressive example at the Museum of Fine Arts, Boston. Also made for the Derby family, this chest-on-chest bears a single carved figure on its pediment, endowed with a wreath, a pike, and a golden sun (all similar to the symbols on the Yale chest), and has carved ornament on the case consisting of baskets of fruit, flower vases, cornucopias, bunches of grapes, and draped putti, all meant to symbolize Abundance and Fertility. For many years, this object has been attributed to Samuel McIntire and a Mr. Lemon, on the strength of a 1796 bill from these

craftsmen to Elizabeth Derby. (The Mr. Lemon in question was long thought to have been upholsterer William Lemon, although it was probably one of the cabinetmaking brothers Charles or John Lemon.) The carved figures on the Yale chest are most closely related stylistically to a bust of Milton on a desk and bookcase owned by Moses Brown and now at the Beverly Historical Society, and to two figures formerly on a desk and bookcase in the Metropolitan Museum. A bombé desk and bookcase in the Winterthur collection bears superbly carved figures representing Justice, Commerce, and Agriculture. These New England examples are paralleled by a larger and earlier group of Philadelphia case furniture with carved finial busts; a few writers have seen this furniture as an influence on the Skillins, some of whom may have worked in the Philadelphia area.[2]

Stephen Badlam, a veteran of the Revolution, operated an extensive cabinetmaking shop, located amid an active community of artisans in Dorchester Lower Mills. His business brought him into contact with many other craftsmen, including Thomas Seymour, who apparently sold Badlam-made furniture in his Boston warehouse.[3] Many documented examples from Badlam's shop are known, including side and lolling chairs, circular and serpentine-front card tables, a sectional dining table, a tripod table, a tall clock, a bed, a cradle, a worktable, a cabinet, and several trays. A number of these objects bear, in addition to Badlam's stamp, a set of initials, such as *WH*, thought to be those of a journeyman or apprentice in Badlam's employ.[4] The Skillin family of carvers, founded by Simeon Skillin (1716–1768), was well known in the last half of the eighteenth century for their work as ship, furniture, and architectural carvers. It is not surprising that they collaborated with Badlam on the Yale chest or that Derby patronized them extensively. Among their other work, the Skillins executed garden figures (such as *Hope* and *Justice* in the Winterthur collection), statuary (including *Mercury* from the Old State House), and architectural carving for Charles Bulfinch's Boston State House and for Derby's mansion.[5]

The Mabel Brady Garvan Collection 1930.2003

1. The possibility remains that Elias Hasket Derby bought and used the Yale chest himself and that it passed to Anstis Derby Pickman after his death. Derby's estate inventory (docket 7571) included "One Chest upon Chest" valued at $60 in the "South East Chamber" as well as other, apparently smaller, chests of drawers.

2. Hipkiss, no. 41. The suggestion that the Lemon was John or Charles is made in Margaret Burke Clunie, "Joseph True and the Piecework System in Salem," *Antiques* 111, no. 5 (May 1977): 1011–1012. For the Milton bust, see Keyes, "Milton, Beverly, and Salem," p. 142; the figures on the Bolles desk and bookcase at the Metropolitan Museum are no longer accepted as an original feature of the object; see Heckscher, no. 181. Montgomery, no. 176. Robert C. Smith, "Finial Busts on Eighteenth-Century Philadelphia Furniture," *Antiques* 100, no. 6 (December 1971): 900–905.

3. For Badlam's career, see Swan, "General Stephen Badlam"; other articles in Bibliography; and *Paul Revere's Boston*, p. 166.

4. Among the objects marked by or attributed to Badlam are side chairs (Montgomery, no. 30, with references to other examples); a lolling chair (Montgomery, no. 110); circular card tables (Swan, "Revised Estimate of McIntire," fig. 2; *Paul Revere's Boston*, no. 270; *Sack Coll.*, 3: 829 no. P3514); serpentine-front card table (Swan, "Revised Estimate of McIntire," fig. 5); a sectional dining table (*Antiques* 73, no. 1 [January 1958]: 15); a tripod table (DAPC 76.3); a tall clock (private collection); a bed (Swan, "Revised Estimate of McIntire," fig. 1); a cradle (*Sack Coll.*, 3: 700 no. P481); a worktable and cabinet (Swan, "Revised Estimate of McIntire," figs. 3, 4); trays (Swan, "General Stephen Badlam," p. 383; *Paul Revere's Boston*, no. 272); and looking glasses (Swan, "Revised Estimate of McIntire," fig. 5; *Antiques* 115, no. 2 [February 1979]: inside front cover). Badlam's shop sign is also known to have survived until the twentieth century; see *Flayderman Coll.*, no. 81; and DAPC 65.853. A shaving mirror with the paper label of Stephen Badlam, Jr., is illustrated in Swan, "Revised Estimate of McIntire," fig. 5.

5. For the Skillin family, see the articles listed in Bibliography; and Leroy L. Thwing, "The Four Carving Skillins," *Antiques* 33, no. 6 (June 1938): 326–328; Mabel Munson Swan, "Simeon Skillin, Senior: The First American Sculptor," *Antiques* 46, no. 1 (July 1944): 21; "John Skillin as Cabinetmaker," *Antiques* 26, no. 1 (July 1934): 7; and "Add to the Skillins' Sculptures," *Antiques* 30, no. 1 (July 1936): 8–9. Sylvia Lahvis of the University of Delaware is at work on a dissertation on the Skillins that promises to add greatly to our knowledge of their work; I am grateful to her for sharing her preliminary research and thoughts on the Yale chest.

83

Chest-on-chest

Newport, Rhode Island, 1755–1785

Description: The chest-on-chest is in two stages. The upper case contains five lipped drawers, two in line over three graduated drawers, and is crowned with a broken-arch pediment with paired applied plaques and an urn and acorn finial mounted on a fluted plinth. There is base molding at the front and sides of the upper case that overlaps the lower case. The lower case contains four graduated lipped drawers and is supported by bracket feet below base molding at the front and sides. Each drawer has a central brass lock escutcheon flanked by matching escutcheons with bail pulls, with the exception of the top two drawers, which are fitted with

83

single escutcheons with bail pulls. Each case is of dovetailed board construction, with the joint of the drawer dividers and the case visible on the front. The horizontal backboards are half lapped and nailed to rabbets. There is a vertical reinforcing strip nailed to the inside of the back of each case. The pediment is closed with slats nailed to the top edge of the back and to the curved moldings. The upper case rests on the lower case, with the midmolding overlapping slightly, and a cleat nailed to the bottom of the upper case fitted to a channel in the center of the top of the lower case. In each drawer, the sides are finely dovetailed to the front and back; the bottoms have slightly beveled edges let into grooves in the front and sides and fastened to the underside of the back with wooden pins and nails. The top two drawers were fitted with wooden spring locks and are supported by a joined framework. There are no dustboards. There are blocks glued behind the bottom front rail in each case and to the front top rail.

Inscriptions: There are numerous pencil shop marks and inscriptions. "Top" is written on the inside of each side of the upper and lower case; "Front Bottom" and another illegible inscription appears on the top side of the bottom of the upper case; "Front Top" appears to be written on the underside of the top of the upper case; "Bottom" is written on the inside of the bottom of the lower case; there is a pencil inscription on the underside of the top of the lower case; and many drawer backs and drawer dividers are numbered. There also are several modern pencil inscriptions, and the modern "318 / Goddard" is written in white chalk on the top side of the bottom of the top drawer in the lower case.

Condition: All four feet are replacements. The lower part of the finial is a replacement, there have been many small repairs to the drawer fronts, and some running strips have been replaced. The right corner of the cornice molding is broken.

Woods: Mahogany; eastern white pine; one drawer divider, blocks, and some other framing elements, chestnut.

Dimensions: H 215.1; W 105.2; UCW 94.3; LCW 97.9; D 52.8; UCD 47.3; LCD 48.8.

Exhibition: YUAG, "Rhode Island Furn."

Bibliography: Kirk, *Early Am. Furn.*, fig. 86.

Provenance: Purchased in 1929 from B. Altman & Co., New York, N. Y., by Francis P. Garvan, New York, N. Y.

THIS chest-on-chest exhibits many features associated with Newport furniture and the work of the Townsend-Goddard families. Among the Newport characteristics are such stylistic attributes as the form of the broken-arch pediment with its applied, shaped panels and such construction details as the presence of a vertical reinforcing strip inside each case, an urn finial without carving on its rear edge, the method of joining the two cases with the midmolding attached to the upper case, and the use of chestnut as a secondary wood. Wooden spring locks in the upper drawers are not an uncommon feature in Rhode Island case furniture. This chest-on-chest is a relatively simple example of the form, although it would still have been costly since it is made of imported mahogany. Similar chests were also made in less expensive

cherry and maple, and more elaborate mahogany versions had fluted quarter columns and finials at the sides as well as in the center or had a blockfront lower case with carved shells.[1] Related chests were also made in nearby New London County, Connecticut, including one made in Lisbon in 1796.[2] The many pencil notations and shop marks on this chest seem to be a characteristic found on many examples of Newport work.

The Mabel Brady Garvan Collection 1930.2162

1. *Sack Coll.*, 7: 1845 no. P5186; Lockwood, fig. 115; *Important XVIII Century American Furniture... Collected by the Late Mrs. J. Amory Haskell ... Part Four*, Sale 599, 8–11 November 1944 (New York: Parke-Bernet Galleries, 1944), no. 832; Ott, no. 55; Comstock, no. 305; Ott, no. 56; Charles Navis, *Tastemaker: A Collection of Early American Furniture* (Richmond, Va.: Valentine Museum, 1967), p. 27D; *Antiques* 119, no. 2 (February 1981): 336; Christopher Monkhouse, "American Furniture Recently Acquired by the Museum of Art, Rhode Island School of Design," *Antiques* 118, no. 1 (July 1980): 126; *Antiques* 100, no. 3 (September 1971): 276. Many Newport examples of the form are conveniently illustrated in Moses.

2. Kirk, *Conn. Furn.*, no. 96; see also no. 97.

84

Chest-on-chest

North Stonington, Connecticut, 1760–1780
(see pl. 8)

Description: The object is in two cases. The upper case is crowned by a scrolled pediment enclosing a central dark-green painted urn-and-flame finial mounted on a fluted plinth, with painted turned balusters at each front corner of the plinth. Similar finials and plinths (without balusters) are at each front corner of the pediment. The tympanum contains applied plaques shaped to echo the curve of the cornice moldings. The upper case holds eight drawers, lipped on three sides, including pairs of superimposed small drawers flanking a deep center drawer carved with a shell. These small drawers stand above a tier of three graduated wide drawers. There is an applied molding at the bottom of the upper case which rests on top of a midmolding applied to the top of the lower case. The lower case holds four graduated drawers. There is applied base molding at the front and sides of the lower case, with a central six-lobed drop on the front. The chest is supported by four bracket feet with scrolled

84

knee brackets. Each wide drawer is fitted with a central brass keyhole liner flanked by dual-disk escutcheons with bail pulls; the four small drawers in the upper case have similar brasses, and the shell-carved drawer has a central brass-button pull. The upper case is of dovetailed board construction. The drawer-divider dovetails are exposed, and the drawer dividers are also pinned in place through the sides of the case. The small drawers are supported by a joined framework, and the wide drawers by runners nailed to the case sides. There are no dustboards. The horizontal backboards are beveled on their sides and top, fitted to grooves in the top

and sides, and nailed to the case bottom. The lower case is fashioned in a similar manner. The top of the lower case consists of two boards running the full width of the case and dovetailed in place at the front and back. The rear feet are curved brackets, and each foot is supported by vertical and horizontal blocks. There is also a block behind the center drop. On each drawer, the sides are dovetailed to the front, the back is dovetailed to the sides, and the bottom is beveled on the front and sides, let into grooves in the front and sides, and nailed to the underside of the back. The top edge of the drawer sides and backs is rounded. The locks are blind on the drawers in the upper case and on the second drawer from the top in the lower case.

Inscriptions: "Appleton" is written on the outside of the right side of the carved drawer in the upper case; "AWR" appears on the inside of the bottom of the same drawer. "Appleton" also appears in pencil on the outside of the back of the middle wide drawer in the upper case. "Back" is written in pencil on the outside of the back of the second drawer from the bottom in the lower case. There are many shop marks and numbers throughout each case. Labels from the 1967 "Connecticut Furniture" exhibition are pasted to the inside of the bottom of the lowest drawer in the upper case and to the top drawer in the lower case.

Condition: Some of the drawer runners in each case have been replaced. The left front foot has been worm eaten, and the right front blocks have been replaced. The finials have been repainted, but the central plinth balusters retain their original green paint.

Woods: Highly figured soft maple; eastern white pine and butternut; some framing elements, soft maple.

Dimensions: H 232.1; W 108.2; UCW 96.5; LCW 101.4; D 52.2; UCD 45.5; LCD 47.8.

Exhibitions: Kirk, *Conn. Furn.*, no. 97; YUAG, "A Wide View for American Art."

Bibliography: John T. Kirk, "The Distinctive Character of Connecticut Furniture," *Antiques* 92, no. 4 (October 1967): 524; Kirk, *Early Am. Furn.*, fig. 87; James P. Walsh, *Connecticut Industry and the Revolution*, Connecticut Bicentennial Series, vol. 29 (Hartford: American Revolution Bicentennial Commission of Connecticut, 1978), p. 32; Kane, "American Furn.," p. 1319.

Provenance: According to tradition, the chest was owned by the Bentley family of North Stonington, Conn. It descended in the family to Mrs. John W. Pearson, Hartford, Conn. Mrs. Pearson sold it in 1929 to dealer Charles Woolsey Lyon, New York, N. Y., who sold it later that year to Francis P. Garvan, New York, N. Y.

THERE seems every reason to believe that this chest-on-chest was made in the area of North Stonington, Connecticut, although its history in the Bentley family of that town has not yet been verified. Similar in form to furniture from neighboring Rhode Island (cat. 83), this rural expression is distinguished by its striped tiger-maple grain, its lower stance, and its central carved shell or "sunburst," echoed in the drop on the base molding in the lower case. The careful choice of wood for the drawer fronts, with the grain used in alternating directions to lead the eye up the chest, has been noted by John T. Kirk. The use of butternut as a secondary wood—here used for some of the drawer linings—is associated in New London County with the work of John Wheeler Geer (1753–1828) of Preston and Griswold (also see cat. 143), who also made use of tiger maple as a primary wood.[1] There is no strong reason, however, to attribute this chest-on-chest to Geer, who is not known to have made an extensive amount of case furniture.

The Mabel Brady Garvan Collection 1930.2212

1. Mayhew and Myers, p. 9, nos. 61, 63, 65, 68.

85

Chest-on-chest
Eastern Connecticut, 1770–1790

Description: The upper case holds seven drawers surrounded by cock beading on the case, three in line over four graduated drawers. The upper center drawer is of greater height and is carved with a gilt-design three-tulip motif containing rosettes and surrounded by leaves. Flanking the drawers of the upper case are fluted pilasters with six flutes, and the case is crowned by a broken-scroll arch flanking a central gilt urn-and-flame finial; the sides are decorated with ball-and-flame finials mounted on square plinths. The upper case rests within molding applied to the top of the lower case. The blockfront lower case contains four graduated drawers surrounded by cock beading on the case, and the

85

chest is supported by unusually shaped feet with thin pads below base molding at the front and sides. The heavy applied cornice molding is a single piece, and the pediment is roofed with thin curved boards nailed to the front and to a notched or V-shaped backboard; the pediment is also closed in its transverse plane to about half of its depth with boards applied to the front and to intermediate shaped longitudinal supports. The top and bottom of each case are dovetailed to the sides, and the horizontal backboards are nailed to rabbets in the sides. There are partial dustboards in the upper case, with wide drawer runners and guides nailed to the top of the runners. The runners for the top center drawer are housed through the backboards. Because of the greater width, the drawer runners within the lower case are thinner, and there are no drawer guides. On each drawer, the sides are dovetailed to the front and back, and the top edge of the sides is rounded. The bottoms are nailed to a rabbet in the front, let into grooves in the sides, and nailed to the underside of the back. In the upper case, the grain of the drawer bottoms runs parallel to the front of the case; in the lower case, the grain of the bottom boards is perpendicular to the front of the chest. The top center drawer is divided internally by partitions into four compartments. The rear feet are triangular, and the feet are supported by vertical blocks. The front feet and base molding conform to the blocking of the lower case.

Inscriptions: There is an illegible, and possibly original, inscription on the underside of the bottom of the upper case. There are chalk drawings of foliate motifs on the inside of the front of the top center drawer and similar drawings in pencil on the upper inside of the right side of the upper case. "N E" is written in pencil on the sides of two of the partitions in the top center drawer of the upper case. The underside of the bottom of the top small drawers in the upper case are each marked "L" in pencil. A modern pencil notation on the underside of the bottom drawer in the lower case reads: "Regult [Reglued?] by / IDS & M / [illegible] 63 [?]." There are columns of addition in pencil on the top edge of the lowest drawer divider in the lower case, and the locations of the upper case drawers have been numbered in white chalk on the inside of the left side of the case.

Condition: New running strips have been added to the drawers, and shrinkage cracks in several drawer bottoms have been pieced. The concave section of the front of the bottom drawer in the lower case has been repaired. There have been minor repairs to the drawer fronts and the cock beading, and the rectangular bases of the pilasters are replacements. The drawer runners on the right side of the lower case have been turned over and reused; some drawer runners have been replaced. The lower backboard of the lower case is a replacement, and the upper backboard has been renailed. All the glue blocks within the case are replacements, and the feet have been reglued and renailed in place. The finials are replacements.

Woods: American black cherry; eastern white pine.

Dimensions: H 223.7; W 103.7; UCW 92.5; LCW 97.5; D 58.6; UCD 49.7; LCD 53.7.

Chest-on-Chests 181

Bibliography: *Important American Antiques from the King Hooper Mansion, Marblehead, Mass.* [*Part Three*], Sale 2300, 7–8 December 1928 (New York: Anderson Galleries, 1928), no. 228; Aaron Marc Stein, "English and American Furniture in the Collection of Mr. and Mrs. Richard De Wolfe Brixey," *Fine Arts* 18 (December 1931): 38 fig. 7.

Provenance: Israel Sack, New York, N. Y.; acquired at auction in 1928 by collector Richard De Wolfe Brixey (1880–1943), New York, N. Y.; by descent to his daughter, Doris M. Brixey (d. 1983).

One of three examples of New England case furniture owned by noted New York collector Richard DeWolfe Brixey and recently bequeathed to the Art Gallery by his daughter, this relatively small cherry chest-on-chest most likely was made in eastern Connecticut, probably in New London County. A related example attributed to that area speaks the same language with only a slightly different accent. Of mahogany, it shares the same drawer arrangement as the Yale chest and has blocking only on the lower case and fluted pilasters in the upper case.[1] Other, bolder, blockfront Connecticut chest-on-chests from Norwich, Colchester, and elsewhere exhibit blocking in both cases.[2] The form of the Yale chest is related to Boston-Salem–area chest-on-chests (cat. 79), but with some significant variations. For example, here the side drawers in the upper case are squared off and do not conform to the scroll of the pediment, although the cornice molding begins to swoop upward directly above the pilasters. The pilasters of this chest terminate in a molded base, a feature atypical for Connecticut work.[3] The unusual, simply curved bracket feet and the carved and gilt decoration on the central drawer in the upper case give this chest-on-chest distinction.

Bequest of Doris M. Brixey 1984.32.40

1. Kirk, *Conn. Furn.*, no. 103; also see Fales, *Deerfield*, no. 446.
2. Kirk, *Conn. Furn.*, nos. 101, 102, 104.
3. Kirk, *Conn. Furn.*, no. 103.

86

86

Chest-on-chest
Connecticut, probably East Granby, ca. 1802

Description: The upper case is crowned by a broken-scroll pediment terminating in carved rosettes and flanking a central carved and pierced asymmetrical cartouche mounted on a fluted plinth. The scrolls of the pediment are supported by pierced fretwork, and the sides are embellished with elongated urn finials mounted on small plinths. The upper case contains five graduated drawers and is decorated at the

sides with applied fluted quarter columns. The upper case rests within restraining molding on the top of the lower case, which contains four graduated drawers and is also decorated with applied fluted quarter columns. Each drawer has a central oval blind brass lock escutcheon flanked by oval escutcheons with bail pulls, and the edges of the drawers are outlined with an incised line to simulate cock beading. There is light base molding at the front and sides over carved gadrooning at the front, and the chest is supported by bracket feet. Each case is constructed in a similar manner. The top and bottom are dovetailed to the sides, and the horizontal backboards are joined with a half lap and beveled on their top and side edges, let into grooves in the top and sides of the case, and nailed to the bottom. The drawer dividers are tenoned to strips at the front and to the case sides, with the quarter columns applied between. There are thick vertical boards (two in the upper case) nailed to the inside of each side of the case, with the drawer runners nailed to these boards. There are no dustboards. The side bracket feet and base molding are a single piece, and the rear foot is formed by a single shaped board running the width of the case and dovetailed to the rear side bracket feet. On each drawer the sides are dovetailed to the front and back; the bottoms are beveled on their front and side edges, let into grooves in the front and sides, and nailed to the underside of the back. The sides and back are unusually thick, and each bottom is a single longitudinal board.

Inscriptions: A silver oval plaque nailed to the front of the upper case above the top drawer is engraved "Hannah Forward / 1802" within a border of bright-cut engraving. A Connecticut Tercentenary (1935) label is tacked to the inside of the right side of the lowest drawer in the upper case.

Condition: The chest retains an old, possibly original, finish and is in excellent condition. Some drawer guides have been added, and the grooved rear edge of the left side of the upper case has been broken and a strip added as a repair. The four feet were once fitted with rectangular wooden platforms with casters; these have been removed. The feet have been broken and reglued, and each corner has been braced with a large iron brace applied with screws.

Woods: American black cherry; eastern white pine.

Dimensions: H 208.9; W 109.7; UCW 98.7; LCW 104.1; D 48.2; UCD 42.6; LCD 45.4.

Exhibition: *Three Centuries of Conn. Furn.*, no. 154.

Bibliography: Robert Rantoul Endicott, "Cherry Was the Mahogany of New England," *American Collector* 5, no. 2 (March 1936): 5; Kirk, *Conn. Furn.*, no. 105 (included in the catalogue but not in the exhibition); Kirk, *Early Am. Furn.*, fig. 81.

Provenance: According to tradition, this chest-on-chest and a nearly identical example were made as part of the wedding furniture of Hannah Forward (1785–1882), who married Horace Clark (1781–1842) of East Granby, Conn., 15 November 1802. The estate inventory of Hannah Forward Clark, who died at age ninety-seven, included two high chests of drawers, one valued at $5 and the other at $8. Presumably the chest stayed in her family until the twentieth century, when it was purchased by Francis P. Garvan, New York, N. Y., along with woodwork from the house in which it stood, the Samuel Clark house (fig. 1), which had been built in the 1730s.[1]

FIG. 1 Samuel Clark house, East Granby, Connecticut, 1730s. Photograph, ca. 1900.

WHEN this chest-on-chest was acquired by Francis P. Garvan it was attributed to Aaron Chapin (1753–1838), an attribution which cannot be supported today. Its matching companion, now in a private collection, was made (according to which modern tradition one prefers to accept) by either Samuel Furgarson or Mark Wilcox of West Granby.[2] (It is interesting to note that Hannah Forward's younger sister Julia, born in 1790, married one Samuel Ferguson.) Oliver Moore (1773–1829), a cabinetmaker of East Granby, is known to have made case furniture, and if the chests were made locally, as indi-

cated by the family tradition of ownership and as seems likely on the basis of their style, construction, and woods, the possibility that he was their maker should be considered.³ A third related object has been published, and somewhat similar scrolls are seen on the pediment of a Connecticut chest-on-chest in the Barbour collection at the Connecticut Historical Society.⁴

The Mabel Brady Garvan Collection 1930.2533

1. For the Clark family, see Albert Carlos Bates, ed., *Sundry Vital Records of and pertaining to the Present Town of East Granby, Connecticut, 1737–1886* (Hartford, 1947), pp. 43, 48, 85, 206; and Henry R. Stiles, *The History and Genealogies of Ancient Windsor, Connecticut*, vol. 2 (Hartford: Case, Lockwood & Brainard Co., 1892), p. 271. The diary of Horace Clark was once owned by the Connecticut Historical Society, and excerpts from it were published in the twentieth century by Albert Carlos Bates, but the diary has been lost or stolen and cannot be located today. Probate records for Horace and Hannah Clark are in the Connecticut State Library, Hartford, and the Probate Court, District of East Granby, respectively. I would like to thank Florence S. Mayer and Betty Guinan for their assistance with the Clark records. For the Samuel Clark house, see Mary Jane Springman and Betty Finnell Guinan, *East Granby: The Evolution of a Connecticut Town* (Canaan, N.H.: Phoenix Publishing for the East Granby Historical Commission, 1983), p. 61. The house was purchased by Francis P. Garvan in 1920, and he later donated the woodwork to Yale. Two upstairs rooms were installed in the Art Gallery in 1928 by J. Frederick Kelly, and the other rooms were placed in storage. In 1953 the staircase and some woodwork were sold to Henry N. Flynt, the founder of Historic Deerfield. When the Garvan Galleries were reinstalled in 1973, the two Granby rooms were dismantled and placed in storage, where they remain today.

2. This chest-on-chest was published in *English and American Furniture . . . Estate of the Late Florence Bates Carter, New York . . . and Other Owners, Including Ralph Carpenter II*, Sale 2299, 16–17 November 1964 (New York: Parke-Bernet Galleries, 1964), no. 401. The various traditions concerning this chest are recorded on five notes pasted at various times to various parts of the object. After Hannah Forward Clark's death in 1882, this chest (according to these notes) passed to Samuel A. Clark of East Granby, who owned it in 1909 and who apparently was the first person to state that it was made by Samuel Furgarson. In about 1909, the chest may have gone to another member of the Clark family, from whom it passed, probably by sale, to Malcolm A. Norton of East Hartford, a noted early collector. Norton's note on the object states: "Old Mr. and Mrs. Clark gave / me the following facts. In 1803 [*sic*], she had two / chest on chests and two / desks made by Mark / Wilcox of West Granby / a cabinet maker of / those old days." In July 1938, Norton sold the chest to Russell S. Carter of Hewlett, Long Island. The chest was acquired at the Carter sale by Mrs. Norman Dudley Johnson of New York City, who retains possession.

3. Oliver Moore Account Book, East Granby, 1808–1819, Connecticut Historical Society, Hartford; Bates, *Vital Records*, pp. 79, 90, 102, 110.

4. "The Editor's Attic," *Antiques* 60, no. 3 (September 1951): 202 fig. 1. Although the text states that this object has never been altered, it assuredly is the upper case of a high chest to which a base has been added. See also *Frederick K. and Margaret R. Barbour's Furniture Collection* (Hartford, Conn.: Connecticut Historical Society, 1963), pp. 54–55.

87

Chest-on-chest-on-frame
New England, possibly Connecticut, 1760–1790

Description: This tall object is in three stages. The upper case has complex cove molding at the top and contains seven lipped drawers, three deep drawers in line over four graduated drawers. The center drawer at the top is carved with a circular shell or pinwheel outlined with an undulating line punctuated with dots. The upper case rests within restraining molding applied to the top of the lower case. The lower case contains three graduated drawers and rests within a supporting framework. The frame has an undulating front skirt, flanking paired reverse curves at the center, and the side skirts are also shaped with paired reverse curves. The frame is supported by four short cabriole legs terminating in pad feet. The upper and lower case are of dovetailed board construction. The drawer dividers and vertical partitions are dovetailed to the frame with exposed dovetails. The horizontal backboards, three for the upper case and two for the lower, are beveled at their sides and fitted into grooves in the sides of the cases. The frame is joined with mortise-and-tenon joints secured with two pegs, and the corner posts continue below the skirt to form the legs and feet. There is a transverse support on each side of the frame housed and nailed to the front and rear rails. In each drawer the sides are dovetailed to the front and back; the bottoms are beveled on their front and side edges, let into grooves in the front and sides, and nailed to the underside of the back.

Inscriptions: "Thomas" or "Thoms" is written in white chalk on the outside of the back of the top right drawer in the upper case. On the outside of the left side of the same drawer are illegible inscriptions in white chalk and in red pencil. The inside of the drawer backs are marked "B" in white chalk, the inside bottom of most drawers are also marked "B," and there are many other shop marks in chalk. Shipping labels, one dated 1930, from the American Railway Express Company are pasted to the underside of the bottom of both the upper and the lower cases. A loan label from the Litchfield Historical Society is pasted to the inside of the left side of the top drawer in the lower case; to its left is another modern label with the typed "#111."

Condition: The midmolding attached to the top of the lower case has been replaced. The edges of several drawers have been repaired, most of the drawer runners are replace-

THE chest-on-chest-on-frame was a popular form in New England, and the Art Gallery collection includes both this example, possibly from Connecticut, and a New Hampshire version probably by a member of the Dunlap family (cat. 88). Here, the carved pinwheel and cherry primary wood suggest a Connecticut origin, although the chest could well have been made elsewhere in rural New England.[1] The placement of a row of deep drawers at the top of the upper case can be found on some Connecticut objects, such as the high chest (cat. 146) attributed to Eliphalet Chapin in the Yale collection.

The Mabel Brady Garvan Collection 1930.2570

1. A more stylish Connecticut chest-on-chest-on-frame is in Downs, fig. 180.

88

Chest-on-chest-on-frame
Attributed to the Dunlap family
Southern New Hampshire, 1790–1815
(see pl. 9)

Description: This chest consists of three stages: an upper and a lower case and a supporting base framework. The upper case is crowned by complex projecting cornice molding that includes a dentil course and the Dunlap-style "flowered ogee" molding. The upper case contains five graduated lipped drawers, with the top drawer fashioned to simulate three small drawers in line. The upper case rests within cove molding applied to the top of the lower case. The lower case contains three lipped drawers; in this instance the middle drawer is fashioned to simulate two superimposed graduated drawers, and the lowest drawer is again shaped to simulate three small drawers in line, with the center section carved with a concave fan. The lower case rests within a molding that includes the "flowered ogee" motif that is applied to the frame. The front skirt of the frame is decorated with a central pair of molded S-scrolls flanked by carved concave fans, and the side skirts are shaped with reverse curves flanking paired scrolls at the center. The four short cabriole legs have sharply arrised knees and applied knee brackets and terminate in pad feet. The chest retains much of its original orange-red paint. The drawers were never fitted with brasses or pulls of any kind. The top and the bottom of each case are dovetailed to the sides, the drawer

87

ments, and there have been many small repairs to the drawer linings. The left front foot has been repaired, the knee brackets on the left front leg are replacements, and the side skirt has been repaired near the left rear leg. The brasses are replacements.

Woods: American black cherry; eastern white pine; back rail, transverse supports of the frame, eastern hemlock.

Dimensions: H 212.2; W 108.5; UCW 89.4; LCW 96.1; D 52.1; UCD 41.7; LCD 44.8.

Provenance: Purchased by Francis P. Garvan, New York, N. Y., from a Mrs. Emmons.

Chest-on-Chests 185

88

divider dovetails are exposed, and the horizontal backboards are nailed to rabbets in the sides. On the simulated drawers, a vertical groove between each "front" is filled with an applied strip. On each drawer, the sides are dovetailed to the front and back; the bottoms are beveled on their front and side edges, let into grooves in the front and sides, and nailed to the underside of the back. There are no dustboards, and the drawer runners are nailed to the sides of the case. The frame is of mortise-and-tenon construction, with a transverse brace at each side housed and nailed in the front and rear rails. The moldings are applied with nails.

Inscriptions: "S H" is written in white chalk on the underside of the bottom of each drawer with the exception of the "double" drawer in the lower case; the letters also appear on the top of the bottom of the upper case. "No 2" appears in white chalk on the inside of the rear rail of the frame and on the top of the top of the lower case, and there are other chalk shop marks on the case and drawers. There are two American Railway Express Company shipping labels pasted to the top of the top of the upper case and one on the top of the top of the lower case; one is dated 1924, and the shipping point was Worcester, Massachusetts. A pattern of nails in both locations indicates that other modern labels were affixed to the chest at one time. "This side up" is written in pencil on the top of the top of the lower case. There are semicircular and concentric compass marks, probably for a shell, on the back of the rear rail of the frame.

Condition: The chest seems to have retained an early and possibly original painted finish; much of the original color can be seen on the undersides of some drawers and drawer dividers and in other scattered and protected locations. The front and rear knee brackets on each side and the right applied strip on the front of the top drawer in the upper case were replaced by Emile Mazzola in 1963.

Woods: Soft maple, probably red maple; eastern white pine.

Dimensions: H 205.1; W 110.7; UCW 93.5; LCW 98.9; D 57.5; UCD 44.9; LCD 47.8.

Exhibition: YUAG, "All That Glisters."

Bibliography: Charles S. Parsons, "The Dunlaps of New Hampshire and Their Furniture," in *Country Cabinetwork and Simple City Furniture*, ed. John D. Morse (Charlottesville: University Press of Virginia, 1969), p. 130 fig. 6; Parsons, *Dunlaps*, fig. 42 (included in catalogue but not in exhibition); Parsons and Brooke, "Dunlap Cabinetmakers," fig. 4; Kirk, *Early Am. Furn.*, fig. 43.

Provenance: Henry V. Weil, New York, N. Y.; by sale in 1924 to Francis P. Garvan, New York, N. Y.

NUMEROUS ornamental details relate this chest-on-chest-on-frame to other examples of the form and to other types of furniture, attributed to members of the Dunlap family.[1] The meaning of the inscribed "S H" is not known; it is possible that they are the initials of an apprentice or a journeyman employed in a Dunlap shop. This chest is unusual in that the drawers were never fitted with brasses or pulls, although other Dunlap-style furniture, including a closely related chest-on-chest-on-frame, and case furniture and tables from

186 *American Case Furniture*

New England and from as far south as Georgia are known that never had hardware.[2] The Art Gallery collection also includes a married Dunlap-style high chest of drawers (Appendix, no. 18), some elements of which appear to be old and may be of interest to students of Dunlap-style furniture.

The Mabel Brady Garvan Collection 1930.2211

1. For related examples, see Parsons, *Dunlaps*, figs. 40, 41, 43–50; ten other examples are listed in Parsons, "More Dunlap," pp. 12–13.
2. Parsons, *Dunlaps*, fig. 47. See also Fales, *Deerfield*, figs. 384, 385; *Neat Pieces*, fig. 91; and *Antiques* 88, no. 3 (September 1965): 304.

89

Chest-on-chest

Philadelphia, Pennsylvania, 1765–1775

Description: This imposing chest-on-chest is in three units: a pediment framework, an upper case, and a lower case. The architrave of the upper section is carved with a blind fret on the front and sides of the upper case; above the fret is heavy projecting cornice molding with a dentil course and a broken-scroll arch terminating in leaf-carved volutes. The center of the pediment is marked by a carved cartouche of a basket of leaves and flowers, resting on a plinth supported by a pierced diamond latticework. The sides of the pediment are marked by ball-and-flame finials supported on square plinths. The upper case contains seven cock-beaded drawers, three in line over four graduated drawers, and the lower case contains three graduated cock-beaded drawers. Each drawer has a central brass lock escutcheon; those on the small drawers are blind and are also fitted with bail pulls, and those on the wide drawers are flanked by matching escutcheons with bail pulls. The sides of each case are decorated with engaged fluted quarter columns, and the chest is supported by bracket feet below a base molding at the front and sides. The pediment is formed of a simple dovetailed-and-blocked framework that fits over cleats applied to the top of the upper case, with the complex moldings applied. The top and bottom of each case are dovetailed to the sides, and the horizontal backboards are nailed to rabbets in the sides and to the top and bottom boards. There are full dust-boards under each drawer, with drawer guides nailed to the dustboards. On each drawer, the sides are dovetailed to the front and back with very fine dovetails; the bottoms are let into rabbets in the front and sides and nailed to the underside of the backs, with running strips applied to the front and sides. Each drawer bottom is a single board with the grain running parallel to the front of the chest. There are horizontal and vertical blocks behind the feet, and the rear feet are triangular.

Inscriptions: The drawers have been numbered in pencil and chalk in modern times, and columns of addition appear in white chalk on the inside of the left side of the upper case.

89

Chest-on-Chests

89a

Condition: The brasses are original, with the exception of the one on the upper right drawer in the upper case. The central cartouche has been broken and repaired and is probably incomplete. The latticework beneath its plinth has been repaired, and new blocks have been added to the pediment frame and to the top of the upper case. One finial has been cracked and repaired. The backboards have been renailed, although some old nails remain, and new screws have been added. There have been many minor repairs, including repairs to the drawer linings and to the cockbeaded edges. The right front and both rear side feet have been repaired, and the blocking of the feet is new.

Woods: Mahogany; drawer linings, backboards, other elements, yellow poplar; top and bottom of each case, rear rail of pediment framework, other elements, southern yellow pine.

Dimensions: H 247.7; W 118.0; UCW 103.8; LCW 108.8; D 60.6; UCD 52.7; LCD 54.8.

Exhibition: YUAG, "All That Glisters."

Bibliography: *Antiquarian* 6, no. 6 (July 1926): 49; Nutting, *Treasury*, no. 199; W. M. Hornor, Jr., "Edward James and 'Philadelphia Chippendale,'" *International Studio* 92 (February 1929): 35 fig. 5; Harold D. Eberlein, "Philadelphia Houses, a Proud Past," *National Geographic Magazine* 118, no. 2 (August 1960): 183; Kirk, *Early Am. Furn.*, fig. 79; Charles F. Montgomery, "A Philadelphia Chest-on-Chest," *Walpole Society Note Book, 1977* (Printed for the society, 1978), facing p. 28.

Provenance: The early history of this chest is unknown, and there is some slight confusion as to how it entered the collection of Francis P. Garvan, New York, N. Y. Mr. Garvan's files

indicate that it was acquired at an American Art Sale of the Huntington collection in 1926, perhaps through the auspices of New York dealer Jacob Margolis. The caption in Nutting, *Treasury* (1928), however, lists Morris Schwartz as the owner (or perhaps merely as the supplier of the photograph).

THIS magnificent chest-on-chest is one of a group of related high-style examples produced by several Philadelphia shops in the 1760s, 1770s, and later.[1] The group varies in its drawer arrangement and in the handling of the carved and molded motifs of the pediment. The Yale chest is most similar to examples now at the Carnegie Institute in Pittsburgh and one illustrated by Hornor, which have the same blind fret and the same arrangement of drawers in the upper case.[2] A related example, now at Colonial Williamsburg, was made by Philadelphia cabinetmaker Thomas Affleck for David Deshler, a Germantown merchant, in 1775, and thus provides a firm basis for dating the Yale example. Although these chest-on-chests were made at the height of the rococo period in Philadelphia, elements of the rococo aesthetic are found only in their pediments. Stripped of its flame finials, carved leafage, blind fretwork, pierced latticework, and wildly asymmetrical finial, the Yale chest would present a rather restrained, architectonic appearance, enlivened primarily by its swirling mahogany drawer fronts.

The large size of these chests must have made their use difficult at times. In 1775, Englishwoman Mary Kenyon noted that in the bedroom of her new house in Lincoln's Inn Fields she had "a large chest upon chest (so high that I must have a step-ladder to look into the five top drawers)."[3] George Smith, in his *Collection of Designs for Household Furniture* (London, 1808), tried to compensate for this unmanageable size. His design (plate 131) for a double chest of drawers was "made lower than is usual, to avoid the disagreeable alternative of getting on chairs to place any thing in the upper drawers."

The Mabel Brady Garvan Collection 1930.2505

1. The best description of the form is found in PMA, *Three Centuries*, cat. 76.
2. David T. Owsley, *The Furniture Collections of the Museum of Art, Carnegie Institute* (Pittsburgh: Carnegie Institute, 1976), fig. 17.
3. Ralph Edwards, *The Shorter Dictionary of English Furniture* (London: Country Life, 1964), p. 208.

90

Chest-on-chest
Pennsylvania, 1760–1790

Description: This massive chest-on-chest is in two stages. The tall upper case is crowned by a broken-arch pediment with deep cove scrolls terminating in carved pinwheels flanking a central plinth for a finial. The center of the pediment is also carved with a shell in low relief. The upper case contains nine lipped drawers, including two pairs of small drawers flanking a deep center drawer all above four graduated drawers. The sides of the case are decorated with engaged fluted quarter columns, and the upper case rests within restraining molding applied to the lower case. The lower case holds six drawers, placed to echo the arrangement used in the upper case. The deep center drawers in each case are carved with a central shell from which scrolled leafage emanates; the concave lobes of the shell are decorated with punchwork, and punchwork is also used to outline the leafage. The deep center drawers and the wide drawers in each case are fitted with central brass lock escutcheons flanked by matching escutcheons with bail pulls; matching escutcheons are used on the small drawers in each case. The chest is supported by bracket feet below cove base molding applied at the front and sides. The top and bottom of each case are dovetailed to the sides, and the vertical partitions are tenoned through the drawer dividers. There are full dustboards under the wide drawers in each case, with drawer guides nailed to the sides of the case and shaped to conform to the vertical blocking behind the quarter columns. The small drawers run on runners nailed in place. There are also full vertical partitions on each side of the deep center drawer in each case. On each drawer, the sides are dovetailed to the fronts and to the backs, with the rounded edges of the sides and backs joined with a miter. The drawer bottoms are beveled on their front and side edges, fitted to grooves in the drawer fronts and sides, and nailed to the underside of the backs. The horizontal backboards are joined with a half lap and are nailed with rosehead nails to rabbets in the sides and to the top and bottom of each case. The pediment is built up of several thicknesses screwed together, and the cornice molding is a single piece nailed to the case.

Inscriptions: The bottom edge of the drawer fronts of the small side drawers in the upper and lower case, and their corresponding drawer dividers, are stamped with the numbers 1–4 and 5–8 respectively. The inside of the same drawer

90a

fronts are also marked with locations in red. Stamped on the back of the brasses is "490," and written in black on the outside of the backboards of the upper case is the modern "X281."

Condition: The finials and their plinths are new, and there have been repairs to the cornice molding. There have been minor repairs to the drawer fronts, and the sides of several drawers have been pieced. Some of the drawer guides within the case are replacements. The four sides of each case are made of two boards joined with a butterfly cleat that may be original. The lock on several drawers is missing, and the backs of all but one of the small drawers have been reduced in thickness. The most significant alteration to the object is the replacement of the bracket feet and their blocking.

Woods: American black walnut; drawer sides, some drawer runners, other elements, white oak; drawer bottoms and backs, other secondary wood, yellow poplar.

Dimensions: H 229.9; W 111.5; UCW 98.8; LCW 103.4; D 57.9; UCD 51.3; LCD 53.7.

Bibliography: *Eighteenth Century American Furniture . . . Sold by Order of Mrs. Gertrude H. Camp, "The Hayloft," Whitemarsh, Pa.,* Sale 2222, 20–21 January 1928 (New York: Anderson Galleries, 1928), no. 273; Nutting, *Treasury,* no. 298; Kirk, *Early Am. Furn.,* fig. 82.

Provenance: Said to have been purchased in 1925 from the Evans family of Philadelphia, Pa., by Mrs. Gertrude H. Camp, Whitemarsh, Pa.; acquired at auction in 1928 by Francis P. Garvan, New York, N. Y.

ON the basis of its ownership in the Evans family, which was reputed to own several examples of Jonathan Gostelowe's work, this enormous and unusual chest-on-chest was once attributed to that Philadelphia cabinetmaker's shop. But as John Kirk has demonstrated in detail, this chest exhibits a

190 *American Case Furniture*

90

misunderstanding of Philadelphia high-style furniture forms and decoration,[1] and it is undoubtedly the work of a rural rather than an urban shop. Its massiveness is a reminder that Germanic influence can also be discerned in the weight and stability of objects, as well as in style and construction.

The Mabel Brady Garvan Collection 1930.2147

1. Kirk, *Early Am. Furn.*, pp. 102–103.

91

Chest-on-chest

Pennsylvania, 1770–1800

Description: This large chest-on-chest is in three units: the pediment is a separate frame resting on top of the upper case, which in turn rests within restraining molding applied to the top of the lower case. The pediment contains a fluted cornice molding and a broken-scrolled arch, with urn-shaped finials at the center and sides mounted on unusual, fluted plinths. The upper case contains six lipped drawers, including two drawers in line over four graduated drawers, and the lower case holds three graduated drawers. The front corners of each case hold engaged fluted quarter columns. Each wide drawer is fitted with a central oval brass lock escutcheon flanked by dual disk escutcheons with bail pulls; the two small drawers in the upper case are fitted with a single matching brass and a brass keyhole liner. There is base molding at the front and sides of the lower case, and the chest is supported on four high bracket feet. The pediment is a separate dovetailed frame, with glue blocks in the corners and applied moldings. It fits over cleats attached to the top of the upper case. Each case is of dovetailed board construction. There are full dustboards in the upper case and three-quarter dustboards in the lower case. The back of each case consists of horizontal half-lapped boards nailed in place. On each drawer, the sides are dovetailed to the front and back; the bottom is fitted to a rabbet in the sides and to a groove in the front and nailed to the underside of the back with rosehead nails; running strips are applied. The rear feet are triangular brackets.

Inscriptions: There are numerous chalk shop marks and numbers on the interior of the cases, and there is an indecipherable word on the underside of the top dustboard in the upper case. The chalk inscription "bk" appears on the inside of the back of the upper and lower case. There are old chalk drawings, probably of a finial, on the inside of the left side of the top wide drawer in the upper case. The modern "130" is written twice in black on the outside of the back of each case and the pediment frame.

Condition: There have been repairs to the left side of the upper case, and the right side of the upper case has been pieced at the rear. There have been minor repairs to the drawer fronts, and the lock mortises on the drawer dividers have been repaired. The drawer runners and guides

Chest-on-Chests 191

91

are replacements. The midmolding attached to the top of the lower case is a replacement. All four feet have been repaired. Holes in the tops of the present finials suggest that they are incomplete and originally may have held an additional ornament.

Woods: American black walnut; top and bottom of cases, other interior elements, southern yellow pine; drawer linings, other secondary elements, yellow poplar.

Dimensions: H 234.6; W 114.7; UCW 103.7; LCW 108.7; D 58.1; UCD 52.5; LCD 54.6.

Bibliography: *Antiquarian* 7, no. 5 (December 1926): 24; *The Jacob Margolis Early American Collection*, 17–19 March 1927 (New York: American Art Association, 1927), no. 447; Wenham, *Collectors' Guide*, no. 204; Miller, 1: no. 621.

Provenance: Jacob Margolis, New York, N. Y.; acquired at auction in 1927 by Francis P. Garvan, New York, N. Y.; by descent in 1937 to Mabel Brady Garvan, New York, N. Y.

This restrained, workmanlike chest-on-chest, sturdily constructed in the Middle Colonies manner, has been attributed to Philadelphia, but it might well have originated anywhere in eastern Pennsylvania. The type of brasses, which appear to be original, and the unusually shaped plinths and finials suggest a date late in the eighteenth century. The practice drawing of a finial inside one of the drawers is an uncommon touch, seen on only a few other examples in the collection.

The Mabel Brady Garvan Collection 1950.698

92

Chest-on-chest
Pennsylvania, 1770–1795

Description: The upper case is crowned by a molded cornice containing a dentil course and holds seven lipped drawers, three in line over four graduated examples. The top three drawers are fitted with brass disk bail pulls, and the lower drawers in both the upper and the lower cases are fitted with central oval brass lock escutcheons flanked by brass disk bail pulls. The front corners of the upper case are fitted with engaged fluted quarter columns, and the upper case has applied base molding that aligns with restraining cove molding applied to the top of the lower case. The lower case contains three graduated lipped drawers and has quarter columns at the corners. There is base molding at the front and sides, and the chest is supported by bracket feet. In each case, the top and bottom are dovetailed to the sides. The cornice moldings are nailed in place. The vertical backboards in each case are pegged to the top, bottom, and rear strips of the drawer support system. In the lower case, the

side backboards continue below the bottom and are shaped to form the rear feet, and the side boards also continue below the bottom to form the side feet at the front and back; they are shaped to conform to the applied base molding and bracket feet. The front feet and base molding are applied to the bottom of the lower case, and the feet are pegged to a vertical block in each corner and rest on thin pads. The drawers are supported on a joined framework, without dustboards, and with drawer guides nailed to the sides of the case. In each drawer, the sides are dovetailed to the front and back with wedged dovetails, the bottoms are beveled on the front and side edges, let into grooves in the front and sides, and secured to the underside of the back with wooden pins. The top three drawers in the upper case are fitted with wooden spring locks.

Inscription: "Samuel" is written in pencil on the outside of the right side of the upper right drawer in the upper case.

Condition: The chest is in excellent condition. There have been minor repairs to the lips of several drawers and to the sides of the lowest drawer in the lower case, and the left rear foot has been pieced. The chest also retains an old finish.

Woods: American black walnut; yellow poplar.

Dimensions: H 190.8; W 108.5; UCW 95.9; LCW 103.5; D 55.9; UCD 50.5; LCD 53.9.

Bibliography: Kirk, *Early Am. Furn.*, fig. 80; Kirk, *Am. Furn. & Brit. Trad.*, fig. 28.

Provenance: Francis D. Brinton, West Chester, Pa.; by sale in 1923 to Francis P. Garvan, New York, N. Y.

THIS rather plain yet sturdily constructed chest-on-chest is of a standard Pennsylvania type that is occasionally attributed specifically to Philadelphia.[1] Similar chests were made in England, including a more horizontal version of ca. 1770–1775 attributed to Thomas Chippendale.[2] Designs for related chests appear in the Gillows papers in the 1780s and 1790s, and Hepplewhite included a related design for a "Double Chest of Drawers" in his *Cabinet-Maker and Upholsterer's Guide* (plate 53).[3] The Yale chest represents an instance where construction techniques in the Germanic tradition, including

92

wedged dovetails and large wooden pins used as fasteners, were used on an essentially Anglo-American form.

The Mabel Brady Garvan Collection 1930.2034

1. For a related example with an inlaid dentil cornice, see *Antiques* 125, no. 4 (April 1984): 724.
2. Christopher Gilbert, *The Life and Works of Thomas Chippendale*, vol. 2 (New York: Macmillan, 1978), fig. 207.
3. Kirk, *Am. Furn. & Brit. Trad.*, figs. 565–568, see also fig. 27.

Dressing and Bureau Tables

Often known today as a lowboy, this form was referred to in period documents as a dressing table, a chamber table, or simply as a table. Usually made en suite with high chests of drawers, dressing tables were used in chambers. English and European prints of the seventeenth and eighteenth centuries often depict them completely covered with a cloth which obscures the form underneath. These prints also usually show the tables used in conjunction with a dressing (or tabletop) mirror or with a looking glass hung above, with candlesticks or candlestands nearby, and with a vast array of toiletries and other accoutrements resting on top. Supported by turned legs in the period from about 1690 to 1730 and by cabriole legs in most cases thereafter, American dressing tables held from one to five drawers, although four seems to have been the most common. The collection contains twenty-nine examples strong in geographic and economic diversity. It is rich in early examples with turned legs from both New England (cats. 93–96) and the greater Delaware Valley (cats. 97–99). Among the important mid and late eighteenth-century examples are tables attributed to Eliphalet Chapin of Connecticut (cat. 108) and to John Shaw and Archibald Chisholm of Annapolis (cat. 121) and the Wynkoop family Pennsylvania dressing table (cat. 116). The bureau table is a related form, more akin visually to a chest of drawers, as its name implies. The collection includes a Philadelphia example (cat. 119) and a Newport block-and-shell example (cat. 109) attributed to John Townsend.

left side *top* *thumbnail molding*

lipped drawer

pegs

side skirt *front skirt* *cabriole leg*

Spanish foot

93

Dressing table

Boston, Massachusetts, area, 1700–1725

Description: The top has thumbnail molding on all four sides and overhangs the case on all four sides. The case contains three drawers in line, the center drawer of greater width and lesser depth, outlined with double half-round molding applied to the case at the front and sides. Each veneered drawer front is bordered with a herringbone band and has a central brass escutcheon with a drop pull. The front skirt is shaped with two simple round arches flanking a higher arch at center set above stepped reverse curves; the side skirts are shaped to double arches. The skirt is outlined by cock beading, and there are two matching drops. The four cup-turned legs are connected by shaped cross-stretchers with a central finial. The turned feet are supported by high pads. The case is of dovetailed construction, and the top is pinned to the four corner posts. The vertical partitions between the drawers are nailed to the front skirt and tenoned through the backboard. There is a medial support for each drawer, and strips are glued to the inside of each side. The drawer sides are dovetailed to the front and back; the bottoms are let into a rabbet in the front and nailed to the underside of all four sides.

Condition: The table was at one time painted black; the paint has been removed except from the top, which originally may have been veneered, and the back, although traces remain elsewhere. The brasses are probably replacements, although no other type of pull was ever used. Most of the cock beading and the drops are replacements, and sections of the double half-round molding around the drawers have been replaced. Half of the molding to the left side of the central drawer is missing. A large piece of veneer on the left side of the same drawer has been replaced, and other small sections of veneer have been replaced. The right rear corner of the top has been replaced, and the stretchers have been repaired with modern screws at their intersection. About half of the back of the center drawer is missing, and small running strips have been added to the tops of the side-drawer supports.

Woods: Front and drawer fronts, walnut veneer on eastern white pine; sides, stretchers, moldings, American black walnut; top, back, drawer linings, drawer supports, vertical partitions, other interior elements, eastern white pine; legs, aspen.

Dimensions: H 77.8; W 84.5; CW 71.5; D 52.3; CD 46.1.

Exhibition: *Forgeries and Restorations*, no. 21.

Bibliography: *The Early American Collection of Mr. and Mrs. G. G. Ernst, Norwalk, Conn.* (New York: American Art Galleries, 1926), no. 606.

Provenance: Mr. and Mrs. G. G. Ernst, Norwalk, Conn.; acquired at auction in 1926 by Francis P. Garvan, New York, N.Y.

ALTHOUGH it has survived in poor condition, this dressing table is one of a group of tables usually assigned a Massachusetts, probably Boston, origin. These tables are characterized by the arrangement of drawers seen here, by simply shaped skirts rising to a high arch beneath the central drawer, and by turned legs related in profile to those on this example. Published examples in public collections include tables at the Museum of Fine Arts, Boston (45.825), and in the Bayou Bend collection (B69.45).[1] These dressing tables also are related in form to the group of slate-top tables associated with the Boston area, including an example in the Dietrich collection

thought to have been owned originally by Thomas Hinckley (1618–1705/06) of Barnstable, Massachusetts, the governor of Plymouth Colony.[2] The shop of Boston cabinetmaker William Howell (d. 1717) was equipped with the tools and materials needed to make a dressing table of this kind, including walnut veneer, a veneering hammer, a toothing plane, glue pots, glue, and lead weights.[3]

The Mabel Brady Garvan Collection 1930.2140

1. Randall, no. 43; Warren, *Bayou Bend*, no. 29. See also Sack, *Fine Points*, p. 189; and Nutting, *Treasury*, no. 395.
2. Fairbanks and Bates, p. 66.
3. Forman, "Urban Aspects," pp. 18–19.

94

Dressing table

Massachusetts, 1700–1730

Description: See Condition. The case contains three drawers in line, with the center drawer of greater width, each outlined with double half-round molding applied to the case. Each drawer has a central brass escutcheon with a bail pull and has strips of herringbone veneer at bottom and sides. The front skirt is cock beaded and is shaped with paired reverse curves flanking a high central rounded arch above stepped reverse curves, and there are two turned drops. The side skirts are also edged with cock beading and are shaped to paired reverse curves. The case is of dovetailed board construction and is supported by four trumpet-turned legs doweled to the case above stretchers shaped to reverse curves on their outer edges. The drawer sides are dovetailed to the front and back and nailed to a rabbet in the front and to the underside of the sides and back. Each drawer has a central support, and the vertical partitions are triangular, nailed to a block glued to the inside of the case above the drops, and tenoned through the back. Small strips are glued to the inside of each side. The cock beading is applied with small rosehead nails.

Condition: This table had survived in poor condition and was extensively restored by Emile Mazzola in 1962. The top was damaged and had lost its veneer; its front edges were pieced with fragments from its side and rear edges, those edges were then pieced, and the top given a new layer of walnut veneer. New blocks were added under the top inside the case. The right front leg, which is maple, was judged to be an early replacement. It was moved to the left rear location, and that leg moved forward to the right front. The veneer on each side of the front above the legs was also repaired, and the cock-beaded strips separating the rear legs from the case were replaced. Prior to this restoration, the stretchers had been pieced near each leg, the bottom of the central drawer had been pieced, and new nails had been added to the drawer dovetails. The two left feet vary in profile from one another and are pine, while the right feet at front and rear are of a third profile and are maple. The pine stretchers originally may have been veneered with walnut.

Woods: Top and front of case, walnut veneer; applied moldings, cock beading, walnut; sides of case, birch; back of case, interior partitions, other elements, southern yellow pine; stretchers, other elements, eastern white pine; left rear leg, right front and rear feet, maple.

Dimensions: H 75.4; W 85.1; CW 73.0; D 49.2; CD 45.2.

Bibliography: Charles Messer Stow, "The Theme of Luxury in the Garvan Collection," *Antiquarian* 15, no. 3 (September

1930): 35; Walter A. Dyer, "The American Lowboy: William & Mary—Queen Anne," *Antiquarian* 17, no. 2 (August 1931): 33; Edward Wenham, "Converting Desks and Lowboys into Dressing Tables," in *Furnishing with Antiques*, ed. Robert Medill McBride (New York: Robert M. McBride, 1939), p. 46 (reprinted in Robert Medill McBride, ed., *A Treasury of Antiques* [New York: Robert M. McBride, 1946], p. 22).

Provenance: Israel Sack, New York, N. Y.; by sale in 1929 to Francis P. Garvan, New York, N. Y.

DESPITE its heavy restoration, commonly encountered in these fragile, early dressing tables, the case of this example remains in basically sound condition. The use of pine for the turned legs and of birch for the case suggests a more rural origin for this table than for the other two Massachusetts examples in the Yale collection (cats. 93, 95). The turnings here also lack the thinness and delicacy often found on the legs of dressing tables, probably because they are pine rather than the more customary maple, which turns more crisply.[1] The straight edge on one side of each stretcher is an unusual feature that may help link this dressing table to others.

The Mabel Brady Garvan Collection 1930.2208

1. For related turnings, see Nutting, *Treasury*, no. 392.

95

95

Dressing table

Massachusetts, 1700–1730

Description: The case contains three drawers outlined with double half-round molding applied to the case. The case is veneered at the front and sides, and the drawer fronts are veneered and outlined at the sides and bottom with a herringbone band. Each drawer has a central brass escutcheon with a bail pull. The front skirt is shaped to a simple central arch above stepped reverse curves, flanked by paired reverse curves; the side skirts are also shaped to paired reverse curves, and cock beading is applied to the front and side skirts. The four trumpet-turned legs terminate in reel and ball feet above a high pad and are joined by shaped cross-stretchers. The case is of dovetailed board construction, with the legs doweled to the carcass. In each drawer, the sides are dovetailed to the front and back, and the bottom is let into a rabbet in the front and nailed to the rabbet and to the underside of the sides and back. The vertical partitions are shaped and tenoned through the backboard; at the front they are housed on a rabbeted block and nailed to the skirt. Each drawer is supported by a central support, and the customary strips are glued to the inside of each side. Small strips are nailed to the back above each drawer support to act as a stop.

Inscriptions: "H M" is carved on the top edge of the central drawer. Each drawer is numbered in chalk on the outside from left to right, 1 through 3 respectively, and there are other illegible chalk inscriptions on the drawers.

Condition: The top has been reveneered. The drops are missing, and the blocks or platforms above their location are replaced. Parts of the case veneer and beading along the skirts have been replaced. The stretchers were probably originally veneered in a manner similar to the top and drawers; their top surface is rough as if it were prepared with a toothing plane. Blocks have been added to each side of the front of the case interior.

Woods: Front and sides of case, drawer fronts, walnut veneer on eastern white pine; legs, feet, American black walnut; drawer sides, backs, bottoms, other interior elements, eastern white pine; stretchers, red oak.

Dimensions: H 75.6; W 84.6; CW 69.6; D 54.5; CD 46.8.

Exhibition: *Forgeries and Restorations*, no. 20.

Bibliography: *Antiques* 11, no. 1 (January 1927): 23; Nutting, *Treasury*, no. 385.

Provenance: Henry V. Weil, New York, N. Y.; by sale in 1924 to Francis P. Garvan, New York, N. Y.

VENEERING, noted Thomas Sheraton in the early nineteenth century, "amongst cabinet makers, is the art of laying down and gluing very thin cut wood, of a fine quality and valuable, upon common wood." He went on to observe, "sometimes the object of veneering is cheapness, and sometimes appearance." On this dressing table, made in Boston when cabinetmaking was just getting under way in this country, about a century before Sheraton was writing, the veneered front facade and the originally veneered stretchers suggest that appearance rather than cheapness was the goal of the maker. Sheraton explained, "in most cases . . . the ground, glue, and extra time [involved in veneering] are equivalent to the expense of solid wood, except it be to save very rich solid boards."[1] Here the maker was able to stretch his rich, reddish-brown burl walnut boards by cutting them into thin veneers and applying them to a white pine carcass and oak stretchers. The solid walnut legs on this example also suggest that it was an expensive object, probably more so than the two preceding dressing tables (cats. 93, 94), which have painted or stained legs. The trumpet-turned legs here are similar to those of a relatively large group of dressing tables and high chests attributed to the Boston area, some of which exhibit variations in the profile of their skirts.[2]

The Mabel Brady Garvan Collection 1930.2993

1. Sheraton, *Cabinet Dictionary*, 2:328.
2. *Sack Coll.*, 2:461 no. 1139; High Museum (1983.45), illustrated in *Sack Coll.*, 7:1991 no. P5415; Singleton, facing p. 390; *Antiques* 63, no. 2 (February 1953): 87; Nutting, *Treasury*, no. 331.

96

Dressing table
New England, 1710–1740

Description: The top has a molded edge on all four sides and is made of three butted boards pinned to the case. The case holds three drawers in line, with the middle drawer of greater width and lesser depth, each outlined with double half-round molding applied to the case. Each drawer has a central brass escutcheon with a bail pull. The front skirt is shaped with a central high arch set above stepped reverse curves, flanked by paired reverse curves. The side skirts are also shaped to paired reverse curves. Cock beading is applied to the front and sides of the skirts, and there are two drops at the front. The four cup-turned legs terminate in reel and bun feet and are joined by shaped cross-stretchers that intersect the legs at a diagonal. The case is of dovetailed board construction, with the legs doweled to the case. In each drawer, the sides are dovetailed to the front and back; the bottom is let into a groove in the front and sides and secured to the underside of the back with wooden pins. The side drawer runners are rabbeted and nailed to the corner posts. The vertical partitions are not shaped and are nailed to the front skirt and nailed with a single rosehead nail through the back. The inner runners for the two side drawers are nailed to the bottom of this partition; the runners for the middle drawer are housed in the front and back. There are drawer stops applied to the inside of the back.

Inscriptions: On the inside of the bottom of the center drawer is a large, octagonal, printed paper label, with notations in ink, which reads: "for [printed] William & Mary period / American 1700–1710 / original and unrestored [ink] / 'THE HAYLOFT' / WHITEMARSH: MONTGOMERY COUNTY: PENNSYLVANIA [printed] / Wood—maple (curly) side / pines, trumpets pine [ink]."

Condition: The left rear leg and foot in pine are replacements, perhaps early ones. The stretchers have been repaired at their intersection, and a maple strengthening brace has been added. The drops are replacements, and the cock beading is a replacement. The present brasses are replacements; evidence of at least two different sets of earlier brasses is visible on the drawer fronts. A small piece has been added at the top of the right rear leg and another small piece to the rear of the left skirt. At one time, screws were inserted from the inside of each corner post to the sides.

96

Woods: Top, front, three legs, drawer fronts, soft maple; sides, drawer sides, backs, bottoms, eastern white pine; left rear leg, southern yellow pine; stretchers, birch.

Dimensions: H 73.0; W 85.7; CW 79.6; D 54.2; CD 46.8.

Bibliography: *Antiques* 11, no. 4 (April 1927): inside back cover; "Gallery Notes," *YUAG Bulletin* 3, no. 2 (December 1928): 34; *Eighteenth Century American Furniture . . . Sold by Order of Mrs. Gertrude H. Camp, "The Hayloft," Whitemarsh, Pa.*, Sale 2222, 20–21 January 1929 (New York: Anderson Galleries, 1929), no. 257.

Provenance: Clarence Allen, Portland, Maine; Gertrude H. Camp, Whitemarsh, Pa.; acquired at auction in 1929 by Francis P. Garvan, New York, N. Y.

EARLY eighteenth-century dressing tables of maple such as this example are relatively rare.[1] This table has been refinished, and although no traces of paint are discernible today, it may have been painted or japanned originally. Or, the use of tiger maple on the top and front may have been an attempt to achieve with less expensive and laborious means the swirling, visually interesting look customarily achieved through the use of walnut veneer. The drawer construction here suggests that it is of a slightly later date than the preceding three examples from Massachusetts (cats. 93, 94, 95), with whom it shares the same drawer arrangement.

The Mabel Brady Garvan Collection 1930.2159

1. A pine table with trumpet turnings is illustrated in *Sack Coll.*, 7: 1916 no. P5283.

97

Dressing table
Philadelphia, Pennsylvania, 1700–1730

Description: The top has thumbnail molding at the front and sides and overhangs the case at the front and sides. Cove molding is applied to the case at the front and sides below the top. The case holds three separated drawers, each bordered with double half-round molding applied to the case at the sides and bottom and with the center drawer of greater width and the side drawers of greater depth. The front skirt has an applied cock beading and is shaped to three pointed arches, with the center arch rising into the case above an arc and a step at each side. The skirt also is decorated with drops. The cock beaded side skirts are shaped to a single pointed arch. The case is supported by four trumpet-turned legs, with turned feet below the curved cross-stretchers. At the intersection of the stretchers there is a fifth foot below and a turned, pointed finial mounted on a diamond-shaped base. The stretchers come to a point where they project beyond the legs and feet, rather than being squared off flush with the front of the case. The top is made of two boards and is pinned to the case; it is also secured with glue blocks. The sides of the case are dovetailed to the front, with the dovetails exposed on the sides, and the back is a single board dovetailed to the sides. The interior corner posts are pinned through the sides and nailed through the back. The drawer runners are rabbeted and nailed to the corner posts and to vertical blocks nailed to the inside of the skirt. Strips are glued to the inside of the back to serve as stops. None of the interior elements are tenoned through the back. The legs are doweled to the corner posts. On each drawer, the sides are dovetailed to the front and back, and the bottoms are nailed to a rabbet in the front and to the underside of the sides and back. The top edge of the sides and back is rounded. The left drawer is divided into two compartments by a single longitudinal partition, about half the height of the drawer, nailed in place through

97

Provenance: According to tradition, this dressing table has a history of ownership in the Frankenfield family of Philadelphia. It was acquired by collector Howard Reifsnyder of Philadelphia, Pa., and purchased at auction in 1929 by Francis P. Garvan, New York, N. Y.

THE separated drawers, cove molding under the top, exposed dovetails, and combination of walnut and southern yellow pine all suggest that this dressing table was made in Philadelphia.[1] At least three other dressing tables are known with the same drawer arrangement and arcaded skirt and with turned legs differing only in detail.[2] One of these related tables is thought to have been made about 1725 for Catherine Johnson of Germantown immediately prior to her marriage in 1726 to Caspar Wistar, and another Philadelphia example is inlaid with the date 1724, each indicating that these tables were made well into the third decade of the eighteenth

the sides; the right drawer is divided similarly by two partitions into three compartments.

Inscriptions: The side drawers are marked "L" and "R" in pencil on the outside of the back. Written in white chalk on the outside of the right side of the left drawer is "#300R"; written in white chalk on the outside of the right side of the right drawer is "R277." A fragment of a modern newspaper, possibly from Philadelphia, is glued to the right rear corner post.

Condition: The brasses are replacements, and holes for earlier brasses or pulls have been plugged on the drawer fronts. The bottom portion of the drops are replaced. The right rear foot and the left rear leg have been repaired, and there have been minor repairs to the cock beading. Some of the glue blocks under the top are replacements, and there are thumbtack holes along the back edge of the top.

Woods: American black walnut; southern yellow pine.

Dimensions: H 73.6; W 86.0; CW 71.5; D 51.1; CD 46.2.

Bibliography: *Reifsnyder Coll.*, no. 631; Walter A. Dyer, "The American Lowboy: William & Mary—Queen Anne," *Antiquarian* 17, no. 2 (August 1931): 34.

97a

century.[3] The foot and finial at the intersection of the stretchers here are probably original; similar details are found on other Philadelphia dressing tables, and the diamond-shaped base is present on the three closely related examples. Like other Philadelphia dressing tables, each drawer on the Yale example originally may have been fitted with more than one brass.

The Mabel Brady Garvan Collection 1930.2056

1. The characteristics of Philadelphia dressing tables of this period are discussed in McElroy, "Furn. in Philadelphia," pp. 69–71.
2. Philadelphia Museum of Art (28.7.13), illustrated in McElroy, "Furn. in Philadelphia," fig. 9; Winterthur Museum (56.38.143); and an example illustrated in *Antiques* 119, no. 4 (April 1981): 713.
3. PMA, *Three Centuries*, no. 22; McElroy, "Furn. in Philadelphia," fig. 7 (Philadelphia Museum of Art, 40.16.28). For other Philadelphia examples, see *Antiques* 111, no. 5 (May 1977): 911 (Colonial Williamsburg); Sack Coll., 1: 162 no. 429; Kirk, *Am. Furn. & Brit. Trad.*, fig. 1463 (Philadelphia Museum of Art, 25.69.1); Robert Bishop, *American Furniture, 1620–1720* (Dearborn, Mich.: Edison Institute, 1975), p. 24. A European, or possibly English, example at Winterthur with similarly separated drawers is illustrated in Kirk, *Am. Furn. & Brit. Trad.*, fig. 1467.

98

98

Dressing table

Pennsylvania, 1700–1730

Description: The top of this single-drawer dressing table has thumbnail molding at the front and sides. The drawer is outlined by single half-round molding applied to the case at the sides and base and has a round blind brass lock escutcheon flanked by brass escutcheons with drop pulls. The front skirt is shaped to double-paired reverse curves, while the side skirts are cut to single-paired reverse curves. Cock beading outlines the case at the front and sides. The four cup-turned legs are joined by a shaped stretcher and terminate in reel and bun feet. The top is of a single board and is pinned to the case. The case is of dovetailed board construction, with the dovetails visible on the sides, and the legs are doweled into the corner posts. The drawer sides are dovetailed to the front and back; the bottom is let into a rabbet in the front and nailed to the rabbet and to the undersides of the sides and back. The drawer runners are rabbeted and nailed with rosehead nails to the corner posts, and drawer guides are fitted between the front and rear posts. An upper drawer guide is nailed on the right side, and small strips are applied to the back to act as stops.

Inscriptions: Chalk shop marks appear on the drawer linings and inside of the back.

Condition: The top has been repaired with a butterfly cleat toward the back and a glue repair about 6 cm from the front. The brasses are attached with new cotter pins and are probably replacements. Evidence of a now-missing block behind the center of the front skirt suggests that originally a central drop may have ornamented the skirt. The cock beading has been damaged, and small pieces have been replaced. The legs retain an old coat of brown paint, and traces of red paint are visible on the underside of the top.

Woods: Top, sides of case, front of case, drawer front, back of case, stretchers, legs, feet, eastern red cedar; corner posts, white oak; drawer sides and back, southern yellow pine; drawer bottom, Atlantic white cedar.

Dimensions: H 76.5; W 78.5; CW 64.6; D 48.6; CD 44.6.

Bibliography: Nutting, *Treasury*, no. 386; Comstock, "Bull Coll.," p. 141; Helen Comstock, "The American Lowboy:

An *Antiques* Survey," *Antiques* 80, no. 6 (December 1961): 570; Kirk, *Am. Furn. & Brit. Trad.*, fig. 1459.

Provenance: Nutting stated in 1928 (see Bibliography) that this table was "from Wilmington, Delaware," but no documentation to substantiate this statement has been found; it may have been based on information transmitted orally by its then owner, C. Sanford Bull, Middlebury, Conn.

ALTHOUGH this dressing table has been attributed to New England, it also has been suggested that it was made in Pennsylvania.[1] A Delaware Valley origin is postulated on the basis of the table's construction of Atlantic white cedar and red cedar and is given some slight added strength by its traditional (yet uncorroborated) history of having been found in Wilmington, Delaware. The use of a single drawer, often cited as evidence of an early date in high chests and dressing tables with turned legs, was probably dictated more by the customer's preferences and pocketbook than date. Single drawers are found on dressing tables attributed to Connecticut, Boston, New York, and elsewhere and were not a regional specialty.[2] Related English examples have been published.[3]

Gift of C. Sanford Bull 1951.56.2.

1. Comstock made the attribution to New England, and Kirk has recently raised the possibility that it was made in Pennsylvania (see Bibliography).
2. Kirk, *Conn. Furn.*, no. 171; Warren, *Bayou Bend*, no. 28; Fairbanks and Bates, p. 67. Also see Nutting, *Treasury*, no. 394. A later Delaware Valley dressing table with a single drawer is in the Yale collection (cat. 113).
3. Kirk, *Am. Furn. & Brit. Trad.*, figs. 1457, 1458, 1460–1462.

99

Dressing table

Pennsylvania, 1720–1740

Description: The overhanging top has thumbnail molding on all four sides and surmounts the case above applied cove molding. The case holds five drawers: three in line, with the center drawer of greater width, over two drawers below flanking the central arch. Each drawer has a central brass escutcheon with bail pull, and the upper three drawer fronts overlap the case at the bottom and sides, while the lower drawer fronts overlap the case at the sides and top. The front skirt rises to a central round arch above stepped reverse curves, flanked by paired reverse curves, and the side skirts are also cut to paired reverse curves. Cock beading is applied to the front and side skirts, and there are two "acorn" drops at the front. The four trumpet-turned legs are connected by shaped cross-stretchers with a disk at their intersection. The turned feet have high pads. The top is pinned to the case, which is of dovetailed board construction, with the legs doweled to the corner posts. The dovetails are exposed on the sides. The drawer sides are dovetailed to the front and back; the bottoms are let into a groove in the front and sides and nailed to the underside of the back. The top edge of each drawer side is rounded. The side drawer runners are rabbeted and nailed to the corner posts; the inner drawer runners for the lower drawers are rabbeted and nailed to blocks nailed to the inside of the back and tenoned and nailed to a rabbeted block nailed to the inside of the front. The vertical partitions between the upper drawers are dovetailed to the case and have transverse partitions behind them. A strip nailed beneath this partition serves as the inner drawer runner for the upper side drawer and as the runners for the central drawer; the strip is tenoned to the back and rabbeted and nailed to the block behind the front.

American Case Furniture

Inscriptions: On the bottom of the central drawer is a printed label that reads: "ADDISON GALLERY / PHILLIPS ACADEMY / ANDOVER, MASSACHUSETTS / 612 f. 1932." An identical label is pasted to the outside of the back of the case, with the exception that the typed number reads "612. 1932f." Written in black on the underside of the bottom of the central drawer is "23/5857."

Condition: In 1977, Peter Arkell undertook conservation to stabilize the table. Small pieces were let in to the top of the left front leg and the left rear leg; new plates were added at the top of each leg; and small pieces were let in where the mitered ends of the curved cock beading meet the plates. A small piece of cock beading also was added to the right of the center arch. An earlier repair to the top right corner of the upper right drawer in yellow poplar was replaced in walnut. Prior to this conservation, the drops had been replaced; the top edge of the central drawer front had been pieced; and the reel turning on the left front foot had been damaged and lost about 1 cm in height.

Woods: American black walnut; southern yellow pine.

Dimensions: H 70.5; W 87.4; CW 75.2; D 55.0; CD 50.0.

Bibliography: *Antiquarian* 12, no. 1 (February 1929): 3.

Provenance: Charles Woolsey Lyon, New York, N. Y.; by sale, probably in 1929, to Francis P. Garvan, New York, N. Y.

THE use of five lipped drawers, common on Delaware Valley dressing tables with cabriole legs (see cat. 110), is unusual for a dressing table with turned legs. Their presence here suggests that this example may have been made toward the end of the turned-leg dressing table's popularity, perhaps as late as 1740. The vertical separation of the drawers, the use of cove molding under the top, and the combination of walnut and southern yellow pine all indicate that this table was made in Pennsylvania rather than New England. The trumpet turnings here are simpler, less well articulated versions of those found on Philadelphia-area tables of the 1720s or earlier (cat. 97).[1] The shape of the feet here is also related to Pennsylvania work.[2]

The Mabel Brady Garvan Collection 1930.2664

1. McElroy, "Furn. in Philadelphia," figs. 7, 9. A Massachusetts dressing table with turned legs also has a later type of drawer arrangement; see *Antiques* 94, no. 4 (October 1968): inside front cover.
2. PMA, *Three Centuries*, cat. 22.

100

100

Dressing table
Boston, Massachusetts, area, 1740–1760

Description: The top has thumbnail molding at the front and sides and overhangs the case on all four sides. The top is divided into two panels of crotch veneer outlined and bordered by light-wood stringing, cross-banding, and herringbone veneer. The case holds four drawers, one wide over three in line, with the lower middle drawer of greater width. The wide drawer and the lower middle drawer are veneered with two panels, and the lower side drawers with one, each edged with light-wood stringing and herringbone veneer. The panels on the lower center drawer are shaped to conform to the recessed center of the drawer, which is inlaid with a stylized shell with eleven lobes and fitted with a brass button pull inserted through an inlaid diamond. The wide drawer has a central blind brass lock escutcheon flanked by larger blind lock escutcheons with bail pulls, and the lower side drawers are fitted with a blind brass lock escutcheon with bail pull. There is no top rail above the wide drawer, which is outlined with cock beading at its sides and bottom;

Dressing and Bureau Tables 205

the lower drawers are surrounded by cock beading. The remainder of the front facade is veneered. The front skirt is shaped to three flathead arches, with the center arch set above stepped reverse curves and recessed to conform to the drawer front. There are two acorn drops on the front skirt, which is without cock beading. The side skirts are shaped to a single flathead arch, and each side has an inlaid eight-point star or compass, formed by alternating strips of light- and dark-wood inlay. The case is supported by four cabriole legs terminating in pad feet, with the knee brackets applied to the skirt. The joint of the top to the case is obscured by veneer. The case is of frame construction, with the corner posts and legs a single piece. The transverse vertical partitions between the lower drawers are triangular and are tenoned through the back. The lower drawers are supported by medial runners joined with a half lap to the front rail and tenoned to the back. Two strips are nailed to the inside of each side of the case. On each drawer, the sides are dovetailed to the front and back, and the bottom is nailed to a rabbet in the front and to the underside of the sides and back.

Inscription: There are modern columns of figures in pencil on the inside of the left interior partition.

Condition: The drops are replacements. The rear 5 cm of the top appears to be a replacement, suggesting that the veneer on the top, which is consistent throughout, also might be replaced. Some drawer runners have been replaced; there has been a repair to the bottom of the wide drawer, which has been renailed. Some of the dovetails joining the drawer sides to the front have been repaired.

Woods: American black walnut; walnut veneer; eastern white pine; light and dark inlaid compasses, two woods, differing from a third used on inlaid shell on lower middle drawer; light-wood stringing, possibly maple.

Dimensions: H 74.7; W 85.7; CW 75.7; D 51.9; CD 45.4.

Provenance: In the collection of Dr. McKnight, Hartford, Conn.; by sale to Charles Woolsey Lyon, New York, N. Y.; by sale in 1929 to Francis P. Garvan, New York, N. Y.

THE inlaid "compasses" on the sides of this dressing table relate it to a group of Boston-area furniture decorated with similar features and often of walnut or walnut veneer and eastern white pine.[1] The lower middle drawer of related dressing tables and high chests usually is recessed and embellished with a carved or an inlaid shell. Two objects in the group are dated 1739: a desk signed by William Parkman (1685–1776) of Boston, and a high chest signed by Ebenezer Hartshorn (1689–1781) of Charlestown.[2]

The Mabel Brady Garvan Collection 1930.2384

1. The objects in this group include Warren, *Bayou Bend*, no. 63; *Boston Furn.*, figs. 14, 16, 17, 70; Fales, *Deerfield*, figs. 427, 428; Rodriquez Roque, *Chipstone*, no. 24; *Antiques* 70, no. 1 (July 1956): 13; *Sack Coll.*, 7:1834 no. P5107, 1997 no. P5392; and the two objects cited in note 2.
2. *Antiques* 107, no. 5 (May 1975): 952, 953; *Boston Furn.*, fig. 19.

101

Dressing table
Connecticut, probably Putnam area, 1740–1760
(en suite with cat. 130)

Description: The top has thumbnail molding on all four sides and overhangs the case on all four sides. The case contains one wide drawer over three in line, with the lower side drawers of greater depth and the lower center drawer of greater width. There is no top rail above the wide drawer. The wide drawer has a central brass escutcheon flanked by escutcheons of varying configuration with bail pulls; the lower side drawers are fitted with single brasses, and the lower center drawer has a blind brass lock escutcheon with a bail pull. The drawers are surrounded with double half-round molding applied to the case, and each drawer is veneered with a central panel of figured veneer with a border of straight-grained veneer. The front skirt is shaped with deep scrolls rising to a central drop; the side skirts are shaped

100a

to reverse curves flanking a central round arch. The case is supported by four cabriole legs terminating in pad feet, with small knee brackets applied to the front of the case. The top is pegged to the case, and the four sides are joined to the legs with mortise-and-tenon joints, with four pegs used to secure the joint of the backboard to the rear legs. The transverse partitions between the lower drawers are triangular and are nailed to the front skirt. The lower drawers have medial runners, with small blocks applied at the rear end of each runner. None of the interior elements are tenoned through the back. Strips are nailed to the inside of each side of the case. On each drawer, the sides are dovetailed to the front and back, and the bottom is beveled on its front and side edges and is let into a groove in the front and sides and nailed to the underside of the back. The top edge of the drawer sides is shaped to a double half round. The top edge of the central brass on the wide drawer has been clipped off.

Inscriptions: There are chalk shop marks and numbers on the drawers. "Trowbridge" is written in white chalk on the outside of the back. A "Connecticut Furniture" (1967) exhibition label is pasted to the inside of the right side of the lower right drawer.

Condition: There are repairs to the veneer on the top of the case. The tip of the center drop on the front skirt and the right rear foot have been repaired.

Woods: Top and front of case, walnut veneer; applied moldings, walnut; sides and back of case, aspen; legs, soft maple; top of case and other elements, eastern white pine; interior partitions, drawer linings, other elements, yellow poplar; drawer fronts, southern yellow pine and yellow poplar.

Dimensions: H 80.9; W 86.7; CW 73.5; D 55.5; CD 46.2.

Exhibition: Kirk, *Conn. Furn.*, no. 181.

Provenance: This dressing table and an accompanying high chest (cat. 130) were purchased from the estate of a member of the Larned family of Putnam, Conn., by the sister of Cornelia B. Trowbridge, Eastford, Conn. The objects were acquired from Trowbridge in 1928 by Henry Hammond Taylor, Bridgeport, Conn., who sold the pair to Francis P. Garvan, New York, N.Y.

SEVERAL factors suggest that this dressing table and its companion high chest (cat. 130) may have been made near Putnam in northeastern Connecticut, in addition to their history in the Larned family of that area. The brasses, which

101

appear to be original, vary in shape among themselves and also differ from those on the high chest. Here, although one lock escutcheon was used, no locks were used on the object, and a further air of provinciality is provided by the clipping of the central brass on the wide drawer, so that it would fit its assigned space. Such mismatching and economical use of imported and expensive brasses is more to be expected from rural, rather than urban, shops. The shape of the skirt, with its central drop, relates to Rhode Island work and probably reflects Rhode Island's pervasive influence in eastern Connecticut. The use of many different woods, five in this instance, is not uncommon on objects from rural eastern Connecticut and other rural areas. The use of walnut and walnut veneer here, however, is unusual in Connecticut work and suggests that the maker of these objects or his client was familiar with more fashionable urban furniture. This dressing table has been assigned a date range beginning as early as 1725, on the basis of the presence of double half-round molding and a style of brasses associated with objects dating from that time.[1] Given its rural origins, however, it seems more probable that it was made in the middle of the eighteenth century.

The Mabel Brady Garvan Collection 1930.2206

1. Kirk, *Conn. Furn.*, no. 181; for a related table, see no. 182.

Dressing and Bureau Tables 207

102

102

Dressing table
Connecticut, 1740–1770

Description: The case contains a wide drawer above two lower side drawers flanking a central carved shell. The upper drawer is fitted with a central blind brass lock escutcheon, flanked by matching escutcheons with bail pulls; the lower drawers have central matching brasses. The drawers are outlined by single half-round molding, and the front is beveled under and to the sides of the lower drawers and above the carved shell. The front and rear skirts are shaped to a simple central arch, slightly recessed in front under the shell, above stepped reverse curves, and are flanked by flathead arches, with drops in front. The side skirts are shaped to a simple central arch above stepped reverse curves. The edges of the front and side skirts are slightly chamfered. The corner posts continue to form four cabriole legs terminating in stylized Spanish feet on thin pads. The case is of mortise-and-tenon construction, with the joints pegged; the lowest peg is driven through the knee of the legs. The drawer divider is dovetailed to the corner posts, with the dovetail exposed on the front. The drawer guides are nailed to the sides of the case; the side drawer runners are rabbeted to posts and nailed to the sides. The runners under the center of the lower drawers are half lapped to the front rail and tenoned to the back, they have an applied wedge nailed to the center of the back to kick the drawers forward to present a flush appearance, and small blocks are applied to the back to serve as stops. The transverse partitions on the inside edges of the lower drawers are dovetailed to the front and tenoned to the back; the dovetails are reinforced with nails. The drawer sides are dovetailed to the front and back, with a single large dovetail on the top drawer, and the top edges of the sides and backs are molded. The drawer bottoms are let into a rabbet in the front and nailed to the rabbet and to the undersides of the sides and back.

Condition: The top and the drops have been replaced, as have the front knee bracket on the left front leg and the side knee bracket on the right front leg. The brasses are probably replacements, although wooden pulls were never installed. The upper portion of the reverse curve on the rear portion of the right side skirt has been replaced. There is much evidence of insect damage throughout. The top edge of the top drawer may have been reduced in height, and the bottom has been repaired. An old note states that the table has been cleaned of original red paint, but traces of such paint are not easily discernible today.

Woods: Soft maple; eastern white pine.

Dimensions: H 72.2; W 83.6; CW 72.4; D 55.4; CD 48.5.

Provenance: Henry V. Weil, New York, N. Y.; by sale in 1929 to Francis P. Garvan, New York, N. Y.

THIS dressing table is unusual in that its backboard is shaped to echo the front skirt. Its use of three drawers, rather than the more customary four, is reminiscent of Newport dressing tables with carved shells that form an integral part of the front skirt.[1] Here, however, the carved shell appears, at first glance, as if it was carved on a lower center drawer. The "Spanish" or carved foot is found on Connecticut objects from Stratford, Woodbury, and elsewhere (cat. 135), although the foot here, with its rather narrow, evenly spaced ribs standing above a flat projecting pad, lacks the boldness found on many examples.[2] Another unusual detail of this dressing table is the beveled edges surrounding the drawers.

The Mabel Brady Garvan Collection 1930.2385

1. Ott, nos. 63, 65.

208 *American Case Furniture*

2. Cooke, figs. 26, 29–31; Edward S. Cooke, Jr., "The Selective Conservative Taste: Furniture in Stratford, Connecticut, 1740–1800" (M.A. thesis, University of Delaware, 1979), figs. 15–20.

103

Dressing table
New England, 1750–1780

Description: The top of this dressing table is molded on its front and side edges and overhangs the case by approximately 10.5 cm at each side and less dramatically on the front and back. The case holds one wide drawer over three in line, with the lower side drawers of greater depth and the lower middle drawer of greater width. The edges of the drawers have thumbnail molding on all four sides but are not lipped. The front skirt is shaped with flathead arches flanking a central rounded arch; no drops were ever present. The side skirts are shaped to a flathead arch. The case is supported by four very slender, quite straight cabriole legs, with tiny knee brackets, that terminate in small pad or "penny" feet. The top, made of two boards, is screwed from underneath through holes in projecting wrought-iron strips that are nailed to two shallow grooves in the top edge of each side of the case. The case is of mortise-and-tenon construction, with the case sides and back pinned to the legs with four pins and the front skirt secured to the front legs with a single peg at each side that projects some 4.5 cm into the case. The transverse partitions between the drawers are dovetailed to the front skirt and nailed through the drawer divider above. None of the interior elements is tenoned through the back. The lower drawers run on medial runners, supported by small strips nailed to the inside of the front. The wide drawer runs on runners nailed to the case sides. The inside face of each case side is not planed off. On each drawer, the sides are dovetailed to the front and back with squarish dovetails; the bottoms are beveled on their front and side edges and let into a groove in the front and sides and nailed to the underside of the back with rosehead nails. The top edge of each drawer side is chamfered, and the pins of the side dovetails extend 2.5 cm beyond the back to act as stops.

Inscriptions: "Eliza B——?" is written in pencil on the top edge of the back of the lower center drawer. Written in

Dressing and Bureau Tables 209

white chalk on the outside of the back of the right lower drawer is "2." A modern printed label bearing the written "3" is pasted to the inside of the bottom of the wide drawer; to its left "3" is painted in red.

Condition: The brasses are replacements, and the right rear foot has been repaired.

Woods: Top, front of case, drawer fronts, mahogany; legs, sides of case, soft maple; eastern white pine.

Dimensions: H 81.5; W 89.5; CW 68.7; D 54.9; CD 44.8.

Bibliography: Miller, 1:fig. 680.

Provenance: Francis P. Garvan, New York, N. Y.

SEVERAL features lend this dressing table an air of individuality, including its mixture of mahogany and maple, its slender legs, its lack of drops, the unusual method of fastening the top to iron strips, and its wide, overhanging top. Such bold projecting tops have been seen as an important characteristic of American design, although here the top is made of imported mahogany rather than native pine or maple.[1] A dressing table related in spirit is in the collection of the Connecticut Historical Society (1975.71.0). Owned by the Latham family of Colchester, this table has a cherry frame, thin maple legs, and a projecting top evocative of the Yale example.

The Mabel Brady Garvan Collection 1930.2677

1. Kirk, *Am. Furn. & Brit. Trad.*, chap. 9.

104

Dressing table
Newtown, Connecticut, 1770–1790

Description: The top is made of two butted boards secured with a spline and has thumbnail molding on all four sides. It overhangs the case on all four sides and is attached to the sides by means of a sliding dovetail, with the groove filled at the rear, and supported by strips nailed to the inside of the case. The case contains four lipped drawers, one wide over three in line, with the lower middle drawer wider and carved with a shell with fifteen concave ribs or lobes. The top drawer is fitted with a central brass escutcheon flanked by matching

104

escutcheons with bail pulls. Matching escutcheons are used on the lower side drawers, with a central brass button pull on the middle drawer. The front skirt is shaped to flathead arches beneath the drawers, with a shallow recess beneath the center drawer and turned drops. The side skirts are shaped to a single flathead arch. The four corner posts extend to form cabriole legs, with beaded scrolls at the knees extending to the knee brackets, terminating in round pad feet. The sides and back are mortised and tenoned to the legs and secured with six and five pegs respectively. The rear corner posts are of a greater depth than the front, and the rear legs are cut flush with the backboard. There is no top rail; the drawer divider is tenoned to the front posts but not pegged; and the bottom rail is tenoned to the posts and held with a single pin. The vertical partitions between the lower drawers are dovetailed to the drawer divider and bottom rail. The side runners for the top drawer are tenoned to the back, rabbeted to the drawer divider, and pinned to a board behind them that is nailed to the sides of the case. The middle support for the top drawer is dovetailed to the drawer divider and tenoned to the back. The side runners for the lower drawers are tenoned to the back and rabbeted to the bottom rail, tapering toward the back. The middle runners

are dovetailed to the bottom rail, are tenoned to the back, and have guides nailed in place at their top centers. There are no dustboards. The sides of the drawers are rounded on their top edges and dovetailed to the drawer fronts. The backs are dovetailed to the sides, and the bottoms are rabbeted on their fronts and sides, let into grooves in the fronts and sides, and nailed to the sides about 10 cm from the front and in some instances also nailed with a rosehead nail to the underside of the back.

Inscriptions: A paper printed label of modern origin is pasted to the inside of the right side of the top drawer and bears the typed "#123." To its right is another printed paper label of the Litchfield Historical Society and the object's loan number.

Condition: The left front knee bracket has been replaced, and the top right corner of the lower left drawer pieced. There is also a small patch to the lower right corner of the top drawer.

Woods: American black cherry; drawer sides and backs, lower drawer runners, strips nailed to sides under top, white oak; back, drawer bottoms, upper drawer runners, other framing elements, eastern white pine.

Dimensions: H 79.9; W 92.6; CW 81.7; D 54.6; CD 46.3.

Provenance: In a letter of 24 September 1929, dealer Henry Hammond Taylor informed Francis P. Garvan that this "cherry lowboy with the C scrolls on legs and original brasses . . . came from the Johnson family on Main St Newtown Conn and has always been in this family." Francis P. Garvan, New York, N. Y.

THIS dressing table once was tentatively attributed to New Haven on the basis of its close relationship to a privately owned example with a history of ownership in the area.[1] However, the family history of that table can only be traced to the mid nineteenth century, and recent research by Edward S. Cooke, Jr., has established that these dressing tables and several other related examples were most likely made in Newtown.[2] These Newtown dressing tables share many characteristics, including oak drawer linings; similarly shaped skirts with flathead arches; distinctive C-scrolls on the knees; rabbeted drawer bottoms (also seen on some Dunlap case furniture, such as cats. 64, 65); and drawers constructed with the backs dovetailed to the sides.[3] Reproductions of the Yale dressing table have been produced by Harden Furniture Company since 1983.

The Mabel Brady Garvan Collection 1930.2075

1. Kirk, *Conn. Furn.*, no. 176.
2. Cooke, pp. 46–51. Other related examples include Cooke, fig. 8; and a dressing table in a private collection undoubtedly from the same shop as the Yale table, illustrated in "Living with Antiques: The William Peters House," *Antiques* 105, no. 1 (January 1974): pl. V. Other related tables are illustrated in Fales, *Deerfield*, no. 442, and in *Antiques and the Arts Weekly* (8 February 1985), p. 10. The Art Gallery Study Collection includes a heavily restored dressing table (Appendix, no. 13) that is probably related to this Newtown group; it was pictured with a matching high chest in *Antiques* 101, no. 5 (May 1972): 757.

105

Dressing table
Connecticut, 1760–1780

Description: The projecting top has a molded edge on the front and sides and is notched at the front corners. The case contains one wide over three drawers in line, with the center drawer of greater width and carved with a concave shell with seventeen ribs contained within an arc. The drawers are lipped. The front skirt is shaped to three flathead arches, with the central arch recessed below the drawer. The side skirts are shaped with paired reverse curves. The four cabriole legs terminate in pad feet. The top is a single board, and the case is framed without the use of pegs. The vertical transverse partitions between the lower drawers are dovetailed to the drawer dividers. The lower part of the front of the lower middle drawer is laminated for depth; a semicircular inner lamination projects into the drawer to the depth of the shell. On each drawer, the sides are dovetailed to the front and back; the bottoms are nailed to a rabbet in the front and to the underside of the sides and back. The top edge of each drawer back is beveled, and the top edge of each side is shaped.

Inscription: A modern printed paper label glued to the inside of the bottom of the top drawer reads: "FROM / MRS. BEEKMAN C. CANNON / 70 HIGH STREET / NEW HAVEN, CONN. 06511 / To [in print] This lowboy was left / to Jonathan Edwards College / with some other goodies / by Mr. Burton Mueller / a descendant of J.E. [in ink] / POST MASTER–This parcel may be opened for postal inspection if necessary [in print]."

Condition: The worn condition of the top of the legs and

Dressing and Bureau Tables 211

A TALL clock (1950.76) by Aaron Miller of Elizabethtown, New Jersey, a New York high chest (cat. 139), and this dressing table have the same history of descent in the Edwards family, but it is doubtful that any of the objects were owned originally by Jonathan Edwards.[1] In rather poor condition, this cherry dressing table is related to many examples from Connecticut with similarly shaped skirts and carved shells of varying configuration (see cat. 104).[2]

Gift of Charles Hoyt 1950.78

1. Edwin A. Battison and Patricia E. Kane, *The American Clock, 1725–1865: The Mabel Brady Garvan and Other Collections at Yale University* (Greenwich, Conn.: New York Graphic Society, 1973), no. 17.
2. Kirk, *Conn. Furn.*, no. 175.

105

the lack of a molded edge on the crisp top of the wide drawer suggest that the dressing table has been reduced in height. The top has been off and reattached with modern nails driven through the top, with screws from underneath, and with new glue blocks. All the knee brackets and the two drops are missing; the plates above the missing drops have been damaged. The brasses are replacements; the wide drawer originally was fitted with a central brass blind lock escutcheon, and the brass pull in the center of the shell has been inserted in a wooden button covering the original hole. Some of the interior glue blocks are replacements, and others are missing. The drawer guides have been renailed, and the interior of the drawers has been finished.

Woods: American black cherry; yellow poplar.

Dimensions: H 78.2; W 91.5; CW 80.7; D 50.1; CD 45.8.

Provenance: Although the inscription suggests otherwise, recent correspondence with Mrs. Beekman C. Cannon indicates that this dressing table and a high chest (cat. 139) were given to Jonathan Edwards College at Yale by Charles Hoyt, a descendant of Jonathan Edwards (1703–1758), perhaps with the assistance of Rowland Burdon-Miller and Charles Beecher Hogan, with the general understanding that the objects had descended in the Edwards family.

106

Dressing table
Connecticut, possibly Norwalk, 1750–1780
(en suite with cat. 136)

Description: The top has thumbnail molding at the front and sides and overhangs the case on all four sides. The case contains four lipped drawers, one very shallow wide drawer over three in line, with the lower side drawers of greater depth and the lower center drawer of greater width. The wide drawer is fitted with a central blind brass lock escutcheon flanked by matching escutcheons with bail pulls. The lower middle drawer has a blind brass lock escutcheon, and the lower side drawers are fitted with matching escutcheons with bail pulls. The front skirt is shaped with deep reverse curves rising to a central, concave, round "sunburst" or shell, with twenty-eight ribs. The side skirts are shaped to single flathead arches. The case is supported by four cabriole legs terminating in pad feet and ridged from the knees to the feet. The top is a single board and is pegged to the case. The case is framed with mortise-and-tenon joints, with two pegs used to secure the back and sides to the legs. The front skirt is pegged to the legs twice above the knees. The posts of the rear legs are considerably thicker than those of the front legs, and the knees of the rear legs are squared off at the back. The dovetails joining the drawer divider to the case sides and the vertical partitions to the drawer dividers are exposed. The drawers are supported by runners at the sides, and there are no dustboards. The runners for the wide drawer are

212 American Case Furniture

106

nailed through the guides to the sides, and the runners for the lower drawers are tenoned to the front and back. No elements are tenoned through the back. On each drawer, the sides are dovetailed to the front and back; the bottoms are beveled on their front and side edges, let into grooves in the front and sides, and nailed to the underside of the back. The top edges of the drawer sides and backs are beveled or chamfered on each side.

Condition: The dressing table has been thoroughly refinished. Some new screws have been added to secure the top to the case.

Woods: American black cherry; yellow poplar; eastern white pine.

Dimensions: H 74.9; W 80.2; CW 75.7; D 51.6; CD 47.9.

Bibliography: Nutting, *Treasury*, no. 414; Charles Nagel, Jr., "Room from the Joel Clark House, East Granby, Connecticut, 1737," *YUAG Bulletin* 4, no. 2 (October 1932): 139.

Provenance: Francis P. Garvan, New York, N. Y.

THIS dressing table's companion high chest (cat. 136) bears an early inscription suggesting that it was owned by a Miss Canfield of Norwalk, Connecticut. Assuredly from Connecticut, it is possible that these objects were made in the Norwalk area. A related dressing table, also in cherry, has the same drawer arrangement and a very similar round carved shell in the center of its skirt.[1]

The Mabel Brady Garvan Collection 1930.2445

1. *Antiques* 89, no. 2 (February 1966): 210. See also a related high chest referred to in the notes to cat. 136.

107

Dressing table

Connecticut, possibly Wethersfield area, 1760–1800

Description: The top of this dressing table is made of two butted boards pegged to the case. It overhangs the case on all four sides and is surrounded on all four sides by applied molding to create a tray top. The case holds four lipped drawers, one wide over three in line of equal size. The upper drawer is fitted with a central brass escutcheon flanked by matching escutcheons with bail pulls. Each lower drawer is fitted with a central brass pull; the side drawers are carved with "pinwheels" in clockwise rotation and the center drawer with a matching "sunburst." The front skirt is shaped to multiple roundheaded arches, and the side skirts have roundheaded arches flanking paired reverse curves. The four corner posts extend to form cabriole legs with scrolled knee brackets terminating in squarish claw-and-ball feet. The case is of mortise-and-tenon construction; the sides and back are pinned to the posts three times, and the front rails and drawer divider once. The vertical partitions between the lower drawers are tenoned through the drawer divider and pinned at top and bottom. The side drawer runners and guides are rabbeted to the posts and nailed to the sides; the center drawer supports are tenoned to the back and nailed to the front rail through the sides. The sides of the drawers are dovetailed to the front and back; the bottoms are beveled on their front and sides, let into grooves in the drawer front and sides, and nailed to the underside of the back. The top edges of the drawer sides are rounded; the top edges of the drawer backs are chamfered.

Inscriptions: On the outside of the left side of the lower right drawer in pencil is the inscription: "Mary Bowen 16 years / 1864 / 12345." A "Connecticut Furniture" (1967)

Dressing and Bureau Tables 213

107

exhibition label is pasted to the inside of the right side of the wide drawer.

Condition: The brasses on the wide drawer are new; originally this drawer may have had only brass button pulls similar to those on the lower drawers, as indicated by old holes under the new escutcheons. The upper edge of each drawer has been pieced.

Woods: American black cherry, including backboard; eastern white pine.

Dimensions: H 80.3; W 78.0; CW 66.8; D 57.7; CD 49.8.

Exhibition: Kirk, *Conn. Furn.*, no. 185.

Bibliography: Robert Rantoul, "Cherry Was the Mahogany of New England," *American Collector* 5, no. 2 (April 1936): 12.

Provenance: Perhaps owned by a Mary Bowen, born ca. 1848, whose identity is not known. Purchased from a H. Hilliker of Derby, Conn., by dealer Henry Hammond Taylor, Bridgeport, Conn., who in turn sold it in 1929 to Francis P. Garvan, New York, N. Y.

Not as wide as most dressing tables, this example is distinguished by its molded tray top (more common on tea tables), the finely carved decoration on all three of its lower drawers, and its superbly articulated legs and claw-and-ball feet. Although few would dispute that it was made in Connecticut, its precise place of origin is less clear. Its feet have been compared with those on a high chest once thought to have been made in the Wethersfield area and now attributed to Newtown and with those on a desk probably from Berlin, which has a similarly shaped skirt featuring several round-headed arches.[1] The construction of the Yale example does not correlate with the methods used in Newtown nor has its style of carving been identified as characteristic of Wethersfield furniture, thus leaving the question open.[2]

The Mabel Brady Garvan Collection 1930.2250

1. Kirk, *Conn. Furn.*, nos. 90, 122; Cooke, fig. 7.
2. Cooke, pp. 46–51; Kevin M. Sweeney, "Furniture and Furniture Making in Mid-Eighteenth-Century Wethersfield, Connecticut," *Antiques* 125, no. 5 (May 1984): 1156–1163.

108

Dressing table
Possibly by Eliphalet Chapin (1741–1807)
East Windsor, Connecticut, 1780–1790
(en suite with cat. 146)

Description: The rectangular top of this high dressing table has astragal molding at the front and sides above cove molding applied to the case. It overhangs the case on all four sides. The case holds four lipped drawers, one wide over three in line, with the middle drawer deeper. The top and bottom side drawers are fitted with brass plate and bail pulls, and the lower center drawer has a brass button pull in the center of a carved flower with eight petals surrounded by a shell with twenty convex ribs. The front corners of the table have fluted quarter columns with four flutes. The front skirt is cut to rising reverse curves with a slight drop at the center, and the side skirts are shaped with scrolls rising to a flathead arch. The four corner posts extend to form cabriole legs with claw-and-ball feet. The top is pocket screwed in place through the back and the front top rail. The case is joined with mortise-and-tenon joints, with pegs used only on the juncture of the back and rear posts. There are small blocks behind each side

of the front top and bottom rails and a line of vertical blocks on the inside of each corner post. The side drawer runners are of a single rabbeted piece nailed to the sides and rabbeted around the blocks and posts. The middle drawer runners, for the lower drawers, are deeply rabbeted on their inside edge to accommodate the deeper middle drawer and have a higher rabbet on their outside edges for the side drawers. They are tenoned through the back, the vertical partitions between the drawers are housed in them, and they are tenoned to the front bottom rail. On each drawer, the sides are dovetailed to the front and back, the bottoms have beveled edges at the front and sides, are let into grooves in the drawer front and sides, and are nailed to the underside of the back.

Inscriptions: A Connecticut Tercentenary label and a "Connecticut Furniture" (1967) exhibition label are pasted to the inside of the right side of the top drawer. The modern "10 / 720" is written in white chalk on the inside of the right side of the case.

Condition: There has been a small repair to the upper edge of the wide drawer. The dressing table has a mahoganized finish that is old.

Woods: American black cherry; eastern white pine.

Dimensions: H 83.2; W 88.4; CW 82.6; D 50.3; CD 43.7.

Exhibitions: *Three Centuries of Conn. Furn.*, no. 87; Kirk, *Conn. Furn.*, no. 186; Jan van der Marck et al., *In Quest of Excellence: Civic Pride, Patronage, Connoisseurship* (Miami, Fla.: Center for the Fine Arts, 1984), no. 71.

Bibliography: Rogers, "Garvan Furn. (1960)," fig. 13.

Provenance: A notation in a ledger kept by William B. Goodwin (1866–1950) of Hartford, Conn., a noted early collector of American furniture, concerns this dressing table and a high chest also at Yale (cat. 146). The page is headed "Cherry High and Low-Boy—to match." Each object is described as having been made in South Windsor, Conn., and as coming "From the same house in South Windsor Conn where I got my pine pannelling & staircase." Goodwin continues: "I tried to interest Mr. H.F. Dupont in these peices but he did not want to even see them. Secord interested Frank Garvan in them and he bought them August 15, 1928.... I did not see my way to buying them myself." The page also has the marginal notation that the two objects are "Now at Yale Art School in Garvan-Brady Collection."[1] Mr. Garvan's files indicate that the objects were purchased from William R. Secord, Hartford, Conn.

108

This dressing table and its matching high chest (cat. 146) are part of a large group of furniture associated with Eliphalet Chapin of East Windsor for many years. The basis of this association, in this instance, is primarily the close relationship between the legs and claw-and-ball feet of the dressing table with those on a pair of chairs, now in the Yale collection (1930.2516a, b), that were part of a set of chairs made by Chapin in 1781 for Alexander King (1749–1831). Unfortunately, the bill of sale for these chairs is now lost, although it survived until the late nineteenth century, long enough to be recorded by pioneering furniture historian Irving W. Lyon.[1] Nevertheless, the attribution of the King family chairs to Chapin has been generally accepted by most writers, although more recent scholars have widened the attribution to recognize the potential contribution of Aaron Chapin (1753–1838), Eliphalet's second cousin who worked in what are now referred to as the Chapin shops in the 1770s and early 1780s.[2] The attribution of this dressing table and the high chest to the Chapin shop is strengthened by the recent discovery that they were found in South Windsor by William B. Goodwin (1866–1950), an active early collector and a benefactor of the Wadsworth Atheneum. Although the dressing table has been a companion to the high chest for many years,

Dressing and Bureau Tables 215

there are several minor differences between the two objects. Each has the same mahoganized finish, but the brasses (original in each instance) are different, there is no rose (or flower) at the center of the carved fan on the high chest, and the tops of the drawer sides are flat on the dressing table but rounded on the high chest. Both the dressing table and the high chest have characteristics that reflect Chapin's years in Philadelphia, particularly the engaged fluted quarter columns, the legs and "claw" feet, and the drawer supports tenoned through the back of the case, a construction feature found on other furniture attributed to the Chapins. Among the most closely related examples is an important dressing table at the Connecticut Historical Society bearing the initials *AL* in a cypher, probably for Amasa Loomis (1737-1793) of East Windsor.[3]

The Mabel Brady Garvan Collection 1930.2125

1. *Great River*, no. 109.
2. *Great River*, nos. 109–112; see also Joseph Lionetti and Robert F. Trent, "New Information about Chapin Chairs," *Antiques* 129, no. 5 (May 1986): 1082–1095. Although nominally focused on seating furniture, this article offers a useful historiographical account of the literature on the Chapins, an analysis of the interrelationships among the Chapin family members and other craftsmen, and an important look at other documented examples of Chapin-shop work.
3. Benjamin Ginsburg, "The Barbour Collection of Connecticut Furniture in the Connecticut Historical Society," *Antiques* 105, no. 5 (May 1974): 1101; see also *Great River*, no. 111. Another example, not examined by the writer, is said to be in the Armstrong-Lockett House in Knoxville, Tenn.

109

Bureau table
Attributed to John Townsend (1732–1809)
Newport, Rhode Island, 1785–1790
(see pl. 10)

Description: The top of this blockfront dressing table has thumbnail molding at the front and sides and is supported below at the sides and front by cove molding applied to the case. The case holds seven drawers, including one wide drawer over two tiers of three graduated drawers flanking a recessed cupboard. The wide drawer has a central concave shell flanked by projecting convex shells. The shells are carved with eleven lobes emanating from a center section containing rows of flutes above cross-hatching and enclosed by a small scroll. The center shell terminates in small incised scrolls at the lower outer ends. The wide drawer is fitted with two brass lock escutcheons, blind on the left, with bail pulls, and the small drawers are fitted with brass escutcheons with bail pulls. The cupboard door is reverse blocked and is carved at the top with a shell echoing that on the center of the wide drawer; the door is hinged on the right, has a lock escutcheon on the left, and opens to a plain interior fitted with two fixed shelves. There is base molding at the front and sides of the case, and the table is supported by six ogee bracket feet, four across the front and two at the rear corners. The blocking continues into the front feet and terminates in a small carved scroll on the inner edge of each front foot. The molding below the cupboard door is notched at the center to echo the form created by the front feet. The true top is placed above a subtop consisting of two longitudinal strips dovetailed to the case sides and the front and back and attached with glue blocks and butterfly-shaped plugs or keys, visible at the rear. The back of the case consists of two horizontal boards nailed to rabbets in the sides, and the case is of dovetailed board construction. The drawer dividers are dovetailed to the case sides, with the dovetails exposed. The convex shells on the wide drawer are applied. The drawer runners are nailed to the sides of the case, and there is a full dustboard under the wide drawer. The feet are braced with three blocks shaped to follow the contours of the bracket and beveled on their inner edges, with the central vertical block applied last and standing above the horizontal blocks. The back bracket on the rear feet is diagonal and is butted against the side bracket, with a glue block added to secure the joint. On each drawer, the sides are finely dovetailed to the front and back; the bottoms are beveled on their front edge, let into a groove in the front, and nailed to the underside of the sides and back, with running strips applied. The top edges of the drawer sides are rounded, while the top edge of the back is flat.

Inscriptions: The drawer dividers are marked on the left, "A," "B," and "C" from top to bottom; on the right, "D," "E," and "F" from top to bottom. "Upper," and other writing which remains illegible, appears on the top of the dustboard below the wide drawer. There is an indecipherable inscription on the bottom of the case. "G198" is written in black on the top of the bottom of the upper right drawer and on the outside of its right side.

Condition: The lower sections of the rear feet are replaced, and two blocks from the back legs are missing. The block

behind the right front foot is a replacement, and the left inside foot has been repaired. The four outside feet once were fitted with casters. The lock on the kneehole cupboard is a replacement, and the lock on the wide drawer is missing.

Woods: Mahogany; drawer linings, yellow poplar; top, bottom, other elements, chestnut; one block, eastern white pine.

Dimensions: H 86.9; W 93.3; CW 87.4; D 51.3; CD 46.9.

Exhibitions: Ward, *Eye of the Beholder*, no. 1; YUAG, "Rhode Island Furn."

Bibliography: Nutting, *Treasury*, no. 272; Ormsbee, *Story Am. Furn.*, fig. 60; Rogers, "Garvan Furn. (1960)," fig. 7; Rogers, "Garvan Coll. (1962)," front cover; Rick Mastelli, "In Search of Period Furniture Makers," *Fine Woodworking*, no. 23 (July–August 1980): front cover, pp. 33, 35; Kirk, *Am. Furn. & Brit. Trad.*, fig. 381; Heckscher, "John Townsend's Block-and-Shell Furniture," *Antiques* 121, no. 5 (May 1982): 1151 fig. 20; Moses, fig. 3.87.

Provenance: In the collection of Francis P. Garvan, New York, N. Y., by 1928; by descent to Mabel Brady Garvan, New York, N. Y.

More than thirty Newport bureau dressing tables of this general type are known, including some two dozen with the four carved shells seen on this example. Recent research by Morrison H. Heckscher has led to the convincing attribution of the Yale table to the shop of John Townsend in the late 1780s, primarily on the basis of "the similarity of the shell and cornice treatment and the construction of the top and feet to those elements of Townsend [four-drawer] chests dated 1790 . . . and 1792." Heckscher cites bureau tables in Winterthur Museum (59.2645), the Bayou Bend collection (B.69.91), the Metropolitan Museum (10.125.83), and at least two others as forming the group of the Townsend-type objects.[1] Even more recently, the attribution to John Townsend has been accepted by Michael Moses, who has called attention to Townsend's distinctive calligraphy found here, a type of handwriting also found on the high chest at Yale (cat. 140) signed by Townsend.[2] Other Newport craftsmen, including Daniel Goddard and Edmund Townsend, produced this form, which seems to have been popular locally.[3] In some instances, the top drawer is fitted as a writing compartment, creating the so-called kneehole desk, a name commonly applied to these objects today. While much attention has been paid to determining the makers of these tables, relatively little concern has been given to the reasons for their popularity. A most intriguing aspect of Newport bureau tables is their radiation of a powerful sensuality. Made to be used primarily by women, they are designed as metaphors of the female form. The two large, projecting shells, each with a central areole, and the lower recessed cavity containing the cupboard, can be seen (on the level of association) as a mirror of the form of their principal users. It is doubtful if Townsend and other makers had this allegorical dimension of the object in mind, of course, although the eighteenth century was permeated with an earthy and frank attitude toward sexual matters. Reproductions of the Yale bureau table have been made by Harden Furniture Company since 1983.

The Mabel Brady Garvan Collection 1957.37

1. See the 1982 article by Heckscher cited in Bibliography and the later discussion in Heckscher, no. 135.
2. Moses, p. 143.
3. Moses, figs. 6.13, 7.22 (Daniel Goddard), figs. 6.10, 6.11, 7.9–14 (Edmund Townsend). Other examples of the form are illustrated throughout Moses.

110

Dressing table
Delaware Valley, probably New Jersey, 1740–1770

Description: The top overhangs the case on all four sides, has thumbnail molding on the front and sides, and is notched at the front corners. The case contains five lipped drawers, three in line over two below on either side of the arched skirt, each with a central brass escutcheon with bail pull. The front skirt is shaped with scrolls and reverse curves rising nearly to the central drawer before dropping at its center. An incised line following the edge of the skirt gives the impression of beading. The side skirts are also elaborately shaped with reverse curves rising to a central pointed arch. The corner posts continue to form squared cabriole legs terminating in Spanish feet. The front legs are molded above the foot on the front and outer edges; the rear legs are similarly ornamented at the outer and rear edges. The moldings above the feet are cut from the solid. The case is framed with mortise-and-tenon joints; the back and sides are secured to the corner posts with four pegs. The drawer sides are dovetailed to the front and back; the bottoms are let into a rabbet in the front and nailed to the underside of all four sides. The top edge of the drawer sides are rounded, and the top edge of the backs are slightly beveled. A vertical strip is applied behind the vertical partitions separating the upper drawers; it extends to the skirt and is shaped at its lower end to conform to a scroll in the skirt. The drawer runners for the upper middle and the lower drawers are rabbeted and nailed to this strip.

Inscription: A Lyman Allyn Museum loan label is glued to the back.

Condition: The table has been cleaned of a reddish mahogany or cherry stain, still visible on the back and in some places on the case and legs, and refinished. The present top is attached with modern countersunk and pocket screws, and is probably new, although the possibility exists that the original top has merely been reset. The brasses are replacements. Some of the drawer runners have been replaced, and shrinkage cracks in the sides have been filled.

Woods: American black walnut; drawer sides and backs, southern yellow pine; drawer bottoms, Atlantic white cedar.

Dimensions: H 77.3; W 86.2; CW 75.8; D 51.7; CD 45.6.

Exhibitions: *Early Furniture Made in New Jersey, 1690–1870* (Newark, N. J.: Newark Museum, 1958), no. 10; *From Lenape Territory to Royal Province: New Jersey, 1600–1750* (Trenton: New Jersey State Museum, 1971), no. 189.

Bibliography: *Duncan Phyfe and Other Fine Early American Furniture and Decorations: The Private Collection of Alexander M. Hudnut, Removed from His Country Residence at Princeton, New Jersey,* 19 November 1927 (New York: American Art Association, 1927), no. 54; "Gallery Notes," *YUAG Bulletin* 3, no. 2 (December 1928): 35; Nutting, *Treasury*, no. 421; *Handbook*, p. 45; Nagel, pl. 7b; Rogers, "Garvan Furn. (1960)," fig. 6; Rogers, "Garvan Coll. (1962)," p. 9; Comstock, no. 222.

Provenance: Alexander M. Hudnut, New York, N. Y., and Princeton, N. J.; acquired at auction in 1927 by Francis P. Garvan, New York, N. Y.

DRESSING tables of this kind are generally associated with the Delaware Valley, and especially with Salem and Cumberland counties of southern New Jersey, where many have been found.[1] Some examples have been attributed to Chester County, Pennsylvania, while others have a Philadelphia history, and the form was in all likelihood a regional one.[2] At least one published example with a long New Jersey

history differs considerably from the Yale table and appears to be a more rural expression of the form, with its straight rear legs, pinched drawers, and widely overhanging top.[3] The Yale table is close in many particulars of design and construction to an example now at the Historical Society of Pennsylvania (X-59) that has a history of ownership in the Logan family of Philadelphia.[4] This table has been attributed to Thomas Tufft (ca. 1740–1788) of Philadelphia, which is surely an error; it probably has been confused with a dressing table Tufft made for Deborah Norris Logan in 1783 that is described in the bill of sale, however, as being carved with fretwork and dentils to match a high chest.[5] The Logan family table has drawer sides and backs of oak, and it has the added embellishment of an incised line outlining its legs as well as its skirt. In an unusual variation of the form in the Winterthur collection (58.1577), the legs are doweled to the frame as they are in dressing tables of the previous generation.[6] Versions of the table in maple have been published.[7] English versions with rather straight legs and rising skirts are also known, and one dressing table that bears a generic relationship has been assigned tentatively to a Continental maker, "possibly Dutch or North German," on the basis of the "exaggerated movement of the skirts, legs, and feet."[8] The movement of the skirt on the Yale table, and others of its kind, is more restrained than this probably European example, and the Yale table has no overt characteristics of German-style construction, yet its undulating skirt may be a pale reflection of Germanic influence in the furniture of the Delaware Valley.[9]

The Mabel Brady Garvan Collection 1931.314

1. *Early Furniture Made in New Jersey, 1690–1870* (Newark, N.J.: Newark Museum, 1958), pp. 8–9; Margaret E. White, "Further Notes on Early Furniture of New Jersey," *Antiques* 78, no. 2 (August 1960): 136–139.

2. Schiffer, *Furn. Chester County*, no. 114; Hornor, pl. 59.

3. *Early Furniture Made in New Jersey*, no. 8.

4. James E. Mooney, "Furniture at the Historical Society of Pennsylvania," *Antiques* 113, no. 5 (May 1978): fig. 5.

5. The bill of sale is reproduced in Clarence W. Brazer, "Early Pennsylvania Craftsmen: Thomas Tufft 'Joyner,'" in *Philadelphia Furniture and Its Makers*, ed. John J. Snyder, Jr. (New York: Main Street/Universe Books, 1975), p. 63.

6. Downs, no. 322.

7. A very closely related example in maple was published in *Discovering Antiques*, vol. 1 (New York: Greystone Books, 1972), p. 59, courtesy of Parke-Bernet; other published related examples in maple include Nutting, *Treasury*, no. 421; and Miller, 1: no. 694. Other related examples in walnut that have been published are Lockwood, fig. 85; and *Antiques* 12, no. 6 (December 1927): 444. A more expensive and perhaps

111

slightly later version, with chamfered fluted corners and shell-carved knees, also was made; see *Sack Coll.*, 1: no. 553; and Chinnery, fig. 4:279.

8. Kirk, *Am. Furn. & Brit. Trad.*, figs. 1470, 1471; quotation from caption to fig. 1471. Also see *DEF*, 3:216, figs. 5, 6, 7.

9. Forman, "German Influences," p. 123, pl. 6.

111

Dressing table
Delaware Valley, probably New Jersey, 1740–1770

Description: The top overhangs the case on all four sides, has thumbnail molding at the front and sides, and is notched at the front corners. The case holds four lipped drawers, two in line over two slightly deeper drawers in line, each with a central brass escutcheon with bail pulls below a brass keyhole liner. The front skirt is shaped with scrolls and semicircular cutouts and drops leading to a central drop; the side skirts have reverse curves rising to a rounded arch and descending to a central drop. The four corner posts continue to form cabriole legs with Spanish feet with high pads below "ankle" moldings applied to the front and sides of the front

Dressing and Bureau Tables 219

legs and to the sides and rear of the back legs. The top consists of two butted boards pegged to the sides and the corner posts. The case is framed with mortise-and-tenon joints, with the sides and back pegged with four pins to the corner posts. The center drawer runners are tenoned to the skirt and back; the side drawer runners are rabbeted and nailed to the corner posts; the lower side drawer runners are shaped on their undersides to conform to the side skirts. There are no dustboards or bottom. On each drawer, the sides are dovetailed to the front and back; the bottoms are beveled on the front and side edges, let into a groove in the front and sides, and nailed to the underside of the back. On one drawer, the bottom consists of two butted boards with the grain parallel to the front; in the others, the grain of the two boards runs perpendicularly to the front.

Inscriptions: There is illegible writing in red on the outside of both sides of a lower drawer.

Condition: The table retains an old finish. The top has been repaired with three butterfly cleats. The brasses, possibly original, may have been lowered when later locks were installed. The side knee bracket on the left rear leg has been replaced, and both "ankle" moldings on the right front legs are replacements. The tip of the center drop on the front skirt has been reattached and may be a replacement. The left rear foot has been pieced, and one of the side drawer runners is a replacement.

Woods: American black walnut; southern yellow pine.

Dimensions: H 73.8; W 85.0; CW 74.1; D 52.5; CD 45.2.

Provenance: Dr. McStevens, Easton, Md.; by sale to Francis P. Garvan, New York, N. Y.

ONCE again, this is a type of dressing table often associated specifically with southern New Jersey, although it was a popular form throughout the Delaware Valley and its production was not circumscribed by colony boundaries. The distinguishing characteristics of this group are a four-square arrangement of drawers of nearly equal size (in the Yale table the lower drawers are only .5 cm deeper than the upper ones) and a rather rectilinear skirt, often with semi-circular notches and drops flanking a center drop of greater or lesser elaboration. On tables with this four-drawer arrangement, positive and negative semicircular arches and drops are relatively rare; they are also seen on a table formerly in the collection of Henry W. Erving that Nutting attributed to New England, and on a table formerly of the Lindens in Washington, D.C.[1] More often, only the positive drops are used.[2] On elaborate tables, the center drop could take the form of a heart-shaped motif, either suggested or completely enclosed, or could contain carving or some other motif.[3] A high chest of the kind that was probably made en suite with the Yale table has been published.[4] The Yale table was acquired from a Maryland source and initially catalogued as a Maryland product, although it does not have the characteristics usually associated with Maryland dressing tables today. A particular preference for this four-drawer arrangement in the Middle Atlantic region, however, may be indicated by its use on a late dressing table in the Yale collection (cat. 121) from Annapolis.

The Mabel Brady Garvan Collection 1930.2275

1. Nutting, *Treasury*, no. 422; *The Contents of the Lindens*, 22 January 1983 (New York: Christie, Manson, and Woods International, 1983), no. 339.
2. As examples, see *Antiques* 13, no. 4 (April 1928): 268; *Antiques* 111, no. 5 (May 1977): 833; Hagler, *American Queen Anne Furn.*, p. 43; Walter A. Dyer, "The American Lowboy: William & Mary–Queen Anne," *Antiquarian* 17, no. 2 (August 1931): 38; *Eighteenth Century American Furniture . . .*, 25 October 1969 (New York: Parke-Bernet Galleries, 1969), no. 106. For a variant with a single drawer in the lower tier, see *Antiques* 12, no. 6 (December 1927): 452.
3. *From Lenape Territory to Royal Province: New Jersey, 1600–1750* (Trenton: New Jersey State Museum, 1971), no. 190; *Antiques* 97, no. 5 (May 1970): 625; Hornor, pl. 17; Downs, fig. 321. For a related high chest, see Elizabeth Meg Schaefer, "Wright's Ferry Mansion," *Antiques* 122, no. 6 (December 1982): 1248.
4. *Important American Furniture and Related Decorative Arts*, Sale 5001, 27–29 January 1983 (New York: Sotheby's, 1983), no. 317, with restorations and repairs.

112

Dressing table
Philadelphia, Pennsylvania, 1745–1775

Description: The rectangular top overhangs the case on all four sides and has thumbnail molding at the front and sides and notched front corners. The case has chamfered and fluted front corners, with four flutes, and holds four drawers with cock-beaded edges. The top wide drawer has a central brass lock escutcheon flanked by matching escutcheons with bail pulls. The lower drawers have matching brasses. The front skirt is shaped with an arch, a scroll, and reverse curves leading to a central shaped drop; the side skirts are shaped to a central drop echoing that on the front; and the rear skirt is

shaped with deep reverse curves to a pointed arch. The four corner posts continue to form cabriole legs with scrolled knee brackets, and all four legs terminate in high, tongued trifid feet with high pads. The front legs are carved with a tripartite shell, with a flower above and three pendant husks below; the rear legs are not carved. The case is framed with mortise-and-tenon joints, with three pegs at the juncture of the sides and back to the corner posts. The drawer fronts and front of the case are veneered with "ripple"-grained mahogany. The vertical partitions are tenoned through the drawer divider. On each drawer, the sides are dovetailed to the front and back, the bottoms are let into grooves in the front and sides and nailed to the underside of the back, and running strips are applied to the bottom at the front and sides. Since the drawers are not lipped, small strips are nailed to the back of the case to serve as stops.

Inscriptions: The undersides of the left and right lower drawers are marked in pencil in a large script hand, "L" and "R" respectively. The same drawers have "I" and "II" scribed on the underside of their fronts. The drawer dividers are also correspondingly marked with roman numerals. A fragment of a modern shipping label is pasted to the inside of the back.

Condition: The top is quite thin, is of a different color from the case, and has been reattached with new blocks and transverse supports; it is probably a replacement. The right rear leg has been broken and repaired. There are minor repairs to the veneer and cock beading. The interiors of the drawers have been stained and varnished. Some of the drawer runners are new, and a new support under the top drawer has been added.

Woods: Mahogany and mahogany veneer; drawer sides and back, other elements, yellow poplar; back, other elements, Atlantic white cedar; drawer bottoms, drawer fronts, front of case beneath veneer, southern yellow pine.

Dimensions: H 74.5; W 83.9; CW 75.6; D 53.5; CD 45.6.

Exhibition: *Forgeries and Restorations*, no. 33.

Provenance: Henry V. Weil, New York, N. Y.; by sale in 1927 to Francis P. Garvan, New York, N. Y.

THIS dressing table is closely related to another example probably from the same shop and now in the collection of the Historical Society of Pennsylvania.[1] That table has an unconfirmed history of ownership by Samuel Taylor of Philadelphia prior to 1781; but the tradition, as attested to by

112a

Dressing and Bureau Tables 221

112

113

several early labels pasted to its drawers, including one dated as early as 1875, may have some validity. The chamfered, fluted corners and the shells carved on the front legs also point toward Philadelphia as the origin of this table. Similar carving seems to appear on two Philadelphia tables illustrated by Hornor.[2] Although this dressing table has been restored, it is still basically sound despite the apparent loss of its top.

The Mabel Brady Garvan Collection 1930.2508

1. James E. Mooney, "Furniture at the Historical Society of Pennsylvania," *Antiques* 113, no. 5 (May 1978): fig. 12. See also *Antiques* 13, no. 4 (April 1928): 274.
2. Hornor, pls. 74–75.

113

Dressing table
Pennsylvania, possibly Lancaster County, 1740–1770

Description: The top overhangs the case on all four sides, has thumbnail molding at the front and sides, and is notched at the front corners. The case encloses a single lipped drawer with a blind brass lock escutcheon flanked by matching escutcheons with bail pulls. The front skirt is elaborately shaped with arches and scrolls rising to a central pointed arch; the side skirts are shaped to paired reverse curves. The corner posts continue to form four cabriole legs, with flattened knees, and terminate in small, pointed, pad feet. The case is framed with mortise-and-tenon joints. The drawer sides are dovetailed to the front and back; the bottoms are let into a rabbet in the front and nailed to all four sides. The top edges of the drawer sides and back are rounded. The drawer runners are rabbeted on their upper edges to serve as guides and are rabbeted and nailed to the corner posts. The top consists of two butted boards and is held in place with glue blocks.

Inscriptions: "Y U" is stenciled in white paint on the inside of the back and underside of the drawer bottom.

Condition: Numerous scratches are evident on the top. The pointed "toe" of the left rear foot was restored in 1964; the side knee bracket on the right front leg is a replacement. Some of the glue blocks have been replaced, and screws have been added to five of them. The brasses are replacements.

Woods: American black walnut; yellow poplar.

Dimensions: H 74.9; W 89.0; CW 78.6; D 50.1; CD 43.0.

Bibliography: *Antiques* 14, no. 3 (September 1928): 189; *Catalogue, Early American Furniture . . . to Be Sold . . . By A. J. Pennypacker* (Pennsburg, Pa.: A. J. Pennypacker, [ca. 1929]), no. 539; Kirk, *Am. Furn. & Brit. Trad.*, fig. 1478.

Provenance: According to Charles Pennypacker, in a 1977 interview, this dressing table was purchased by him for his brother A. J. Pennypacker in 1924 or 1925 from a private home in Lititz, Pa.[1] It was acquired in 1929 from A. J. Pennypacker, Pennsburg, Pa., probably at auction, by Francis P. Garvan, New York, N. Y.

THIS dressing table is nearly identical to an unpublished example in a private collection that also was found in Lancaster County, Pennsylvania, in the early 1920s. These tables share the same exuberantly shaped skirts, rather straight cabriole legs with pointed "slipper" feet, and the somewhat unusual feature of a single drawer.

The Mabel Brady Garvan Collection 1930.2207

1. John J. Snyder to the writer, 24 March 1977.

114

Dressing table
Delaware Valley, possibly New Jersey, 1750–1780

Description: The top overhangs the case on all four sides and has thumbnail molding at the front and sides and notched front corners. It is pegged to the corner posts and the sides and stands above a cove molding nailed to the front and sides. The case holds four lipped drawers, one wide over three in line, with the lower center drawer wider and not as deep as the side drawers. The top drawer has a central brass lock escutcheon flanked by matching escutcheons with bail pulls. The lower drawers are fitted with matching lock escutcheons with bail pulls. The bottom section of all but two of the brasses has been clipped off, and the screws holding the pulls have been threaded into the drawer fronts without the use of nuts. The front skirt is shaped with round arches with a stepped, rounded top flanking reverse curves leading to a central rounded arch; the side skirts are shaped with paired reverse curves forming a stepped, central rounded arch. The four corner posts continue to form cabri-

114a

114

ole legs with trifid, tongued feet; the front knees are carved with a shell with a pendant below. The case is of mortise-and-tenon construction; the sides and back are pegged three times to the corner posts, the front rails only once. The skirt is a single shaped board, and the vertical partitions between the lower drawers are tenoned through the drawer divider. The knees of both front legs and of the left rear leg are built up with an added piece pegged in place, which was then, in the case of the front legs, carved en suite with the rest of the leg. In each drawer, the sides are dovetailed to the front and back; the bottoms are beveled on their front edge, let into a groove in the front and rabbets in the side, and nailed to the underside of the back, with running strips applied to each side of the bottom.

Condition: The table retains an old finish, with the exception of the recently refinished top. The right side and the back of the top drawer have been reglued. Both front feet have been repaired.

Woods: American black walnut; back, southern yellow pine; drawer sides and backs, yellow poplar; drawer bottoms, Atlantic white cedar.

Dimensions: H 75.6; W 88.5; CW 73.4; D 51.5; CD 46.8.

Bibliography: *Antiques* 11, no. 3 (March 1927): 172; *Antiquarian* 9, no. 2 (September 1927): 11; Nutting, *Treasury*, no. 408; Thomas Hamilton Ormsbee, "Antique Furniture with Double Uses," *American Collector* 12, no. 1 (February 1943): 11; Nagel, pl. 10b.

Provenance: Frances Wolfe Carey, Haddonfield, N. J., stated in a letter of 8 August 1927 to A. W. Clarke, Mr. Garvan's agent: "I am enclosing a photograph of the little low-boy which I procured near here recently. . . . This piece has been in one family for generations, and I procured it personally from the owner." Francis P. Garvan, New York, N. Y., purchased the table in 1927.

DRESSING tables with this drawer arrangement, shell carved legs, and trifid feet are usually assigned a Philadelphia origin. Here, although the quality of the carving is high, the use of ill-fitting brasses gives the table an air of provinciality that suggests it may have been made near where it was found in New Jersey. Other related versions are known, some without carving on the knees, others with chamfered fluted corners, and many with slightly varying skirt arrangements.[1] The use of the tongued trifid foot is usually cited as evidence of an Irish influence in furniture of the Delaware Valley.[2] The building up of three of the knees on this table with added facings pegged in place is an unusual feature.

The Mabel Brady Garvan Collection 1930.2088

1. For related tables, see Nutting, *Treasury*, no. 403; Miller, 1:nos. 687–689; a more elaborate table in *Sack Coll.*, 6:1635 no. P4805, with voluted knee brackets; Hornor, fig. 58; and a more loosely related version possibly made in Delaware, illustrated in *Sack Coll.*, 5:1288 no. P4283.
2. David Stockwell, "Irish Influence in Pennsylvania Queen Anne Furniture," *Antiques* 79, no. 3 (March 1961): 269–271.

115

Dressing table
Delaware Valley, 1750–1780

Description: The rectangular top overhangs the case on all four sides, has thumbnail molding at the front and sides, and is notched at the front corners. The case holds four lipped drawers, one wide drawer over three in line, with the lower side drawers deeper. The front skirt is shaped in a repetitive pattern of scrolls and drops; the side skirts are shaped to

224 *American Case Furniture*

simple paired reverse curves forming a pointed arch. The four corner posts continue to form cabriole legs terminating in tongued trifid feet. The top consists of two butted boards and is pegged to the four corner posts. The case is of mortise-and-tenon construction, with the back and sides pegged three times to the corner posts and the top front rail and drawer divider once. The skirt is pinned twice. The vertical partitions between the lower drawers are tenoned through the drawer divider, and a horizontal board is applied between them and the skirt to elevate the lower middle drawer. The side drawer runners are rabbeted and nailed to the corner posts; the runners for the center lower drawer are rabbeted and nailed to the vertical partitions at the front and housed in the back; the side drawer runners for the lower drawers are rabbeted around the partition, let into a groove in the skirt, and housed in the back. On each drawer, the sides are dovetailed to the front and back; the bottoms are beveled on their front and side edges, let into a groove in the drawer front and a rabbet in the sides, and nailed to the underside of the back, with running strips nailed to the bottom at the sides and front. The top edges of the drawer sides are rounded.

Inscriptions: Written in red ink on the inside of the top drawer is "37" next to a modern printed label bearing the same number in ink.

Condition: New screws and glue blocks have been added to secure the top. The front edge of the top has been repaired at the center. The brasses are replacements.

Woods: American black walnut; drawer sides and backs, yellow poplar; drawer bottoms, Atlantic white cedar.

Dimensions: H 72.4; W 87.3; CW 77.2; D 51.5; CD 45.6.

Exhibition: *Early Furniture Made in New Jersey, 1690–1870* (Newark, N. J.: Newark Museum, 1958), no. 13.

Bibliography: *Antiques* 11, no. 5 (May 1927): 354; *Antiques* 12, no. 6 (June 1927): 499; *Eighteenth Century American Furniture . . . Sold by Order of Mrs. Gertrude H. Camp, "The Hayloft," Whitemarsh, Pa.*, Sale 2222, 20–21 January 1928 (New York: Anderson Galleries, 1928), no. 43; Nutting, *Treasury*, no. 416; Miller, 1:fig. 695.

Provenance: Probably firm of Winick & Sherman, New York, N. Y.; probably by sale to Mrs. Gertrude H. Camp, Whitemarsh, Pa.; acquired at auction in 1928 by Francis P. Garvan, New York, N. Y.

115

ALTHOUGH this dressing table has been exhibited as a New Jersey object, which it may well be, there is as yet no firm evidence on which to conclude that it was made on one side of the Delaware River or the other. The common combination of walnut, cedar, and yellow pine suggests the Delaware Valley, and the simple repetitive shaping of the skirt lacks the vitality of some other related tables and may point toward its being an example of simple city or rural furniture. A closely related table appeared on the market in 1984, but without an early history.[1]

The Mabel Brady Garvan Collection 1930.2627

1. Correspondence, YUAG object file.

116

Dressing table
Philadelphia, Pennsylvania, 1760–1780
(en suite with cat. 147)

Description: The top of the case has thumbnail molding at the front and sides and overhangs the case on all four sides. It stands above a cove molding applied to the case at the front and sides. The case holds four lipped drawers, including one wide drawer over three in line, with the lower center drawer of greater width and depth. The wide drawer is fitted with a central brass lock escutcheon flanked by pierced escutcheons with bail pulls, the lower side drawers are fitted with pierced escutcheons with bail pulls, and the lower center drawer has a brass button pull. The lower middle drawer is carved with a shell containing a central flower contained within an arc and flanked by scrolled acanthus leafage. The front corners of the case have engaged fluted corner columns with three flutes, and the front skirt is shaped to deep scrolls and a central drop, with the scrolls carved with leafage and the drop containing a stylized carved shell. The case is supported by four cabriole legs terminating in claw-and-ball feet, with knee brackets shaped to reverse curves; the knee brackets and knees of the front legs are carved with acanthus leafage; and the rear legs are not carved. The front edge of the top and the flutes of the quarter columns are painted black, and black paint is used on the legs, in the interstices of the carving, and on the claw-and-ball feet. The top consists of two butted boards and is secured to the case with multiple horizontal glue blocks and with vertical glue blocks in the corners. The case is of mortise-and-tenon construction, with the back secured to the rear legs with three pegs. The partitions between the lower drawers extend the depth of the case and are housed in a groove in the back and nailed through the back. There is no dustboard below the wide drawer, which is supported by side runners. There are full dustboards below the three lower drawers, supported by strips nailed to the case sides. The vertical partitions between the lower drawers are tenoned through the drawer divider. On each drawer, the sides are dovetailed to the front and back; the bottoms are let into grooves in the front and sides and nailed to the underside of the back, with running strips applied to the front and sides of the bottom.

Inscriptions: The modern "H. G. BARNES / 100 / 6 DIST PA" in a circle appears on the underside of one of the modern lids

116

to the new compartments in the wide drawer; there is a modern drawing on the underside of the other lid.

Condition: There have been losses to the applied acanthus scrolls on the lower middle drawer; the outline of the original pattern is still visible. The pierced lock escutcheon on the wide drawer is a replacement made in 1974, cast from the escutcheon on the lowest drawer in the upper case of the matching high chest (cat. 147); it replaces a solid escutcheon which was not original to the object. The other brasses on the wide drawer appear to be replacements. The wide drawer has been partitioned at the front into small compartments, two of which have lids with white ceramic pulls screwed in place. Some of the glue blocks securing the top are replacements, as are some of the drawer guides. New strips have been nailed to the insides of the two lower drawers, to act as supports for trays, now missing.

Woods: American black walnut; drawer sides, other elements, yellow poplar; drawer bottoms, backs, other elements, Atlantic white cedar.

Dimensions: H 78.5; W 84.6; CW 78.9; D 52.7; CD 44.7.

Bibliography: *Antiques* 7, no. 6 (June 1925): 303; Charles Over Cornelius, *Early American Furniture* (New York:

D. Appleton-Century Co., 1926), pl. 28; Nutting, *Treasury*, no. 427; *YUAG Bulletin* 4, no. 2 (December 1930): front cover; Halsey and Tower, *Homes of Our Ancestors*, fig. 54; Rogers, "Garvan Furn. (1960)," fig. 12; Robert Bishop, *How to Know American Antique Furniture* (New York: E. P. Dutton, 1973), fig. 69; "American Arts and the American Experience," *Museum News* 53, no. 3 (November 1974): 39; Montgomery, "1776—Furniture," p. 59; Montgomery and Kane, *American Art, 1750–1800*, fig. 34; Montgomery, "Regional Preferences and Characteristics," fig. 7; Charles F. Montgomery, "Francis P. Garvan: He Would Educate the Nation," *Arts in Virginia* 19, no. 3 (Spring 1979): 15.

Provenance: This dressing table and its matching high chest (cat. 147) have a history of ownership by Henry Wynkoop (1737–1816) and his wife Susanna Wanshaer Wynkoop (d. 1776), who were married in 1761, of Bucks County, Pa. In Wynkoop's will, dated 7 October 1813, he bequeathed to his daughter Christina several objects including his "black walnut chest with drawers, dressing table & chairs."[1] Christina Wynkoop (1763–1841) married Dr. Reading Beatty (1757–1831) in 1786, and according to tradition the objects passed to their daughter Mary (b. 1798). Mary Beatty married the Reverend Robert Steel (1794–1862) of Abingdon, Pa., and was still living in 1873. By tradition, the objects passed to her daughter Mary (b. 1839), who married Dr. Samuel D. Harvey of Jenkintown, Pa., in 1863. Objects then passed to their daughter in the fifth generation, Mary Steel Harvey (b. 1864), of Baltimore, Md. Miss Harvey sold the dressing table and high chest to dealer Henry V. Weil, New York, N. Y., possibly in 1925; Weil sold the pair to Francis P. Garvan, New York, N. Y.

This dressing table and its matching high chest (cat. 147) are representative of the best high-style Philadelphia furniture of the third quarter of the eighteenth century. They take on additional importance through their strong history of ownership by Judge Henry Wynkoop, a leading figure in Bucks County, Pennsylvania, who served for many years as associate justice of the county court. Among his many other acts of public service, Wynkoop represented Pennsylvania in the Continental Congress from 1779 to 1783 and was a delegate to the House of Representatives during the first United States Congress (1789–1791). A portrait of Wynkoop painted by Rembrandt Peale about 1810 survives, although his house burned in the early twentieth century. Wynkoop is buried in the cemetery of the Low Dutch Reformed Church in Richboro, Pennsylvania.[2] Like the high chest, this dressing table exhibits the rich vocabulary of ornament found on Philadelphia furniture, with some of the carved details organized and highlighted through the use of black paint. A closely related example, formerly in the Jacob Paxson Temple collection, is now at Winterthur.[3] A nearly identical skirt can be seen on an example in the Museum of Fine Arts, Boston, which, like the Winterthur table, is made of the more expensive imported mahogany.[4]

The Mabel Brady Garvan Collection 1930.2001

1. Docket 4308, estate papers of Henry Wynkoop, Bucks County Courthouse, Doylestown, Pa.
2. For biographical information on Wynkoop and his descendants, see John Sparhawk Wurts, "Judge Henry Wynkoop," in *A Collection of Papers Read before the Bucks County Historical Society*, vol. 3 (1909), pp. 197–217; Joseph M. Beatty, Jr., "Letters of Judge Henry Wynkoop," *Pennsylvania Magazine of History and Biography* 38 (1914): 39–45; Virginia B. Geyer, "Further Notes on Henry Wynkoop," *Bucks County Historical Society Journal* 1, no. 10 (Fall 1976): 1–12; *Who Was Who during the American Revolution* (Indianapolis: Bobbs-Merrill, 1976), p. 390; and *Record of the Family of Charles Beatty, Who Emigrated from Ireland to America in 1729* (Steubenville, Ohio: W. R. Allison, 1873), pp. 69–77.
3. Downs, no. 334.
4. Hipkiss, no. 54.

117

Dressing table
Pennsylvania or Maryland, 1760–1780

Description: The top overhangs the case on all four sides and has thumbnail molding at the front and sides and canted front corners. It rests above cove molding applied to the case. The case has chamfered and fluted front corners, with four flutes, and lightly stop-chamfered rear corners. There is one long drawer over three in line, the center lower drawer being of greater depth. The top drawer has a brass lock escutcheon, flanked by matching escutcheons with bail pulls; the lower drawers have matching brasses. The front skirt is elaborately shaped with paired reverse curves flanking scrolls and a central drop; the side skirts are shaped to simple pointed arches with a fillet at the apex. The four corner posts continue below the case to form cabriole legs with claw-and-ball feet; the front knees are carved with a lambrequin motif. The top is attached with glue blocks, the case is of frame construction, and the back consists of two butted boards.

117

There is no dustboard below the top drawer, but dustboards are used under the bottom drawers. The vertical partitions between the lower drawers are tenoned through the drawer divider; the transverse interior partitions between the lower drawers are tongue and grooved to the vertical partitions. The dustboards are rabbeted to the skirt and supported at the rear by strips nailed to the case; the middle dustboard is also nailed to the transverse partitions. The drawer sides are dovetailed to the front and back; the bottoms are beveled on their front and side edges, let into grooves in the drawer front and sides, and nailed to the underside of the back. The rear feet are carved from two butted blocks.

Inscriptions: The modern "304" is written in yellow chalk on the inside of the left side of the top drawer; another modern "#223R" is written in white chalk on the outside of the right side of the same drawer.

Condition: This dressing table has had several repairs. The top has been pieced at the rear and reattached with new glue blocks and new supports at the sides. The cove molding is crisp and clean and may be a replacement. The dustboard under the lower right drawer is a replacement, and all four front knee brackets are new. The upper left corner of the top drawer front has been repaired, the left side of the same drawer is a replacement, and the bottom has been pieced and renailed; it may also be a replacement. New running strips have been added to some drawers. The brasses are replacements, as is the bottom of the center lower drawer.

Woods: American black walnut; southern yellow pine; drawer bottoms, Atlantic white cedar.

Dimensions: H 76.8; W 91.8; CW 81.4; D 54.1; CD 47.0.

Bibliography: "Early Furniture of Pennsylvania: The Notable Reifsnyder Collection," *Good Furniture* 30 (February 1928): 88 fig. 5; *Reifsnyder Coll.*, no. 618.

Provenance: Howard Reifsnyder, Philadelphia, Pa.; acquired at auction in 1929 by Francis P. Garvan, New York, N. Y.

THIS heavy, sturdy walnut dressing table exhibits several characteristics found on related examples made both in the Philadelphia area and down into Maryland. The drawer arrangement, the elaborately scrolled and arched skirt, and the fluted chamfered corners are characteristic of these large Middle Colonies tables.[1] The lambrequin motif on the front knees raises the specter of William Savery (1721/22–1787), but this table differs from documented Savery examples in several important particulars, and any association with his shop is at best tenuous.[2] A related table is in the collection of Gunston Hall.

The Mabel Brady Garvan Collection 1930.2062

1. Hummel, *American Chippendale Furn.* fig. 107, see also fig. 82; Elder, *Maryland Queen Anne and Chippendale Furn.*, pp. 67–74.
2. PMA, *Three Centuries*, pp. 50–51, cat. 40. Savery's preferred drawer arrangement was three drawers in line above two below flanking the kneehole, and his treatment of the front skirt was also different.

118

Dressing table
Delaware Valley, ca. 1769

Description: The top of this dressing table overhangs the case on all four sides and has thumbnail molding at the front and sides. The case contains one wide drawer over three in line, with the center lower drawer being both wider and deeper, and the drawers are lipped. The front skirt is shaped

118

with multiple reverse curves leading to an arch at the center; the side skirts have paired flathead arches flanking a central drop. The corner posts continue below the case to form cabriole legs that terminate in trifid feet. The top is pocket screwed to the case on all four sides, and there are glue blocks behind the top front rail. The case is of mortise-and-tenon construction with three pegs used to secure the sides to the legs. The drawer sides are dovetailed to the front and back. The bottoms are let into a rabbet in the sides and a groove in the front and are nailed to the underside of the back with rosehead nails. Runners are applied to the drawer bottoms. The side drawer runners within the case are nailed; runners for middle drawers are nailed to vertical partitions.

Inscriptions: Scratched in old script on the outside of the back of the lower center drawer is "1769." The right side of the left drawer has a pencil inscription, partially illegible, on the outside, which includes "Davis." Written in white chalk on the outside of the back is "3."

Condition: The side knee brackets on the right front and rear legs are replacements, as are the brasses. The rear 12 cm of the top has been pieced, and there are many small dents and scratches on the object. The top edges of the lower side drawers have been pieced, and the upper right corner of the central lower drawer has been repaired. The top edge of the back of the left lower drawer has been replaced.

Woods: American black cherry; southern yellow pine.

Dimensions: H 72.6; W 87.7; CW 78.1; D 50.5; CD 47.5.

Provenance: Francis P. Garvan, New York, N. Y.

"Davis" may be the name of an owner or possibly of the maker; in either case, it remains only a clue that so far has not yielded any convincing results. The use of cherry for a Delaware Valley dressing table was not customary but was by no means unknown; cherry appears in the stock of Philadelphia cabinetmakers, in less quantity than with the more desired walnut, but with some regularity.

The Mabel Brady Garvan Collection 1930.2037

1. Hornor, p. 45.

119

Bureau table
Philadelphia, Pennsylvania, 1760–1790

Description: The rectangular top overhangs the case on all four sides and has a complex applied molding on its front and sides that extends to the front and sides of the case. The case holds a wide lipped drawer at the top above banks of three graduated lipped drawers flanking a central recess. A single blind drawer is at the top of the recess, which encloses a fielded paneled door leading to an interior fitted with a single shelf. There are engaged fluted quarter columns at the front corners of the table and below an applied base molding at the front and sides. The table is supported by six bracket feet. The top is dovetailed to the sides and is supported by blocks attached to the outside of the back, by transverse braces nailed to the underside of the top, and by horizontal blocks glued to the top rail. The bottom also consists of two boards dovetailed to the sides. The back is made of two horizontal butted boards fitted to a rabbet in the case sides and the bottom and nailed with rosehead nails. There are full thin dustboards rabbeted to the drawer dividers and fitted to grooves in the sides of the case, with applied drawer guides on their edges. The base molding is applied with pegs, and the triangular rear brackets are dovetailed to the rear side

Dressing and Bureau Tables 229

119

Woods: Mahogany; drawer bottoms, other elements, Atlantic white cedar; drawer sides, back, other elements, yellow poplar; large block at left rear foot, white oak.

Dimensions: H 86.1; W 90.4; CW 86.5; D 54.0; CD 47.2.

Exhibition: *Forgeries and Restorations*, no. 28.

Bibliography: Evans, "Bureau Table," fig. 3; Kirk, *Am. Furn. & Brit. Trad.*, fig. 534.

Provenance: The table was purchased by Henry Hammond Taylor, a dealer from Bridgeport, Conn., from a Miss Anne Seegee, also of Bridgeport. According to tradition, the table was owned by Ruth (Fry) Buckley, Miss Seegee's great-great-grandmother, and was the work of John Goddard of Newport, R.I. The table was purchased from Taylor by Francis P. Garvan, New York, N.Y.

KNOWN in the mid eighteenth century as a bureau table or bureau dressing table, this form was most popular in Philadelphia, although examples were also made in Massachusetts, Rhode Island (cat. 109), and elsewhere.[1] Designs for the form, which is thoroughly English, were published by Chippendale, and many English examples are known, including some attributed to Chippendale's workshop.[2] The Yale bureau table was probably in the middle economic range of Philadelphia examples. More elaborate versions were embellished with carving on the feet, blind drawer, and moldings or had a second set of engaged fluted quarter columns flanking the prospect door.[3] An example at Winterthur (66.138) is fitted with a slider above the top wide drawer and has banks of only two small drawers, rather than the more customary three.[4] Less expensive models lacked the quarter columns, which added £1 to the cost according to the 1786 Philadelphia price book, and the blind drawer in the kneehole; such a basic version is in the collection of the Metropolitan Museum (51.126), which also has restored feet.[5] Although Chippendale's designs for this form show four feet across the front, some drawings in the Gillows estimate books do not include the two center feet, and no doubt a percentage of American tables were made in this fashion.[6]

The Mabel Brady Garvan Collection 1930.2316

feet. The feet have horizontal and vertical shaped blocking nailed to the bottom; small shims are used at the top of the feet so that they meet the height of the base molding. The drawer sides are dovetailed to the front and back; the bottoms are fitted to a groove in the front and sides, are beveled on their front and side edges, and are nailed to the underside of the back.

Inscriptions: There is an illegible chalk inscription on the underside of the base and a column of added figures in chalk on the inside of the right side.

Condition: When the table was acquired by Mr. Garvan, it was missing the two front center feet. Based on evidence visible at the time, these feet were replaced by Emile Mazzola in 1961. The right front foot is a replacement. There have been many repairs to the edges of the drawers and to the drawer dividers, and new running strips have been added. The brasses are replacements, and the table has been thoroughly refinished. One transverse brace under the top is missing. The bottom of the right side rear foot has been pieced, and the side feet on the left have been repaired. The base molding on the right side has been replaced from the front to the beginning of the rear foot; the replaced piece is nailed to a little strip glued to the bottom.

1. Evans, "Bureau Table," pp. 24–36, discusses the origins and evolution of this form in detail.
2. See Christopher Gilbert, *The Life and Works of Thomas Chippendale*, vol. 2 (New York: Macmillan, 1978), figs. 415–417. For other English examples, see Kirk, *Am. Furn. & Brit. Trad.*, fig. 535; and R. W. Symonds,

230 American Case Furniture

English Furniture from Charles II to George II (New York: International Studio, 1929), p. 95 fig. 60.

3. *Sack Coll.*, 7:1877 no. P5097; Hornor, fig. 197; Nutting, *Treasury*, no. 613.

4. Hummel, *American Chippendale Furn.* fig. 109.

5. Evans, "Bureau Table," fig. 2; Fitzgerald, p. 293.

6. Kirk, *Am. Furn. & Brit. Trad.*, figs. 533, 537; *Antiques* 95, no. 4 (April 1969): 483.

120

Dressing table
Pennsylvania, 1765–1795

Description: The rectangular top projects at the front and sides and has half-round molding at the front and sides above cove molding applied to the case at the front and sides. The case is of mortise-and-tenon construction, with the sides secured to the legs with three pegs and the top and bottom front rails with a single peg. The case holds one wide drawer over three in line, the center one deeper, with brass escutcheons and bail pulls. The corner posts continue to form four straight legs, with scrolled knee brackets. The bottom front rail is shaped to paired reverse curves flanking scrolls with a drop at center; the sides are shaped to paired reverse curves. The top is a single board pegged to the case, with triangular glue blocks on the inside as reinforcements. The back and sides are single boards; the vertical partitions between the lower drawers are tenoned through the drawer divider. The drawers are lipped, and the drawer sides are dovetailed to the front and back. The drawer bottoms are let into grooves in the front and sides and pinned to the underside of the back. There are mortises cut in the rear face of each rear leg.

Condition: All the knee brackets except the right side rear example have been replaced. The brasses are replacements, and a lock, now missing, was once fitted to the lower right drawer. The dustboards under the bottom drawers, which are nailed to a rabbet in the front rail and to a strip, possibly original, pegged to the back, are replacements. A large shrinkage crack in the top has been repaired and glued. All four legs were once fitted with stem casters. The bottom edges of the drawer sides have been pieced, and the bottom of the wide drawer has been pieced and renailed.

120

Woods: American black walnut; drawer sides and backs, yellow poplar; drawer bottoms, Atlantic white cedar; back, white oak.

Dimensions: H 75.7; W 86.6; CW 80.7; D 53.8; CD 50.5.

Bibliography: Kirk, *Am. Furn. & Brit. Trad.*, fig. 1480.

Provenance: Francis D. Brinton, West Chester, Pa.; by sale to Francis P. Garvan, New York, N. Y.

A PENNSYLVANIA origin for this simple dressing table is suggested by its construction of walnut, yellow poplar, white cedar, and white oak. The attribution is buttressed by the acquisition of the dressing table from Francis D. Brinton, a noted collector and dealer from West Chester, Pennsylvania, who specialized in objects from Chester County and the surrounding area. The drawer arrangement found here is common to many dressing tables, both high-style and otherwise, from eastern Pennsylvania and Maryland. The straight legs on the Yale example were probably simply a less expensive alternative to cabriole legs, although there may have been an attempt to evoke the feeling of the so-called Marlborough legs.[1] Related English examples have been published.[2]

Dressing and Bureau Tables 231

The Mabel Brady Garvan Collection 1930.2387

1. An unusual example of a Philadelphia dressing table with Marlborough legs is illustrated in Hornor, pl. 283.
2. Kirk, *Am. Furn. & Brit. Trad.*, pls. 1479, 1481; Christopher Gilbert, *An Exhibition of Town and Country Furniture Illustrating the Vernacular Tradition* (Leeds, England: Temple Newsam House, 1972), no. 10.

121

Dressing table
Attributed to John Shaw (1745–1829) or
Archibald Chisholm (d. 1810) or both
Annapolis, Maryland, ca. 1780–1785

121

Description: The rectangular top overhangs the case slightly on all four sides and has cyma molding at the front and sides. The case holds four drawers with cock-beaded edges, two in line over two slightly deeper drawers in line. The top drawers are fitted with brass keyhole liners, and each drawer contains a dual brass disk and bail pull. There is applied bead molding at the base of the front and sides. The four posts continue to form square tapered legs. The top is pegged to the corner posts and reinforced with small blocks inside the case on all four sides. The bead molding is run on strips that are rabbeted to overlap the corner posts, which have a shallow groove to accept the molding, and nailed to the front and sides from underneath. There is a board fitted to each side of the case on the interior to which the side drawer runners are nailed. The case is constructed with mortise-and-tenon joints without pegs. The middle drawer runners are housed in the drawer divider and bottom rail and tenoned to the back, with a drawer guide nailed in turn to them. There are no dustboards, and there is no bottom to the table. The drawer sides are dovetailed to the front and back; the bottoms are beveled on their front and side edges, let into grooves in the drawer front and sides, and nailed to the underside of the back; blocks, mitered at the front corners, are glued to the bottom at the front and sides.

Condition: It has been suggested that cove molding may have been applied to the case below the top, but since the table has been refinished and there are no nail holes present, this supposition, based on the presence of such molding on other Shaw/Chisholm objects, must remain conjectural.

Woods: Mahogany; yellow poplar.

Dimensions: H 73.6; W 86.6; CW 83.8; D 44.5; CD 41.4.

Exhibitions: *Charles Carroll of Carrollton (1737–1832) and His Family: An Exhibition of Portraits, Furniture, Silver, and Manuscripts at the Baltimore Museum of Art, September 19–October 30, 1937* (Baltimore, Md.: United States Commission for the Celebration of the Two Hundredth Anniversary of the Birth of Charles Carroll of Carrollton, 1937), p. 126; Elder, *Maryland Queen Anne and Chippendale Furn.*, no. 52; YUAG, "Southern Furn.," no. 8; Elder and Bartlett, *John Shaw*, no. 12.

Bibliography: Henry J. Berkley, "Early Maryland Furniture," *Antiques* 18, no. 3 (September 1930): fig. 5; William M. Hornor, Jr., "John Shaw, of the Great Days of Annapolis," *International Studio* 98, no. 406 (March 1931): fig. 5.

Provenance: For more than half a century it has been said that this object was owned originally by Charles Carroll (1737–1832) of Carrollton, Md., but to date no firm evidence to substantiate this tradition has been discovered. It also has been stated that the table was owned by Dr. Henry J. Berkley, an early collector of Maryland furniture, but this does not seem to have been the case. Berkley was the first to publish the table, in *Antiques* in 1930, and he probably lent his photograph of the table to William MacPherson Hornor,

who published it the next year in *International Studio*, "courtesy of Dr. Henry J. Berkley," whereby the tradition began. Mr. Garvan's records indicate that the table was purchased from R. T. Haines Halsey, New York, N. Y., and make no mention of Dr. Berkley.

WHEN acquired by Mr. Garvan, this object was catalogued as a serving table. It does resemble lift-top cellarettes attributed to Shaw that are somewhat similar in size and have facades decorated with inlay to simulate drawers, suggesting (perhaps) that the cellarettes were made to resemble objects like the Yale table because both were used simultaneously in drawing or dining rooms.[1] But it is more likely that it was made as a late example of the dressing- or chamber-table form.[2] The most recent research has indicated that while this table is undoubtedly from the shop of John Shaw or his sometime partner Archibald Chisholm, either working alone or in partnership, there is not enough evidence to assign the table to either of them individually.[3]

The Mabel Brady Garvan Collection 1930.2994

1. Elder and Bartlett, *John Shaw*, nos. 23, 32. A similar but much wider form, described as a sideboard table and attributed to Newport, has been published; see *Antiques* 107, no. 5 (May 1975): 785. See also Nutting, *Treasury*, no. 1070.
2. Another late example of the form, made in Connecticut, is illustrated in Kirk, *Conn. Furn.*, no. 187.
3. Elder and Bartlett, *John Shaw*, pp. 69–70 and passim.

High Chests of Drawers

Generally made to match dressing tables and also used in chambers, high chests of drawers (generally referred to today as highboys) consist of a lower case resembling an enlarged dressing table surmounted by an upper case that is, in essence, a chest of drawers. The upper case occasionally contains a blind frieze drawer, and the flat tops of early examples were often used for the display of small and valuable articles. A few high chests were originally fitted with special steps for the display of these goods (cat. 137). Introduced in this country by the 1690s, the earliest high chests were the products of cabinetmakers who had the ability to dovetail boards and to veneer carcasses of native woods with highly figured veneers of more exotic and visually interesting species. More vertical in stance than seventeenth-century furniture, less stable, and often with swirling, active surfaces of rich veneer, the high chest was the prime example of the new aesthetic that is generally referred to today as the William and Mary style. The collection includes seven early examples, each supported by six turned legs joined with stretchers shaped in conformity with the skirt of the lower case. Of particular interest are two veneered examples (cats. 122, 126) and a rare walnut high chest from Pennsylvania (cat. 128). New England high chests dominate the collection in the period from 1730 to 1790, with some seventeen examples included. By this time, high chests were supported by four cabriole legs terminating in various types of feet, and most examples were embellished with a scrolled pediment. An unusual example, made of ten woods and two veneers and possibly from Rhode Island (cat. 132), a Salem high chest with painted graining (cat. 134), a high chest signed by John Townsend of Newport and dated 1759 (cat. 140), and an example attributed to Eliphalet Chapin (cat. 146) are among the most notable New England examples at Yale. A cherry high chest (cat. 139) from Long Island is a rare example of New York–area case furniture in the collection. The Philadelphia area is represented by only three examples, including the walnut high chest owned originally by Judge Henry Wynkoop and made in Philadelphia (cat. 147) and a massive example with bird-carved knees from a more rural area of Pennsylvania (cat. 149).

- pulvinated frieze with blind drawer
- cornice moldings
- upper case
- midmolding
- lower case
- double half-round molding
- cup-turned leg
- stretcher
- turned foot

122

High chest of drawers
Boston area or New York area, 1700–1720
(see pl. 11)

Description: The high chest is in two cases. The upper case is crowned at the front and sides with complex cornice molding above a pulvinated frieze containing a blind drawer. The upper case contains six drawers: three in line, with the center drawer of greater width, above three graduated drawers, each separated by double half-round molding applied to the case. The upper middle drawer and each of the three wide drawers contain a central brass lock escutcheon flanked by matching escutcheons with drop pulls and are divided into two panels of burl veneer outlined by herringbone veneer. The two upper side drawers contain a central brass and are veneered with a single burl panel outlined by herringbone veneer. There is base molding at the front and sides of the upper case, and the upper case rests within midmolding applied to the top of the lower case. The lower case contains three drawers in line, with the outer drawers of greater depth and the center drawer of greater width, again outlined and separated by cock beading applied to the case. These drawers are veneered and fitted with brasses in a manner parallel to the three drawers in line in the upper case. The front skirt is edged with cock beading and is shaped to a central rounded arch above stepped reverse curves and flanked by reverse curves forming a pointed arch. The cock-beaded side skirts are shaped to a single pointed arch. The chest is supported by six cup-turned legs joined by flat stretchers shaped in conformity with the skirt at the front and sides and straight across the back and by six turned feet. The top and bottom of the upper case are dovetailed to the sides. The vertical backboards are butted together and nailed to a rabbet in the top and sides and to the bottom; they extend slightly below the bottom. The front face of the case and the drawer fronts are veneered. There is a full dustboard under the blind frieze drawer and under the three small drawers in line. The drawer runners are let into grooves in the case sides; the vertical partitions between the drawers in line are tenoned through the drawer divider. Small blocks are glued to the inside of the back as stops. The applied base molding rests within the projecting midmolding of the lower case, and there is no top to the lower case. The back of the lower case is a single horizontal board dovetailed to the sides. The front posts are tapered, being thicker at the bottom, and they extend the full height of the case; the rear posts are only half the height of the case. There is a center runner for each drawer in the lower case, tenoned in place and with a block applied as a stop to its rear end. The vertical transverse partitions between the drawers are triangular, nailed to the front rail, and tenoned through the back. The cock beading on the front and side skirts is applied with rosehead nails. The legs in each corner are doweled to the corner posts; the two legs in the center of the front are doweled to rabbeted blocks applied to the inside of the skirt. Strips are nailed to each side of the lower case. Each of the front and side stretchers is made from two boards. On each drawer, the sides are dovetailed to the front and back, and the bottoms are nailed to a rabbet in the front and to the underside of the sides and back, with running strips used on

High Chests of Drawers 237

the wide drawers. The lock escutcheon on the small center drawer in the upper case is blind.

Condition: One backboard and one drawer runner in the upper case are replacements. The right brass on the lowest drawer in the upper case is a replacement; the other brasses appear to be original, although their locations may have been switched. There have been repairs to the platforms above the legs and minor repairs to the veneer.

Woods: Drawer fronts, front face, walnut veneer and a burl veneer on eastern white pine; applied moldings, cock beading, walnut; legs, feet, stretchers, sides of upper and lower case, soft maple; top and bottom of upper case, aspen; drawer linings, dustboards, drawer dividers, back of upper case, dowels in feet, other elements, chestnut.

Dimensions: H 167.6; W 102.8; UCW 91.8; LCW 94.8; D 54.3; UCD 47.2; LCD 50.6.

Exhibition: *Girl Scouts Exhibition*, no. 510.

Bibliography: Ormsbee, *Story Am. Furn.*, fig. 111a; Nagel, pl. 6b; Sack, *Fine Points*, p. 175; Comstock, *Concise Encyclopedia*, p. 34 pl. 6b (as Henry Ford Museum); Kirk, *Early Am. Furn.*, fig. 68; "American Arts and the American Experience," *Museum News* 53, no. 3 (November 1974): 37–38; Kirk, *Am. Furn. & Brit. Trad.*, fig. 546.

Provenance: Israel Sack, New York, N. Y.; by sale in February 1921 to Francis P. Garvan, New York, N. Y.

ALTHOUGH it has been published and catalogued for many years as a Massachusetts high chest, probably from the Boston area, more recent research by Benno M. Forman raised the strong possibility that this object was made in the New York area. As cited by John T. Kirk, Forman's suggestion of a New York origin was based on the following line of reasoning: "the brasses are a type used in New York; the drawer arrangement at the top of the upper case is not a Massachusetts pattern; the low-hanging ogee curves of the skirt are found in New York; flat bottom turnings on the legs above the ankle baluster combined with a flare under the cup are New York features; and finally, the veneer panel down the center of the cases again indicates New York."[1] The same use of three drawers in line at the top of the upper case—sometimes of equal size and sometimes with the center drawer of greater width, as on the Yale example—is found on a core group of related high chests, most of which have been linked to the New York area. This group includes the signed and dated high chest made in 1726 by Samuel Clement

122a

(w. ca. 1698–1726) of Flushing, in the Winterthur collection (57.512); the Ten Eyck and Bowne family high chests; examples in the Metropolitan Museum (50.228.2), Art Institute of Chicago (1977.177), and Stone (1953.2) collections; and other published examples.[2] The division of the drawer fronts into veneered panels, creating a veneered panel down the center of the case, represents an organization of the facade that perhaps is a better clue to regional preferences.[3] This arrangement is seen on several of the New York–style high chests cited above and on other published examples attributed to New York.[4] At least two members of the New York group have the same pattern of brasses as the Yale example, although as these brasses were imported, their use need not have been restricted to a single area, and it is difficult to see their use as conclusive evidence. The shaping of the front skirt of the Yale example is similar to that found on many high chests of this period from New York and New England, and the turnings of the legs, which do include the features seen by Forman as characteristic of New York, differ considerably from the cup turnings on the documented New York examples and are not sufficiently distinct from the cup turnings found on examples attributed to New England to warrant any conclusions. Some features of the Yale chest do leave open the possibility of a New England origin, however. Its combination of secondary woods, including soft maple, aspen, chestnut, and eastern white pine, seem to point toward New England, and the red gum used on some (but by no means all) of the New York chests is lacking here. An upper tier of three drawers in line is found on the high chest originally owned by Edward Holyoke (1689–1769) and presumably made in Boston, now in the Metropolitan Museum (1975.132.1), and on other examples attributed to New England (cats. 124, 125), although two drawers in line seems to have been the most popular choice in New England.[5] The blind frieze drawer is found on examples attributed to both New York and New England and probably was simply an option available at extra cost in both regions.[6]

The Mabel Brady Garvan Collection 1930.2197

1. Kirk, *Am. Furn. & Brit. Trad.*, fig. 546, p. 381 n. 11.
2. Failey, *Long Island*, no. 39; *Antiques* 103, no. 4 (April 1973): 599; Failey, *Long Island*, no. 41; Marvin D. Schwartz, *American Furniture of the Colonial Period* (New York: Metropolitan Museum of Art, 1976), fig. 30; Milo M. Naeve, *The Classical Presence in American Art* (Chicago: Art Institute of Chicago, 1978), fig. 5; Rodriguez Roque, *Chipstone*, no. 11; *Antiques* 94, no. 1 (July 1968): 56.
3. Hewitt, pp. 84–87, cautions that in the case of federal-period card tables, when production methods presumably were even more standardized, "facade designs in general are only suggestive of regional origin."
4. Also see Miller, *Furn. New York Cabinetmakers*, no. 21.
5. Cooper, *In Praise of America*, fig. 109.
6. The frieze drawer is found on two of the New York examples cited above and is found on Massachusetts high chests often compared with the Yale example, including examples at Bayou Bend (in Warren, *Bayou Bend*, no. 39) and Winterthur (66.1306), which is inscribed "J M / 1720" on the back, possibly for a Boston craftsman.

123

High chest of drawers
Essex County, possibly Ipswich, Massachusetts, 1710–1730

Description: The upper case is crowned by a complex projecting cornice molding above deep cove molding concealing a blind drawer. The upper case also holds five other graduated drawers, two in line over three below, that are surrounded and flanked by double half-round molding on the case. Cove base molding on the upper case is contained within the projecting molding applied to the top of the lower case. The lower case contains three drawers in line, with the side drawers of greater depth and the center drawer of greater width, and again the drawers are outlined with double half-round molding. The front skirt is shaped to flathead arches at the sides flanking stepped reverse curves leading to a round arch below the middle drawer. The side skirts are shaped to simple flathead arches. The chest is supported by six cup-turned legs and turned feet, connected by stretchers shaped to a simple segmental curve. The wide drawers are fitted with a central blind stamped brass lock escutcheon flanked by matching escutcheons (also with blind keyhole piercings) with bail pulls; the top two drawers in the upper case and the three drawers in the lower case also have a single blind lock escutcheon fitted with a bail pull attached with snipe-bill hinges. The joint of the top and bottom of the upper case to the sides is obscured by applied moldings, but it is likely that they are simply nailed together. There is a full dustboard under the top two drawers in the upper case, and the drawer runners are nailed to grooves in the sides of the case. Two of the drawer dividers in the upper case are through-dovetailed to the sides. The two horizontal backboards of the upper case are secured with large rosehead nails to rabbets in all four sides. In the lower case, the back is a single horizontal board rabbeted and nailed to thick (about 4 cm) sides with large rosehead nails. The top molding is formed of deep strips molded on their outer edges and

123

extending into the case beyond the front and sides to form a support for the upper case; there is no top board to the lower case. The drawer runners are nailed to the sides of the case, and vertical partitions on each side of the middle drawer are housed in grooves in the back and nailed to the front skirt, with runners in turn nailed to these partitions. Thin facing strips are nailed to the front edge of each side of the lower case, probably to conceal the nailed joint between the front skirt and the sides. The legs at each corner are doweled to and pinned through the sides; the two front center legs are doweled to the front skirt and to small blocks screwed to the inside of the front skirt which may be new. The stretchers are a single board on each side joined together with a half lap. On each drawer, the sides are dovetailed to the front, but are rabbeted to accept the back, which is nailed in place through the back. The bottoms are a single longitudinal board nailed to a rabbet in the front and to the underside of the sides and back.

Inscriptions: There is an old but illegible inscription on the underside of the top of the upper case. The outside of the back of two of the wide drawers in the upper case is inscribed "Back Side" in white chalk, and other chalk shop marks appear on the chest. A paper label pasted to the inside of the left side of the left drawer in the lower case reads in ink: "Dr. I.W. Lyon's Note Book—p. 67 says / 'I bought, Sept. 14, 1883, of Mr. James T. / Moulton, dealer, West Lynn, Mass.: / 1 six legged highboy—' / This piece is Fig. 28—page 83, Colonial Furn- / iture. / Lyon says on p. 98 of same note book regarding / this highboy that he bought from Moulton, / 'Capt. Samuel Brown, of Newburyport, / dealer, says saw the photo of my Moulton / 6-legged high Chest of drawers—know / the piece—It was first picked up, / he said, at Ipswich, Mass. / Jan. 7, 1922." A blank medical prescription form, printed with the name and address of Dr. Irving P. Lyon of Buffalo, N. Y., is pasted to the inside of the left side of the top wide drawer in the upper case and bears the following notation by Dr. Lyon in ink: "Dr. I.W. Lyon's Note Book, p. 67. Says / 'I bought, Sept. 14, 1883, of Mr. James T. / Moulton, dealer, West Lynn, Mass.,' / 1 six legged highboy.' / This piece is Fig. 28, Colonial Furniture, / described on p. 83. / Paste this on your piece! / First picked up at Ipswich, Mass. I.P.L. / over." A third notation, this time on the printed letterhead of Lyon, is pasted to the outside of the back of the lower case, and reads: "Referring to this highboy! / [gives the same information as on the other two labels, and concludes with the statement that the high chest] is in the possession of his daughter, / Mrs. Chester B. Albree, of Pittsburgh."

Condition: The high chest has lost its original paint and has been refinished. Traces of red paint remain, suggesting the original color. The brasses may be original, although they have been disturbed, perhaps when the chest was refinished. The center drawer in the lower case is a replacement, and the cock beading on the front skirt is new and may be an added feature rather than a replacement. New running strips have been added to several drawers, and strips of cloth have been pasted over holes in several drawers and to the inside and outside of the back of the upper case to cover shrinkage cracks. The legs and feet have been secured with new small nails.

Woods: Drawer fronts, sides and front of lower case, legs, feet, soft maple; sides of upper case, stretchers, front of frieze

240 *American Case Furniture*

drawer, eastern white pine; facing strips on front of sides of lower case, possibly cherry.

Dimensions: H 170.0; W 102.5; UCW 88.5; LCW 96.6; D 53.1; UCD 45.1; LCD 50.7.

Bibliography: Lyon, fig. 28; Kirk, *Early Am. Furn.*, fig. 190; Elizabeth Stillinger, *The Antiquers* (New York: Alfred A. Knopf, 1980), p. 75.

Provenance: This high chest was purchased on 14 September 1883 by collector Irving W. Lyon, Hartford, Conn., from dealer James T. Moulton of West Lynn, Mass.[1] A Captain Samuel Brown, a dealer from Newburyport, Mass., later informed Lyon that the chest originally had been found in Ipswich. The chest descended to Lyon's daughter, Mrs. Chester B. Albree, Pittsburgh, Pa., who sold it in 1929 to Francis P. Garvan, New York, N. Y.

LIKE so much early furniture, this high chest has suffered from the loss of its original paint that would have covered and blended its exterior of maple and pine. Due to the note-taking habits and penchant for documentation of the Lyon family, both father and son, we know that this high chest was found in Ipswich, Massachusetts, in the late nineteenth century, and there is a good possibility that it was made in that vicinity. The construction of the chest is atypical in several respects, and the object probably was not produced by a sophisticated urban shop. The maker of the chest used dovetails for the joint of the drawer sides to the drawer fronts, but relied on simple nailed construction for the rest of the drawer joints and for the carcass of each case. The unusual thick sides of the lower case made the use of the customary four corner posts generally found in high chests and dressing tables of this period superfluous. It is also unusual to find the stretchers shaped to patterns that do not correspond to the shaping of the front and side skirts.

The Mabel Brady Garvan Collection 1931.1227

1. The purchase price, omitted by Irving P. Lyon in his notes pasted to the chest, is given in Lyon's notebook; Irving W. Lyon Papers, Winterthur Library, 76 x 99.17.

124

124

High chest of drawers
Massachusetts, 1700–1730

Description: The upper case has cornice molding at the front and sides formed by bead, fillet, and cyma molding. The case contains six drawers, three in line with the center drawer of greater width, over three graduated drawers, all surrounded and flanked by half-round molding on the case. The upper case has base molding that rests within projecting molding on the top of the lower case. The lower case contains three drawers in line, with the side drawers of greater depth and the center drawer of greater width, and again the drawers are outlined by half-round molding on the case. The front and side skirts are edged with cock beading nailed

High Chests of Drawers 241

in place; the front skirt is shaped with paired reverse curves below the side drawers and stepped reverse curves flanking a central rounded arch below the middle drawer. The chest is supported by six cup-turned legs and turned feet, and the stretchers are shaped in conformity with the lower edge of the case sides. In the upper case, the top side drawers are fitted with stamped brass escutcheons with drop pulls; the top center drawer and the wide drawers, as well as the center drawer in the lower case, are fitted with central brass lock escutcheons (blind on the small center drawers) flanked by matching escutcheons with drop pulls. The side drawers in the upper case are fitted with pulls, and the side drawers in the lower case with blind lock escutcheons above pulls. In the upper case, the bottom is dovetailed to the sides with very square through-dovetails, and the top is blind dovetailed to the sides. The two horizontal backboards are joined with a half lap and nailed to a rabbet in all four sides. The cornice and base molding are applied with nails. The drawer runners are housed in grooves in the sides and nailed in place, and the drawer dividers are also housed in grooves in the sides. The runners for the top center drawer are tenoned through the backboards. In the lower case, the back is dovetailed to the sides, and the four corner posts are nailed to the sides with rosehead nails. The top of the lower case consists of a framework of strips at the front and sides, mitered together at the front corners, shaped to form the projecting molding on their outer edges, and grooved on their inner edges to accept two longitudinal boards with beveled edges, thus creating in effect a paneled top; the strips are then nailed to the lower case. The side drawer runners are rabbeted and nailed to the posts; there are vertical partitions on each side of the center drawer that are rabbeted and nailed to the front skirt, are housed in grooves in the backboard, and stand above shaped blocks glued to the skirt above the two center legs. Runners for the drawers are nailed to each side of these partitions. The stretchers are a single board on each side, joined with a half lap at the corners. The legs are doweled to the corner posts and the stretchers, and the feet are doweled to the stretchers. On each drawer, the top edges of the sides and back are rounded; the sides are dovetailed to the front and back, and the dovetails are reinforced with nails; the bottoms are beveled on their front and side edges, let into grooves in the front and sides, and nailed to the underside of the back. In the lower case, the pins of the rear dovetails extend slightly to act as stops.

Inscriptions: A modern shipping label pasted to the outside of the backboards of the upper case reads: "[in ink] Mr C.E. Albree / 189 Western Ave / Alleghany / Pa / [printed] From ROBBINS BROTHERS, / Cabinet Furniture, Bedding, Curtains, Etc., / 209 MAIN STREET, / HARTFORD,—CONN." The side drawers in the upper and lower cases have been marked in pencil in modern times "Left" and "Right." One of Irving Lyon's tags labeled "245" is pasted to the inside of the bottom of the center drawer in the lower case.

Condition: What may be early or original painted graining is discernible under a coat of dark varnish, probably applied in the nineteenth century. There have been minor repairs to the stretchers, and running strips have been added to some drawers. The feet were once fitted with stem casters. Paper strips were used to cover shrinkage cracks in the upper case. The brasses appear to be original in most instances.

Woods: Yellow poplar; some drawer bottoms and one board used for top of lower case, southern yellow pine; legs, feet, probably soft maple; second front foot from the left, beech.

Dimensions: H 157.7; W 99.8; UCW 90.2; LCW 94.8; D 55.9; UCD 49.9; LCD 53.4.

Bibliography: Kirk, *Early Am. Furn.*, fig. 192.

Provenance: Irving W. Lyon, Hartford, Conn.; by descent to his daughter Mrs. John P. Penney (Mamie P. Lyon), Pittsburgh, Pa.; by sale in 1929 to Francis P. Garvan, New York, N. Y.

THE active surface decoration achieved on other high chests of this period through the use of expensive veneers may have been simulated on this example through painted graining on a yellow poplar case, graining that is now obscured by a later coat of varnish.[1] One wonders if this graining, if original, was applied in a manner designed to simulate the division of each wide drawer and the center drawers in the upper and lower case into two visual panels, as seen on the veneered high chest attributed to the New York or Boston area (cat. 122). This high chest shares several features with that example, including the same drawer arrangement, virtually the same skirt profile, and the same type of brass lock escutcheon, all features that pointed toward a New York origin. Here, however, the turned legs lack the element above the ankle baluster found on cat. 122, and the lower half of the cup turning is not swelled in the same manner.

The Mabel Brady Garvan Collection 1930.2264

1. An illustration of a high chest in the collection of Old Sturbridge Village that retains its original brown painted graining is in Fales, *Am Painted Furn.*, p. 33.

125

125

High chest of drawers
New England, 1700–1730

Description: The upper case is crowned by light cyma cornice molding, and it contains eight drawers in the unusual arrangement of three in line over two in line over three graduated drawers. The drawers are divided and flanked by double half-round molding. The upper case rests within molding on the top of the lower case, and the lower case contains three drawers in line, with the side drawers of greater depth and the middle drawer of greater width, and again the drawers are outlined with applied double half-round molding. The front and side skirts have cock-beaded edges; the sides of the front skirt are shaped to round arches, with the center shaped with stepped reverse curves rising to a rounded arch. The side skirts are shaped with paired reverse curves. The chest is supported by six cup-turned legs, and the flat stretchers are shaped to conform to the skirt, with the exception of the center portion of the front stretcher, which is shaped to paired reverse curves. The top and bottom of the upper case are simply nailed to the sides with large rosehead nails, and the three horizontal backboards are nailed to rabbets in all four sides. The drawer runners are housed in grooves and nailed to the sides of the case; the vertical partitions between the two tiers of small drawers are nailed in place through the back and from underneath through the drawer dividers. The bottom front rail is tenoned through the sides, and the half round moldings are applied. In the lower case, the four sides are nailed to the corner posts. Each drawer is supported by a medial runner that is tenoned through the single horizontal backboard. The vertical partitions are also nailed in place through the back, and the guides for the side drawers are nailed to grooves in the corner posts. The midmolding on the lower case is applied, and there are two longitudinal butted boards nailed in place forming the top of the lower case. The four legs at the corners of the case are doweled to the corner posts; the two front center legs are doweled to small blocks that are dovetailed and glued to the front skirt. The drawer sides are dovetailed to the fronts, and in most instances they are butted to the back and nailed with two nails through the back (in some drawers, the rear edge of the drawer side is beveled and is nailed to the back through the sides). The drawer bottoms are nailed to a rabbet in the front and to the underside of the sides and back; in the lower case, the bottoms project slightly beyond the back to act as stops.

Inscriptions: There are a few of what appear to be original shop marks in white chalk remaining, and numerous modern pencil shop marks can be found throughout the case and drawers. A fragment of an American Railway Express Company label, with the shipping point given as Boston, remains on the underside of the bottom of the upper case, along with the penciled "H V Weil / 126 E 57th / NY City." A fragment of another shipping label remains on the underside of the bottom of the center drawer in the lower case. On the top of the bottom of the same drawer is a modern oval white label with a red border and "17" written in ink; the same number is written in red ink on the drawer bottom beside the label. The modern "C1430" is written in pencil on the inside of the bottom of the lowest drawer in the upper case.

High Chests of Drawers

Condition: The chest has been stripped of its original paint and refinished; traces of red and possibly of white paint remain. All the feet and the brasses are replacements, and the rear section of the front stretcher has been pieced. The right rear leg has been damaged extensively by insects, and the other legs have been slightly damaged; it may be that these insects destroyed the original feet. The cock beading on the skirts is probably a replacement in its entirety, and the double half-round molding has been damaged and repaired in several places.

Woods: Yellow poplar; legs, soft maple, possibly silver maple; four corner posts, red oak; blocks above the two center legs, eastern white pine; restored feet, chestnut or ash.

Dimensions: H 176.8; W 102.8; UCW 90.5; LCW 95.1; D 56.8; UCD 49.5; LCD 52.9.

Bibliography: Miller, 1:no. 633.

Provenance: Henry V. Weil, New York, N. Y.; by sale to Francis P. Garvan, New York, N. Y.

UNDOUBTEDLY a rural object, with its cases constructed almost entirely with nails and with dovetails used only to join the drawer sides to the drawer fronts, this high chest suffers from the loss of its original paint and the replacement of its feet. Its upper case seems exaggerated in height, due to the presence of five tiers of drawers, rather than the more customary four. In high-style examples (cat. 122), if the upper case contains five tiers of drawers, the uppermost drawer is usually a blind frieze drawer. The arrangement of three drawers in line above two drawers in line above three wide drawers is reminiscent of Philadelphia-area furniture of the later eighteenth century.

The Mabel Brady Garvan Collection 1930.2614

126

High chest of drawers

Boston, Massachusetts, area, 1700–1720

Description: The high chest is in two cases. The upper case is crowned with light cornice molding at the front and sides and contains five drawers: two in line over three graduated drawers. The drawers are outlined and separated by applied half-round molding, and each is veneered with veneer bordered by feather banding. The three wide drawers are fitted with a central brass lock escutcheon flanked by pierced, round escutcheons with drop pulls; the two small drawers in line have matching escutcheons with drop pulls. There is base molding applied to the front and sides of the base of the upper case, which rests within the midmolding applied to the top of the lower case. The lower case contains a single wide drawer, veneered in the same manner as those in the upper case, although it lacks the upper border of feather banding, and again bordered with applied half-round molding at the sides and bottom. It is fitted with a central blind brass lock escutcheon flanked by escutcheons with drop pulls. The front skirt is shaped to a triple arcade of three equal, round arches; the side skirts are shaped to a pair of round arches. Neither the front nor side skirts were protected with cock beading. The case is supported by six cup-turned legs, joined by stretchers that echo the shape of the front and side skirts and are straight across the back, and by

244 *American Case Furniture*

six turned feet. The top and bottom of the upper case are dovetailed to the sides. The vertical backboards are nailed to a rabbet in all four sides. There is a full dustboard under the drawers in line, and the drawer dividers are quite deep. The vertical partitions between the drawers in line are tenoned through the drawer divider. Cleats are applied to the bottom of the upper case and rest on the top of the lower case. The top of the lower case is made of several transverse butted boards nailed to a rabbet in the midmolding and to the top edge of the back of the case. The back of the lower case is dovetailed to the sides of the case. The legs in each corner are doweled to short, fat, blocks, with the runners for the drawer applied on top of these blocks. The two legs in the center of the front are doweled to blocks that are pinned in place through the front of the case. Drawer guides are applied to the sides of the case. On each drawer, the sides are dovetailed to the front and back, and the bottoms are nailed to a rabbet in the front and to the undersides of the sides and back. The arches of the stretchers were formed by semicircular strips glued to the straight rear edge of the main stretcher.

Condition: The lock mortises on the drawer dividers in the upper case have been repaired. The rear of the middle drawer divider in the upper case has been pieced, and paper has been used to cover a knothole in the back. The drawer runners are replacements, and there have been repairs to the veneer and moldings. The rear blocks above the legs are replacements, and the blocks above the four front legs may be replacements as well; new screws have been added to the blocks above the two feet in the center of the front. The legs have been painted a dark brown. Minor repairs were made to the high chest by Edward Hoepfner in 1952.

Woods: Drawer fronts, front facade, irregular-grained walnut veneer; borders, plain-grain walnut veneer; applied moldings, sides, case, American black walnut; legs, feet, aspen; eastern white pine.

Dimensions: H 148.2; W 104.5; UCW 91.7; LCW 96.7; D 59.6; UCD 52.6; LCD 56.1.

Bibliography: Nutting, *Furn. Pilgrim Century* (1921), p. 78; Nutting, *Furn. Pilgrim Century* (1924), p. 136 no. 108; Nutting, *Treasury*, no. 330; Kane, "Hadley Chest," p. 108 fig. 25.

Provenance: According to Nutting, before 1921 he acquired this high chest "in Boston," and it was "taken to the Webb House, Wethersfield," Conn. It apparently was then acquired by dealer Jacob Margolis of New York, N.Y., who sold it in 1924 to Francis P. Garvan, New York, N.Y.

A SOPHISTICATED example of Boston work, veneered with bold flitches of black walnut veneer, this high chest is most closely related to an example at Winterthur (58.579).[1] Although the Winterthur and Yale chests appear to be nearly identical in their drawer arrangement, the shaping of their skirts, and the profile of their turned legs, unpublished research by Benno M. Forman revealed that the legs and stretchers of the Winterthur example have been altered. To summarize his carefully reasoned argument, he hypothesized that the rear legs and stretchers of the Winterthur example are replacements and that the object may have begun life as a four-legged chest of drawers on frame, with the skirts simply arched between the legs in each corner. The unaltered upper case of the Winterthur chest is more elaborate than that of the Yale example in that the sides of the case and the top are veneered, while the sides of the Yale chest are solid walnut boards and the top is undecorated. The legs of the Winterthur example were painted with swirling decoration in simulation of burl veneer, and the legs of the Yale chest are painted brown; although the paint has been retouched, the legs may have been painted originally. Another high chest with a single drawer in the lower case, attributed to Connecticut, is in the Yale collection (cat. 127), and it seems that the form was produced in both urban and rural areas. Other examples, with a variety of turned legs and surface ornament, including paint and japanning, are known. On some examples, attributed to New England, New York, and Philadelphia, there are only five legs in the lower case, and there is no shaped skirt below the single drawer.[2] A six-legged veneered example, attributed to New York, shares the triple arcading of the skirt found on the Yale chest, and is supported by twist-turned legs.[3] Twist-turned legs are also seen on a five-legged high chest made of red gum in the Metropolitan Museum's collection and made in New York.[4] An important high chest with five scrolled legs is signed by Edmund Titcomb (d. 1723) of Newbury, Massachusetts.[5] English prototypes for the form have been published.[6]

The Mabel Brady Garvan Collection 1930.2148

1. Illustrated in Fairbanks and Bates, p. 55. See also a related veneered example in Comstock, fig. 70; and a more rural version in sycamore in Nutting, *Treasury*, no. 333.
2. Kirk, *Am. Furn. & Brit. Trad.*, fig. 543; Fales, *Deerfield*, fig. 421; Fales, *Am. Painted Furn.*, fig. 43; Schwartz, *Amer. Interiors*, fig. 6; Nutting, *Treasury*, no. 334; Schwartz, *Amer. Interiors*, fig. 33; McElroy, "Furn. in Philadelphia," fig. 13. See also Nutting, *Treasury*, no. 325, for a five-legged example with a shaped skirt.
3. Kirk, *Am. Furn. & Brit. Trad.*, fig. 540.
4. Failey, *Long Island*, no. 38.
5. Fairbanks and Bates, p. 53; see also Nutting, *Treasury*, fig. 327.

6. Lockwood, fig. 53 (with replaced legs); Kirk, *Am. Furn. & Brit. Trad.*, figs. 538, 541, 542; Nutting, *Treasury*, no. 328; Lockwood, fig. 52.

127

High chest of drawers
Connecticut, 1700–1730

Description: The upper case is crowned by light cyma molding and contains five drawers, two in line over three graduated drawers below. The drawers are flanked and separated by heavy half-round molding on the case. The base molding of the upper case rests within a molding on the top of the lower case, forming a complex and projecting midmolding. The lower case contains a single wide drawer outlined by half-round molding at the sides and bottom. The chest is supported by six cup-turned legs and small turned feet below stretchers shaped in conformity with the case sides. The front skirt is shaped to segmental arches of equal size between the front legs, and the side skirts are shaped to pairs of segmental arches. The joint of the top and bottom of the upper case to the sides is obscured by the cornice and base moldings and by cleats nailed to the front and sides of the underside of the bottom. The three horizontal backboards are nailed to rabbets in all four sides with rosehead nails. The drawer runners are housed in grooves and nailed to the sides; a runner serving the top two drawers is tenoned through the upper backboard. In the lower case, the back is a single horizontal board dovetailed to the sides, with the dovetails reinforced by nails, and the back is also nailed with rosehead nails to the corner posts. The sides and front of the lower case appear to be nailed to the corner posts; the right side is composed of two butted boards nailed together. The front skirt is given an arcaded appearance with applied horizontal strips above the arches and vertical strips above the legs. The drawer runners are rabbeted and nailed to the corner posts. The four corner legs are doweled through plates into the corner posts; the two center legs are doweled to blocks glued to the inside of the front skirt. There is no top to the lower case; the upper case is supported by extensions of the midmolding at the front and sides. The flat stretchers are of a single board on each side joined with a half lap at the corners. On each drawer, the sides are dovetailed to the front, rabbeted to accept the back, and nailed through the sides. The bottoms are nailed to a rabbet in the front and to the underside of the sides and back. Running strips have been applied in recent times and may have been present originally. Each drawer is fitted with a blind brass lock escutcheon flanked by round brass escutcheons with wide drop pulls.

Inscriptions: Written in black on the underside of the bottom of the upper case is the enigmatic "Land on / Lan don." There are numbers in white chalk on the inside of the sides of the upper case, and some chalk shop marks are present.

Condition: The chest retains an old finish. The brasses are probably original, but they have all been reattached with new wire staples. The rear feet have been damaged by insects. New running strips have been added to the drawers, and the bottom of the drawer in the lower case has been pieced.

Woods: American black cherry; legs, feet, soft maple; drawer linings, other elements, yellow poplar; corner posts, blocks above two center legs, red oak and white oak; drawer runners in upper case, chestnut.

127

246 *American Case Furniture*

Dimensions: H 144.5; W 106.2; UCW 91.4; LCW 105.1; D 58.9; UCD 51.0; LCD 57.9.

Bibliography: *American and English Furniture & Decorations ... from Various Private Collections and Other Sources*, Sale 3791, 19–21 November 1929 (New York: American Art Association/Anderson Galleries, 1929), no. 600; Kirk, *Conn. Furn.*, no. 73 (included in catalogue but not in exhibition).

Provenance: Acquired at auction in 1929 by Francis P. Garvan, New York, N. Y.

Unusually broad, this cherry high chest can be seen as a rural counterpart to the preceding urban example (cat. 126). The drawer arrangement, the triple-arcaded skirt and stretchers, and the general profile of the legs are similar in the two objects, but the verticality, rich walnut veneers, and crisp turnings of the Boston example are not present here. Attributed to Connecticut for many years, this example is related in stance and feeling to an example in a private collection from the Suffield area and to the magnificent painted high chest from the Guilford-Saybrook area in the Winterthur collection.[1] Like these two examples, the Yale high chest retains something of a conservative air. John T. Kirk has called attention to the rectangular plaques set into the lower case above the two middle legs in an apparent attempt to suggest that the legs are one continuous piece up to the height of the drawer. The almost casual reference to structural stability and the horizontal orientation of the high chest suggest that its maker and owner were reluctant to leave the seventeenth-century emphasis on stability and sense of proportion behind. The use of red oak and white oak as structural elements in the lower case also can be seen as evidence of a lingering conservatism.

The Mabel Brady Garvan Collection 1930.2312

1. Kirk, *Conn. Furn.*, nos. 72, 74.

128

High chest of drawers
Philadelphia, Pennsylvania, 1700–1730

Description: The upper case contains five drawers, two in line over three graduated drawers below, outlined by heavy half-round molding on the case. There is a cyma molding

128

cornice, and the upper case rests within a molding on the top of the lower case. The lower case contains three separated drawers in line, with the side drawers of greater depth and the middle drawer of greater width and each outlined at the bottom and sides with applied half-round molding. This molding continues from the bottom of each drawer to the sides of the front and along the sides of the case. The front and side skirts are decorated with cock beading; the front skirt is shaped with stepped reverse curves rising to a central rounded arch below the middle drawer and with simple segmental arches below the side drawers; the side skirts are shaped to pairs of segmental arches. The chest is supported by six cup-turned legs and turned ball feet, with flat stretchers shaped in conformity to the case. Each drawer has a central brass lock escutcheon (blind on the top two drawers in the upper case and on the lower case drawers) flanked by round escutcheons with drop pulls. The top and bottom of

High Chests of Drawers 247

the upper case are dovetailed to the sides, and the cornice molding is formed of two pieces and nailed in place. The horizontal backboards are nailed with rosehead nails to rabbets in all four sides. The drawer runners are shaped at the rear edge and are nailed to the sides, as are the drawer guides. Thin vertical strips are applied to the inside of each side of the case at the front to give the front edges of the sides greater width. A vertical partition between the top two drawers is nailed in place through the top. In the lower case, the back is dovetailed to the sides, and the sides are dovetailed to the front, with the dovetails exposed on the sides. The top consists of four transverse boards, joined with a tongue-and-groove joint and nailed in place. The midmolding is again made of several pieces and is nailed in place. The side drawer runners and guides are rabbeted and nailed to the corner posts; the inside drawer runners are nailed to posts above the center legs and applied to strips nailed to the inside of the backboard. On each drawer, the sides are dovetailed to the front and back and the bottoms are nailed to a rabbet in the front and to the underside of the sides and back. The upper left drawer in the upper case is approximately 7 cm shallower than the other drawers in the upper case. Both top drawers in the upper case were fitted with wooden spring locks.

Inscriptions: There are numerous original shop marks in white chalk on the drawers. Written in white chalk on the top of the top of the lower case is "210." The modern "137," relating to the chest's sale at auction, is written in black on the outside of the back of the upper and lower cases. "L" is written in pencil on the underside of the bottom of the upper left drawer in the upper case.

Condition: The wooden spring lock on the upper left drawer is missing, as is the metal lock on the top wide drawer in the upper case. The brasses are probably replacements. Some drawer guides in the upper case are replacements, new running strips have been added to most of the drawers, and blocks have been glued to the back of the wide drawers in the upper case to act as stops. The backboard of the lower case was damaged by insects and has been filled and repaired. There have been repairs to the midmolding on the left side of the lower case, and shrinkage cracks in the sides of the upper case have been filled.

Woods: American black walnut; drawer bottoms, other elements, Atlantic white cedar; drawer sides, backs, other elements, southern yellow pine.

Dimensions: H 167.3; W 108.4; UCW 97.1; LCW 105.1; D 60.3; UCD 53.3; LCD 58.6.

Bibliography: *Eighteenth Century American Furniture . . . Sold by Order of Mrs. Gertrude H. Camp,"The Hayloft," Whitemarsh, Pa.*, Sale 2222, 20–21 January 1928 (New York: Anderson Galleries, 1928), no. 137; Kirk, *Am. Furn. & Brit. Trad.*, fig. 553.

Provenance: Mrs. Gertrude H. Camp, Whitemarsh, Pa.; acquired at auction in 1928 by Francis P. Garvan, New York, N. Y.

THE separation of the lower drawers, the use of two pulls on each drawer, and the combination of walnut, southern yellow pine, and Atlantic white cedar all point toward a Pennsylvania, and probably Philadelphia, origin for this deep high chest. Like much eighteenth-century furniture from Pennsylvania, the greater depth and weightiness of this high chest may reflect a Germanic concern for solidity and stability. The mass of the high chest is accentuated here by thin strips placed to the sides of the drawers, giving the effect of greater width. High chests of this style from Pennsylvania are far rarer than their counterparts from farther north in New York and New England. Trumpet-turned legs are found on three related examples, which share the use of separated drawers in the lower case, including high chests in the Philadelphia Museum of Art (28.7.12) and the Chester County Historical Society (61–76Fchst2).[1] Each of these high chests is of solid walnut, in conformity with the continuing Pennsylvania preference for solid surfaces, and two of the examples make use of multiple brasses on the small drawers. Two of the high chests also have three drawers in line at the top of the upper case, while the third has the two drawers in line found on the Yale example. Three drawers in line in the upper case and separated drawers in the lower case are also found on a high chest veneered in walnut and attributed to New York (Art Institute of Chicago, 1977.177). With secondary woods of southern yellow pine and Atlantic white cedar, a Pennsylvania origin for this high chest might be considered, for although veneering was not popular in Philadelphia, at least one craftsman and probably more were equipped with the proper tools.[3] A related example with decorative Bermuda-style dovetailing has been published.[4]

The Mabel Brady Garvan Collection 1930.2311

1. PMA, *Three Centuries*, no. 22; Schiffer, *Furn. Chester County*, fig. 111; Hornor, fig. 14. Separated drawers in the lower case are found on Philadelphia-area dressing tables (cat. 97) and on some spice chests from there as well (PMA, *Three Centuries*, no. 7).
2. Milo M. Naeve, *The Classical Presence in American Art* (Chicago: Art Institute of Chicago, 1978), fig. 5.
3. McElroy, "Furn. in Philadelphia," p. 108.
4. *Antiques* 85, no. 2 (February 1964): 169.

129

High chest of drawers

Boston, Massachusetts, area, 1730–1750

Description: The high chest is in two cases. The upper case is crowned by a projecting complex molded cornice at the front and sides above deep cove molding concealing a blind frieze drawer. The upper case contains five drawers, three in line over three graduated drawers, separated and outlined by double half-round molding applied to the case. Each drawer is veneered with flitches of figured walnut bordered by herringbone veneer. There is a base molding at the front and sides of the upper case which rests within the projecting midmolding applied to the top of the lower case. The lower case also contains five drawers, veneered as in the upper case and outlined with double half-round molding, including two drawers of equal size in line over three drawers in line, with the lower side drawers of greater depth and the center drawer of greater width. The front skirt is shaped to a central rounded arch above stepped reverse curves flanked by drops and by pointed arches formed by paired reverse curves under the side drawers. The side skirts are shaped to a single pointed arch by paired reverse curves. The chest is supported by four cabriole legs with sharply pointed knee brackets and arrised knees; the legs terminate in pad feet, each with a distinctive ring and thick pad. The top and bottom of the upper case are dovetailed to the sides, and the horizontal backboards are nailed to a rabbet in the top and sides and to the bottom. There is a full dustboard under the frieze drawer, and the drawer divider is deeper under the two drawers in line. The vertical partition between the drawers in line is tenoned through the drawer divider. The drawer runners are housed in grooves in the case sides, and small strips are glued to the inside of the back as stops. The lower case is constructed with mortise-and-tenon joints, with the joints of the case sides secured to the legs with six pegs. The posts of the rear legs are of greater thickness than those of the front legs, and the rear knees of the rear legs are squared off. The top of the lower case consists of several transverse butted boards nailed to the top edge of the back and to the midmolding. There are full rectangular transverse partitions between the two drawers in line and full triangular partitions between the three lower drawers. The upper drawers run on top of the partitions for the lower drawers, and the lower drawers are supported by center runners. Two strips are nailed to the inside of each side of the case. On each drawer, the sides are dovetailed to the front and back, and the bottoms are nailed to rabbets in the front and sides and to the underside of the back. The lower center drawer in the lower case is divided by partitions into six small compartments. No locks were installed in the drawers in the lower case.

Inscriptions: "B" is written in white chalk on the inside of the back of the two drawers in line in the upper case. An inscription, mostly illegible, but beginning with "D" followed by several more letters, is written on the underside of the top of the upper case. "M M" is written in chalk on the bottom of the upper case. There are many white chalk shop marks and numbers and scratched numbers throughout the case.

High Chests of Drawers 249

Condition: The brasses are replacements, and the original cock beading on the front and side skirts is missing. The knee bracket on the left rear leg is a replacement, and the right rear foot has been repaired. The left drop, the platform above it, and its block within the case, are replacements. Running strips have been added to the drawers, and there have been minor repairs to the veneer.

Woods: Front of case, crotch walnut veneer; sides of each case, legs, applied moldings, American black walnut; eastern white pine.

Dimensions: H 179.0; W 104.3; UCW 91.5; LCW 96.0; D 57.2; UCD 49.5; LCD 52.8.

Bibliography: *Antiquarian* 11, no. 4 (November 1928): 3; Nagel, fig. 14.

Provenance: Charles Woolsey Lyon, New York, N. Y.; by sale in 1929 to Francis P. Garvan, New York, N. Y.

ONLY the use of cabriole rather than turned legs and the presence of an additional pair of drawers in the lower case significantly distinguish this high chest from examples made earlier in the eighteenth century, such as cat. 122. In form, this high chest is related to similar examples from the Boston area with japanned decoration and to other high chests from eastern Massachusetts and southern New Hampshire.[1] The distinctive pad feet, raised above a flattened ring and a disk, are found on a small tea table (Museum of Fine Arts, Boston, 1974.484), originally owned by Gideon White (1717–1779) of Plymouth and attributed to Plymouth County, and on a japanned high chest from the Boston area in the Winterthur collection.[2] The "M M" and the illegible inscription on the top of the upper case may yet prove helpful in determining the maker of this high chest.[3]

The Mabel Brady Garvan Collection 1930.2483

1. Randall, no. 52; Fairbanks and Bates, p. 133; Downs, no. 187; Fitzgerald, fig. 111–12.
2. *Antiques* 120, no. 3 (September 1981): 596; Downs, no. 187. The writer would like to thank Wendy A. Cooper for bringing the Gideon White tea table to his attention.
3. No individual with the initials "M M" appears in the list of eighteenth-century Boston furniture craftsmen included in *Boston Furn.*, although several possibilities exist if the initials are read as "W W."

130

130

High chest of drawers
Connecticut, probably Putnam area, 1730–1760
(en suite with cat. 101)

Description: The upper case is crowned by complex projecting cornice molding that includes shallow cove molding concealing a blind frieze drawer. The upper case contains five other drawers, two in line over three graduated drawers below, outlined and flanked by double half-round molding. The upper case rests within the midmolding applied to the top of the lower case. The lower case contains one wide drawer over three in line, with the side drawers of greater depth and the middle drawer of greater width. The front

American Case Furniture

skirt is shaped with deep reverse curves flanking a central drop; the side skirts are shaped with deep reverse curves flanking a central roundheaded arch. The chest is supported by four cabriole legs terminating in pad feet. The drawer fronts are veneered with panels of figured veneer outlined by borders of plain veneer. The wide drawers are fitted with central stamped brass lock escutcheons (blind in the lower case) flanked by matching escutcheons with bail pulls. The small drawers have a single brass escutcheon with bail pull. In the upper case, the top and bottom are dovetailed to the sides, and the two horizontal backboards have beveled edges, are joined with a half lap, and are fitted to a groove in the top and sides and nailed to the bottom. There is a dustboard under the two drawers in line, and the vertical partition between these drawers is tenoned through the drawer dividers. The runners are nailed to the sides of the case. The lower case is framed with mortise-and-tenon joints, with five pegs used to secure the single horizontal backboard and the sides to the legs. There are center runners for the lower drawers, with stops applied to their rear edges. The vertical partitions between the lower drawers are triangular and are nailed to the front skirt and tenoned to the back. Strips are nailed to each side of the case, and the upper case rests on strips applied to each side of the case. On each drawer, the sides are dovetailed to the front and back, with the top edge of the sides rounded. The bottoms are beveled on their front and side edges and are let into grooves in the front and sides and nailed to the underside of the back.

Inscriptions: The drawers are numbered in white chalk, and "B" is written on the inside of the back of the frieze drawer. "Trowbridge" is written in white chalk on the outside of the back of the lower case and on the inside of the bottom of the wide drawer in the lower case. A "Connecticut Furniture" exhibition label is pasted to the inside of the right side of the lowest drawer in the upper case and to the same location in the wide drawer in the lower case.

Condition: The side knee bracket on the left rear leg is a replacement. There have been minor repairs to the veneer, some drawer runners have been replaced, and new blocks have been added as stops in the upper case.

Woods: Drawer fronts, walnut veneer; applied half-round moldings, walnut; sides and bottom of upper case, sides of lower case, aspen; legs, cornice moldings, including front of frieze drawer, soft maple, probably red maple; back of lower case, southern yellow pine; drawer fronts, drawer dividers, eastern white pine; back and top of upper case, drawer sides, bottoms, and backs, other elements, yellow poplar.

Dimensions: H 173.4; W 100.1; UCW 89.0; LCW 94.8; D 54.5; UCD 48.2; LCD 51.4.

Exhibition: Kirk, *Conn. Furn.*, no. 79.

Provenance: See cat. 101.

As is true of another set of matching high chest and dressing table in the collection (cats. 108, 146), the brasses on this high chest and its dressing table (cat. 101) do not match, although in both instances they appear to be original. The multiplicity of woods used here has come to be expected in furniture from rural parts of New England, especially eastern Connecticut (see cats. 132, 143, for example).

The Mabel Brady Garvan Collection 1930.2205

131

High chest of drawers
Connecticut, possibly New Haven, 1740–1765

Description: The upper case is crowned by light cornice molding above deep cove molding concealing a blind drawer. The case holds an additional five drawers, two in line over three graduated drawers below, each outlined and flanked by single half-round molding on the case. The base molding of the upper section fits within the projecting midmolding on the lower case. The lower case holds one wide drawer over three in line, with the middle drawer of greater width and recessed in the center. The front skirt is shaped to flathead arches below each drawer, with the center arch recessed, and with turned drops. The side skirts are shaped to single flathead arches. The case is supported by four rather straight cabriole legs terminating in pad feet; the rear knees of the rear legs are squared off. Each drawer is decorated with a rectangle of triple-line stringing; the sides of the upper case have a similar line of inlay; the front and skirt of the lower case are outlined with a line of stringing that conforms to the shape of the skirt; the sides of the lower case are similarly decorated; and the middle drawer in the lower case has an inlaid shell with ten lobes in the recessed section. In the upper case, the top and bottom are dovetailed to the sides, and the three vertical backboards are joined with a half lap and nailed to the top and bottom; scribe lines were used to mark the location of the rosehead nails. The side drawer runners are nailed to the case; the middle runner for

the two drawers in line is applied to a horizontal strip applied to the inside of the back. Cleats are nailed to the front and sides of the bottom of the upper case. The lower case is framed with mortise-and-tenon joints, with six pegs used to secure the single horizontal backboard to the rear legs and the sides to the front and rear legs. The top of the lower case is a single horizontal board fitted to a groove in the top front rail and in strips at each side that are nailed to the sides of the case and nailed to the top edge of the back. The knee brackets are applied to the skirt. On each drawer, the sides are dovetailed to the front and back, and the top edge of the sides is rounded. The bottoms are fitted to grooves in the front and sides and nailed to the underside of the back. The top two drawers in line in the upper case were originally fitted for wooden spring locks.

Inscriptions: A paper label pasted to the inside of the bottom of the middle drawer in the lower case reads in ink: "This highboy belonged to / President Clap of Yale, de / descending through Temperance / (Clap) Pitkin, Anna (Pitkin) / Perkins, Emily (Perkins) / Baldwin, to Simeon E. Baldwin. / [in pencil] and then to his grand daughter Charlotte Gilman Penfield in 19[??]." A brass plaque once affixed to the outside of the left side of the upper case is stamped "owned by / S.E.B.—1908" and contained two paper cards with ink inscriptions. One card reads "President / Thomas Clap / of Yale / 1703–1767," and the other card, the back of a calling card, reads "Clap Highboy inherited / by Simeon E. Baldwin / 1840–1927 / Inherited by Charlotte Gilman / Penfield his granddaughter / Thomas Clap was 1st Pres.

131a

of Yale." The plaque and its cards have been removed and are stored in the object file. "Joe" and some columns of figures are written in pencil on the top of the top of the lower case, and "R" is written on the drawer divider under the top right drawer in the upper case and on the corresponding drawer bottom.

Condition: At one time the upper case was fitted with legs and used separately as a chest of drawers; a round hole in each corner of the underside of the bottom remains. The bottom of the lowest drawer in the upper case has been replaced, and the top 2 cm of the front of the same drawer have been pieced. New running strips have been added to most of the drawers. The brass escutcheons with bail pulls are replacements; the lock escutcheons may be original. The feet and legs have been damaged by insects and have been repaired. The side knee brackets on the rear legs are replacements, and the top element of the cornice molding on the left side is a replacement.

Woods: Sycamore; drawer fronts, with one exception, drawer dividers, with one exception, sides of lower case, sycamore; top, bottom, and sides of upper case, yellow poplar; legs, birch; back of upper case, top of lower case, chestnut; front rail of lower case, front of middle drawer in lower case, soft maple; inlaid stringing, apparently all soft maple; drawer sides and backs, upper drawer divider in upper case, eastern white pine; drawer bottoms, Atlantic white cedar.

Dimensions: H 175.8; W 103.2; UCW 90.7; LCW 97.7; D 52.4; UCD 47.2; LCD 51.3.

Provenance: According to a family tradition, this high chest originally belonged to Thomas Clap (1703–1767), president of Yale College from 1740 to 1766. It descended to his daughter by his first wife, Temperance (Clap) Pitkin (b. 1732), who married the Reverend Timothy Pitkin of Farmington, Conn., in 1753; to their daughter, Anna (Pitkin) Perkins; to her daughter, Emily (Perkins) Baldwin (1796–1874) and her husband Roger Sherman Baldwin (1793–1863) of New Haven; to their son Simeon E. Baldwin (1840–1927) by 1908; to his granddaughter Charlotte Gilman Penfield by 1927. Mrs. Penfield gave the chest to the Yale University Library in 1968.

THOMAS Clap was a graduate of Harvard College (class of 1722) who served in the ministry in Windham, Connecticut, before being called to Yale to serve as rector in 1740.[1] In that same year, he took as his second wife one Mary Saltonstall

silver, and his extensive library. He owned a "Case of Drawers, & dressing Table" valued together at £2.10.0, and probably located in his north front chamber. The "Case of Drawers" may well be the high chest now at Yale. Interestingly, he also owned a "Japan'd Case of Drawers, & dressing table" valued at the same amount of £2.10.0. Although the seventeenth-century furniture of the New Haven area has been studied somewhat thoroughly, little work has been done to date on eighteenth-century objects from the area. The simple shaping of the skirt seems typical of Connecticut work, and stringing is used on a dressing table found in the Plattsville area of Trumbull, Connecticut, by Henry Hammond Taylor.[4] The inlaid shell on the center drawer of the lower case recalls the use of similar motifs on Boston-area furniture of the period (cat. 100).

Gift of Mrs. Paul L. Penfield 1968.9

1. For Clap, see Louis Leonard Tucker, *Puritan Protagonist: President Thomas Clap of Yale College* (Chapel Hill: University of North Carolina Press, 1962); and Ebenezer Clapp, comp., *Record of the Clapp Family in America* (Boston: David Clapp & Son, 1876), pp. 130–137 and passim.
2. Clifford K. Shipton, *Biographical Sketches of Those Who Attended Harvard College in the Classes of 1722–1725*, Sibley's Harvard Graduates, vol. 7 (Boston: Massachusetts Historical Society, 1945), p. 31.
3. Docket 2629, New Haven Probate District, New Haven County Records, on file in the Connecticut State Library, Hartford.
4. Kirk, *Conn. Furn.*, no. 172.

131

(d. 1769), a wealthy widow from Branford, and he lived in New Haven until his retirement from Yale in 1766 and his death the year after. If the strong family tradition linking this high chest to Clap is correct, and it seems more plausible than many such histories, it probably was made during Clap's New Haven years, perhaps shortly after his marriage in 1740. As one of Clap's biographers noted, Mary Clap's "family connections provided important alliances, her wealth made possible many popular benefactions, such as the gift of a new bell to the college, and her social training and personality made her an excellent mistress of the large house on College Street."[2] If Mary did not bring the high chest with her at marriage, which is a distinct possibility, she may have been responsible for selecting this stylish object. The inventory of Clap's estate, taken in February 1768, totaled £6,656 and included many fine furnishings, substantial amounts of

132

High chest of drawers
Eastern Connecticut or Rhode Island, 1740–1760
(see pl. 12)

Description: The object is in two cases. The upper case is crowned by light complex projecting cornice molding and holds seven drawers in an unusual arrangement: a top wide drawer surmounts three drawers in line, with the center drawer of greater width, with three graduated drawers below. The wide drawers have a central panel of dark burl veneer flanked by panels of the same dark veneer outlined with rectangles of a lighter herringbone veneer, while the middle small drawer is veneered in the same pattern as the wide drawers. The wide drawers and the middle drawer are fitted with a central brass lock escutcheon flanked by matching escutcheons with bail pulls; the small side drawers are

fitted with a single brass with bail pull. The drawers are flanked and separated by applied double half-round molding on the case. The sides of the upper case are decorated with a central vertical panel flanked by vertical strips of dark veneer, a thin strip of another dark veneer, and a strip of the light-colored veneer. The base molding on the upper case rests within the projecting midmolding on the lower case. The lower case contains one wide drawer above three in line, with the side drawers of greater depth and the center drawer of greater width. These drawers are veneered with the same materials and in the same manner as the upper case drawers, and they are fitted with brasses in the same fashion, with the exception that the lock escutcheons are blind. The drawers are again outlined with applied double half-round molding. The sides of the lower case are decorated in a manner similar to the sides of the upper case, although here the thin strip of the second dark veneer is not present, and the grain of the light colored veneer runs vertically rather than horizontally. The front of the lower case is veneered with the dark burl veneer, and the front and side skirts are edged with applied cock beading. The front skirt is shaped with flathead arches at the sides flanking a deep center arch that contains a central pendant section with a turned drop flanked in turn by pendant sections with matching turned drops at the sides. The side skirts are shaped with reverse curves rising to a central flathead arch. The chest is supported by four slender, straight cabriole legs terminating in pad feet. In the upper case, the top and bottom are dovetailed to the sides, and the three horizontal butted backboards are beveled at their top and side edges and nailed with rosehead nails to the top and bottom and to rabbets in the sides. The three drawers in line are supported by a joined framework; the side drawer runners are rabbeted to the drawer dividers and nailed to the sides of the case. The drawer dividers are of unequal depth, and there are no dustboards. The vertical partitions between the drawers in line are tenoned through the drawer dividers. The sides of the upper case are formed of three vertical butted boards. In the lower case, the single horizontal backboard and the sides are joined to the legs with mortise-and-tenon joints secured with four pegs. There is no top to the lower case; the upper case merely rests on the applied midmolding. Vertical blocks are nailed to the inside faces of the legs and the drawer runners, and guides are applied to these strips. The vertical partitions between the lower drawers are nailed to glue blocks on the skirt. The lower drawers are supported by a medial runner, and small blocks are glued to the inside of the back as stops. On each drawer, the sides are dovetailed to the front and back, and the top edge of the sides is rounded; the drawer bottoms are nailed to a rabbet in the front and to the underside of the sides and back, with running strips applied in the upper case. The drawer linings in the lower case are quite thin.

Inscriptions: A blank American Express Co. shipping label dated 1914 is pasted to the outside of the back of the lower case. A museum accession number, "20.843," is painted in red on the outside of the back of the upper and lower case and in a drawer. "Sabotnik" and "Sabot——" and "Hippi——" are scratched on the top of the top of the upper case; the scratching appears to be modern.

Condition: There are traces of red paint, probably original, on the midmolding. The outer drops on the front skirt are replacements, as are two of the brasses on the lowest drawer in the upper case. The right front leg has been broken and repaired, one-third of the right rear foot is a replacement, and the backs of the lower side drawers in the lower case have been pieced; there have been other small repairs to the drawers. The center runners for the top wide drawer in the upper case, the middle small drawer in the upper case, and the wide drawer in the lower case are missing. There have been minor repairs to the inlay.

Woods: Varieties of woods are used almost interchangeably within this object. Dark burl veneer on exterior, maple, probably soft maple; light-colored veneer, staghorn sumac (*Rhus typhina*); thin strips of dark stained veneer on sides of upper case, probably maple; legs, cornice, midmoldings, soft maple; half-round moldings, drops, American black walnut; top and bottom of upper case, some drawer fronts, some drawer dividers, some drawer bottoms and backs, chestnut; backboards of upper case, southern yellow pine and eastern white pine; one drawer divider in upper case, red oak; sides of upper case, formed by a central panel of hard maple, probably sugar maple, flanked by panels of sycamore; drawer fronts and linings, mixture of eastern hemlock, chestnut, maple, eastern white pine, southern yellow pine, and either Atlantic white cedar or northern white cedar.

Dimensions: H 182.6; W 95.1; UCW 86.8; LCW 91.1; D 54.0; UCD 49.1; LCD 51.5.

Exhibition: YUAG, "Rhode Island Furn."

Bibliography: *Sack Coll.*, 1:20 no. 67; "Recent Gifts and Purchases," *YUAG Bulletin* 30, no. 2 (March 1965): 34; Ruth Davidson, "In the Museums," *Antiques* 88, no. 3 (September 1965): 356; Kirk, *Early Am. Furn.*, fig. 26.

Provenance: This high chest was once in the collection of the Museum of Art, Rhode Island School of Design, Provi-

132

Several features suggest that this unusual and outstanding high chest was made in Rhode Island, or perhaps in eastern Connecticut, where Rhode Island influence was pronounced. Among the Rhode Island–style features present are the central drop on the front skirt and the drawer construction, featuring thin drawer linings in the lower case and running strips in the upper but not the lower case.[1] In contrast to Rhode Island practice, however, the midmolding here is applied to the lower rather than the upper case, and the legs are framed as an integral part of the lower case, rather than glued in place. The multiplicity of woods used to make this chest—more woods than used in any other object in this catalogue—also suggests a rural maker, and other objects from eastern Connecticut have been found to contain many different woods. Yet the maker of this object was not an unsophisticated craftsman, for the design is complex and rich, and the veneered side panels are an unusual embellishment not frequently encountered even in urban objects. The use of staghorn sumac as a veneer has not been recorded as yet on other eighteenth-century American furniture. The pattern of veneered panels and the multiple brasses on the drawers are reminiscent of early eighteenth-century high chests associated with the New York area (see cat. 122).

The Mabel Brady Garvan Collection 1964.46

1. There are no known close counterparts to this high chest; for examples related in feeling, see Nutting, *Treasury*, no. 346 (which has three drops on the front skirt) and no. 347; Lockwood, fig. XV; Fairbanks and Bates, p. 112 (a Massachusetts or New Hampshire example with veneered panels); and *Antiques* 48, no. 4 (October 1945): 221. An English example with veneered panels of related design is illustrated in *Antiques* 91, no. 2 (February 1967): 147. Center drops are found on a Boston-area dressing table (Fitzgerald, fig. III-10) and on objects from eastern Long Island, where Rhode Island influence was also strong (Failey, *Long Island*, nos. 136, 137).

dence, R. I. (20.843). Museum records indicate that it is one of several high chests owned by well-known Providence collector Mrs. Eliza Greene Metcalf Radeke (1855–1931), one of the museum's principal benefactors. It is probably the "really remarkable highboy" with "walnut burl inlay" and "features . . . that make it wholly unique" that dealer Arthur Leslie Green of Newport found in the Boston shop of Israel Sack and urged Mrs. Radeke to buy for $600 in November 1916. Whatever its source, it was given to RISD by Mrs. Radeke on 6 April 1920. The museum sold the chest in 1957 to dealer Harry Arons, Ansonia, Conn., who sold it to Israel Sack, Inc., New York, N. Y. The Sack firm in turn sold it to collector Richard Tishman, New York, N. Y., who later sold it back to the Sacks. It was acquired from the Sacks by exchange in 1964.

133

Chest-on-frame
Newport, Rhode Island, 1740–1760

Description: The chest is in two stages. The upper case has applied molding of a single piece nailed to the edges of the top and the case at the front and sides. The case holds five lipped drawers, two in line over three graduated drawers. The top two drawers are fitted with central brass escutcheons with bail pulls; the lower three drawers have central brass

High Chests of Drawers 255

133

lock escutcheons flanked by matching escutcheons with bail pulls. A complex base molding is applied to the bottom edge of the upper case at the front and sides. The front skirt is shaped with deep reverse curves rising at the center to an acorn drop; the side skirts are cut to a serpentine shape. The four cabriole legs have applied knee brackets and terminate in pad feet with large pads. The upper case is of dovetailed board construction; the two horizontal butted backboards are nailed to a rabbet in the top, sides, and bottom. There are three glue blocks behind the bottom front rail of the upper case and two behind the top rail, and the top drawers are supported by a strip across the back into which their medial runner is housed. In each drawer, the sides are dovetailed to the front and back, and the bottom is nailed to a rabbet in the front and to the undersides of the sides and back and runs on applied running strips (with the exception of the top two drawers, which are without running strips). The underside of the bottom of the top two drawers has a groove at center for a tab or spring lock, and these drawers vary by 2 to 3 cm in depth. The upper case rests on the frame, with battens or cleats nailed to the underside of the bottom fitting within the frame and the applied molding at the front and sides overlapping the frame. The frame consists of four dovetailed boards, with the dovetails exposed on the front and back. The four legs are detachable and are housed in rabbets cut in these boards. They extend about half the height of the frame and are glued and blocked to the corners.

Condition: The lip of the upper most drawer has been pieced, and there are other minor repairs to the drawer fronts and moldings. The spring locks on the upper drawers are missing.

Woods: Soft maple; chestnut.

Dimensions: H 144.3; W 95.5; CW 89.6; D 49.6; CD 44.3.

Exhibition: YUAG, "Rhode Island Furn."

Bibliography: *Flayderman Coll.*, no. 415.

Provenance: Philip Flayderman, Boston, Mass.; acquired at auction in 1930 by Francis P. Garvan, New York, N. Y.

THE shape of the skirt, the detachable legs terminating in crisply outlined pad feet with high pads, and the fitting of the upper case on top, rather than within, the lower section all suggest that this object was made in Rhode Island, and possibly in Newport. Maple was commonly used for furniture there, being slightly more costly than pine but far less expensive than walnut or mahogany, and chestnut as a secondary wood is often found in Rhode Island objects.[1] Other Rhode Island chest-on-frames of the same period are found with one additional wide drawer in the upper case.[2] Reproductions of this chest-on-frame have been made by Harden Furniture Company since 1983.

The Mabel Brady Garvan Collection 1930.2313

1. Ott, pp. 174–175.
2. *Sack Coll.*, 2: 461 no. 1140; Ott, no. 58, with a frame of varying configuration; *Antiques* 91, no. 1 (January 1967): 44.

134

High chest of drawers
Salem, Massachusetts, 1740–1760
(see pl. 13)

Description: The upper case is crowned by a complex projecting cornice at the front and sides and contains seven lipped drawers. There are three deep drawers in line at the top, with the middle drawer of greater width and carved with a convex shell, above four graduated drawers below. The upper case rests within midmolding on the top of the lower case. The lower case contains one wide lipped drawer over three lipped drawers in line, with the middle drawer again being of greater width and carved with a convex shell. The front skirt is carved with a central shell with a diamond piercing that is flanked by scrolled drops and is shaped with reverse curves. The side skirts are shaped to paired reverse curves. The chest is supported by four cabriole legs with sharply arrised knees and scrolled knee brackets, and the legs terminate in pad feet with high pads. The surface of the chest is decorated with painted graining to simulate walnut or mahogany. The carved drawers are painted to simulate straight grain, with their shells decorated with a rainbow pattern of alternating bands of light and dark; the other drawers are painted to simulate figured grain. The wide drawers in each case are fitted with central brass lock escutcheons flanked by matching escutcheons with bail pulls; the

134a

134b

High Chests of Drawers 257

134

small side drawers are fitted with escutcheons with bail pulls; and the middle small drawers in each case are fitted with brass button pulls. The top of the upper case is dovetailed to the sides, and the sides are dovetailed to the bottom. The back consists of two vertical boards fitted to grooves in the top and sides and nailed to the bottom. The drawer-divider dovetails are exposed, and the vertical partitions between the drawers in line are tenoned through the top. The drawer runners are nailed to the sides of the case, and the three drawers in line are supported by a joined framework, with the side elements housed in grooves that pierce the backboard. Kickers are nailed to the sides of the case and to the top above the top drawers. There are three small glue blocks behind the bottom front rail of the upper case. In the lower case, the back is a single horizontal board joined to the rear legs with mortise-and-tenon joints secured on one side with six pegs and on the other with five. The rear posts are of greater depth than the front posts, and the knees of the rear legs are squared off. The drawer divider is dovetailed to the sides with the dovetail exposed, and the drawer runners are tenoned to the front skirt and to the back, with drawer guides nailed to the sides. The upper case rests on two thick boards nailed to the sides of the lower case and on the deep top rail of the lower case. The knee brackets are pinned in place. On each drawer, the sides are dovetailed to the front, and the back is dovetailed to the sides, with the top edges of the sides rounded. The bottoms are let into grooves in the front and sides and nailed to the underside of the back; in the wide drawers, the front and side edges of the bottoms are beveled.

Inscriptions: There are columns of figures on the outside of the left side of the upper left drawer in the upper case in white chalk. Some compass scribe lines appear on the outside of the right side of the same drawer. "L 49 66 / C 15" appears in white chalk on the outside of the back of the middle drawer in the lower case.

Condition: The high chest retains its original painted graining and finish. The front knee bracket of the right front leg is a replacement, as are the brass button pulls. The center runner for the wide drawer in the lower case is missing, and the upper part of the back of the lower left drawer in the lower case is missing. The kicker above the middle drawer in the top of the upper case is loose, and several knotholes in the top and in a drawer bottom have been patched.

Woods: Soft maple, including backboard of lower case; drawer fronts, moldings, soft maple with tiger-maple grain; eastern white pine.

Dimensions: H 198.5; W 107.2; UCW 96.7; LCW 101.7; D 51.3; UCD 45.7; LCD 49.2.

Bibliography: Kirk, *Early Am. Furn.*, fig. 76; Kirk, *Am. Furn. & Brit. Trad.*, figs. 383, 384.

Provenance: Found in Rowley, Mass.; acquired by exchange from Israel Sack, Inc., New York, N. Y.

THE sharply arrised knees, the scrolled knee brackets, the high pads of the feet, and the distinctively shaped front skirt, with its diamond cutout flanked by scrolls, of this high chest found in Essex County are all features associated with Salem-area furniture.[1] The most remarkable feature of this example

is its painted graining, probably in imitation of walnut or mahogany, on a surface of tiger maple.

The Mabel Brady Garvan Collection 1966.63

1. See, for example, a scroll-top high chest with claw-and-ball feet attributed on the basis of its family history to Elijah Sanderson (1752–1825) of Salem in *Antiques* 113, no. 5 (May 1978): 1079. A related dressing table, with a carved shell of a more flowing and less rigid nature on its lower middle drawer, is illustrated in Cooper, *In Praise of America*, fig. 229. See also high chests illustrated in Nutting, *Treasury*, no. 377; *Antiques* 82, no. 5 (November 1962): 461; 107, no. 5 (May 1975): 963; and 111, no. 5 (May 1977): 898; and *Sack Coll.*, 1: 111 no. 321, 2: 557 no. 1301, vol. 3: 631 no. 1420.

135

High chest of drawers

Connecticut, 1740–1770

Description: The upper case is crowned by complex projecting cornice molding and contains five lipped drawers, two in line over three graduated drawers below. The upper case rests within the midmolding applied to the top of the lower case, and the lower case contains four lipped drawers, one wide over three in line, with the middle drawer of greater width and carved with a concave shell. The front skirt is shaped with flathead arches below each drawer, with the arch under the middle drawer recessed, and with pointed drops below a line of beading. The chest is supported by four straight cabriole legs terminating in Spanish feet. In the upper case, the top and bottom are dovetailed to the sides, and the dovetails joining the drawer dividers and vertical partitions to the case are exposed. The cornice molding is applied with large round wooden pins. The three vertical backboards are joined with a half lap and nailed to a rabbet in the sides and to the top and bottom. The drawer runners within the case are housed in grooves in the sides; some grooves for runners were apparently cut initially in the wrong position and then filled. There is no top to the lower case, which is framed primarily with mortise-and-tenon joints. The single horizontal backboard and the sides are secured to the legs with six pegs, but the top front rail is dovetailed to the front legs with an unusually long slot dovetail. The drawer divider is also dovetailed in place, but the bottom front rail is held with a mortise-and-tenon joint to the legs secured with two pins. The side drawer runners

135

are nailed through drawer guides to the legs. The knee brackets are applied to the skirt and secured with wooden pins, as is the midmolding. The drops are shaped rather than turned and are braced from behind with shaped blocks nailed to the inside of the skirt. On each drawer, the sides are dovetailed to the back, while the back is dovetailed to the sides; the bottoms are beveled on their front and side edges and let into grooves in the front and sides and nailed to the underside of the back. In the upper case, the top two drawers are fitted with single brass escutcheons with bail pulls; the top wide drawer has a central brass escutcheon flanked by matching escutcheons with bail pulls, while the two wide drawers below have a central blind lock escutcheon flanked by matching brasses. The wide drawer in the lower case also has a blind lock escutcheon flanked by brasses, while the lower side drawers have single escutcheons with bail pulls, and the middle drawer is fitted with a brass button pull.

Condition: The chest was refinished by Emile Mazzola in 1962. The right rear leg has been severely damaged by insects and has been extensively repaired; insect damage to the other legs and feet has also been repaired to a lesser extent. An iron brace has been added between the backboard of the lower case and the left rear leg. Shrinkage cracks in the sides of the lower case have been pieced. The brasses appear to be original.

Woods: American black cherry; backboards of upper case, sides, backs, and bottoms of three wide drawers in upper case, sides and backs of top two drawers in upper case, bottoms and backs of drawers in lower case, aspen or cottonwood (*Populus* spp.); top and bottom of upper case, sides of drawers in lower case, eastern white pine; bottom of top two drawers in line in upper case, red oak.

Dimensions: H 181.1; W 104.9; UCW 91.1; LCW 99.8; D 55.0; UCD 45.0; LCD 50.6.

Provenance: Harry Arons, Ansonia, Conn.; by sale to Henry Hammond Taylor, Bridgeport, Conn.; by sale to Francis P. Garvan, New York, N. Y.

As its squarish, blocky stance suggests, several unusual details of this high chest confirm that it is the product of a rural craftsman's shop. For example, its moldings and knee brackets are applied with wooden pegs rather than nails, and its drops are shaped from the solid, rather than being separate turned elements, implying that the chest's maker was without a ready supply of nails and that his shop lacked a lathe. The small brasses, which appear to be original, do not scale well with the object and may have been used out of necessity rather than choice if only a small supply of brasses was available to the isolated rural maker. Although it is difficult to pinpoint a precise place of origin for this chest, perhaps it was made in the western part of the state, since its carved shell, Spanish or web feet, simply shaped skirt with a recess below the middle drawer, and rather straight legs bring to mind the more sophisticated (in Connecticut terms) products of several shops in the Housatonic Valley.[1]

The Mabel Brady Garvan Collection 1930.2309

1. Edward S. Cooke, Jr., "Craftsmen-Client Relations in the Housatonic Valley, 1720–1800," *Antiques* 125, no. 1 (January 1984): 272–280.

136

High chest of drawers
Connecticut, possibly Norwalk, 1750–1780
(en suite with cat. 106)

Description: The high chest is in two cases. The upper case is crowned by complex cornice molding at the front and sides above deep cove molding. The upper case contains five lipped drawers, including two in line over three graduated drawers, and it rests within a midmolding applied to the top of the lower case. The lower case contains four lipped drawers, including one wide drawer over three in line, with the lower side drawers of greater depth and the middle drawer of greater width. The wide drawers in each case are fitted with central brass lock escutcheons (blind in the lower case) flanked by matching escutcheons with bail pulls; the two small drawers in the upper case and the two lower side drawers in the lower case are fitted with a single escutcheon with bail pull; and the lower middle drawer in the lower case is fitted with a blind brass lock escutcheon. The front skirt is shaped with deep reverse curves flanking a round central shell with twenty-two lobes, and the side skirts are shaped to a single flathead arch. The case is supported by four rather straight cabriole legs, with small applied knee brackets, terminating in pad feet. The top and bottom of the upper case are each a single board dovetailed to the sides, and the three horizontal backboards are joined with a half lap and nailed to rabbets in the top and sides and to the bottom with rosehead nails. The cornice moldings are formed of four elements applied with nails. The dovetails joining the drawer dividers to the case sides and the vertical partition between the drawers in line to the top rail and the drawer divider are exposed. The two drawers in line are supported by a nailed framework, and the runners for the other drawers are nailed to the case sides; there are no dustboards. The bottom front rail is nailed to the bottom of the case with rosehead nails. The upper case rests on transverse strips nailed to the inside of each side of the lower case; the nails are countersunk and there is no top to the lower case. The lower case is framed with mortise-and-tenon joints, with three pegs used to secure the case sides to the legs. The bottom front rail is double pegged to the legs, and the dovetails of the drawer dividers and vertical partitions are exposed. The posts of the rear legs are thicker than those of the front, and the rear face of the rear legs is squared off. On each drawer, the sides are dovetailed to the front and back; the bottom is beveled on its

136

front and side edges, let into grooves in the front and sides, and nailed to the underside of the back. The top edges of the sides and back are beveled.

Inscriptions: "Miss Canfield / Norwalk" is written in pencil on the bottom of the lower right drawer in the lower case. The first *s* in *Miss* is the old-fashioned long *s*, suggesting that the inscription was written in the eighteenth century and is perhaps original. The lower side drawers in the lower case are marked "1" and "2" in white chalk on the outside of the back, and there are other shop marks in pencil and white chalk on the object, including columns of addition on the inside of the back of the upper case.

Condition: The high chest has been refinished, and the brasses are possibly original. In each corner of the underside of the bottom of the upper case there is a hole, surrounded by three small holes and contained within an impressed circle, suggesting that the upper case was once fitted with casters and used as a separate chest of drawers. The lip of the wide drawer in the lower case is pieced.

Woods: American black cherry; eastern white pine; yellow poplar.

Dimensions: H 180.5; W 101.3; UCW 90.8; LCW 97.2; D 53.6; UCD 49.7; LCD 52.8.

Bibliography: Nutting, *Treasury*, no. 349; Ormsbee, *Story Am. Furn.*, fig. 114b.

Provenance: The inscription would lead one to believe that the high chest, and perhaps its accompanying dressing table (cat. 106), were owned at an early date and possibly originally by a Miss Canfield of Norwalk, Conn. It is not known how the high chest was acquired by Francis P. Garvan, New York, N. Y.

THIS high chest shares many construction as well as design similarities with its companion dressing table (cat. 106). The recently discovered inscription, "Miss Canfield / Norwalk," raises the possibility that these objects were made in that vicinity. A related cherry high chest, with a broken arch pediment and a round carved shell in the upper case, was once owned by Miss Katrina Kipper of Queen Anne Cottage Antiques, Accord, Massachusetts.[1]

The Mabel Brady Garvan Collection 1930.2444

1. DAPC, 67.479.

137

High chest of drawers
Connecticut, possibly Waterbury or Woodbury, 1750–1800

Description: The object is in three units, with a separate frame of three graduated steps resting on top of the upper case which in turn is supported by the lower case. The upper case is crowned by a complex molded cornice at the front and sides above deep cove molding concealing a blind frieze drawer. The upper case contains five other lipped drawers, two in line over three graduated drawers, and rests within the midmolding applied to the top of the lower case. The

High Chests of Drawers 261

137

lower case contains five lipped drawers, including two in line over three lower drawers in line, with the center drawer of lesser width. The front skirt is shaped to three flathead arches corresponding in width to the drawers; the side skirts are shaped to single flathead arches. The case is supported by four rather straight cabriole legs terminating in pad feet raised on small disks. The steps are a dovetailed framework, with the treads molded on their front and side edges and with the dovetails joining the sides to the risers exposed on the sides; longitudinal braces under the lowest and middle steps are tenoned through the sides. The dovetails are reinforced with nails. In the upper case, the top and bottom consist of two longitudinal boards, one across the front and another at the back, which are dovetailed to the case sides; at the top, a wide board is then nailed in place over these framing elements. The back consists of three vertical backboards, two wide boards flanking a narrow center strip, nailed in place. The dovetails of the drawer dividers to the case sides and of the vertical partition between the drawers in line are exposed. The drawer runners are nailed to the sides of the case, and there are no dustboards; the runner between the drawers in line is tenoned through the back. The lower case is framed with mortise-and-tenon joints. The drawer runners in the case interior are tenoned through the back. On each drawer, the sides are dovetailed to the front and back and are nailed to the back through the sides. The top edge of the sides is rounded. The bottoms are let into a groove in the front and to rabbets in the sides and nailed with rosehead nails to the underside of the back. On most of the drawers, the sides extend beyond the back to act as stops. The upper and lower dovetails on the drawer sides are reinforced with nails.

Condition: As noted in *Antiques* in 1937, "When first seen by Mr. and Mrs. [C. Sanford] Bull, this highboy's lower frame and upper chest had been separated and were doing individual duty in an old homestead in Woodbury, Connecticut. The steps, whose function had long since been forgotten, were reposing in the attic." Evidence remains of where round feet were doweled into the bottom of the upper case when it was used as a separate chest of drawers. A top was fitted to the lower case so that it could be used as a dressing or side table, and in the process the midmolding was lost; it subsequently has been replaced. The brasses are replacements, and the drops on the front skirt are missing. The chest has been stripped of its original paint and given a dark stain.

Wood: Yellow poplar.

Dimensions: H (including steps) 205.5; H (without steps) 179.5; W 103.3; UCW 92.9; LCW 101.1; D 51.5; UCD 45.7; LCD 50.3.

Bibliography: Nutting, *Treasury*, no. 345; "The Editor's Attic," *Antiques* 31, no. 4 (April 1937): 172–174; "Living with Antiques: The Connecticut Home of Mr. and Mrs. C. Sanford Bull," *Antiques* 45, no. 4 (April 1944): 190; Edith Gaines, "The Step-top Highboy," *Antiques* 72, no. 4 (October 1957): 333.

Provenance: Found in Woodbury, Conn., by C. Sanford Bull, Middlebury, Conn., prior to 1928.

THIS flat-top high chest has the distinction of being the only example in the Yale collection to retain its original "steps" for the display of ceramics, glass, and other precious and costly household articles. The earliest reference to such steps

found by Irving Lyon was in a Boston inventory of 1733, and documentary references continue to appear for the next half century.[1] Although it is often said that steps are more frequently found on Connecticut high chests, it is likely that they were used throughout New England and in other areas as well. It is also thought that such steps are a characteristic of American work, as English examples have not been published to date. Surviving examples of high chests with their original steps are rare today, although without question many sets of steps have become separated and lost over the years, as nearly happened with this example.[2] Steps were either permanently attached to the top of the high chest or, more commonly, were separate objects which slid over cleats attached to the top of the high chest or, as here, simply rested on the chest. Although this example was found in Woodbury, it is related in style and construction to privately owned objects with Waterbury histories examined by Edward S. Cooke, Jr.[3]

Gift of C. Sanford Bull 1949.244

1. Lyon, pp. 102–105; Edith Gaines, "The Step-top Highboy," *Antiques* 72, no. 4 (October 1957): 332–334.
2. In addition to the examples illustrated by Gaines, see Lockwood, fig. 86; *Antiques* 111, no. 1 (January 1977): 51; Lyon, fig. 42; Fales, *Deerfield*, fig. 384; Frances Clary Morse, *Furniture of the Olden Time* (New York: Macmillan Co., 1908), fig. 13.
3. Cooke to the author, 1 July 1984.

138

138

High chest of drawers

Connecticut, possibly Wethersfield, ca. 1787

Description: The upper case is crowned by a complex molded cornice that includes deep cove molding. The case contains nine lipped drawers, including a deep upper middle drawer carved with a concave shell and flanked by pairs of superimposed small drawers, all above four graduated drawers. The upper case rests within the midmolding on the top of the lower case. The lower case contains one wide lipped drawer over three lipped drawers in line, with the side drawers wider and the middle drawer carved with a concave shell. The front skirt is shaped to flathead arches below the drawers but was never fitted with drops. The side skirts are shaped to a single flathead arch. The chest is supported by four cabriole legs with arrised knees but without knee brackets terminating in ridged or arrised pad feet. In the upper case, the top and bottom are dovetailed to the sides, with some of the dovetails reinforced with rosehead nails. The two vertical backboards are joined with a half lap and nailed to the top and bottom and to rabbets in the sides with rosehead nails. The dovetails joining the drawer dividers to the sides are exposed. The side drawer runners are housed in grooves in the sides. The lower case is framed with mortise-and-tenon joints, with the single horizontal backboard joined to the rear legs with five pegs. The front rails and drawer divider are also pegged to the legs. The top of the lower case is a single board dovetailed to the sides and only extending about a third of the depth of the case. The drawers are supported by runners at the sides. On each drawer, the

sides are dovetailed to the front and back, and the top edges of the sides and back are molded. The bottoms are beveled on their front and side edges, let into grooves in the front and sides, and nailed to the underside of the back.

Inscriptions: Written in chalk on the outside of the back of the upper right drawer in the upper case is "1787." Written in white chalk on the outside of the back of the lowest drawer in the upper case is "1787 then was ———" An illegible inscription in white chalk appears on the outside of the back of the upper left drawer of the upper case. The inside bottom of the top wide drawer in the upper case has been patched with a piece of paper that reads: "SAND PA[torn] / EMERY PAPER an[torn] / Ground F[torn] / GLUE an [torn]."

Condition: The high chest was refinished by Emile Mazzola in 1964. The wide drawer in the lower case is a replacement, and the brasses are replacements. The lips of other drawers have been pieced, and there have been minor repairs to the drawer linings. The skirt on the left side of the lower case has been repaired near the rear leg.

Woods: Soft maple, probably red maple; eastern white pine.

Dimensions: H 187.4; W 100.3; UCW 88.8; LCW 96.6; D 54.4; UCD 45.9; LCD 50.8.

Provenance: Charles Stetson, Boston, Mass.

THIS high chest is related to a group of furniture linked to Wethersfield, Connecticut, although it shows variations from the core group of documented examples, suggesting that it was made in another shop or perhaps elsewhere in the Connecticut Valley.[1] This chest originally had brasses located above the shells in the middle drawers of each case, like the other members of the Wethersfield group, but the shaping of the skirt and the profile of the legs differ slightly. The date 1787 appears twice on this chest, and there seems to be no good reason not to accept this late date as the date of manufacture. A similar high chest in the same style was made by a member of the Dominy family of Long Island in 1796.[2]

Bequest of Charles Stetson 1954.37.28

1. Kevin M. Sweeney, "Furniture and Furniture-Making in Mid-Eighteenth-Century Wethersfield, Connecticut," *Antiques* 125, no. 5 (May 1984): 1156–1163. For other related examples, see *Antiques* 106, no. 5 (November 1974): 731; *Antiques* 93, no. 5 (May 1968): 625; and *Fine American Furniture, Silver and Decorative Arts*, 22 January 1983 (New York: Christie's, 1983), lot 461.
2. Hummel, *With Hammer in Hand*, cat. 193.

139

139

High chest of drawers
Eastern Long Island, New York, 1740–1800

Description: The high chest is in two cases. The upper case is crowned by a complex molded cornice containing deep cove molding and contains five lipped drawers, including two in line over three graduated drawers. The upper case rests within a midmolding applied to the top of the lower case. The lower case contains four lipped drawers, including one wide drawer over three in line, with the lower side drawers of greater depth and the lower middle drawer of greater width. The front skirt is shaped with deep reverse curves flanking a central drop, and the side skirts are shaped with paired reverse curves. The chest is supported by four

cabriole legs terminating in high pointed pad feet; the pads are approximately 3.1 cm high. The top and bottom of the upper case are dovetailed to the sides, and the three horizontal backboards are nailed in place. The dovetails joining the drawer dividers to the case sides are covered with a thin facing strip. The two drawers in line in the upper case are supported by a joined framework, and there are side drawer runners for the wide drawers; there are no dustboards. The lower case is framed with mortise-and-tenon joints, with four pegs used to secure the sides to the front and rear legs, a single peg used to secure the drawer divider, and two pegs to secure the skirt to the front legs. There is no top to the lower case; the upper case rests on transverse strips nailed to the front and rear legs. On each drawer, the sides are dovetailed to the front and back, with the top edge of the sides rounded; the bottoms are beveled on their front and side edges, let into grooves in the front and sides, and nailed to the underside of the back. The two drawers in line in the upper case are fitted with a brass lock escutcheon; the three wide drawers in the upper case and the wide drawer in the lower case have a central brass lock escutcheon flanked by matching escutcheons with bail pulls; the lower middle drawer in the lower case has a single brass lock escutcheon, and the flanking drawers are fitted with a single matching escutcheon with bail pull.

Inscriptions: A large "IIIX" is gouged into the inside of the left side of the lower left drawer in the lower case; a "VII" is similarly carved on the outside of the back of the upper left drawer in the upper case; and a "XII" appears on the outside of the back of the lowest wide drawer in the upper case. A modern printed paper label pasted to the inside of the bottom of the wide drawer in the lower case reads: "FROM / MRS. BEEKMAN C. CANNON / 70 HIGH STREET / NEW HAVEN, CONN. 06511 /*To* [printed] This Tallboy was left / to Jonathan Edwards College / by Mr. Burton Mueller / a descendant of / Jon[a]than Edw[ards] [script] / [POST] MASTER–This [parcel] may be ope[ned for insp]ection if necessary. [printed]." A fragment of another label, probably identical, also remains in the same drawer, and there are small fragments of another modern label remaining on the underside of the bottom of the upper case. "YALE" is written in black near the center of the outside of the back of the upper case.

Condition: The left front knee bracket and the bottom part of the central drop in the skirt have been repaired. A small section of the right midmolding has been replaced near the joint with the front midmolding. Some of the drawer runners have been renewed, and the backboards of the upper case have been renailed. Two small boards have been added to the sides of the lower center drawer in the lower case, perhaps to accommodate a sliding tray.

Woods: American black cherry; legs, birch; yellow poplar; eastern white pine.

Dimensions: H 195.5; W 114.7; UCW 103.4; LCW 111.5; D 55.1; UCD 49.0; LCD 53.6.

Provenance: See cat. 105.

THE very high, thick pads of the pointed slipper feet of this high chest are a detail found on much furniture attributed in recent years to Long Island.[1] The broad proportions and massive quality of this high chest also suggest its affinity to New York–area furniture. High chests appear more frequently in estate inventories for the eastern counties of Long Island than for the western sections, reflecting the influence of New England preferences for this form.[2] The central drop of the skirt—here simply a rounded arch rather than an applied, turned drop—echoes Rhode Island design (cat. 141). Related high chests were made on Long Island by members of the Dominy family of East Hampton as late as 1796 and possibly into the early years of the nineteenth century, indicating a stylistic conservatism in the area.[3]

Gift of Charles Hoyt 1950.77

1. Failey, *Long Island*, nos. 138–140.
2. Failey, *Long Island*, no. 141; other related high chests are illustrated as nos. 136–138; see also a high chest in Winterthur Museum (53.105), of red gum.
3. Hummel, *With Hammer in Hand*, cat. 193.

140

High chest of drawers
John Townsend (1733–1809)
Newport, Rhode Island, 1759

Description: The upper case is crowned by a broken-scroll pediment flanking a central fluted plinth, with five flutes at its front and sides, for a finial. The sides of the pediment are decorated with fluted plinths for finials; the bonnet is closed behind the arch by a board painted black; the scrolled edges of the arch are molded; and the pediment contains two applied plaques. The upper case contains five lipped draw-

ers, two in line over three graduated drawers, flanked by quarter columns at the side. The midmolding is attached to the base of the upper case in the Rhode Island fashion. The lower case contains four lipped drawers, one wide over three in line, with the side drawers of greater depth and the center drawer of greater width. The front skirt is shaped with deep reverse curves flanking a central concave carved shell; the side skirts are shaped with round arches flanking a central rounded drop. The case is supported by four cabriole legs; the knees of the front legs are carved with an acanthus and a shell and terminate in claw-and-ball feet with undercut talons. The rear legs are not carved and terminate in pad feet. The top and bottom of the upper case are dovetailed to the sides; the horizontal backboards are joined with a half lap and nailed to rabbets in the sides. The drawer dividers are dovetailed to the sides with the dovetails exposed, and the bottom front rail is blocked behind. The top two drawers in line are supported on a joined framework; there are no dustboards and no vertical reinforcing strip. The runners for the other drawers are nailed to the sides. In the lower case, the back is dovetailed to the sides, and the legs are housed within the case in the Newport fashion and supported by blocks. There is no top to the lower case; the upper case is cleated and rests within the midmolding and applied strips. The wide drawer and lower drawers in line are supported by center runners; the vertical partitions are housed in grooves in the drawer divider and nailed to the skirt, with guides for the center drawer tenoned to them. The bonnet is roofed with curved boards nailed in place to the front rail and to an arched backboard. In each drawer, the sides are dovetailed to the front and back; the bottoms are let into grooves in the front and nailed to the underside of the sides and back, with running strips applied. The top edge of the sides is rounded.

The lower drawers in line in the upper case, however, have bottoms that are nailed to rabbets in the front and sides and to the underside of the back and are without running strips. The top two drawers in line in the upper case were fitted with wooden spring locks. The wide drawers are all fitted with central stamped brass lock escutcheons flanked by matching escutcheons with bail pulls; the small drawers at the sides in the lower case and the two drawers in line in the upper case are fitted with escutcheons with bail pulls; and the middle drawer in the lower case is fitted with a blind lock escutcheon with bail pull.

140b

Inscriptions: "N⁰ 28 / Made By / John Townsend / Newport / 1759" is written in pencil on the inside of the bottom of the top wide drawer in the upper case. The outside of the back of the left and right drawers in line in the upper case are marked in white chalk "A" and "B" respectively, with the lower drawers marked "C," "D," and "E," from top to bottom respectively. The outside of the back of the wide drawer in the lower case is marked "A" in white chalk; "August 1 day" is scratched on the inside of the left side of the same drawer.

Condition: There have been many breaks and repairs to the cornice moldings, and the lips of some of the drawers in each case have been pieced. Shrinkage cracks in the sides of the upper case have been repaired with glue blocks, some of which subsequently have been lost. The cleats on the underside of the upper case are replacements. Most of the glue

140a

blocks on the legs are replacements, and the front legs have been screwed in place through the sides of the case, with the screw heads covered with filler. Glue blocks on the apron are missing, and some drawer runners and guides in each case are replacements. The side knee bracket on the left front leg is a replacement. In 1984, Peter Arkell replaced the inner talon on the left front foot; this had been lost earlier and poorly repaired. He also replaced a poorly repaired rear talon on the right front leg and carved a replacement for the missing outside talon on the same leg. The center talon on that foot has been broken and repaired. The wooden spring locks are missing.

Woods: Mahogany; drawer linings, mixture of chestnut, eastern white pine, and cottonwood (upper case: sides and backs, cottonwood; bottoms, chestnut; wide drawer in lower case: sides, cottonwood; back and bottom, chestnut; lower side drawers in lower case: sides and backs, chestnut; bottoms, eastern white pine; middle drawer in lower case: sides, cottonwood; back and bottom, eastern white pine); eastern white pine; chestnut; replaced cleats on bottom of upper case, southern yellow pine.

Dimensions: H 225.7; W 100.1; UCW 93.8; LCW 98.5; D 56.2; UCD 49.4; LCD 52.6.

Exhibition: *Girl Scouts Exhibition*, no. 659.

Bibliography: Walter A. Dyer, "The American Highboy: Chippendale," *Fine Arts* 17, no. 1 (July 1931): 37; Moses, figs. 3.99a–e; *Antiques* 127, no. 1 (January 1985): 133; *YUAG Bulletin* 39, no. 3 (Winter 1986): 40.

Provenance: Richard DeWolfe Brixey (1880–1943); by descent to his daughter Doris M. Brixey (d. 1983).

First published in 1929 as the work of an anonymous Newport craftsman, this high chest remained in a private collection for more than fifty years, out of sight to most collectors and students. It reemerged in 1984 as part of the generous bequest by Doris M. Brixey to Yale of part of the collection gathered by her father, Richard DeWolfe Brixey. Upon examination by the Art Gallery staff and Michael Moses, then completing his monograph on Newport furniture, it was discovered that the high chest is signed by John Townsend of Newport and dated 1759 and is thus "the only documented bonnet-top [high chest] extant" among John Townsend's rather large group of labeled and signed objects. (The meaning of "28" in the inscription remains unclear.) What was already a superb example of Newport furniture instantly became a landmark in the history of American eighteenth-century furniture as a whole. The many distinctive characteristics of John Townsend's shell, knee, and foot carving, his typical construction characteristics, and his distinctive calligraphy are discussed at length by Moses, who was able to attribute confidently (and, as it turned out, correctly) this object to Townsend's shop prior to the discovery of the signature.[1] In addition to its usefulness as a document against which one can compare unlabeled examples, much of the importance of this high chest lies in its early date. It is the second earliest dated example of John Town-

140

send's work (the earliest being two objects dated 1756), and it indicates that Townsend was already using in his midtwenties a full-blown Newport high style, a style and vocabulary of ornament and design that he would embrace for nearly four decades. The consumers of Newport were clearly confident in Townsend's abilities at an early age: the joinery work for a mahogany high case of drawers was valued at £90 in 1756 (revised upward to £100 in 1757) in a Providence cabinetmaker's agreement.[2] No other type of furniture was more expensive. Townsend's reputation must have spread quickly in a town with only 888 dwellings in 1760.[3] The frequency with which his furniture is signed and labeled is testimony to Townsend's large production for other markets, since any sort of identifying mark would probably be redundant in his own town.

Bequest of Doris M. Brixey 1984.32.36

1. Moses, chap. 3.
2. Ott, pp. 174–175.
3. Carl Bridenbaugh, *Cities in Revolt: Urban Life in America, 1743–1776* (New York: Alfred A. Knopf, 1955), p. 17.

141

High chest of drawers
Newport, Rhode Island, 1760–1780

Description: The upper case is crowned by a broken-scroll pediment, with the open arches flanking a gilt urn finial mounted on a fluted plinth with three flutes. The pediment is decorated with applied plaques; the cornice molding extends to the rear on either side of the opening, with the bonnet closed at the rear. The upper case contains five lipped drawers, two in line over three below, and the midmolding is applied to the base of the upper case. The lower case contains four lipped drawers, a single wide drawer over three in line, with the side drawers of greater depth and the middle drawer of greater width. The front skirt is shaped with reverse curves flanking a central reel and acorn drop that is partially reeded. The side skirts are shaped with reverse curves. The chest is supported by four cabriole legs terminating in claw-and-ball feet; the knees of all four legs are carved with scrolled leafage. In the upper case, the top and bottom are dovetailed to the sides, and the horizontal backboards are joined with a half lap and nailed to rabbets in the

141

sides and to the top and bottom with rosehead nails. The drawers in line are supported by a joined framework; runners for the other drawers are nailed to the sides. There is a vertical reinforcing strip nailed to the center of the inside of the back; there are no blocks behind the bottom front rail. The dovetail that joins the drawer dividers to the side is exposed. The vertical partition between the drawers in line is nailed through the drawer divider. The bonnet is roofed with boards nailed to the front and to the semicircular backboard. There are no transverse partitions within the bonnet. The top of the lower case consists of a longitudinal board at

the front dovetailed to the sides, with several butted transverse boards fitted to it and nailed to the back. The back is dovetailed to the sides, and the legs are fitted in the usual Newport manner, supported by glue blocks and extending to only about half the height of the lower case. There are side drawer runners for the wide drawers and central runners for the small drawers in line. The vertical partitions are again nailed through the drawer dividers. On each drawer, the sides are dovetailed to the front and back, and the top edge of the sides is rounded. In most of the drawers, the bottoms are let into grooves in the front and nailed to the underside of the sides and back, with running strips applied; however, on the three drawers in line in the lower case, the bottoms are let into a rabbet in the front, and running strips are not used. The four wide drawers are fitted with a central brass lock escutcheon flanked by matching escutcheons with bail pulls; the small drawers in each case are fitted with matching brasses with bail pulls.

Inscriptions: Strips of newspaper, probably a New York City paper of April 1885, are pasted across several shrinkage cracks and holes in the backboards of the upper case. Written in pencil on the underside of the bottom of the upper case is "153"; "G 153" appears in black on the inside of the bottom of the wide drawer in the lower case; and "C 53" appears in black on the inside of the back and bottom of the lowest drawer in the upper case.

Condition: Most of the vertical reinforcing strip in the upper case is missing. The legs have been screwed in place through the sides and back of the case, and the screw heads covered with filler on the sides. There have been minor repairs to the drawer dividers and cornice moldings, and the running strips on the drawers are replacements. The right rear leg has been broken at the knee and reattached to the case, perhaps at an early date. The other legs also have been repaired.

Woods: Mahogany; drawer linings, in most instances, yellow poplar; back of lower side drawers in lower case, chestnut; sides and back of middle drawer in lower case, chestnut; bottom of wide drawer in lower case, eastern white pine; chestnut; small vertical partition between the two drawers in line in upper case, soft maple; some blocks and other small framing elements, eastern white pine.

Dimensions: H 218.9; W 97.0; UCW 90.8; LCW 95.6; D 52.7; UCD 49.1; LCD 52.1.

Exhibitions: Carpenter, no. 42; YUAG, "Rhode Island Furn."

141a

Bibliography: *Important American Furniture . . . Collected by . . . Mr. Herbert Lawton, Boston, Mass.*, Sale 2214, 6–7 January 1928 (New York: Anderson Galleries, 1928), no. 275.

Provenance: A marginal note in a copy of the Lawton sale catalogue (see Bibliography) by A. W. Clarke, Mr. Garvan's agent, indicates that Mr. Garvan bought this high chest "of Lyon" (probably Charles Woolsey Lyon of New York). Mr. Garvan then sold the object to dealer Charles Morson "when he bought several pieces." Morson, in turn, sold the chest, but took it back again in trade and then sold it again, this time to Herbert Lawton. The chest probably was acquired at the Lawton sale by the Brooks Reed Gallery, Inc., Boston, who sold it to Mr. Garvan in 1929.

THIS Newport high chest differs from the other two examples (cats. 140, 142) in the Yale collection by having a turned drop rather than a carved shell in the center of its front skirt and by having four claw-and-ball feet. Another variation here is that the pediment is enclosed at the rear of the case rather than the front. The carving on the front knees is quite restrained here, and the distinctive large knuckles of the webbed feet are unusual. The balls of each foot have been stained black, perhaps to make the carved talons stand out in greater relief. Central drops are found on a flat-top Newport high chest made in 1748 by Christopher Townsend and on a related example at Historic Deerfield which has a broken-scroll pediment; each of these high chests has pointed slipper feet.[1]

The Mabel Brady Garvan Collection 1930.2310

1. Ott, no. 57; Fales, *Deerfield*, fig. 436.

142

High chest of drawers
Newport, Rhode Island, 1760–1780

Description: The high chest is in two cases. The upper case is crowned by a broken-scroll pediment flanking a central finial shaped to an acorn above an urn. The pediment is enclosed by a longitudinal partition behind the finial and between the scrolls and contains two shaped panels above the drawers. The upper case contains five lipped drawers, two in line above three graduated drawers. There is a mid-molding applied to the bottom of the upper case. The lower case contains four lipped drawers, including one wide drawer over three in line, with the lower side drawers of greater depth and the lower center drawer of greater width. The wide drawers in each case are fitted with a central brass lock escutcheon flanked by matching escutcheons with bail pulls, and the small drawers in each case have a brass escutcheon with bail pull. The front skirt is shaped with reverse curves flanking a central carved shell, and the side skirts are shaped

142a

to pairs of reverse curves. The chest is supported by four cabriole legs; the two front legs terminate in webless claw-and-ball feet with undercut talons, and the two rear legs terminate in pad feet with high pads. The pediment is roofed with thin transverse boards nailed in place; there are two thicker transverse supports near the top of the arch that are housed in the back and front of the case and blocked within. In the upper case, the two small drawers in line are supported by a joined framework, and the runners for the wide drawers are nailed to the sides of the case; there are no dustboards. The panels on the pediment are applied. The top and bottom of the case are dovetailed to the sides, and the horizontal backboards are butted and nailed to a rabbet in the sides and to the case bottom. The dovetails joining the drawer dividers to the case sides are exposed. The bottom front rail is blocked behind. In the lower case, the back and front are dovetailed to the case sides, with the legs applied separately in the Rhode Island manner. The legs extend about half the height of the case, are fitted into shallow grooves in the case sides, and are glued and blocked in place. The wide drawer is supported by side runners and guides; there are central runners below the three lower drawers in line. There is no top to the lower case; the midmolding, applied to the upper case, rests on top of the lower case. There are deep vertical partitions between the lower drawers, nailed to the front skirt; guides for the middle drawer are tenoned to them and dovetailed to the drawer divider. On each drawer in the upper case and the wide drawer in the lower case, the sides are dovetailed to the front and back, and the bottoms are let into grooves in the front and nailed to the underside of the sides and back, with running strips applied. On the two small drawers in line in the upper case, the drawer sides are nailed in place through the sides to the backs, and each drawer was originally fitted with a wooden spring lock. In the three drawers in line in the lower case, the drawer bottoms are let into a rabbet in the front, and no running strips are used.

Inscriptions: There is an illegible inscription, probably original, on the outside of the back of the upper case; it may contain "1778." There are numerous shop marks and numbers in pencil and white chalk. A modern paper label with a red border inscribed with "20" is pasted to the inside of the bottom of the wide drawer in the lower case; the same number is painted in red next to this label.

Condition: The top and bottom of the finial have been repaired. The front inner talon on the right front foot is missing, and the rear outer talon on the left front foot is also

142

missing. The spring lock on the upper left drawer has been broken and repaired. Some drawer runners within the case and some running strips on the drawers have been replaced. There have been minor repairs to the cornice moldings and drawer fronts.

Woods: Mahogany; chestnut; top front rail in lower case, eastern white pine; spring lock on upper right drawer in upper case, white oak; replaced spring lock on upper left drawer in upper case, black locust.

Dimensions: H 209.6; W 99.5; UCW 91.2; LCW 95.1; D 51.1; UCD 46.8; LCD 49.5.

Exhibitions: Ralph E. Carpenter, "The Newport Exhibition," *Antiques* 64, no. 1 (July 1953): 43 fig. 20; Carpenter, no. 41; YUAG, "Rhode Island Furn."

Bibliography: Miller, 1:no. 656; Ralph E. Carpenter, Jr., "Schemes for an Exhibition House," *Antiques* 70, no. 1 (July 1956): 57; Kirk, *Early Am. Furn.*, fig. 90; Robert Bishop, *How to Know American Antique Furniture* (New York: E. P. Dutton, 1973), fig. 71; Kirk, *Am. Furn. & Brit. Trad.*, fig. 352; Moses, fig. 3.103.

Provenance: Henry V. Weil, New York, N. Y.; by sale to Francis P. Garvan, New York, N. Y.

LIKE the two previous examples, numerous details of construction and ornament firmly link this high chest to Newport, although the handling of these details varies slightly on each object. One significant difference here is the lack of carving on the knees of the legs, reflecting the pocketbook and perhaps the taste of the owner. This example has recently been associated with the family of John Townsend, although the lack of calligraphy, the shell with an open center, and other differences from Townsend's documented work (cat. 140) make a definite attribution impossible.[1] The inscription on the back of this chest, as yet undeciphered (although it may contain the date 1778), may indicate which member of the Newport cabinetmaking community executed this particular expression of a popular form. The circle of makers was wider than just the Townsend and Goddard families, as a high chest signed by Benjamin Baker attests.[2]

The Mabel Brady Garvan Collection 1930.2678

1. Moses, p. 146. See fig. 3.104 for a closely related example. Another related high chest has been acquired recently by the Worcester Art Museum (1986.36).

2. Cooper, *In Praise of America*, fig. 25.

143

High chest of drawers
Preston, Connecticut, area, 1770–1790

Description: The high chest is in two cases. The upper case is crowned above simple cornice molding by a broken-scroll pediment terminating with carved rosettes, painted red,

143

flanking a central pinecone finial, painted black, mounted above a molded plinth. The upper case holds seven lipped drawers, including an upper tier of three in line over four graduated drawers below. The center drawer of the drawers in line is of lesser width and is carved with a small shell enclosed within an arc. The front corners of the upper case have freestanding rope-turned columns. The upper case rests within a midmolding on the top of the lower case. The lower case holds three lipped drawers in line, with the side drawers of greater depth and the center drawer of greater width. The wide drawers in the upper case are fitted with a

272 *American Case Furniture*

central brass lock escutcheon (blind on the lowest drawer) flanked by matching escutcheons with bail pulls. The plain small drawers in each case have a single brass with bail pull, and the shell-carved drawer is fitted with a brass button pull. The front skirt is shaped with reverse curves leading to rounded arches flanking a large central carved shell; the side skirts are formed to a rounded arch flanked by reverse curves. The chest is supported by four cabriole legs terminating in rather small claw-and-ball feet. The scrolls of the pediment are roofed to their full depth with thin transverse slats; the pediment is closed at the rear by a shaped backboard. The top and bottom of the upper case are dovetailed to the sides. The vertical backboards are joined with a half lap and nailed to the bottom, and they are nailed in place through the case sides and top in an unusual manner. The dovetails joining the drawer dividers to the case sides and the vertical partitions flanking the small carved drawer to the drawer dividers are exposed. The drawers run on side runners and guides that are tenoned to vertical strips nailed to the front and back of the case; there are no dustboards. The upper case rests on a rabbet in the midmolding applied to the top of the lower case. The lower case is of dovetailed board construction, with the legs being glued in place in the Rhode Island manner. The legs extend about half the height of the case, and there are additional blocks glued in place above each leg. There is a distinct notch or gap at the top of each leg, just below the edge of the case. On the small carved drawer in the upper case, the sides are dovetailed to the front, and the back is dovetailed to the sides. The bottom of this drawer is beveled on its front and side edges, let into grooves in the front and sides, and nailed to the underside of the back. On the other drawers in each case, the drawer bottoms are flat and are rabbeted to a groove in the front and sides and nailed in place through the sides, as well as being nailed to the underside of the back.

Inscriptions: "Top" is written in white chalk on the inside of the back of the upper case. "Edward" is written twice on the outside of the right side of the shell-carved drawer, above earlier but illegible writing, and to the left of a column of added figures. "E" is written on the outside of the other side of the same drawer. "Aaron" followed by an illegible letter or name appears on the outside of the back of the wide drawer second from the top in the upper case. On the outside of the left side of the lower case is "Herbert West" and "[Herbert?] West" along with two childish drawings of a stick figure riding an animal of indeterminate species. A "Connecticut Furniture" (1967) exhibition label is pasted to the inside of the right side of a side drawer in the lower case,

143a

High Chests of Drawers 273

and another is pasted in the same location on the lowest wide drawer in the upper case.

Condition: Both knee brackets on the right front leg, the side knee bracket on the right rear leg, and the side knee bracket on the left rear leg are replacements. Both rear legs have been broken below the knee and repaired, perhaps at an early date. A later half-round molding at the base of the upper case at the front and sides has been removed; it seems likely, however, that a molding was present there originally. New strips have been added under the current midmolding at each side. In 1963, the chest was cleaned of a nineteenth-century varnish by Emile Mazzola, revealing red paint on the carved rosettes and black paint on the finial. There have been minor repairs to the drawer fronts, and all four feet have been damaged by insects and repaired. Some of the drawer runners in the upper case have been replaced.

Woods: Cornice moldings, pediment, drawer fronts (with one exception), drawer dividers (with one exception), sides of lower case, midmolding, American black cherry; front of lowest wide drawer, top drawer divider in upper case, birch; sides of upper case, columns, four legs, soft maple; top of upper case, chestnut; back of each case, drawer linings, probably finial, yellow poplar; roof of pediment, eastern white pine; some replaced drawer runners in upper case, oak.

Dimensions: H 210.2; W 99.1; UCW 90.5; LCW 95.8; D 50.4; UCD 45.0; LCD 48.3.

Exhibitions: Kirk, *Conn. Furn.*, no. 87; Mayhew and Myers, no. 61.

143b

Bibliography: Charles Messer Stow, "The Theme of Luxury in the Garvan Collection," *Antiquarian* 15, no. 3 (September 1930): 35; Kirk, *Early Am. Furn.*, fig. 91; Minor Myers, Jr., "Furniture and Growth of American Cultural Society," *Connecticut College Alumni* 53, no. 1 (Fall 1975): 7; Montgomery and Kane, *American Art, 1750–1800*, p. 61 fig. 36; Montgomery, "Regional Preferences and Characteristics," p. 1205 fig. 9.

Provenance: Charles Woolsey Lyon, New York, N. Y.; by sale in 1929 to Francis P. Garvan, New York, N. Y.

THERE are at least five other examples related to this high chest in their use of freestanding rope-turned columns in the upper case and in the profile and shape of their legs and claw-and-ball feet. Two of the related published examples, one with a broken-scroll pediment and another with a flat top, share the same distinctive large shell in the center of the front skirt.[1] Three other flat-top examples lack this shell and simply have an undulating skirt without carving.[2] Mayhew and Myers have suggested that this group was made in the Preston area of New London County, where Rhode Island influence was strong. The "detachable" legs, the carved shell on the skirt, and the exposed dovetails of this high chest, for example, mirror Rhode Island practices. The other examples in the group retain a base molding at the front and sides of the upper case, perhaps another reflection of a Rhode Island custom. Mayhew and Myers also discuss the possible attribution of this group to a cabinetmaking tradition that included John Wheeler Geer (1753–1828) and Abishai Woodward (1752–1809) of Preston and their as yet unknown master, possibly Daniel Denison II (b. 1740). The use of butternut, which Geer is known to have used, is cited as one factor linking the Yale example to this shop tradition; however, butternut is *not* used in this high chest. Several idiosyncracies of construction, including the unusual manner of nailing the backboards of the upper case in place through the sides and top of the case and the unusual construction of the drawer bottoms, should help to identify the members of this group more securely. The architectural nature of the Yale chest has been noted by many writers; Mayhew and Myers suggest plate XXVI of William Salmon's *Palladio Londonensis*, an architectural pattern book and builder's guide published in London in 1734, as a possible design source.

The Mabel Brady Garvan Collection 1930.2055

1. *Three Centuries of Conn. Furn.*, no. 151; *Antiques* 60, no. 3 (September 1951): 174.
2. *Antiques* 123, no. 2 (February 1983): 339; *Antiques* 92, no. 2 (August 1967): 147; Kirk, *Early Am. Furn.*, fig. 92.

144

High chest of drawers
Connecticut, probably Hartford area, 1770–1790

Description: The high chest is in two cases. The upper case is crowned by a broken-scroll pediment with circular piercing flanking a central finial and with turned finials mounted on plinths at each side. The upper case holds seven lipped drawers, including an upper tier of three drawers in line, with the center drawer of greater height and carved with a shell, above four graduated drawers below. The upper case rests within a midmolding applied to the top of the case. The lower case holds four lipped drawers, including one wide drawer over three in line, with the lower middle drawer of greater width and again carved with a shell. The wide drawers in each case are fitted with a central blind brass lock escutcheon flanked by matching escutcheons with bail pulls. The plain small drawers in each case are each fitted with a single blind brass lock escutcheon with bail pull, and the two shell-carved drawers are fitted with a brass button pull. The front skirt is shaped to three flathead arches conforming in size to the drawers and separated by turned drops; the side skirts are shaped to a single flathead arch. The chest is supported by four cabriole legs terminating in pad feet. The roof of the pediment consists of strips nailed to the top front rail and to a shaped backboard, and there are vertical transverse boards extending the depth of the case behind each scroll and enclosing the pediment. There is a top above the middle drawer, but no top above the upper side drawers. The bottom of the upper case is dovetailed to the sides, and the horizontal backboards are joined with a half lap and nailed to rabbets in the sides; the upper backboard is shaped in conformity with the closed portions of the pediment. There is a full dustboard under the drawers in line, but there are no other dustboards in either case. Guides for the drawers in line are nailed to the dustboard, and the side runners for the wide drawers are nailed to the case sides. The dovetails joining the drawer dividers to the case sides, and those joining the vertical partitions flanking the upper middle drawer to the top front rail and the drawer divider, are exposed. The upper case rests on strips nailed to the sides of the lower case, on the four corner posts, and on the top front rail of the lower case. The lower case is joined with mortise-and-tenon joints, with three pegs used to secure the joints of the sides to the legs. The side drawer runners and guides in the lower case are nailed to the sides. The interior

144

runners are tenoned to the front and back of the case; their mortises in the backboard were initially cut too high. On each drawer, the sides are dovetailed to the front and back, with the top edge of the sides rounded. The bottoms are beveled on their front and side edges, fitted to a groove in the front and sides, and nailed to the underside of the back with rosehead nails.

Inscriptions: "According to Mr E Simons / this case of drawers, (English bureau) / is about 125 years old now / 1877— I W Lyon" is written in pencil on the underside of the bottom of the upper left small drawer in the upper case. There are also chalk shop marks on the case.

High Chests of Drawers 275

Condition: One of the large side finials and the smaller center finial are replacements; originally, all three finials may have been of the same size as the surviving large example.

Woods: American black cherry; eastern white pine; back of second wide drawer from bottom in upper case, southern yellow pine, possibly pitch pine.

Dimensions: H 208.3; W 101.0; UCW 90.2; LCW 94.9; D 52.3; UCD 43.5; LCD 47.0.

Bibliography: Kirk, *Early Am. Furn.*, fig. 15.

Provenance: Irving W. Lyon's notebook (page 182), now in the Art Gallery collection, indicates that he bought this high chest and a set of four chairs on 3 July 1877 from Mrs. Mehitable (Stratton) Dayton (1787–1892) of South Glastonbury, Conn., who was then ninety years old and who told Lyon that the objects had belonged to her grandmother. Mrs. Dayton was the wife of Ezra Dayton (1774–1849) and the daughter of Samuel Stratton (1758–1807) and Mary (Hollister) Stratton (1764–1840). Her grandparents were Samuel Stratton (1728–1810), a blacksmith, and his wife Mehitable (Hollister) Stratton, and Elijah Hollister (1729–1785), a mill owner, and his second wife, Mary (Pratt) Hollister. The Hollisters were an old Glastonbury-area family; the Strattons apparently arrived in the middle of the eighteenth century.[1] The high chest was eventually purchased from Irving Lyon's descendants by Francis P. Garvan, New York, N. Y.

THIS high chest is of a standard, almost generic, New England type, made for many years during the eighteenth century. Its large finials, its carved shells, and its use of cherry as a primary wood all suggest that this example was made in Connecticut. Its strong history in the South Glastonbury area in the Stratton or Hollister family confirms a Connecticut attribution and points toward an origin in the vicinity of Hartford. A high chest related in form has a history in the Wethersfield area.[2] Reproductions of the Yale high chest have been made since 1983 by Harden Furniture Company.

The Mabel Brady Garvan Collection 1930.2443

1. For Mrs. Dayton's genealogy, see Harriet Russell Stratton, comp., *A Book of Strattons*, 2 vols. (New York: Grafton Press, 1907), 1:178–181, 2:34, 59–60; Donald Lines Jacobus and Arthur Bliss Dayton, *The Early Daytons and Descendants of Henry, Jr.* (New Haven: New Haven Colony Historical Society, 1959), pp. 55, 63–67; Lafayette Wallace Case, comp., *The Hollister Family of America* (Chicago: Fergus Printing Co., 1886), pp. 84–86; and Alonzo B. Chapin, *Glastenbury for Two Hundred Years* (Hartford: Case, Tiffany, 1853), pp. 102, 200. Mrs. Dayton achieved some notoriety as the "Oldest Woman in the State" as she advanced beyond the century mark. A Chinese export porcelain tea set owned by Mrs. Dayton is also in the Art Gallery collection (see *Great River*, cat. 293).

2. Bayou Bend (B.28.1), illustrated in Warren, *Bayou Bend*, no. 69. See also Kirk, *Early Am. Furn.*, fig. 14; and a high chest in the collection of the Minneapolis Institute of Arts (24.66) for related examples. A Massachusetts variation of the form can be found in Fales, *Deerfield*, fig. 435.

145

High chest of drawers
Connecticut, 1760–1790

Description: The upper case is crowned by a high-arching broken-scroll pediment flanking a central finial with an unusual reel and flattened ball form; the sides of the pediment are decorated with turned finials with a reel and possibly a stylized flame form that are doweled to the pediment without plinths. The upper case contains seven lipped drawers, three in line at the top, with the center drawer of greater width and depth above four graduated drawers. The middle upper drawer is carved with a center rectangle with notched edges and a stippled background that contains asymmetrical leafage and a central eight-petaled rosette. The upper case rests within the midmolding applied to the top of the lower case. The lower case contains four lipped drawers, with one wide drawer over three deeper drawers in line, with the middle drawer being of greater width and carved with a convex shell with twenty lobes notched at each end. The front skirt is shaped to flathead arches below each drawer, with acorn drops; the side skirts are shaped to a single flathead arch. The chest is supported by four cabriole legs terminating in pad feet with high pads; the rear feet are unusually small versions of the front feet. In the upper case, the pediment is roofed with curved boards nailed in place with rosehead nails and closed with transverse boards nailed in place. The front of the pediment is dovetailed to the sides; the rear board is shaped to a U form. The drawer dividers are dovetailed to the sides with the dovetails exposed. The three horizontal backboards are nailed to rabbets in the sides and to the bottom; the upper backboard is shaped to conform to the closed pediment. The vertical partitions are dovetailed to the drawer dividers and dovetailed and nailed to the pediment. The back of the lower case is a single horizontal board, and the back and sides are joined to the legs with mortise-and-tenon joints secured with three pegs. The rear legs are squared off on the back. The drawer divider is again dovetailed with the dovetail exposed, and the vertical

145

partition is dovetailed in place. The drawers are supported by runners at the sides tenoned to the front and back. The drops are doweled through small platforms to the skirt. In each drawer, the sides are dovetailed to the front and back, and the top edge of the sides is molded. The bottoms are beveled on their front and side edges, let into grooves in the front and sides, and nailed to the underside of the back with rosehead nails.

Inscriptions: "A Brown[?]" is written in white chalk on the outside of the left side of the upper right drawer in the upper case. Written in pencil on the inside of the front of the wide drawer in the lower case is "1866 Bought at Reuben Jennison's Auction / March 27th I [?] D——" There are shop marks and numbers in pencil. A "Connecticut Furniture" (1967) exhibition label is pasted to the inside of the bottom of the lowest drawer in the upper case and to the same location in the wide drawer in the lower case.

Condition: The brasses are replacements, and the lips of several drawers have been pieced. The drawer runners in the upper case are replacements, and a shrinkage crack in the left side of the upper case has been repaired with a butterfly cleat. The left rear leg has been pieced near the top. The bottom edges of most drawer sides have been repaired, there are new runners for the wide drawer in the lower case, and the runners for the lower middle drawer have been pieced. New braces have been added to the inside of the lower case to help support the upper case.

Woods: American black cherry, including backboard of lower case; eastern white pine; some elements, including upper backboard of upper case, southern yellow pine.

Dimensions: H 222.2; W 98.1; UCW 90.8; LCW 96.8; D 50.3; UCD 46.0; LCD 49.4.

Exhibition: Kirk, *Conn. Furn.*, no. 91.

Bibliography: *Antiques* 8, no. 5 (November 1925): inside front cover; David G. De Long, Helen Searing, and Robert A. M. Stern, eds., *American Architecture: Innovation and Tradition* (New York: Rizzoli International Publications, 1986), p. 11 fig. 12.

Provenance: Owned in 1925 by Israel Sack, Inc., Boston, Mass.; by sale to Brooks Reed Gallery, Inc., Boston, Mass.; by sale in 1929 to Francis P. Garvan, New York, N. Y.

This Connecticut high chest is distinguished by its unusual finials, characteristic of the idiosyncratic finials often found on Connecticut case furniture, and by the rather unusual carving found on the top middle drawer of the upper case, with its petaled rose and vines against a matted background. The inscriptions on the chest provide inconclusive clues as to its origins within Connecticut. There was a craftsman named Asher Brown who died in Lisbon in 1815 possessed of joiner's tools, turning chisels, and lumber in his shop, but Brown is a common name.[1] Members of the Jennison family were living in Norwich, New London, Hartford, and Middletown by the time of the 1850 Connecticut census.[2]

The Mabel Brady Garvan Collection 1930.2228

1. Mayhew and Myers, p. 111.

High Chests of Drawers 277

2. Ronald Vern Jackson and Gary Ronald Teeples, *Connecticut 1850 Census Index* (Bountiful, Utah: Accelerated Indexing Systems, 1978), p. 168.

146

High chest of drawers
Possibly by Eliphalet Chapin (1741–1807)
East Windsor, Connecticut, 1780–1790
(en suite with cat. 108)

Description: The high chest is in two cases. The upper case is crowned by cornice molding at the front and sides and surmounted by a broken-scroll pediment terminating in leaf-carved volutes flanking a central pierced cartouche mounted on a plinth carved with blind fretwork. The scrolls are supported by pierced fret- or latticework, and the sides of the pediment are fitted with turned finials mounted on small plinths. The upper case contains seven lipped drawers, including three deep drawers in line at the top, with the center drawer of lesser width and carved with a shell, above four graduated drawers. The front corners of the upper case

146a

146

have fluted quarter columns, and the upper case rests within a midmolding applied to the top of the lower case. The lower case contains four lipped drawers, including one wide drawer over three in line, with the lower middle drawer of lesser width and greater depth and again carved with a shell, echoing but slightly different in handling from the shell in the upper case. The front corners of the lower case are again fitted with engaged fluted quarter columns. The wide drawers in each case are fitted with a central brass lock escutcheon (blind on the top wide drawer in the upper case and the

278 *American Case Furniture*

drawer in the lower case) flanked by matching escutcheons with bail pulls. The shell-carved drawers in each case are fitted with a blind lock escutcheon above the shell and a brass button pull; the small drawers in each case have a brass escutcheon with bail pull. The front skirt is shaped with reverse curves, and the side skirts are shaped with reverse curves flanking a straight center. The chest is supported by four cabriole legs terminating in claw-and-ball feet. The top and bottom of the upper case are dovetailed to the sides, and the horizontal butted backboards have beveled edges and are fitted to grooves in the top and sides and nailed to the bottom. The cartouche (which is a replacement) is fitted to a slot in the plinth and tilts forward at a slight angle. There is a full dustboard under the top wide drawer, and the interior runners for the drawers in line are tenoned through the back. The side drawer runners and guides are each a single strip and are nailed to the case sides. The upper case rests within the midmolding applied to the lower case and is supported by strips nailed to the sides of the lower case; there is no top to the lower case. The lower case is framed with mortise-and-tenon joints. The legs are blocked on their inner faces. The T-shaped runners for the lower middle drawer are tenoned through the back. On each drawer, the sides are dovetailed to the front and back, with the top edge of the sides shaped with a half-round molding. The bottoms are beveled on their front and side edges, let into a groove in the front and sides, and nailed to the underside of the back.

Inscriptions: Written in white chalk on the inside of the back of the upper left drawer in the upper case is "O 4-2 mony." There are chalk inscriptions on the sides of the lower side drawers in the lower case and other chalk shop marks. A Connecticut Tercentenary (1935) label is pasted to the inside of the right side of the upper right drawer in the upper case and in the same location on the wide drawer in the lower case.

Condition: The present cartouche is a replacement, carved by Paul Koda of Hartford in 1966–1967, based on the original cartouche on a related high chest in the collection of the Wadsworth Atheneum (1964.146; illustrated in Kirk, *Conn. Furn.*, no. 93). The high chest has an old mahoganized finish.

Woods: American black cherry; eastern white pine.

Dimensions: H 220.3; W 102.1; UCW 92.2; LCW 97.9; D 51.9; UCD 44.0; LCD 47.0.

Exhibition: *Three Centuries of Conn. Furn.*, no. 161.

Bibliography: Ormsbee, *Story Am. Furn.*, fig. 117; Rogers,

146b

High Chests of Drawers

"Garvan Furn. (1960)," fig. 13; Helen Comstock, "The American Highboy," *Antiques* 80, no. 3 (September 1961): 231 fig. 11; Comstock, no. 314; Kirk, *Early Am. Furn.*, fig. 84.

Provenance: See cat. 108.

ALTHOUGH its brasses and carved shells vary, this high chest was acquired as a companion piece to an otherwise closely related dressing table (cat. 108) in the Yale collection. The many Philadelphia-area stylistic characteristics of this Connecticut Valley object, reflecting the Philadelphia training of its presumed maker, Eliphalet Chapin, have been discussed by many writers and most eloquently by John T. Kirk.[1] Related high chests with similar carved shells are known, including an example at Historic Deerfield, as are other Chapin-style high chests with paired S-scroll leafage on the drawers rather than shells.[2]

The Mabel Brady Garvan Collection 1930.2124

1. Kirk, *Early Am. Furn.*, pp. 103–105.
2. Fales, *Deerfield*, fig. 440; *Antiquarian* 12, no. 5 (June 1929): 3; Kirk, *Conn. Furn.*, no. 93; *Antiques* 110, no. 5 (November 1976): 4; *The American Heritage Society Auction of Americana*, Sale 4180, 16–18 November 1978 (New York: Sotheby Parke Bernet, 1978), no. 1006.

147

High chest of drawers

Philadelphia, Pennsylvania, 1760–1780
(en suite with cat. 116; see pl. 14)

Description: The high chest is in two cases. The upper case is crowned by a broken-scroll pediment with moldings terminating in carved floral rosettes with crosshatched centers flanking a large canted central cartouche in the form of a shell surrounded by leafage. The center of the pediment has an applied canted shell flanked by scrolling acanthus leafage, and the sides of the pediment are fitted with large urn-and-flame finials mounted on plinths. The upper case contains eight lipped drawers: three in line, with the center drawer of greater width, and the right drawer of slightly greater width (27.5 cm) than the left drawer (25.1 cm), above two drawers in line, above three graduated drawers. The front corners of the upper case have fluted quarter columns, and the upper case rests within the midmolding applied to the top of the lower case. The lower case holds four lipped drawers, including one wide drawer over three in line, with the lower middle drawer of greater depth and carved with a central shell. The shell has a rosette at center, is contained within an arc, and is flanked by scrolled and intertwining acanthus leafage. The wide drawers in each case have a central brass pierced lock escutcheon flanked by matching escutcheons with bail pulls. The three drawers in line in the upper case and the two lower side drawers in the lower case are fitted with a single escutcheon with bail pull; the two drawers in line in the upper case have a pierced brass lock escutcheon

147

147a

with a bail pull; and the shell-carved drawer is fitted with a brass button pull. The front corners of the lower case also have engaged fluted quarter columns. The front skirt is shaped to reverse curves edged with acanthus carving and flowing toward a central carved shell; the side skirts are shaped to a simple rounded arch. The chest is supported by four cabriole legs terminating in claw-and-ball feet; the front legs are carved with acanthus leafage. Black paint is used to decorate the fluted quarter columns, the midmolding, the upper and lower edge of the cornice molding on the pediment scrolls, parts of the pediment shell and leafage, and parts of the central cartouche and side finial urns; the small bead molding in the center of the cornice molding on the pediment scrolls is gilt. The left rear leg is made of pieced construction, apparently original. The top and bottom of the upper case are dovetailed to the sides, and the horizontal backboards are nailed to rabbets in the sides. There are full dustboards in the upper case, with guides nailed to them at the sides. The vertical partitions between the small drawers are double tenoned through the drawer dividers, and there are multiple vertical blocks behind the quarter columns. The lower case is framed with mortise-and-tenon joints secured with pegs and includes a full top of three boards. The vertical partitions between the lower drawers are

tenoned once through the drawer divider. There is a full dustboard below the wide drawer, and the dustboards below the lower drawers are nailed to strips that in turn are nailed to the case and to internal partitions. On each drawer, the sides are dovetailed to the front and back; the bottoms are let into a groove in the front and sides and nailed to the underside of the back, with running strips applied at the front and sides.

Inscriptions: A chalk inscription, only partially legible, on the top of the top of the lower case appears to contain three separate words: the first word ends in " ... bet," the second word is illegible, and the third word begins with "Dome...." The inside of the drawer fronts of the row of three drawers in line in the upper case are marked I, II, and III from left to right. There are chalk shop marks on the case.

Condition: Large corner blocks have been added to each corner of the lower case. The side knee brackets on the front legs and the knee brackets of the rear legs are replacements. The button pull on the shell-carved drawer is a replacement. Some drawer runners have been replaced, and small pieces of carving have been lost. The left rosette in the pediment is secured with a modern screw.

Woods: American black walnut; drawer sides, dustboards, other elements, yellow poplar; drawer bottoms, backs, Atlantic white cedar; bottom of upper case, a backboard of lower case, southern yellow pine.

Dimensions: H 245.7; W 115.5; UCW 105.0; LCW 110.2; D 60.1; UCD 52.4; LCD 55.4.

147b

147c

282 *American Case Furniture*

Bibliography: *Antiques* 7, no. 6 (June 1925): 303; Halsey and Tower, *Homes of Our Ancestors*, fig. 53; Charles Over Cornelius, *Early American Furniture* (New York: D. Appleton-Century Co., 1926), pl. XXVIII; Holloway, pl. 35; Nutting, *Treasury*, no. 363; Theodore Sizer, "The Mabel Brady Garvan Collection," *YUAG Bulletin* 4, no. 2 (December 1930): 110; *Handbook*, pp. 49, 62; "Outstanding Examples from the Mabel Brady Garvan Collection," *YUAG Bulletin* 8, no. 2 (February 1938): 44; Rogers, "Garvan Furn. (1960)," fig. 12; Meyric R. Rogers, "Philadelphia via Dublin: Influences in Rococo Furniture," *Antiques* 79, no. 3 (March 1961): 275 fig. 9; Kirk, *Early Am. Furn.*, figs. 17, 18; Robert Bishop, *How to Know American Antique Furniture* (New York: E. P. Dutton, 1973), fig. 96; "American Arts and the American Experience," *Museum News* 53, no. 3 (November 1974): 39; Montgomery, "1776—Furniture," p. 59; Montgomery and Kane, *American Art, 1750–1800*, fig. 34; Montgomery, "Regional Preferences and Characteristics," p. 1204 fig. 7; Virginia B. Geyer, "Further Notes on Henry Wynkoop," *Bucks County Historical Society Journal* 1, no. 10 (Fall 1976): 4; *Fine Woodworking*, no. 9 (Winter 1977): front cover, 31, 38, 42; Charles F. Montgomery, "Francis P. Garvan: He Would Educate the Nation," *Arts in Virginia* 19, no. 3 (Spring 1979): 14; Kane, "American Furn.," p. 1320 pl. VII; Rick Mastelli, "In Search of Period Furniture Makers," *Fine Woodworking*, no. 23 (July–August 1980): 35; Kirk, *Am. Furn. & Brit. Trad.*, fig. 386.

Provenance: See cat. 116.

DURING the course of the last sixty years, this high chest owned by Judge Henry Wynkoop has been published more than twenty times and, along with its matching dressing table (cat. 116), has been attributed to William Savery, Thomas Affleck, and other leading Philadelphia cabinetmakers. In light of the interrelationships between shops and the frequent use of specialist carvers and other craftsmen, it seems best at present not to link a maker's name to these objects. Superbly proportioned, this high chest is firmly supported by its massive lower case, an expanded version of the dressing table. The upper case, framed like the lower case with engaged fluted quarter columns enriched with black paint, rises to its richly carved pediment topped by its large "peanut" finial, the only truly asymmetrical ornament on the object. The thin bead molding in the scrolled arches is picked out in gilt, further defining and highlighting the organization of the design. The arches terminate in carved rosettes that may have been known as sunflowers, a term used in a 1772 bill from Philadelphia carver Hercules Courtenay to John Dickinson.[1] An unusual and no doubt unintended feature of this high chest is the difference in size between the two small side drawers in the top row of the upper case; the larger size of the drawer on the right is not easily explained except through a mistake in workmanship. The most closely related example, also of walnut, is in the Winterthur collection.[2] A limited number of reproductions of the Yale chest were made in 1966 by Kittinger Company of Buffalo, New York, as part of the celebrations commemorating their hundredth anniversary.

The Mabel Brady Garvan Collection 1930.2000

1. Hornor, p. 92.
2. Downs, no. 197. See also *Important American Furniture, Folk Art and Related Decorative Arts*, Sale 5094, 21–22 October 1983 (New York: Sotheby's, 1983), lot 315. Some related features also appear on an example illustrated in *Antiques* 87, no. 4 (April 1965): 365. More elaborate versions of the form can be seen in Heckscher, nos. 165, 166.

148

Lower case of a high chest of drawers
Philadelphia, Pennsylvania, 1760–1780

Description: This object is the lower case of what originally must have been a large and imposing high chest. The top of the case is decorated with complex molding including a guilloche band, a cove molding, and fretwork course. The case holds four lipped drawers, one wide drawer over three in line, with the lower center drawer of greater depth and carved with a concave shell containing a central floral motif and flanked by scrolled and intertwined leafage. The front corners of the case hold quarter columns carved with trailing flowers and leaves; the front skirt is shaped with reverse curves and carved with leafage and a central shell motif; and the side skirts are shaped with reverse curves flanking a central rounded arch. The four corner posts continue below the case to form cabriole legs with a central floral motif at their top flanked by acanthus carved knees and knee brackets. All four legs terminate in claw-and-ball feet, but only the sides of the rear knees are carved with a few lines of leafage. The case is framed with mortise-and-tenon joints, with three pegs used to secure the two horizontal butted backboards to the rear posts. There is a full vertical partition on each side of the lower center drawer, with the mahogany facing tenoned through the drawer divider and with the rear edge housed in a groove in the back. Thin dustboards under

148

the lower drawers are supported by strips nailed to the front skirt and the back of the case, by strips nailed to the underside of the vertical partitions, and by blocks glued to the case sides. The top drawer is supported by runners at the sides and by the vertical partitions. Drawer guides are applied on top of the runners and dustboards and are shaped to fit within the posts. The inside faces of the corner posts are fitted with glue blocks within the case and are also blocked below the dustboards. On each drawer, the top edges of the drawer sides are rounded, and the sides are dovetailed to the front and back. The bottoms are let into grooves in the sides and front and nailed to the underside of the back, with running strips applied to the sides and front.

Inscriptions: "Top of frame" is written in white chalk on the underside of the top. There are many modern pencil notations, including columns of figures on the underside of the bottom of the lower center drawer.

Condition: At some time, probably prior to 1900, a mahogany board was placed on top of the original top of this lower case, in order to make a flush surface with what originally was a restraining molding applied to the lower case. This board is glued and is screwed in place through the original top both within the case and through pocket screws in the backboards. A pull was once located in the center of the floral motif on the lower center drawer; the present brasses are replacements. The knee brackets on the rear legs and on the right side of the right front leg are replacements; the surviving brackets have been reattached with large modern screws. Pieces of the fret motif are missing, and others have been repaired and replaced.

Woods: Mahogany; drawer sides, backs, other elements, yellow poplar; drawer bottoms, other elements, Atlantic white cedar; backboards, other elements, southern yellow pine.

Dimensions: H 95.1; W 115.6; CW 110.5; D 60.1; CD 54.4.

Exhibition: *Girl Scouts Exhibition*, no. 611.

Bibliography: *Illustrated Catalogue of the Rare and Extremely Choice Collection of Early American and English Furniture . . . Formed . . . by . . . Mr. Louis Guerineau Myers* (New York: American Art Association, 1921), no. 651; Nutting, *Treasury*, no. 434.

Provenance: Louis Guerineau Myers, New York, N. Y.; acquired, probably at auction in 1921, by Francis P. Garvan, New York, N. Y.

As Hornor phrased it, large case pieces, like this example, that have lost one or the other case, are in a "crippled condition," yet they are worthy of preservation in their altered states.[1] The earliest known photographs of this object, dating to 1919, show it in its present condition. When whole, it probably resembled a Philadelphia high chest now in the Metropolitan Museum of Art (18.110.6), with which it shares some details of carving and moldings, including the guilloche band and Greek fret motif.[2] A related dressing table is in the Minneapolis Institute of Arts (31.21).[3]

The Mabel Brady Garvan Collection 1930.2193

1. Hornor, p. 106; see also pl. 153, another surviving high-chest base.
2. Nutting, *Treasury*, no. 361; see also the matching dressing table, no. 423.
3. Nutting, *Treasury*, no. 429.

149

High chest of drawers
Pennsylvania, 1760–1780

Description: The upper case of this enormous high chest is crowned by a broken-scroll pediment terminating in carved

284 *American Case Furniture*

floral rosettes on each side of a central gilt urn-and-flame finial. The sides of the pediment are decorated with gilt flame finials mounted on plinths fluted at the front and outer side and with shaped brackets applied to the pediment at their front and sides. The front of the pediment is inlaid with three initials and contains a lipped drawer carved with a concave shell with scrolls and a floral pendant flanked by applied flowers and leafage. The drawer is flanked by larger flowers and leaves applied to the pediment and echoing the carving on the drawer. The upper case also contains eight lipped drawers, three in line over two in line over three graduated drawers below, and the sides are decorated with applied fluted quarter columns terminating in a lamb's-tongue chamfer. The upper case rests within a broad restraining molding applied to the lower case. The lower case contains four more lipped drawers, including one wide drawer over three in line, with the middle drawer of greater depth and carved with a concave shell similar to the shell on the pediment drawer. The sides of the lower case are also decorated with applied fluted quarter columns terminating in a lamb's-tongue chamfer. The front skirt is shaped with scrolls and arches on each side of a drop at center; the side skirts are shaped with reverse curves flanking a central round arch. The chest is supported by four massive cabriole legs with the head and neck of a bird holding leafage in its beak on each knee bracket, with feathers trailing below, and terminating in claw-and-ball feet. The side knees of the rear legs are carved, while the rear knees are left in reserve. In the upper case, the top and bottom are dovetailed to the sides, and the horizontal backboards are nailed to rabbets in all four sides. The pediment drawer runs on the top of the case and is housed within vertical transverse partitions on the sides and a horizontal one at the top that are nailed in place. The scrolls of the pediment and the form of the plinth supporting the center finial are carried the full depth of the case, and the entire pediment is roofed with thin boards nailed in place and covered with cloth that may originally have been dyed red. The backboard of the pediment is shaped in conformity with the scrolls and center section. Within the upper case, there are full dustboards beneath the drawers, with guides applied to them. There are vertical blocks at the front corners behind the quarter columns; the vertical partitions are tenoned through the drawer dividers. The lower case is joined with mortise-and-tenon joints, with the sides and back joined to the legs with six large square wooden pins. The top of the lower case consists of two longitudinal butted boards. There are no dustboards in the lower case; the drawers are supported by runners at the sides, with those for the middle lower drawer nailed to vertical parti-

149

tions that run the depth of the case and are nailed in place through the back. The rails and drawer divider are pegged to the case, and the knee brackets are applied with nails. In each drawer, the sides are dovetailed to the front and back, and the top edge of the sides is rounded. The bottoms are beveled on their front and side edges, let into grooves in the front and sides, and nailed to the underside of the back with rosehead nails. The carved drawers are fitted with brass button pulls; the wide drawers are fitted with central brass lock escutcheons flanked by matching escutcheons with bail pulls; the small drawers in the upper case are fitted with blind lock escutcheons with bail pulls; the lower side drawers

149a

in the lower case are fitted with escutcheons with bail pulls. The pediment drawer originally may have been fitted with a lock mechanism consisting of a pin housed in a hole in the top edge of the drawer front and connected to the center finial which would be released when the finial was lifted.

Inscriptions: "N V M," probably the initials of the original owner or owners whose identity is today unknown, is inlaid, probably in sulfur, on the pediment. There are several inscriptions on the top of the top of the lower case, including "C" painted in black; "John Hill Coffin T M" scratched very faintly; "BARBOUR" in pencil; and possibly a longer inscription, mostly illegible, that may read in part "by Samuel ———." There are shop marks in white chalk. "Centre" is written in pencil on the underside of the bottom of the middle drawer in line in the upper case. "C" is also painted in black on the outside of the back of the upper case. There is a shell outlined with compass scribe marks and chalk on the inside of the front of the pediment drawer that relates to the shell carved on the outside. The top edge of the drawer fronts of the five small drawers in the upper case, and the drawer dividers beneath them, are marked with roman numerals. A round green paper label pasted to the inside of the bottom of the left drawer in the row of three drawers in the upper case is printed in gold "ELEPHANT ORCHARDS / REDLANDS, CAL." in a circle around a depiction of an elephant with "TRADE MARK" below.

Condition: The chest retains an old, possibly original finish. A plinth for the center finial is missing. Portions of the applied carving on the pediment are missing; some of the original pieces from the right side, primarily, were found in Mrs. Garvan's effects by her descendants in 1983 and have been reapplied. The lips of some drawers have been repaired, and there has been minor damage to the moldings. Both front feet have been damaged by insects. The legs were once fitted with casters, and there is a small repair to the backboards in the upper case.

Woods: American black cherry; drawer sides and backs, dustboards, other elements, southern yellow pine; drawer bottoms, other elements, Atlantic white cedar.

Dimensions: H 240.1; W 111.8; UCW 100.2; LCW 105.6; D 58.5; UCD 51.2; LCD 54.9.

Bibliography: Kirk, *Am. Furn. & Brit. Trad.*, fig. 1154.

Provenance: Charles R. Morson, New York, N. Y.; by sale in 1925 to Francis P. Garvan, New York, N. Y.

WHILE echoing the form and ornamental pattern of a Philadelphia high-style example (such as cat. 147), this massive cherry high chest retains an air of provinciality that suggests it was made outside of the city, possibly in Lancaster County. Its weight and sturdiness is matched in the Yale collection only by a chest-on-chest (cat. 90) also from rural eastern Pennsylvania. An extra drawer in the pediment is found occasionally on high chests from eastern Pennsylvania, and inlaid initials and other decoration in sulfur are found on Pennsylvania German case furniture emanating from the Lancaster area.[1] The quality of the carved leafage, shells, and finials on this high chest is quite high, and the object gains added distinction from the presence of the carved birds on the knees, possibly a unique feature on American case furniture. Their meaning, if they are not purely decorative, remains obscure. Although they could be interpreted as doves or eagles holding olive branches in their beaks, it seems unlikely that they are patriotic symbols. Carvings of this kind are found on English furniture and on rare examples of American seating furniture, but a more likely source of design for these particular birds can be found in related birds depicted in Pennsylvania German Fraktur.[2] Of English form but of Germanic mass, with decoration derived from both English and Germanic traditions, this high chest is an important document of the blending of cultures that was taking place to some degree in eastern Pennsylvania during the last half of the eighteenth century. Despite the loss of some of the applied carving, the chest has survived in superb condition, retaining its original brasses and an old finish.

The Mabel Brady Garvan Collection 1930.2632

1. Fabian, p. 51. John J. Snyder, Jr., in correspondence in the Yale Furniture Study files, indicates that the high chest was most likely made in the Lancaster area or elsewhere in inland Pennsylvania, but also raises the possibility that it may have originated in Maryland or the Shenandoah Valley of Virginia or West Virginia.
2. An easy chair in the Metropolitan Museum of Art (18.110.26) is carved with griffins on the knees in a similar fashion; the arm terminals of some eighteenth-century American chairs are carved with a bird's head and wing; see a Massachusetts example in Robert Bishop, *Centuries and Styles of the American Chair, 1640–1970* (New York: E. P. Dutton, 1972), fig. 220. Examples of English furniture with birds carved on the knees can be seen in R. W. Symonds, *English Furniture from Charles II to George II* (New York: International Studio, 1929), figs. 15, 22; see also J. D. U. Ward, "Animal Carvings in English Furniture," *Antiques* 38, no. 6 (December 1940): 282–285. For a related drawing, see Fabian, fig. 143.

149b

Desks

First produced in this country about 1720, the desk remained largely unchanged in form until the end of the eighteenth century. Known variously as a bureau desk, as an escritoire, and by other names, the desk held an upper compartment fitted with pigeonholes and drawers, and often one or more secret drawers, designed to hold pens, ink, paper, and other writing materials and to store cash and small valuable items. The lower portion of the desk contained several wide drawers, functioning in the fashion of a chest of drawers. A slight variation on the form is the desk-on-frame: examples from Connecticut (cats. 154, 155) and Pennsylvania (cat. 164) are included in the collection. The desk form seemed to reach the height of its expression in Boston blockfront examples of rich mahogany and with large claw-and-ball feet (cat. 158). Other Massachusetts desks in the collection have histories in Maine (cat. 159) and on Nantucket (cat. 157), suggesting that the form was exported with some frequency and had a high degree of regional popularity. The collection also includes an important New London County desk with carved shells in the Rhode Island manner and a superb interior (cat. 160). Pennsylvania work is represented by objects from both early (cat. 152) and later in the century (cats. 163, 165). Federal-period desks at Yale include a tambour desk (cat. 166), a small desk-on-stand (cat. 167), and two portable writing desks (cats. 169, 170). Two small desks for children (cats. 151, 156) are significant documents of the production of specialized furniture for children in the eighteenth century.

150

Desk

Massachusetts, probably Leicester, 1720–1740

Description: Below the slant front, the case contains four drawers, two in line above two graduated drawers. The lipping on the case drawers is simulated on the sides and bottom. There is applied base molding at the front and sides, and the desk is supported by four turned feet. The cleated lid is supported by lopers and is flanked at the sides by small brackets applied to the front edge of the case sides. It opens to an interior divided into three units. The recessed center section contains three small drawers in line over two open compartments flanking three small superimposed drawers over two tiers of three drawers in line. The front edge of the platform of the center section is molded. To each side of the center section are stepped units consisting of, from top to bottom, a small drawer, an open compartment, another small drawer, and a larger drawer. The edges of the partitions between the three units of the interior are rounded and shaped. There are three secret compartments located behind the two drawers in line in the case, each designed to hold a small drawer. The secret compartments are reached by removing the large lower drawers on each side of the desk interior and by removing the lowest drawer divider in the middle section of the center section of the interior. The top of the case is dovetailed to the sides with the dovetails exposed on the top. The back consists of horizontal boards joined with a half lap and nailed to rabbets in all four sides. The drawer-divider dovetails and those joining the vertical partitions to the drawer dividers are exposed. The slant front is attached with wrought-iron butterfly hinges. The top two drawers in line in the case are supported by a joined framework with a longitudinal compartment at the rear housing the secret drawers. The highest wide drawer is supported by a longitudinal strip at the back to which the drawer runners are tenoned. The base framework of strips is applied to the underside of the bottom at the front and sides. The feet are screwed to a separate threaded dowel which in turn is screwed to this base framework and the bottom of the case. On the drawers in the case, the sides are dovetailed to the front and back, with the top edge of the sides rounded, and the bottoms are beveled on their front and side edges, let into grooves in the front and sides, and nailed to the underside of the back. The sides of the desk interior drawers are dovetailed to the front and back with the top edge of the sides rounded; the bottoms are glued to a V-shaped rabbet in the front and to the underside of the sides. The bottom edge of the top drawers in all three units is molded and lipped. The secret drawers are simple nailed boxes.

Inscriptions: "Uncle Ira Bryant bought this Desk of / Samuel Denny of / Leicester / Mass" is written in pencil on the underside of the bottom of the upper left drawer in the center section of the desk interior. The same inscription appears on the outside of the right side of one of the small drawers in the center section of the desk interior. "Samuel Denny of Leicester this Acct Rec^d" is written in pencil on the top of the drawer dividers below the upper right drawer and the top wide drawer in the case. A partially illegible inscription scratched on the inside of the right loper reads "Mary [?] Denny aged [?] . . . Year end [?] August 21 1787." There is an inscription on the surviving original secret drawer that may read "Illy." The drawer guides for the two small drawers in line in the case are incised "I," "II," and "III" from left to right. There is a fragment of a modern label tacked to the outside of the back.

Condition: The brasses are replacements, and the locks are missing. Two of the original three secret drawers are missing; one of the existing drawers is a replacement. The upper left drawer in the desk interior is a replacement, and four small drawers in the center unit of the desk interior are missing. A small bracket originally located on the front edge of the right side of the case at the level of the lid is a replacement. Traces of red and black paint suggest that the desk was painted originally, and probably more than once. A butterfly cleat has been added to the left side of the case.

Woods: Soft maple; two bottom backboards, bottom of case, chestnut; drawer bottoms in case, eastern hemlock; drawer sides and backs in case, drawer linings in interior, eastern white pine; feet, birch; threaded dowels in feet, hickory.

Dimensions: H 107.6; W 94.9; CW 91.1; D (closed) 53.2; D (open) 91.5; CD 50.7.

Provenance: The inscriptions strongly suggest that this desk was owned at an early date by a Samuel Denny of Leicester, Mass., a small community near Worcester. The earliest member of the Denny family in Leicester by that name is Samuel Denny (1731–1817), the son of Daniel Denny (1694–1760), an English immigrant via way of Boston who settled there in 1717. The inventory of this Samuel Denny's estate, recorded in 1817, included his "home farm . . . situated in . . . Leicester containing 190 acres with the building thereon" valued at $3,000, and "desk and books" appraised at $3. There is no evidence discovered to date to indicate that this Samuel Denny was the maker of the desk, and its style leaves open the possibility that he was not the original owner. He apparently did not inherit the desk from his father, however, who left him only half of his wearing apparel, "the Negro boy named Richard," and land. The desk may have entered the family through one of Samuel Denny's three marriages. His will specified that his executors should "make sale of All My Real and Personal Estate for the most it will fetch at Publick Auction, preference being given to my Heirs in the sales Excepting all such Articles as my present wife brought with her when I married her." The handwriting on the desk is not a close match to the signatures of Samuel Denny recorded on several documents, however, raising the distinct possibility that "the" Samuel Denny involved here is his son Samuel (1762–1832).[1] Ira Bryant (born in Leicester in 1791) acquired the desk in the nineteenth century from one of the Samuel Dennys, and it presumably was owned later by Bryant's nephew. The desk was acquired in the twentieth century by dealer Jacob Margolis, New York, N. Y., who sold it in 1925 to Francis P. Garvan, New York, N. Y.

ALTHOUGH its precise history remains somewhat unclear, there is every reason to believe that this desk was made in or near Leicester. Several features suggest that it may have been made slightly later than its general style and form might indicate. The simulated lipping on the drawers may represent an attempt to mimic the lipped drawers found on case furniture from about 1730 and eliminated the need for half-round or double half-round applied molding found on many early examples. The desk interior, although of an early arrangement, lacks the well with a sliding cover often found on examples made in the first decades of the eighteenth century (cats. 151, 152). Its construction of several woods, unusual feet threaded to the case, and general stance are consistent with a maker working in a rural area such as Leicester. Although the primary wood is a striped or tiger maple considered desirable today, this desk probably was painted red originally, with a later, sloppily applied coat of black. A similar maple desk at Historic Deerfield, attributed to eastern Massachusetts, retains its original red paint.[2] A good description of this type of desk is given by Sheraton in his *Cabinet Dictionary*. Writing in 1803, he noted that in England *bureau* "has generally been applied to common desks with drawers under them, such as are made very frequently in country towns. They run from 3 to 4 feet long, and have three heights of common drawers under them, the upper one divided into two in length. The desk flap turns down to 30 inches perpendicular height from the ground, or a little less, for sitting to write at [here the flap slopes from 30¼ to 29¼ inches]. The inside of the desk part is filled up with small drawers, and holes for letters."

The Mabel Brady Garvan Collection 1930.2389

1. Sources for the Denny family include C. C. Denny, *Genealogy of the Denny Family in England and America* (Leicester, Mass.: C. C. Denny, 1886), pp. 20–21, 47–51, 80–82, 89–90, and passim; Emory Washburn, *Historical Sketches of the Town of Leicester, Massachusetts* (Boston: John Wilson and Son, 1860), pp. 248, 354–358, and passim; and Samuel Denny's will and inventory, Probate Court, Worcester, Mass., docket 16647 (true copy in the object file).
2. Fales, *Deerfield*, figs. 460, 460a. Another curly maple Massachusetts desk of this period is illustrated in *Antiques* 78, no. 6 (December 1960): 531.

151

Child's desk
New England, 1715–1735

Description: The case of this slant-front child's desk contains a single drawer in the lower section, beneath a well space flanked by lopers, all of which are outlined with double half-round molding. The desk is supported by four high turned feet below applied molding at the front and sides. The cleated lid has thumbnail molding on all four sides and is attached to the desk with brass butt hinges. The interior contains an upper tier of four pigeonholes with valances shaped to flathead arches above a lower tier of plain pigeonholes flanking a wide center drawer. The well space has a fielded panel as its sliding cover, operated with a thumb depression. The top is dovetailed to the sides, with the dovetails exposed on the top, and the bottom is dovetailed to the sides. The back consists of two horizontal butted boards nailed to a rabbet on all four sides. The feet are doweled to a base framework at the front and sides that is pinned and nailed to the bottom. On the large drawer, the sides are dovetailed to the front, and the back is dovetailed to the sides; the bottom is let into a groove in the front and sides and nailed to the underside of the back. The top edge of the sides and back are shaped to a double half round, and the sides stand slightly above the back. On the interior drawer, the sides are dovetailed to the front and back, the bottom is secured in the same fashion, and the top edges of the sides and back are flat and of the same height.

Condition: The desk has been refinished; traces of red paint remain. The right side of the lid was damaged and repaired in 1946. Portions of the double half-round molding have been replaced, and there are many other patches and repairs

151

151a

throughout the desk. The interior has been refitted, and the valances are replacements or additions. The brass escutcheons and wooden pulls are of a later date. The bottom of the large drawer has been pieced, and the running strips replaced. The backboards have been renailed.

Woods: Soft maple; eastern white pine.

Dimensions: H 66.8; W 60.8; CW 56.9; D (closed) 36.5; D (open) 67.5; CD 34.5.

Bibliography: Nutting, *Treasury*, no. 641; Schiffer, *Miniature Antique Furn.*, fig. 180; Kirk, *Impecunious Collector's Guide*, fig. 92.

Provenance: Francis P. Garvan, New York, N.Y.

BECAUSE this desk, which probably was painted originally, has been refinished in modern times, it has been lamented that it is "now only a record that small desks, similar to larger ones, were made for children during the early years of the eighteenth century."[1] But what an important document it is, especially in the light of recent comments that specialized furniture for children was a phenomenon of the nineteenth century and very rare in the eighteenth century. This desk is thus important three-dimensional evidence of patterns of child rearing, evidence that is often overlooked by those who study only printed or written documents.

The Mabel Brady Garvan Collection 1930.2398

1. Kirk, *Impecunious Collector's Guide*, p. 101.

152

Desk
Pennsylvania, 1710–1740

Description: Below the slant front the case contains five drawers, three in line, with the center drawer of slightly greater width, above two graduated wide drawers. There is applied molding at the front and sides above the top tier of drawers, and the drawers are flanked and separated by double half-round molding on the case. There is base molding at the front and sides, and the desk is supported by five turned feet. The front skirt is shaped to paired reverse curves between the front feet, and the side skirts are shaped with deep paired reverse curves. The cleated slant lid, framed with mitered joints at the corners, is supported by lopers at the sides and has a strip of applied molding to serve as a book rest. The interior contains a central recessed section behind the sliding well cover fitted with a brass ring pull. The center section consists of a central wide pigeonhole with a fixed valance shaped with stepped reverse curves leading to a round arch; this pigeonhole is flanked on each side by three smaller pigeonholes with fixed valances shaped with paired reverse curves. The pigeonholes stand above three drawers in line fitted with brass button pulls, with the center drawer of greater width. The front edge of the base of the center section is molded, and the well cover slides on rabbets in the floor of the interior. A small lid located in front of the well lifts out to provide access to a secret compartment containing three narrow boxes of nailed construction. The sides of the interior are each fitted with a tier consisting of a drawer below two stepped pigeonholes, with the upper pigeonhole fitted with a fixed valance shaped to paired reverse curves. The vertical partitions at the inner side of each tier are rounded and shaped with reverse curves; the floor of the upper pigeonhole is shaped with paired reverse curves. The top of the desk is dovetailed to the sides, with the dovetails exposed on the top, and the bottom is also dovetailed to the sides. The horizontal backboards are joined with a half lap and nailed to rabbets in the top and sides and to the bottom. There are no dustboards within the case; the top rail above the well is dovetailed to the case sides with the dovetail exposed. The feet are doweled to large square blocks, with the base moldings applied to the bottom and sides. On each drawer in the case, the sides are dovetailed to the front

152a

152

and back, and the bottoms are nailed to a rabbet in the front and to the underside of the sides and back, with running strips applied. The small drawers in the desk interior are made in the same fashion but without running strips.

Inscriptions: There are original shop marks in white chalk and later shop notations in pencil. There are numbers in white chalk on the outside of the right side of the bottom drawer in the left side of the desk interior.

Condition: All five feet are old but not original, and the skirt on the right side is a replacement. New blocks have been added to the right rear foot. The brasses are replacements. The drawer runners within the case and the running strips on the case drawers are replacements, and small blocks have been added to the back of some drawers as stops. The lid has been repaired, and its interior surface once may have been covered with baize. Cracks in each side of the case have been filled, and a strip added to the top edge of the upper backboard.

Woods: Mahogany; eastern white pine; lopers, drawer linings of desk interior, yellow poplar; feet, blocks, red gum or black gum.

Dimensions: H 106.9; W 102.2; CW 98.4; D (closed) 55.4; D (open) 94.3; CD 53.0.

Provenance: Jacob Margolis, New York, N. Y.; by sale in 1929 to Francis P. Garvan, New York, N. Y.

ALTHOUGH the feet of this desk are replacements, it is probable that it originally was fitted with five turned feet in the arrangement now present of a foot in each corner and a central front foot. The Yale desk is related to a desk at Winterthur that has a history of ownership in the Richardson family of Philadelphia.[1] The Winterthur desk also has five feet, and its slanting lid has an applied book rest, but it differs in many particulars from the Yale desk, precluding any thought that they might be from the same shop. The interior of the Winterthur desk differs markedly from the Yale example, its drawer construction is different, and it has dustboards.[2] Although walnut was the preferred fashionable wood in Philadelphia until about 1730, mahogany furniture was owned there at the opening of the eighteenth century, and the imported wood appears in cabinetmakers' inventories from shortly after 1700.[3]

The Mabel Brady Garvan Collection 1930.2323

1. McElroy, "Furn. in Philadelphia," pp. 75–76 fig. 15; see also the lower case of fig. 18.
2. An open view of the Winterthur desk is in Nutting, *Treasury*, no. 610.
3. McElroy, "Furn. in Philadelphia," p. 72.

153

Desk
New England, 1740–1760

Description: Below its inlaid slant lid, the front of this unusual desk is decorated to simulate four graduated lipped drawers, with a simulated drawer at the top fashioned from applied moldings shaped to accommodate the lopers, and with three working drawers below. Each drawer is fitted with a brass lock escutcheon (blind on the middle drawer, which is fitted with a wooden spring lock) flanked by matching escutcheons with bail pulls. There is a cove base molding at the front and sides, and the desk is supported by short, straight cabriole "hock" legs with pad feet at the front and by reel-and-ball feet at the rear. The cleated lid is supported by small lopers with brass button pulls that are flanked by brackets pinned to the case. Each corner of the lid has an inlaid ornament, resembling a large quarter fan, and there is a large inlaid shell in the center beneath a brass lock escutch-

153

eon. The desk interior contains at each side a pair of superimposed pigeonholes above a drawer; the upper pigeonhole has a fixed valance, and its shelf is shaped with a round arch. The center section of the interior is recessed to allow for the sliding cover of the well behind the simulated case drawer. This center section contains three vertical pigeonholes with shaped valances flanked by document drawers faced with colonnettes; to each side of the center section are three pigeonholes over a single drawer. The desk interior drawers are fitted with turned wooden pulls and decorated with rectangles of light- and dark-wood inlay. The case is of dovetailed board construction, with the joint of the top to the sides exposed on the top and with the drawer dividers through-dovetailed to the sides. The dovetails of the top and bottom drawer dividers are also pegged; the drawer runners within the case are pegged, as is the base molding. The framework of the desk interior is also pegged in place through the sides of the case. There are three butted vertical backboards, still rough and possibly pit sawn, nailed in place. The feet are doweled through blocks pinned to the underside of the bottom and through the bottom, with the dowels wedged. The rear feet are square on their rear faces, and there is a strip pegged to the underside of the bottom behind the base molding. In the wide case drawers, the sides are dovetailed to the front and back; the bottoms are let into grooves in the front and sides and pegged to the underside of the back. The top of the drawer sides are shaped to a double half round, and the top edge of the back is beveled. The sides of the desk interior drawers are dovetailed to the front and back; the bottoms are let into rabbets in the front and sides and glued to all four sides. The document drawers are of simple nailed construction.

Condition: The lip of the well cover is a replacement. There have been minor repairs to the drawer fronts, to the backboards, and to the bottom edges of the drawer sides. The pigeonhole valances are probably replacements. The rear feet have been questioned and may be replacements, although the same type of rear foot was used on the only known related desk.

Woods: American black walnut; eastern white pine; light- and dark-wood inlays, including (possibly) a maple burl, white oak, and walnut, and a light-colored diffuse porous fine textured hardwood; spring lock, hickory.

Dimensions: H 99.9; W 102.1; CW 88.5; D (closed) 46.8; D (open) 75.7; CD 44.3.

Provenance: Francis P. Garvan, New York, N. Y.

This desk was catalogued initially in Mr. Garvan's files as a Pennsylvania example, probably because it is made of walnut and because of the extensive use of wooden pins in its construction. It is more likely, however, that it was made in

153a

rural New England. The only known related example is a very similar desk in maple that was purchased from a family in Maine along with examples of Maine furniture.[1] The inlaid decoration found on these two objects is similar to that used on Massachusetts furniture of the middle decades of the eighteenth century (see cat. 100, for example), and these two desks are probably rural expressions of an urban style. The front feet are particularly distinctive, with their unusual hocked form, probably a version of the Massachusetts "horsebone" feet introduced about 1730.

The Mabel Brady Garvan Collection 1930.2634

1. *Antiques* 58, no. 2 (August 1950): 91.

154

Desk-on-frame
Connecticut, probably East Granby, 1740–1770

Description: The case contains four graduated lipped drawers below the slant-front lid, with the upper drawer flanked by the lopers. The lid opens to an interior with a wide central pigeonhole with a shaped valance, containing a blind drawer, and with a drawer below. The center section is flanked on each side by four smaller pigeonholes with fixed shaped valances; each pair of the flanking pigeonholes stands above a drawer. The upper case rests within a restraining molding applied to the top of the supporting frame. The front skirt of the frame is shaped with deep reverse curves flanking a central drop, and the side skirts are shaped with paired reverse curves. The frame is supported by four short cabriole legs terminating in squared and pointed pad feet. The top of the desk is dovetailed to the sides with the dovetails exposed on the top, the bottom is dovetailed to the sides, and the horizontal backboards are joined with a half lap and nailed to rabbets in the top and sides and to the bottom. The dovetails joining the drawer dividers to the case sides are exposed. On each drawer, both in the interior and in the case, the sides are dovetailed to the front and back; the bottom is beveled on the front and side edges and is let into a groove in the front and sides and nailed to the underside of the back. The bottom of one of the wide drawers is riven. The frame is joined with mortise-and-tenon joints secured with two pegs. It contains diagonal cross braces, with the top brace housed and nailed to the lower and the four corners nailed to the legs.

Inscriptions: A shield-shaped silver plaque engraved "Joel Clark 1746" was once attached to the center of the lid; it was

stolen while the desk was on exhibition. "Back" is written on the back of the wide drawers in the case; the desk interior drawers are numbered in chalk; and there are columns of figures on the back and sides of one of the desk interior drawers. Other shop marks in chalk are also present.

Condition: The brasses and hardware are replacements installed in 1962. The pigeonhole valances are all restored, with the exception of the center valance drawer, which has been pieced. The drawer runners within the case are replacements, and running strips have been added to some drawers. All the knee brackets on the frame are replacements, and there have been many other minor repairs.

Woods: American black cherry; eastern white pine.

Dimensions: H 108.9; W 99.3; UCW 91.6; LCW 96.5; D (closed) 46.5; D (open) 76.1; UCD 41.9; LCD 44.4.

Bibliography: Charles Nagel, Jr., "Room from the Joel Clark House, East Granby, Connecticut, 1737," *YUAG Bulletin* 4, no. 3 (October 1932): 139; Kirk, *Conn. Furn.*, no. 114 (included in catalogue but not in exhibition).

Provenance: According to tradition, this desk was built and owned by Joel Clark (1717–1777) of East Granby, Conn., who married Lydia Forbes (d. 1796) in 1742. The desk presumably stayed in the Clark family, and it was one of the furnishings acquired by Francis P. Garvan when he purchased the Samuel Clark house in 1920 (see cat. 86).

ALTHOUGH it seems likely that this simple desk-on-frame descended in the Clark family of East Granby, along with a chest-on-chest in the Yale collection (cat. 86), the tradition that it was made by Joel Clark in 1746 has yet to be confirmed. Clark's estate papers, including a detailed inventory of his household goods, include no mention of a desk, nor has it been determined that he was a woodworker.[1] Several related desk-on-frames from the Connecticut Valley have been published.[2]

The Mabel Brady Garvan Collection 1930.2546

1. Estate papers of Joel Clark, docket 730, Simsbury Probate District, Connecticut State Library, Hartford.
2. *Antiques* 105, no. 1 (January 1974): 18; Kirk, *Conn. Furn.*, no. 115.

155

155

Desk-on-frame
Possibly by Eliphalet Chapin (1741–1807)
Connecticut, possibly East Windsor, 1771–1775

Description: The desk section contains a single wide lipped drawer below the slant front. The cleated lid has mitered joints at the front corners, is attached to the case with brass butt hinges, and is supported by lopers. It opens to an interior with ten pigeonholes with fixed shaped valances above five drawers. The vertical partitions between the pigeonholes are also shaped, and four of the drawers are fitted with brass button pulls, while the middle drawer is fitted with an oval stamped brass lock escutcheon. The desk, or upper case, rests within a restraining molding applied to the frame, or lower case. The lower case contains three lipped drawers in line, with the side drawers of greater width and the middle drawer carved with a convex fan. The front skirt is shaped with reverse curves; the side skirts are shaped to flathead arches. The desk is supported by four cabriole legs terminating in pad feet. The top and bottom of the upper case are dovetailed to the sides with the rather square dovetails used throughout this object, and the dovetails are exposed on the

298 *American Case Furniture*

top. The desk interior drawers have sides dovetailed to the front and back, with the bottoms glued to rabbets in all four sides and with small strips glued to the outside of the back as stops. The wide drawer in the upper case and the three drawers in the lower case have the sides dovetailed to the front, with the bottoms beveled on the front and side edges, let into grooves in the front and sides, and nailed to the underside of the back. The back of the upper case is a single horizontal board with beveled edges fitted to grooves in the top and sides and nailed to the bottom. Two transverse cleats are screwed to the underside of the bottom. The lower case is framed with mortise-and-tenon joints, with two pegs used to secure the horizontal backboard to the rear legs. There is no top to the lower case; the upper case rests on the frame, with a restraining strip nailed to the top edge of the back and strips nailed to each side of the inside of the case. The inner faces of the legs are blocked; the side supports and runners are housed around these blocks and nailed in place. The runners for the middle drawer are T-shaped and tenoned through the back. The wide drawer is fitted with a central brass lock escutcheon flanked by escutcheons with bail pulls, the side drawers in the lower case with a single brass escutcheon with bail pull, and the middle drawer with a brass button pull in the center of the fan and a brass lock escutcheon above. There is a secret compartment drilled out in the center of the back frame that contains a removable compartment that is merely a hollowed-out block. The sides of this compartment became thin when being hollowed out and were covered with pages from an almanac. The compartment once was fitted with a pull on its lower edge; it can be released by pushing down through a hole chiseled away where the drawer runner is tenoned through the back (see illustration).

155b

Inscriptions: The drawers were numbered originally in white chalk; later numbers have been added in pencil. A "Connecticut Furniture" (1967) exhibition label is pasted to the inside of the right side of the wide drawer in the upper case. The pages from the almanac used to reinforce the secret compartment are dated 1770.

Condition: The brasses are replacements. The right and left corners of the wide drawer in the upper case have been repaired, and the bottom of the same drawer has been pieced. New running strips have been added to the drawers, and new screws have been added to the cleats on the underside of the bottom of the upper case. The tops of the middle and right drawer fronts in the lower case have been pieced.

Woods: American black cherry; eastern white pine; back of frame, secret compartment, other elements, butternut.

Dimensions: H 97.8; W 97.6; UCW 87.4; LCW 92.4; D (closed) 52.5; D (open) 77.5; UCD 45.2; LCD 47.5.

Exhibition: Kirk, *Conn. Furn.*, no. 117.

155a

Bibliography: Kirk, *Early Am. Furn.*, fig. 146; Elaine Ulman, "'I'm Perfectly Willing to Write Bold Statements, Be Wrong, and Be Corrected . . . the True Emphasis in My Work Is Learning to See," *Antiques World* 2, no. 10 (October 1980): 64.

Provenance: C. Sanford Bull, Middlebury, Conn.

THE possibility that this diminutive desk-on-frame was made by Eliphalet Chapin is raised by the close relationship between several details of its ornament and construction to those on other objects attributed to Chapin, including a dressing table (cat. 108) and a high chest (cat. 146) in the Yale collection. Among these details are the distinctive shaping of the skirt, the carved fan or shell, and the use of rabbeted drawer runners tenoned through the backboard. Variations on this form include desks mounted on similar high frames without drawers and at least two unusual examples with a bookcase or cupboard section rising above the desk unit.[1] The secret compartment in the backboard of the frame, conveniently covered with an almanac dated 1770, is a detail rarely encountered. A related desk-on-frame has been attributed to Newbury, or Newburyport, Massachusetts.[2]

Gift of C. Sanford Bull 1953.50.1

1. Kirk, *Conn. Furn.*, no. 113; [Homer Eaton Keyes], "The Individuality of Connecticut Furniture," *Antiques* 28, no. 3 (September 1935): 112; Kirk, *Conn. Furn.*, no. 123 (Wadsworth Atheneum).
2. Fales, *Deerfield*, figs. 463, 463a.

156

Child's desk
New England, 1760–1790

Description: The case below the slant front contains three graduated lipped drawers. The upper drawer is flanked by lopers, and each drawer is fitted with a central blind brass escutcheon flanked by matching escutcheons with bail pulls. The cleated lid has a brass lock escutcheon and thumbnail molding on all four sides; it is attached to the desk with brass butt hinges. The desk interior contains a central stepped section consisting of an upper recessed tier of three drawers flanked on each side by a pair of pigeonholes above a drawer, all above a single wide drawer and flanked on each side by a pigeonhole above a drawer. The interior drawers and the lopers have brass button pulls. The vertical partitions in the interior are rounded and shaped, except those on the sides of the upper bank of drawers, which have beaded edges, as does the horizontal partition above the wide center drawer. The top is dovetailed to the sides, with the dovetails exposed on the top. The bottom is let into a groove in the sides, and the sides continue below the bottom and are shaped to a flathead arch, thus forming the support for the desk. At the front and sides, both the simple base molding and the bracket feet are shaped from a single board and applied to the bottom front rail and the sides. The back consists of three horizontal butted boards nailed to a rabbet in the top and sides and to the bottom. The drawer dividers are dovetailed to the sides, with the runners housed in grooves and nailed to the sides. The top drawer, between the lopers, has an additional support across the back that is rabbeted to the runners. There are no dustboards. On each large drawer in the case, the sides are dovetailed to the front and back; the bottom is beveled on its front and side edges, let into a groove in the drawer front and sides, and nailed to the underside of the back. The sides of the desk interior drawers are dovetailed to the front and back; the bottoms are let into a rabbet in the front, butted to the back and sides, and glued in place; the bottom

156a

156

of the wide center drawer is also pinned through the sides and back.

Inscriptions: Possibly "Long" is written in white chalk on the outside of the back of the center wide drawer in the interior. "X" in white chalk appears on the outside of several drawer backs and sides and on other interior elements.

Condition: The desk probably was painted originally; it has been refinished. The brasses are replacements, and new running strips have been added to many of the drawers. The bottom of the top drawer in the case has been pieced, and the left rear applied bracket foot has been repaired.

Wood: Eastern white pine.

Dimensions: H 77.3; W 71.2; CW 66.6; D (closed) 40.8; D (open) 67.4; CD 38.2.

Bibliography: *Third Sale of Fine Early American Furniture Gathered during the Last Seven Months by Jacob Margolis, Cabinet Maker of New York City*, Sale 1770, 16–17 November 1923 (New York: Anderson Galleries, 1923), no. 85; Schiffer, *Miniature Antique Furn.*, fig. 190.

Provenance: Jacob Margolis, New York, N. Y.; acquired at auction in 1923 by Francis P. Garvan, New York, N. Y.

An unusual feature of this desk is the way in which its sides continue below the bottom board (which is grooved rather than dovetailed in place) to form the actual support for the desk, much as they do in a six-board chest (cat. 34). Perhaps the maker felt that this method, which saved him the trouble of cutting a number of dovetails, was adequate for a desk of this small size. The desk is, however, large enough to have been used by a child and shows evidence of having been so employed. Like cat. 151, it is thus in a different class of furniture than true miniatures or dollhouse furniture, such as the toy desk sold by Abraham Forst of Philadelphia in 1816.[1] The Art Gallery collection also includes another child's desk (Appendix, no. 21) of related date and size.

The Mabel Brady Garvan Collection 1930.2397

1. Nancy Goyne, "A Miniature Desk Sold by Abraham Forst," in *Winterthur Portfolio* 2 (Winterthur, Del.: Henry Francis du Pont Winterthur Museum, 1965), pp. 82–83. Other miniature desks are illustrated in Schiffer, *Miniature Antique Furn.*, figs. 187, 189; and Fales, *Deerfield*, figs. 468, 469.

157

Desk
Boston, Massachusetts, area, ca. 1768

Description: Below the slant front the case contains four graduated lipped drawers. There is base molding at the front and sides, and the case is supported by four short cabriole legs terminating in claw-and-ball feet. The center of the front base molding is decorated with a shaped drop. The cleated lid is supported by lopers and opens to an interior arranged in two tiers. The upper tier has a central prospect door with concave blocking topped with a convex carved shell, and the door is flanked by document drawers faced with colonnettes with unusual rounded finials. The door opens to an interior with three superimposed drawers with rounded blocking and with the upper drawer of greater depth. To each side of the center section is a unit with three pigeonholes with valances shaped to roundheaded arches, all above a single block-front drawer. To the sides of the upper tier are three superimposed drawers, with concave blocking, with the upper drawer of greater depth and carved with a shell to echo the

Desks 301

prospect door. The lower tier is fitted with two drawers flanking a wide central open compartment that may have been fitted originally with a drawer. The partitions between the pigeonholes are shaped; the other vertical partitions and the platform of the upper tier have cock-beaded edges; and the front edge of the platform for the lower tier is molded. The top is dovetailed to the sides with the dovetails exposed on the top; the bottom is dovetailed to the sides. The vertical backboards are joined with a half lap and nailed to rabbets in the top and sides and to the bottom. The joint of the drawer dividers to the case is covered with an applied facing strip; the dovetails joining the vertical partitions to the drawer dividers are exposed. The drawer runners within the case are nailed to the sides. The sides of the case drawers are dovetailed to the front and back, with the top edge of the sides molded. The bottoms are beveled on their front and side edges, let into grooves in the front and sides, and nailed to the underside of the back. The sides of the desk interior drawers are dovetailed to the front and back; the bottoms are let into rabbets in the sides, are flush with the front and back, and are nailed in place through the sides. The sides of the document drawers are tenoned to the front and glued to the back.

Inscriptions: On the outside of the right side of the left document drawer are several inscriptions, including, in pencil, "Wm Butler / September ye 10, 1768" enclosed in a circle; "Wm C Wyer / April 28th 1838 / Lydia C. Wyer do Do" enclosed in a circle; and to the left, "1861 / –1768/ 93" twice in pencil. These inscriptions are written over one in white chalk that reads "Note / T——." On the outside of the left

157

157a

side of the same document drawer is, in pencil,"Wm Clisby Desk from / Huldah Crosby June 1830," with "0" written over an original "3." On the outside of the right side of the lowest left drawer in the upper tier of the interior is "this Desk from / Nantucket" in pencil. On the outside of the back of the shell-carved drawer on the right side of the upper tier is "Wm Clisby Oct 9 1874 / Nantucket / CW [inverted]" in pencil. In pencil on the underside of the bottom of the top drawer in the case is the modern "Made 1711 ye——."

Condition: The brasses and the hinges are replacements. The lower edge of the lid has been pieced, and there have been repairs to the right rear corner of the top and to the upper front edge of the right side of the case. The fronts of the case drawers have been repaired. The side knee brackets on the front and rear feet and the blocks behind them are replacements.

Woods: Mahogany; eastern white pine.

Dimensions: H 112.6; W 114.1; CW 106.4; D (closed) 56.5; D (open) 89.4; CD 51.5.

Provenance: The earliest inscription on this desk suggests that it was acquired, perhaps on 10 September 1768, by William Butler (d. 1791) of Nantucket, Mass. Butler, orig-

inally from Martha's Vineyard, married Mary Jenkins of Nantucket in 1742. There is no inventory of his estate; his will directs that his goods be left to his wife, who died in 1811. The history of the desk after 1811 is confused, although it appears to have been owned on Nantucket until late in the century and perhaps longer. The inscriptions seem to indicate that the later owners may have included Huldah Crosby (1750–1833), the daughter of Matthew and Mary (Butler) Pease who thus might have been a relation to William Butler. Huldah Crosby seems to have bequeathed the desk to William Clisby II (1790–1871) in 1830 or 1833. The date 1838 is associated in another inscription with the names of William C. Wyer and his wife Lydia (Coffin), who were married in 1823. The latest inscription, with the name of William Clisby and the date 1874, may refer to a later ownership by the earlier William Clisby or may be a misprint for his date of death (1871). The desk was acquired in the twentieth century by dealer Jacob Margolis, New York, N. Y., who sold it on 6 March 1926 to Francis P. Garvan, New York, N. Y.[1]

ALTHOUGH this desk has a strong history of ownership on Nantucket as early as 1768, it is unlikely that it was made there, where little furniture of this quality appears to have been produced.[2] The desk probably was imported from mainland Massachusetts, perhaps from the Boston area, for it shares an affinity with many desks produced there.[3] However, William Butler does appear in Nantucket documents of the eighteenth century as a housewright, and it is possible that his woodworking skills extended to the making of furniture. The straight front of this example stands in contrast to the two blockfront examples in the collection (cats. 158, 159).

The Mabel Brady Garvan Collection 1930.2036

1. The writer would like to thank Charles H. Carpenter, Jr., and Mary Carpenter for their assistance in tracing the names inscribed on this desk. Sources for birth and death dates include the vital records of Nantucket and the Pollard Papers, Nantucket Atheneum; see letters to the author of 22 July 1983, 24 August 1983, and 4 August 1985, object file, Yale Furniture Study.
2. While conducting research for a forthcoming book on the decorative arts of Nantucket, the Carpenters found no case furniture that could be attributed conclusively to a Nantucket maker, although joiners and chairmakers were at work there in the eighteenth century.
3. Lovell, "Boston Blockfront Furn.," pp. 112–117.

158

Desk

Boston, Massachusetts, area, 1755–1775

Description: Below the slant front the case holds four blockfront graduated drawers outlined by cock beading on the case. Each drawer is fitted with a central brass lock escutcheon flanked by matching escutcheons with bail pulls, and there are large carrying handles on the sides. There is base molding at the front and sides, with a central drop at the front, and the desk is supported by short cabriole legs with large knee brackets and terminating in large claw-and-ball feet. The blocking of the drawers is carried through the base molding and brackets. The cleated lid has mitered joints at the front corners and a lip applied to the front and sides; it is supported by lopers and has a central brass lock escutcheon. It opens to an interior with two tiers. The center section of the upper tier consists of a prospect door with concave blocking and a carved convex shell contained within a line. The door is flanked by document drawers faced with colonnettes with urn-and-flame finials and opens to an interior with a pigeonhole over a drawer. The valance of the pigeonhole is shaped with reverse curves and works like a drawer. Next to the center section on each side is a pair of pigeonholes with fixed shaped valances over a blockfront drawer; the vertical partition between the pigeonholes is shaped. And at each side of the upper tier are a pair of superimposed drawers with recessed blocking, with the upper drawer of greater depth and carved with a convex shell echoing that on the

158a

158

prospect door. The lower tier consists of three drawers in line, with the center drawer of greater width. The front edges of the platforms of each tier are molded, and the vertical partitions between the lower tier of drawers and on the sides of the document drawer have cock-beaded edges. The drawers are fitted with brass button pulls (two are on the wide drawer in the lower tier) and the prospect door has a brass lock escutcheon. The top and bottom of the case are dovetailed to the sides, and the horizontal backboards are nailed to rabbets in the top and sides and to the bottom. The joint of the drawer dividers to the case sides is covered by an applied facing strip. The drawer runners within the case are applied to the sides; the runner for the second drawer from the top is interrupted by the posts for the carrying handles. The case bottom is flush with the base molding, which is attached by means of a "giant" dovetail. The blocks for the feet are beneath the case. There are thin strips applied to the bottom of the sides of the case, horizontal shaped blocks behind the knee brackets, and rectangular horizontal blocks for the triangular rear supports, which also have vertical blocks behind them. The rear claw-and-ball feet are created from two blocks. On the case drawers, the sides are dovetailed to the front and back, and the bottoms are nailed to rabbets in the front and sides and to the underside of the back. The blocking is cut from the solid. The desk interior drawers are fashioned in the same manner, with the exception of the document drawers, where the sides are nailed to a rabbet in the front and to the back. There are central runners for the drawers in the lower tier.

Inscriptions: "Boston" and some figures are written in white chalk on the outside of the right side of the left document drawer. The left and right document drawers are numbered respectively "1" and "2" in pencil. "To / Boor / P/B/258" is written in pencil on the underside of the bottom of the interior drawer behind the prospect door. There are chalk and pencil numbers of varying dates on the drawers and case.

Condition: The hinges are replaced, although the brasses may be original. The lock escutcheon on the lowest case drawer varies from those on the other drawers. The side bracket on the right rear foot is a replacement, and one horizontal block for that foot has been replaced. The lipped edges of the slant front have been pieced. The interior of all the drawers has been varnished.

Woods: Mahogany; eastern white pine; lopers, probably cherry.

Dimensions: H 112.8; W 117.9; CW 105.2; D (closed) 59.5; D (open) 87.9; CD 53.1.

Exhibition: YUAG, "Rhode Island Furn."

Bibliography: *Colonial Furniture: The Superb Collection of Mr. Francis Hill Bigelow of Cambridge, Mass.* [Part One], Sale 1795, 17 January 1924 (New York: Anderson Galleries, 1924), no. 136; Kirk, *Early Am. Furn.*, fig. 153; Lovell, "Boston Blockfront Furn.," fig. 80.

Provenance: According to tradition, originally owned by the Winthrop family of Boston; acquired by Francis Hill Bigelow (1859–1933), who began to collect furniture as early as 1875; acquired at auction in 1924 by Francis P. Garvan, New York, N.Y.

BIG, bold desks such as this example are characteristic of the best in Boston blockfront furniture in the third quarter of the eighteenth century. Many feature the large claw-and-ball feet found here, although hairy-paw feet are found on some examples.[1] The square-topped blocking on the drawer fronts of the Yale desk is not as common as the more typical rounded blocking usually found on Boston desks, but the interior of this desk conforms to "the classic formula for

304 *American Case Furniture*

Boston blockfront interiors."[2] These interiors were designed to be useful, for a desk was a place of business, where letter writing, record keeping, and filing would be conducted. An Englishman, H. Purefoy, ordered an interesting custom-made feature for the pigeonholes in his desk. Writing to a London stationer in 1751, he specified: "The little nests [pigeonholes] in my Burow [desk] are six in number & each of the nests is 3 inches & a quarter wide, 4 inches & an half high, & 7 inches & an half deep. Now I want six little black boxes made of pasteboard covered with leather (to hold notes & receipts) to be made of these Dimensions, so as to go each black box into one of these nests."[3]

The Mabel Brady Garvan Collection 1930.2506

1. For related examples, see Fales, *Deerfield*, fig. 465; St. Louis Art Museum (184.1929), in Springer, p. 11; Museum of Fine Arts, Boston, in Hipkiss, nos. 24, 25 (an example with hairy-paw feet and square-topped blocking); Lovell, "Boston Blockfront Furn.," figs. 78, 81.
2. Lovell, "Boston Blockfront Furn.," p. 115.
3. G. Eland, ed., *Purefoy Letters, 1735–1753*, vol. 2 (London: Sidgwick & Jackson, 1931), p. 287.

159

Desk

Boston, Massachusetts, area, 1760–1790

Description: Below the slant front the case holds four graduated blockfront drawers outlined by cock beading on the case. Each drawer is fitted with a central brass lock escutcheon flanked by matching escutcheons with bail pulls, and the blocking is rounded at the top. There is base molding at the front and sides, marked at the center with a shaped drop, and the desk is supported by ogee bracket feet, with the blocking carried through the base molding and brackets. The cleated lid is supported by lopers and has a central brass lock escutcheon at the top. It opens to an interior with a single tier. The center section contains a prospect door holding a looking glass within a frame shaped with reverse curves. The door opens to an interior with a pigeonhole with a valance drawer above a drawer with concave blocking, and the door is flanked by document drawers faced with colonnettes with urn-and-flame finials. To each side of the center section is a unit of two pigeonholes with fixed valances shaped with reverse curves above two superimposed graduated drawers with convex blocking. To the sides of these units are three drawers, with the upper drawer of greater depth and carved with a convex shell contained within an arc, above two graduated drawers, all with concave blocking. All the interior drawers have brass button pulls; the prospect door is fitted with a brass keyhole escutcheon. The drawers are raised on a platform with a molded edge that is contoured to the fronts of the drawers. The vertical partitions between the pigeonholes are shaped. The top is dovetailed to the sides, with the dovetails exposed on the top, and the bottom is dovetailed to the sides. The horizontal backboards are joined with a half lap and nailed to a rabbet in the top and sides and to the bottom. There is an applied facing strip over the joint of the drawer dividers and the case. The drawer runners within the case are nailed to the sides; the upper drawer is flanked by the lopers and has both a runner and a guide. The base molding is flush with the bottom and is joined with the "giant" dovetail found in Boston-area work. A vertical block is in each corner, and strips are applied to the underside of the bottom at the front and sides above horizontal blocks shaped for the brackets and rectangular blocks in front of the rear triangular feet. The sides of the case drawers are dovetailed to the front and back, with the top edge of the sides molded. The bottoms are nailed to a rabbet in the front and sides, with

running strips applied, and nailed with rosehead nails to the underside of the back. The desk interior drawers are fashioned in the same manner, with the exception of the document drawers, which are made in the usual nailed-board method. Small blocks are glued to the rear sides of the case as stops.

Inscriptions: There are numerous pencil and chalk inscriptions on the desk interior drawers. "E Wasgatt" is written on the underside of the bottom of the lower drawer below the pigeonholes on the left side. "Sarah Hays Wasgatt / Draw / D" is written in pencil on the outside of the back of the shell-carved drawer on the left side, and "Sarah H Wasgatt" followed by an illegible word is scratched on the outside of the left side of the same drawer. There are illegible words and numbers in chalk on the outside of the right side of the middle drawer in the left tier of three drawers. "Mary / Wasgatt" is written in pencil on the outside of the right side of the shell-carved drawer on the right side of the interior. There is an illegible chalk inscription on the inside of the right side of the lowest drawer in the right-side tier of three and on the outside. There is illegible writing in pencil on the outside of the left loper. There are chalk shop marks on the backs of the case drawers.

Condition: The hinges are replacements, and there have been patches to the right lip of the slant front. The feet have been cracked and reglued.

Woods: Mahogany; eastern white pine; lopers, soft maple, with stop pins, probably replacements, of hickory.

159a

Dimensions: H 109.3; W 111.3; CW 105.2; D (closed) 55.8; D (open) 93.3; CD 52.5.

Bibliography: *Eighteenth Century American Furniture... Sold by Order of Mrs. Gertrude H. Camp, "The Hayloft," Whitemarsh, Pa.*, Sale 2222, 20–21 January 1928 (New York: Anderson Galleries, 1928), lot 261; Kirk, *Early Am. Furn.*, fig. 152.

Provenance: The desk was owned at an early date by members of the Wasgatt family of Mount Desert, Maine. Eunice, Sarah, and Mary Wasgatt were the daughters of Thomas Wasgatt of Maine. Eunice married David Bradstreet of Mount Desert in 1792, suggesting that the desk was made prior to that event.[1] The desk was owned in the twentieth century by Mrs. Gertrude H. Camp of Whitemarsh, Pa., and was acquired at auction January 1928 by Francis P. Garvan, New York, N. Y.

THE inscriptions on this desk have led to the conclusion that it was owned at an early date in Maine, and thus, like the Boston-area desk in the Yale collection (cat. 157) owned originally on Nantucket, represents the diffusion of a Boston form to outlying parts of New England. After chairs, desks were the form most commonly made for export to the South by Boston and other New England furniture makers in the eighteenth century, and it is not surprising to find them turning up with histories in other parts of New England.[2] The presence of a mirrored prospect door is an important embellishment on this example.

The Mabel Brady Garvan Collection 1930.2158

1. Lovell, "Boston Blockfront Furn.," p. 112.
2. Greenlaw, p. 3.

160

Desk

Connecticut, probably Norwich area, 1755–1795

Description: Below the slant front, the case contains three blockfront graduated drawers outlined by cock beading on the case. The top drawer is flanked by lopers and contains applied carved convex shells flanking a concave shell carved from the solid. There is a base molding at the front and sides, with the front skirt shaped with a series of ascending S-scrolls. The desk is supported by large bracket feet, and the blocking

306 American Case Furniture

160

of the drawers is carried through the base molding and feet. The cleated lid opens to an elaborate interior containing nineteen drawers and eight pigeonholes arranged in two tiers. The center section of the upper tier is flanked by document drawers faced with reeded pilasters and contains two superimposed drawers with concave blocking, with the upper drawer of greater depth and carved with a convex shell. To each side of this center section are four pigeonholes with valance drawers shaped with recessed half circles and paired reverse curves. The vertical partitions between the pigeonholes are shaped with C-curves, and the edges are rounded. The pigeonholes stand above two drawers with serpentine fronts in line, with the inner drawers recessed. The lower tier contains three drawers in line; the wide center drawer has a concave front decorated with horizontal shaping outlined with incised scrolls at the corners; the side drawers have serpentine fronts. The front edge of the platform for each tier is molded. The valance and document drawers are blind; the other drawers are fitted with brass button pulls, with the exception of the shell-carved drawer, which has a brass ring pull. The top and bottom of the case are dovetailed to the sides, with the dovetails exposed on the top. The two horizontal backboards are joined with a half lap and nailed to rabbets in the top and sides and to the bottom. The joint of the drawer dividers to the case is covered with an applied facing strip. The drawer runners are nailed to the sides of the case; the top drawer is fitted with runners tenoned to the drawer divider and with guides. Blocks are nailed to the inside rear of the sides and to the underside of the bottom of the desk section to serve as stops. A sturdy framework supports this heavy desk. The front base molding is applied in horizontal layers. There is a large triangular horizontal board nailed to each corner of the underside of the bottom; the four corners have large vertical blocks, with smaller horizontal blocks behind the brackets. The rear feet are triangular. The sides of the wide case drawers are dovetailed to the front and back, with the top edge of the sides and back chamfered. The bottoms are nailed to rabbets in the front and sides and to the underside of the back, with running strips applied. The blocking is applied to the drawer fronts. The desk interior drawers are fashioned in the same manner, with the exceptions that the bottoms of the valance drawers are only glued in place and that the sides of the document drawers are nailed to the back, with the top edge scalloped with reverse curves. Strips are glued to the back of the document drawers as stops; the sides are rabbeted to grooves in the front.

Inscriptions: "Botom" is written on the underside of the bottom in a large florid hand. Another inscription in white chalk is on the top edge of the bottom front rail of the case and appears to read "Lor P" or "For P" or possibly "Tor P";

160a

Desks 307

it may merely say "Top" in an indecipherable fashion. The desk interior drawers are marked with scratched roman numerals; the lower drawer in the center section of the upper tier is inscribed "m" in white chalk; the inside of the left loper is marked "L" in white chalk; and there are other shop marks. A Connecticut Tercentenary label is pasted to the inside of the right side of the top case drawer.

Condition: The lower edge of the feet and some of the scrolled decoration have been replaced (see cat. 160b). The brasses and hinges are replacements. In 1974 and 1975, the desk was refinished by Peter Arkell in an attempt to achieve the appearance of mahoganized cherry. There have been other minor repairs.

Woods: American black cherry; eastern white pine.

Dimensions: H 120.9; W 114.0; CW 107.2; D (closed) 66.1; D (open) 108.0; CD 61.1.

Exhibitions: *Three Centuries of Conn. Furn.*, no. 216; Mayhew and Myers, no. 47; YUAG, "Rhode Island Furn."

Bibliography: Charles Messer Stow, "The Theme of Luxury in the Garvan Collection," *Antiquarian* 15, no. 3 (September 1930): 36; *Handbook*, p. 59; Walter A. Dyer, "The American Scrutoire-Desk: Chippendale-Empire," *Fine Arts* 18, no. 6 (May 1932): 28; Symonds and Ormsbee, *Antique Furn.* p. LXX; Kirk, *Conn. Furn.*, no. 118 (included in catalogue but not in exhibition); Jobe and Kaye, figs. 1-45, 1-45a.

Provenance: Said to have been owned by the Carpenter family of Swansea, N. H.; by sale to Israel Sack, Inc., New York, N. Y.; by sale in 1929 to Francis P. Garvan, New York, N. Y.

THIS mammoth desk is closely related to at least four desks from the Norwich area that exhibit similar Rhode Island influence and that share the same type of scrolled front skirt, carved shell on the top drawer in the case, and superb stepped interior.[1] More elaborate desks from the same area are known, including a mahogany example at the Art Institute of Chicago (1948.122) which has zebrawood drawer fronts on its interior, and an example signed by Benjamin Burnham and now at the Metropolitan Museum of Art.[2]

The Mabel Brady Garvan Collection 1930.2277

1. Nutting, *Treasury*, no. 629; *Colonial and Early Federal Furniture . . . Acquired from Notable Collections by Israel Sack*, Sale 3940, 9 January 1932 (New York: American Art Association, Anderson Galleries, 1932), no. 69, with a history in the Dickinson family of Rhode Island; and *Sack Coll.*, 5: 1315 no. P4374, formerly in the collection of Charles K. Davis. A desk and bookcase formerly in the Maryland Historical Society and now in a private collection is related to this group; see *Antiques* 98, no. 2 (August 1970): 216. The nine-shell chest of drawers in the Winterthur collection (Mayhew and Myers, no. 49) is not of the period.
2. Mayhew and Myers, nos. 58, 31; see also no. 32, attributed to Benjamin Burnham and Samuel Loomis working together, and nos. 36 and 38, for other impressive desks from New London County.

161

Desk-on-frame
Connecticut, probably Hartford, 1770–1800

Description: Below the slant front, the case holds four graduated lipped drawers. The drawer fronts are shaped with reverse blocking, with the side sections recessed rather than projecting, and the blocking terminates in Ionic capitals on the top case drawer. The lid is molded with elliptical arches that carry the blocking upward. The case has a brass carrying handle on each side and rests within a supporting frame. The front skirt of the frame is shaped with deep reverse curves flanking a central concave shell and is reverse

160b Before restoration, ca. 1929

blocked in conformity with the drawer fronts. The side skirts are shaped with reverse curves flanking a central stepped round arch. The slant front is supported by lopers and opens to reveal an elaborately shaped interior. On each side of a central compartment, there are four pigeonholes with drawer valances shaped to flathead arches surmounting two drawers in line with shaped fronts. The center compartment contains two pigeonholes with fixed valances, shaped to a "keyhole" effect, over a single drawer with a carved concave shell echoing that on the skirt, and the compartment is flanked by colonnettes. The center compartment can be drawn forward to reveal secret document drawers housed behind the colonnettes and the lidded secret entrance to a well beneath the interior drawers and behind the top case drawer, which is shallow. The vertical partitions between the the interior drawers are shaped, and the drawers rest on a stepped board with a molded front edge following the shape of the drawers. The desk is of dovetailed board construction, with the dovetails joining the top to the sides and the drawer dividers to the case exposed. There is a full dustboard underneath the top case drawer (to accommodate the secret well), but there are no dustboards below the other drawers. The drawer sides are dovetailed to the front and back with squarish dovetails; the bottoms are beveled on their front and side edges and let into grooves in the front and sides and nailed to the underside of the back (with the exception of the valance drawers, which are not nailed). The drawer fronts are all cut from the solid. The horizontal backboards are nailed to a rabbet on all four sides. The front, sides, and back of the frame are joined to the corner posts with mortise-and-tenon joints; the corner posts extend below the skirt to form the

cabriole legs and stylized Spanish feet with pads. The legs have applied knee brackets, and there are applied moldings at the front and sides of the frame. A strip is nailed behind the front of the skirt, and three transverse supports are nailed to the underside of this strip and to the top of blocks attached to the back of the frame.

Inscriptions: Most of the case drawers and the valance drawers are carved with roman numerals. A "Connecticut Furniture" exhibition label is pasted to the inside of the right side of the frame and to the inside of the bottom of the top case drawer.

Condition: This desk is made of extremely dense and heavy mahogany, and as one might expect the weight has taken its toll on the object. The frame has been extensively repaired. New corner blocks have been screwed in each corner; new supports have been nailed to the sides; the back left corner post has been replaced; both right legs have been repaired; the side moldings have been replaced; and the transverse supports may be additions. There also have been many

Desks 309

repairs to the desk drawer fronts, lid, and sides. The brasses are replacements, as are the hinges that attach the lid to the case; the original hinges were probably a victim of the great weight of the lid. Several drawer bottoms have been pieced, some drawer runners have been replaced, and unusual corner blocks have been added to the corners of the drawers as a later addition necessitated by the weight of the drawer fronts. The top edge of the lopers and the edges of the lid have been covered with modern green baize. The desk has been refinished to a light, somewhat greenish, color.

Woods: Mahogany; eastern white pine; lopers, rear rail of frame, yellow poplar; small blocks in corners of drawers, transverse supports in frame, and additions to drawer bottoms, butternut; other repairs, yellow poplar.

Dimensions: H 112.1; W 103.5; CW 92.3; D (open) 82.9; D (closed) 54.1; CD 45.9.

Exhibitions: Kirk, *Conn. Furn.*, no. 116; *Great River*, cat. 107.

Bibliography: "A Fresh Chip Hewn from the Block," *Antiques* 21, no. 5 (May 1932): fig. 5; Ormsbee, *Story Am. Furn.*, illus. 58; Comstock, "Bull Coll.," p. 140; Kirk, *Early Am. Furn.*, fig. 167; Minor Myers, Jr., "The Migration of a Style," *Art & Antiques* 3, no. 2 (March–April 1980): 86.

Provenance: The early history of the desk is unknown. It was owned by C. Sanford Bull's uncle from New Haven in the late nineteenth century and was in the collection of C. Sanford Bull, Middlebury, Conn., by 1932.

THIS desk has been attributed to the Hartford area on the basis of the relationship of its shaped skirt with a central carved shell to that on related desks with a Hartford provenance.[1] One of the related desks, now at the Brooklyn Museum (64.87), also is made of very heavy and dense mahogany.[2] Mahogany was not used frequently for furniture made in Connecticut or western Massachusetts, but one recent survey has found at least twenty examples of Connecticut eighteenth-century furniture made of mahogany in public collections.[3] The most unusual and distinctive feature of this desk is its reverse-blocked facade with Ionic capitals. The reverse blocking has been likened to the serpentine shape popular in the late eighteenth and early nineteenth centuries, and the capitals have been seen as another element of the classical revival pointing to a late date for this desk.[4] The effectiveness of the secret well in this desk is compromised by the top drawer's being the only case drawer without a lock; one has only to remove it to gain access to the "secret" compartment behind it.

Gift of C. Sanford Bull 1951.56.1

1. Kirk, *Conn. Furn.*, no. 116.
2. Kirk, *Conn. Furn.*, no. 115.
3. "Williams Family High Chest Acquired," *Historic Deerfield Quarterly* 22, no. 2 (April 1983): 1; this brief article discusses a mahogany high chest acquired by Historic Deerfield that is linked to these desks. See also *Great River*, cat. 107.
4. Kirk, *Conn. Furn.*, no. 116.

162

Desk
Attributed to Samuel Dunlap (1752–1830)
Possibly Salisbury, New Hampshire, 1790–1810

Description: The top board is through-dovetailed to the sides and has a beveled front edge. Beneath the slant front the case contains four graduated lipped drawers with brass bail pulls. There is applied molding at the base and sides, and the chest stands on four claw-and-ball feet with S-scroll leg brackets at the front and sides. The slant front, which has an oval brass escutcheon, opens to an interior containing three rows of drawers. The top row of five deep drawers stands above another row of five drawers; these two rows are slightly stepped back and supported by a drawer divider with a front molded edge beneath which there are three drawers in line, the center one somewhat wider than those on the sides. The slant front has cleats pegged in place at each

162a

162

end and is attached with brass butt hinges. It is supported in the open position by lopers with molded ends pinned in place. The interior desk drawers have sides dovetailed to the front and back, with the characteristic deep kerf marks visible on the insides of the front; the bottoms are beveled on their front and side edges, fitted to grooves in the drawer front and sides, and attached to the backs with wooden pins. Small strips are glued behind each drawer to act as stops. Beneath the desk interior, the frame and drawers are constructed in the same manner as the two Dunlap chests of drawers in the collection (see cats. 64–65). Here, the drawer sides are shaped to a central bead, and the drawer bottoms are attached with sprigs rather than machine-cut nails.

Inscriptions: "B" is written in chalk on the inside of the back of each of the lower three wide drawers in the desk. There are numbers and letters in chalk on the inside bottom of an interior drawer, and the left and right side interior drawers in the lower level are marked "L" and "R" respectively, as are the top edges of the lopers.

Condition: The desk has been refinished; traces of red paint remain on the desk interior. The wide center drawer in the lower level of the desk interior is a replacement made by Emile Mazzola in 1961. The tip of the inner S-scroll on the right front foot is a replacement.

Woods: Soft maple; eastern white pine.

Dimensions: H 105.3; W 100.5; CW 96.2; D (closed) 49.8; D (open) 84.9; CD 47.7.

Exhibitions: Parsons, *Dunlaps*, fig. 74; Parsons and Brooke, "Dunlap Cabinetmakers," fig. 8.

Provenance: Francis P. Garvan, New York, N. Y.

Desks were another furniture form made in relatively large numbers by members of the Dunlap school, and at least twenty-five surviving examples have been recorded.[1] The Yale example is one of the simpler versions, lacking the flowered ogee base molding and carved shells on the desk interior drawers.[2] A similar desk has a strong history of ownership that suggests Samuel Dunlap was its maker, and this desk is attributed to him on the basis of that relationship.[3] That desk lacks a drawer in the center of the lowest tier of the interior, and it has been suggested that this place was used for an account book; the conjectural restoration of a middle drawer on the Yale example thus may have been unwarranted.[4] Samuel Dunlap's account book records nine desks made between 1785 and 1810, although he may well have made more.[5]

The Mabel Brady Garvan Collection 1930.2272

1. Parsons, *Dunlaps*, p. 9; Parsons, "More Dunlap," p. 113.
2. For illustrations of related examples, see Parsons, *Dunlaps*, figs. 64–73, 75.
3. Parsons, *Dunlaps*, fig. 71; letter of Charles S. Parsons, 10 January 1969, accession files.
4. Parsons, "More Dunlap," p. 114.
5. Parsons, *Dunlaps*, p. 41. Charles Parsons has recorded more Dunlap-school desks than are recorded in the account books of John and Samuel, suggesting that the documentary record is incomplete; Parsons, "More Dunlap," p. 113.

163

Desk
Delaware Valley, 1755–1795

Description: The case holds four graduated lipped drawers below the slant front, and the sides of the case are embellished with fluted quarter columns. The case is supported by

Desks 311

163

bracket feet below cove base molding at the front and sides. The cleated lid has mitered joints at the front corners, with side moldings glued in place. It is supported by lopers and opens to an unusual interior. Here, the document drawers are at the sides of the interior and are faced with fluted columns with unusual bases and capitals of double rows of dentils. Between the document drawers the pigeonholes and drawers are arranged in three levels. The upper level has an unusual center drawer, with the front shaped in a reverse curve and with two rows of the dentil motif at the top; the drawer is flanked on each side by three pigeonholes with fixed shaped valances, with the vertical partitions between the pigeonholes shaped with reverse curves to match the drawer front. The middle level consists of three drawers in line, and the lower level also consists of three drawers in line, with the side drawers being very small and square and the wide middle drawer decorated with an applied vertical molding and brass button pull to simulate three drawers in line. The document drawers can be pushed forward through notches cut in the rear of the vertical partitions on their inside edges. The platform under the wide lower drawer is notched at the back and slides forward and out to reveal a shallow secret well underneath. The vertical partitions on each side of the wide middle drawer also slide forward in grooves, providing access to small square secret drawers housed behind the little side drawers; these are pulled out with leather tabs nailed to the drawers. The vertical partition on the right side of the pigeonhole to the immediate right of the middle drawer in the upper level slides forward in a similar manner, allowing access to two small superimposed secret drawers housed behind the middle drawer, with the lower secret drawer being of greater depth. The top of the case is dovetailed to the sides, with the dovetails exposed on the top; the bottom is dovetailed to the sides. The horizontal backboards are joined with a half lap and nailed to rabbets in all four sides. The drawer dividers are pinned to the case sides, and the drawer guides are nailed to full dustboards below each drawer in the case. The base framework consists of strips nailed to the underside of the bottom on all four sides, molded on their outer edges on the front and sides to form the base molding. Each corner has a large rectangular block and small shaped horizontal blocks behind the brackets. The rear feet are triangular braces nailed to the case. The sides of each drawer in the case are dovetailed to the front and back; the bottoms are beveled on the front and side edges, let into grooves in the front and sides, pinned with wooden pins to the underside of the back, with little glue

163a

312 *American Case Furniture*

blocks attached to the sides and front of the bottom. The middle row of drawers in the desk interior are fashioned in the same manner as the large case drawers, but without the glue blocks. In the bottom row of three drawers, the bottoms are pinned to a rabbet in the front and to the underside of the sides and back with wooden pins. The moldings on the wide drawer are let into grooves in the drawer front. In the upper middle drawer and the document drawers, the sides are nailed to a rabbet in the front and pegged to the back, with the bottoms pegged through a rabbet in the sides and (in the upper middle drawer) nailed to the underside of the sides and back. In the deep secret drawer in the upper level, the sides are pinned to a rabbet in the front and to the back, with the bottoms pinned to a rabbet in the front and to a rabbet in the sides; in the smaller drawer in that level, the bottom is pinned to the underside of all four sides. In the lower secret drawers, the sides are dovetailed to the front and back, with the bottoms let into rabbets in the front and sides and pinned; small blocks are glued to one side to act as stops for the drawers in front of them.

Inscriptions: The right and left lower secret drawers are marked "L" and "R" respectively in pencil on the underside of the bottom. There are columns of added figures in white chalk on the outside of the right side of the left document drawer. There are some shop marks throughout the desk.

Condition: The brasses and hinges are replacements. The left lower drawer in the interior is a replacement. The depth of the second drawer from the bottom has been reduced, and the lid has been repaired.

Woods: American black walnut; dustboards, yellow poplar; bottom, southern yellow pine; most drawer sides, backboards, large vertical blocks behind feet, red gum; drawer bottoms, one drawer side, horizontal blocks on base, Atlantic white cedar; front of upper middle and lower right drawers in desk interior, American black cherry; replaced block at right rear foot, eastern white pine.

Dimensions: H 105.2; W 77.9; CW 71.1; D (closed) 53.6; D (open) 84.6; CD 49.4.

Bibliography: *Antiques* 13, no. 3 (March 1928): 181.

Provenance: Purchased in 1928 from dealer Frances Wolfe Carey, Haddonfield, N. J., by Francis P. Garvan, New York, N. Y.

UNUSUALLY small, this desk was purchased by Mr. Garvan from a New Jersey dealer who advertised it as a "little local desk." It is made of a veritable vocabulary of woods commonly used in Delaware Valley furniture, including walnut, yellow poplar, southern yellow pine, red gum, Atlantic white cedar, and cherry. The desk is distinguished additionally by the uncommon decoration of the document drawers and the central upper drawer in the interior and its cleverly concealed secret drawers. Its thick boards, dustboards, and use of pins to secure the drawer dividers to the case sides are all evidence of a Middle Atlantic origin.

The Mabel Brady Garvan Collection 1930.2174

164

Desk-on-frame
Pennsylvania, 1755–1795

Description: The upper case of this two-unit object contains the desk section and two graduated lipped drawers, with the lipping on the drawers simulated. The upper drawer is flanked by the lopers, and the front corners of the case are decorated with fluted applied quarter columns. The slant front is cleated and opens to reveal an interior fitted with a central prospect door with an arched panel flanked by document drawers faced with fluted pilasters. To each side of this central section are units consisting of four pigeonholes with shaped valance drawers over two tiers of two drawers in line. The prospect door opens to reveal four drawers, with the bottom drawer of greater depth. The sides and rear of the top

164a

of the desk have applied molding with raised plinths in the rear corners to form a low gallery. The outer edges of the canted sides of the desk have incised molding. The desk rests within restraining molding applied to the front and sides of the frame. The frame is supported by four cabriole legs; the two front legs have shell-carved knees and terminate in claw-and-ball feet, while the rear legs terminate in pad feet. There is incised molding on all four sides of the base of the frame. The upper case is of dovetailed board construction, and there is a full dustboard between the two wide drawers in the case. The back is made of two horizontal boards nailed in place with rosehead nails. The quarter columns are applied in three pieces: base, column, and capital. The small drawers in the desk interior are constructed with the sides dovetailed to the front and back and the bottoms let into grooves in the front and sides and secured to the underside of the back with wooden pins. The two large drawers in the case are made in the same fashion, although rosehead nails are used in place of wooden pins. The prospect door gives the appearance of being a framed panel, but it is a single board with strips applied to its outer face to simulate panel construction. The frame is of mortise-and-tenon construction, with the front, rear, and side rails secured to the corner posts with two pins. Support for the desk is a platform of three transverse boards let into grooves in the front and side rails and to a rabbet in the rear rail. The middle board (now missing) was fitted with a tongue-and-groove joint to the side boards, and the boards were nailed to the rabbet in the rear rail.

Inscriptions: The inside of the bottom of the wide drawer in the upper case is marked "Samuel Feite" or "Feike" in pencil. An inscription in red pencil in the top left lower drawer in the left interior of the desk reads "Samuel T." Other drawers in the desk interior have letters and numbers in red pencil, and most of the drawers have scribe marks in red pencil. A modern shipping label is pasted to the underside of the bottom of the upper case.

Condition: The rear knee brackets on the back legs are missing, and the brasses are replacements. The bottom right side of the lower drawer in the upper case is replaced. A piece has been lost from the bottom right corner of the top drawer in the upper case. There has been much wear to the desk interior. The capital of one of the document drawers is a replacement. The valance drawer next to the document drawer on the left side is a replacement. Substantial oxidation on the underside of the upper case above the missing board in the frame indicates that this board has been missing for some time.

164

Woods: American black cherry; southern yellow pine.

Dimensions: H 108.8; W 107.0; UCW 98.0; LCW 102.5; D (closed) 61.8; D (open) 95.9; UCD 54.2; LCD 57.4.

Bibliography: Kirk, *Early Am. Furn.*, fig. 147; Elaine Ulman, "I'm Perfectly Willing to Write Bold Statements, Be Wrong, and Be Corrected . . . the True Emphasis in My Work Is Learning to See," *Antiques World* 2, no. 10 (October 1980): 64; Kirk, *Am. Furn. & Brit. Trad.*, fig. 621.

Provenance: Samuel Whitacker Pennypacker (1843–1916), Philadelphia, Pa.; Jacob Margolis, New York, N. Y.; by sale in 1930 to Francis P. Garvan, New York, N. Y.

DESK-ON-FRAMES were not a popular form in Pennsylvania during the last half of the eighteenth century, although several other examples are known, including two more elaborate desks in the Winterthur collection.[1] The drawer arrangement and applied quarter columns of this example are found on other Pennsylvania case furniture of the same period. The use of claw-and-ball feet in the front and pad

feet in the rear is a combination that is customarily associated with case furniture from Rhode Island (cat. 142).

The Mabel Brady Garvan Collection 1930.2388

1. Hummel, *American Chippendale Furn.*, figs. 84, 85.

165

Desk

Pennsylvania, 1790–1800

Description: Below the slant front the case contains four graduated veneered drawers with cock-beaded edges flanked by fluted quarter columns at the front corners of the case. Each drawer is fitted with a central stamped brass oval lock escutcheon flanked by dual disk escutcheons with bail pulls. There is base molding at the front and sides, and the desk is supported by bracket feet. The cleated lid has mitered joints at the front corners and is supported by lopers that are fitted with brass button pulls and have cock-beaded edges, and the lid has a central oval brass lock escutcheon at the top. The interior contains a veneered central prospect door, hinged at the right, which contains an inlaid eagle against a *bois verte* ground and outlined with light-wood stringing; the door is bordered by cross-banding and a single line inlay and has a brass lock escutcheon at the left. It opens to an interior with two pigeonholes with fixed shaped valances in line above two graduated veneered drawers bordered with cross-banding and stringing. The door is flanked by rounded document drawers faced with tooled and gilt leather to simulate book spines. Each side of the center section contains four pigeonholes with fixed shaped valances in line above two veneered drawers in line in turn above a single wide veneered drawer. The vertical partitions between the pigeonholes are shaped to roundheaded arches, and the drawers are fitted with brass button pulls (two on the wide drawers) and are bordered with stringing and cross-banding. The document drawers are flanked by vertical partitions with molded edges; the other vertical partitions have rounded edges; and the front edge of the platform is molded. The top and bottom of the case are dovetailed to the sides; the dovetails on the top are blind. The vertical partitions to the inside of the lopers are double tenoned through the drawer divider. There are full dustboards within the case, with guides applied to them. The horizontal backboards are nailed to a rabbet in the top and sides and to the bottom; the bottom of the desk section is nailed through the back. On each case drawer, the sides are dovetailed to the front and back; the bottoms are let into a groove in the front and sides, with small blocks sandwiched in the sides beneath running strips, and nailed to the underside of the back; there are also small blocks glued to the

Desks 315

165b

bottom behind the front. The sides of the desk interior drawers are dovetailed to the front and back, with the bottoms nailed to a rabbet in the front and sides and to the underside of the back. The document drawers, which can be pushed forward through a notch in the vertical partitions on their outside edges, have the sides nailed to the front and back, with a deep scalloping at the top and with the bottoms glued in place. The rear feet are triangular braces nailed to the bottom; the bottom framework includes strips nailed to the front and sides and to the back above the feet, with large vertical blocks in each corner and thin triangular horizontal blocks behind the brackets.

Inscriptions: The document drawers are labeled "Left" and "Right" respectively in red pencil or chalk; there are other red shop marks throughout the case. The leather facings of the document drawers read in gilt lettering, "PENN'S WORKS" at the top against a red ground, with "VOL. 1." and "VOL. 2" against a green background on the left and right drawers respectively; the other panels of the "spines" are decorated with gilt floral decoration.

Condition: The front edge of the top has been repaired at its junction with the lock. The valance above the pigeonhole to the immediate right of the right document drawer is a replacement. There have been minor repairs to the veneer. The bottom of the right front foot is a replacement, and the left front foot has been broken and repaired. Some of the running strips on the drawers have been replaced. The right front corner of the top is pieced.

316 *American Case Furniture*

Woods: Mahogany and mahogany veneer; desk interior drawers, prospect door, bordered with satinwood crossbanding and light-wood stringing; case drawer sides and backs, dustboards, yellow poplar; case drawer bottoms, drawer dividers, bottom, sides of document drawers, bottoms of wide drawers in interior, eastern white pine; fronts, sides, and backs of desk interior drawers, mahogany; bottoms of six small interior drawers, Atlantic white cedar.

Dimensions: H 109.4; W 111.1; CW 105.4; D (closed) 56.5; D (open) 90.4; CD 52.7.

Provenance: Francis P. Garvan, New York, N.Y.

THE use of simulated leather book spines on the interior of this desk follows a custom practiced in English furniture and occasionally encountered in American work.[1] Hornor quotes a document of 1791 indicating that David Evans, a Philadelphia cabinetmaker, made "a Walnut Desk with Prospect and Cullum Draws made in the shape of Books."[2] The most extensive use of *faux-livres* on an American desk appears on an example of ca. 1770 with titles of ten actual eighteenth-century books and five account books, including a daybook, a journal, a ledger, a cashbook, and an invoice book, simulated on an elaborate interior.[3] The title "PENN'S WORKS" undoubtedly refers to the collected works of William Penn and strongly suggests a Pennsylvania origin for the Yale example.

The Mabel Brady Garvan Collection 1930.2317

1. Christopher Claxton Stevens and Stewart Whittington, *18th Century English Furniture: The Norman Adams Collection* (Woodbridge, England: Antique Collectors' Club, 1983), nos. 154, 189, 237.
2. Hornor, p. 121.
3. Joan Sayers Brown, "A Desk Associated with George Washington," *Antiques* 113, no. 5 (May 1978): 1084–1085. See also B. Garvan, *Pennsylvania German Coll.*, p. 34; Miller, 1:nos. 808, 828, 835, 867; *Antiques* 96, no. 6 (December 1969): 806; and Miller, *Furn. by New York Cabinetmakers*, no. 48.

166

Tambour desk
Salem, Massachusetts, area, 1790–1815

Description: The rectangular top of the upper section overhangs the upper case at the front and sides, and its edge is decorated at the front and sides with a line of patterned inlay.

The upper case is divided into three units, with a central veneered door, hinged at the right, flanked by sliding tambour doors fitted with brass button pulls. The door is decorated with a rectangle with hollow corners of stringing enclosing an inlaid oval formed by patterned inlay, and the sides of the case are decorated with a vertical line of patterned inlay. The door opens to an interior with two superimposed drawers fitted with brass button pulls above a pair of pigeonholes in line, with fixed valances shaped to paired reverse curves; the tambours slide open to similar interiors. The upper case rests on the rear half of the lower case within restraining molding applied to the lower case. The hinged writing surface falls forward and is supported by lopers with brass button pulls; its surface is covered with green baize, and the center section of the midmolding is applied to it. The lower case contains two graduated drawers with cockbeaded edges and bordered with rectangles of patterned stringing. Each is fitted with a central oval lock escutcheon flanked by stamped brass escutcheons with bail pulls, each depicting an eagle with a shield-shaped breast grasping a thunderbolt and an olive branch and in its beak a trailing banner with the motto "E PLURIBUS / UNUM" with sixteen stars used as a border. The drawers are flanked by light-wood stringing on the legs, forming a rectangle with an incurved top leading to a white bellflower above a black pellet and drop. The lower edge of the lower case is decorated with patterned inlay at the front and sides, and the bellflower and pendant motif is repeated on the square tapered legs, with a

166a

Desks 317

166

line of patterned inlay at the cuffs of the front legs. The overhanging edges of the top are formed by applied molding; the joint of the top to the sides is obscured by veneer on the top. The bottom front rail is dovetailed to the sides. The back of the upper case is a single horizontal board nailed to a rabbet in the top and sides and to the bottom. The four sides project beneath the bottom, with cleats nailed to the inside of each side. The tambour slides are backed with cloth and run in grooves. The sides of the interior drawers are dovetailed to the front and back; the bottoms are beveled on their front and side edges, let into grooves in the front and sides, and nailed to the underside of the back. The lower case is framed with mortise-and-tenon joints, with the horizontal top boards fitted with a tongue-and-groove joint to the sides and nailed to the back. There are no dustboards, and the drawer runners are applied to the side of the case. The two wide drawers are fashioned in the same manner as the small interior drawers. The backboards, the interiors of the pigeonholes, and the back of the prospect door are stained red. Many drawer bottoms show evidence of pit sawing.

Inscriptions: "March" is written above an illegible word in pencil on the inside of the bottom of the upper drawer behind the central door in the upper case. Modern "R.H.Y." and "1772" are written in pencil on the inside of the bottom of the upper drawer behind the left tambour slide; an illegible pencil inscription appears on the outside of the right side of the same drawer.

Condition: The central door has been repaired with butterfly cleats, and its lock escutcheon is a replacement. There has been a good deal of damage and loss to the patterned inlay and veneer. The hinges of the fall front are replacements, and the baize lining the writing surface is new.

Woods: Mahogany and mahogany veneer, with light- and dark-wood inlays; eastern white pine.

Dimensions: H 107.4; W 92.8; UCW 90.8; LCW 91.5; D (closed) 48.2; D (open) 70.2; UCD 27.3; LCD 47.4.

Bibliography: *Antiquarian* 12, no. 3 (April 1929): 135; *American Furniture . . . Collection Formed by Fred Wellington Ayer, Bangor, Maine, 3–4 May 1929* (New York: American Art Association, 1929), no. 438.

Provenance: Fred Wellington Ayer, Bangor, Maine; acquired at auction in 1929 by Francis P. Garvan, New York, N. Y.

CHARLES F. MONTGOMERY noted that "tambour desk" is a modern term for objects of this kind, which were produced in large quantities in New England during the federal period. Without an exact English prototype, tambour desks bear the closest resemblance to the "Lady's Cabinet and Writing Table" published by Sheraton and in English price books of the period.[1] The Seymours of Boston, the acknowledged masters of the form, were only one of many shops in Boston, Salem, and elsewhere to produce these small desks, although the few labeled and firmly attributed Seymour products are superior in quality to more representative desks like the Yale example.[2] With two drawers in the lower case, and with its sliding tambour shutters flanking a central door, this desk represents only one variation of the form. Other tambour desks have one, three, or four drawers, or shutters that are not separated by a drawer; a few elaborate examples have triangular pediments.[3] The white bellflowers and black, ebonized pellets of the Yale desk are of the type occasionally associated with the work of Edmund Johnson of Salem, although a documented Johnson tambour desk differs considerably from the Yale example.[4]

The Mabel Brady Garvan Collection 1930.2083

1. Montgomery, p. 218.
2. Montgomery, no. 184; and Fairbanks and Bates, p. 231, for a labeled and an attributed Seymour example.

3. The gamut of tambour desk variations is well covered in Stoneman, *Seymour*, nos. 4–43.
4. Fales, *Essex County Furn.*, no. 23.

167

Desk-on-stand

Massachusetts, 1790–1815

Description: This object consists of a portable writing desk supported by a stand containing a single drawer. The desk has brass carrying handles at the sides, and it is edged at its corners with light-wood stringing. The desk is hinged at the center of the front and contains a brass keyhole liner in the center of the top. It falls open to form a slanting writing surface covered with crimson baize. Each half of the writing surface can be lifted to reveal the well below; the halves are glued to a single sheet of baize rather than hinged. The back of the desk contains three small drawers in line, with the right drawer divided into three small compartments at its front, with the right compartment having a sloping transverse partition. The desk rests within a midmolding applied to all four sides of the frame. The single veneered drawer is bordered by light-wood stringing on each side of crossbanding. The lower edge of the frame is decorated on all four sides with light- and dark-wood stringing, and the desk is supported by four square tapered legs. Most of the joints of the desk section are obscured by veneer, but the front of the fall front is dovetailed to the sides with the dovetails exposed. The bottom is nailed to a rabbet in all four sides. The drawers within the desk are mahogany; the sides are dovetailed to the front and back, and the bottoms are let into grooves in the front and sides and nailed to the underside of the back. The stand is framed with mahogany rails joined to the legs; strips of pine are added to the inside of each side to help support the desk. The runners for the drawer are applied to the sides, small blocks are nailed to the inside of the back as stops, and there is no bottom to the frame. On the drawer, the sides are dovetailed to the front and back; the bottom is let into a groove in the front and sides and nailed to the underside of the back; running strips may have been used originally, and small blocks are glued to the underside of the bottom at the front. Red stain appears on the underside of the writing flaps and at the base of the rear well. The bottom of the wide drawer shows evidence of pit sawing.

Desks 319

Inscriptions: Modern "E.337.66" is written in red on the outside of the left side of the drawer in the stand. The bottoms of the drawers in the desk are numbered in pencil.

Condition: The brasses on the drawer and the baize are replacements. There have been minor repairs to the back edge of the top of the desk and to each edge of the fall front, and there have been minor repairs to the veneer and inlay.

Woods: Mahogany; mahogany veneer; light- and dark-wood inlays; eastern white pine.

Dimensions: H 91.3; W 65.4; UCW 63.2; LCW 65.4; D (closed) 45.5; D (open) 69.8; UCD 43.5; LCD 45.5.

Bibliography: Meyric R. Rogers, "The American Rooms," *Bulletin of the City Art Museum of St. Louis* 16, no. 4 (October 1931): 58.

Provenance: Jacob Margolis, New York, N. Y.; by sale in 1924 to Francis P. Garvan, New York, N. Y.

KNOWN today as a "captain's desk" or a "lady's desk," this form consists in essence of a portable desk, such as cats. 169, 170, supported by a separate small frame with a drawer. In some instances, a third section consisting of a bookcase or cupboard was added to the top of the object.[1] Similar examples consisting of a single case are known.[2]

The Mabel Brady Garvan Collection 1930.2061

1. Montgomery, no. 192; *Sack Coll.*, 6: 1568 no. P4689. For related examples without this superstructure, see Stoneman, *Supplement*, no. 11 (Henry Ford Museum); and *Antiques* 104, no. 4 (October 1973): 519.
2. Comstock, fig. 488 (Museum of Fine Arts, Boston).

168

Desk

Northeastern Massachusetts or New Hampshire, 1800–1820

Description: The rectangular top of the upper case overhangs slightly at the front and sides and is decorated with lunette inlay at the front and sides. There is a band of patterned inlay above the two doors, which are veneered with a large panel of crotch mahogany veneer and a vertical panel of light-wood veneer, probably satinwood, at the outer edges, separated and bordered by light-wood stringing and mahogany cross-banding. The doors open to an interior with a central section of three ledger compartments, with the vertical partitions shaped with reverse curves, flanked by units consisting of two superimposed drawers with brass button pulls above three pigeonholes in line with fixed valances shaped to rounded arches. The upper case rests on the rear half of the lower case within restraining molding. The fall front of the lower case slopes and is veneered with mahogany bordered by light-wood stringing and cross-banding. It is supported in the open position by lopers with brass button pulls and borders of light-wood stringing, and its writing surface is covered by green baize with a Greek key border. The lower case contains three graduated veneered drawers with cock-beaded edges, each bordered with light-wood stringing and cross-banding and each with a central brass keyhole liner flanked by wooden pulls. There is a bead molding at the front and sides above the shaped skirts, and the desk is supported by four short ring- and vase-shaped legs terminating in rounded feet. In the upper case, the bottom is dovetailed to the sides, and the horizontal backboard is nailed to rabbets in the top and sides and to the bottom. The case rests on top of small blocks and cleats attached to the top of the lower case. The joints of the lower case are obscured, but it is probably of dovetailed board construction. The horizontal backboards are nailed to rabbets in the sides and top and to the bottom. The drawer runners are applied to the sides of the case, and there is no dustboard or bottom to the lower case. There are vertical blocks on each face of the legs and multiple horizontal blocks behind the skirts at the front and sides. Shaped brackets are nailed to each side of the

168a

168

rear. In the case drawers, the sides are dovetailed to the front, with the joint covered by cross-banding, and dovetailed to the back; the bottoms are beveled on their front and side edges, let into grooves in the front and sides, and nailed to the underside of the back. The desk interior drawers in the upper case are made in the same fashion, with the exception that their fronts are solid rather than veneered, the bottoms are not beveled, and no running strips or blocks were used. The interior of the upper case has been stained red.

Inscriptions: Chalk inscriptions on the underside of the bottom read "Bottom," "John / Dole," and "W:T——." There are original shop marks, numbers, and letters in white chalk on the drawers and later numbers and marks in pencil.

Condition: Round press marks on the veneer underneath the present wooden pulls suggest that round brasses were used originally and that the present pulls are additions. The blocking on the underside of the bottom has been reglued more than once; some of the blocks are additions, and others have been nailed. The left skirt has been nailed in place. The top edge of the backboard of the lower case has been pieced. There has been minor damage to the veneers and inlays. The valances of the pigeonholes on each side of the central ledger section have been replaced.

Woods: Mahogany; American black cherry; mahogany veneer; light- and dark-wood inlay; vertical panels on outer edges of doors in upper case, probably satinwood; framing elements on edges of each door, fronts of interior drawers, front edges of interior partitions, pigeonhole valances, top, some of cockbeading on drawers in lower case, American black cherry; eastern white pine.

Dimensions: H 123.9; W 101.5; UCW 97.6; LCW 101.1; D (closed) 49.5; D (open) 65.3; UCD 26.5; LCD 46.7.

Provenance: The desk may have been owned originally or may have been made by a John Dole, whose identity remains elusive. The illegible inscription also on the underside of the bottom, where Dole's name appears, may be a town name, perhaps "West" something, but this cannot be determined. Research has not revealed as yet a cabinetmaker with the name of John Dole in the late eighteenth or early nineteenth centuries; there were men named Dole active in the furniture trades in Newburyport, Mass., and in Maine. Several men named John Dole appear in the 1800 census index for both Massachusetts and New Hampshire. In the twentieth century, the desk was in the collection of Charles Stetson, Boston, Mass.

THIS desk, or small secretary, is decorated with lunette and other patterned inlay that often is found on New England furniture from Boston and Essex County.[1] The form also was made in New Hampshire, and the use of carefully selected veneers of mahogany and possibly satinwood provides the dramatic color contrast associated with furniture from northeastern Massachusetts and coastal New Hampshire.[2] An interesting variation of the "blind-front tambour desk" has doors decorated with strips of alternating light and dark wood simulating tambour.[3] The form also was produced in the Maritimes provinces of Canada in strikingly similar fashion.[4] The inscriptions on the Yale desk may yet prove fruitful in determining its origin with greater precision.

Gift of Charles Stetson 1954.37.24

1. The lunette inlay, associated with the Seymour shop but widely used by others, was found on card tables from the Boston area and Salem by Hewitt, while a patterned inlay (Montgomery, inlay 16) was used on a northeastern Massachusetts lady's secretary and bookcase at Winter-

Desks 321

thur (Montgomery, no. 190) and on a north-of-Boston card table (1930. 2700) in the Yale collection. Hewitt, however, (p. 81) cautions against the use of relying on patterned inlays, which were widely available, as an indicator of regional origin.

2. A closely related example was published in *Flayderman Coll.*, no. 344. For other examples, see Stoneman, *Seymour*, nos. 43A, 43B, 44A, 44B. An example branded "w.w. NOLEN" has been published; *Antiques* 115, no. 3 (March 1979): 453. See also *Antiques* 65, no. 5 (May 1954): 364.

3. Stoneman, *Supplement*, nos. 6, 10.

4. Donald Blake Webster, "The Identification of English-Canadian Furniture, 1780–1840," *Antiques* 115, no. 1 (January 1979): 168 fig. 7.

169

Portable writing desk
New England, 1790–1815

Description: Of board construction, this rectangular portable desk has a top and bottom section hinged together which open to form a slanting writing surface covered with green baize. The top section is decorated with a rectangle of light inlay with hollow corners and has brass braces screwed to each corner. When in the closed position the front of the desk has a rectangle of light inlay at the edges and an inlaid keyhole. The bottom section houses a drawer on the right side which is released by means of a brass draw pin located on the inside. In the open position, the two boards of the writing surface are attached with a leather hinge; each is supported by thin strips nailed to the sides; each has cleats on the ends held with a tongue-and-groove joint and with mitered veneer on the sides and front edge; and each opens to an open compartment below. Above the writing surface are five compartments for writing accoutrements, one lidded and another with a removable dished tray for pens, with loose partitions fitted into grooves. The drawer is housed below the upper writing surface and storage compartments. The drawer has a bail handle for a pull, matching the carrying handle on the other side. The drawer sides are finely dovetailed to the front and back; the bottom is a single board fitted to a rabbet in the front and to V-shaped grooves in the sides and nailed to all four sides.

Inscriptions: Some numbers in pencil appear on the underside of the upper writing compartment.

Condition: New green baize has been applied to the writing surfaces and to the bottom. Two of the partitions for the storage compartments are missing. The front edge of the top has been replaced.

Woods: Mahogany and mahogany veneer; a light inlay; writing surface panels, cherry; drawer sides, bottom, and back, desk bottom, other interior elements, eastern white pine.

Dimensions: H (closed) 16.5; H (open) 13.0; W 53.3; D (closed) 27.9; D (open) 55.8.

Provenance: According to a family tradition, this portable writing desk was owned originally by the Reverend Elisha Williams (1694–1755), rector of Yale College from 1726 to

1739. It became known in the family as "The Rector Williams Desk," but it was made a generation after the rector's death and surely was not owned by him. It was owned in the nineteenth century by his granddaughter Miss Susan Buck, Wethersfield, Conn., who gave it to the grandmother of the donor, Robinson D. Buck of Hartford. It passed to Buck's mother, who gave the desk to the university in 1940, although the credit line bears the name of her son.

SMALL portable writing desks of this kind were very popular in the late eighteenth and early nineteenth centuries, in an age when letter writing was a more common form of communication than it is today. Designs for them were published by Thomas Shearer, and specifications for their construction were given in the English and American price books of the period. The small storage compartments were for ink, sand, and wafers, and the 1796 New York price book listed a "stained hollow for pens," such as is present in this example, as an extra obtainable for one shilling. Another shilling was charged for "Lining the writing part of the desk with cloth," and that was an option that seems to have been exercised frequently, as it probably was here.[1] In 1803 and 1804, cabinetmakers Nehemiah Monroe and John Clap of Roxbury, Massachusetts, valued "small portable desks" of their making at $5 and $7, while "portable desks with brasses on the corners," such as this example, were valued at $8.[2] Such brasses can be seen on a portable desk depicted in a portrait by English artist John Hoppner.[3] The family history of this object is a good example of the common phenomenon wherein the tradition of ownership gets pushed back a generation or so and assigned to a family member of some renown.

Gift of Henry Robinson Buck, PH.B. 1896 1940.54

1. Ralph Fastnedge, ed., *Shearer Furniture Designs from the Cabinet-Makers' London Book of Prices, 1788* (London: Alec Tiranti, 1962), pl. 14; *The Journeymen Cabinet & Chair Makers' New-York Book of Prices* (New York: T. & J. Swords, 1796), p. 69.
2. Inferior Court of Common Pleas, Suffolk County, Mass., July 1805, case no. C-457. The writer would like to thank Thomas S. Michie for bringing this reference to his attention. A brass-bound example of ca. 1832 is published in *Documented New Hampshire Furn.*, no. 49.
3. Present location unknown; published in Roger Fry et al., *Georgian Art (1760–1820)*, Burlington Magazine Monograph III (London: B. T. Batsford, 1929), advertisement of Ainslie Galleries, Inc., New York. See also John Vanderlyn's *Sampson Vryling Stoddard Wilder* in the Worcester Art Museum (1981.331).

170

170

Portable writing desk

Southern New England or Middle Atlantic states, 1790–1815

Description: This portable writing desk is constructed and operates on very similar lines to the preceding example. Here, the exterior is veneered with tiger maple, and there is no drawer. The partitions in the storage compartment, with the exception of the removable pen tray, are fixed, and no use was made of brass braces. The bottom of the desk is a single board nailed to a rabbet on all four sides.

Condition: Fragments of the original green baize remain on the writing surfaces; three of the four leather hinges holding them in place have worn through, and an iron hinge has been added to the left side of the lower panel. There have been repairs to the veneer at the lower left and right front corners, and the veneer on the top is in poor condition.

Woods: Front, sides, top, back, tiger-maple veneer; top, yellow poplar; storage compartments, cleats, veneer on edges of writing panels, soft maple; bottom, writing panels, red gum; sides, eastern white pine; keyhole surround, possibly rosewood.

Dimensions: H (closed) 19.6; H (open) 15.1; W 50.8; D (closed) 28.2; D (open) 56.4.

Provenance: Francis P. Garvan, New York, N.Y.

THE shimmering tiger-maple veneer on this example makes it one of the more visually interesting examples of this small form. The use of red gum suggests that this example was made in southern New England or in the Middle Atlantic states.[1]

The Mabel Brady Garvan Collection 1931.1271

1. Montgomery, pp. 36–37.

171

Desk

Designed by Donald Deskey (b. 1894);
cabinetwork by Schmieg, Hungate, and Kotzian
New York, New York, 1929

Description: The horizontal writing surface is straight across the back and curved at its right front side. It contains a lidded well to the left, raised by means of a brass handle and attached to the case with Soss hinges, and a wide blind drawer in the front. A smaller blind drawer is housed in the rear of the curved end and opens in the back. The curved end is supported by an open brass brace screwed to the case. To the left of the writing surface is a vertical unit extending above and below the horizontal section of the desk. The upper part of this unit contains two superimposed open compartments, the lower one of greater height, and each extending about half the depth of the case. The rear half of this unit contains another open compartment set above and facing the writing surface. The top edge of the unit is bordered with a brass strip screwed in place at its front, left side, and rear; the strip extends beyond the front and rear of the top and holds a swinging, curved, brass lampshade housing a 15-watt fluorescent tube. There is a brass strip below the lower open compartment on the front, extending to the right to meet the handle on the lidded well, and on its left side. The lower half of the vertical unit, below the writing surface, is curved at its left side and straight across the back. It contains at the front a curved door hinged with Soss hinges and opening to reveal a plain compartment. There are two triangular boxes screwed to the inside of the door. On the left side of the lower part of the vertical unit is a tall vertical compartment with a rectangular door opening to a plain compartment. The door has a brass pull screwed in place, and it is attached to the case with Soss hinges. The base of the vertical unit is bordered on its curved side with a wide brass band screwed in place. The joints of the case are hidden by veneer. On the wide blind drawer on the front, the sides are dovetailed to the front, and the back is joined to the sides with a tongue-and-groove joint. The bottom is let into a groove in the front and sides and nailed to the underside of the back. The top of the drawer front and the corresponding section of the case are beveled, and the lower edge of the case is chamfered beneath the drawer so that the drawer may be pulled out by grasping the bottom of its front. The small drawer on the rear of the case is made in the same fashion; its side is curved to conform to the shape of the curved portion of the desk, and it has a transverse medial runner glued to its bottom that runs in a groove in the bottom of the case.

Inscriptions: The keys to the desk are stamped "EAGLE LOCK CO / TERRYVILLE, CONN. U.S.A." on one side and "6W9" or "9W6" on the other. The light fixture is marked "A.H. & H / MADE IN U.S.A."; the light switch is marked "LEVITON / 3A–125V 1A–250V." The electrical component inside the open compartment on the upper level of the vertical unit is marked "GE" in script within a circle and "CAT./ 58G680" on the front, and "SERIES BALLAST / FOR USE WITH 15 WATT FLUORESCENT LAMP / 118 VOLTS 32 AMPS. 60-CYCLES A. C." on the back.

171a

324 *American Case Furniture*

Condition: There has been damage to the veneer, and the hinges on the curved cupboard of the lower vertical unit have been replaced. The brass mounts have been cleaned and lacquered. There are screw holes and shadow marks on the underside of the bottom of the horizontal writing surface at the right.

Woods: Ebony, probably Macassar ebony, veneer on a core of yellow poplar; one drawer front core wood, chestnut; runner on small curved drawer, ash; drawer bottoms, plywood faced with mahogany on inside and yellow poplar on outside; other elements, mahogany.

Dimensions: H 106.4; W 122.4; D 50.5.

Bibliography: Richard Guy Wilson, Dianne H. Pilgrim, and Dickran Tashjian, *The Machine Age in America, 1918–1941* (New York: Brooklyn Museum in association with Harry N. Abrams, 1986), p. 282 fig. 8.11.

Provenance: Purchased in 1929 by Mr. and Mrs. Arthur D. Berliss, Sr., for their apartment at 1185 Park Avenue, New York, N. Y.

IN 1927, designer Donald Deskey and Phillip Vollmer established Deskey-Vollmer, Inc., a firm that continued into the early 1930s.[1] Their products were custom made for patrons interested in modern design, such as Mr. and Mrs. Arthur D. Berliss, Sr., who commissioned Deskey-Vollmer to decorate their Park Avenue apartment in 1929. Designed to be freestanding, the desk was used by its owners in a study and guest room. A shelf clock (1984.23.1), designed by Paul T. Frankl for Warren Telechron Co., was acquired by the Berlisses at the same time as the desk, and signs of wear on top of the vertical unit suggest that the clock was located there for many years. According to tradition, an aluminum ash tray (1984.22.2), also recently given to the Art Gallery, was used in association with the desk as well.[2] This type of ash tray appears in period photographs of the Deskey-Vollmer studio. Deskey, best known today for his design of the interiors of Radio City Music Hall, was influenced by trends in nonobjective painting and sculpture of the 1920s. His choice of Macassar ebony veneer for this desk is in keeping with the use of this exotic wood on much expensive European and American furniture of the 1920s and 1930s. The Berlisses may have been influenced in their selection of Deskey as their interior decorator by Mrs. Berliss's father, Samuel R. Karpen of the Chicago furniture company S. Karpen & Bros.[3]

Gift of Mrs. Arthur D. Berliss, Sr. 1984.23.2

1. Karen Davies, *At Home in Manhattan* (New Haven: Yale University Art Gallery, 1983), nos. 30, 76. Recent research by Jennifer C. Toher of David A. Hanks and Associates, Inc., has identified the cabinetmaking firm responsible for executing some of Deskey's designs.
2. A silk wall hanging by Ruth Reeves, also from the Berliss apartment, is now part of the Art Gallery collection.
3. S. Karpen & Bros. introduced a line of modern furnishings in the late 1920s by such designers as Kem Weber, Eugene Schoen, and Edwin Josselyn; see Sharon Darling, *Chicago Furniture: Art, Craft, and Industry, 1833–1983* (New York: Chicago Historical Society in conjunction with W. W. Norton, 1984), p. 281.

Desk and Bookcases, Library Bookcases, and Secretaries

The desk and bookcase of the eighteenth century is simply a desk with an enclosed bookcase surmounted on its top. The bookcase was often embellished with architectural ornament, such as fluted columns, and crowned with a broken-scroll or triangular pediment. Its interior was fitted for shelves, pigeonholes, and small drawers in many possible combinations. The so-called Jonathan Edwards desk (cat. 172) is perhaps the most unusual example of the form, representing an uncommon instance where an early eighteenth-century desk was expanded through the addition of flanking cupboards and stacking book boxes above. The collection is particularly strong in New England examples and is dominated by the most beautiful of the Newport block-and-shell desk and bookcases attributed to the Townsend-Goddard families (cat. 177). By the federal period, virtually the same form was referred to most commonly as a secretary (cats. 182, 183); a large variation on the form was known as a gentleman's secretary (cat. 184) and was made in the Salem, Massachusetts, area. The collection also includes large library bookcases, each with a secretary drawer, from New York (cat. 186), Philadelphia (cat. 187), and Charleston (cat. 188). The later nineteenth century is represented by an enormous empire example (cat. 189), a Gothic-revival example labeled by the New York firm of J. and J. W. Meeks (cat. 190), and a pair of large bookcases probably from Baltimore, also in the Gothic-revival style (cat. 192). The Osborn family wall shelf (cat. 193), possibly designed by Dan Cooper, is the sole twentieth-century example of this type of furniture in the collection.

172

Desk with later bookcases
New England, 1700–1730 and later

Description: This unusual object consists of an early eighteenth-century desk, flanked by matching cupboards and surmounted by three long bookcases, added at a later date, perhaps in the eighteenth century. Below the slant front, the desk contains four drawers, two in line over two graduated drawers. The drawers are flanked and separated by double half-round molding that continues up the canted sides of the desk and around the sides and rear of the desk top. There is applied base molding at the front, and the desk is supported by four turned feet. The lid is supported by lopers housed on each side of a well, and it opens to an interior with a center section fitted with five pigeonholes with fixed valances, the center one of greater width and depth, above three corresponding drawers in line. This center section is flanked by open stepped compartments with shaped partitions, and the front area of the desk interior houses a well covered by a sliding lid. The desk is flanked by two cupboards. Each cupboard is surmounted by a large bookcase with two sliding doors above an open compartment. The lower section of each cupboard contains a single drawer above a cupboard enclosed by paired doors with fielded panels. There is a base molding at the front and sides of the cupboards, and they are each supported by four turned feet. The desk and cupboards are topped by three wide stepped bookcases, each a separate unit simply resting on top of the one below; they decrease in height as well as depth from bottom to top. (The lowest bookcase unit is slightly deeper than the built-in bookcase section of the cupboards.) Each bookcase is divided into two sections by a central transverse vertical partition, and each half is enclosed by a pair of sliding doors. The front edges of the cupboards and bookcases and one vertical edge of each pair of sliding doors, have applied double half-round molding. The desk is of dovetailed board construction. The backboards are beveled on their edges and fitted to a rabbet in the case sides. The turned feet are doweled through large, roughly triangular boards nailed to the underside of the desk bottom. On the desk interior, the sides are dovetailed to the front and back, and the bottoms are let into a rabbet in the front and nailed to all four sides; a small tab projects from the rear of the bottom to act as a stop. The drawer dividers are nailed into place through the case sides. The large drawers in the desk are made in a similar manner. The cupboards are also of dovetailed board construction and are made in a fashion similar to the desk. The cupboard doors are fitted with wrought-iron hinges and open to an undifferentiated space. The drawers in the cupboards are divided by partitions into two and four compartments respectively. The three bookcases or book boxes are of dovetailed board construction. Their doors slide in grooves and are opened by handholds created by a small circular sinkage on one end and a strip of double half-round molding at the other end of each pair. The doors of the bookcases on the cupboards operate in the same manner.

Condition: The object was heavily restored in the mid 1930s, when it was transferred from the Divinity School to the Art Gallery. These restorations were described by Charles Nagel in 1934: "The lid itself was missing, having been replaced in rough pine so crudely as to be obviously a makeshift [and it was therefore replaced]. The pigeonhole partitions were split in some cases beyond repair, but were reproduced exactly, and the scalloped arches above the pigeon holes were a restoration copied from contemporary models. The double arch molding was replaced where needed in walnut on all sections alike, since the pine molding was so badly split and broken that it was evidently not a practical material for the purpose. One of the smaller sliding

panels, the two pieces of molding on the lower front of the side cupboards, the sliding cover to the well in the desk proper, and a few minor patchings completed the necessary cabinetmaking repairs. All were executed with the greatest care and in old wood. The brasses being in an utterly fragmentary condition except for the small drawer pulls, and of the desk lid support knobs, it was most fortunate that a complete set of fine contemporary desk brasses of a stamped pattern almost identical with the old design was found." Although the six front feet appear to be original, the rear feet appear to be replacements. There have been, as Nagel indicates, many other minor repairs.

Woods: Central desk, top, drawer fronts, moldings, American black walnut; desk sides, soft maple, probably red maple; eastern white pine; front feet, eastern white pine and aspen; cupboards, bookcases, eastern white pine, with some moldings replaced in walnut.

Dimensions: H 198.8; W 197.5; D 48.3.

Bibliography: Charles Nagel, Jr., "The Jonathan Edwards Desk," *YUAG Bulletin* 6, no. 2 (June 1934): 27–29; Gerald W. R. Ward, "Yale Memorabilia," *Antiques* 117, no. 6 (June 1980): 1311 fig. 1.

Provenance: It has been thought for the last fifty years that this object was owned originally by Jonathan Edwards (1703–1758), although there is no conclusive evidence to support this tradition. As stated by Charles Nagel in 1934: "When the Yale Divinity School Buildings on the corner of Elm and College Streets were about to be demolished in 1931 there was removed from the basement of one of them an ancient desk.... While no actual proof exists, and even those longest connected with the School had no memory of any such proof, tradition as to original ownership was always strong enough so that, even after its somewhat dilapidated condition had consigned it to the cellar, the desk was still known as the Jonathan Edwards desk."

JONATHAN EDWARDS, the great New England divine, entered Yale in 1716 and stayed for six years, four as an undergraduate and two as a student of theology. He returned to the college in 1724 and served as a tutor until 1726. If he was the owner of this desk and its bookcases, he might have acquired them during either period of residence in New Haven, or they could have found their way to Yale at any time after Edwards's death in 1758. There is some rather slight evidence supporting the traditional history of ownership by Edwards, evidence that suggests that the desk may have been in Stockbridge, Massachusetts, in the late nineteenth century. A reference in the diary of Thomas Robbins (1796–1854) makes mention of an unsuccessful attempt to "procure any of the study furniture of Pres. Edwards" in 1833. Increase N. Tarbox, the editor of Robbins's diary when it was published in 1887, indicates in his annotation to this entry that "there were such relics in existence" and that he had seen Edwards's "writing-desk" in Stockbridge, Massachusetts, where Edwards lived in the 1750s.[1] (A loose piece of walnut, now stored in the desk, bears a paper label pasted on it with the notation in a nineteenth-century hand, "From Pres. Edwards / Meeting House in / Stockbridge," lending some circumstantial support to Tarbox's siting of Edwards's desk there.) The issue is clouded somewhat because a closely related object, a pine dresser with nearly identical stacking bookcases above, was owned by John Sergeant (Yale 1729), who had been Edwards's student at Yale and who preceded him as a missionary to the Stockbridge Indians.[2] While the Sergeant dresser appears to have been created as an integrated whole from the very beginning, with its four tiers of bookcases above a lower case containing six drawers and a cupboard, the Edwards object evolved over time. Evidence of the presence of applied moldings, now removed, on the sides of the desk indicates that the flanking cupboards, and therefore the wide bookcases above, are later additions, although their construction suggests that they were made in the eighteenth century. Despite its poor condition and only tentative association with Edwards, this object remains an important document in the history of book-storage furniture in this country. Today, it is kept in the Fellows Common Room of Jonathan Edwards College at Yale.

172a

Yale University Art Gallery 1800.3

1. *Diary of Thomas Robbins, D.D., 1796–1854*, ed. Increase N. Tarbox, vol. 2 (Boston: Beacon Press, 1887), p. 319. The writer is grateful to Robert F. Trent for this reference.
2. Susan Clendon Storer Edwards, "The Mission House, Stockbridge, Massachusetts," *Antiques* 123, no. 3 (March 1983): 558 fig. 2; "A Colonial Restoration," *Antiques* 18, no. 3 (September 1930): 217.

173

Desk and bookcase
Connecticut or New York, 1700–1730

Description: This desk and bookcase is in two units. Below the slant front the desk contains three graduated drawers located below a well that is masked in its front face to simulate a pair of drawers in line. The drawers, both real and simulated, are outlined by thick half-round molding; the simulated drawers are fitted with a central round brass escutcheon with a drop pull, and the three wide drawers are fitted with central blind lock escutcheons flanked by round brass escutcheons with drop pulls. Below base molding at the front and sides, the desk is supported by four large turned feet. The slant front is framed to a horizontal fielded panel and is decorated with two inlaid diamond motifs on its lower edge above the hinges. The lid is supported on lopers housed on each side of the well, and the sides of the case are shaped to each side of the lower edge of the lid. The lid opens to an interior with an upper tier of five pigeonholes with fixed valances shaped to pointed arches. The pigeonholes are above a row of five small drawers in line, each with a central wooden pull. The outer drawers are flanked by scalloped transverse partitions that extend to the front of the desk. The sliding well cover is edged with double half-round molding on its front and triple half-round molding on each side. There are secret drawers located behind the two side drawers. The partitions within the interior have rounded edges. The bookcase rests within a molding applied to the top of the desk. It is surmounted by a complex molded cornice and contains a pair of doors with arched fielded panels. The doors open to an interior with two fixed shelves. The desk is of dovetailed board construction. The horizontal backboards are joined with a half lap and nailed to rabbets in all four sides. The platforms of the side compartments in the interior are housed through the back. The drawer dividers above and below the simulated drawers are tenoned through the sides of the desk case. The drawer runners within the case are nailed to grooves in the sides, and shaped blocks are nailed to the inside of the back as stops. There are applied longitudinal strips above the bottom of the case at the front and the back. The feet are doweled through the bottom board. The slant front is attached to the case with wrought-iron hinges. The joints of the doors in the bookcase are pegged twice on the bottom and four times on the upper. The horizontal backboards of the bookcase also are joined with a half lap and nailed to rabbets in all four sides. On both the large case drawers and the small interior drawers, the sides are dovetailed to the front and back, and the bot-

173

tom is beveled on all four sides and let into a groove on all four sides.

Inscriptions: There are numerous chalk marks on the inside of both bookcase doors and columns of addition on the top of the desk interior. A fragment of what appears to be a modern recipe for soup is pasted to the inside of the front of the lowest drawer in the desk.

Condition: The brasses and the hardware appear to be original, with the exception of the catch on the bookcase doors, the lower hinge on the left bookcase door, and the round escutcheons on the upper left simulated drawer and on the right side of the lowest drawer. An escutcheon on the lid is missing. The molding applied to the inner edge of the right bookcase door is a replacement. Many of the applied moldings are replaced in walnut, including the base molding at the front and sides, the cornice moldings on the left side of the bookcase, the midmolding on the left side of the desk, and probably the half-round molding on the front edges of the desk sides. The drawer runners within the desk and two of the stops are replacements, as is the rear longitudinal brace above the bottom.

Woods: American black cherry; yellow poplar; drawer fronts in desk interior, feet, eastern red cedar; replaced moldings, walnut.

Dimensions: H 182.9; W 96.0; UCW 86.9; LCW 92.1; D (closed) 55.1; D (open) 85.3; UCD 27.3; LCD 52.0.

Bibliography: Sack, *Fine Points*, p. 157.

Provenance: Henry V. Weil, New York, N. Y.; by sale in 1927 to Francis P. Garvan, New York, N. Y.

SPECIALIZED objects made for the storage of books, ledgers, and writing materials are rare in early eighteenth-century American furniture. Two of the more interesting examples, fall-front cabinets from New York and Philadelphia, are closely based on English and Continental prototypes.[1] The Philadelphia example, now at Colonial Williamsburg, is signed by cabinetmaker Edward Evans and dated 1707. The Yale example is of the more conventional slant-front type that, once introduced, was made throughout the eighteenth century with only stylistic changes. Some elaborate walnut and walnut veneered examples from Philadelphia are known, and desks of this period attributed to Massachusetts generally have richly figured burl walnut veneers.[2] The Yale desk and bookcase is a sturdy, amply proportioned example of cherry and yellow poplar, with bold cedar feet. While its precise place of origin is not known, it may have been made in Connecticut or New York. A desk similar in appearance, now in the Wadsworth Atheneum (1926.324), probably is married.[3] A related English example of ca. 1705 with the label of John Gatehouse of London has been published.[4]

The Mabel Brady Garvan Collection 1931.1233

1. These are conveniently illustrated in Fairbanks and Bates, pp. 58–59.
2. Fairbanks and Bates, p. 60; McElroy, "Furn. in Philadelphia," fig. 18; Fairbanks and Bates, p. 61.
3. Illustrated in Nutting, *Treasury*, no. 681.
4. Gilbert, *Furn. at Temple Newsam*, no. 26.

173a

174

Desk and bookcase
Boston or Salem, Massachusetts, area, 1770–1790

Description: The bookcase is crowned by a broken-scroll pediment terminating in floral carved rosettes. The pediment is fitted with a central ball finial mounted on an urn and with urn-and-flame finials mounted on small plinths at each side. The bookcase contains a pair of doors with arched fielded panels flanked by fluted pilasters with five flutes. There are candle slides with brass button pulls below each door. The bookcase rests within a restraining molding applied to the top of the desk. Below the blockfront slant-front lid of the desk, which is fitted with a brass lock escutcheon and supported by lopers with brass button pulls, the desk contains four graduated blockfront drawers outlined by cock beading on its case. Each drawer is fitted with a central brass lock escutcheon flanked by matching escutcheons with bail pulls. There is base molding at the front and sides, with a central drop at the center of the front, and the object is supported by four short cabriole legs with claw-and-ball feet. The bookcase doors open to an interior with carved shells behind the arches of the doors. The interior contains, at the top, a row of eight pigeonholes with fixed shaped valances that are separated by shaped partitions. Below this row, there is a wide open compartment for books and ledgers, flanked by pigeonholes. Below this level, there is a central open space fitted with a single loose shelf that can be adjusted to one of three positions, flanked by a pair of superimposed pigeonholes above a small drawer with a brass button pull. The bottom of the interior contains four drawers in line, with the small outer drawers fitted with a single pull and each of the inner drawers with two pulls. The desk interior contains a central prospect door with reverse blocking, carved with a shell contained within an arc. The door opens to reveal a compartment with a valance drawer above a pigeonhole and another drawer. The door is flanked by simulated document drawers faced with columns or pilasters with urn-and-flame finials. A small hole in the roof of the center compartment, accessible when the valance drawer is removed, provides access to a wooden spring lock. When the lock is released, the whole center section can be removed. There are secret drawers with leather pulls housed behind the simulated document drawers, and behind the center compartment is a nest of four superimposed secret drawers with leather pulls. The center section is flanked by units consisting of a small drawer with a brass button pull, above

174

three pigeonholes in line (with the valances of the side pigeonholes fixed and that of the center pigeonhole a working drawer), above a blocked drawer with a brass button pull. Each side of the desk interior contains three reverse-blocked superimposed drawers, graduated in reverse, and with the upper drawer carved with a shell. The interior of the lid is lined with baize. The pediment is roofed with transverse boards and enclosed at the rear by the upper backboard. The bookcase is of dovetailed board construction, with the horizontal backboards nailed to rabbets in all four sides. There are nineteen lobes to the shells within the

bookcase doors, and the valances below the shells are shaped in accordance with the curve of the shells. On the small drawers in the bookcase, the sides are dovetailed to the front and back, and the bottoms are glued in place; the top edges of the drawer sides are molded. The desk is also of dovetailed board construction, with the backboards again nailed in place. There are partial dustboards below the wide drawers in the case, and the base molding is joined to the case bottom with a giant "Boston-style" dovetail. An applied strip covers the dovetails on the front of the case sides. Horizontal blocks are behind the brackets and drop, and a framework of strips is applied to the underside of the case bottom at the front and sides. The legs are large blocks tenoned into the case bottom. On the large desk drawers, the top edges of the sides are shaped to double half-round molding, and the sides are dovetailed to the front and back. The bottoms are nailed to rabbets in the front and sides and to the underside of the back, with running strips applied. The desk interior drawers are fashioned in the same manner as those in the bookcase.

Inscriptions: The secret drawers housed behind the simulated document drawers are numbered "1" and "2" respectively. Some of the desk interior drawers are also numbered. The shell-carved drawer on the upper left of the desk interior is numbered "98" in pencil, and its counterpart on the right side of the interior bears a fragment of a modern paper label with "A.6" in ink. In the drawer below the pigeonholes on the right of the interior, there is an octagonal modern paper label, white with a red border, glued to the inside of the right side, with "1905/614503" in ink. "William C. [or H.] Allen" is written above illegible writing on the right wide drawer, marked "2" on the outside of the back, of the four drawers in line in the bookcase interior. Written in pencil on the outside of the back of the upper and lower cases is "33769"; "1905" is written in blue chalk on the inside of the bottom of the top wide drawer in the desk.

Condition: The four feet are spliced to the cabriole legs just below the knees and are undoubtedly replacements. There have been many small repairs to the moldings in both the bookcase and the desk, and the midmolding on the sides at the top of the desk is a replacement. The locks and hinges in the bookcase are replacements; the top of the lock escutcheon on the third wide drawer from the top in the desk has been repaired, and the escutcheon is missing on the prospect door. A partition in the left wide drawer of the four drawers in line in the bookcase interior is missing, and one of the nest of four secret drawers in the desk interior has been lost. New screws have been added to the top of the center,

removable compartment in the desk interior. There are new drawer runners in the desk, and a new block or brace has been added to the inside of the back of the desk.

Woods: Mahogany; eastern white pine.

Dimensions: H 253.3; W 109.2; UCW 97.2; LCW 101.9; D (closed) 58.4; D (open) 94.4; UCD 29.4; LCD 33.7.

Bibliography: Nutting, *Treasury*, nos. 696, 698; Lovell, "Boston Blockfront Furn.," fig. 88.

Provenance: According to the records of Francis P. Garvan, he acquired this desk at the "Travers sale," possibly that of C. M. Traver Company of New York, but this has not been confirmed. It has been suggested that the inscribed name "William C. [or H.] Allen" is that of a nineteenth-century owner of the desk.

174a

This desk and bookcase, one of three related eastern Massachusetts examples in the Yale collection (cats. 175, 176), exhibits a combination of Boston- and Salem-area characteristics. Although its blocked desk lid is often considered a Salem feature, the slightly rounded corners of the blocking on the top drawer in the desk are not similar to the squared corners associated with Salem examples. Here, the giant Boston dovetail at the bottom of the desk is used, rather than the Newport method common in Salem work, and while there is a center drop in the front base molding, it does not take the form of a three-dimensional, realistic scallop shell found on many Salem objects. The desk interior loosely follows the Newport style, as do many Salem and Boston desks. The center ball-and-urn finial here is reminiscent of one found on a desk and bookcase attributed to Salem, but the verticality and spring of the pediment seems more characteristic of Boston furniture.[1] Unfortunately, the feet of this example are new and thus cannot provide additional stylistic evidence. On balance, one might suggest that this object was probably made closer to Boston than to Salem. However, the differences between Boston and Salem work are not nearly as important as the similarities, a fact often overlooked in the desire to pinpoint shop traditions and places of origin. Clearly, Salem was looking to Boston, as well as to Newport and perhaps other places, for patterns to follow in the decorative arts in the eighteenth century. As a "micropolitan" center, Salem was within the sphere of influence of Boston in markets and patronage patterns. The symbiotic relationship between the two communities is the key point to be emphasized in this period, rather than minor differences in the handling of ornamental features or construction techniques.[2]

The Mabel Brady Garvan Collection 1930.2241

1. Lovell, "Boston Blockfront Furn.," pp. 120–125, figs. 84–89.
2. For a discussion of this relationship between Boston and Salem in terms of silver objects, see Gerald W. R. Ward, "Silver and Society in Salem, Massachusetts, 1630–1820: A Case Study of the Consumer and the Craft" (Ph.D. diss., Boston University, 1984).

175

Desk and bookcase
Boston, Massachusetts, area, 1770–1790

Description: The desk and bookcase is in two units. Below the slant front, the desk contains four graduated blockfront drawers surrounded by cock beading on the case. Each drawer is fitted with a central brass lock escutcheon flanked by matching escutcheons with bail pulls. There is base molding at the front and sides, and the desk is supported by four carved claw-and-ball feet. The cleated lid has a central brass lock escutcheon and is supported by lopers that flank the top drawer. The lid opens to an interior with a central prospect door or "locker" carved with a shell and flanked by document drawers faced with colonnettes with urn-and-flame finials. The prospect door opens to a pigeonhole with a valance drawer above a single small drawer with a concave front. Flanking the center section are two pigeonholes with fixed shaped valances above a drawer with projecting blocking, and at each side of the interior is a bank of three drawers with recessed blocking, the top drawer being of greater depth and carved with a shell contained within an arc. The main vertical partitions in the desk interior are shaped to a double half-round molding. The bookcase is flanked by fluted pilasters with five flutes and surmounted by a broken-scroll pediment with center and side urn-and-flame finials. The bookcase doors are paneled with continuous reverse curves, and there is a candle slide below each door. The doors open to an interior with a row of eight pigeonholes with fixed shaped valances at the top, above a wide center section fitted with two adjustable bookshelves and flanked by units with a pigeonhole above a ledger compartment, all above three corresponding drawers in line. The vertical partitions between the pigeonholes are shaped. The desk is of dovetailed board construction, and the base molding is joined to the desk bottom at the front with a giant dovetail. Facing strips are not used to cover the joint of the drawer dividers and the desk sides. The back of the desk consists of horizontal boards nailed in place. The rear sides of the back feet are not carved. On each drawer in the desk, the sides are dovetailed to the front and back; the bottoms are nailed to a rabbet in the front, let into rabbets in the sides, and nailed to the underside of the back, with running strips applied. The blocking is cut from the solid, the top edge of each drawer side is rounded, and the top edge of each drawer back is beveled. On the drawers in the desk interior, the sides are dovetailed to the

Desk and Bookcases 335

175

front and back, and the bottoms are glued to rabbets in the front and sides and to the underside of the back. The prospect door is fitted with a lock at its top edge and a pin in its lower edge and falls forward when released, rather than swinging open on hinges. The bookcase is also of dovetailed board construction, and the backboards are again nailed to rabbets in the top and sides and to the bottom of the case. There is an incised line around the pierced opening of the pediment. The scrolls of the pediment are supported by transverse braces. The ledger compartments contain pairs of grooves allowing five possible positions for ledger dividers. The small drawers are constructed in the same manner as those on the desk interior.

Inscriptions: There are columns of addition, probably modern, in pencil on the top of the lower case.

Condition: On the upper case, the right finial is probably a replacement, there is a new molding on the plinth for the left finial, and there have been repairs to the cornice moldings. The small drawer on the right of the bookcase interior is missing, as are all the ledger dividers. The stops for the candle slides are missing, and their runners have been renewed. On the desk, the lid has been reattached with modern hinges and is placed too low on the case. The drawer runners within the case have been replaced or renailed, and a new support has been added under the top drawer. The drawer stops are replacements. Although the feet and brackets appear to be original, there is a good deal of wear on the front and side base moldings beneath where the feet and brackets are attached, even though there is no corresponding wear on the feet and brackets themselves. This suggests that the feet and brackets, and the supporting blocks, were at one time removed, sanded, refinished, and then reattached. In the desk interior, the pigeonhole valances are all replacements, and the upper part of the colonnette on one document drawer has been repaired. New nails have been added to all the drawer bottoms. There have been many other minor repairs to the object, including the piecing of several brasses on the desk drawers.

Woods: Mahogany; eastern white pine.

Dimensions: H 243.6; W 114.7; UCW 98.7; LCW 103.7; D (closed) 61.5; D (open) 90.5; UCD 28.1; LCD 55.7.

Bibliography: *Flayderman Coll.*, no. 455; Aaron Marc Stein, "English and American Furniture in the Collection of Mr. and Mrs. Richard deWolfe Brixey," *Fine Arts* 18 (December 1931): fig. 5; F. Lewis Hinckley, *A Directory of Antique Furniture* (New York: Crown Publishers, 1953), p. 342 fig. 1076; F. Lewis Hinckley, *A Directory of the Historic Cabinet Woods* (New York: Crown Publishers, 1960), p. 123 fig. 118.

Provenance: Philip Flayderman, Boston, Mass.; acquired at auction in 1929 by Richard DeWolfe Brixey (1880–1943), New York, N.Y.; by descent to his daughter Doris Brixey (d. 1983).

THIS recent addition to the Yale collection is distinguished by the richly figured mahogany panels on its bookcase doors. The blocking and construction of this example suggest that

it is a Boston rather than Salem product, but the differences between the two schools are minor in comparison with the strong similarities found in urban Massachusetts furniture of this period. Doors with these double-ogee or continuous reverse curve panels are common on Boston-area desk and bookcases and are also seen on cat. 176. Equally impressive desk and bookcases were made in New York and Philadelphia during the second half of the eighteenth century, but are not represented in the Yale collection.[1]

Bequest of Doris M. Brixey 1984.32.29

1. As examples for comparison, see Hummel, *American Chippendale Furn.*, figs. 19, 86; Fairbanks and Bates, pp. 184, 185, 188.

175a

176

Desk and bookcase

Boston or Salem, Massachusetts, 1770–1790

Description: In two units, this desk and bookcase is in many respects similar to the two preceding Massachusetts examples. Here, however, the desk contains four graduated reverse-serpentine drawers outlined by cock beading on the case. Each drawer is fitted with a central brass lock escutcheon flanked by matching escutcheons with bail pulls. Below the base molding at the front and sides, which is shaped to follow the reverse-serpentine form, the desk is supported by four short cabriole legs with arrised knees, pointed knee brackets, and carved claw-and-ball feet. The cleated lid has a central brass lock escutcheon and is supported by lopers housed on each side of the upper desk drawer. The lid opens to an interior with a central unit of three superimposed drawers with recessed fronts, with the top drawer of greater depth and carved with a shell. The central section is flanked on each side by a unit consisting of four pigeonholes with fixed shaped valances above a pair of drawers in line over a single wide drawer. Each small drawer is fitted with a brass button pull, the vertical partitions between the middle pigeonholes and the two drawers in line are shaped with double half-round molding, the other partitions between the pigeonholes are shaped, the drawer divider has double half-round molding, and the platform of the interior is molded on its front edge. The bookcase rests within molding applied to the top of the desk that projects slightly at the front corners. The bookcase contains a pair of paneled doors with panel edges of continuous reverse-curve form, flanked by fluted pilasters. The pilaster capitals and entablature project at the sides; the entablature contains a row of dentils, as does the broken triangular pediment which flanks a central fluted plinth that is not fitted for a finial. The doors open to an interior containing a row of ten pigeonholes with fixed shaped valances at the top. The center section is fitted with two adjustable bookshelves, flanked by side units containing, from top to bottom, a drawer with a recessed front and a carved shell, a pigeonhole with a fixed shaped valance, another shell-carved drawer, another pigeonhole, and a small plain drawer. The bottom of the interior contains five drawers in line: small drawers at the sides under the side units, and three drawers of equal size beneath the bookshelf section. The front edges of the bookshelves have double half-round molding, the small drawers are fitted with brass

Desk and Bookcases 337

176

button pulls, and the vertical partitions between the upper row of pigeonholes are shaped as on the desk interior. The desk is of dovetailed board construction, with the back consisting of three horizontal boards nailed to rabbets in all four sides. A facing strip is used to cover the joint of the drawer dividers and desk sides. The drawer runners within the desk are housed in grooves, and small blocks are nailed to the inside of the back as stops. The base molding at the front stands above the desk bottom and projects below, with a row of multiple horizontal glue blocks behind its lower edge. There are shaped horizontal blocks behind the knee brackets and a large square block on the inside edge of the rear feet. On each drawer in the desk, the sides are dovetailed to the front and back; the bottoms are beveled on their front and side edges, let into grooves in the front and sides, and nailed to the underside of the back, with running strips applied. Each top edge of the sides is rounded. The desk interior drawers are made in the same fashion, with the top edge of the sides flat. The lowest drawer in the center section of the interior is divided by partitions into three small transverse compartments at the front and a larger compartment at the back. The bookcase also is of dovetailed board construction, and its horizontal backboards also are nailed to rabbets. The front and sides of the bookcase extend below the bookcase bottom, and there are applied cleats at the sides and blocks at the front that rest on top of the desk. There are six pairs of grooves for the adjustable shelves in the center section of the interior. The pediment is braced with a single longitudinal strip applied to the top of the bookcase. The drawers are fashioned in the same manner as those on the desk interior.

Inscriptions: The drawers in the bookcase were numbered initially in ink and have later pencil numbers. Written in white chalk on the outside of the back of each case is "84" in a circle. A modern label with "192" written in ink is pasted to the outside of the back of the bookcase.

Condition: A new strip has been let in at the top of the backboards in the bookcase, and the pediment is not original to the object. There are cloth patches on the outside of the back of the bookcase and over shrinkage cracks in the drawers. The running strips on the drawers are replacements. The left rear leg has been repaired, and the blocks on the left front leg have several new screws.

Woods: Mahogany; eastern white pine.

Dimensions: H 242.6; W 114.6; UCW 101.7; LCW 106.0; D (closed) 65.3; D (open) 96.8; UCD 30.5; LCD 58.5.

Bibliography: *Early American Furniture: The Collection of Jacob Margolis*, 5–6 November 1926 (New York: American Art Association, 1926), no. 292.

Provenance: Jacob Margolis, New York, N. Y.; acquired at auction in 1926 by Francis P. Garvan, New York, N. Y.

THE three Massachusetts desk and bookcases in the Yale collection are a good illustration of the various design options available to the consumer on essentially the same form. Here, for example, the desk section has a reverse-serpentine

(sometimes called an "oxbow" or "yoke-front") shape, rather than the blocked form seen on cats. 174 and 175. Similar examples attributed to both Boston and Salem have been published.[1] The elaborate interior here, fitted with fourteen pigeonholes, eleven drawers, and space for three shelves of books, is reminiscent of the elaborate interior on an English desk and bookcase of ca. 1745 at Temple Newsam House.[2] The English example is fitted with sixteen small drawers and twenty-four blockfront alphabet drawers; it contains a dozen pigeonholes and three compartments for ledgers and books, as well as other fittings.

The Mabel Brady Garvan Collection 1930.2487

1. *Antiques* 124, no. 2 (August 1983): inside front cover; Fitzgerald, fig. IV–60, with a broken-scroll pediment. A combination of an upper case with a broken-scroll pediment and fielded arched panel doors and a desk with a reverse-serpentine front has been attributed to Abraham Watson of Salem and illustrates another combination of designs used in this Massachusetts desk and bookcase form, which also was popular, of course, in the bombé form.

2. Gilbert, *Furn. at Temple Newsam*, no. 29.

177

Desk and bookcase
Attributed to the Townsend-Goddard families
Newport, Rhode Island, 1760–1790
(see pl. 15)

Description: The bookcase is crowned by an open broken-scroll pediment terminating in carved rosettes flanking a central ball-and-flame finial mounted on a fluted plinth. The sides of the pediment are fitted with matching finials mounted on square plinths. The tympanum contains a pair of applied plaques shaped to follow the arch-opening moldings. The blockfront bookcase is enclosed by three paneled doors, each capped with a carved shell, concave in the center and convex at each side. The center and right doors are hinged together and open as one. There are small incised triangles at the top corners of each door above the shell. Each side of the center door is fitted with a brass lock escutcheon, blind on the left. The front corners of the bookcase hold fluted quarter columns with turned capitals and bases. The bookcase rests within restraining molding applied to the top of the desk. Below the slant lid, the desk contains a writing slide and three graduated drawers outlined by cock beading on the case. The slant lid has a molded edge and is carved with three large shells echoing those on the bookcase. Each desk drawer is fitted with a central brass lock escutcheon flanked by matching escutcheons with bail pulls. The lid is fitted with two brass lock escutcheons, blind on the left. The writing slide is flanked by lopers; each loper is fitted with a brass button pull, and the slide with a pair of pulls. There is base molding at the front and sides of the desk, and the object is supported by four ogee bracket feet; the blocking continues through the base molding and feet. The slant front opens to an interior divided into five sections. At the center is a concave-blocked door carved with a shell and enclosing two concave-blocked drawers. This door is flanked by units containing three pigeonholes with concave-shaped valance drawers and shaped vertical partitions, all above a convex-blocked drawer with a brass button pull. These units, in turn, are flanked by the outermost units containing a tier

176a

Desk and Bookcases 339

177

of three drawers; the top drawer is of greater depth and is carved with a shell. Each drawer is concave blocked and fitted with a brass button pull. All the interior compartments rest on a shelf with a molded front edge. The interior of the bookcase is divided by two vertical partitions faced with double half-round molding, thus forming three vertical compartments. Beginning at a height of 40 cm, the sides of each compartment are grooved for adjustable shelves at intervals of 3 cm on center. Nine adjustable shelves remain. The center unit of the three compartments is slightly wider than the side compartments. The roof of the bonnet top is enclosed with boards nailed to the vertical backboards of the bookcase, and the bookcase is of dovetailed board construction. There is a full dustboard behind the center finial. The desk is of dovetailed board construction, with the backboards applied horizontally. The drawer dividers are dovetailed to the desk sides, with the joints exposed; they are faced with mahogany, with a thin pine strip and then a full chestnut dustboard behind. The ends of the lopers are rabbeted to accommodate the front of the top drawer, which extends beneath it. The base moldings are applied to a front rail that is located above the desk bottom. The rear feet are diagonal brackets; each foot is reinforced with a central vertical block and horizontal blocks shaped in conformity with the brackets. On the large desk drawers, the blocking is applied and reinforced with blocks within the drawers. The sides are dovetailed to the front and back, the bottoms are beveled on their sides, nailed to a rabbet in the front, fitted to a groove in the sides, and nailed to the underside of the back, with small chestnut blocks located behind the front. The top edges of the drawer sides are rounded, and the top edges of the backs are beveled. On the top and middle drawers, the grain of the chestnut bottom board runs from side to side; on the bottom drawer, the grain of the white pine board runs from front to back. On the small drawers in the desk interior, the sides are dovetailed to the front and back, and the bottoms are let into a rabbet in all four sides and secured with glue and, occasionally, nails. The top edge of their sides is rounded, and the top edge of the backs beveled.

Inscriptions: "Bottom" is written in white chalk on the underside of the desk bottom. The valance drawers on the desk interior are numbered on the inside of the back "I" through "VI" from left to right; the other drawers are numbered in pencil, possibly later, in Arabic numerals; and there are numerous chalk shop marks throughout the interior. An octagonal modern paper label with a blue border is pasted to the underside of the bottom of the middle desk drawer; it reads, in blue letters on a white ground: "COLLINGS & COLLINGS / *Antiques* / 528 Amsterdam Ave. / NEW YORK." The same label appears on the top of the dustboard below this drawer; on the inside of the left side of the desk, at the level of the bottom drawer; and on the underside of the desk bottom.

Condition: The desk and bookcase has survived in excellent condition. There is a small repair to the top left corner of the pediment; there is a new edge on the left bookcase

340 *American Case Furniture*

door and a small patch near the keyhole escutcheon on the bookcase doors. The top molding of the desk has been repaired, and the lips of the slant lid have also been patched. The bottoms of two desk interior drawers ("8" and "9") have been replaced. The writing surface of the desk interior has been pieced beneath the hinges. The drawer runners have been replaced in the desk. The bottom of the top and middle desk drawers has been pieced, with new running strips and blocks applied. The left rear foot has been pieced; the right front foot has been pieced and repaired. There have been other minor repairs.

Woods: Mahogany; light-colored, possibly Honduran or Santo Domingan, mahogany; fluted quarter columns, cornice moldings, finials, front of writing slide and drawer dividers, base molding, feet, much darker, possibly Cuban, mahogany; interior of bookcase and sides, backs, and bottoms of pigeonhole valance drawers, American black cherry (previously published many times as yellow poplar); drawer linings, with one exception, other elements, chestnut; bottom of bottom desk drawer, other elements, eastern white pine; some repairs, yellow pine.

Dimensions: H 272.4; W 113.5; UCW 100.7; LCW 105.8; D (open) 94.9; D (closed) 64.0; UCD 32.1; LCD 58.9.

Exhibitions: *Girl Scouts Exhibition*, no. 638; Montgomery and Kane, *American Art, 1750–1800*, no. 100; YUAG, "Rhode Island Furn."; YUAG, "A Wide View for American Art."

Bibliography: Lockwood, no. 271; Nutting, *Treasury*, no. 708; Ormsbee, *Story Am. Furn.*, no. 59; Miller, 1: no. 897; Nagel, pl. 15; Rogers, "Garvan Furn. (1960)," fig. 10; Rogers, "Garvan Coll. (1962)," p. 10; Louis B. Wright et al., *The Arts in America: The Colonial Period* (New York: Charles Scribner's Sons, 1966), pl. 233; Kirk, *Early Am. Furn.*, fig. 19; Andrew Carnduff Ritchie and Katharine B. Neilson, *Selected Paintings and Sculpture from the Yale University Art Gallery* (New Haven: Yale University Art Gallery, 1972), intro.; Wendy A. Cooper, "The Purchase of Furniture and Furnishings by John Brown, Providence Merchant," *Antiques* 103, no. 2 (February 1973): pl. 2; Sydney V. James, *Colonial Rhode Island: A History* (New York: Charles Scribner's Sons, 1975), p. 246; Montgomery, "1776—Furniture," p. 62; Barbaralee Diamonstein, "What Would You Choose if You Could Choose Any Object?" *ARTnews* 74, no. 8 (October 1975): 49; Charles F. Montgomery, "And of Early American Art," *Yale Alumni* 39, no. 7 (April 1976): 14; Montgomery, "Regional Preferences and Characteristics," pl. I; Christopher Gilbert, "The Victoria and Albert Museum, American Art, 1750–1800: Towards Independence," *Decorative Arts Society Newsletter* 2, no. 3 (Summer 1976): 6; John Cornforth, "The Birth of American Art," *Country Life* (22 July 1976): 221; Simon Jervis, "The Americanization of American Art?" *Apollo* (September 1976): 186; *Antiques* 115, no. 1 (January 1979): 40; Robert Bishop and Patricia Coblentz, *Furniture 1, Prehistoric through Rococo*, Smithsonian Illustrated Library of Antiques (New York: Cooper-Hewitt Museum, 1979), fig. 93; Gerald W. R. Ward et al., *Francis P. Garvan, Collector* (New Haven: Yale University Art Gallery, 1980), fig. 5; Kane, "American Furn.," pl. IV; Charles F. Montgomery, "Francis P. Garvan," *Antiques*

177a

Desk and Bookcases 341

177b

121, no. 1 (January 1982): 248; Kirk, *Am. Furn. & Brit. Trad.*, fig. 3; Bill Dulaney, "Wallace Nutting: Advocate of the Pilgrim Century," *Fine Woodworking*, no. 39 (March/April 1983): 72; Shestack, *Selections*, p. 46; John T. Kirk et al., comps., "Giving an Elephant to Blind Men? The Cross-Disciplinary Role of a Desk and Bookcase," *Arts* 59, no. 2 (October 1984): 87–99; Moses, figs. 8.16a–c.

Provenance: According to family tradition, generally accepted today, this desk and bookcase was owned originally by wealthy Providence merchant John Brown (1736–1803). It descended in Brown's family until 1918, by which time it was in the possession of his great-granddaughter, Caroline L. H. Chesebrough of Bristol, R. I. Mrs. Chesebrough noted in a letter of 14 September 1918: "It [the desk and bookcase] belonged to my great-grandfather John Brown of Providence, one of the 'four Brown brothers,' for whom it was made in 1785. Each of his brothers ordered one at the same time, Nicholas, Moses & Joseph, all noted men in their day." Mrs. Chesebrough, who had recently lost her son, sold the desk and bookcase to the firm of Collings and Collings, New York dealers, in September 1918. A. W. Clarke, Francis P.

Garvan's agent, apparently went to see the desk, and reported back to Mr. Garvan on 21 September: "Collings says it is the finest and most stately looking of any of these desks—in fine condition. Never repaired except slightly reinforced on inside of drawers, it was done over before Mrs. Cheeseboro owned it—it came to her from her Mother many years ago—Mrs. C is now 81 & a sister of Nat Herreshof —the Yacht designer. The house that it came from was her great grandfathers home in Providence which was purchased & now occupied by J. Marsden Perry. Collings took the desk to Brightenstein of Prov. to be packed—he has been in the business 40 years & C[ollings] says a splendid judge—Says it is the finest in existence—much better than #270 [in Lockwood] owned by Brown & Ives—on account of the interior which is very much superior." On the strength of these recommendations, Mr. Garvan purchased the desk in 1918; it passed by descent to Mabel Brady Garvan in 1937, who in turn presented it to Yale in 1940.

THIS desk and bookcase is one of ten related examples, each with carved shells in both the bookcase and the desk, attributed to Newport, Rhode Island, usually to a member of the Goddard-Townsend families. Thought to have been owned by John Brown, the Yale desk is most closely related to three other examples in the group: the unique nine-shell example owned originally by John's brother Joseph (1737-1785) and now at the Rhode Island Historical Society, a six-shell example at the Museum of Fine Arts, Boston (39.155), and another with six shells thought to have been owned originally by a third brother, Nicholas Brown (1729-1791), and still in the possession of a descendant. (Another example made for brother Moses [1738-1836] has not survived.) The other six examples, each with six shells, include two at the Museum of Art, Rhode Island School of Design, and single examples at Winterthur (59.2646), the Metropolitan Museum of Art (15.21.2), the Museum of Fine Arts, Boston (40.790), and Bayou Bend (B.69.22). Other Newport desk and bookcases with only two carved shells, or without shells, are known, and a related example with three carved shells in the desk by Grindall Rawson (1719-1803) of Providence has been published.[1]

The subgroup that includes the Yale desk shares several distinguishing features, including open pediments, cornice moldings terminating in petaled rosettes, similar finials, and a sense of verticality in the bookcase sections, each fitted with three vertical compartments. The Yale example is the only one fitted with a writing slide, and it is further distinguished by its contrasting colors of mahogany. The entire object is framed in dark Cuban mahogany, giving a sense of definition and outline to the warmer, light-colored mahogany it encloses. A famous object in the Yale collection, the John Brown desk and bookcase has been attributed on occasion to John Goddard (1723-1785), but as yet no maker's name can be linked to it with any degree of confidence. Many writers have praised the design of the Yale desk, extolling its proportions, sensitive handling of wood, and carved details; John T. Kirk, in particular, has explicated the design characteristics of the object and most recently has linked the form to Germanic and other Continental design sources, while suggesting that the Yale desk represents a conscious rejection by Newport craftsmen of the English rococo aesthetic.[2]

The precise dating of the Yale desk, like the question of its maker, remains somewhat problematic. While it has been given a wide date range here from 1760 to 1790, more than one writer has suggested that the desk was made at about the time John Brown was completing his magnificent three-story mansion on Power Street in Providence (now the Rhode Island Historical Society) between 1786 and 1788. However, Brown ordered furniture from Newport as early as 1760, the year he married Sarah Smith, a Quaker, and set up housekeeping on Water Street (now South Main Street) in a brick house measuring forty by thirty-six feet. Wendy A. Cooper has analyzed in detail the furnishings acquired by Brown for these houses, without finding conclusive evidence concerning the purchase of the desk and bookcase. She has called attention, however, to a document of 1782 that does refer to a bookcase with drawers. On 19 December of that year, John Brown wrote to his daughter, "Your Mar told me the pieces

177c

Desk and Bookcases 343

like Your Brocade frock is in the Lore Draw of the Book Case[;] if they can be found [they] shall be sent you with this."³ Such a letter does little to link the Yale desk with Brown, but it does serve to suggest the multiple functions served by a desk and bookcase in the eighteenth century. It was not a form solely for literary or business pursuits; it united the storage of textiles in the desk drawers with the shelving of books, ledgers, and business papers in the tall bookcase above. Thus the Yale desk and others like it stand as a representation of the wholeness of life in the eighteenth century, prior to the separation of work from domestic life common in the next century. Reading this desk and bookcase in this manner is only one of many different ways of trying to squeeze as much information from it as possible. An unusual and provocative analysis of the object is offered in the article cited in the Bibliography above entitled "Giving an Elephant to Blind Men?" John T. Kirk's class in the American and New England Studies Program at Boston University prepared information concerning the desk and bookcase and circulated it to some twenty-six individuals, including scholars in several different fields (history, art history, material culture, folklore, and literature) and museum professionals, collectors, craftsmen, and a dealer. These people were then asked "to speculate on the usefulness of a particular piece of furniture to their disciplines." While the answers as recorded and published reveal as much or more about the respondents as they do about the desk (especially in the case of a few historians who revealed their prejudices and blind spots through their inability to deal with the desk), the project served to illustrate the manifold meanings and layers of information that an object can embody.

A reproduction of the Yale desk and bookcase was commissioned by the Garvans (Appendix, no. 24), and Harden Furniture Company has made reproductions since 1983.

The Mabel Brady Garvan Collection 1940.320

1. The other members of the subgroup including the Yale desk are conveniently illustrated in Moses, figs. 8.21, 8.17, 8.18. For the other six examples, see Moses, figs. 8.10, 11; Moses, fig. 8.12 (Downs, no. 232); Moses, fig. 8.14 (Heckscher, no. 184); Moses, fig. 8.5 (Randall, no. 62); and Moses, fig. 8.13 (Warren, *Bayou Bend*, no. 135). For other Newport desk and bookcases, see Moses, figs. 8.1–4, 8.27, 28; the Rawson desk and bookcase is illustrated in Ott, no. 66.
2. The group has been discussed most recently and effectively by Heckscher, no. 184; see also Moses, chap. 8. Kirk, *Am. Furn. & Brit. Trad.*, pp. 4–6.
3. "The Purchase of Furniture and Furnishings by John Brown, Providence Merchant, Part I: 1760–1788," *Antiques* 102, no. 2 (February 1973): 328–339 (quotation p. 339); "Part II: 1788–1803," *Antiques* 102, no. 4 (April 1973): 734–743. For the John Brown house, see the notes by Antoinette F. Downing in Ott, pp. xix–xxiv.

178

Desk and bookcase
Connecticut, probably New London County, 1760–1790

Description: The bookcase is crowned by a broken-scroll pediment with a fretwork course and a deep cove molding, terminating in carved pinwheels flanking a central carved and pierced asymmetrical cartouche. The bookcase contains two paneled doors, arched at their upper ends, which open to an interior with three bookshelves on each side of a central vertical partition. The bookcase rests within restraining molding on the top of the desk. The desk contains below the slant front four graduated lipped drawers. The cleated slant front is supported by lopers and opens to a two-tiered interior. The upper tier is slightly recessed and contains a central section of two superimposed open compartments flanked on each side by pairs of pigeonholes with fixed valances shaped to pointed arches. The upper center section is flanked on each side by two superimposed drawers, with the upper drawer of greater depth and carved with a shell. The lower tier contains three drawers in line, with the center drawer of greater width. The drawers and pigeonholes are outlined by half-round molding, and the vertical partitions are shaped. Below

177d

The desk is probably of dovetailed board construction, with the joint of the drawer dividers to the sides blind. There are no dustboards, and the drawer runners are nailed to the sides of the case. Drawer guides are used only for the top wide drawer, and these are housed through the backboards. The back consists of three vertical boards joined with a half lap and nailed to the bottom; the floor of the desk is dovetailed to the sides and is nailed through the back. Butterfly cleats are used to join the two boards used to form the sides of the bookcase and the desk; these may be original. The base framework consists of strips nailed to the front and sides of the underside of the bottom, with large vertical shaped blocks in the corners and shaped horizontal blocks behind the brackets; the rear of the framework consists of a single shaped board rabbeted around the strips and dovetailed to the rear side brackets. (This form of construction is also seen on the East Granby chest-on-chest, cat. 86.) On the desk drawers, the sides are dovetailed to the front and back, with the top edge of the sides rounded and the top edge of the backs chamfered. The bottoms are beveled on their front and side edges, let into grooves in the front and sides, and nailed to the underside of the back. The desk interior drawers are fashioned in the same manner.

Inscriptions: The desk interior drawers are labeled in white chalk with locations on the inside of the back and were numbered later in pencil, along with the drawer compartments. "LOVE / ANITA / '61'" and "1960" are written in ink on the underside of the bottom of the middle drawer on the left side of the desk interior.

178

178a

base molding at the front and sides the desk is supported by bracket feet with scrolled knee brackets. The top and bottom of the bookcase are dovetailed to the sides; the three horizontal backboards are joined with a half lap and nailed to rabbets in the top and sides and to the bottom. The vertical partition in the bookcase section is nailed in place through the top and back and pegged through the front. The pediment is supported at each side by two shaped transverse brackets nailed to the top. The joints of the doors are double pegged, and the rails and stiles are molded on their panel edges. Each side of the bookcase is fitted with three shelves housed in grooves in the sides and in the vertical partition.

Desk and Bookcases

Condition: The upper portion of the finial has been replaced, and the brasses and hinges for the slant front are replacements. A brace was once added to join the upper and lower cases at the rear, because the shallow bookcase has an alarming tendency to fall forward when the bookcase doors are opened. The drawer runners within the desk are replacements, and the bottom edges of some drawer sides have been pieced. The vertical blocks on the left front and rear feet are replacements.

Woods: American black cherry, including bookshelves and lopers; eastern white pine.

Dimensions: H 229.6; W 106.1; UCW 93.5; LCW 97.4; D (closed) 52.5; D (open) 83.9; UCD 21.6; LCD 47.7.

Exhibition: *Three Centuries of Conn. Furn.*, no. 231.

Provenance: William Tynan, Middletown, Conn.; by sale in 1928 to Francis P. Garvan, New York, N. Y.

ALTHOUGH simpler than most published examples, this workmanlike desk and bookcase is undoubtedly of Connecticut origin. Its Colchester-type foot and distinctive scrolled-cornice terminating in rosettes with pinwheels suggest that it shares an affinity with other, more elaborate examples from New London County.[1] The shaping of the panels of the bookcase doors to conform to the pediment is a refinement not generally encountered.[2] The bookcase section here is unusually shallow and hence somewhat precariously balanced.

The Mabel Brady Garvan Collection 1930.2276

1. Mayhew and Myers, no. 39; Fales, *Deerfield*, fig. 478.
2. It is seen on the Deerfield example cited above and on a desk and bookcase illustrated in Nutting, *Treasury*, no. 691, which is similar to the Yale example in other respects.

179

179

Desk and bookcase
Connecticut, possibly New London County, 1760–1790

Description: The desk and bookcase is fashioned in three units: an upper case, a lower case, and a separate frame. The upper case, or bookcase, is crowned by a broken-scroll pediment containing a dentil course and a cove molding at the front and sides. The scrolls flank a central urn-and-flame finial mounted above a carved rosette; the sides of the pediment hold unusual ball and ring-turned finials mounted on small, square plinths. The bookcase contains a pair of arched doors, each framed to six fielded panels. The front corners of the bookcase hold three-quarter fluted columns, and the upper case rests within a molding applied to the top of the lower case, or desk. Below the slant front, the desk contains four graduated lipped drawers; the highest drawer is flanked by lopers. The front corners of the desk contain

spiral-turned, fluted engaged columns, bordered by cock beading on their inner edges. The desk rests within a molding applied to the top of the frame. The front skirt of the frame is shaped to six flathead arches; the side skirts are arcaded with three similar arches. The frame is supported by four short cabriole legs terminating in squarish claw-and-ball feet. The desk interior contains a central section with a double-valance drawer, above a pair of pigeonholes, above a deep drawer carved with a round shell, flanked by simulated document drawers faced with unusual applied columns or balusters. This entire center section can be removed to provide access to a secret compartment running the width of the case at the level of the lopers. (To reach this secret compartment, the double-valance drawer and the partition between the pigeonholes, a loose board housed in a groove, are first removed. Then, a short, thin object, such as a nail, can be inserted through a hole in the dustboard below the double-valance drawer, and through a hole in the top of the compartment, to release a metal spring lock. When released, the entire center compartment can be drawn forward. It contains on each side of the rear a pair of simple, superimposed secret drawers with gouged grips. With the center compartment removed, a blind lid or cover at the rear of the interior can be removed, providing access to the longitudinal compartment holding two secret drawers or boxes with leather pulls.) Each side of the desk interior holds four pigeonholes with fixed valances above a wide drawer that in turn is above a pair of drawers in line. The pediment scrolls are roofed with transverse boards, and the arched opening is enclosed at the back of the case by an extension of the upper backboard and is partially roofed. There are transverse walls flanking the arched opening. The bookcase doors are housed in the three-quarter columns, which in turn are pintle hinged in an unusual manner to the case. The joints of the door frames are secured with two pegs, and the doors open to a plain interior with two adjustable shelves that can be housed in the three pairs of grooves in the case sides. The front edge of the shelves is beaded. The edges of the bookcase door panels are decorated with applied moldings. The horizontal backboards of the upper case are nailed to rabbets in the case sides and bottom. The sides of the upper case are dovetailed to the bottom; the pins on the side dovetails extend below the bottom and are housed in dovetail-shaped mortises in the top of the lower case. The desk is of dovetailed board construction, and the horizontal backboards are joined with a half lap and secured with rosehead nails. The lopers are enclosed by a transverse partition on their inner sides, so as to seal and protect fully the secret compartment at the rear of the case that houses the secret drawers. The frame is joined with mortise-and-tenon joints secured with two pegs. Supporting strips are nailed to the front and sides of the frame. On the interior drawers and the desk drawers, the sides are dovetailed to the front and back; the bottoms are beveled on their front and side edges, let into grooves in the front and sides, and nailed to the underside of the back.

Inscriptions: "Monday / Jan 1825" is written in black ink on the inside of the right side of the bookcase. "Clark" and many illegible words and numbers are written in white chalk on the inside of the back of the bookcase. There are chalk shop marks on the drawers and case and illegible writing in pencil on the inside of the bottom of the double-valance drawer in the desk interior. There are figures in pencil on the underside of the bottom of the lowest case drawer. The numbers "65"

179a

Desk and Bookcases

and "601" and illegible writing in pencil appear on the top of the top of the desk. A "Connecticut Furniture" (1967) exhibition label is pasted to the inside of the right side of the top wide drawer in the case.

Condition: The brasses are replacements. The frame has been repaired at the left rear corner, once with metal strips, and new blocks have been added to the corners of the frame. The drawer runners have been replaced.

Woods: American black cherry; yellow poplar; eastern white pine.

Dimensions: H 229.9; W 102.9; UCW 88.3; LCW 92.7; W (frame) 97.2; D (closed) 54.5; D (open) 76.3; UCD 30.1; LCD 45.9; D (frame) 48.8.

Exhibition: Kirk, *Conn. Furn.*, no. 126.

Bibliography: Nutting, *Treasury*, no. 709; "Living with Antiques: The Connecticut Home of Mr. and Mrs. C. Sanford Bull," *Antiques* 45, no. 4 (April 1944): 191.

Provenance: Acquired before 1928 by C. Sanford Bull, Middlebury, Conn.

THE Connecticut features of this desk and bookcase have been discussed at length by John T. Kirk, who suggested that it may have been made in New London County. The most unusual aspects of its construction, almost certainly denoting a rural origin, are the use of the columns in the upper case as hinges for the bookcase doors and the method of additionally securing the bookcase to the desk by extensions of the case-side dovetails. The paneled doors of the bookcase are another unusual feature of this distinctive object. The name "Clark," recently discovered on the bookcase interior, may yet help to establish a precise origin for this object, which entered the Yale collection without an early provenance. The system of secret compartments and drawers in this example, requiring five separate steps to reach them, is perhaps the most complex such system found on a desk in the Yale collection.

Gift of C. Sanford Bull 1949.243

180

Desk with later bookcase
Desk attributed to Isaac Fitch (1734–1791)
Lebanon, Connecticut, ca. 1769 and later

Description: This object in its present form consists of a desk of ca. 1769 to which a bookcase section was added at some later date. Below the fall front, the desk contains four graduated blockfront drawers, with the blocking on the top drawer rounded. The blocking of the drawers is carried through base molding and bracket feet. The cleated lid is supported by lopers and opens to an elaborate interior. The center section contains a prospect door with concave blocking and a carved shell at the top. The door is flanked by document drawers faced with colonnettes with vase-shaped finials and opens to an interior with a pigeonhole with a vallance drawer shaped with scrolls above a drawer with concave blocking. The center section is flanked on each side by a pair of pigeonholes in line with fixed valances shaped to pointed arches above a single drawer with convex blocking. The sides of the interior contain a tier of three drawers with concave blocking, with the upper drawer carved with a shell to match the prospect door. The platform for the fittings is molded on its front edge and is shaped in conformity with the drawer fronts. The elements of the interior are decorated with half-round molding, and the edges of the shaped partitions between the pigeonholes are rounded. The desk is of dovetailed board construction, with blind dovetails used to join the top to the sides. The three horizontal backboards are joined with a half lap and nailed to rabbets in the top and sides and to the bottom. The bracket feet, including shaped brackets at the rear, are nailed to the base moldings and bottom, and there are vertical blocks in the corners. On each of the desk drawers, the sides are dovetailed to the front and back; the bottoms are nailed to a rabbet in the front and sides, with running strips applied, and nailed to the underside of the back, with the top edge of the sides rounded. The drawers in the desk interior are fashioned in the same way. The drawer runners within the case are nailed to the sides. The bookcase section has a cornice and base molding, and it rests directly on the top of the desk. It is of dovetailed board construction, with three horizontal backboards butted together, fitted to grooves in the sides, and nailed to the top and bottom and to the vertical partitions within the case. Both the side and the recessed center sections have glazed doors that open to an interior with three fixed shelves.

cousin of the 2d. Gov. / Trumbull, at Lebanon Ct. / prior to 1777. — & belonged to 2d. / Gov. Trumbull used by his widow / during her life & then given to her / daughter Harriet Trumbull (/Mrs. Silliman) & at her death / given to her daughter Faith / W. Silliman (Mrs. Hubbard) '49."

Condition: See Description. The date of the added bookcase is problematical. Rosehead nails are used in its construction, and its glass appears to be of an early type, suggesting that it could have been added as early as ca. 1800. The top board of the bookcase is a later addition, and one of the panes of glass is cracked. The top of the desk is scratched considerably by the bookcase. The brasses on the desk are replacements, and some of the runners on the drawers have been replaced. The backboards in each case have been extensively renailed.

Woods: Desk: mahogany; eastern white pine; lowest backboard, chestnut; drawer fronts on desk interior, Spanish cedar (*Cedrela odorata*); bookcase: mahogany; top, bottom, red oak; backboards, shelves, added top, American black cherry.

Dimensions: H 198.1; H (desk) 106.1; W 102.9; CW (desk) 95.6; CW (bookcase) 92.6; D (closed) 55.2; D (open) 85.7; CD (desk) 50.6; CD (bookcase) 26.3.

Exhibition: Mayhew and Myers, no. 60.

Bibliography: William Lamson Warren, "Isaac Fitch Revisited (as Cabinetmaker)," *Connecticut Antiquarian* 31, no. 1 (June 1979): figs. 2A, 2B.

180

Inscriptions: "Isaac" is written vertically in white chalk on the upper rear of the inside of the left side of the desk, hidden by the loper when in the closed position. "F T" is carved on the rear edge of the top of the desk, and "2nd Story Back" is written in white chalk on the outside of the back of the upper backboard of the desk. "OPH / 32" and "OPH / 28" are painted in black on the outside of the back of the desk and bookcase respectively. There are chalk shop marks on the case drawers, and the desk interior drawers were numbered originally, with later pencil numbers also present. A paper label pasted to the inside of the lid has an ink inscription in the handwriting of Faith Wadsworth Silliman Hubbard which reads: "[Th]is Desk was made [by ——] / Elliott,

180a

Desk and Bookcases 349

Provenance: According to tradition, the desk was owned originally by Governor Jonathan Trumbull, Jr. (1740–1809). It is thought that it descended to his wife, Eunice Backus Trumbull (1749–1826), and to have been brought by her to New Haven in 1814 when she came to live with her daughter and son-in-law, Harriet (1783–1850) and Benjamin (1779–1864) Silliman. The desk was inherited by Harriet Silliman in 1826 and then passed on to her daughter Faith Wadsworth Silliman Hubbard (1812–1887), wife of Oliver Payson Hubbard (1809–1900). The desk eventually descended, in 1923 or 1924, to Mrs. Hubbard's niece, Maria Trumbull Dana (1867–1962), who gave it to the Art Gallery in 1955.

ALTHOUGH the family history of this desk states that it was made for Jonathan Trumbull, Jr. (1740–1809), governor of Connecticut, by a J. Elliott, possibly one Jacob Eliot, Mayhew and Myers attributed it to Isaac Fitch on the grounds that while Eliot is not known to have made furniture for Trumbull, Fitch made a desk for him in 1769. (The bookcase, clearly a later addition, may have been made by Eliot, they suggest, and thus be the source of the family tradition.) The attribution of the desk to Fitch is considerably strengthened by the recent discovery of the name "Isaac" written on the left side of the case, presumably before the desk was assembled. The use of imported Spanish cedar, a hardwood from the tropical West Indies, for the drawer fronts of the desk interior lends an even greater air of importance to this mahogany desk made for a Connecticut statesman.

Gift of Maria Trumbull Dana 1955.50.1

181

181

Doctor's cabinet
Connecticut, probably Norwich, 1770–1800

Description: The upper case of this unusual cabinet has a complex molded cornice at the front and sides, including a dentil course, and contains a pair of paneled doors shaped with stepped reverse curves to a rounded arch. The doors open to an interior with two fixed bookshelves. Below the doors are a pair of lipped drawers in line. The upper case rests within a molding on the rear half of the lower case. At the top of the lower case there is a small flap, with scrolled ends decorated with notches and an incised line, hinged to the case. It has a central oval brass lock escutcheon and can be lifted to reveal six small drawers. The remainder of the lower case contains ten drawers, made to appear as three graduated rows of four small lipped drawers in line; the bottom row actually consists of only two drawers in line. The front corners of the case are embellished with fluted chamfered quarter columns. There is base molding at the front and sides, and the cabinet is supported by bracket feet with double cusp knee brackets. The upper case is of dovetailed board construction; the top is joined to the sides with wedged dovetails. The horizontal backboards are beveled on their side edges and let into grooves in the sides. The joints of the upper case doors are double pegged, and the rails and stiles are molded on their panel edges. There is a vertical partition at the front of the interior that is housed through the top and

dovetailed to the floor of the upper case with an exposed dovetail. The floor of the upper case and the board below the drawers are dovetailed to the case sides with exposed dovetails. The shelves are housed in grooves in the case sides and vertical partition; the maker originally cut these grooves in a different location and located the door hinges in a different position. The sides of two drawers in the upper case are dovetailed to the front and back; the bottoms are beveled on their front and side edges, let into grooves in the front and sides, and nailed to the underside of the back. The drawer runners are nailed to the bottom of the case. On the lower case, the horizontal backboards have beveled edges and are fitted to a groove in the sides and top. The board forming the front part of the top of the case is pegged in place; the bottom is dovetailed to the sides. There are full dustboards between the drawers, with drawer guides nailed to them. The shaped rear brackets are housed in grooves in the side brackets. The drawers of the lower case are constructed in the same manner as those in the bookcase.

181a

Inscriptions: "Charles ———" is written in red on the outside of one of the drawers in the lower case. The drawers under the flap are numbered "1" through "6" from left to right respectively; the other drawers in the lower case are numbered, from left to right, "T1" through "T4" on the top row, "M1" through "M4" on the middle row, and "B1" through "B4" on the bottom row (even though there are only two drawers here). A modern label was once pinned to the underside of the bottom of the upper case.

Condition: The second drawer from the left under the flap is a replacement. Some drawer guides have been replaced and nails added to several joints. A strip has been added to the top of the backboards of the upper case, and the blocks on the base are replacements. Some of the scrolls on the feet are replacements. There are inexplicable nail holes on the underside of the top board of the lower case, suggesting it originally was used for another purpose or is a replacement.

Woods: American black cherry; butternut and eastern white pine; replaced drawer under flap, cherry front (other drawers here, butternut fronts), chestnut back, yellow poplar sides.

Dimensions: H 183.5; W 101.1; UCW 89.3; LCW 95.9; D 47.3; UCD 25.9; LCD 46.9.

Exhibition: Mayhew and Myers, no. 57.

Provenance: Francis P. Garvan, New York, N. Y.

CABINETS such as this with many small drawers are generally considered to have been made for the use of a doctor or an apothecary. This example has the important feature of a flap covering six small drawers which can be locked for security. Primarily on the basis of its scrolled feet, this cabinet has been considered to be from New London County. The use of full dustboards and wedged dovetails in at least one instance raise the possibility that it may have been made by a craftsman with a Pennsylvania background, if not in Pennsylvania itself, where such construction techniques were more common.

The Mabel Brady Garvan Collection 1950.784

1. Apothecaries' cabinets of varying form are published in Fales, *Deerfield*, figs. 425, 426; and Greenlaw, no. 78.

Desk and Bookcases 351

182

182

Secretary

Northeastern Massachusetts, 1790–1815

Description: The upper case is crowned by a pediment with urn-shaped finials mounted on reeded plinths at the corners and with a larger urn-shaped finial mounted above a central block flanked by C-scrolls. Below the pediment is cornice molding at the front and sides above a plain veneered entablature with bead molding at the front and sides. The upper case contains two glazed doors, each with mullions arranged to form three panels with rounded arches superimposed above three below. The mullions are decorated with double half-round moldings. The doors open to an interior with two adjustable bookshelves. A horizontal line of triple half-round molding separates the glazed doors from a pair of veneered doors below. These doors have brilliant center panels of bird's-eye maple outlined by light- and dark-wood stringing and surrounded by a mahogany border. They open to an interior containing two wide drawers in line (each simulated to appear as two in line) above four actual drawers in line, all above seven pigeonholes with fixed valances shaped to roundheaded arches. The drawer dividers and the vertical partitions (both real and simulated) are edged with light- and dark-wood stringing, and the vertical partitions between the pigeonholes are shaped. The drawers are fitted with brass button pulls, and each pair of doors in the upper case is fitted with brass keyhole liners. The upper case rests on the rear portion of the lower case within restraining molding. The fall front is veneered with a panel of bird's-eye maple surrounded by cross-banding of a dark, highly figured veneer, probably rosewood. It is supported by lopers fitted with brass ring pulls and edged with cock beading and is hinged to the case. It opens to form a slanting writing surface covered with green baize. The lower case contains three graduated veneered drawers, each with a panel of bird's-eye maple and rosewood cross-banding. The sides of the front are decorated with reeding of an unusual sort; the individual reeds are divided and flanked by channeling. There is

182a

352 *American Case Furniture*

double half-round base molding at the front and sides, and the secretary is supported by four turned and reeded legs. The pediment is applied to the top of the upper case at the front and sides and is secured with multiple horizontal glue blocks. The back of the upper case consists of two vertical panels with beveled edges fitted to grooves in center and side boards, with the whole assembly nailed to rabbets in the top and sides and to the bottom. The floor of the upper case is also nailed in place through the back. The four sides of the upper case extend below the base; blocks affixed to the top of the lower case and to these extensions of the upper case mesh together when the cases are united. The two shelves of the upper case are rectangular boards faced with mahogany; they simply slide into grooves cut in the case sides. There are two sets of three grooves in the sides, allowing for some adjustment. In the drawers in the interior, the sides are dovetailed to the front and back; the bottoms are beveled on their front and side edges, let into grooves in the front and sides, and nailed to the underside of the back. The lower case is framed with mortise-and-tenon joints, with four pegs used to secure the horizontal backboard to the rear legs. The drawer runners are nailed to the sides through the guides, and there are multiple vertical blocks behind each leg. There are no dustboards and no bottom to the lower case. The wide case drawers are fashioned in the same manner as those in the interior of the upper case, although here small blocks are glued to the sides and running strips have been applied. Small horizontal blocks are also glued to the outside of the back to serve as stops. Each drawer has a central brass keyhole liner flanked by round brass pulls.

Inscriptions: There are large inscriptions in black paint on the outside of the back of the upper and lower case that read, respectively, "Bookcase / B R Nº 4" and "Secretaria & Bookcase / B R Nº 6." The interior drawers in the upper case and the drawer dividers are numbered in pencil; "246" is written on the inside of the right veneered door in the upper case.

Condition: A pattern of nail holes on the top and bottom of the inside of the glazed doors suggests that they were fitted with curtains at one time. Fragments of green cloth remain beneath some nails on the left door. Old blue baize and a leather border were removed from the writing surface in 1975 and the present green baize installed. The right edge of the right glazed door has been pieced, and there have been repairs to the mullions. At least some of the pulls on the interior drawers in the upper case are replacements. The backboards of the upper case have been extensively damaged by insects. The running strips on the case drawers are replacements or possibly additions. There have been minor repairs to the moldings and veneers.

Woods: Mahogany, mahogany veneer, maple veneer with bird's-eye grain, probably rosewood veneer; eastern white pine.

Dimensions: H 230.4; W 102.0; UCW 98.2; LCW 101.3; D (closed) 51.5; D (open) 73.0; UCD 28.1; LCD 50.8.

Provenance: Mrs. Clark McIlwaine, West Hartford, Conn., and Washington, D.C.

KNOWN in their own day as a lady's secretary and bookcase or a lady's desk and bookcase, among other terms, this secretary and the following example (cat. 183) are typical in many respects of this popular Massachusetts form.[1] This example makes effective use of beautiful bird's-eye maple veneer on its drawer and door fronts, providing a sharp color contrast to the darker mahogany. This use of bird's-eye maple combined with the vertical proportions of this secretary can be found on other examples of the period, which have been attributed to the Boston and Salem areas.[2]

Gift of Mrs. Clark McIlwaine in memory of her mother, Margaret Tyler Clark 1946.4

1. Montgomery, nos. 186, 189, 190.
2. Stoneman, *Seymour*, nos. 53, 54, 55; Stoneman, *Supplement*, no. 14; see also Stoneman, *Seymour*, no. 52.

183

Secretary
Northeastern Massachusetts, 1790–1815

Description: The pediment is decorated with urn-shaped finials mounted on plinths reeded at their front and outer sides and flanked by C-scrolls at their front and sides. A slightly larger finial is mounted above a central veneered plaque again flanked by C-scrolls. There is cove and bead cornice molding at the front and sides above a veneered entablature with molding at the front and sides. The upper case contains two glazed doors, each with mullions arranged to form pairs of Gothic arches and decorated with a double half-round molding. They open to a bookcase section fitted with two adjustable shelves. Below the glazed doors are

decorated with two panels of bifurcated crotch veneer. The sides of the front are decorated with panels formed by applied moldings. The drawer dividers and the vertical partitions are veneered with mahogany cross-banding. There is double half-round base molding at the front and sides, and the secretary is supported by four turned legs. The pediment consists of a separate dovetailed frame, with the moldings applied and the raised moldings reinforced with glue blocks. The pediment frame rests on top of the upper case, fitting over a series of glue blocks on each side. The top and bottom of the upper case are dovetailed to the sides. The vertical backboards consist of two panels housed in grooves in a center and side boards, with the whole assembly nailed to the top and bottom and to rabbets in the sides. The floor of the upper case is also nailed in place through the back. There are two sets of three grooves for the adjustable shelves, which are pine boards faced with mahogany on their front edges. The interior compartments of the upper case have been stained red. The upper case rests on transverse cleats and longitudinal glue blocks applied to the top of the lower case, and it has been screwed to the lower case. The lower case is probably framed with mortise-and-tenon joints, although no pins are used. There is a transverse partition nailed to the underside of the top, and blocks are glued to the underside of the top along the rear edge. There are multiple vertical blocks behind the legs; the drawer runners are applied at the sides, and the guides stand above them. There are no dustboards, but there is a bottom nailed to rabbets in the sides and butted to a deep bottom front rail.

183

three doors in line, with the outer doors of greater width, each with a central panel of figured veneer outlined by borders of mahogany veneer. The side doors enclose two superimposed drawers over three pigeonholes in line with fixed valances shaped to rounded arches. The center door encloses a single drawer above a plain open compartment. The doors in the upper case are fitted with brass keyhole liners and the drawers with brass ring pulls. The upper case rests on the rear portion of the lower case within restraining molding. The fall front is supported by lopers outlined with cock beading, and it opens to form a sloping writing surface covered with green baize. The lower case contains three graduated veneered drawers with cock-beaded edges, each

183a

354 American Case Furniture

There are small strips of mahogany applied to each side of the upper edge of the drawer dividers. On each of the small drawers in the upper case, the sides are dovetailed to the front and back, and the bottoms are beveled on their front and side edges and glued to the underside of the back. The wide drawers in the case are fashioned in a similar manner, with the exception that the front edges are only slightly beveled and the bottoms are nailed to the underside of the back.

Inscriptions: The interior drawers and drawer dividers are numbered in pencil.

Condition: The brasses and the baize on the writing surface are replacements. One glue block is missing from the top of the upper case. The tops of the finials appear to have been broken and repaired. There are minor repairs to the moldings and veneer.

Woods: Mahogany, mahogany veneers; eastern white pine.

Dimensions: H 222.3; W 102.8; UCW 98.5; LCW 101.9; D (closed) 50.2; D (open) 70.1; UCD 27.9; LCD 49.9.

Bibliography: *Flayderman Coll.*, no. 184.

Provenance: Philip Flayderman, Boston, Mass.; acquired at auction in 1930 by Francis P. Garvan, New York, N. Y.

ANOTHER characteristic Massachusetts secretary, this example has striking veneers of swirling crotch mahogany providing great visual interest. Here, there are three doors in the lower part of the upper case, and the glazed doors have pointed rather than rounded arches. The small C-scrolls flanking the central plinth are repeated here on the side plinths.

The Mabel Brady Garvan Collection 1930.2315

184

Gentleman's secretary
Salem, Massachusetts, 1790–1815

Description: The upper case consists of a bookcase with a central projecting section with two glazed doors flanked by side units, each with a single glazed door. The upper case is crowned with a pediment containing brass ball finials mounted on reeded plinths, with a center finial mounted

184

above a plaque with a central panel of burl veneer outlined by dark- and light-wood stringing, cross-banding, and patterned inlay. The horizontal element of the plinth is shaped between the finials, and the pediment continues on the sides of the case to rear plinths with finials. There is a complex cornice molding at the front and sides, with a bead molding at the front and sides above the glazed doors. The mullions of the glazed doors are shaped to form tall Gothic arches with capitals and bases, and the vertical mullions are decorated with quadruple half-round molding and the horizontal mullions with double half-round molding. The tall arched panels stand above a pair of clear square panels, in turn above a pair of square panels decorated with reverse paintings on glass, arranged from left to right in an A-B-C-D-D-C-B-A pattern. The vertical columns are supported on projecting bases faced with burl veneer and outlined by light- and dark-wood stringing, while beneath the glazed panels are panels

Desk and Bookcases 355

184a

of burl veneer outlined by dark- and light-wood stringing and cross-banding. Each door in the upper case is fitted with a brass keyhole liner, and each section contains three adjustable shelves. The upper case rests within restraining molding on the rear portion of the lower case. The lower case contains a projecting center section of two superimposed veneered drawers with cock-beaded edges flanked by side compartments, each with a veneered cock-beaded drawer above a cupboard with a veneered cock-beaded door. The front and side edges of the top of the lower case are decorated with patterned inlay, and each drawer and cupboard door is bordered with light-wood stringing and cross-banding. The fronts of each leg have inlaid rectangles of light-wood stringing, round at the top and hollow at the bottom. The top drawer in the middle section is a secretary drawer with a fall front with quadrant stay hinges, and an interior with a baize-lined writing surface and two drawers in line over six pigeonholes with fixed valances shaped to flathead arches. The base

of the center section is shaped to a high rounded arch, and the lower edge of the lower case is decorated at the front and sides with the same patterned inlay used above, laid in an opposite direction. The secretary is supported by six turned legs ending in brass wheeled cup casters. The upper case is a single unit, probably of dovetailed board construction, with the pediment an integral part. The back is framed to four large vertical panels and nailed in place. Within each upper-case section, there are twelve sets of grooves for the shelves, which are pine boards faced on their front edges with mahogany. The upper case rests on top of small blocks applied to the top of the lower case. The top of the lower case is a tongue-and-groove frame pocket screwed through the back. The drawers in the side sections have dustboards underneath, and the cupboards contain a single fixed shelf supported by glue blocks. The center drawers are supported by side drawers and guides, and there is no bottom to the center section. Bottoms for the cupboard sections are supported by

356 *American Case Furniture*

glue blocks. The horizontal backboards are shaped at the rear to conform to the arched front. There are multiple horizontal and vertical blocks on the lower frame. On each case drawer and interior drawer, the sides are dovetailed to the front and back; the bottoms are beveled on the front and sides, let into grooves in the front and sides, and nailed to the underside of the back.

Inscriptions: There are shop marks and numbers in the lower case. There is an illegible chalk inscription on the underside of the top of the lower case. The upper case doors have been marked in modern times.

Condition: The brasses are replacements, and at least several of the finials are also replacements. The far right painted panel was broken in 1949 while the secretary was on intra-university loan, and it was replaced based on photographs and surviving fragments, which have been retained. There have been many losses and repairs to the inlays and veneers. The right rear leg was replaced in 1962, and other legs have been repaired. Several of the many blocks in the lower case have been replaced, and some of the drawer runners are also replacements. Pieces of wallpaper are pasted to the outside of the rear of the pediment.

Woods: Mahogany, mahogany veneer, a burl veneer, light- and dark-wood inlays; eastern white pine; some drawer runners, replaced, yellow poplar.

Dimensions: H 229.3; W 169.4; UCW 165.8; LCW 167.3; D 50.7; UCD (side section) 30.9; UCD (center section) 35.9.

Exhibition: "Exhibition of Georgian Art," *Pennsylvania Museum Bulletin* 26, no. 138 (January 1931): 10.

Provenance: Ipswich Historical Society, Ipswich, Mass.; by sale to Francis P. Garvan, New York, N.Y.

More than a dozen "gentleman's secretaries" of this type have been published, including documented examples by Nehemiah Adams (1769–1840) and Edmund Johnson (active ca. 1793–1811) of Salem.[1] The form is known today as a "Salem secretary," although it undoubtedly was made in other parts of Massachusetts and New England. The Yale example is distinguished by several features, including its lack of the undulating cornice found on most examples, its bookcase doors framed to pointed arches by mullions with capitals and projecting veneered bases, and its eglomise panels. Only one of the published examples seems to be directly related to the Yale example, lacking only the eglomise paintings.[2] Similar muntins are found on smaller secretaries that may be related to these two gentleman's secretaries.[3] Sheraton noted that the gentleman's secretary "is intended for standing to write at," and in his design, "the door on the right incloses a cupboard for a pot and slippers, and the left side contains a place for day book, ledger, and journal, for a gentleman's own accounts."[4] The library bookcase form also was made in the Salem area, although extant examples are not as numerous.[5]

The Mabel Brady Garvan Collection 1930.2016

1. For a discussion of the form, see Fiske Kimball, "Salem Secretaries and Their Makers," *Antiques* 23, no. 5 (May 1933): 168–170; Montgomery, nos. 179–182; Randall, no. 67; Warren, *Bayou Bend*, no. 167.
2. *Antiques* 106, no. 4 (October 1974): 503. Eglomise panels of a quite different character can be found on an example at Winterthur (Montgomery, no. 182).
3. *Sack Coll.*, 6:47 no. P4640, 5:1337 no. P4375; Stoneman, *Seymour*, no. 51.
4. *Cabinet Dictionary*, 2:303.
5. Fitzgerald, fig. V-6.

185

Writing table and bookcase
New York, New York, 1800–1820

Description: The upper case has a shallow cove molding and a bead at the top at the front and sides, and its fall front is locked at the center of the top and hinged and tenoned to the case at the bottom. It is framed with two panels, veneered with mahogany and bordered with cross-banding to create the appearance of two arched panels. The panel edges of the rails, stiles, and muntin of the fall front are molded, and there is a vertical line of cross-banding in the center of the muntin. There are horizontal lines of cross-banding above and below the fall front on the case; the upper line is continued around the sides. The writing surface of the fall front is covered with a large rectangle of blue baize outlined with a Greek-key border. The fall rests on top of the lower case, creating a sloping surface, and opens to an interior with pigeonholes, ledger compartments, and drawers. There is an upper row of six plain pigeonholes at the top, with three plain pigeonholes flanking a center section for ledgers with six adjustable vertical partitions shaped and fitted to V-shaped grooves. Below the pigeonholes and ledger compartment are three drawers in line, with the center drawer of

greater width, above two small drawers flanking an open center compartment. The drawers are fitted with brass button pulls stamped with lion masks, the vertical and horizontal partitions are decorated with half-round molding, and the adjustable ledger dividers have rounded edges. The upper case rests on top of the rear portion of the lower case. The lower case contains a pair of veneered cock-beaded drawers in line, each with a central brass keyhole liner. The front edge of the top of the lower case is rounded, and the lower edge of the front of the case is edged with crossbanding. The top of each of the four turned legs is veneered with a panel of flame veneer; the legs are reeded and terminate in bulbous feet with brass casters. The cornice of the upper case, or bookcase, is a joined framework attached to the top with glue blocks that have also been screwed in place. The horizontal backboards are nailed to a rabbet in the top and sides and to the bottom. The sides and front project beneath the bottom, and the horizontal partitions within the bookcase are nailed through the back. Rabbeted cleats screwed to the underside of the bottom slide over similar rabbeted cleats screwed to the top of the lower case. The top of the lower case consists of a central board joined with a tongue and groove to strips at the front and sides, and the top is pocket screwed from underneath to the frame. The lower case is probably joined with mortise-and-tenon joints. The side drawer runners are nailed through guides to the sides, and there are vertical blocks in the corners. There is a central transverse brace on the underside of the top, and the runner for the drawers is dovetailed to the bottom front rail and to the back. In the upper case, the drawer sides are dovetailed to the front and back; the bottoms are half lapped to the front and sides and nailed to the underside of the back. The upper left drawer is divided by partitions into smaller compartments, and the interior of each drawer is stained red. The sides of the drawers in the lower case are dovetailed to the front and back; the bottoms are beveled on their front and side edges and are let into grooves in the front and sides and nailed to the underside of the back, with small blocks glued to the sides of the bottom.

Condition: The pull on one of the drawers in the upper case is a replacement, and the keyhole liner for the fall front is missing. There have been many minor repairs to the veneer and cross-banding, and the upper right corner of the cornice molding has been repaired. The fall front shows signs of having been dropped, and the top of the lower case is heavily scratched from having the upper case brought forward to be separated. There is a fragment of wallpaper pasted to the outside of the back of the upper case.

185

Woods: Mahogany, mahogany veneer; sides and backs of small drawers in upper case, mahogany; drawer bottoms in upper case drawers, drawer sides, bottoms, backs in lower case, backboards, other elements, yellow poplar; drawer fronts in lower case, other elements, eastern white pine; transverse brace, lower case, American black cherry.

Dimensions: H 158.8; W 80.2; UCW 78.5; LCW 78.8; D (closed) 66.5; D (open) 101.8; UCD 30.2; LCD 63.3.

Provenance: The early history of the writing table and bookcase was unknown when it was transferred from Silliman College at Yale to the Art Gallery in 1970. A fragment of a receipt dated 1901 recently was found wedged behind the pigeonholes in the upper case, and it may provide a clue to the early if not original owners. The bill is made out

358 *American Case Furniture*

185a

published.³ Later versions of this form are referred to occasionally as "plantation desks."⁴

Yale University Art Gallery 1970.98.4

1. See the New York price books for 1802, 1811, and 1817; Hewitt, pp. 156–157.
2. Hewitt, no. 43.
3. McClelland, fig. 167.
4. Fairbanks and Bates, p. 331.

186

Library bookcase
New York, New York, 1790–1815

Description: In five units, this large library bookcase has a separate pediment which overhangs the case at the front and sides and projects in the center in conformity with the cases below. The bookcase consists of three separate units: a central, projecting case with paired glazed doors flanked by smaller cases with a single glazed door, all with the mullions forming a rectangular pattern terminating at the top in pointed arches. In the lower case, a single unit, the center section contains a deep secretary drawer at the top above three graduated drawers, all with cock-beaded edges and

on the letterhead of Louis J. Goodman, "Dealer in Wood, Coal, Hay, Straw, Fertilizer, Farming Implements, & Champion W[agons?]," in Litchfield, Conn., and it is addressed to a Mrs. M. D. F. McLaughlin. From this slim evidence, one might surmise that it was owned at an early date by Mrs. McLaughlin.

A NEW YORK origin for this desk is strongly suggested on several grounds. The form, a writing table and bookcase, is described in detail in the New York price books of the early nineteenth century, and the shape of the turned legs is characteristic of the turnings found on New York card tables of the 1790–1820 period.¹ Those on this example are quite close to those on a card table with the label of John T. Dolan of New York, which also has the same style of brass casters.² A related example attributed to Duncan Phyfe has been

186a

Desk and Bookcases 359

186

with a central brass keyhole liner flanked by round brass pulls decorated with rosettes. The secretary drawer is veneered with a panel of figured mahogany with hollow corners, bordered by cross-banding. The front of the secretary drawer falls forward and is supported by quadrant stay hinges to form a flat writing surface covered with green baize. The drawer interior contains a central drawer that opens to a plain compartment. The door is flanked on each side by two wide horizontal compartments, which originally housed drawers, above a row of five pigeonholes, in turn above wide open compartments that meet below the door and are flanked by small drawers at the sides. Each side of the lower case contains a cupboard enclosed by a door with a panel of figured mahogany surrounded by cock beading. The doors are fitted with a brass keyhole liner and open to an interior fitted with eleven pairs of grooves for adjustable shelves. The front edge of the top of the lower case is molded, and the case is supported by a straight base below base molding at the front and sides. The cornice is a simple dovetailed open frame, with three evenly spaced transverse braces tenoned through the back rail, and it rests on top of the three bookcase units. The bookcases are screwed to each other through the sides and to the lower case through their bottoms and rest on the lower portion of the top of the lower case. The backs of the side bookcases are framed to a single panel, and that of the center unit to two vertical panels. The sides of each bookcase are grooved with seventeen pairs of grooves for shelves. The vertical backboards of the lower case are joined with a tongue and groove. The sides of the three lower drawers are dovetailed to the front and back; the bottoms are beveled on their front and side edges, fitted to grooves in the front and sides, and nailed to the underside of the back, with running strips applied. The drawer beneath the secretary drawer and the next lower drawer were fitted with two transverse partitions. The secretary drawer is of dovetailed construction and is held in the case by wooden spring locks. There are no dustboards between the case drawers.

Inscriptions: There are four circular printed labels pasted to the object, each with an open space in the middle containing an ink notation, and printed with "W. & J. Sloane / FLOOR / COVERINGS / FURNITURE / Fifth Avenue & 47th St. / New York." Two of these labels are pasted to the outside of the back on the left side; the upper one has "M 249/S" and the lower one "M 245/ W. SR." A label pasted to the outside of the back on the right side is annotated "M 249/S." There is a fragment of the label pasted to the secretary drawer. Written in pencil on the top of the top of the lower case and on the outside of the back of the upper case in the center is "33–770"; "33" is written on the upper right corner of the outside of the back of the upper case.

Condition: The two small drawers in the secretary drawer are replacements, while two wide drawers are missing. The baize has been renewed. The shelves for the side compartments in the lower case are missing, and the bookshelves in the upper case are replacements. The drawer runners in the lower case are replacements, and the partitions in two case drawers are missing.

Woods: Mahogany, mahogany veneer; drawer fronts, other elements, eastern white pine; drawer linings, other elements, yellow poplar; replaced drawers, mahogany; replaced bookshelves, rosewood.

Dimensions: H 239.3; W 247.6; UCW 241.6; LCW 244.5; D 57.2; UCD (sides) 31.7; LCD (sides) 49.5.

Provenance: Purchased, probably from W. & J. Sloane, New York, N. Y., by Francis P. Garvan, New York, N. Y.

IN his commentary on a much more elaborate example of this form in the Winterthur collection, dated 1796, Charles F. Montgomery quoted the relevant entry in *The Journeymen Cabinet and Chair Makers' New-York Book of Prices* for that year

that aptly describes a large, expensive "Library Book-case with wings" and a secretary drawer. The specifications described "flat pannel'd doors to the upper and lower part... the lower part made in one carcase, three clothes press shelves in the center, and one book-shelf in each wing; the upper part made in three carcases, with 9 bookshelves in ditto, framed backs, loose cornice and fast plinth, all solid."[1] Like the Winterthur example, this bookcase has the more expensive glazed doors in the upper case and is fitted with the additional option of a secretary drawer.

The Mabel Brady Garvan Collection 1930.2093

1. Montgomery, no. 183.

187

Library bookcase
Philadelphia, Pennsylvania, 1800–1810

Description: The library bookcase is fashioned in three units: an upper bookcase, a lower case containing drawers and cupboards, and a separate framed pediment. The center section of the pediment is shaped to a pointed arch rising to a center urn-shaped finial. This center section is inlaid with what may be a covered urn, from which scrolls of light-wood stringing flow to each side. The cover of the urn may be a

187

187a

liberty cap; the urn holds fifteen ornaments that may represent stars; and the body of the urn is inlaid with fifteen alternating light- and dark-wood strips. The center section is flanked by finials mounted above plinths inlaid with panels containing a tall stalk emerging from an urn and is bordered by cross-banding and stringing. These plinths are flanked in turn by shaping leading to small plinths and finials of related design at the front corners of the pediment. The cornice moldings include a dentil course and cove and bead molding at the front and sides of the case. The upper case contains three vertical bookcase sections, each fitted with adjustable shelves. The center section is of greater width and projects slightly. Each section is fitted with a glazed door with mullions arranged in a pattern of interlaced scrolls above a series of rounded arches. The bookcase sections are separated by inlaid pilasters bordered with light-wood stringing. The four flutes of each pilaster are rounded on their upper ends, hollow on their lower ends. There is a line of patterned inlay

Desk and Bookcases 361

187b

below the flutes, and the base of each pilaster is an applied, pointed plaque. The upper case rests within a molding applied to the top of the lower case. The lower case is also divided into three vertical units. The center section is again of greater width and projects slightly; it also is wider than the center section of the upper case. It contains a single wide secretary drawer above a pair of paneled doors; each side section contains a single drawer above a single paneled door. There is bead molding applied to the front and sides of the case between the drawers and the doors. The drawers are bordered with light-wood stringing and light cross-banding, with inlaid quarter fans at the corners. The cupboard doors are similarly decorated. Each drawer contains a central brass keyhole liner; the secretary drawer is fitted with two and the side drawers with one round stamped brass escutcheon with bail pull. The cupboard doors are fitted with brass keyhole liners. There is molding at the front and sides below the cupboard doors, and the case is supported by a plinth base. The front of the secretary drawer is attached to the drawer with quadrant stay hinges. It opens to reveal an interior containing a central section of a wide drawer over four pigeonholes with fixed shaped valances, flanked by four superimposed drawers. The wide drawer is fitted with two and each of the smaller side drawers with one brass stirrup pull. The pediment is a separate dovetailed frame that rests on top of the upper case. The back of the upper case is framed to three pairs of superimposed panels, with the center panels of greater width, and the back of the lower case is framed to four vertical panels. The bookcases are fitted with fifteen pairs of grooves for shelves. The secretary drawer is fitted with quadrant stay hinges. The sides of its small drawers are dovetailed to the front and back; the bottoms are let into grooves in the front and sides and nailed to the underside of the back. On the large drawers on each side of the secretary

362 *American Case Furniture*

drawer, all mahogany, the sides are very finely dovetailed to the front and back; the bottoms are let into grooves in the front and sides and nailed to the underside of the back, with running strips and small blocks applied. There are three-quarter dustboards below the drawers. The large drawer to the left is divided by partitions into nine compartments. The lower center cupboard holds one loose shelf, fitted to one of three pairs of grooves.

Condition: There have been minor repairs to the veneers, inlays, and moldings and to the base of the lower case. A line of patterned inlay appears to be missing at the base of the pilasters on the bookcase. Nail holes on the inside of the bookcase doors suggest that they were once backed with cloth curtains. The stops on the secretary drawer are missing.

Woods: Mahogany, mahogany veneer, with light- and dark-wood inlays; light-wood inlays may be maple; drawer linings of large drawers, mahogany; eastern white pine.

Dimensions: H 283.8; W 186.1; UCW 179.6; LCW 183.2; D 58.1; UCD 31.0; LCD 51.6.

Exhibitions: *Girl Scouts Exhibition*, no. 723; *Charles Carroll of Carrollton (1737–1832) and His Family: An Exhibition of Portraits, Furniture, Silver, and Manuscripts at the Baltimore Museum of Art, September 19–October 30, 1937* (Baltimore: United States Commission for the Celebration of the Two Hundredth Anniversary of the Birth of Charles Carroll of Carrollton, 1937), p. 130; PMA, *Three Centuries*, no. 165.

Bibliography: *Illustrated Catalogue of . . . Early American and English Furniture . . . Formed . . . by . . . Mr. Louis Guerineau Myers of New York* (New York: American Art Association, 1921), no. 652; Rogers, "Garvan Coll. (1962)," p. 15.

Provenance: According to a tradition, this bookcase and its mate were owned originally by Thomas Willing (1731–1821) of Philadelphia, first president of the Bank of the United States. Research by Beatrice Garvan of the Philadelphia Museum of Art determined that the original owner was Thomas Willing's son, Richard Willing (1775–1858), also of Philadelphia, and that the bookcases then descended to Edward Shipping Willing (1810–1906) and then to J. Rhea Barton Willing (d. 1913). They were acquired "at the sale of the effects of the late Barton Willing" by collector Louis Guerineau Myers, New York, N. Y., and then they were acquired at the Myers sale of 1921 by Francis P. Garvan, New York, N. Y. In 1962, one of the pair, identical except for its lack of a secretary drawer, was given to the White House by Yale Corporation as a contribution toward Jacqueline Kennedy's redecorating of the presidential residence. It was given in memory of Francis P. Garvan, "honoring his long and active appreciation of early American arts and his generosity to the university."

This bookcase and its mate were used in the chamber of Richard Willing at the time of his death in 1858. By then unfashionable, the bookcases were valued at $30, while the books in them were appraised at three times that amount. A smaller bookcase in the Philadelphia Museum of Art appears to be by the same shop, and an even larger, three-unit library bookcase that appears to be related has been published.[1] One of Hepplewhite's designs for a "library case" (pl. 45) illustrates a glazing pattern of arches and shields that may have provided the inspiration for the arrangement of mullions in these examples. Another large Philadelphia library bookcase of varying style and with restored doors (Metropolitan Museum of Art, 67.203) was made for Maskell Ewing, Jr. (1758–1825).[2]

The Mabel Brady Garvan Collection 1930.2346

1. PMA, *Three Centuries*, no. 165, is an excellent and detailed entry on the Yale example by Beatrice B. Garvan; see also Hornor, pl. 400.
2. Marshall B. Davidson, *The American Wing: A Guide* (New York: Metropolitan Museum of Art, 1980), fig. 100.

188

Library bookcase
Charleston, South Carolina, 1790–1815

Description: This large library bookcase is made in nine units. The upper case, made of three vertical units, is crowned by a separate framed pediment; the lower case, also of three vertical units, has a separate top and is supported by a separate plinth base. The pediment contains cornice molding at the front and sides; the center section is of greater width and projects slightly. It holds thin broken-arch scrolls flanking a center finial supported by a fluted plinth; the front corners of the pediment hold similar finials. The upper case contains three vertical bookcases, each fitted with grooves for two adjustable shelves. The center section is of greater width and projects slightly and is fitted with a pair of glazed doors; each side bookcase is fitted with a single glazed door. The mullions of the doors form a geometric pattern consist-

Desk and Bookcases

188

ing of superimposed, interlocking octagons with rectangles at their centers. Each corner of the veneered doors is marked with an inlaid husk. Each bookcase stands above a drawer of corresponding width. The veneered drawers are bordered with cross-banding and light- and dark-wood inlay. Each drawer is fitted with a central brass keyhole liner; the side drawers have a single oval stamped brass escutcheon with bail pull, while the center drawer is fitted with a pair of matching escutcheons. The center drawer is fitted like a secretary drawer and opens with quadrant stay hinges. The interior contains a central section with a prospect door enclosing four superimposed compartments and flanked by blind document drawers. (The document drawers can be drawn forward by reaching into the pigeonhole to their outside and pushing them forward through a hole in the partition; they are rectangular boxes open at the top.) Each side of the interior contains a single wide drawer fitted with a pair of brass button pulls, over a pair of drawers in line, each with a single pull, over six pigeonholes with fixed shaped valances.

The upper case rests within restraining molding on the rear portion of the lower case. The top of the lower case has a molded edge at the front and sides and is shaped in conformity with the case below. The lower case is divided into three vertical sections. The center section is serpentine in shape, is of greater width, and contains a pair of paneled doors below a slider fitted with a pair of brass button pulls. The doors are decorated with an inner panel of veneer containing inlaid quarter fans in each corner, bordered by light- and dark-wood stringing and cross-banding, with husk inlays in the corners. The edges of the doors are bordered with light-wood stringing, and each door is fitted with a brass keyhole liner. Each side section of the lower case holds four superimposed serpentine drawers below a slider fitted with a single brass pull. The drawers are fitted with a central brass keyhole liner and a round, stamped brass escutcheon with a ring pull. The sliders are veneered with cross-banding outlined by light-wood stringing; the drawer fronts are veneered and bordered with light-wood stringing and cross-banding. The plinth base conforms in shape to the lower case and has canted corners. The outer sections are decorated with light-wood stringing and inlaid husks; the center section also has light-wood stringing, husks, and a central inlaid oval star. The constituent parts of this large object are held together with screws. The backs of the upper and lower case are framed to large vertical panels, and the cases are of dovetailed board construction. On the two side drawers in the upper case, the sides are dovetailed to the front and back; the bottoms are beveled on their front and side edges, let into grooves in the front and sides, and nailed to the underside of the back. Small glue blocks are sandwiched between the drawer bottom and an applied running strip. Small trapezoidal blocks are nailed to the case as stops. On the little drawers in the secretary drawer, the sides are dovetailed to the front and back; the bottoms are glued to rabbets in the front and sides and tacked to the underside of the back. The top of the sliders in the lower case are lined with baize. The serpentine drawer fronts in the lower case are formed of horizontal laminations and otherwise constructed like the upper-case drawers. There are three-quarter dustboards below the drawers, with runners housed in grooves. The center section of the lower case contains three wide drawers with low fronts and shaped sides. The sides are dovetailed to the front and back; the bottoms are nailed to rabbets in the front and sides and to the underside of the back. The bottoms project slightly beyond the sides and run in grooves in the partitions to each side. These drawers are additionally supported by strips of cypress nailed in place at each side. There are no dustboards in this section. The outer edge of each

364 *American Case Furniture*

cupboard door has been grooved in the appropriate places to allow the projecting drawer bottoms to pass through.

Inscriptions: There is an illegible inscription in white chalk on the outside of the back of the upper case. The secretary drawers and large case drawers and drawer dividers have been numbered in modern times.

Condition: Old photographs of the object indicate that it has undergone some restoration. It appears that at one time there was an additional base, perhaps 4–5 cm in height, below the present plinth base. Examination of the underside of the present base by Patricia E. Kane ca. 1970 confirmed that the underside of the present base is very clean, shows no wear whatsoever, and retains evidence of screw holes where another base was attached. Other restorations include the reversal of the central panels of veneer in the lower cupboard doors, so that the swirls in the grain now point inward rather than outward. Large cracks in these panels were also repaired. Perhaps at an early date, the right drawer in the upper case was replaced; this early replacement retains its original oval stamped brass. The other two drawers in the upper case originally were fitted with round brasses, probably matching those in the lower case; these were probably replaced with the present oval brasses when the right drawer was built. There have been many repairs to the veneer in each case. The canted corners of the plinth base were originally decorated with triglyph inlay (see cat. 71). One small drawer in the desk interior is a replacement. One of the small side finials has been repaired, and some of the glass in the bookcase doors has been replaced.

Woods: Mahogany; doors, drawer fronts, mahogany veneer with light- and dark-wood inlays; drawer linings, red cedar (*Juniperus* spp.), probably southern red cedar (*J. silicola*); drawer runners in center cupboard of lower case, bald cypress (*Taxodium distichum*); framing of pediment, eastern white pine; drawer fronts and valances in secretary drawer, holly (*Ilex opaca*); some repairs in lower case, hard maple.

Dimensions: H 320.9; W 253.0; UCW 240.0; LCW 251.3; D 66.0; UCD 35.4; LCD 64.3.

Bibliography: Nutting, *Treasury*, no. 797; E. Milby Burton, "The Furniture of Charleston," *Antiques* 61, no. 1 (January 1952): 45; Burton, *Charleston Furn.*, fig. 2; Hayward, *World Furn.*, p. 195 fig. 727; Anthony Livesey, ed., *A Treasury of World Antiques* (New York: Crescent Books, 1979), p. 149.

Provenance: This library bookcase and a sideboard (cat. 222) were purchased in 1928 by Francis P. Garvan, New York, N.Y., from Elizabeth D. Allston, Marion, S.C., who provided the following family history: "These two pieces . . . were owned by Wm. Alston . . . and probably bought by him for his plantation house on Clifton, his beautiful estate on the Waccamaw river, So. Carolina. . . . The furniture has remained in the possessions of his descendants [including herself] up to the present time."

IF the family history is correct, and there appears to be no reason to doubt its validity, this imposing library bookcase and a sideboard (cat. 222), also now at Yale, were originally owned by William Alston (1756–1839), a wealthy South Carolina planter. The family tradition indicates that these objects were used by Alston at Clifton, a country house on the Waccamaw River near Georgetown, one of several family plantations operated by Alston. It is equally possible, and perhaps even more likely, however, that they were part of the furnishings of Alston's town house on King Street in Charleston, now known as the Miles Brewton house, which he had purchased in 1791. Alston's will refers to his "books

188a Before restoration, 1931

both in Charleston and in the Country"; the inventory of his estate does not specify individually the articles of furniture in his Charleston residence but does include a listing at Clifton of a bookcase valued at $100 and a "Library Containing about 250 books." Alston, at his death, was a large slaveholder in South Carolina. He had served as a captain in the "Swamp Fox" brigade under Colonel Francis Marion during the Revolution and served briefly as a state legislator, but he was known in his own day primarily as a Carolina planter. One of his children, Joseph (1778–1816), became governor of South Carolina and married Theodosia Burr (1783–1813), daughter of Aaron Burr.[1] A closely related library bookcase, probably from the same shop, was owned in Charleston and is now at the Heyward-Washington house, a branch of the Charleston Museum. Another large example, again with a Charleston history, is also at the Heyward-Washington house and has been attributed to Charleston cabinetmaker Robert Walker. An earlier Charleston example, based almost directly on a plate in Chippendale's *Director*, is in the MESDA collection.[2] The red cedar drawer linings, the bald cypress as a secondary wood, and the canted corners of the base are further indications of a Charleston origin for the Yale example. Sheraton referred to this form as a "Library Case," indicating, "the lower middle part contains clothes-press shelves, and every other part may be fitted up for books." He added, "the young workman should observe, that the whole is to be made in six carcases, and screwed together, and then the plinth should be made to fit it, of one entire frame, and screwed down on the carcases; as also is the cornice and its freeze."[3]

The Mabel Brady Garvan Collection 1930.2023

1. For Alston, see his will, 29 November 1838, in Charleston County Wills, 41:939–946, and inventory, 1842, Charleston County Inventories, H:433–434, 470–471, in the South Carolina Department of Archives and History, Columbia (copies in the Yale Furniture Study object files); and Joseph A. Groves, *The Alstons and Allstons of North and South Carolina* (Atlanta: Franklin Printing and Publishing Co., 1901), pp. 75–80. George Washington was entertained at Clifton in 1791 by Alston; see *The Diaries of George Washington*, ed. John C. Fitzpatrick, vol. 4 (Boston: Houghton Mifflin Co. for the Mount Vernon Ladies' Association of the Union, 1925), p. 169.
2. Burton, *Charleston Furn.*, frontis., p. 61 fig. 35.
3. *The Cabinet-Maker and Upholsterer's Drawing-Book* (3d ed.; London: T. Bensley, 1802), app., pp. 7–8.

189

Library bookcase
American, possibly New York, New York, 1830–1850

Description: This tall object is in two cases. The upper case is crowned with a projecting cornice containing a deep cove molding above a wide arch. The front corners of the upper case hold freestanding columns flanking a bookcase section enclosed by two glazed doors with mullions forming six panels on each door. The bookcase holds four adjustable shelves supported by a system of toothed slips. The upper case rests on the rear part of the lower case. The center of the top of the lower case contains a writing compartment fitted with a wooden pull on its top. It opens in the manner of a portable desk to form a sloping writing surface covered with green baize. Each half of the writing surface lifts via a leather pull to reveal a well, and at the top of the compartment there are lidded compartments at each side (with the removable lids fitted with a leather pull), a black pen tray, and four small open compartments, one with a sloping partition. The lower case also has projecting columns at each side, flanking a recessed center section containing a pair of paneled doors at the center and a single paneled door at each side. The panels of the doors are of figured mahogany, and the side doors and the right door of the center are fitted with wooden pulls; each door has a brass keyhole liner. The center doors open to a compartment with a single loose shelf. Behind the right door there is an open compartment above a drawer with a brass ring pull; the left door opens to a compartment with a single fixed shelf. The case rests on a straight plinth base. The pediment is a dovetailed framework, reinforced with multiple glue blocks, and screwed to the top of the bookcase section. It is fitted with several metal hook eyes, presumably so that the bookcase could be tied to the wall. The back of each case consists of a series of boards of alternating width, with the wider boards beveled on their vertical edges and fitted to grooves in the narrower boards; the assembly is then nailed to the top and bottom and to rabbets in each side. The lower case is supported by thick blocks at each corner, with skids nailed to their undersides. There are multiple horizontal glue blocks behind the bottom front rail of the lower case. Each shelf in the bookcase is faced with mahogany veneer on its front edge. The shelves in the side compartments are fixed, while that in the center section is loose; all are supported by strips applied to the sides of the case. The shelves, inside back of the bookcase, and compartments in the lower case are stained red. On the drawer in the

right compartment, the sides are dovetailed to the front and back, with the top edge of each side rounded; the bottom is beveled on its front and side edges and let into a groove in the front and sides, without nails.

Inscriptions: "XXC" is written in white chalk on the outside of the back of the lower case. "*HESN / 5000*" is written in white chalk on the top of the bottom of the lower well in the writing compartment. There are columns of added figures in pencil on top of the lower case.

Condition: The baize on the writing surface is a replacement. There have been minor repairs to the veneer. The keyhole liner on the left door in the lower case is missing.

Woods: Mahogany, mahogany veneer; eastern white pine; backboards of lower case, basswood; sides and back of drawer, mahogany.

Dimensions: H 278.0; W 199.0; UCW 183.5; LCW 183.4; D 54.5; UCD 27.2; LCD 43.3.

Provenance: According to a family tradition, this bookcase was acquired in the last quarter of the nineteenth century, possibly in Philadelphia, by Thomas Bertrand Bronson (1851–1948), for many years a member of the faculty at Lawrenceville School, Lawrenceville, N. J. It descended to his son, Bertrand H. Bronson, Berkeley, Calif., and was purchased from him by Herman W. Liebert, New Haven, Conn.

REMINISCENT of more elaborate secretaries and wardrobes from New York with similar columns and projecting cornices containing a wide arch, this tall library bookcase might have been made in that city as well.[1] Unlike the other library bookcases in the collection, which are fitted with secretary drawers, this example has a folding writing compartment equivalent to a portable desk.

Gift of Herman W. Liebert 1976.99.1

1. Tracy, *19th-Century America*, no. 70; Otto, fig. 233; Comstock, figs. 605, 665 (advertisement of Joseph Meeks and Sons); *Antiques* 125, no. 4 (April 1984): 794.

Desk and Bookcases

of paneled doors decorated with applied moldings forming a quatrefoil. Each door is again fitted with a wooden lock escutcheon, again blind on the left. There is base molding at the front and sides of the lower case, and the object is supported by bracket feet. The front corners of each case are rounded. The sliding lid of the cylinder desk is flanked by moldings on the case, and the front of the desk drawer is faced with applied molding and fitted with a wooden lock escutcheon. The sliding lid is fitted with a pair of wooden pulls that serve as stops when the lid is lifted. The lid lifts to reveal an interior containing, at the rear, a center section of three superimposed drawers with round wooden pulls, flanked on each side by five pigeonholes with partitions shaped to reverse curves. When the desk drawer is pulled forward, it provides a sloping writing surface at the center, covered with green baize. This can be lifted with a brass ring pull to reveal an open compartment below. The writing surface is flanked at the front by compartments with loose lids that slide in grooves or open to the sides and provide access to open compartments below. On the right, behind this compartment, are a pen tray with a removable lid and three small wells, the center one with a sloping partition. The top and bottom of the upper case are dovetailed to the sides, and the back of the upper case is framed to three vertical panels; the panels have beveled edges, and the joints are reinforced with screws. The bookcase holds three adjustable veneered shelves supported by a ratchet system. The back of the lower case is framed to two vertical panels. The cupboard doors open to an interior with one fixed

190

190

Desk and bookcase

John (1801–1875) and Joseph W. (1806–1878) Meeks
New York, New York, 1836–ca. 1855
(see pl. 16)

Description: The bookcase is surmounted by a plain plinth cornice above deep cove molding and a bead. The bookcase contains two glazed doors decorated with mullions forming Gothic arches containing quatrefoils. Each door is fitted with a wooden lock escutcheon, blind on the left. The bookcase rests within molding applied to the top of the desk. The lower case contains a cylinder desk and drawer, above a pair

190a

shaped shelf supported by strips nailed to the case sides. Large blocks are glued under the bottom of the desk drawer. The doors are secured with a metal spring lock. There are small square blocks in each corner of the base, and the backboard of the base is dovetailed to the sides. On the desk interior, the small drawers increase in depth from top to bottom, in order to fit into the cylinder. The drawer sides are dovetailed to the front and back; the bottoms are let into a groove in the front and sides and nailed to the underside of the back. There are no dustboards; the drawers are supported on small runners housed in grooves, and little blocks are glued in place as stops. Thy cylinder is housed within the case, and its sides are formed of both wood and metal elements.

Inscriptions: "J. & J.W. MEEKS / MAKERS / No 14 Vesey Street / NEW YORK" is stenciled on the inside of the bottom of the lowest drawer in the desk interior. The brass lock for the desk drawer is stamped "NETTLEFOLD" on the left and "V / PAT[ENT]" on the right, with a symbol above the V. Written in blue chalk on the outside of the back of the upper and lower case is "2000/86." There is a fragment of a paper label on the outside of the back of the top rail of the upper case.

190b

Condition: A hole at each front corner and a glue outline and residue extending across the front and sides indicate that the bookcase was originally surmounted by some sort of additional pediment, now lost. Evidence that the bookcase doors were originally fitted with curtains on the inside led to the restoration of such curtains in green in 1979 by Elite Decorating Service of New Haven. The right side molding on the writing surface has been broken and reglued. The molding on the right and left side of the cylinder has been repaired, and the right bookcase door has been repaired around the hinges. There has been a repair to the pigeonhole partition on the right nearest the center drawers, and there is a patch below the outermost pigeonhole on the same side. At one time, the upper and lower cases were joined at the back with metal strips attached with screws.

Woods: American black walnut, walnut veneer; inside of bookcase, much of desk interior, satinwood (*Cholroxlyon* spp.), probably *C. swietenia*, Ceylon satinwood, veneer; pulls on cylinder and desk interior drawers, probably rosewood; writing surface, sliding covers of wells, mahogany; yellow poplar; eastern white pine.

Dimensions: H 235.1; W 135.6; UCW 121.5; LCW 122.0; D 61.1; UCD 30.5; LCD 57.1.

Exhibition: YUAG, "A Century of Tradition and Innovation," checklist no. 2.

Bibliography: John Pearce and Lorraine W. Pearce, "More on the Meeks Cabinetmakers," *Antiques* 90, no. 1 (July 1966): 70 fig. 2; "Acquisitions 1971," *YUAG Bulletin* 34, no. 1 (November 1972): 54; Marvin D. Schwartz, "Tradition and Innovation," *Antiques World* 2, no. 3 (January 1980): 126; Kane, "American Furn.," p. 1325 fig. 13.

Provenance: According to tradition, this desk and bookcase was owned originally by Henry Griswold Hubbard (1814–1891), president and general manager of Russell Manufacturing Company, Middletown, Conn. The object descended in his family, to his daughter Margaret Sill Hubbard (d. 1908) and her husband Elijah K. Hubbard, Middletown; to his grandson, T. M. Russell, Sr. (d. 1935), Middletown; to Mrs. T. M. Russell, Sr., and her daughter, Margaret Hubbard Russell (1905–1963), Philadelphia, Pa., and North Haven, Conn.; to T. M. Russell, Jr., North Branford, Conn. It was purchased from the family by Jerrold N. Moore, Woodbridge, Conn., in 1964, and acquired by purchase by the Art Gallery in 1971.

ALTHOUGH other examples have subsequently come to light, in 1964 "this handsome piece of walnut and satinwood [was] the first signed Meeks piece to be found with Gothic revival details."[1] A closely related desk and bookcase, veneered in rosewood, is in the Metropolitan Museum of Art (69.19), and an unusual desk and bookcase in a combination of Elizabethan and Stuart revival styles, also of rosewood and with the same stenciled label, is in a private collection.[2]

The Meeks firm was at 14 Vesey Street between 1836 and 1847 and at 14 and 16 Vesey Street until about 1855.³ The presumed original owner of the desk, Henry G. Hubbard, spent some time in New York City in the early 1830s, when he may have become acquainted with the Meekses' work, before returning to Middletown, his place of birth, in 1833. A pioneer in the manufacture of elastic webbing in the United States, Hubbard assumed his position as general manager of Russell Manufacturing Company in 1836, suggesting one possible date for the manufacture of the desk. His marriage to Charlotte Rosella McDonough came in 1844, suggesting another possible, and perhaps more likely, date for the purchase of the desk. With its Gothic details, the desk and bookcase probably lent a romantic and picturesque air to the library of this locally prominent Episcopalian, politician, and businessman.⁴ In creating their design, the Meekses may have looked for inspiration to an English design, such as George Smith's 1808 illustration of a cylinder desk and bookcase in the Gothic style. Smith's notes on his design indicate that it contains a "gentleman's wardrobe" below the cylinder, and he suggests, "the upper doors may be backed with lustring [a plain glossy silk] in flutes, if it is required to screen the books."⁵ The Meekses also appear to have drawn on an English design and, in this case, manufacturer for the lock that secures the desk. The lock, marked "NETTLEFOLD," is probably "the lock invented by Mr. Nettlefold [and] so constructed, that when the bolt is shot out by the key, two teeth or quadrants are projected from the sides of the bolt, which take a firm hold of the plate fixed on the door-post or edge. This construction is said to answer well for sliding-doors."⁶

The Mabel Brady Garvan Collection 1971.70

1. John Pearce and Lorraine W. Pearce, "More on the Meeks Cabinetmakers," *Antiques* 90, no. 1 (July 1966): 70 fig. 2.
2. MMA, *19th-Century America*, no. 100; Karen Jones, ed., "Collector's Notes," *Antiques* 123, no. 5 (May 1983): 1074–1075, 1080. An unmarked Gothic revival desk and bookcase with mahogany veneer (Metropolitan Museum of Art, 67.262.1), also a New York product, is related to the Meekses' work; see MMA, *19th-Century America*, no. 98. See also a closely related bookcase, now in a private collection, in *Fine American Furniture, Silver, and Decorative Arts*, 11 April 1981 (New York: Christie, Manson, & Woods International, 1981), lot 437.
3. John Pearce, Lorraine W. Pearce, and Robert C. Smith, "The Meeks Family of Cabinetmakers," *Antiques* 85, no. 4 (April 1964): 414–420.
4. William F. Moore, *Representative Men of Connecticut, 1861–1894* (Everett: Massachusetts Publishing Co., 1894), pp. 407–410.
5. *A Collection of Designs for Household Furniture and Interior Decoration* (London: J. Taylor, 1808), p. 18 pl. 100.
6. Robert Mallet, *The Construction of Locks: Compiled from the Papers of A. C. Hobbs, Esq., of New York*, ed. Charles Tomlinson (1868; reprint, Bath, England: Kingsmead Reprints, 1970), pp. 60–61.

191

191

Desk with later bookcase
Desk possibly by John Hambly
Portsmouth, Rhode Island, ca. 1780 and ca. 1850

Description: This object consists of a simple late eighteenth-century desk to which a bookcase section in the Gothic revival style has been added, probably in the mid nineteenth century. The desk contains three graduated drawers below

the slant front, with cock beading applied to the edges of the drawers. The desk is supported by bracket feet below applied base molding at the front and sides; the rear feet are triangular braces. The top of the desk is dovetailed to the sides, with the dovetails exposed on the top. The cleated lid is supported by lopers and attached to the desk with brass butt hinges. It opens to a plain interior of three drawers in line over two drawers below flanking a central open compartment. The horizontal backboards of the desk are half lapped and nailed to a rabbet in the sides and to the top and bottom. The feet are supported by horizontal and vertical blocks and strips. On each drawer in the case, the sides are dovetailed to the front and back, and the bottoms are let into grooves in the front and sides and nailed to the underside of the back. On the interior drawers, the sides are dovetailed to the front and back; the bottoms are rabbeted on all four sides and let into grooves in all four sides, with the exception of the wide upper drawer, where the bottom is beveled on its front and rear edges and nailed to the underside of the back. The vertical partitions in the interior have double half-round molding, while the horizontal partitions are rounded; the top drawers run on their bottoms, while there are runners for the lower drawers to raise them to the height of the horizontal strip. The bookcase rests on top of the desk. Its two roundheaded doors have applied moldings to form Gothic tracery, and they open to an interior with two fixed shelves. The sides of the bookcase also have applied moldings in the Gothic style, and the case has a heavy base and cornice molding. It is surmounted by a Gothic arch pediment flanked by large, heavy, urn-shaped finials. The bookcase is framed; the backboards are nailed to the frame, and the doors are attached with brass butt hinges. An outline of the pediment is scribed on the outside of the upper backboard. The pediment is closed with curved boards nailed in place.

Inscriptions: Written in pencil on the outside of the back of the desk is "John Hambly / Portsmouth R I / for Mr[?] M[?] / ring [?]." "Back" is written in pencil on the inside of the back and on the inside of the back of the top case drawer.

Condition: The object has been refinished and given a red stain. The desk has been extensively repaired and is considerably scratched and worn. The brasses are replacements; the valance in the desk interior is new; the base molding has been repaired; the backboards have been renailed; and there is a new glue block at the left rear foot. The drawer bottoms in the desk drawers have been pieced; their backs have been beveled off, probably with a band saw, and then the backs have been reduced in thickness and squared off by being run over a jointer. New running strips have been added to the top desk drawer, and the cock beading on the lowest drawer has been pieced on the right side. There are small repairs above the doors in the bookcase, and the tip of one finial has been replaced and its base repaired.

Woods: Eastern white pine; finials, probably cottonwood; one replaced glue block, mahogany.

Dimensions: H 197.4; W 85.9; UCW 77.4; LCW 84.5; D (open) 92.0; D (closed) 57.1; UCD 27.9; LCD 56.1.

Provenance: According to tradition, this object was found in an old church in New London, Conn., by dealer Florian Papp, New York, N. Y., who sold it in 1928 to Francis P. Garvan, New York, N. Y.

THE inscription on the back of this desk would lead one to believe that it was made by a John Hambly of Portsmouth, Rhode Island. Unfortunately, the greater part of the inscription, which was discovered only recently, remains undeciphered, refusing to yield to infrared photography, ultraviolet light, magnification, and other attempts to understand its meaning. Various documents record the presence of the Hambly family in Portsmouth and Tiverton, Rhode Island, in the eighteenth century. A John Hambly was born in Portsmouth in 1745, the son of Benjamin Hambly and his first wife, Mary (Burrington) Hambly, who were married in 1737, and it may be that this man is connected with the desk.[1] The Gothic revival style bookcase, clearly later, was with the desk when it was acquired by Francis P. Garvan.

The Mabel Brady Garvan Collection 1930.2322

1. James N. Arnold, *Vital Records of Rhode Island, 1636–1850*, vol. 4, *Newport County* (Providence: Narragansett Historical Publishing Co., 1893), pt. 1, "Portsmouth," pp. 26, 79. John Hambly's grandfather left him £1,000 in his will, dated 1759, when John was to reach twenty-three years of age; see John Osborne Austin, *The Genealogical Dictionary of Rhode Island* (Baltimore: Genealogical Publishing Co., 1969). The 1774 census lists only Benjamin Hambly's household; John may have been one of the two males over sixteen still living at home then, or he may have left the area; see John R. Bartlett, *Census of the Inhabitants of the Colony of Rhode Island and Providence Plantations, 1774* (1858; reprint, Baltimore: Genealogical Publishing Co., 1969), p. 187. There are references to Benjamin and Peleg Hambly in *The Early Records of the Town of Portsmouth*, ed. Clarence S. Brigham (Providence: E. L. Freeman & Sons, 1901), pp. 328, 352, 368.

192

192

Library bookcase (one of a pair)
American, possibly Baltimore, Maryland, 1840–1850

Description: Each of this large pair of identical bookcases, of which only one example (1972.79.1) is illustrated, has a pair of glazed doors fitted with locks and decorated with Gothic motifs. The front corners of the case contain projecting pilasters terminating in pointed spires. The front section of the gallery rises in a series of arches with carved crockets to a central carved finial; each side gallery consists of an arcade of rounded arches. Each side of the case interior is fitted with six adjustable shelves, and there is a full vertical transverse partition between the sides. The bookcase is of dovetailed board construction and is screwed to a dovetailed base. The corner pilasters are applied, and the gallery elements are screwed in place from underneath. The back is framed with four large panels, with the rails and stiles screwed to the case. The interior of each bookcase is stained red; the exterior and the front edge of each bookshelf are grained in imitation of rosewood.

Inscriptions: The bookcases contain many shop marks and numbers, and the shelf supports bear stamped numbers. Modern paper labels are pasted to the gallery elements identifying their respective locations, and were probably added to aid reassembly at some time when the galleries were dismantled for moving.

Condition: The bookcases have seen much use, and the galleries of each example are weakened and loose. Some of the shelf supports are replacements, and the mullions on 1979.72.2 have been repaired.

Woods: Eastern white pine; yellow poplar.

Dimensions: H 290.3; W 175.3; CW 164.6; D 50.5; CD 43.1.

Bibliography: John F. Fulton, *Harvey Cushing: A Biography* (Springfield, Ill.: Charles C. Thomas, 1946), facing p. 244.

Provenance: What he called "ecclesiastical bookcases" were acquired by Dr. Harvey Cushing (1869–1939) in the early twentieth century from a Madame Carroll of Baltimore, Md. Cushing, later of Boston, Mass., gave them to the Historical Library of the Yale Medical School, and they were transferred to the Art Gallery in 1972.

LARGE Gothic bookcases related at least in form to these examples were made for the libraries and studies of several houses in the 1840s, suggesting a date for their production. A much more elaborate pair, for example, were made ca. 1847 for the Gothic revival study of the Enoch Pratt house in Baltimore, possibly by a cabinetmaker named Robert Renwick, and one was made for Daniel Webster's Gothic library, remodeled in 1843, in his Marshfield, Massachusetts, home.[1] A nearly contemporary cabinetmaker's guide noted in reference to other large bookcases of different styles but of similar concept, "the ornamental parts are mechanically non-essential, but are superadded for the purposes of beauty and effect."[2] The same manual described a method of supporting bookshelves which was used in these bookcases: the system "consists of pairs of toothed slips...exactly similar to, and equidistant from, each other, that are glued on along the insides of each pair of gables [sides of the case], and flush with

their fore and back edges. Cross bars ... of the same thickness, bearing the shelves, ... are fitted between the slips, and made to rest on the projecting teeth. The slips are prepared from a single piece by a plane for the purpose."[3]

Yale Medical School Library Transfer 1972.79.1, .2

1. Katherine S. Howe and David B. Warren, *The Gothic Revival Style in America, 1830–1870* (Houston: Museum of Fine Arts, 1976), no. 90; see also *Antiques* 109, no. 5 (May 1976): 988. "Mementos of Daniel Webster," *Antiques* 25, no. 5 (May 1934): 177. See also Ruth Ralston, "Nineteenth-Century New York Interiors," *Antiques* 43, no. 6 (June 1943): 268, illustrating a library at 41 Fifth Avenue, New York, of 1847.

2. Blackie and Son, *The Victorian Cabinet-Maker's Assistant* (1853; reprint, New York: Dover Publications, 1970), p. 30.

3. Blackie and Son, *Victorian Cabinet-Maker's Assistant*, pp. 30–31.

193

Wall shelf
Design attributed to Dan Cooper (1901–1965)
New York, New York, ca. 1954

Description: This wall shelf or display cabinet is designed to hang flush against the wall. The rectangular frame encloses at the left a fixed horizontal shelf butted to a vertical partition. At the right is a fixed vertical partition running the height of the frame, with one adjustable shelf supported by wooden pegs. The vertical partitions and the sides of the case have drilled holes at regular intervals to accommodate movable shelves. The back is covered with fabric and consists of a sheet of plywood screwed to the frame and the fixed partitions.

Condition: When acquired by the Art Gallery in 1977, the silk that covered the back of this object had faded considerably from sunlight and was frayed and worn in several places (see illustration). It subsequently became wet while in storage at the Furniture Study, and in 1982 the original back was removed and stored and replaced with a new plywood panel covered with new silk chosen to match the original material as closely as possible. It is likely that there originally were more adjustable shelves than the one that survives today.

Woods: Frame, dark veneer, possibly kingwood; base, yellow poplar; shelves, partitions, holly; pegs, birch; back, plywood.

Dimensions: H 133.1; W 107.0; D 13.4.

193

Provenance: Mr. and Mrs. James Marshall Osborn, New Haven, Conn.

AMONG their other interests, the Osborns were collectors of African art. In 1954, they purchased the collection of the late Dr. Ralph Linton, Sterling Professor of Anthropology at Yale, after the collection had been on view at the Art Gallery.[1] Mrs. Osborn stated in a letter of 25 May 1954 to the New York designer Dan Cooper, "We are leaving most of the items on loan at the Yale Art Gallery, but expect to gradually give them the whole collection over a period of years... but we are also keeping certain pieces around the house, and shall change them as occasion makes desirable. This calls for some sort of shelf arrangement for display of pieces that cannot be hung on the wall. I should like your help in designing this shelf or wall form, and would want you to have it made up for me." It is thought that this object resulted from Mrs. Osborn's request. An undated photograph shows the cabinet in use in the Osborn's residence, with masks hung against the back and standing figures arrayed on the shelves, which were arranged as they appear in the photograph in this volume. Cooper's simple design, however, was flexible and allowed Mrs. Osborn to adjust the shelves if necessary when the collection was rotated.

Gift of J. Marshall & Thomas M. Osborn in memory of Mr. and Mrs. James M. Osborn 1977.40.8

1. See *The Linton Collection of African Sculpture: An Exhibition*, 13 March–18 April 1954 (New Haven: Yale University Art Gallery, 1954).

Cupboards and Presses

Cupboards (often designated in period documents by a bewildering variety of names, such as press cupboard, plate cupboard, court cupboard, and livery cupboard) were among the most prestigious and expensive forms of furniture in the houses of the well-to-do in the seventeenth century. They were usually located in areas where eating took place, and they fulfilled several specific functions: they supplied interior storage space for textiles and utensils, and provided flat surfaces for the display of eating and drinking wares of silver, pewter, glass, and ceramic. The Yale collection is exceedingly rich in examples of seventeenth-century Connecticut cupboards, including an example from the New Haven area with rare inlaid decoration (cat. 194); two of the seven known examples of cupboards attributed to Peter Blin of Wethersfield, including the only one to have survived in a relatively untouched state (cat. 195); and two Guilford-area cupboards with drawers (cats. 197, 198). The survival of the form in rural areas well into the eighteenth century is documented by the New Hampshire example (cat. 199) of board construction and with fanciful painted decoration. Related in size but varying in function, clothespresses are fitted with doors opening to an interior fitted with pegs for hanging clothes. The collection includes an unusual New England example (cat. 200), more typical examples from Pennsylvania (cats. 201, 202), and a rare and unusual southern clothespress (cat. 203).

194

Cupboard

Coastal Connecticut, probably New Haven, 1670–1700

Description: The cupboard is in two stages. The upper case has a simple cornice decorated with corbels, each with three vertical incised lines, at the center and sides of the front and at the front and rear of each side. It is supported by turned balusters at each corner of the front. The cupboard section of the upper case is trapezoidal in shape and contains a door with a wooden pull on its front face and cruciform panels on its canted sides. The door is flanked by applied split spindles with "acorn" caps, and its rails are molded and painted black. The door contains a central projecting rectangular panel of light and dark diamonds of walnut, framed by raised, beveled moldings and surrounded by four L-shaped panels formed by applied moldings. Each panel on the canted sides is flanked by applied split spindles and contains an oval ebonized boss at its center. The rails of these side panels are also molded and ebonized. The upper case rests on top of the lower case. The lower case contains a wide drawer, decorated to simulate a pair of drawers in line, over two doors leading to a lower cupboard. The drawer contains two panels separated and flanked by corbels. Each panel is outlined by applied moldings, contains a central wooden pull, and is decorated with alternating light and dark diamonds of walnut. The doors of the lower cupboard are separated and flanked by applied split spindles conforming to those on the upper case, with the addition of a small round boss above and below the spindle. Each door contains a central projecting square of "checkerboard" parquetry, outlined by raised moldings, and a panel of oak framed by applied moldings at the top, bottom, and each side, with the corners of each panel filled with squares of walnut. There is a horizontal applied split spindle on the rails of each door. Each side of the lower case is framed to a single panel with applied moldings on the panel edges, with a corbel at the front and rear at the height of the drawer. There is deep cove molding at the front and sides, and the cupboard is supported by straight feet formed by continuation of the stiles. The present top of the upper case is a replacement (see Condition) and is attached to the frame with screws. The cupboard is joined with mortise-and-tenon joints, and the side panels of the upper case are formed of two butted boards. The balusters are doweled to blocks at the top, with the front rail of the upper case tenoned to these blocks. The back of the upper case is framed to three vertical panels, and each joint is secured with two pegs. No moldings or chamfering are present on the rear of the object. The back of the lower case is also framed to three vertical panels, with the rails double pinned and the muntins only single pinned to the rails. The doors to the lower cupboard are double pegged, and the bottom of the lower case consists of several transverse boards beveled on their edges, joined with a tongue-and-groove or V-shaped joint, and nailed with rose-head nails to the four sides. The drawer is side hung; the drawer sides are dovetailed to the front, with the dovetails reinforced with nails. The sides are rabbeted to accept the back and nailed above and below the channel for the runner with rosehead nails. The drawer bottom consists of four transverse boards joined with a tongue-and-groove or V-shaped joint and is nailed to a rabbet in the front and to the underside of the sides and back with rosehead nails.

Inscriptions: A Connecticut Tercentenary label is pasted to the inside of the right side of the drawer; a "Connecticut

194

Cupboards and Presses 377

Furniture" (1967) exhibition label is pasted to the inside of the upper case.

Condition: Edward Comfort Starr's memorandum on the history of the cupboard (see Provenance) indicates that in the early 1860s his uncle Burgis P. Starr "had it repaired by Robbins & Winship at Hartford, for $50." This restoration included the replacement of the top of the upper case and the top of the lower case, repairs to the cupboard doors and the replacement of their hinges, and the replacement of the platforms and blocks above the turned columns. Each side of the drawer has been repaired, the rail above the drawer is a replacement, and the drawer runners within the case also probably are replacements. The base molding has been repaired at the rear on both sides, and there have been minor repairs to the corbels and applied moldings. The applied spindles and other ornaments apparently were removed during restoration and replaced. The large turned columns were removed and apparently replaced upside down; they appear in this reversed position in all earlier photographs of the cupboard. In the 1970s, they were placed in their present, presumably original, orientation, which is more in keeping with seventeenth-century practice. Lockwood stated that the front feet "should have been of the ball variety," but evidence for such a restoration is hidden by the applied base molding. It is likely that the front stiles continued to form the front feet in the manner now seen.

Woods: Frame, white oak; light and dark "checkerboard" inlays, raised, beveled moldings, American black walnut (dark heartwood and light sapwood); applied spindles, bosses, soft maple; other applied moldings, eastern red cedar; side panels of lower case, lower left back panel of lower case, chestnut; some replaced elements, yellow poplar.

Dimensions: H 143.8; W 110.0; UCW 100.5; LCW 104.9; D 58.5; LCD 53.9.

Exhibitions: *Three Centuries of Conn. Furn.*, no. 57; Kirk, *Conn. Furn.*, no. 110; Kane, *Furn. New Haven Colony*, no. XXIII.

Bibliography: Lyon, no. 18; Luke Vincent Lockwood, *The Furniture Collectors' Glossary* (New York: Walpole Society, 1913), p. 20 (as a line drawing); Nutting, *Furn. Pilgrim Century* (1924), fig. 223; Nutting, *Treasury*, no. 469; Lockwood, fig. 165; *Handbook*, p. 58; Ormsbee, *Story Am. Furn.*, fig. 102; Kettell, *Early American Rooms*, facing p. 59 (as line drawing); "Outstanding Examples from the Mabel Brady Garvan Collection," *YUAG Bulletin* 8, no. 2 (February 1938): 44; Nagel, pl. 1; Rogers, "Garvan Coll. (1962)," p. 6; *Antiques* 92, no. 4 (October 1967): 506; Kane, "New Haven Colony Furn.," pp. 956–957; "American Arts and the American Experience," *Museum News* 53, no. 3 (November 1974): 38; Chinnery, fig. 4:225; Kirk, *Am. Furn. & Brit. Trad.*, fig. 163; Trent, "Postscript," p. 36 fig. 9.

Provenance: In a statement written in the 1920s, the Reverend Edward Comfort Starr (Yale College, 1866; Yale Theological Seminary, 1870) traced the descent of the cupboard through four generations of his family back to the late eighteenth century. When his grandfather Deacon Comfort Starr (ca. 1770–1862) was married in 1808, he lived in the "Old Starr House" in Guilford, Conn., which had been purchased by his father, William (ca. 1730–1816), in 1786. Edward's grandmother, according to Edward, recalled, "the old cupboard ... was in the house and called 'the old ark' when she came there to live, but [she] did not, I think, know whence it came. It might have been his [William's] wife, who was a Burgis; or he might have inherited it from his ancestors, Starr, Hopson, or others unnamed; or it is possible that it was left in the house by other occupants, Collins, Wright, Lee, &c." (The Starr family came to Guilford from Middletown in the late seventeenth century.) Later owners included Comfort Starr's sons, Henry B. Starr and his younger brother, Burgis P. Starr, who was the owner in the early 1860s. About 1880, Burgis P. Starr gave the cupboard to his nephew, Edward Comfort Starr, apparently reserving a life interest for his wife, who was still the owner when Lyon pictured the cupboard in 1891. After the death of Mrs. Starr, her adopted daughter, Christine (Mrs. Harvey Brainerd), effected the transfer to Edward Comfort Starr, who in turn gave the cupboard about 1925 to his daughter Mabel E. Starr of Cornwall, Conn. It was purchased from Miss Starr 27 January 1930 by Henry Hammond Taylor, acting as agent for Francis P. Garvan, New York, N. Y.

PART of a group of furniture recently attributed to the "Russell-Gibbons shops" of New Haven on somewhat tenuous grounds (see cat. 33), the Starr family cupboard (with its Guilford history) is related to cupboards with histories in the Treat (the Metropolitan Museum of Art, 1953.197.1) and Andrew (Virginia Museum of Fine Arts, 77.75) families of Milford and to a chest of drawers with doors (Museum of Fine Arts, Boston, 1980.274) without an early provenance.[1] A related chest, also decorated with parquetry, was found in Middletown and is now in a private collection.[2] Although none of the traditional histories associated with these objects should be regarded as conclusive, it is curious that no member of the group has a New Haven provenance.[3] The frontal emphasis and economical construction of this "Russell-

Gibbons" group are said to be "characteristic of a specifically urban mentality probably found nowhere but in London," and the use of parquetry on the Starr cupboard and other members of the group also suggests that they were produced by a relatively sophisticated urban shop.[4] This type of construction, however, might well have been practiced in smaller English urban centers outside of London, and the houndstooth and "checkerboard" inlay on the group also is found (in conjunction with carving) on English objects from the Leeds area.[5] The possibility that these traditions of ornament and construction were brought to New Haven by craftsmen from outside of London cannot be discounted on the basis of the available evidence. The Starr family cupboard is a good instance of an early restoration by the Hartford firm of Philomen F. Robbins (1807–1890) and Joseph Winship (d. 1889), where cabinetmakers such as Walter Hosmer and Edwin Simons performed work for the early circle of Hartford collectors, including Henry Wood Erving, Irving Lyon, and others.

The Mabel Brady Garvan Collection 1930.2271

1. The three cupboards are illustrated and thoroughly compared in Kane, *Furn. New Haven Colony*, nos. XXI–XXIII. For the chest of drawers with doors, see Fairbanks and Trent, *New England Begins*, no. 482, wherein the attribution to the Russell-Gibbons shops is made in the context of an excellent discussion of the group's characteristics and English background.
2. For an illustration, see Kane, *Furn. New Haven Colony*, no. XXIII. This chest was offered to Francis P. Garvan in the 1930s; he turned it down on the grounds of its close similarity to the Starr cupboard.
3. For the Starr family history, see also Ralph D. Smith, *The History of Guilford, Connecticut, from Its First Settlement in 1639* (Albany, N. Y.: J. Munsell, 1877), pp. 28, 104, 106, 145–146.
4. Fairbanks and Trent, *New England Begins*, no. 482.
5. Chinnery, p. 471. Two examples attributed to London are referred to in Fairbanks and Trent, *New England Begins*, no. 482. See also Perry Macquoid, *The History of English Furniture: The Age of Oak* (London: Lawrence and Bullen, 1904), fig. 205, for an English chest of drawers with doors closely related to the American example at the Museum of Fine Arts, Boston.

195

Cupboard
Possibly by Peter Blin (d. 1725)
Wethersfield, Connecticut, 1675–1690
(see pl. 17)

195

Description: Unlike the preceding example (cat. 194), this cupboard is built as a single unit. The top of the case has a thumbnail molding at the front and sides and overhangs the cornice and sides of the case slightly. The cornice overhangs the recessed upper cupboard and is supported at its front corner by turned ebonized balusters. The front of the cornice is decorated at its center and each side with a plaque carved with tulips against a background painted black, thus dividing the front into two panels. Each panel then contains a row of diagonal dentils, centering from left to right to a central triangular block carved with incised vertical lines, placed above an oval ebonized boss. The sides of the cornice also contain carved plaques at the front and rear, and there is applied molding at the lower edge of the cornice. The front of the recessed upper cupboard is divided into three panels. At each side is a door decorated with applied moldings in a geometric pattern with reentrant sides, top, and bottom and with five applied bosses. The applied moldings of the doors are painted a white-yellow color with black painted squiggles. The rails and stiles of the doors have central molding

Cupboards and Presses 379

painted black. The central panel has applied moldings forming L-shaped panels around a central rectangle, with small flattened bosses in each panel. Again, the applied moldings are painted white-yellow with black squiggles. The center panel is flanked by pairs of applied ebonized split spindles. The top rail and stiles of the recessed cupboard have a central molding painted black. The shelf separating the upper and lower section has a thumbnail molding at the front and sides. Below the shelf there is a row of diagonal dentils, again centered on a small triangular carved block, this time located above the center of the drawer. The lower section contains a single wide drawer above a cupboard. The drawer is flanked by ebonized triglyphs on the stiles and is divided at its center by a triglyph into two panels, simulating a pair of drawers in line. Each simulated drawer contains a central wooden pull flanked by diagonal oval bosses and has applied moldings in a rectangle with cut corners. The applied moldings are painted red with black squiggles, and the inlaid corners are painted black. The rail below the drawer and the bottom front rail are decorated with a central channel molding painted black. The paneled door to the lower cupboard is carved with a "sunflower" or marigold motif outlined by a rectangle with cut corners formed by applied moldings. The moldings are painted with the white-yellow ground with black squiggles, with the inlaid corners again painted black. Each fixed side panel is carved with a central vertical stem terminating in a notched flower at the top, with three scrolled flowers and a lower "thistle" extending to each side. The moldings surrounding these side panels are painted red with black squiggles. The three panels in the lower section are flanked and separated by applied split spindles below a strapwork-applied heart motif on the stiles and muntins. The rails above and below the panels have central molding painted black. The four stiles continue to form the feet. Each side of the upper section contains a single panel with a central oval boss and applied moldings painted red forming a rectangle with cut corners; the inlaid corners are painted black. The lower section of each side is framed to two vertical panels, outlined with applied moldings painted red, and each contains a central boss. The middle and lower rails and the muntin on each side contain central molding painted black. The top of the cupboard is a single board with thumbnail molding at the front and sides, and it is nailed to the four corners of the case. The cupboard is joined throughout with mortise-and-tenon joints. The rear stiles extend the full height of the cupboard and are joined at their tops to the rails of the overhanging cornice. The balusters are doweled to the middle shelf at their lower ends and to large blocks at their upper ends. The top side rails of the case extend beyond the stiles of the recessed cupboard and are tenoned to the blocks above the balusters. The front rail of the cornice also is tenoned to each block, while the front rail of the recessed cupboard is tenoned to the front stiles. A thin board is then nailed to the top of these two front rails, forming a roof for the overhang. The molding on the lower edge of the cornice is applied with nails. The doors to the upper cupboard are hinged with wooden pintles at their outside edges; each is fitted with a wooden pull and secured with a wooden catch nailed to the frame. The joints of each door frame are secured with two pegs. Inside the upper cupboard there is a longitudinal shelf across the rear, supported by shaped brackets nailed to the stiles. A central vertical transverse partition divides the cupboard in half; it is made of two boards nailed in place and is notched to allow the shelf to pass through. The cupboard door in the lower section is pintle hinged on the right and opens to a plain interior. The rails and stiles of the lower section are secured with a single pin, while the muntins between the panels are double pinned. On the case sides, the middle rail is double pegged; the bottom rail and the mun-

195a

tin are single pegged. The bottom of the upper cupboard consists of several transverse boards joined with a V-shaped groove, beveled on their front edge, and nailed to the top of the back rail and fitted to a groove in the front rail. The bottom of the lower cupboard is a single board beveled at each side and nailed to the frame. The three vertical backboards extend the full height of the case, are beveled on their sides, and are nailed with large rosehead nails to all four sides of the case. The drawer is sidehung on runners rabbeted and nailed to the stiles. The drawer front is rabbeted to accept the sides, which are nailed with T-head nails above and below the channel for the runner. The back is rabbeted to accept the sides and is nailed in place through the back above and below the runner channel with rosehead nails. The drawer bottom is a single longitudinal board beveled on all four sides, let into a groove in the front, and nailed to the underside of the sides and back with rosehead nails.

Inscriptions: A Connecticut Tercentenary label and a "Connecticut Furniture" (1967) exhibition label are pasted to the inside of the right side of the drawer; a typewritten note thumbtacked to the outside of the back reads "Bequeathed to Yale University by / Mr. Charles Wyllys Betts / of the Class of 1867."

Condition: The cupboard has survived in an extraordinary condition, retaining almost all of its applied ornament and original painted decoration. Four "satellite" bosses once surrounded the large boss on the upper panels of each side. A turned drop in the center of the frieze is missing, and the top element of the spindle on the left side of the lower section is larger than the other three and may be a replacement. A new interior catch has been added to the door in the lower cupboard; the original wooden catch located at the top of the door is missing. Iron braces have been added to the inside of this door at the joint of the rails and the right stile. Two dentils on the right and left above the drawer are missing; in old photographs, one additional dentil on the right was missing, as was the small boss in the upper right corner of the central panel in the upper section. John T. Kirk, citing nail holes on the underside of the top, has suggested recently that the current top was used originally as a chest top.[1]

Woods: Frame, white oak; drawer back, bottom of upper and lower cupboard, shelf in upper cupboard, other elements, southern yellow pine; backboards, drawer bottom, yellow poplar; balusters, bosses, spindles, possibly a maple; applied moldings, dentils, probably eastern red cedar.

Dimensions: H 142.6; W 123.1; CW 119.2; D 53.7; CD 51.1.

Exhibitions: *Three Centuries of Conn. Furn.*, no. 30; Kirk, *Conn. Furn.*, no. 106; Ward, *Eye of the Beholder*, no. 84; Fairbanks and Trent, *New England Begins*, no. 257; *Great River*, cat. 78.

Bibliography: Nutting, *Furn. Pilgrim Century* (1921), p. 127; Nutting, *Furn. Pilgrim Century* (1924), fig. 202; Nutting, *Treasury*, no. 449; Dyer, "Press Cupboard," fig. 4; *Antiques* 49, no. 2 (February 1946): front cover; Kirk, *Early Am. Furn.*, fig. 27; Kane, "Joiners of Hartford County," fig. 2; Fales, *Am. Painted Furn.*, fig. 14; Joseph T. Butler, *American Furni-*

ture from the First Colonies to World War I (London: Triune Books, 1973), p. 12; James P. Walsh, *Connecticut Industry and the Revolution*, Connecticut Bicentennial Series, XXIX (Hartford: American Revolution Bicentennial Commission of Connecticut, 1978), p. 29; Chinnery, fig. 4:213; Kane, "American Furn.," pl. I; Michael Goldman, "Curators in Wonderland: A Survey of Wishful Thinking," *Antiques World* 3, no. 5 (March 1981): 40; Kirk, *Am. Furn. & Brit. Trad.*, fig. 227; Christopher Wilk, *The Art of Wood Turning* (New York: American Craft Museum II, 1983), fig. 11; Shestack, *Selections*, p. 36.

Provenance: Charles Wyllys Betts, New York, N.Y.

OF the several Wethersfield cupboards discussed by Walter A. Dyer in 1935, this example has survived in the best condition and is the best guide to the original applied and painted decoration of the entire Wethersfield group. No other examples have come to light in the half century since Dyer's survey appeared in *Antiques*. Among the other examples that he published are another cupboard at Yale (cat. 196); cupboards in the Wadsworth Atheneum (26.288), the Museum of Fine Arts, Boston (32.273, formerly in the Tyler collection), and the Lancaster Public Library, Lancaster, Massachusetts; and two privately owned examples, one then in the collection of Henry W. Erving of Hartford, and another, formerly in the collection of Mr. Garvan, then in the collection of Harold M. Lehman of Tarrytown, New York. One example published by Dyer (fig. 7), now in the New Haven Colony Historical Society, is not of the period. Like the two Wethersfield chests with drawers in the Yale collection (cats. 26–27), this cupboard and the following example are attributed to the shop of Peter Blin and his followers in Wethersfield and the surrounding area. The cupboards are unique in American workmanship of this period in being constructed of a single unit, although smaller, later board cupboards (cat. 199) also are made in this fashion. For every Wethersfield cupboard to survive, there are about seven or eight surviving chests, suggesting the rarity and importance of the cupboard form in its own time. The cupboard now in the Lancaster Public Library was owned originally by the Reverend Joseph Rowlandson (d. 1678) and his wife Mary, and the other cupboards probably were owned originally by individuals of similar high social status.

Bequest of Charles Wyllys Betts, B.A. 1867 1887.7

1. John T. Kirk, "American Furniture in an International Context," in *Perspectives in American Furniture*, ed. Gerald W. R. Ward (forthcoming).

196

Cupboard
Possibly by Peter Blin (d. 1725)
Wethersfield, Connecticut, 1675–1690

Description: This cupboard varies from the preceding example (cat. 195) only in small details of construction and ornament and in its condition. There are variances in the carved panels on the lower section: for example, here the tulips at the top of the panels have long, thin vertical carved lines rather than the short gouges found on the other cupboard, and the "thistles" at the lower end of the side panels are lacking on this example. The molding at the lower edge of the cornice of this cupboard is in a reversed position, and this cupboard has four small "satellite" bosses surrounding the larger boss on the upper panels of each side of the case. The door to the lower cupboard is hinged on the opposite side here as well, and there are no brackets supporting the shelf in the upper cupboard.

Condition: This cupboard has been refinished, and the painted decoration heavily restored. The central drop in the cornice, the round bosses on the central panel in the upper section, the applied strapwork hearts in the lower section, and other applied elements are replacements. The bottom of the right front leg is pieced, and new screws have been added to the drawer sides and front. There is a new lock on the upper right cupboard door, and a new catch on the lower cupboard door. There are burn marks on the underside of the projecting cornice.

Woods: Frame, white oak; southern yellow pine; balusters, bosses, spindles, strapwork hearts, a maple; applied moldings, dentils, a cedar.

Dimensions: H 142.4; W 126.0; CW 120.3; D 52.7; CD 50.9.

Bibliography: Lyon, fig. 19; [George T. Robinson], "The Colonial Furniture of New England," *Building News* (London), 13 May 1892; *Sun* (New York), 10 July 1892; Dyer, "Press Cupboard," fig. 3.

Provenance: Lyon states that he purchased this cupboard from an old Connecticut family, and Dyer gave the family name as Kircombe. However, in a letter to Francis P. Garvan dated 6 October 1935 from a Miss Grace E. Hine of Dedham, Mass., Miss Hine suggests that the family's name was Kirkham. She wrote, with reference to the illustration of the Lyon cupboard in the Dyer article, "This cupboard is of special

196

interest to me because I have heard all my life of the old Atwood sunflower cupboard which my grandmother, Mrs. John S. *Kirkham*, not *Kircombe*, once sold for a hundred dollars. She had brought it from the old Atwood homestead in Newington when she was married.... My mother and two uncles have told about crawling into the lower cupboard when they were small children." Miss Hine's grandmother was Hannah Prudence Atwood (1827–1882), who married J. S. Kirkham in 1859.[1] She was a direct descendant of Thomas Atwood (d. 1682), a physician of Wethersfield, Conn., and his wife Abigail. Their youngest son, Josiah Atwood, settled in Newington parish and established the family homestead. Irving W. Lyon purchased the cupboard, probably in 1882 after the death of Hannah Atwood Kirkham, and it descended to Lyon's son Charles Woolsey Lyon, New York, N. Y., who sold it to Francis P. Garvan, New York, N. Y.

THE first Wethersfield cupboard to be published, this example takes on additional importance because of its recently discovered history of ownership in the Atwood family of Wethersfield and Newington, a small town just to the southwest of Wethersfield. Unfortunately, the estate papers of the presumed original owner, one Thomas Atwood, physician, do not include an inventory of his personal goods; his total estate, both real and personal, was valued at £148.6.9.[2] Perhaps even more unfortunately, this cupboard has not survived in the virtually untouched state of cat. 195. Its condition is testimony to the late nineteenth- and early twentieth-century taste for heavily refinished objects that would shine like reproductions. An even more dramatic example of this philosophy is another cupboard (Appendix, no. 26), once owned by collector Henry Waters of Salem and even more thoroughly rebuilt.

The Mabel Brady Garvan Collection 1942.255

1. Henry R. Stiles, *The History of Ancient Wethersfield, Connecticut*, vol. 2 (New York: Grafton Press, 1904), pp. 38–40.
2. Docket 225, Hartford Probate District, Connecticut State Library.

197

Cupboard
Guilford, Connecticut, 1670–1700

Description: The cupboard is in two cases. The top of the upper case is molded at the front and sides and overhangs the case slightly. The cornice contains an ebonized corbel at the center and each side of the front and at the front and rear of each side. The upper edge of the cornice is molded, and the face of the cornice, between the corbels, is carved with foliated S-scrolls against a matted or punched ground. The base of the cornice is fitted with applied ebonized molding. The front of the upper case is divided into three units. The center section is framed to a single panel, decorated with applied moldings and a center ebonized strip to simulate a pair of superimposed panels. Each simulated panel contains a raised diamond-shaped ebonized boss. The center section is flanked by pairs of tall applied ebonized spindles, which are repeated on the stiles flanking the cupboard doors. Each door contains a central panel decorated with applied cruciform moldings, with ebonized squares in the corners and with a large ebonized boss and four small bosses in the center of each panel. The sides of the upper case are framed to a single large panel, edged with applied moldings and with a large, rather flat diamond-shaped boss at center, flanked by an applied spindle. The bottom of the upper case has heavy V-shaped pro-

Cupboards and Presses

197

jecting molding at the front and sides. The lower case has dentil molding at the top and contains three graduated drawers. Each drawer has a central wooden pull, flanked by carved glyphs and panels of carved foliated S-scrolls. The drawers are separated by heavy ebonized moldings and flanked by pairs of ebonized spindles on the stiles. The sides of the lower case are framed to a single panel decorated with bosses and applied moldings to simulate three superimposed panels. The center panel conforms to the size of the middle drawer, while the bottom panel is slightly smaller, and the top panel is smaller still, barely accommodating the pair of bosses. There is heavy base molding at the front and sides of the lower case, and the four stiles extend below to form the feet. The top of the upper case consists of two longitudinal butted boards extending the width of the case, edged with strips at the front and sides, and nailed and pegged to the case. Each case is heavily framed with mortise-and-tenon joints, with the heavy moldings and spindles applied with wooden pegs. The back of each case is framed to a pair of large panels. The upper case rests on top of the lower case, with tenons projecting from the bottom rear rail of the

upper case inserted into mortises in the top rear rail of the lower case. The side and rear panels in each case are formed of several butted boards. The joints of the cupboard doors are double pegged, and the bottom of the upper case consists of several half-lapped transverse boards nailed in place. There is no bottom to the lower case. The drawers are side hung on runners rabbeted and nailed to the stiles. (The right drawer runner for the lowest drawer initially was placed too high on the stile.) There is a longitudinal support for the bottom drawer nailed to the inside of the back, and the lower left drawer runner also is braced with a small support, all possibly original. The drawer fronts taper in thickness from top to bottom (being thicker at the bottom) and are rabbeted to accept the sides. The outer face of each side is rabbeted, and the sides are nailed to the front with rosehead nails above and below the groove for the drawer runner. The drawer bottoms consist of several longitudinal boards nailed to the underside of the sides and back, beveled on the front edge, and fitted to a groove in the front. The wood used throughout the cupboards appears to be riven, and the rough surfaces were not planed off. The cupboard doors are pintle

197a

hinged to the case. The right door is fitted with an iron escutcheon and lock; the left with a wooden pull. There is a wooden turn button for each door. There is much variation in the sizes of the various elements used to compose the tall spindles in the upper case.

Inscriptions: A small fragment of a late seventeenth- or early eighteenth-century document, possibly a bill of sale or list of articles including bushels of salt, recently was found wedged in the upper case, between the top and the front of the case.

Condition: A shelf and a central vertical transverse partition, originally nailed to the inside of the cupboard, are missing. The rear corbels on the left and right sides of the upper case and the outer spindles on the far right of the stile opposite the middle and lowest drawers are replacements. The bosses on the side panels of the upper case have been scored with concentric circles, and circles have been scored on the outside and inside of the right cupboard door. In 1967, an original spindle was discovered in storage and was reinstalled in its original location on the far right of the stile opposite the top drawer, where a replacement had been located.

Woods: Frame, red oak and white oak; drawer bottoms, bosses, spindles, light applied moldings, Atlantic white cedar; strip nailed to inside of back below bottom drawer, yellow poplar.

Dimensions: H 146.1; W 130.4; UCW 121.3; LCW 120.8; D 60.7; UCD 55.9; LCD 55.9.

Exhibition: Kane, *Furn. New Haven Colony*, no. XII.

Bibliography: Lyon, fig. 20; Nutting, *Furn. Pilgrim Century* (1924), fig. 219; Nutting, *Treasury*, no. 454; Kirk, *Conn. Furn.*, no. 107 (included in catalogue but not in exhibition); Kirk, *Early Am. Furn.*, figs. 148, 182; Kane, "New Haven Colony Furn.," pl. I; Kirk, *Am. Furn. & Brit. Trad.*, fig. 219; Trent, "Postscript," p. 39 fig. 12.

Provenance: Found in Durham, Conn., in the early 1880s by collector Charles Wyllys Betts, New York, N.Y.

THIS cupboard and the succeeding example (cat. 198), presumably from the same workshop, are part of a larger group of objects identified with the Guilford-Madison area of Connecticut with related foliated S-scroll carving (also see cats. 21, 23).[1] The other cupboard now at Yale has a history of ownership in the Stone family, at least raising the possibility that their maker was Lieutenant Nathaniel Stone (1649–1709), a woodworker of Guilford.[2] The Stones were a large family in Guilford, however, tracing their origins to the mid seventeenth century, and thus an attribution to Nathaniel Stone must remain tentative without further evidence. The Betts bequest to Yale also included another cupboard (Appendix, no. 27), possibly English, that has been heavily restored and altered.

Bequest of C. Wyllys Betts, B.A. 1867 1887.6

197b

1. Four related cupboards are known, as well as chests, chests with drawers, and boxes (see Kane, *Furn. New Haven Colony*, nos. VIII–XX). Also see Lyon, fig. 8 (Metropolitan Museum of Art, 30.120.378), and St. George, *Wrought Covenant*, fig. 77 (Old Dartmouth Historical Society, Taunton, Mass.).
2. Kane, *Furn. New Haven Colony*, p. 90.

198

Cupboard
Guilford, Connecticut, 1670–1700

Description: This cupboard is distinguished from the preceding example (cat. 197) only by minor variations of ornament and construction. Here, the cornice is shallower and is decorated with triglyphs rather than corbels. There are no small bosses used in the center of the paneled doors, and the cruciform moldings are laid in a more vertical pattern. Large spindles are not used on the sides of the upper case. In the lower case, there is no dentil course above the top drawer,

and single spindles (rather than pairs) are used on the stiles. The simulated panels on the sides of the lower case lack the applied moldings found on the other example, and only single bosses are used in each panel. On the top drawer, on the right side, the carver reversed the orientation of the foliated S-scroll. The cupboard doors are fitted with wooden pulls, but without the use of an iron lock. Here, the shelf and central partition within the cupboard have survived. The grain of the boards used to form the panels in the backs and sides of the upper case is reversed from the preceding example. The spindles here are a somewhat simpler form, lacking some of the elements found on cat. 197, and there are other minor differences.

Inscriptions: Labels from the Connecticut Tercentenary and "Connecticut Furniture" (1967) exhibition are pasted to the inside of the right side of the top drawer.

Condition: The drawer runners in the case are replacements, and the grooves for the drawer sides have been repaired. The drawer bottoms have been renailed, and the top edge of some drawer sides has been pieced. Some of the black paint has been retouched. The spindle to the right of the middle drawer, attached only with a nail, may be a replacement. The applied moldings on the side panels of the upper case are replacements.

Woods: Frame, primarily red oak; top of upper case, chestnut; spindles, bosses, triglyphs, light moldings, eastern red cedar.

Dimensions: H 141.1; W 130.3; UCW 121.8; LCW 121.5; D 58.9; UCD 55.1; LCD 55.3.

198

198a

Exhibitions: *Three Centuries of Conn. Furn.*, no. 3; Kirk, *Conn. Furn.*, no. 108.

Bibliography: *Antiquarian* 12, no. 4 (May 1929): 48 (see also *Antiques* 121, no. 1 [January 1982]: 275; Walter A. Dyer, "The American Press & Court Cupboard," *Fine Arts* 19, no. 3 (December 1932): 19; Kirk, *Early Am. Furn.*, fig. 149; Kane, *Furn. New Haven Colony*, no. XIII (included in catalogue but not in exhibition).

Provenance: Purchased from the Stone family, "in which it had descended for generations," in 1883 in Madison, Conn., by a Mrs. Leete on behalf of Irving W. Lyon.[1] The cupboard descended to Lyon's son Charles Woolsey Lyon, New York, N.Y., who sold it in 1929 to Francis P. Garvan, New York, N.Y.

THIS cupboard and cat. 197 are the only two examples in the Yale collection of cupboards with only drawers in the lower case or section. This form, certainly uncommon and perhaps unknown in English furniture, also was made in Massachusetts.[2] Its use in this country represents a mixture of the

cupboard, a form dating to medieval times, with the more modern chest of drawers, and thus may be indicative of the tension in the New World between old traditions and new modes. The broad, projecting midmolding on the two Yale cupboards is seen on two-part English chests of drawers of the mid seventeenth century, to which these cupboards also bear an affinity in their two-stage construction and front facades in a single plane, lacking the recessed upper section supported by balusters.[3] Of the two examples, this cupboard is less richly ornamented, and therefore probably cost less, than its more elaborate counterpart. The owner of this cupboard chose not to have a lock on either cupboard door, perhaps as another cost-cutting measure.

The Mabel Brady Garvan Collection 1930.2192

1. Irving P. Lyon Papers, Winterthur Museum, 78 x 314.578.
2. Chinnery, p. 373; St. George, *Wrought Covenant*, nos. 35, 36, 59. For an earlier, related example from south Germany, see Eric Mercer, *Furniture 700–1700* (London: Weidenfeld and Nicolson, 1969), fig. 99.
3. Chinnery, fig. 4:46; Percy Macquoid, *A History of English Furniture: The Age of Oak* (London: Lawrence and Bullen, 1904), figs. 210, 211.

199

Cupboard

New Hampshire, probably Hampton, 1700–1740
(see pl. 18)

Description: This small cupboard of board construction is made as a single unit. The top is molded on its front and side edges and overhangs the recessed upper cupboard. It is supported at the front corners by turned ebonized balusters. The front of the upper cupboard is divided into three simulated panels by applied moldings painted black, with the side panels of greater width. The central panel, a door, is hinged on the right with a pair of snipe-bill hinges, and each panel has a round brass escutcheon with a drop pull; the pull is placed higher on the door. The panels are painted with many black squiggles against the "tiger" stripe of the maple. The shelf between the upper and lower sections is molded on its front and side edges and painted black. The lower section contains a cupboard faced with three panels over a drawer, with the central panel again being a door, of greater width, hinged on the right with snipe-bill hinges. It bears a brass placed high in the center. The door is painted with a central tree rising from the bottom to the height of the brass, with small birds roosting in its branches, and with many black squiggles; each side panel is painted with a large stylized branch emanating from its lower inner edge and forking into three branches, and with a smaller branch or vine beginning at the outer lower corner and moving toward the center. The middle of the drawer is painted with "SR" flanked by trees with scrolling vines moving to the sides, and the drawer is fitted with two brasses. Each side of the drawer has an applied vertical molding continuing the line of the panel moldings above, and there is a base molding at the front below the drawer. The front skirt is shaped with rather jagged brackets and a central drop and is painted with scrolls and a branch or leaf form on the drop. The sides of the case are painted with large leaves and branches, including a roosting bird, and the lower edge of each side is shaped to a simple bracket to form the front and rear feet. The top is a single board, and the balusters are nailed in place through

Cupboards and Presses 387

the top. The back of the case consists of three vertical boards fitted together with beveled edges and nailed to the case. The middle shelf and bottom of the lower cupboard are single boards nailed to a framework of strips applied to the case sides and front. The boards forming the front of the case are nailed to the case sides and to these longitudinal strips. The front apron consists of three separate boards nailed in place. The drawer is supported by runners nailed to the sides and by strips at the front and back of the case. On the drawer, the sides are slot dovetailed to the front, which projects slightly beyond the sides. The sides are rabbeted to accept the back and nailed in place through the back. The drawer bottom is a single longitudinal board nailed to all four sides. The back of the drawer is riven and remains rough hewn in the center. The drawer sides taper from a height of 11.5 cm at the front to 8.5 cm at the rear, and the drawer runners are nailed to the case at a corresponding angle.

Inscriptions: "Sarah / Rowell" is written in black paint on the top of the cupboard, and "SR" is painted in black in the center of the drawer front. Sawmill marks appear on the underside of the drawer bottom.

Condition: Four of the brasses are replacements.

Woods: Front of case, drawer front and sides, balusters, soft maple; sides of case, bottom of drawer, eastern hemlock; drawer back, backboards, shelf, other secondary wood, eastern white pine.

Dimensions: H 133.5; W 93.9; CW 90.9; D 48.2; CD (upper section) 32.2; CD (lower section) 46.6.

Bibliography: Nutting, *Treasury*, no. 472; Esther S. Fraser, "Pioneer Furniture from Hampton, New Hampshire," *Antiques* 17, no. 4 (April 1930): 313; Nina Fletcher Little, "Country Furniture: A Symposium," *Antiques* 93, no. 3 (March 1968): 348; Kirk, *Early Am. Furn.*, fig. 77; Fales, *Am. Painted Furn.*, fig. 56; Chinnery, fig. 4:228; Marshall B. Davidson, *The Bantam Illustrated Guide to Early American Furniture* (New York: Bantam Books, 1980), p. 8; Kirk, *Am. Furn. & Brit. Trad.*, fig. 589.

Provenance: According to a tradition recorded in the 1920s, this cupboard was redecorated as a dower chest for Sarah Rowell, who married Benjamin Moulton (b. 1721) at an unspecified date, possibly in the 1740s. The Rowell family was located in Hampton, Hampton Falls, and South Hampton, N. H., and the surrounding area from the seventeenth century. The name Sarah was a popular family choice, making identification of the owner of the cupboard difficult. She may have been the Sarah Rowell born in 1722 in nearby Salisbury, Mass., the daughter of Job and Bethiah (Brown) Rowell. The cupboard descended in the family to a Miss Smith of Exeter, N. H., who sold it to Mr. Charles W. Arnold, a leather manufacturer of Haverhill, Mass. After placing the cupboard on loan to the Museum of Fine Arts, Boston, for several years, Arnold sold the cupboard in 1929 to Francis P. Garvan, New York, N. Y., through Henry Hammond Taylor, Bridgeport, Conn.

DESPITE the traditional family history, the painted decoration on this cupboard is probably original to it, rather than a later embellishment. This would hold true even if the cupboard was made for Sarah Rowell's wedding of about 1740 (which remains unclear), for such a late date is not

199a

inconsistent with this late expression of the seventeenth-century cupboard form. The black painted decoration here is related to that on a chest dated 1719 and signed by Samuel Lane (1698–1776) of Hampton, New Hampshire, further strengthening the attribution to that area, although not necessarily to that maker.[1] There are several related American examples, and English board cupboards of this type have been published.[2] The balusters of the Yale example, reminiscent of the front stretchers on early eighteenth-century chairs, are particularly bold.

The Mabel Brady Garvan Collection 1930.2189

1. Esther S. Fraser, "Pioneer Furniture from Hampton, New Hampshire," *Antiques* 17, no. 4 (April 1930): 312–316, fig. 1.
2. Related American cupboards include examples at the Metropolitan Museum of Art (Nutting, *Treasury*, nos. 470, 471), the Museum of Fine Arts, Boston (Randall, no. 24), the Wadsworth Atheneum (Nutting, *Treasury*, no. 473), and other published examples in *Antiques* 93, no. 3 (March 1968): 361, *Antiques* 110, no. 1 (July 1976): 97, and Nina Fletcher Little, *Little by Little: Six Decades of Collecting American Decorative Arts* (New York: E. P. Dutton, 1984), pp. 196–197. See also *Sack Coll.*, 6: 1624 no. P2419. For an English example, see Kirk, *Am. Furn. & Brit. Trad.*, fig. 590.

200

200

Clothespress

Connecticut, probably Middletown, 1660–1690

Description: The press has a flat rectangular top above an applied dentil course and a heavy applied molding on the front of the case. Each door flanking a central stile is framed to four panels, each decorated to simulate a pair of superimposed panels. Each simulated panel has a rabbeted edge and a raised central rectangle, molded on its vertical sides and notched on its horizontal edges, with an inlaid diamond (elongated on the lower panels) surrounded by inlaid pegs at the corners of the diamond, and with stamped punchwork in each corner. The rails, stiles, and muntins of the doors have central channel molding. The right door is fitted with an iron lock, and the doors are attached to the case with wrought-iron butterfly hinges. Heavy molding is nailed to the front of the case below the doors, and the front is framed to four horizontal panels at this level. The stiles and muntins at this level have central channel molding, and the muntins are molded on their panel edges. The four stiles continue below applied base molding to form the legs. The sides of the case are framed to echo the front, with a pair of vertical panels above another pair of vertical panels at the height of the doors, with a single horizontal panel below. The doors open to a plain interior; the top rear rail is fitted with five pegs for clothes, and the middle rail is also fitted with turned pegs. Three pairs of battens or strips are nailed to the sides. The back consists of five vertical boards joined with a tongue and groove and nailed to the rear rails. The bottom consists of five boards, again fitted with a tongue and groove and nailed in place.

Condition: The front and side edges of the top have been planed, and its color underneath is fresh, suggesting that it is a replacement. The outer dentils on each side are replacements. The four stiles have been pieced to about the height of the base molding, which itself is a replacement. The backboards and bottom boards are early replacements, perhaps dating to the eighteenth century. The supports for shelves

Cupboards and Presses 389

added to the interior have aged, but are not original to the press. The row of turned pegs in the middle rail is a later addition, and some of them in turn have been replaced. The lock is a later addition, the hinges on the left door are replacements, and a new hook and eye has been added to the left door. According to tradition, the cupboard was at one time painted red, which was stripped off in the nineteenth century. The backboards were stained by water in 1980.

Woods: Red oak; inlaid diamonds, pegs, probably cedar; replaced backboards, bottom boards, eastern white pine.

Dimensions: H 158.8; W 120.4; CW 112.6; D 46.1; CD 42.2.

Exhibitions: Kirk, *Conn. Furn.*, no. 111; Fairbanks and Trent, *New England Begins*, no. 258.

Bibliography: *The Story of an Old Oaken Cupboard: 125 Years of Progress, 1825–1950* (Middletown, Conn.: Middletown Savings Bank, 1950); Kane, "Joiners of Hartford County," fig. 13.

Provenance: According to tradition, the press was owned prior to 1825 by Samuel Southmayd, Middletown, Conn., who used it in his apothecary store as a place to safeguard valuable papers and money for his friends, prior to the founding of the Middletown Savings Bank in 1825. It passed by descent to Horace Southmayd, New York, N. Y.; by descent, ca. 1877, to Stephen Southmayd, Middletown, Conn.; by descent to his wife, Sarah A. Southmayd; by descent, ca. 1890, to Alice G. Southmayd, Derby, Conn.; by sale to Sam Wineck, Hartford, Conn.; by sale to Wallace Nutting, Framingham, Mass.; by sale to Henry Hammond Taylor, Bridgeport, Conn.; by sale in 1929 to Francis P. Garvan, New York, N. Y.

T**his** unusual New England clothespress is one of three related objects, including another rare press, attributed by Patricia E. Kane to the hand of John Hall, Sr. (1584–1673), of Middletown, or to his sons John, Jr. (1619–1694), or Samuel (1626–1690), all of whom were carpenters.[1] The cornerstone of the attribution is a chest, now in the collection of Old Sturbridge Village, that descended in the Hall family, and it is given added strength by all three objects' having traditional histories in the Middletown area.[2] The clothespress was not a popular form in early New England, where people preferred to keep their clothes and other goods in the enclosed, more tightly organized and controlled interior spaces of cupboards and chests. Although the form was not popular there, several English examples related to the Yale press have been published.[3]

The Mabel Brady Garvan Collection 1930.2232

1. Kane, "Joiners of Hartford County," pp. 82–85. A more recent discussion of the "Hall shops" is included in Fairbanks and Trent, *New England Begins*, no. 258. Both writers emphasize that although the press is joined, its construction and ornament reveal several gaucheries that indicate these objects were made by carpenters rather than accomplished joiners. The other press is illustrated by Nutting (*Treasury*, no. 474), who stated that it has a Glastonbury history; its present whereabouts are unknown.
2. Illustrated in Kane, "Joiners of Hartford County," fig. 12.
3. Chinnery, figs. 3:284–288.

201

Clothespress

Pennsylvania, probably Chester County, 1750–1770
(see pl. 19)

Description: The press is crowned by large complex cornice molding that projects at the front and sides. There is secondary molding at the front and sides above the pair of doors. Each door is framed with two superimposed fielded panels, with the raised center section surrounded by applied molding in a geometric pattern. There is a vertical strip with central half-round molding applied to the inner edge of the right door. The doors are flanked by pairs of superimposed panels with the rails and stiles molded on their panel edges. There is applied molding beneath the doors, and the lower section contains three blind lipped drawers in line, with the center drawer of lesser width. There is complex projecting base molding at the front and sides, echoing the cornice molding, and the press is supported by turned feet in each corner and a fifth foot at the center of the front. The right door is fitted with an iron escutcheon and lock, and the doors open to an interior with three superimposed shelves on the left. The shelves have canted front edges and rest on thin strips pinned to the front and rear of the case. They are enclosed on the right at the rear by a transverse vertical board that is braced at the bottom, scrolled on its upper edge, and tenoned to a board that runs the width of the case and acts as an upper shelf. The interior also includes a longitudinal strip nailed with rosehead nails to the upper part of the back, below the shelf, and fitted with five shaped pegs for clothes. The press is made in several separate sections joined together by wooden pegs or keys. The sections include the

201

cornice, the sides of the case, the backboards, and the base section with the drawers. The cornice and base are dovetailed frameworks with the moldings applied with wooden pins. The backboards of the case are loosely fitted together with a half lap or simply butted and rest in grooves in the cornice and base. The feet are doweled to the base. On the drawers, the sides are dovetailed to the front and back, and the bottom is pinned to a rabbet in the front and to the underside of the sides and back. On the left and center drawers, the bottom is a single transverse board, while the bottom of the right drawer consists of two outer boards grooved on their inner edges as if for a central spline. The drawer runners are pegged in place.

Inscriptions: Small fragments of a modern Philadelphia newspaper are pasted to the inside of the front and right side of the case.

Condition: The H-hinges on the right door and the rattail hinges on the left door are replacements. Originally the doors were fitted with H-hinges attached to a vertical strip pegged to the case; the strip is still present on the right. The foot at the center of the front is smaller than those in the four corners and may be a replacement. The left front edge of the cornice has been repaired, and there have been other minor restorations.

Woods: American black walnut; yellow poplar.

Dimensions: H 204.7; W 192.5; CW 158.5; D 73.0; CD 56.0.

Provenance: The press is said to have been found in Chester County, Pa., by dealer Philip Platt; it was purchased from Platt about 1950 by dealer Richard French of Old Lyme, Conn., from whom it was acquired by purchase.

KNOWN as a *Kleiderschrank* or simply *Schrank* in German, or as a *kast* or *kas* in Dutch, architectonic clothespresses of this kind reflect the ethnic diversity found in many parts of early America and Canada outside of New England.[1] These *Schranks*, used for the storage of clothing and other textiles, were more mobile than one might imagine, due to their construction in several units that could be quickly and easily disassembled.[2] The Yale example is a rather simple example of the form, without the sulfur and other inlays often found on walnut presses. *Schranks* of softwood often were painted, and an important group of early kas are painted with grisaille decoration of fruit and foliage.[3]

The Mabel Brady Garvan Collection 1971.51

1. Forman, "German Influences," pp. 160–164.
2. An "exploded" *Schrank* is illustrated, along with several examples of the form, in Vernon S. Gunnion, "The Pennsylvania-German *Schrank*," Antiques 123, no. 5 (May 1983): 1026 fig. 7; see also Forman, "German Influences," fig. 102.
3. Patricia Chapin O'Donnell, "Grisaille Decorated *Kasten* of New York," Antiques 117, no. 5 (May 1980): 1108–1111.

202

Clothespress
Pennsylvania, 1770–1800

Description: The upper case is crowned at the front and sides with heavy projecting cornice molding and contains two doors with fielded panels flanking a center vertical paneled partition. The doors are attached to the case with wrought-iron rattail hinges, and each has six fielded panels, a pair of square panels over two pairs of vertical rectangular

201a

panels. The center partition is paneled in a similar manner with a tier of single panels. The upper case rests within a mid-molding applied to the lower case. The lower case contains five lipped drawers: three in line, with the side drawers of greater width, over two deeper and wider drawers in line. The cupboard doors are fitted with brass lock escutcheons, blind on the right side, and the right door is locked by means of a wooden throw passing through a cleat on the rear of the center partition and the right door and released through the left side. The left door opens to an interior with strips nailed near the top at the sides and rear and fitted with turned hanging pegs for clothes; there is a center vertical transverse partition, and the right cupboard (now similarly fitted with hanging pegs) originally contained three fixed shelves. Each case is constructed in a similar sturdy manner. The sides are dovetailed to the top and bottom, with the dovetails at the joint of the lower-case sides and top exposed on the sides. The front frame is pegged to the sides and top, and the vertical backboards are joined with a half lap and pegged to the sides and top, with some nails also used. The joints of the paneled doors are secured with pairs of large wooden pegs, like those used elsewhere on the case, and they can be lifted off their hinges. There is a three-quarter dustboard between the tiers of drawers, with guides and runners pegged in place. The vertical partitions in the lower case are tenoned through the drawer divider and pegged. The cornice and midmoldings are nailed and pegged in place. On each drawer, the sides are dovetailed to the front and back with wedged dovetails; the bottoms are beveled on their front and side edges, let into grooves in the front and sides, and nailed to the underside of the back. The top edge of each drawer side is rounded. The middle drawer in the upper tier is divided into two small compartments at the back.

Inscription: Written in black on the outside of the back of the upper case is "1357."

Condition: At one time the cupboard was painted, possibly green; the paint has been removed, and the object given a cherry stain. The feet and base molding are replacements. The shelves in the right side of the cupboard interior have been removed, the grooves that housed them filled, and new strips with hanging pegs installed. The interior of the cupboards has been stained. There have been minor repairs to the drawer fronts and the moldings. The bottom of the lower left drawer is a replacement, and running strips have been added to several of the drawers. The brasses are replacements; the cupboard originally may have been fitted with cast brass escutcheons of an earlier style.

202

Woods: Yellow poplar; most drawer linings, chestnut.

Dimensions: H 206.4; W 166.4; UCW 150.0; LCW 156.7; D 55.6; UCD 47.1; LCD 49.1.

Provenance: Francis P. Garvan, New York, N. Y.

LESS bold than the preceding example (cat. 201), and slightly later in date, this clothespress also reflects Continental woodworking traditions in its extensive use of wooden pegs as fasteners and of wedged and exposed dovetails. Here, although the doors lift off their hinges, the case itself is composed of only two stages. Once again, shelves and hanging pegs in the upper part of the case are combined with drawers in the lower section, although here there are a total of five drawers. This blending of a clothespress with a chest of drawers represents a significant merger of Continental and Anglo-American traditions for the storage of clothing and textiles. Some related examples are decorated with quarter

Cupboards and Presses 393

columns on the front corners of the case.[1] Unlike the previous, walnut clothespress, this yellow poplar example undoubtedly was painted, perhaps with polychrome decoration, originally.

The Mabel Brady Garvan Collection 1930.2278

1. Lockwood, fig. 177; Hagler, *American Queen Anne Furn.*, p. 51. See also *Antiques* 114, no. 5 (November 1978): 962; *Antiques* 90, no. 4 (October 1966): 475; and an unpublished example in the collection of Bartram's Garden, Philadelphia.

203

Clothespress
Southern, possibly Virginia, 1680–1710

Description: The joined press has a cyma molding at the front and sides of the top, and its two doors open to an interior fitted with four pegs in the top back rail and a single peg in the center of each side top rail; the pegs are doweled through the top back rail. The doors are attached to the case with wrought-iron H-hinges and are secured with an iron-chain catch. Each door is framed to two superimposed panels of equal size, decorated with diagonal applied moldings meeting at the center, where a square panel is formed with additional heavy applied moldings. The front of the case below the doors is framed to two horizontal panels in line with applied moldings echoing those on the doors. Each side of the case is framed to three superimposed horizontal panels edged with applied moldings, and the back is framed to six panels with beveled edges. There is applied base molding at the front and sides. The bottom consists of several transverse half-lapped boards nailed in place. The case is joined with mortise-and-tenon joints secured with a single peg.

Condition: The press has been stripped of its paint and refinished. There are traces of white and a brick color on the front and sides and of later blue-green paint on the back. The interior retains traces of an old reddish stain. The top has been replaced with three old boards originally used for another purpose which are nailed to new supporting strips nailed to the sides of the case between the front and rear stiles. A center post originally separating the doors has been removed, and the bottom rail pieced. The right door originally had a catch, now lost, at its upper edge; a new wooden catch has been added to the bottom of the left door. Two pairs of supports for shelves are nailed to the front and rear stiles, probably at an early date, and shelves consisting of two boards were placed on top of these supports; half of the bottom shelf is now missing. Although it has been said that the press originally stood on ball feet, no evidence of the existence of such feet remains today. The four stiles do not appear to have been cut recently, and the press may have stood originally on its bottom, or the stiles may have continued below the base molding to form the feet. The inside of the top front rail is lined with old paper and contains a wasp nest of indeterminate age.

Wood: Southern yellow pine.

Dimensions: H 168.8; W 129.5; CW 124.1; D 74.3; CD 71.3.

Exhibition: YUAG, "Southern Furn.," no. 2.

Bibliography: Lockwood, fig. XXXIX; Burroughs, *Southern Antiques*, p. 133; Chinnery, fig. 3:289.

Provenance: J. K. Beard, Richmond, Va.; by sale to Francis P. Garvan, New York, N. Y.

An interesting counterpart to the Middletown press (cat. 200), this southern example is an equally rare survival. Although it has been suggested that this press might possibly be from Georgia, a Virginia origin is more likely. Clothes-presses or hanger presses were popular on the eastern shore of Virginia in the mid eighteenth century, and another late seventeenth-century example attributed to eastern Virginia has also survived.[1] It is unfortunate that the Yale press has lost its original paint, which would have articulated the design of the applied moldings and panels more clearly.

The Mabel Brady Garvan Collection 1930.2660

1. Melchor et al., *Raised-Panel Furn.*, pp. 13–50; Fairbanks and Bates, p. 20.

Buffets

In the eighteenth century, buffet (also spelled beaufit, beaufat, boffit, and in many other ways) was the name most commonly applied to the built-in cupboard, often fitted with glazed doors, that was used for the storage and display of glass, ceramics, and other small articles. Most examples, including all of those at Yale, have shaped shelves in the upper section and enclosed cupboards below, occasionally separated by drawers. Generally known today as corner cupboards (a term also found in some early documents), these objects were not always designed for the corner of a room, but rather were built as an integral part of the interior trim and might be found, for example, flanking a fireplace. The collection includes a good geographical cross section, although some important regional variations, such as the turkey-breast cupboards from Virginia, Maryland, and Delaware, are not represented. The large number of buffets at Yale, all but one from the Garvan collection, probably reflects Garvan's own use of these objects to display the small wares in his collection. The documented examples include a buffet that can be traced to the Williams house in Wethersfield (cat. 204) and the even more elaborate cupboard from the Rose house in Branford (cat. 205). The Rose house cupboard is the only buffet in the collection that still remains in a simulation of its original context, as part of the woodwork in the Art Gallery's only period-room installation.

- fluted keystone
- inverted heart motif
- hinge
- glazed door
- cornice moldings
- carved rosette
- fluted pilaster
- mullion
- door with arched fielded panel
- base molding

204

Buffet
Wethersfield, Connecticut, ca. 1760

Description: A single unit, this architectural buffet gives the appearance of being a two-stage cupboard. The upper section has a large open arch flanked on its front and inside faces by projecting columns with high molded capitals. The arch molding supports a central triglyph between fielded paneled spandrels and is crowned by a heavy cyma cornice that projects at the front sides and center. The semicircular upper storage section has three shaped shelves with molded front edges and small steps at the rear below a large central shell with scalloped edges and a pendant drop. The lower section has paired doors with fielded panels which open to a plain interior. The counter shelf is a single board, and the back of the upper section is formed of five curved vertical boards. The shelves are set in grooves in the backboards and nailed with large rosehead nails through the back. The shell is built up of seven curved laminations, nailed together through the back. Traces of red or orange paint remain in the upper section, and there are traces of blue paint throughout the buffet.

Condition: The buffet has undergone significant modifications since its removal about 1890 from its original location. An early illustration (Lockwood, fig. 188) shows the buffet, then in the home of Mr. and Mrs. Albert Hastings Pitkin of Hartford, enclosed within a paneled exterior with glazed doors on the upper section and with what appear to be the present paneled doors visible on the lower section. Lockwood, on page 108 of the first edition of his book, published in 1901, notes, "the cupboard portion is made separate from the outer portion, to which the doors, panelled like it, are attached, leaving a space of about four inches between the two." This outer framework has been lost. The lower doors have been retained and moved back to be flush with the surviving upper section, and new vertical stabilizing boards have been nailed to the outside edges of the buffet. The lower doors have been pieced on their outside edges, and new hinges added; these alterations, however, had already taken place when the buffet was pictured by Lockwood. The buffet appears to have been painted white when illustrated by Lockwood; it subsequently was stripped and refinished.

Wood: Eastern white pine.

Dimensions: H 239.1; W 111.8; D 53.3.

204

Bibliography: Luke Vincent Lockwood, *The Colonial Furniture of America* (New York: Charles Scribner's Sons, 1901), pp. 107–108, fig. 71; Lockwood, fig. 188; Ormsbee, *Story Am. Furn.*, no. 104b.

Provenance: The buffet, according to correspondence between Mrs. Albert Hastings Pitkin and Francis P. Garvan in 1919, was removed from the "old Williams place in Wethersfield" about 1890 by her husband, of Hartford, Conn. The "old Williams place" almost assuredly was the home of merchant Sheriff Ezekiel Williams (1729–1818), erected about 1759 on Broad Street and still standing,

Buffets 399

FIG. 2 Ezekiel Williams house, Wethersfield, Connecticut, ca. 1759. Drawn by Edwin Whitefield (1816–1892), ca. 1875. Watercolor, ink, and pencil on paper; H 10.5, W 17.1. (Society for the Preservation of New England Antiquities.)

although greatly modified (fig. 2). The buffet descended to Mrs. Pitkin, who sold it in 1927 to Francis P. Garvan, New York, N.Y.

THE inventory of Ezekiel Williams's estate made mention of three cupboards, one of which is the buffet now at Yale. In his parlor, Williams kept "sundry articles in the Beaufit" valued at $20.58, and in his "Front Room" there were "sundry articles in the East Cupboard" valued at $4.50 and "Crockery, glass, &c. in the West Cupboard" worth a total of $15.49.[1] Related in style to the cupboard in the north parlor of the Joseph Webb, Sr., house in Wethersfield, built in 1752, and to other cupboards in the area, this example undoubtedly was painted originally, perhaps with the bright and contrasting colors used on the Webb house cupboard and recently restored.[2] A related example was made for the Major Elisha Williams house on the common in Deerfield, Massachusetts, built ca. 1755-1762.[3]

The Mabel Brady Garvan Collection 1930.2347

1. The writer would like to thank Kevin M. Sweeney and C. Douglass Alves, Jr., for their assistance in determining the provenance of this buffet. A copy of Williams's inventory, on file in the Connecticut State Library, Hartford, was provided by Mr. Sweeney.
2. Susan Finlay Watkins, "The Webb-Deane-Stevens Museum," *Antiques* 109, no. 3 (March 1976): 536; see also Nutting, *Treasury*, no. 526.
3. Fales, *Deerfield*, no. 495. This cupboard has what are described as later "flame" finials; similar "flames" may once have been used on the Yale buffet (although no evidence of their presence is readily discernible today). A memo from A. W. Clarke, Mr. Garvan's agent, concerning the buffet noted "Photo does not do it justice—ought to have been taken with doors thrown back—then it would show 2 fluted columns fluted inside with flames on top."

205

Buffet

North Branford, Connecticut, 1750–1775
(see pl. 20)

Description: This architectural buffet has a single glazed door in the upper section, hinged at the right, with mullions forming a simple rectangular grid below an arched top with an inverted heart motif. The arch has a fluted keystone and supports heavy cornice molding that projects at the corners and center. The door is flanked by fluted pilasters that extend to the canted sides, with carved rosettes with six petals above the pilasters. Heavy molding separates the upper from the lower section. The lower section contains a pair of doors with arched fielded panels which again are flanked by fluted pilasters. There is heavy base molding at the front and sides of the buffet. The glazed door opens to an interior with a large shell at the top and a central rosette. There are four shaped shelves, stepped at the rear, grooved for plates, and flanked by fluted pilasters with rosette capitals. The lower doors open to a plain interior with a single fixed shelf. The outer framework of the buffet is joined with mortise-and-tenon joints with the moldings applied. The lower section is trapezoidal in plan, with vertical riven backboards. The curved or "barrel" back of the upper section supports the shell, which is made up of several laminations. The shelves are nailed in place through the backboards.

FIG. 3 Rose house, North Branford, Connecticut, 1720s and later. Photograph, ca. 1924.

400 *American Case Furniture*

205

ments, and new locks have been added to each door. A brass lock escutcheon was once added to the lower right door. Some new reinforcing boards were added to the back, probably during reinstallation, and iron braces were added at an earlier date to the arch on the glazed door.

Woods: Eastern white pine; yellow poplar.

Dimensions: H 235.5; W 146.0; D 66.0.

Bibliography: "Yale's Branford Rooms," *Christian Science Monitor* (18 October 1930); *Handbook*, p. 44; "Pictorial Supplement," *Yale Daily News* (15 October 1932); Walter A. Dyer, "American Corner Cupboards: 1710–1810," *Fine Arts* 20, no. 1 (May 1933): 26; Kettell, *Early American Rooms*, pp. 47–58; *Yale Alumni* 4, no. 11 (January 1941):2.

Provenance: The buffet was located originally in the so-

205a Buffet in situ, 1924

Inscriptions: A modern pencil inscription written on the outside of the back of the upper section reads "1742 / J. Carey / McManus / 1714," and "J Carey McManus" is written in the same hand on the outside of the back of a shell lamination. McManus may have been a workman involved in the installation of the buffet and other woodwork in the Art Gallery.

Condition: The buffet was removed, along with other woodwork, from its original location in the Rose house and reinstalled as an exhibit in the Art Gallery in 1928–1929. Based on colors found under layers of later paint, it was repainted a light blue-green on the exterior, with the rosettes and keystone picked out in red, and red on the interior of the upper section. The hinges on the lower doors are replace-

Buffets 401

called Rose-Curtiss house of North Branford, Conn., built in the 1720s by Jonathan Rose, Jr. (d. 1768), and his wife Abigail (Barker) Rose. The house was inherited by their son Justus Rose (d. 1810), who in turn passed it to his son, Jonathan Rose (d. 1862). The house was owned later by the Reverend William B. Curtiss and was acquired in 1922 by New Haven Water Company. Some of the woodwork from the first floor of the house, including this buffet, was purchased by Yale in 1926 and subsequently installed as two period rooms in the Art Gallery, then under construction, in 1928–1929; the rooms remain on view today. The Rose house was destroyed prior to the flooding of the land by the water company for a reservoir known as Lake Gailliard.

THE Rose house (fig. 3), from which this buffet was removed in the 1920s, was built in the 1720s and subsequently enlarged at least once.[1] Although the buffet has been considered a part of the original features of the house, it dates to a later expansion or redecoration, perhaps undertaken when the house passed from father to son in 1768. Related to many buffets from houses in the New Haven area in its use of fluted pilasters and rosettes, the buffet is distinguished by the unusual inverted heart motif in the arch of its glazed door. Similar inverted hearts are present on some heart-and-crown chairs made along the Connecticut coast in the eighteenth century.[2] A heart-and-crown chair (1950.694) in the Art Gallery collection, with its crest rail pierced with a heart in the normal orientation, is thought to have been part of the furnishings of the Rose house.[3]

Yale University Art Gallery 1926.114

1. The writer is indebted to a research file on the Rose house, compiled principally by Sheila Rideout, maintained by the American Arts Office. A summary of the history of the Rose house and the installation of the Rose house period rooms prepared by Ms. Rideout and Patricia E. Kane appears on page 10 of the tabloid issued in 1973 as an introductory guide, "The Mabel Brady Garvan Galleries: American Arts and the American Experience," and published as a supplement to the Arts & Antiques section of the *Newtown Bee*. See also Leslie Richardson, "An Early Connecticut Interior," *Antiques* 16, no. 6 (December 1929): 500–501, in addition to the sources cited under Bibliography.
2. Robert F. Trent, *Hearts & Crowns: Folk Chairs of the Connecticut Coast, 1710–1840* (New Haven: New Haven Colony Historical Society, 1977), figs. 7, 26.
3. Patricia E. Kane, *300 Years of American Seating Furniture: Chairs and Beds from the Mabel Brady Garvan and Other Collections at Yale University* (Boston: New York Graphic Society, 1976), no. 87.

206

206

Buffet
Connecticut, ca. 1760

Description: The buffet is in two stages. The upper case rests on the lower and is crowned with a molded cornice that projects at the front sides and center. The paired glazed doors to the interior are flanked by fluted pilasters with carved rosettes on the capitals. The interior of the upper section has four shaped shelves, each with an applied plate rail, flanked by pilasters echoing those of the front. The lower case is divided into three panels by applied moldings; the middle section contains a small door with a fielded panel leading to a plain interior. There is a straight horizontal baseboard. The upper case front is framed with mortise-and-tenon joints; the backboards are half lapped and form a

semicircle; the shelves are nailed in place through the back with rosehead nails. The lower section is trapezoidal in shape and has vertical half-lapped backboards. The doors in the upper and lower case are attached with H-hinges with shaped tops and are constructed with mortise-and-tenon joints that are both pinned and wedged.

Condition: The buffet has been stripped of paint and refinished. In 1967, it was reglued, new blocks were added to the base, and small sections of molding were restored. The left glazed door was missing when the object was illustrated by Nutting, but the original door seems to have survived and been reattached. Both glazed doors have been repaired, and some of the panes of glass replaced; others are cracked. The brass pulls are replacements, and the door to the lower section has been repaired.

Woods: Eastern white pine; southern yellow pine.

Dimensions: H 215.3; W 135.3; D 89.5.

Bibliography: Nutting, *Treasury*, no. 488.

Provenance: Francis P. Garvan, New York, N. Y.

ALTHOUGH this buffet was acquired without provenance, its carved rosettes and exterior and interior fluted pilasters suggest that it originally was part of the woodwork in a Connecticut house of the mid eighteenth century. Rosettes of this kind (here with eight petals) are most closely identified with the Connecticut Valley, but are also found on woodwork in Litchfield and other parts of the area.[1] This buffet is related to the more elaborate example from the Rose house in Branford, also in the Art Gallery collection (cat. 205). The use of wedged through-tenons on the doors of this buffet is an interesting instance of a technique more commonly associated with the Germanic woodworking tradition in Pennsylvania, although also found on Chapin chairs.[2]

The Mabel Brady Garvan Collection 1930.2736

1. Peter Benes, *Two Towns: Concord & Wethersfield* (Concord, Mass.: Concord Antiquarian Museum, 1982), fig. 270 (Litchfield, 1762).
2. Forman, "German Influences," p. 123.

207

207

Buffet
New England, 1810–1840

Description: This single-unit buffet is of simple nailed-board construction. The tall arched opening is surrounded by molding that continues down each side of the door in the lower section. Small rosettes are applied to the spandrels at the break of the arch. The outer edges of the buffet are canted to meet the room paneling. The interior of the upper section

Buffets 403

contains three shaped shelves, each made with two boards, with grooves for plates. The lower door has a fielded panel, is attached to the cupboard with iron butt hinges fastened with screws, and has a metal turnbuckle. It opens to a plain interior with one shelf. The backboards are two tiers of half-lapped vertical boards, breaking at the counter shelf; the shelves are nailed in place through the back. The exterior of the buffet retains an old coat of blue-green paint over layers of white and what might be nineteenth-century painted graining.

Condition: The inside of the lower section contains an old coat of yellow paint. The door catch is old but not original. Several rat holes in the backboards have been patched with scraps of metal. Base molding was probably present originally at the front and sides.

Wood: Eastern white pine.

Dimensions: H 230.8; W 110.2; D 69.9.

Provenance: Frank W. MacCarthy, Longmeadow, Mass.; by sale in 1929 to Francis P. Garvan, New York, N. Y.

ALTHOUGH its provenance was not recorded, this simple buffet was catalogued initially in Mr. Garvan's files as a Connecticut object, perhaps on the basis of information passed along orally by the dealer from whom it was acquired. Frank W. MacCarthy, of Longmeadow, Massachusetts, specialized in New England objects and sold many objects to Mr. Garvan in the late 1920s, including a good deal of wrought iron. Perhaps because of its unexceptional nature, this buffet has managed to retain its various layers of paint and has not been stripped to the bare pine, as occurred with some of the earlier cupboards in the collection (see cat. nos. 204, 206). A Massachusetts cupboard has been published in which the molding continues down each side of the lower door, as it does here.[1]

The Mabel Brady Garvan Collection 1931.1232

1. Kettell, fig. 149.

208

Buffet
Delaware Valley, possibly Salem, New Jersey, 1760–1800

Description: This tall buffet is a single unit, crowned by a broken-arch pediment with a carved floral cartouche. The arched opening of the upper section is enclosed with two glazed doors, above a pair of lipped drawers in line, in turn placed above a pair of doors with fielded panels in the lower section. The front sides are embellished with unusual tapered and fluted columns, rounded at the base and pointed at the top, supporting a fluted pilaster surmounted by a carved shell. The arch is surrounded by molding with a central keystone, and there are carved scrolls of stylized leafage in each spandrel. The cupboard has canted sides and is supported by rather plain bracket feet below base molding. The glazed doors open to an interior with three shaped shelves grooved for plates, a fluted center backboard, and a large laminated shell at the top, with lath-and-plaster ribs radiating from a central carved disk. The rounded back consists of two tiers of vertical backboards, joined with a tongue and groove in the upper section and butted together in the lower section. The top, bottom, dustboard, counter shelf, and shelves are nailed in place through the backboards. The front of the case and the doors are joined with mortise-and-tenon joints, with the tenons on the doors wedged. The canted sideboards are nailed to the front frame assembly. The heavy cornice molding is blocked behind and nailed in place. On each drawer, the sides are dovetailed to the front and back, and the bottoms are secured with wooden pins to a rabbet in the front and to the undersides of the sides and back. The lower doors open to a plain compartment without a shelf. The center backboard of the lower section continues below to form the rear center foot and is both blocked and braced. There is also a brace nailed from each front corner to the backboards of the lower section.

Condition: All the hardware on the buffet has been replaced, and the lock on the glazed doors is missing. The lower doors were once fitted with pulls. The front feet and base molding are replacements. The outside edges of the buffet had been damaged by insects, and new reinforcing blocks were added between the canted sideboards and the front frame in 1967, when new blocks were also added to the base. The bottom of the right drawer is a replacement, and the upper right corner of the front of the same drawer has been pieced. The central cartouche has been repaired, and it

208

is probably incomplete. There have been minor losses and repairs to the cornice molding; in particular, a section of molding is missing above each projecting side of the cornice molding. The cupboard interior has been painted a light yellow in modern times; this paint has been removed from the interior shell, revealing traces of reddish paint, possibly original, and green paint.

Woods: American black walnut; shell laminations, backboards of upper case, drawer bottom, other elements, Atlantic white cedar; drawer sides and backs, bottom, other elements, southern yellow pine; backboards of lower case, other elements, yellow poplar.

Dimensions: H 244.3; W 127.5; CW 112.7; D 48.3.

Bibliography: *Antiquarian* 3, no. 4 (November 1924): 36; *Antiquarian* 9, no. 1 (August 1927): 39; Wenham, *Collectors' Guide*, no. 266; Walter A. Dyer, "American Corner Cupboards, 1710–1810," *Fine Arts* 20, no. 1 (May 1933): 25.

Provenance: According to statements published when this buffet was first offered for sale in 1924, it came from the "Johnson House" in Salem, N. J., although it was believed to be of Philadelphia manufacture. The house in question may have been the Robert Gibbon Johnson house on Market Street in Salem, built in 1806, although there were several other "Johnson" houses in or near Salem.[1] The buffet was owned in 1924 by dealer Renwick C. Hurry, New York, N. Y., and was purchased in 1929 from Israel Sack, New York, N. Y., by Francis P. Garvan, New York, N. Y.

THIS curious buffet is perhaps more ornamental than attractive. It was said to have been removed from a house in Salem, New Jersey, a small town across the Delaware River from Philadelphia, and although the design is ambitious and the quality of some of the carving is good, several factors suggest that it may have been made in Salem rather than in a Philadelphia shop. A rural origin is indicated by the odd arrangement of thin columns supporting broad pilasters, certainly an unusual if not unique feature, and by the profuse yet poorly integrated carved ornament also found on the buffet. It is possible that some of the carved motifs, such as the shells surmounting the pilasters, were purchased from a Philadelphia carver and applied by a local Salem cabinetmaker.

The Mabel Brady Garvan Collection 1931.1311

1. The writer would like to thank Julie A. Riesenweber for her assistance in attempting to determine the house from which this buffet was removed.

209

Buffet
Eastern Pennsylvania, 1775–1800

Description: This large imposing cupboard is in two cases. The upper case contains a central round arched opening with a pair of glazed doors flanked by fluted pilasters (with six

Buffets 405

209

flutes) and with a corbel at the top of the arch molding. The case is crowned with heavy cornice molding that projects at the sides, and is raked at the corners to follow the canted sides of the cases. Below the projecting front sides of the cornice are fluted pilasters with the flutes filled with a rope or twist carving that alternates direction from flute to flute. The interior of the upper case contains four fixed shaped shelves with grooves for plates, with the upper shelf being simply curved rather than elaborately shaped. The upper case rests on top of the lower case. The lower case contains a pair of drawers in line surrounded by cock beading on the case above a pair of doors with reverse-curved panels. The drawers and doors are flanked by sunken pilasters formed by applied molding. There is top and base molding at the front and sides of the lower case, and the case is supported in the front by applied bracket feet. The interior of the lower case contains a single fixed shelf. The front of each trapezoidal case is framed with mortise-and-tenon joints secured with large wooden pins. The vertical backboards of each case are joined with a half lap and mitered and nailed to a center backboard parallel to the front of the case. The shelves are pegged and nailed in place through the backboards, and scribe lines on the back mark their location. The center backboard of the lower case extends to form the rear foot. The complex and heavy cornice is nailed and pegged in place, and built up with blocking in behind. The two drawers are made entirely of walnut and are shaped with canted outer sides to fit the cupboard's trapezoidal shape. The long inner side of each drawer is wedge dovetailed to the front and to the short, straight side of the back; on the short outer side of each drawer, the side is again wedge dovetailed to the front and is mitered and nailed to a canted board, which in turn is mitered and nailed to the straight section of the back. The drawer bottoms are beveled on their sides, fitted to a groove in the sides, and nailed to the underside of both the canted and the straight portions of the back. There is a full dustboard below the drawers, and drawer guides are nailed to the dustboard.

Condition: The brasses and hinges are replacements, and the lock on the glazed upper doors and the pulls on the lower doors are missing. A transverse brace has been added to the bottom of the lower case, and the buffet was reglued in 1962. There have been repairs to the left side of the cornice molding; on the right drawer, the straight and canted portions of the back and part of the bottom have been replaced. The central drawer guide is a replacement, and there is a metal patch to the left side of the back of the lower case.

Woods: American black walnut, including shelves in upper case and drawer linings; southern yellow pine.

Dimensions: H 238.3; W 145.5; D 72.0.

Provenance: Charles Woolsey Lyon, New York, N. Y.; by sale to Francis P. Garvan, New York, N. Y.

THE combination of walnut and southern yellow pine, the use of large wooden pins and wedged dovetails, and the architectural nature of this buffet all suggest that it was made by a craftsman working in eastern Pennsylvania. It is thought that glazed cupboards such as this example were not made there until the last quarter of the eighteenth century.[1] A very

similar cupboard has been attributed to North Carolina, where Germanic influence also was strong.[2]

The Mabel Brady Garvan Collection 1931.1310

1. Forman, "German Influences," p. 159; see also fig. 99 for a related cupboard. See also Nutting, *Treasury*, no. 496.
2. Burroughs, *Southern Antiques*, chap. XIX, pl. III.

210

Buffet

Eastern Pennsylvania, 1760–1790

Description: The buffet is a single unit with canted corners and is crowned by a dentil cornice that projects at the center. The upper section contains a pair of doors with fielded panels enclosed within arch molding scored to simulate dentiling and with a central keystone fluted and pierced to echo the dentil motif. The doors also are outlined with an incised line. The doors open to an interior with two shaped shelves and a counter shelf grooved for plates; the center board of the back is fluted, and the edges of the backboards are molded. An applied midmolding separates the upper from the lower section, which contains two doors with fielded panels enclosing an interior with a single fixed shelf with a straight rather than shaped edge. There is base molding with a central shaped drop above the large bracket feet. The front, sides, and doors are framed with mortise-and-tenon joints, with some of the tenons on the doors wedged. The complex cornice molding consists of six boards, and it and the other moldings are applied. The curved back is formed by vertical boards running the full height of the buffet, joined with a tongue and groove, and nailed to the top, bottom, and shelves. The cupboard rests at the rear on a large block, with an extra brace nailed to the center backboard and to the block at the rear. The front and canted sideboards continue to form the front supports, with the base molding and bracket feet applied. The cupboard doors are attached with brass butt hinges; blind brass escutcheons are applied to the doors; and each is fitted with an exterior brass pierced drop pull and an interior wooden turn button.

Condition: The buffet has lost its original, probably red, paint and has been refinished. Traces of red paint remain on the interior of the lower section. There have been minor repairs to the moldings, and the brass pull on the upper

210

right door has been relocated above rather than below the escutcheon.

Woods: Southern yellow pine; panels, other elements, yellow poplar.

Dimensions: H 221.6; W 128.3; D 60.3.

Exhibition: YUAG, "A Wide View for American Art."

Bibliography: Holloway, pl. 14A; *Reifsnyder Coll.*, no. 395; Miller, 1:no. 927.

Provenance: Howard Reifsnyder, Philadelphia, Pa.; acquired at auction in 1929 by Francis P. Garvan, New York, N. Y.

THE solid paneled doors, rather than a glazed door or doors, distinguish this buffet from most of the other examples in the collection. These solid doors, found on many cupboards from all regions, probably reflect only an economic or aesthetic decision on the part of the consumer, but their selection also may be indicative of the owner's attitude toward privacy and security. Objects stored in a cupboard with solid doors could be seen only when the doors were thrown open. When company was present, the decision to open the doors or leave them closed thus became a comment on the owner's attitude toward their guests. This all-or-nothing option stands in contrast to the compromise offered by a glazed door, which allowed the cupboard's interior and its contents of china, glass, metalware, and other articles to be seen while remaining covered. A related buffet in walnut, of more vertical proportions but lacking the well-articulated cornice of the Yale example, is in the Henry Ford Museum.[1] Buffets were a favorite of Francis P. Garvan, whose collection included many examples in addition to those now at Yale.[2]

The Mabel Brady Garvan Collection 1930.2721

1. Hagler, *American Queen Anne Furn.*, p. 50.
2. Nutting, *Treasury*, nos. 490, 534, 545, 552, 555, 558 are buffets then in Mr. Garvan's collection that are not at Yale.

211

Buffet

Southern, possibly Virginia or North Carolina, 1790–1820

Description: The buffet is a single unit with canted corners and is crowned by a heavy cornice with an undulating line of light-wood stringing and a dentil course. The upper section contains an arched opening with a single glazed door hinged on the right and flanked by fluted pilasters supported by plinths with inlaid hearts and surmounted by capitals inlaid with four-pointed star motifs. The door is also surrounded by an incised line on the case. Curved strips with an undulating line of inlay spring from the capitals to form the arch and terminate on either side of a two-handled urn with light-wood handles. The upper section is separated from the lower by molding above a paneled strip decorated with alternating inlaid diamond and star motifs. The lower section contains two doors with raised panels decorated with rectangles of light-wood stringing with hollow corners and inlaid keyhole escutcheons. The doors are flanked by applied panels with a round-arch top and pointed bottom. The glazed door opens to an interior with three shaped shelves, and the lower doors enclose an interior with one fixed shelf with a straight edge. The front of the cupboard is framed with mortise-and-tenon joints secured with large, square wooden pins, which are used throughout as fasteners. The shelves are housed in grooves in the backboards and pegged in place. The vertical backboards run the full height of the trapezoidal case, are joined by a half lap on the canted sides, and are mitered to a central backboard. The framing elements continue below the case bottom to support the cupboard.

408 *American Case Furniture*

Inscriptions: A fragment of a modern newspaper, possibly from Georgia, is pasted to the top of the bottom of the buffet. The modern "242" appears in white paint on the lowest shaped shelf in the upper section and on the top of the right door in the lower section.

Condition: The hinges are the third set the buffet has had, and the lock on the glazed door and the catch on the frame are missing. The upper-section shelves and the counter shelf once had applied plate rails which are now missing. The base molding is a replacement, and there have been many losses and repairs to the inlay and moldings, including the replacement of the right handle of the urn. Several of the panes in the arched section of the glazed doors are cracked, and iron braces have been added to the back of the curved section. Holes in several of the backboards have been patched with metal, and new blocks have been added to the base.

Woods: American black walnut, light wood inlay; shelves, other elements, southern yellow pine; backboards, other elements, yellow poplar.

Dimensions: H 223.7; W 133.3; D 65.4.

Provenance: Purchased in 1930 from Florence Booker, Old Point Comfort, Va., by Rhea Mansfield Knittle, Ashland, Ohio; by sale to Francis P. Garvan, New York, N. Y.

FOUND in Virginia, this buffet may have been made there or by a craftsman working in a rural area farther south or west. Rural southern buffets, such as those from the eastern shore of Virginia or from the piedmont area of Georgia, generally were made as a single unit, as is the case here. Many examples from Georgia, Kentucky, western Pennsylvania, and North Carolina were decorated with simple line inlay of the kind used here, which was in all likelihood fashioned by the maker of the buffet rather than being purchased from a specialist. The consistent use of wooden pegs in this example and its construction of walnut, yellow poplar, and southern yellow pine also suggest that its maker may have had training or experience in Pennsylvania. The naive form of the neoclassical urn here relates in feeling to some of the motifs used on the work of rural cabinetmakers such as Jesse Needham of Randolph County, North Carolina, one of many southern cabinetmakers with a Pennsylvania connection.[1]

The Mabel Brady Garvan Collection 1931.1236

1. John Bivins, Jr., "A Piedmont North Carolina Cabinetmaker: The Development of Regional Style," *Antiques* 103, no. 5 (May 1973): 968–973.

212

212

Buffet

Southern, possibly Virginia, 1770–1800

Description: The buffet is in two stages; the upper case rests within restraining molding on the top of the lower case, which is of slightly greater width. The upper case has heavy complex molding at the top and a trapezoidal interior flanked by fluted pilasters with five flutes on the outer faces and a single flute on each side. The interior is edged with

Buffets 409

scalloping at the sides and top and contains three shaped shelves. The shelves have two grooves for plates, the lowest shelf is also notched for cutlery, and the center backboard of the upper case is also fluted. The lower case is again flanked with pilasters, each with a small scrolled bracket on the inner edge of its capital, and has top molding that projects at the sides. The case contains two paneled doors over a bracket-foot base; the doors open to a plain interior with a single shelf with a straight front. The sides of the cupboard are canted, and the front is framed with mortise-and-tenon joints secured with large wooden pins. The vertical backboards in each case are joined with a tongue and groove, are set into grooves in the backboards, and in the upper case are molded on their inside edges. They are nailed in place through the back with large rosehead nails. The doors in the lower case are attached with brass H-hinges, and there is an iron catch on both the upper and the lower case. The center backboard of the lower case continues to form the rear foot.

Condition: The doors to the upper case are missing. The interior of the buffet retains traces of red paint. There have been small replacements and repairs to the scalloping, moldings, and right front foot, and a lock and pull on the lower doors is missing. In 1967 new glue blocks were added to the base, and the buffet was reglued.

Woods: Southern yellow pine; pilasters and canted corners of upper case, some moldings, other elements, yellow poplar; scalloping, American black walnut.

Dimensions: H 207.0; W 117.5; D 57.1.

Exhibition: YUAG, "A Wide View for American Art."

Provenance: Francis P. Garvan, New York, N. Y.

THIS buffet was acquired by Francis P. Garvan as a New England example, but it has been catalogued by the Art Gallery staff in more recent years as a southern object. It bears an affinity to cupboards made on the eastern shore of Virginia, although it differs in being constructed in two stages rather than as a single unit and in several other particulars.[1] Another buffet in the Art Gallery collection (cat. 210) is also made of a mixture of yellow pine and yellow poplar, has a fluted center backboard and canted backboards with molded edges, and is attributed to Pennsylvania.

The Mabel Brady Garvan Collection 1930.2764

1. Melchor et al., *Raised-Panel Furn.*, pp. 89–131.

213

213

Buffet
Maryland, possibly Baltimore, 1790–1820

Description: The buffet is in two units, with the upper case resting within restraining molding applied to the lower case. The upper case contains a pair of glazed doors with mullions arranged in a geometric pattern including an octagon. The mullions are edged with light-wood stringing, and the door frames are outlined with a double line of stringing. The upper case is crowned by cornice molding surmounted by a

thin broken-scroll pediment terminating in carved rosettes flanking a central plaque inlaid with an eagle. The lower case contains a pair of paneled doors decorated with inlaid rectangles with hollow corners. The cupboard is supported by bracket feet at the front. The doors in each case are flanked by light-wood interlaced stringing on both the facing of the case and the canted sides. The glazed doors open to an interior with three shelves shaped with serpentine fronts; the lower doors enclose a plain interior with one fixed shelf with a straight front. The case is trapezoidal in shape, and the vertical backboards are butted on the canted sides and mitered to a center backboard, with the top, bottom, and shelves nailed in place. The center backboard of the lower case continues below the bottom to form the rear foot. The doors are attached to the case with brass butt hinges.

Inscriptions: In pencil on the outside of the backboards is the modern "L Steinberg[?] / South Norfolk / Va." A similar inscription, partially illegible and crossed out, appears on the outside of the center backboard of the upper case. An American Railway Express Co. shipping label is pasted to the outside of the backboards of the upper case.

Condition: The cupboard has been extensively repaired at its upper and lower extremities. The scrolled molding on the left side of the pediment is a replacement, the left side has been damaged and repaired, and there have been other repairs to the right side of the pediment and to the cornice molding. The finial, originally located over the central plaque in the pediment, has been lost, and new blocks have been added behind the pediment. The facing and the vertical corner blocks of the front feet have been replaced, and the molding on the right lower door is also a replacement. A transverse brace has been added under the bottom of the cupboard. The most troublesome aspect of the buffet, however, is the poor, almost crude, quality of the inlaid stringing and eagle; its lack of quality suggests that it may not be original to the piece.

Woods: Mahogany, mahogany veneer, light-wood stringing; yellow poplar.

Dimensions: H 239.9; W 132.4; D 61.0.

Bibliography: Miller, 1:no. 928.

Provenance: Purchased in Annapolis, Md., by R. T. Haines Halsey, New York, N. Y.; by sale in 1930 to Francis P. Garvan, New York, N. Y.

THIS cupboard was purchased in Annapolis by antiquarian R. T. H. Halsey and was acquired by Francis P. Garvan as a Baltimore example, presumably on the basis of its light and thin pediment, inlaid decoration, and provenance. Many of its distinguishing features, however, have been damaged or repaired, and the age of the geometric and pictorial inlay is somewhat suspect; thus, assigning a more precise place of origin is difficult. Buffets were made in Baltimore, such as the "mahogany Corner cupboard" valued at $30 in the inventory of cabinetmaker Gerrard Hopkins, but they were not commonly produced there.[1] The geometrical arrangement of the glazed doors is related to the double-hexagon pattern known as "Chinese doors" in the Philadelphia price books.[2] Similar cupboards with and without a scrolled pediment have been published.[3]

The Mabel Brady Garvan Collection 1930.2996

1. John Henry Hill, "The Furniture Craftsman in Baltimore, 1783–1823," vol. 1 (M.A. thesis, University of Delaware, 1967), p. 206.
2. Montgomery, no. 446.
3. *Antiques* 107, no. 1 (January 1975): 99; Miller, 1:no. 929.

Sideboards, Cabinets, and Cellarettes

A new form introduced in the federal period, the sideboard was descended from the seventeenth-century cupboard. It was usually located in the dining room of the house, occasionally in an architectural niche designed especially for it. With drawers and cupboards designed to hold silver plate, dishes, glasses, tablecloths, bottles, chamber pots, and other articles, the sideboard held all the accoutrements necessary for dining. Although some examples are relatively small, such as the two Rhode Island examples in the collection (cats. 214, 215), most federal-period sideboards tend to be large and capacious. An eight-legged example labeled by James Tabele of New York City (cat. 217), a Baltimore sideboard elegantly decorated with inlaid ovals and bands of zebrawood (cat. 220), and a mammoth Charleston sideboard owned originally by Colonel William Alston (cat. 222) are among the most important examples at Yale. The period from 1850 to the present is represented more thoroughly in the collection in this form than in any other type of case furniture. Among the five examples are a magnificent rococo-revival sideboard (cat. 223), a cabinet produced by the shop of Alexander Roux (cat. 224), a labeled sideboard by Gustav Stickley (cat. 225), and a modern example designed by Dan Cooper (cat. 227). The cellarette, designed to hold wine bottles and often placed at the side or between the legs of a sideboard, is represented by two widely divergent objects: a rich, high-style New York City example in the French taste (cat. 229) and a much simpler, yet no less functional, example from the South (cat. 230).

light-wood stringing

inlaid quarter fan

top

drawer

cupboard door

patterned inlay

cuff

bottle drawer

cupboard with sliding tambour

pictorial inlay

tapered leg

214

214

Sideboard
Providence, Rhode Island, 1795–1810

Description: The rectangular top of this small sideboard overhangs the case slightly, and its front edge is veneered with mahogany cross-banding and edged with light-wood stringing. The case contains a central cupboard enclosed by paired doors, flanked by a pair of superimposed drawers on the left and a single deep drawer on the right decorated to simulate a pair of superimposed drawers. The cupboard doors and the drawers (both real and simulated) are bordered with light-wood stringing and mahogany banding, and each is fitted with a brass keyhole liner (blind on the simulated drawer and the left door). Each drawer also is fitted with an oval stamped brass escutcheon with bail pull. The front face of each corner post opposite the drawers is embellished with a panel of highly figured light inlay bordered with light- and dark-wood stringing. There is a crossed vine and leaf motif in light and dark inlay beneath the cupboard doors on the serpentine-shaped apron. The edge of the apron contains a light and dark patterned inlay that also extends onto the front of the legs. The sideboard is supported by four tapered legs decorated with stringing, a flower or husk at the top, and with light-wood cuffs edged with stringing on the front and side faces of all four legs. The cupboard doors open to a plain interior, and the drawers are not divided internally in any fashion. The top of the sideboard is screwed in place from underneath to all four sides. The back of the case is a single horizontal board; the horizontal framing elements of the front are mahogany boards backed with wider pine boards. The cupboard is enclosed with full vertical transverse partitions housed in grooves in the back; the bottom of the cupboard is nailed from underneath to these partitions and supported with glue blocks. The sides of the cupboard bottom extend beyond this partition to form a runner for the lower left and the right drawer. The drawer runners and guides within the case are nailed to the sides; there are multiple vertical blocks on the inside faces of the legs. The drawer divider on the left side is double tenoned through the vertical partition on its right. On the drawers, the sides are dovetailed to the front and back; the bottoms are beveled on their front and side edges, let into grooves in the front and sides, and nailed to the underside of the back. Small glue blocks are affixed to the bottom along the sides.

Condition: There have been minor repairs to the inlay and veneer.

Woods: Top and drawer fronts, mahogany veneer on eastern white pine; doors, mahogany veneer on American black cherry; inlays, light and dark woods; legs, sides of case, other exterior framing elements of front, mahogany; back, drawer linings, other elements, eastern white pine.

Dimensions: H 96.9; W 125.7; CW 121.5; D 54.4; CD 53.2.

214a

Sideboards 415

Exhibition: YUAG, "Rhode Island Furn."

Bibliography: Sack, *Fine Points*, p. 225.

Provenance: Israel Sack, New York, N. Y.; by sale in 1929 as a pair with cat. 215 (1930.2171) to Francis P. Garvan, New York, N. Y.

A GROUP of about a dozen or more small sideboards of this type, including a second example in the Yale collection (cat. 215), have been attributed since 1964 to Thomas Howard, Jr. (1774–1833), of Pawtuxet and Providence, Rhode Island, because many of the sideboards had histories in the Providence area and many of them were decorated with "a characteristic Howard feature: a simple and rather crude crossed branch and leaf inlaid design" found on documented examples from Howard's shop.[1] In all likelihood the form was made by more than one shop in the area, although the preference for the form seems to have been restricted to the Providence area.[2] The eagle brasses on this sideboard are the same as those on a Massachusetts tambour desk in the Yale collection (cat. 166).

The Mabel Brady Garvan Collection 1930.2172

1. Eleanore Bradford Monahon, "Providence Cabinetmakers," *Rhode Island History* 23, no. 1 (January 1964): 12–13, with reference to an example in the collection of the Rhode Island Historical Society (fig. 7).
2. For other published examples, see Greenlaw, no. 111 (Colonial Williamsburg); *Antiques* 107, no. 5 (May 1975): 935 (Rhode Island School of Design); *Antiques* 111, no. 4 (April 1977): back cover; *Sack Coll.*, 2: 408 no. 1031, 4: 1044 no. P3682; *Important American Furniture . . . from the Estate of the Late Cornelius C. Moore*, Sale 3259, 30 October 1971 (New York: Parke Bernet Galleries, 1971), no. 79; *Fine American Furniture*, Sale 5208, 28–30 June 1984 (New York: Sotheby's, 1984), no. 702; and *Fine Americana*, Sale 4692, 26 September 1981 (New York: Sotheby's, 1981), no. 424. A few somewhat smaller New England serving or dressing tables are known; see, for example, Penny J. Sander, ed., *Elegant Embellishments* (Boston: Society for the Preservation of New England Antiquities, 1982), no. 57.

215

Sideboard

Providence, Rhode Island, 1795–1810

Description: Of the same general form and style as the preceding example (cat. 214), this sideboard differs in a number of details, suggesting that it may be from another shop. There are visible differences in the use of stringing and patterned inlay here, of course, and the brasses, which appear to be original here as well, are of a different pattern. There are other, more significant differences in construction which may indicate another shop's practices. Here, for example, the vertical partitions enclosing the cupboard section are tenoned through the backboard with four tenons; the cupboard bottom is supported on strips nailed to the front and back of the case and does not extend to serve as a runner; the horizontal mahogany framing members of the front are not backed with pine; and the drawers, while made in a somewhat similar manner, differ markedly in the angle and profile of the dovetails.

Condition: Many unexplained screw or nail holes and glue outlines indicate that the top, which is made of three boards of varying thicknesses (two veneered pine boards flanking a

214b

215

solid mahogany plank) is a replacement. New strips have been let into the top of each side of the case. The cupboard doors have been braced with a diagonal strip let into the inside. The bottom edges of the drawer sides have been pieced, and the drawer runners in the case are probably replacements. The right door has a new inlaid diamond.

Woods: Mahogany, mahogany veneer, as on the preceding example (excepting the replaced top); light- and dark-wood inlays; eastern white pine.

Dimensions: H 96.7; W 126.6; CW 121.7; D 54.6; CD 53.0.

Provenance: See cat. 214.

The pattern of stringing use on the doors and drawer fronts of this example is more common on sideboards in the "Thomas Howard" group than the decoration used on cat. 214. Although the two sideboards were acquired as a pair, it is likely that they were an assembled rather than a "natural" pair. They were initially catalogued in Mr. Garvan's files as being from Newburyport, Massachusetts.

The Mabel Brady Garvan Collection 1930.2171

215a

215b

Sideboards 417

216

216

Sideboard

American, 1800–1820

Description: The top of this sideboard with ovolo front ends and serpentine middle overhangs the case slightly on all four sides, and has a line of patterned inlay (Hewitt, no. 67) in the center of its edge at the front and sides. The case is divided into five vertical sections. The center section contains a single wide drawer above a slightly recessed cupboard enclosed by a pair of doors flanked by convex panels. The center section is flanked by a pair of superimposed drawers, including a small square drawer over a deep bottle drawer, and each side of the case holds a large cupboard enclosed by a door decorated with veneer and inlay to simulate a drawer superimposed above a door. Each drawer and door, both real and simulated, and the panels flanking the center cupboard, is bordered with light-wood stringing. Each drawer and door, both real and simulated, contains a circle or oval of patterned inlay (again Hewitt, no. 67), and the lower center cupboard is bordered with the same inlay applied to the case. The convex panels flanking the middle cupboard contain ovals of light- and dark-wood stringing. The center drawer and the simulated upper side drawers each also contain a central inlaid eagle with eighteen stars (Hewitt, no. 129) against a green background and with shading in red and black. Each door to the center cupboard contains an inlaid urn with flowers in an oval, and each outer cupboard door contains a more hori- zontal inlaid urn filled with leaves and flowers in an oval (Hewitt, no. 136). The front face of each of the four corner posts holds, at the level of the top drawers, a vertical rectangle of striped inlay containing an inlaid shell or conch (Hewitt, no. 123) against a green background; the shell on the far left corner post, however, is of a different form than the other three. Below, the corner posts contain a rectangle with

216a

418 *American Case Furniture*

216b

rounded top and hollow end of light- and dark-wood stringing. The front skirt is decorated with a patterned inlay (Hewitt, no. 70); the inlay does not continue around the sides of the case. The sideboard is supported by six tapered legs. The front face of each of the four front legs contains an inlaid cone outlined by light- and dark-wood stringing that terminates in the cuff. The side faces of the two center legs and the inside face of the two outer legs also have light-wood stringing terminating in the cuff. All six legs are cuffed at the front and sides with broad bands of light-wood inlay bordered at the top and bottom with patterned inlay (Hewitt, no. 70). The top consists of one wide and one narrow board attached to a framework and screwed to the case. The sides and back of the case are joined to the legs in each corner, and the front rails are joined to the four front legs. The bottom of the case is nailed in place. There are full dustboards under the upper small drawers, and full vertical transverse partitions on the outer sides of each bottle drawer and small square drawer. These partitions are nailed in place through the back with rosehead nails, as are the dustboards, and the partitions are also nailed in place through the case bottom. Two transverse braces under the top are tenoned through the back. The bottle drawers are divided by partitions into five compartments. Each side cupboard contains a single fixed shelf nailed to strips that in turn are nailed to the case; the middle cupboard is simply an open interior. The interiors of the drawers and cupboards have been given a reddish stain. On the drawers, the sides are dovetailed to the front and back; the bottoms are beveled on their front and side edges, let into grooves in the front and sides, and nailed to the underside of the back.

Inscriptions: Written on the outside of the back is "695/1" in yellow chalk and "33773" in pencil.

Condition: The present oval brasses are replacements installed in 1982 to replace wooden knobs that had in turn replaced earlier brasses. The bottom boards, due to shrinkage, have been moved forward, and a small strip has been added to the bottom at the rear. Braces have been added under the top, and ball catches have been added to the cupboard doors. The dustboard below the center drawer is missing. There have been many minor repairs to the veneer and inlays.

Woods: Mahogany; case front, mahogany veneer with light- and dark-wood inlays; case back, some drawer linings, other framing elements, southern yellow pine; some framing elements, white oak; some drawer linings, other framing elements, yellow poplar.

Dimensions: H 101.9; W 215.1; CW 212.0; D 75.6; CD 57.0.

Bibliography: *Handbook*, p. 61; Walter A. Dyer, "The American Sideboard: 1780–1820," *Fine Arts* 20, no. 3 (July 1933): 31.

Provenance: According to tradition, this sideboard was owned by the Apperson family of Richmond, Va., as early as 1860. It was purchased from Mrs. A. H. Apperson of Richmond by Francis P. Garvan, New York, N. Y.

BECAUSE of its history in a Virginia family, and because of the extensive use of southern yellow pine in its construction, this cavernous sideboard was once tentatively attributed to Virginia; however, the patterned inlays and, more significant, the pictorial inlays used in such abundance to decorate the object are found almost exclusively on card tables of this period from various regions of New England, suggesting its origin there.[1] The inlaid two-handled urn, found here on the side cupboard doors, is also used on a sideboard labeled by William Lloyd (1779–1845) of Springfield, Massachusetts, while the eagle inlay on the center and simulated side drawers is associated most closely with Boston-area objects.[2] Both inlays, however, as well as the other pictorial inlays on the sideboard, were probably made by specialists and used by many different craftsmen. This use of purchased inlays is underlined here because three of the conch shells match, while the fourth (on the far left corner post), which also appears to be original, is of a similar but varying pattern.

Had these inlays been made in the same shop where the sideboard was produced, they no doubt would have been made to match. The low stance and rather bulky proportions of the sideboard suggest a maker working in a minor urban center. The same form and massive size are seen, for example, on a more elegant eight-legged sideboard thought to have been made in 1804 by Aaron Chapin (1753–1838) of Hartford, and the low stance is mirrored by the proportions of three sideboards made by Silas E. Cheney (1776–1821) of Litchfield.[3]

The Mabel Brady Garvan Collection 1930.2111

1. One patterned inlay (Hewitt, no. 67) appeared on card tables from rural Massachusetts–New Hampshire and the Boston area (tables 15 and 212 in Hewitt's study); it also appears on a Massachusetts work table at Winterthur (Montgomery, no. 393). The other patterned inlay (Hewitt, no. 70) appears on a table labeled by Joseph Short of Newburyport and on a Baltimore table (Hewitt, tables 54, 339). The three matching conch shells are of a type (Hewitt, no. 123) found on card tables from Newburyport and the Boston area (Hewitt, tables 74, 156, 189); the two-handled urn inlay on the outside cupboard doors (Hewitt, no. 136) was found on tables from urban New Hampshire, Newburyport, the Boston area, and Connecticut (Hewitt, tables 2, 51, 182, 262). The eagle inlay (Hewitt, no. 129) appeared on four tables from the Boston area and on a Providence table (Hewitt, tables 150, 156, 178, 180, 245); it also appears on a table branded by William Leverett of Boston (*Sack Coll.*, 6: 1446 no. P4539). The urns on the center cupboard doors and the fourth conch shell did not appear on tables in Hewitt's study.

2. Lloyd's sideboard is also of mahogany and exhibits the same plentiful use of inlay as found on the Yale sideboard; it is illustrated in *Sack Coll.*, 6: 1483 no. P4291. An urn of similar but nevertheless varying character is found on another sideboard labeled by Lloyd; see *Sack Coll.*, 7: 1807 no. P5020.

3. Comstock, no. 512; Page, *Litchfield County Furn.*, nos. 51–53.

217

Sideboard
James Tabele (w. 1794–1803)
New York, New York, ca. 1799–1803

Description: This sideboard is in the form described in the 1796 New York price book as "A Celleret Side-board with Elliptic Middle and Ogee on each Side." The top is nearly flush with the case at the front and sides but has a pronounced overhang at the rear. Its edge is bordered with light-wood stringing at the front and sides, and the top is shaped in conformity with the case. The case is divided into five vertical sections. The center section contains a wide drawer above a cupboard enclosed with a sliding tambour that moves from

217

left to right and is flanked by hollow recesses at each side. The center section is flanked by pairs of superimposed drawers, including a small drawer above a deep bottle drawer, and each side of the case has a shallow drawer superimposed above a deep cupboard enclosed by a door hinged at its outside edge. Each drawer (except the bottle drawers), the cupboard doors, the hollow recesses in the center section, and the upper section of the six front legs are decorated with rectangles with hollow corners of light-wood stringing; each drawer (including the bottle drawers) is bordered with light-wood stringing. Each bottle drawer is divided visually by inlay into two superimposed panels; the upper panel contains a rounded arch with inlaid quarter fans in the spandrels and a round patera; the lower panel contains a pictorial inlay of an oak leaf enclosed within a rectangle with hollow corners. The wide center drawer, the outer cupboard doors, and the bottle drawers have inlaid keyhole escutcheons. The front skirt is decorated with a patterned inlay (Hewitt, nos. 2, 5) which does not carry around the sides. The sideboard is supported by eight tapered legs, decorated with tapered rectangles of light-wood inlay and with cuffs of the same type of patterned inlay as that used on the skirt at the front and sides. The top is screwed and blocked to the case. The back of the case is a single board, and the inner partitions are tenoned three times through the back. The back and sides of the case are joined to the legs in each corner, and the front rails are joined to the six front legs. The bottom is nailed in place, and

420 *American Case Furniture*

the interior partitions are nailed in place through the bottom. There are full vertical transverse partitions on each side of the bottle drawers, and the sliding tambour is enclosed by an additional partition. The tambour strips are laid on a white cloth decorated with a design of red flowers and green leaves. The cupboard doors and the drawer fronts are built up of horizontal laminations; the bottle drawers initially were divided by partitions into five compartments. There are no dustboards under the drawers. On each drawer, the sides are dovetailed to the front and back; the bottoms are beveled on their front and side edges, let into grooves in the front and sides, and nailed to the underside of the back, with small glue blocks applied.

Inscriptions: A printed paper label pasted to the inside of the bottom of the wide center drawer reads: "JAMES TABELE / Cabinet and Chair Maker, / At No. 39 [in ink] Fair Street and No. 37 Ann-Street, New-York, / M[akes] and sells all kinds of Cabinet Work, at / [torn] est notice, and of the most rea- / [torn] arranted equal to any made in / [remainder torn]." A modern label pasted to the outside of the back of the same drawer, with a red border and blue letters against a white ground, reads: "Antique Furniture / Refinishing, Upholstering, Cabinet Work / Mattress Making Picture Framing / FRANK J. HOLMES / 282–284 Milton Avenue / BALLSTON SPA, - N.Y."

Condition: The brasses are replacements, and the framework of the top has been reinforced by several new transverse braces. There have been repairs to the wide center drawer and to the left bottle drawer. The partitions in each bottle drawer are missing. There have been many minor repairs to the veneers and inlay. The sideboard was refinished by Emile Mazzola in 1962.

Woods: Mahogany; top, drawer and door fronts, case front, mahogany veneer with light- and dark-wood inlays; drawer sides and backs, other elements, yellow poplar; drawer fronts and backs, other elements, eastern white pine; top front rail at each side, ash.

Dimensions: H 103.6; W 201.2; CW 199.9; D 75.9; CD 56.9.

Bibliography: Charles Messer Stow, "Labels: Parcel of Serious Collecting," *Antiquarian* 14, no. 2 (February 1930): 53.

Provenance: The sideboard may have been owned in the 1920s by the family of a Mrs. F. C. Adler of Gansevoort, N.Y. It was sold by dealer Charles Woolsey Lyon, New York, N.Y., to Francis P. Garvan, New York, N.Y.

217a

217b

Sideboards 421

As Charles F. Montgomery noted in his discussion of a related sideboard in the Winterthur collection (57.580), the initial cost of £9.12.0 for "A Celleret Side-board with Elliptic Middle and Ogee on each Side" given in the 1796 New York price book is the second highest figure given in that volume for any type of sideboard.[1] The presence of an additional two legs, making a total of eight rather than the more customary six, and the abundant use of inlaid decoration would have made both the Winterthur sideboard and the Yale example even more expensive. James Tabele, the presumed maker of the Yale sideboard, remains a shadowy figure. He is listed in New York directories as a joiner and cabinetmaker at 39 Fair Street beginning in 1794. In 1795, he is joined at that address and at that occupation by Jacob Tabele, Jr., possibly his brother. In 1799, both James and Jacob are listed at 39 Fair Street and 36 Ann Street, and they continue at this address through 1803. In 1804, Jacob is still listed as a cabinetmaker at that address, but James is now listed as a merchant at Nassau and Fair streets. This would suggest a fairly narrow date range of 1799–1803 for the Yale sideboard, even though the object's label gives James's address as 37 (rather than 36) Ann Street. The only other object by James Tabele known to the writer is a mahogany table bearing a label that gives his address as 15 Fair Street and 37 Ann Street, but which is otherwise identical to the label on the sideboard.[2] The number "39" on the Yale label is written in ink, perhaps over a printed number "15," suggesting that Tabele used the label after his address had changed. The directories list a Jacob Tabele, possibly the father of James and Jacob, Jr., as a shoemaker at 15 Fair Street between 1789 and 1793.[3]

The Mabel Brady Garvan Collection 1930.2204

217c

1. Montgomery, no. 360.
2. DAPC, 75.113. This table was owned in 1975 by Samuel T. Freeman & Company of Philadelphia; its present whereabouts are not known to the writer.
3. A Jacob Tabeley and Hannah Pettenger were married in 1763; see *New York Marriages previous to 1784* (1860; reprint, Baltimore: Genealogical Publishing Co., 1966), p. 382. The Winterthur Library owns a manuscript inventory of the estate of a Jacob Tabele, taken in 1831 (54.90.61) and an undated inventory of a William Tabele (54.67.204).

218

Sideboard
New York, New York, 1790–1815

Description: This sideboard has a square or straight front and ovolo front ends. The top overhangs the case slightly at the front and sides and is edged with cross-banding bordered at the top and bottom with light-wood stringing. The case is divided into three vertical units. The center unit contains a row of three drawers in line, with a wide center drawer flanked by small, square drawers. The drawers stand above a recessed center cupboard flanked by canted panels and deep bottle drawers. Each side of the case holds a drawer above a cupboard enclosed by a door hinged at its outside edge. The seven drawers and the canted panels flanking the center cupboard are bordered with light-wood stringing and inlaid with rectangles with astragal ends of light- and dark-wood stringing. The four cupboard doors are similarly bordered and inlaid with rectangles with hollow corners. The five upper drawers are fitted with brasses; the bottle drawers and cupboard doors are fitted with brass keyhole liners. The front face of the four corner posts and the outside face of the two center posts, contain, from top to bottom, a square of vertical light- and dark-wood inlay, an inlaid panel with astragal ends of light wood surrounded by stringing at the height of the upper drawers, and an inlaid panel of mahogany surrounded by stringing at the level of the bottle drawers and cupboards. The front skirt is marked with horizontal lines of light- and dark-wood stringing. The sideboard is supported by six legs. The front face of all six legs and the outside face of the two center legs each contains a rectangle of light-wood stringing with hollow corners at the top that terminates in the cuffs. All six legs are cuffed on their front and side faces with horizontal bands of light- and dark-wood inlay. The top of the case is a thin mahogany board applied to

218

a joined framework and screwed to the case. The back and sides of the case are joined to the four outer legs, and the front rails are joined to the four front legs; the curved rails at the sides of the front are dovetailed to vertical posts placed behind the two center legs. The bottom boards are joined with a tongue and groove and nailed in place. The internal transverse partitions separating the cupboard sections are tenoned through the back. The drawer runners are nailed to the frame, and small blocks are glued to the inside of the back to act as stops. The drawer fronts and cupboard doors are horizontally laminated. The drawer sides are dovetailed to the front and back, with the top edge of the backs beveled. The drawer bottoms are beveled on their front and side edges, let into grooves in the front and sides, and nailed to the underside of the back; running strips are wedged into the grooves on the drawer sides below the bottoms. The bottle drawers are divided by partitions into five compartments. The cupboard interiors have been given a reddish stain.

Inscriptions: There is an illegible pencil inscription, beginning with "A," on the underside of the bottom. There is an illegible inscription on the outside of the right side of the small drawer above the left bottle drawer. This drawer, its right counterpart, and the two bottle drawers are marked in pencil "L" and "R" respectively several times.

Condition: The brasses are replacements. Supporting brackets have been added to the outer front legs. There have been many minor repairs to the veneer, including the replacement of the veneer on the drawer divider below the wide center drawer by Edward Hoepfner in 1965.

Woods: Mahogany; case front facade, mahogany veneer with light- and dark-wood inlays; drawer linings, yellow poplar; a bottom front rail, soft maple; top front rail, chestnut; a drawer divider, hard maple, probably sugar maple; drawer fronts, case bottom, eastern white pine; some drawer front laminations, southern yellow pine.

Dimensions: H 112.5; W 189.4; CW 187.7; D 72.7; CD 48.1.

Provenance: Francis P. Garvan, New York, N. Y.

WITHOUT the pictorial and patterned inlay found on the previous example, with only six legs, and of a far more rectilinear nature, this sideboard is decorated with triple-line stringing, inlaid flutes or reeds, and astragal end panels characteristic of New York–area furniture.[1] Here, the hollow corners of the panels on the cupboard doors are left empty, while on the succeeding New York example they are filled with inlaid quarter fans.

The Mabel Brady Garvan Collection 1930.2999

1. Montgomery, no. 360.

219

Sideboard
New York, New York, 1790–1815

Description: The top of this serpentine sideboard overhangs the case slightly on all four sides, and its front and side edges are bordered with light-wood stringing. The projecting center section of the case contains a single wide drawer with a bowed front overhanging a recessed cupboard section enclosed by paired doors flanked by concave recesses. Each side section of the case is formed of a single drawer superimposed over a deep drawer, each with a concave front. The deep drawer on the left is divided by partitions into nine bottle compartments. Each drawer and cupboard door is edged with light-wood stringing and contains a rectangle of light- and dark-wood stringing; the deep drawers and cupboard doors have the additional embellishment of an inlaid quarter fan in the corners of these rectangles. The recesses

219

flanking the cupboard doors have rectangles with hollow corners of light- and dark-wood stringing. The wide center drawer has a central brass keyhole liner flanked by oval brass escutcheons with bail pulls; matching brasses are used on the small side drawers and the deep drawers, which also have brass keyhole liners. The cupboard doors have paired brass keyhole liners, blind on the left. The lower edge of the front skirt has light- and dark-wood stringing. The sideboard is supported by six tapered legs; the front and rear legs on each side are squared and decorated on their front face, while the two center legs are five sided, to follow the contour of the case, and are decorated on two faces. At the top of each leg there is an inlaid motif consisting of alternating vertical bands of light and dark wood, with a rectangle with hollow corners of light- and dark-wood stringing below. Below the case, the legs are decorated with light- and dark-wood stringing that comes to a point at the top, is rounded at the bottom, and points at a round ball of inlay, with the top half of the circle in dark wood and the bottom half light. The legs are also decorated with cuffs of banding on their front faces. The top is a veneered framework screwed to the case. The back and sides of the case are joined to the legs, and the front rails are also joined to the four front legs. The bottom boards are nailed to the underside of the back and rest on strips nailed to the sides and front of the case; the vertical internal partitions are nailed in place through the bottom. The internal partitions are not tenoned through the horizontal backboards. Small blocks are glued to the inside of the back to act as drawer stops and are glued to the underside of the drawer runners and the front posts. There are half dustboards below the upper drawers, nailed to the drawer runners, and there are full vertical transverse partitions separating the center section from the side sections. There is a transverse brace under the top at the center. The cupboard doors and the drawer fronts are built up of horizontal laminations and veneered; the laminations of the cupboard doors are of mahogany, while those of the drawers are eastern white pine. The interior of the three upper drawers has been given a reddish stain. On the drawers, the sides are dovetailed to the front and back; the bottoms are fitted to grooves in the front and sides and nailed to the underside of the back with cut nails.

Inscriptions: Two modern labels pasted to the outside of the back read "3A" in ink.

Condition: The two center legs in the front have been broken and are braced with metal supports. The right rear leg has also been broken and repaired. There are new running strips on the drawers, and the drawer runners within the case are replacements. There have been repairs to the inlay and veneers.

Woods: Mahogany; top, drawer fronts, case front, mahogany veneer with light- and dark-wood inlays; drawer linings, bottom, other elements, yellow poplar; top rail, other elements, ash; bottom rail, other elements, American black cherry; back, other elements, eastern white pine.

Dimensions: H 108.0; W 186.9; CW 184.8; D 75.2; CD 46.3.

Provenance: According to a tradition, this sideboard was owned originally by the Reverend Isaac Lewis (1765–1840). It belonged in the twentieth century to Theodore E. Blake (d. 1949), Greenwich, Conn., who bequeathed it to the university along with a cane also thought to have been owned by Lewis.

THE 1796 New York price book describes this type of sideboard as a "serpentine front celleret sideboard," and the form was commonly produced in the New York area. The form closely resembles that of sideboards with an elliptic middle and hollow ends, an equally popular New York–area form, differing only in the unbroken sweep of the serpentine facade and in the attitude and position of the two center legs, which here are decorated on only one face rather than two.[1] Structural variations on the serpentine form include two small drawers, rather than one, above the center cupboard, and a single cupboard, rather than drawers, in the side sec-

tions. Ornamental variations are numerous, although most examples include the inlaid quarter fans, triglyphs, and pattern of stringing found on the rather plain Yale example. A serpentine sideboard, now in the collection of the High Museum in Atlanta, bears the label of William Whitehead (w. 1792–1800) and has survived with its original knife cases.[2]

Gift of Theodore E. Blake 1950.65

1. A sideboard of this type, otherwise nearly identical in style to the Yale example, is in the collection of the Metropolitan Museum of Art (23.80.1) and is illustrated in Verna Cook Salomonsky, *Masterpieces of Furniture* (1931; reprint, New York: Dover Publications, 1953), no. 66. Labeled New York sideboards of this form include examples by Elbert Anderson (Comstock, no. 510); Matthew Egerton, Jr., of New Jersey (Comstock, no. 511); William Mills and Simeon Deming (Fairbanks and Bates, p. 237); and Thomas Burling (*Antiques* 46, no. 6 [December 1944]: inside front cover).
2. *Sack Coll.*, 5: 1254 no. P4286. For other related examples, see *Sack Coll.*, 6: 1664 no. P4756, 1669 no. P4775; *Antiques* 42, no. 5 (November 1942): 225; Hipkiss, no. 44; and Berry B. Tracy, *Federal Furniture and Decorative Arts at Boscobel* (New York: Boscobel Restoration and Harry N. Abrams, 1981), no. 38.

220

220

Sideboard
Baltimore, Maryland, 1790–1810
(see pl. 21)

Description: The sideboard is in the form of a straight-front sideboard with ovolo ends. The top overhangs the case slightly at the front and sides and is edged with cross-banding and bordered with light-wood stringing. It is shaped in conformity with the case, with the addition of an extra canted corner on the outside edges. The case is divided into three vertical units. The center section contains a wide drawer above a slightly recessed cupboard enclosed by paired doors flanked by concave panels. The right side of the case contains a deep bottle drawer, and the left side contains a cupboard enclosed by a door hinged at its outside. The drawers and cupboard doors are edged with light-wood stringing. The wide center drawer contains a center square panel with hollow sides of veneer bordered by a broad band of light-wood stringing enclosed within thinner bands of dark-wood stringing. It is flanked by similar oval panels enclosing a stamped oval brass with bail pull. The lower cupboard doors contain similar ovals, and the right drawer and left cupboard door fronts also have similar ovals which enclose a brass. The recessed panels flanking the center cupboard are outlined with rectangles of the same stringing. The front face of each of the four front legs, as well as the outside face of the two center legs, is decorated with a panel of highly figured wood, again bordered by stringing. The front skirt is decorated with a band of patterned inlay (Hewitt, no. 11). The sideboard is supported by six tapered legs. The front face of each of the four front legs, and the outside face of the two center legs, is decorated with light-wood stringing terminating at the top with a double-round end, terminating at the bottom in the cuff, and enclosing four pendant bellflowers (Hewitt, no. 115). All six legs are cuffed on all four sides with bands of light-wood inlay. The top is braced and framed and is pocket screwed to all four sides of the case. The case is framed with mortise-and-tenon joints, with very deep top and bottom front rails. The case bottom is housed in the bottom front rail and additionally secured with numerous small glue blocks. The transverse vertical partitions flanking the center cupboard are held in place with rosehead nails driven through the case bottom and back and are tenoned through the backboard four times. The outside of the back and the interior of the center cupboard are stained red. The cupboard doors and drawer fronts are made up of horizontal laminations. The left and center cupboard interiors consist of undifferentiated open space; the deep drawer on the right lacks partitions. On this drawer and on the wide center drawer, the sides are dovetailed to the front

Sideboards 425

and back; the bottom is let into a groove in the front and sides, and nailed to the underside of the back, with applied running strips on each side. There is a full dustboard beneath the center drawer.

Inscriptions: The brasses, which are original, are stamped "H J" probably for the Birmingham, England, firm of brass founders organized by Thomas Hands and William Jenkins.

Condition: The drawer runners have been replaced, and the bottom boards have been damaged by insects. There have been minor repairs to the veneer, and some glue blocks are replacements.

Woods: Mahogany; case front, mahogany veneer with light- and dark-wood inlays; highly figured wood on front posts is often called zebrawood, but it has not been subjected to microanalysis; frame, eastern white pine; drawer linings, yellow poplar.

Dimensions: H 101.3; W 191.3; CW 182.9; D 68.4; CD 39.7.

Bibliography: Comstock, no. 513; Rogers, "Garvan Furn. (1960)," fig. 17; Rogers, "Garvan Coll. (1962)," p. 13; Kirk, Early Am. Furn., fig. 16; Jules David Prown, "Style as Evidence," Winterthur Portfolio 15, no. 3 (Autumn 1980): 206 fig. 10.

Provenance: Purchased from C. Watson, Princess Anne, Md., by dealer Charles R. Morson, New York, N. Y., who sold it to Francis P. Garvan, New York, N. Y.

NUMEROUS characteristics indicate that this sideboard was produced in Baltimore. The patterned inlay on its skirt was seen by Charles F. Montgomery as "almost a signature for Baltimore workmanship," and the bellflowers on the legs are also typical of Baltimore work.[1] The repeated use of ovals formed by stringing is another characteristic of many objects from the Baltimore area.[2] The highly figured wood used on the front posts here, with its irregular stripes of light and dark grain, may have been known in its own time as zebrawood, as it is often called today.[3] Sheraton, in his Cabinet Dictionary, noted that zebrawood "is streaked with brown and white as the animal is" and that it is "a beautiful wood for cross-banding," although it was "extremely scarce" in England in the early nineteenth century.[4] The "brilliantly conceived" design of this example, a visually successful sideboard of the federal period, has been analyzed extensively by John T. Kirk.[5]

The Mabel Brady Garvan Collection 1930.2492

220a

1. Montgomery, no. 444. Hewitt also found this inlay on a card table labeled by John Shaw of Annapolis (table no. 371). The bellflowers (Hewitt, no. 115) were found by Hewitt on four Baltimore card tables, and they also appear on a Baltimore pier table at Winterthur (Montgomery, no. 351), among other objects.

2. See many examples of objects, including sideboards, illustrated in *Baltimore Furniture: The Work of Baltimore and Annapolis Cabinetmakers from 1760 to 1810* (Baltimore, Md.: Baltimore Museum of Art, 1947).

3. Zebrawood is a term applied to several species of wood with light and dark markings from Central America, South America, and western Africa. It seems to be most commonly used as a term for zebrano (*Microberlinia brazzavillensis* and *M. sulcata*), a wood used for decorative veneers and usually quarter cut to show its markings to the best advantage; see B. J. Rendle, *World Timbers: Volume 1, Europe & Africa* (London: Ernest Benn, 1969), pp. 176–177.

4. Vol. 2, p. 334.

5. Kirk, *Early Am. Furn.*, pp. 29–30.

221

221

Sideboard

Baltimore, Maryland, area, 1790–1815

Description: This form of sideboard was described in price books of the period as "a Celleret Sideboard with an Eliptick Middle, [and] an Eliptick Hollow on each Side."[1] The top is shaped in conformity with the case and overhangs the case slightly on all four sides. It has a border line of light-wood stringing at the front and sides, and its front edge is faced with banding and bordered with light-wood stringing at the top and bottom. The case is divided into three units. The center section contains a wide drawer above a pair of cupboard doors, and there is a door at each side hinged to the case on its outside edge. The four cupboard doors and the drawer front are inlaid with rectangles with hollow corners of light-wood stringing and bordered with light- and dark-wood stringing. Each also has an inlaid keyhole escutcheon of light-wood inlay. The front face of each post is inlaid with rectangles of cross-banding bordered with patterned inlay and light-wood stringing. The sides of the case are inlaid with rectangles with hollow corners of light-wood stringing. There is a band of patterned inlay (Montgomery, inlay no. 79) around the bottom of the case at the front and sides. The case is supported by six tapered legs; the two legs in the center of the front have inlaid rectangles with rounded upper ends on their front faces; those at the corners of the front have the same decoration on their front and outside faces; and the two rear legs have this stringing only on their outside faces.

Each leg has a cross-banded cuff bordered with stringing on all four sides. The top is a veneered framework, with strips at the front and sides and two transverse braces, screwed to the case. The sides of the case are joined to the front and rear legs; the front of the case consists of top and bottom rails joined to the four front legs and a rail below the drawer. There is a full dustboard under the drawer, and full vertical transverse partitions separate the center section from each side compartment; these partitions are tenoned four times through the backboard and nailed in place through the bottom. The back is a single horizontal board joined to the rear legs. The bottom is fitted to the lower front rail and to the sides of the case and additionally secured with multiple small horizontal glue blocks attached behind the front rail. The cupboard doors are horizontally laminated and open in each instance to a plain interior. The drawer sides are dovetailed to the front and back, with the top edge of the sides rounded; the drawer bottom is beveled on its front and side edges, let into a groove in the front and sides, and nailed to the underside of the back, with running strips applied. There are many small glue blocks attached to the bottom behind the drawer front.

Condition: The brasses are replacements. The left door and some of the inlays were repaired by Emile Mazzola in 1961, and there have been many other repairs to the veneer and inlay. The lock is missing on the center cupboard door, there are new running strips on the drawer, and there is a patch to

Sideboards 427

the top at the rear of the center. The center and side compartments have been given a reddish stain.

Woods: Mahogany, mahogany veneer with light- and dark-wood inlays; drawer linings and other elements, yellow poplar; drawer divider, other elements, eastern white pine.

Dimensions: H 102.4; W 183.3; CW 179.0; D 63.8; CD 43.8.

Bibliography: Miller, 1: no. 964.

Provenance: Purchased from Dr. McStevens, Easton, Md., by Francis P. Garvan, New York, N. Y.

WITH its concave sides and convex middle, this relatively small sideboard is of the type described in the Philadelphia price book of 1811 as "A Celleret Sideboard with an Eliptick Middle, [and] an Eliptick Hollow on each Side." The form appears to have been derived from plate 29 of Hepplewhite's *Cabinet-Maker and Upholsterer's Guide*, which illustrates the same shape but without the cupboard below the middle drawer and with drawers rather than cupboards on each end, and it was used in several regions of America. The Yale example, with plain cupboards, lacks the internal fittings for bottles, silver plate, cloths, and napkins and the lead-lined cistern "for the convenience of holding water to wash glasses" suggested by Hepplewhite. Purchased in Maryland, this sideboard probably was made in the Baltimore area, although it lacks the exuberance and rich veneers of the finest Baltimore work (see cat. 220). One of the patterned inlays used here, on the lower edge of the case at the front and sides, is found on other objects attributed to Baltimore and Annapolis.[2] The simple inlaid rectangles with hollow corners and the general stance of this sideboard also are reminiscent of small sideboards made in Delaware, including an example labeled by George Whitelock (working 1810–1822) of Wilmington.[3]

The Mabel Brady Garvan Collection 1930.2606

1. *The Journeymen Cabinet and Chairmakers' Pennsylvania Book of Prices* (Philadelphia: Printed for the society, 1811), p. 51.
2. Montgomery, no. 444; and Hewitt, no. 371.
3. Deborah Dependahl Waters, *Delaware Collections in the Historical Society of Delaware* (Wilmington: Historical Society of Delaware, 1984), no. 3. See also *Antiques* 78, no. 5 (November 1960): 391.

222

222

Sideboard

Charleston, South Carolina, 1790–1810

Description: This mammoth sideboard is surmounted by a gallery at the sides and back that is supported by a dozen small columns or "pillars" rising from square plinths. The lower front edge of the support for the gallery's shelf is bordered by light- and dark-wood stringing; the front edge of the shelf is molded and holds two lines of dark-wood stringing. (The shelf is not grooved for plates.) The gallery's railing is composed of a pierced fretwork design, stained or painted black, with gilt columns with turned button finials at the front and rear of each side and flanking a central plaque of pictorial floral inlay. The plaque is bordered by patterned inlay, cross-banding, and light- and dark-wood stringing. The sideboard is shaped with a hollow center flanked by ovolo units in turn flanked by ovolo corners. The top overhangs the case slightly on all four sides and has a band of light- and dark-wood stringing conforming to the shape of the top and inset slightly from the edge. The top of its front edge is bordered with light-wood stringing above dark-wood stringing, and the lower edge is bordered with dark-wood stringing. The case is divided into five vertical sections. The center section contains a single wide drawer above a cupboard enclosed by tambour shutters. This center

428 *American Case Furniture*

section is flanked by units containing a shallow drawer above a deep bottle drawer. The upper left drawer is divided by partitions into five sections, and each bottle drawer is similarly divided by partitions (slightly hollowed to accommodate bottles) into fourteen compartments. Each side unit holds a single door (decorated to simulate two superimposed drawers) enclosing a cupboard divided by a single shelf. The drawer in the center section contains a slightly projecting central plaque of pictorial floral inlay, similar to but varying from the related plaque at the center of the gallery and bordered by the same combination of patterned inlay, cross-banding, and stringing. The plaque is flanked by panels, each containing a central pull with bail handle enclosed within a horizontal diamond formed by light- and dark-wood stringing and surrounded by triangles created by mitering pieces of cross-grained veneer at the four corners. The drawer is bordered on all four sides by light- and dark-wood stringing. The arch for the center cupboard is bordered with patterned inlay, and the spandrels contain inlaid shaded oak leaves against a green background. The tambour is composed of alternating vertical strips of light and dark wood and is formed in two sections, which slide in grooves to the left and right to open. There are fixed sections of tambour at each side of the opening. Each small drawer flanking the center drawer contains a central pull placed over and cut to accommodate a brass keyhole liner. Each of these drawers is decorated in the same manner as the side panels of the center drawer. Each large, deep bottle drawer contains a brass keyhole liner at the top and a central escutcheon with bail pull. These drawers are decorated in the same manner as the drawers above, with the substitution of an oval for the

222b

222a

diamond shape. Each side cupboard door has a brass keyhole liner on its inner edge, is hinged on its outer edge, and is otherwise decorated to simulate the working drawer to its inside. The front face of each of the six front legs contains a vertical diamond of dark mahogany veneer enclosed by light- and dark-wood stringing at the height of the small drawers above a larger oval of dark mahogany veneer again enclosed by light- and dark-wood stringing at the height of the bottle drawers. The skirt is decorated with patterned inlay at the front and sides of the case. The case is supported by eight turned legs with carved capitals that originally may have been gilt, fluted shafts, a reeded, drumlike base, and a plain, tapered foot. (Part of the rear face of each leg is not fluted.) The supports for the gallery pierce the top of the case; they are threaded below the top and secured with large wooden nuts. The top framework is screwed to the case, and the case is framed with mortise-and-tenon joints. There are full dustboards under the top drawers supported by thin strips nailed to the case. The vertical transverse partitions separating the internal units of the case are tenoned through the back four times and are secured with a rosehead nail driven through the back above the upper through-tenon and by screws and nails through the bottom front rails and case bottom. Each side compartment is fitted with a single loose shelf, shaped at its front to conform to the case, resting on thin strips nailed to the case. There is no bottom to the case below the bottle drawers. The bottom under the side compartments consists of several diagonal boards joined with a tongue and groove; these are supported at the rear by a strip

Sideboards 429

nailed to the inside of the back of the case and are joined to the curved bottom front rail with a tongue and groove. The drawer and door fronts are formed of multiple horizontal laminations. On the drawers, the sides are dovetailed to the front and back; the bottoms are beveled on their front and side edges, let into grooves in the front and sides, and nailed to the underside of the back. The "brasses" are made of a silvered base metal, probably copper.

Inscriptions: The bail handles on each pull are stamped "H J," probably for the firm of Thomas Hands and William Jenkins, brass founders of Birmingham, England. "R.80 7667 1" is painted in red on the outside of the rear edge of the top. Some of the drawer sides have been marked (inaccurately) in modern times with the names of various woods.

Condition: There have been many repairs to the veneers, patterned inlays, and stringing. The bottom of each drawer side has been repaired; the outer edges of the center drawer are replaced; one of the partitions in the right bottle drawer has been lost; and the back of the same drawer has been pieced. The gilding on the upper gallery columns is worn; that on the capitals of the legs is even more so; and the original silvering on the pulls has largely worn away, revealing the base metal, probably copper, underneath. There are many stains on the top of the sideboard, including one in the image of a candle snuffer, on the left.

Woods: Mahogany, mahogany veneer with light- and dark-wood inlays; tambour, alternating dark strips of mahogany and light strips, probably of satinwood; gallery, mahogany (with inlays), secured by nuts of red gum or black gum (*Nyssa* spp.); laminations of drawer and door fronts, yellow poplar; drawer backs and bottoms, southern yellow pine; drawer sides, southern red cedar (*Juniperus silicicola*); framing elements, southern red cedar, southern yellow pine, red gum or black gum; partitions in right bottle drawer, dustboard under center drawer, other small elements, eastern white pine.

Dimensions: H (to top of gallery) 145.4; H (to top of case) 102.9; W 228.0; CW 225.6; D 77.8; CD (sides) 35.9.

Exhibition: YUAG, "Southern Furn.," no. 13.

Bibliography: Nutting, *Treasury*, no. 750; Burton, *Charleston Furn.*, fig. 65; E. T. Joy, "English Furniture in America in the Georgian Period and Some hitherto Unpublished Trading Figures," *Connoisseur* 146, no. 587 (September 1960): 72 fig. 9.

Provenance: See cat. 188.

THE design for this eight-legged sideboard is loosely based on plate 29 in Sheraton's *Cabinet-Maker and Upholsterer's Drawing-Book* (1803), dated 1791, and on plate 70 in volume 2 of his *Cabinet Dictionary* (1802). The form of the case, for example, is derived from that suggested in the *Drawing-Book*, while the form of the gallery is related to that depicted in the *Dictionary*, although varying in detail. Sheraton states that the shelf of the gallery, supported in his design by brass pillars, should have "a groove to receive the edges of plates, when it is thought proper to place them in such a manner." The shelf in the Yale example is not grooved, although the upper level of columns are gilt, possibly in imitation of brass. In addition, Sheraton explains, the shelf "serves to place any small silver ware upon, according to the custom or fancy of a family."[1] Sheraton also notes that the hollow front, not customarily present on sideboards, had several practical advantages. "If a sideboard be required nine or ten feet long, as in some nobleman's houses [the Yale example is about seven and a half feet wide], and if the breadth of it be in proportion to the length, it will not be easy for a butler to reach across it." The hollow front would remove this difficulty, "and at the same time have a very good effect, by taking off part of the appearance of a great length of such a sideboard." Moreover, "if the sideboard be near the entering door of the dining-room, the hollow front will sometimes secure the butler from the jostles of the other servants."[2] Such an elaborate sideboard was well suited to the life-style of its original owner, wealthy planter Colonel William Alston of South Carolina, reputedly a large slaveholder in the state. Like the large library bookcase in the Yale collection (cat. 188), also originally owned by Alston, this object was probably used in his house on King Street in Charleston, although tradition maintains that it was used in his plantation house, Clifton, in Georgetown on the Waccamaw River. No specific reference to either object has been found as yet in Alston's estate papers. Alston was noted for his hospitality, however, and his estate included goodly quantities of silver plate, table linen, and various wines, all of which probably found a home in this cavernous sideboard.[3] Although it has been stated that the two inlaid plaques on this sideboard depict "the cotton plant in bloom as well as the cotton boll," examination of the designs by members of the Yale School of Forestry and Environmental Studies indicated that although cotton may be one of the four or more plant species depicted in these inlays, along with (possibly) sweet potato and nasturtiums, the flowers depicted "are so stylized or altered by artistic license that none can be identified with any certainty."[4] A related sideboard, also with a history in Charleston, has been published.[5]

430 *American Case Furniture*

The Mabel Brady Garvan Collection 1930.2308

1. Sheraton, *Cabinet-Maker and Upholsterer's Drawing-Book*, p. 366.
2. Sheraton, *Cabinet Dictionary*, 2: 304.
3. Inventory of the estate of William Alston, Charleston, S. C., Inventories, vol. H, pp. 433-434, 470-472 (xerox copy in YUAG object files).
4. Burton, *Charleston Furn.*, p. 56; letter of David M. Smith, professor of Silviculture, 27 October 1978, YUAG object files.
5. Burton, *Charleston Furn.*, fig. 62.

223

Sideboard
New York, New York, 1855-1865
(see pl. 22)

Description: This large sideboard is in three units. The high upper case rests on the rear portion of the lower case. The upper unit is crowned by a detachable carved pediment with a large central cartouche flanked by scrolls and leafage. The unit is divided into two panels by a shelf with a molded front edge that projects in an arch at its center. Each panel is flanked by longitudinal and transverse supports decorated with scrolls, fruits, bosses, and, above the shelf, carved chimera on the transverse supports. The upper panel contains a rectangle of applied moldings arched at its top in conformity with the pediment and holds a carved fox hanging by a hind leg and surrounded by a grapevine. The lower panel contains a rectangle of applied moldings, with a central cluster of grapes, fruit, and leaves encircled by a vine. The top of the lower case is molded on its front edge. The lower case is shaped with a straight front and ovolo corners and holds four small drawers in line above four cupboard doors. The drawers are decorated with rectangles of applied moldings, hollow on their inner sides, and with circular molding around the lock or pull. The two center drawers are fitted with locks, and the two side drawers with turned wooden pulls. The drawers are separated and flanked by rectangular faceted bosses enclosed within applied moldings, and there is a course of applied moldings below the drawers. The four doors, each fitted with a lock, contain panels formed by applied moldings with hollow upper corners, each enclosing a carved motif. The left center door is carved with two fish suspended on a line with aquatic vegetation on each side; the right center door holds a hare suspended by a hind paw and surrounded by leaves, branches, and vines; and the curved side doors are fitted with clusters of fruit, nuts, and foliage. The cupboard doors are separated and flanked by pilasters with scrolled and strapwork capitals and bases and with pendant carvings of fruit and foliage. There is complex base molding below the doors, and the sideboard is supported on a plinth base. The two sections of the sideboard are sturdily framed. The upper section, which can be secured to the wall, is a paneled frame that merely rests on the top of the lower case. The detachable pediment is secured with four dowels to the rest of the upper unit. The back of the lower case is framed to four large panels. The four cupboard doors are pivot hinged. The center doors open to an interior divided by a central vertical transverse partition; each side holds a single loose adjustable shelf supported at its sides by strips placed in other, toothed strips. The curved side doors open to compartments containing a single loose shaped shelf supported in one position by strips screwed to the case. On the

drawers, the sides are dovetailed to the front and back, and the bottom is let into grooves in the front, sides, and back. The drawer backs are notched to accommodate a runner screwed to the full dustboards below each drawer. The side drawer fronts are curved to meet the drawer back, thus forming a drawer with only three sides.

Condition: The sideboard has survived in superb condition, with only very minor losses and repairs to the veneer and carved elements.

Woods: Frame, primarily walnut, probably American black walnut; panels in upper section, top of lower case, drawer and door fronts, and plinth base, burl walnut veneer; drawer linings, walnut; some framing elements, American black ash (*Fraxinus nigra*); some elements of upper section, shelves behind center cupboard doors, yellow poplar.

Dimensions: H 259.1; W 201.4; CW 184.4; D 60.4; CD 56.0.

Bibliography: Martha Blythe Gerson, "Furniture," in *Antiques: An Encyclopedia of the Decorative Arts*, ed. Paul Atterbury (London: Octopus Books, 1979), p. 40; Kenneth L. Ames and Michael Ettema, "Unseating Style," *Art & Antiques* (March 1984): 76.

Provenance: According to tradition, this sideboard was located in the home of Joseph Earl Sheffield (1793–1882) and his wife Maria (St. John) Sheffield (1801–1899) at 6 Hillhouse Avenue in New Haven, Conn., and was part of the Sheffields' bequest to Yale. After Mrs. Sheffield's death in 1889, the sideboard was removed to the Sheffield Memorial Room of the Yale Sheffield Scientific School. When that room was subsequently converted to a seminar room, the sideboard was placed in storage at 285 Prospect Street. It was removed from storage to the Art Gallery in 1971.

REPLETE with carved images of dead fish and game and of fruit and other verdure, as well as with Renaissance revival ornament, this sideboard probably owes its ultimate inspiration to the monumental, prize-winning sideboard designed by Hugues Protat, manufactured by the Parisian firm of Alexandre Georges Fourdinois (1799–1871), and exhibited in 1851 at the Crystal Palace in London.[1] There were several sideboards exhibited at the New York exhibition of 1853 which were indebted to the Fourdinois sideboard and other French and English examples for their design and ornament. That exhibited by the firm of Alexander Roux of New York perhaps bears the closest relationship to the Yale example, although the sideboards exhibited by Rochefort & Skarren of New York and Eliars of Boston are also related in feeling.[2]

223a

432 *American Case Furniture*

223b

An even more elaborate American example of this form, also decorated with the iconography of mid nineteenth-century dining, has been acquired recently by the Museum of Fine Arts, Houston (83.46.1-16), and less ornate sideboards are also in the collection of the Currier Gallery of Art (1981.56) and the Margaret Woodbury Strong Museum.[3] Large sideboards in the Renaissance revival style similar in form but lacking the carved game and fish were made in the 1860s by Daniel Pabst (1827–1910) of Philadelphia, including examples now in the Philadelphia Museum of Art and the Virginia Museum of Fine Arts.[4] Many period photographs illustrate sideboards such as these groaning with the family silver. Sideboards of a single type of wood, such as the carefully selected walnut and burl walnut veneer used here, were particularly suited for the display of these silver articles. The London firm of Blackie and Son noted in 1853, "having to contrast with plate, the sideboard should have a species of richness that looks well alone, and, at the same time, sets off the service of plate to the best advantage. Positive contrasts of various-colored woods, gilding, decorations in brass work or ormolu, tend to interfere with unity of design, and disturb the effect of plate; such modes of ornament should therefore be avoided. Sufficient effect may be obtained by the use of beautiful woods, carefully wrought, and enriched occasionally by carving, inlaying, or fret-cutting."[5]

Bequest of Joseph Earl Sheffield, M.A. (Hon.) 1871 1971.115

1. Kenneth L. Ames, "The Furniture of Fourdinois," *Antiques* 110, no. 2 (August 1976): 336–338, figs. 1–2.
2. B. Silliman and C. R. Goodrich, *The World of Science, Art, and Industry Illustrated from Examples in the New-York Exhibition, 1853–1854* (New York: G. P. Putnam's, 1854), pp. 111, 114, 162. The writer is indebted to an unpublished paper by Benjamin A. Hewitt in the YUAG object files in which the Yale sideboard is visually compared with examples exhibited in the 1851 and 1853 exhibitions. A labeled Roux sideboard with carved fish and game is illustrated in Eileen and Richard Dubrow, *American Furniture of the 19th Century, 1840–1880* (Exton, Pa.: Schiffer

Sideboards 433

Publishing, 1983), p. 168. See also a pair of sideboards, one of which is stamped "A. Roux," in *Maine Antique Digest* 13, no. 2 (February 1985): 26A.

3. The Houston example is illustrated on the front cover of *Decorative Arts Society Newsletter* 10, no. 2 (March 1984); the Strong Museum example in Fitzgerald, fig. XI-1. Other examples are in the collection of the Baltimore Museum of Art and the Cleveland Museum of Art. See also Henry Hawley, "American Furniture of the Mid-Nineteenth Century," *Bulletin of the Cleveland Museum of Art* 74, no. 5 (May 1987): 202-212.

4. David A. Hanks and Page Talbott, "Daniel Pabst—Philadelphia Cabinetmaker," *Philadelphia Museum of Art Bulletin* 73, no. 316 (April 1977): 10 fig. 4.

5. Blackie and Son, *The Victorian Cabinet-Maker's Assistant* (1853; reprint, New York: Dover Publications, 1970), p. 10.

224

Cabinet
Alexander Roux (ca. 1813–1886)
New York, New York, 1850–1870
(see pl. 23)

Description: The cabinet is surmounted by a central rectangular pedestal. The top of the pedestal is edged with applied egg-and-dart molding above deep cove molding decorated with incised ornament. Below the cove molding the pedestal is decorated with a central ebonized and incised ornament and flanked by rectangles of herringbone veneer (curved on their inner edges to conform to the circular shape of the ornament) which are flanked in turn at the ends by small squares of inlay. There are ormolu moldings above and below this decoration. The moldings and inlay are repeated on the sides of the pedestal and on a rear rail or gallery, which terminates at each end in a projecting plinth decorated with an ebonized geometrical ornament surmounted by an inverted floral ebonized finial. The cabinet itself is a large rectangle with hollow corners. Its cornice consists of ebonized and ormolu moldings and a broad central guilloche band of inlaid woods. The front of the case contains a pair of arch-panel doors flanked and separated by engaged three-quarter ebonized and turned columns with palmette capitals. The side columns support blocks with chamfered edges and an applied ormolu caryatid mount; the center column supports a block with a bronze plaque of a female figure in classical garb. Each door is mounted with a painted porcelain plaque enclosed by an oval ormolu frame and surrounded by inlaid scrolls, flowers, and other ornaments. There are ormolu mounts in the spandrels of the doors, and the molded panel edges are ebonized. Each door is fitted with a lock on its inner edge. The hollow sides of the case have vertical rectangular panels containing colorful floral marquetry and incised ornament. The sides of the case are fitted with freestanding ebonized columns with Corinthian capitals, reeded shafts, bands of ormolu molding, and incised, vase-shaped bases. There is an ebonized cyma molding above the plinth base, and the cabinet is supported by five ebonized, flattened ball feet decorated with incised lines. The cupboard doors open to an interior containing a single fixed shelf. The cabinet is sturdily constructed with heavy framing elements. The top of the case is screwed to the sides of the pedestal, and the pedestal itself is fastened together with screws and glue. The top of the cabinet is dovetailed to a board below that terminates at each end in large blocks. The back of the case consists of four panels screwed to the case sides and the bottom. The hollow sides of the case are formed of a vertical scored plywood. The heavy base frame has several tenoned transverse supports. The feet are doweled to the frame, and its joints are reinforced with screws and glue. The doors are fastened to the case with pivot hinges; the frames for the porcelain plaques are screwed in place through the doors. The other metal mounts are nailed or tacked in place.

Inscriptions: "ROUX" is stamped on the pair of keys to this object. "L" and "r" are written in black on the back of the

434 *American Case Furniture*

left and right porcelain plaques respectively, and the right plaque also has "68" or possibly "681." "V 18/6" is written in pencil on the outside of the back of the pedestal. Stamped on the outside of the back and written in pencil twice on the outside of the back is "2676."

Condition: There have been minor repairs to and replacements of the moldings and veneers; the pedestal has also been repaired.

Woods: Rosewood veneer (*Dalbergia* spp.), probably Brazilian rosewood (*D. nigra*); marquetry, other inlaid decoration, light and dark woods; curved and scored sides of cabinet, plywood with exterior rosewood facing and interior soft maple facing; columns, framing elements, American black cherry; chestnut; eastern white pine; yellow poplar; interior of cupboard section, shelf, doors, curly maple veneer.

Dimensions: H 129.2; W 176.6; CW 150.2; D 41.1; CD 35.8.

Exhibition: YUAG, "A Century of Tradition and Innovation," no. 6.

Bibliography: "Recent Gifts and Purchases," *YUAG Bulletin* 33, no. 1 (Summer 1971): 34; Kane, "American Furn.," pl. XIV.

Provenance: Purchased in 1970 from dealer Peter Hill, Washington, D.C.

Perhaps known in its own day as a French cabinet or drawing room cabinet, this large object was one of the key examples of display furniture during the third quarter of the nineteenth century.[1] Although it provides a modest amount of enclosed storage space in its stunning interior veneered with brilliant curly maple, this cabinet served primarily as a decorative support for a clock or bronze sculpture. Examples were made by many urban shops, particularly those operated by immigrant French craftsmen in New York. Alexander Roux operated one of the largest and most fashionable of

224a

224b

Sideboards 435

these establishments, producing a large quantity of objects in a variety of styles for nearly half a century.² Several other labeled Roux cabinets in this Renaissance revival style, with porcelain plaques and metal mounts in a Louis XVI style, share some of the motifs and general feeling of the Yale example and help to provide a date range for its production. These include cabinets in the Metropolitan Museum of Art (68.100.1) and the Museum of Art, Rhode Island School of Design (78.052), each dated to about 1866; an example in the Virginia Museum of Fine Arts, Richmond (77.39), dated 1848–1857; and an example in the Bowdoin College Museum of Art (1974.42), dated on the basis of its label to ca. 1867–1877.³ Other large cabinets of this form, but differing in motifs and style, were made by Roux and the New York firms of Léon Marcotte, Nelson Gustafsson, and Herter Brothers.⁴

The Mabel Brady Garvan Collection 1970.55

1. Ulysses G. Dietz, *Century of Revivals: Nineteenth Century American Furniture in the Collection of the Newark Museum* (Newark, N. J.: Newark Museum, 1983), no. 36; MMA, *19th-Century America*, no. 164.
2. Dianne D. Hauserman, "Alexander Roux and His 'Plain and Artistic' Furniture," *Antiques* 93, no. 2 (February 1968): 210–217; MMA, *19th-Century America*, nos. 99, 120, 144, 149, 164.
3. MMA, *19th-Century America*, no. 164; *Antiques* 118, no. 1 (July 1980): 131; *Antiques* 113, no. 5 (May 1978): 1061; DAPC, 74.6148. A large cabinet in this style is in the collection of the Margaret Woodbury Strong Museum, Rochester; and a cabinet attributed to Roux but bearing the label of Thomas Godey of Baltimore is in the collection of the High Museum, Atlanta (DAPC, 79.897). A cabinet by Roux in varying style is in the collection of the Museum of the City of New York; see *Antiques* 107, no. 5 (May 1975): 832. Large cabinets of this period are often attributed to Roux; see, for example, Ann Perry, *Renaissance Revival Victorian Furniture* (Grand Rapids, Mich.: Grand Rapids Art Museum, 1976), no. 2.

4. An example by Marcotte is in the Newark Museum (34.110); see Dietz, *Century of Revivals*, no. 36. An example attributed to Marcotte and now in the collection of the Los Angeles County Museum of Art is illustrated in *Antiques* 115, no. 1 (January 1979): 48. A cabinet by Nelson Gustafsson, working in the 1870s, is now in the Museum of Fine Arts, Boston (1981.400); it is illustrated in Fairbanks and Bates, p. 419. An example, dated by a bill of sale to 1871, was made by Herter Brothers; see *Antiques* 123, no. 1 (January 1983): 80.

225

Sideboard
Gustav Stickley's (1857–1942) Craftsman Workshops
Eastwood, New York, 1909–1912

Description: This rectangular sideboard is surmounted by a plate rail formed by vertical extensions of the rear corner posts, a horizontal bottom rail, a middle rail pegged to the front of the posts, and a slightly arched upper rail. The top overhangs the case slightly on all four sides. The case holds three small graduated drawers at its center, flanked by a pair of cupboard doors, all above a single wide drawer. Each small drawer is fitted with a wrought-copper escutcheon with bail pull, and the top drawer is also fitted with a lock. The wide drawer is fitted with a pair of escutcheons; the cupboard doors are fastened to the case with wrought-copper strap hinges and are fitted with a wrought-copper lock escutcheon with bail pull. The sideboard is supported by four slightly tapered legs. The right cupboard door opens to a plain interior, while the left cupboard is fitted with a single loose shelf. The top small drawer is lined with brown ooze leather. The top of the case consists of four boards joined with a tongue and groove; these are pegged to the interior partitions and secured to the case with pocket screws from underneath. The sides of the case are framed to a single panel. The top back rail extends above the case top to form the lower element of the plate rail and is screwed to the case top. The back panels are also screwed to rabbets in the corner posts, to the bottom rail, and to the interior vertical partitions. There is no top rail on the front of the case; the lower front rail is joined to the corner posts and secured with a single peg. The bottom of the case is a large panel supported by multiple horizontal glue blocks behind the bottom front rail. The top edges of

224c

the rear posts are beveled and taper slightly. Vertical transverse partitions separate the small drawers from the outer cupboards. On the drawers, the sides are dovetailed to the front and back; the plywood bottoms are let into grooves in the front and sides and nailed to the underside of the back. A medial runner is screwed to the bottom of each drawer and runs on strips screwed to the full dustboards below each drawer. Wooden pegs applied to the drawer dividers act as stops. The wrought-copper hardware is fastened with round-headed copper screws.

Inscriptions: A red Stickley decal, of the type illustrated in Cathers, page 63, is applied to the inside of the bottom of the middle small drawer. A paper label, now obscured by later varnish, is pasted to the outside of the back of the case. It is the type of label illustrated in Cathers, page 66, and is marked in ink with the catalogue number "814½." Written in black on the outside of the back is "5–48x30¼"; "19¾ scant" is written in pencil on the underside of the dustboard below the middle small drawer; and "18" is written in pencil on the outside of the back of the wide drawer. A notation, largely illegible but containing words and numbers, is written in pencil on the underside of the bottom of the lowest small drawer. The lock on the top small drawer is stamped on the inside "EAGLE LOCK CO / TERRYVILLE, CONN, U.S.A." and "4K17."

Condition: There have been repairs to the veneer on each cupboard door, and the mahogany shelf in the interior of the left cupboard may be a replacement. There is a reddish stain below the bottom hinge on the left cupboard door. The cupboard interiors show many signs of wear, including evidence that they were used extensively for the storage of bottles. The ooze leather has deteriorated slightly.

Woods: White oak; cupboard doors, quarter-sawn white oak veneer; case bottom, chestnut; drawer runners, birch; drawer bottoms, oak plywood.

Dimensions: H 121.2; W 142.5; CW 126.4; D 54.0; CD 52.4.

Exhibition: YUAG, "A Century of Tradition and Innovation," no. 14.

Bibliography: Kane, "American Furn.," p. 1326 fig. 14; "Acquisitions 1979," *YUAG Bulletin* 38, no. 1 (Fall 1980): 65.

Provenance: Purchased at the New Haven Antiques Show in spring 1979 from Handlebar Antiques, Los Angeles, Calif.

A 56-inch-wide sideboard of this type was introduced for the first time in the 1909 catalogue of Gustav Stickley's Craftsman Workshops. The decal and paper label applied to the object are of the type used by Stickley until 1912, suggesting a rather tight date range for this sideboard. A further detail indicating a date close to 1909 is that the side rails are not tenoned through the front posts; this type of construction appeared only on later examples of the 56-inch sideboard.[1] Stickley's 1909 catalogue offered six types of sideboard, ranging in price from $84 to $28, and in width from 70 to 48 inches. This example, given the catalogue number 814½, was priced at $50, placing it in the middle range in terms of both cost and size.[2] It represented an option to catalogue number 814, which was 10 inches wider and $18 more expensive. The top small drawer, fitted with a lock for security and lined with ooze leather, probably was meant for the storage of table silver. The lower wide drawer (which in some Stickley designs is located at the top of the case) was designed to be "deep and long enough to hold table-cloths."[3] Many Stickley catalogues and advertisements illustrate related sideboards with examples of metalwork, also produced in the Craftsman Workshops, displayed on the plate rail. A nearly identical example is in the collection of the Virginia Museum of Fine Arts, and related examples in various sizes can be found in the Museum of Fine Arts, Houston, the St. Louis Art Museum, and the High Museum in Atlanta.[4]

Gift of Dr. and Mrs. Matthew Newman 1979.27

Sideboards 437

1. Cathers, pp. 206, 63, 66.
2. *Catalogue of Craftsman Furniture Made by Gustav Stickley at the Craftsman Workshops, Eastwood, New York* (1909; reprint, Watkins Glen, N.Y.: American Life Foundation, 1978), nos. 800, 814, 814½, 816, 817, 819.
3. *Collected Works of Gustav Stickley*, ed. Stephen Gray and Robert Edwards (New York: Turn of the Century Editions, 1981), p. 103.
4. *Antiques* 113, no. 5 (May 1978): 1063; Cathers, pp. 198–199; David A. Hanks and Donald C. Peirce, *The Virginia Carroll Crawford Collection: American Decorative Arts, 1825–1917* (Atlanta: High Museum, 1983), p. 94.

226

Living room case
Designed by Oskar G. Stonorov (1905–1970) and
Willo von Moltke (b. 1911)
American, 1940–1941

226

FIG. 4 Prototype of living-room storage units from "Organic Design in Home Furnishings," 24 September–9 November 1941. (Museum of Modern Art, New York.)

Description: The object consists of three interchangeable rectangular units mounted on a supporting framework with two shaped feet at each end. Each unit is fitted with a series of drilled holes to accommodate pegs supporting adjustable shelves. One unit has two shelves and was never enclosed; another unit has paired doors with wooden pulls echoing the shape of the feet; and the third unit is fitted with a vertically sliding tambour door with a matching wooden pull. Cleats are screwed to the underside of the front and back of each case to fit over the support; the front edge of the front cleat is molded. The joint of each case side is obscured by veneer; the bottoms of the open unit and the unit with doors are nailed to rabbets in all four sides; the bottom of the tambour section is elevated to allow the tambour to run under it in a groove. The back of each unit is screwed to rabbets in all four sides. The visible portions of the exterior are veneered with walnut. The base framework consists of a single longitudinal board fitted to front and rear feet at each end, which are shaped to extend upward and over the board. A transverse brace is housed in the feet, and the support is screwed in place through the underside of this brace. Holes in the baseboard correspond to holes in the underside of the side of each case, allowing the units to be screwed in position. Metal strips affixed to the outside of the back of each unit allow them to be screwed together there as well. The cupboard doors are attached with brass butt hinges and ball catches.

Inscriptions: The outside of the back of the open unit has "E3/606/550/240" written in black, is stamped "2," and has other black shop marks. One edge of its adjustable shelves is marked "RF" in pencil. Written on the outside of the back of the tambour section is "575/240 LT/ D2." The outside of the back of the cupboard unit with doors is stamped "1" and has the written "D3/606/550/240 L D" and "51 R" in black. The top of the supporting baseboard has the written "E3 606 550" in black.

438 *American Case Furniture*

Condition: An additional supporting brace of red oak had to be added to the underside of the supporting framework in 1982 to strengthen the object. The brace is rabbeted to the existing transverse braces in the feet and screwed in place through the baseboard. At the same time this brace was added, Peter Arkell also made a new wooden pull for the tambour door. There has been some damage to the veneer, and the shelves for the tambour section have been lost.

Woods: Exterior, "gray" walnut veneer on yellow poplar core plywood; pulls, feet, cleats, other elements, walnut.

Dimensions: H 87.3; W 215.5; D 35.8; each unit, H 68.7; W 68.7; D 35.7.

Exhibition: Eliot F. Noyes, *Organic Design in Home Furnishings* (New York: Museum of Modern Art, 1941), p. 23.

Bibliography: "Organic Design in Home Furnishings," *Pencil Points* 22, no. 10 (October 1941): 635.

Provenance: Acquired at the end of the "Organic Design" exhibition by Mr. and Mrs. Andrew C. Ritchie, then of New York, N. Y., and used by them in their homes in Buffalo (1942–1949), New York (1949–1957), New Haven (1957–1971), and Canaan, Conn. (1971–1981).

On 1 October 1940, the Museum of Modern Art's Department of Industrial Design opened a competition in an attempt "to discover good designers and engage them in the task of creating a better environment for today's living."[1] Prizes were awarded in a dozen categories of home furnishings, and objects by the winning designers were included in an exhibition entitled "Organic Design" held at the Museum of Modern Art in 1941. (Organic design was defined, rather nebulously, as "a harmonious organization of the parts within the whole, according to structure, material, and purpose.") The partnership of two Philadelphia architects, Stonorov and von Moltke, was awarded first prize in Category D, Furniture for a Bedroom. As described in the catalogue, their designs included a system of unit cases in walnut, made with a depth of 20 inches for the bedroom but only 12 inches for the living room. (The object now at Yale, however, has a depth of 14 inches.) The units were consistently 27 inches high and 27 inches wide, and they could be grouped in any desired combination of two or three units resting directly on the floor or mounted on a base of corresponding size (fig. 4). Oxidation marks on the base of this example indicate that the tambour section (or "roler-cabinet," as its designers called it) always was placed on the right side. In addition to the three types of units in this example, three other units were available, including a cabinet with tie racks mounted on the inside of the doors, a roler-cabinet fitted with butler trays, and another unit housing three drawers. A competition drawing also illustrates the units fitted with metal pulls and with aluminum supports.[2] The living room case now at Yale was acquired at the end of the exhibition by Andrew C. Ritchie (1907–1978), who in 1942 was appointed director of the Albright Art Gallery in Buffalo, New York.[3] Mr. Ritchie was later director of the Department of Paintings and Sculpture at the Museum of Modern Art (1949–1957) and director of the Yale University Art Gallery (1957–1971). Strongly interested in modern design, he organized during his tenure at the Albright Art Gallery the 1947 "Good Design Is Your Business" exhibition. Several objects from that show, this living room case and a prize-winning lamp by Peter Pfisterer (b. 1907) also from "Organic Design," and other examples of twentieth-century furniture from their collection were given to Yale in 1981 in memory of Mr. Ritchie by his wife Jane. Mrs. Ritchie recalls using the case in both the living room and the dining room of their several houses over the years, to hold books or china. Its relatively shallow yet still adequate depth was a great convenience in comparison to deeper, more cumbersome sideboards.[4] Thus the versatility inherent in the object's design met the test of time, as it served several functions equally well on a daily basis during a span of nearly forty years.

Gift of Jane Ritchie
in memory of Andrew C. Ritchie 1981.53.8

1. Eliot F. Noyes, *Organic Design in Home Furnishings* (New York: Museum of Modern Art, 1941), p. 4. The Stonorov-Moltke designs are illustrated and discussed on pp. 22–25, and biographical data on the two European immigrants is provided on p. 48. Other award-winning furniture designers in the exhibition included Eero Saarinen and Charles Eames. Also see the Stonorov Collection, American Heritage Center, University of Wyoming.
2. Competition drawing, 1940, from "Organic Design in Home Furnishings," 23 September–9 November 1941, Museum of Modern Art, New York.
3. *YUAG Bulletin* 37, no. 2 (Summer 1979): 13.
4. Telephone conversation with the writer, 27 September 1984.

227

227

Sideboard

Designed by Dan Cooper (1901–1965)
New York, New York, ca. 1950
(see pl. 24)

Description: The rectangular sideboard is supported by four square legs and has two sliding doors covering the interior. The doors are painted a flat red and decorated with applied latticework. The left side of the case contains ten drawers, and the right side holds two adjustable shelves. The compartments are separated by a vertical transverse partition. On the left side, the top two drawers are lined with a blue-gray cloth and are grooved for transverse partitions. Although there are seventeen possible positions for the partitions, one drawer is fitted with seven, and the other with nine. The drawer fronts are low and rounded at their top edges; the drawer sides are reduced in height at their fronts with C-shaped cutouts in order to meet the fronts. The top eight drawers are the same size, and the lowest two drawers are graduated. The two shelves are rounded on their front edges and are supported by round, pierced copper pins inserted in a series of sixteen drilled holes placed 3 cm on center. The case is framed with a blind mitered joint, and brass braces are used at the joint of the sides and bottom as reinforcements. The plywood back is screwed to rabbets in all four sides, and the vertical partition within the case also is screwed in place through the back. The top and bottom edges of the sliding doors are grooved to run on thin strips screwed to the top and bottom of the case. The scored outline of the latticework appears on the inside of the doors. The sides of the case extend below the bottom, and there are small horizontal glue blocks affixed to the sides. There is a longitudinal strip behind the bottom front rail; the two front feet are rabbeted to this, with the front portion of each foot extending upward and covering the front rail. The drawer sides are dovetailed to the front and joined to the back with a boxlike tongue and groove. The drawer bottoms project slightly on all four sides and are screwed to the underside on all four sides. The drawer bottoms serve as runners, sliding on small strips screwed to the case and to the vertical partition.

Inscriptions: There are pencil shop marks on the drawers.

Condition: There has been some paint loss on the doors. The fabric lining the top two drawers is worn.

Woods: All four sides of case, feet, shelves, American black walnut; back, walnut veneered plywood; drawers, doors, red oak; strip behind bottom front rail, strips used as guides for doors, maple.

227a

Dimensions: H 96.0; W 162.5; D 46.4.

Provenance: Mr. and Mrs. James Marshall Osborn, New Haven, Conn.

In March 1950, designer Dan Cooper opened a showroom on the 67th floor of the RCA building in Rockefeller Plaza, New York. Publicity photographs of the space show a sideboard that appears to be identical to the one now at Yale.[1] Cooper, perhaps best known today for his fabric and wallpaper designs, had a long association with Mr. and Mrs. Osborn (see cat. 193), and this sideboard was only one of several objects they owned that were either designed by Cooper or upholstered with Cooper-designed material. Although Cooper designed furniture to be produced by manufacturers, much of his work entailed the creation of custom-made pieces, and it seems likely that this sideboard was one such custom-made design. Its stability, use of thick walnut boards, and rather conservative approach gives no foreshadowing of the emphasis on light, modular components with metal fittings that were to be a popular solution to storage problems as the 1950s progressed.[2]

Gift of J. Marshall and Thomas M. Osborn in memory of Mr. and Mrs. James M. Osborn 1977.40.7

1. *Interiors* 109, no. 9 (April 1950): 10. For details on Cooper, the writer is indebted to Shelley A. Schaenen, "Dan Cooper: Designer with a Plan" (Seminar paper, Yale University, 1976). The Yale Art & Architecture Library owns a copy of Cooper's *Inside Your Home* (New York: Farrar, Straus, 1946) inscribed by Cooper to the Osborns.
2. Philippe Garner, *Twentieth-Century Furniture* (New York: Van Nostrand Reinhold Co., 1980), pp. 158–175.

228

228

Cabinet

Designed by Edward Wormley (b. 1907) in 1952; manufactured by Dunbar Furniture Corporation of Indiana Berne, Indiana, ca. 1955

Description: The cabinet has a rectangular mitered case; the slightly projecting top, sides, and bottom have rounded edges. The case holds a single drawer, with a central leather-covered pull, above paired doors, each also fitted with a leather-covered pull. Each door opens to a cupboard section fitted with two adjustable shelves; there is a full vertical transverse partition between the cupboard sections. The case is supported by a recessed rectangular leather-covered base. The cabinet is constructed in a manner consistent with the Dunbar long chest (cat. 77). Here, horizontal glue blocks are used on the base, and the rear of the base framework is screwed to the case. The adjustable shelves are supported by metal pins inserted into a series of drilled holes in the case sides and the middle partition; four positions are possible for both the upper and the lower shelf. The doors are attached to the case with brass butt hinges, and there is a ball catch at the base of each door. The drawer is partitioned into a wide compartment at the left and three smaller compartments at the right; it retains its coin tray.

Inscriptions: The same type of metal label used on the Dunbar long chest (cat. 77) also is nailed to the inside of the left side of the drawer. "N 1 3" is stamped on the underside of the left door; the right door is similarly stamped "N 2 3." "N 3" is stamped on the bottom edge of the drawer front and on the inside of the left side of the case. Stamped on the outside of the back is "0-11." There are many pencil shop marks.

Woods: Case, a grained hardwood plywood, dark in color; drawer front, cupboard doors, a light, bleached walnut veneer; back of case, a plywood with an inner facing of sugar

maple; four adjustable shelves, a sugar maple veneer, some with bird's-eye figure, over a yellow poplar core; coin tray, walnut; base frame, elm on front and back, yellow poplar on sides; hard maple; mahogany; possibly ash.

Dimensions: H 81.5; W 91.5; D 46.2.

Provenance: See cat. 77.

THIS cabinet model was no. 666 in Dunbar's "Career Group" and was also available with 7-inch walnut legs or imported Japanese metal pulls. The top drawer is "partitioned for silver and has a removable sap walnut coin tray," according to the Dunbar literature. The Dunbar firm, according to tradition, traces its origins to 1919, when Aloysius Dunbar of Riney Dunbar's Buggy Works, left with idle time because of the horseless carriage, made a rocking chair for his wife. His creation proved popular and led to the formation of a furniture company which remains in business today. Edward Wormley, after experience with the Marshall Field Department Store and the firm of Berkey and Gay in Chicago, joined Dunbar as director of design in 1931.[1] His association with the company continued until his retirement, and over the years he designed a vast amount of furniture in a wide variety of modern styles. Among his many designs of the mid 1950s was a much more elaborate cabinet than this example, incorporating drawers, trays, shelves, and two electric hot plates.[2]

Gift of Mr. and Mrs. Gifford Phillips, B.A. 1942 1984.14.2

1. For Wormley, see *The Britannica Encyclopedia of American Art* (Chicago: Encyclopaedia Britannica Educational Corp., 1973), pp. 605–606.
2. Illustrated in George Nelson, ed., *Storage*, Interiors Library 4 (New York: Whitney Publications, 1954), p. 96; for other Wormley case furniture, see pp. 59, 94, 98, and 111.

229

Cellarette
New York, New York, 1810–1820
(see pl. 25)

Description: The stepped lid of the cellarette is decorated at its top and lower edge at the front and sides with applied bands in varying design of patterned brass and (probably) ebony inlay, separated by deep cove molding. The case is fitted with a brass keyhole liner surrounded by a horizontal applied ormolu mount cast as waterleafs. Below the ormolu is a border at the front and sides of five alternating bands of brass and ebony stringing. The sides of the case are shaped with deep reverse curves, giving the cellarette the form of a sarcophagus. The cellarette is supported by a small turned baluster at the center of the rear flanked by simulated supports of gold painted fruit and flowers housed in a black and gold painted urn. It is supported at the front by a pair of black and gold painted sphinxes with lions' bodies and women's heads. These supports rest in turn upon a base platform with hollow sides and canted corners. The top and bottom edge of the platform are fitted with applied strips holding a center line of brass stringing. The platform is supported at the front with two gold and black painted paw feet with gold painted acanthus carved knees and gold painted wing brackets and at the rear with two black and gold painted turned legs. All four feet are fitted with metal casters which move in only a forward-backward direction. The lid is hinged to the case at the rear with two sets of brass butt hinges and is supported in the open position by a brass folding hinge at the left side. The lid opens to reveal an interior divided by partitions into six bottle compartments. The joints of most of the object are obscured by veneer. The sphinxes are screwed in place through the bottom of the bottle compartment and with large threaded posts through the base platform. The turned rear feet are doweled to the base platform.

Condition: When acquired by the Art Gallery in 1966, there had been substantial losses of the patterned brass and ebony inlay and stringing; these losses had been replaced in

228a

American Case Furniture

some locations with mahogany veneer. The folding hinge supporting the lid had also been broken. In 1975, Peter Arkell undertook an extensive restoration and conservation treatment which included the refinishing of the cellarette; the replacement of the brass and ebony inlay and stringing with reproductions fashioned after surviving original pieces of each design by Ball & Ball of Exton, Pennsylvania; the repair of the brass folding hinge; the replacement of small portions of each sphinx's tail; and many other minor repairs. (An illustrated restoration report is on file in the YUAG object files.) Small repairs were also made by Peter Arkell in 1982 after the cellarette had been damaged by water. The presence of nail holes on the canted front corners of the base platform indicates that ornaments were originally mounted here and subsequently have been lost.

Woods: Exterior, rosewood veneer; interior, mahogany veneer; sphinxes, other elements, eastern white pine; rear legs, soft maple; original inlay, stringing, brass and a black dense hardwood, probably ebony; left rear flower, fruit basket, alder (*Alnus* spp.).

Dimensions: H 76.6; W 87.5; D 54.5.

Exhibition: Berry B. Tracy and William H. Gerdts, *Classical America, 1815–1845* (Newark, N. J.: Newark Museum, 1963), no. 14.

Bibliography: Richard H. Randall, Jr., "Sources of the Empire Style," *Antiques* 83, no. 4 (April 1963): 452 fig. 1; *Sack Coll.*, 1: 212 no. 544; Joseph Aronson, *The New Encyclopedia of Furniture* (New York: Crown Publishers, 1967), fig. 86; Fales, *Am. Painted Furn.*, fig. 256; Kane, "American Furn.," pl. XII; Fairbanks and Bates, p. 276; John S. Bowman, *American Furniture* (New York: Exeter Books, 1985), p. 72.

Provenance: According to tradition, this object and a card table (1966.127), also now at Yale, were owned originally by merchant Stephen Ball Munn (1766–1856) of New York, N. Y. They descended in the Munn family until they were acquired by dealer Paul Cooley of Hartford, Conn. Cooley sold them to Israel Sack, Inc., New York, N. Y., in 1962, from whom they were acquired by exchange in 1966.

THIS cellarette, an ambitious American example, has been attributed by several writers to French immigrant craftsman Charles-Honoré Lannuier (1779–1819) of New York City, on the basis of its Egyptian-inspired sphinxes, French-style ormolu mounts, and exotic woods including rosewood and probably ebony. In addition, as Richard H. Randall, Jr., noted in 1963, the sphinxes appear to be rather closely based

229

on a design for garden sphinxes published by Jacques-François Blondel in his *De la distribution des maisons de plaisance et de la décoration des édifices en général*, published in Paris in 1738. To date, however, no conclusive evidence has been discovered that will support a firm attribution to Lannuier's shop, and the cellarette might well have been made in another high-style New York shop—perhaps even that of Duncan Phyfe. The clusters of fruit and flowers at the rear of this object are fashioned from alder (*Alnus* spp.), either red alder (*A. rubra*) from the western United States, gray alder (*A. incana*) from northern Europe, or common alder (*A. glutinosa*) from Europe, including the British Isles. This raises the possibility that the wood for these ornaments was imported, or, more interesting, that the ornaments themselves were imported from abroad in finished form. An identical cluster is found on a New York pier table in a private collection.[1] Although related American cellarettes of sarcophagus form from New York, Boston, and Maryland are known, the Yale example was considered unique until the emergence in 1983 of a nearly identical cellarette, now in a private collection.[2] Varying only in ornamental detail, this cellarette is surely from the same shop as the Yale object. It too holds only six bottles, a strong indication that these cellarettes were valued more as examples of conspicuous

Sideboards 443

consumption than as practical storage devices. The irony in selecting the ancient sarcophagus form, with its overtones of death and immortality, as a container for wines and spirits has been noted by several writers.[3] Thomas S. Michie, recalling that the word *sarcophagus* originally referred to a type of limestone used by the Greeks for the construction of coffins and thought to disintegrate the flesh of bodies deposited in it, finds a rich symbolism in this sarcophagus form: the ancient sarcophagus-coffin contained the body yet was reputed to consume it, while the modern sarcophagus-cellarette was used to store alcohol, which preserves flesh but destroys the body.[4] If the tradition is correct that this cellarette was owned originally by Stephen Ball Munn, it may have been made at the time he moved into an elaborate residence on Broadway in the mid 1810s. A wholesale dry-goods merchant, Munn was reputed to be one of the wealthiest men in New York during the first half of the nineteenth century. It is said that in early life he was "excessively dissipated, but he afterwards reformed and became not only an extremely good business man, but a leading man in the Broome street Baptist Church." No doubt the cellarette now at Yale is a document of his period of dissipation.[5]

The Mabel Brady Garvan Collection 1966.126

1. Katherine Gross Farnham, "Living with Antiques: The Gordon-Banks House in the Georgia Piedmont," *Antiques* 102, no. 3 (September 1972): 438.
2. For other New York examples, see Celia Jackson Otto, *American Furniture of the Nineteenth Century* (New York: Viking Press, 1965), fig. 161 (Metropolitan Museum of Art); Warren, *Bayou Bend*, no. 197; Berry B. Tracy, *Federal Furniture and Decorative Arts at Boscobel* (New York: Boscobel Restoration and Harry N. Abrams, 1981), fig. 42; McClelland, pl. 107; and *Antiques* 79, no. 5 (May 1961): 465 (Museum of the City of New York). For Boston examples, see Fairbanks and Bates, p. 276 (Museum of Fine Arts, Boston, 1978.125); and *Antiques* 120, no. 6 (December 1981): back cover. A Maryland example is illustrated in Romains S. Somerville, "Furniture at the Maryland Historical Society," *Antiques* 109, no. 5 (May 1976): 985 fig. 26. For a Philadelphia example of ca. 1825 with a history in the Gratz family, see PMA, *Three Centuries*, no. 221. This cellarette has survived with its accompanying sideboard and knife boxes.
3. Fairbanks and Bates, p. 276.
4. Draft catalogue entry, YUAG object files.
5. For Munn, see Walter Barrett (alias Joseph A. Scoville), *The Old Merchants of New York City*, vol. 2 (New York: Worthington Co., 1885), pp. 20–30 (quotation, p. 27); and William Frederick Cornell, *The Munn Family* (Freeport, N. Y., 1941), p. 10.

230

230

Cellarette
North Carolina, possibly Alamance County, 1785–1820

Description: The top is a single board with applied molding at the front and sides that overlaps the case. It is attached to the back with iron butt hinges. The interior is divided into twelve compartments for bottles by a framework tenoned to the stiles about halfway down the case. The top of the front has a brass keyhole escutcheon, and there is applied molding and scalloping at the front and sides of the bottom.

444 American Case Furniture

The four corner posts continue to form squared tapered legs. The base molding is of two pieces and is applied with sprigs. The bottom of the cellarette consists of three butted boards, two narrow strips flanking a wider center board, that are nailed in place. The case is joined with mortise-and-tenon joints that are double pegged; the inside top edges of the stiles are chamfered.

Inscription: "Mr John Bentl" is written in pencil on the underside of the lid.

Condition: The lock, perhaps significantly, is missing. The scalloped molding is broken in several places.

Woods: Top, sides, bottom, southern yellow pine; four legs, ash, probably white ash; scalloped base molding, eastern white pine.

Dimensions: H 87.8; W 54.3; CW 50.9; D 41.3; CD 39.5.

Exhibition: YUAG, "Southern Furn.," no. 19.

Provenance: W. S. Ahern, Richmond, Va., by sale to Francis P. Garvan, New York, N. Y.

WILDLY dissimilar in appearance from the preceding example, this rural cellarette nevertheless performed the same function as its fancier urban counterpart. In fact, it served it better, for it could hold twelve bottles in a much smaller space than the New York *garde-de-vin* required to store only six. It has been repeated endlessly that the cellarette is a particularly southern piece of furniture; this example may be from the Piedmont area of North Carolina, where related scalloping was used as a decorative device.[1] The cellarette was most commonly used when sideboards with deep bottle drawers were not; the chest section of this cellarette is smaller than either of the commodious bottle drawers in the Yale Charleston sideboard (cat. 222). Cellarettes of slightly more elaborate form contained a mixing slide or perhaps a drawer or two in a stand below.[2]

The Mabel Brady Garvan Collection 1930.2438

1. Note in YUAG object files from Frank Horton and Brad Rauschenberg of MESDA.
2. Helen Comstock, "Furniture of Virginia, North Carolina, Georgia and Kentucky," *Antiques* 61, no. 1 (January 1952): 62–64. Two more elaborate cellarettes from North Carolina are illustrated in *North Carolina Furniture, 1700–1800* (Raleigh: North Carolina Museum of History, Division of Archives and History, Department of Cultural Resources, 1977), nos. 3, 4. See also Marleine Reader Harris, *Virginia Antiques* (New York: Exposition Press, 1953), p. 107.

Pianos and Radio

The production of musical instruments such as the piano (cats. 231, 232) or electronic devices such as a cabinet radio (cat. 233) involve the skills of the instrument maker or technician as well as those of the cabinetmaker. The limited examples in the Art Gallery collection were acquired, however, as works of art rather than as functional, operating devices. The two early nineteenth-century pianos entered the collection as examples of stylish New York cabinetwork, and the Philco radio was acquired in the 1970s as an example of the art deco style of the 1930s. Since the early nineteenth century, however, musical instruments have played important roles in the domestic interior, serving as a focal point of family entertainment, as a means of social interaction, and in other symbolic roles. The Yale University Collection of Musical Instruments, inaugurated in 1900, contains nearly a hundred American instruments in its holdings, including other pianos of the nineteenth and twentieth centuries.

- hinged lid
- reeding
- turned and reeded pedestal
- leg
- lyre-shaped pedal post
- stretchers
- brass hairy-paw feet with casters
- drawer

231

Piano

John Geib, Jr. (working 1815–1822)
New York, New York, 1815–1820

Description: The rectangular case of this piano has rounded front corners. The top is bordered on all four sides with a line of dark-wood stringing, brass inlaid stringing, and mahogany banding, with an additional edging of light-wood inlay at the front and sides. The front facade is divided into three units, consisting of a wide, slightly bowed center section flanked by symmetrical side units. The upper part of the center section is decorated with an oval of brass stringing contained within a rectangle of brass stringing and bordered with mahogany banding. Below this panel is a line of applied, molded brass, beneath which is a horizontal course of reeds, with the six reeds stopped shy of the end of the panel. Below the reeds is an arched lower section that is inlaid with brass stringing curved on its lower edge to follow the contour of the arch and edged with light-wood stringing. This central unit is flanked by vertical elements consisting of, from top to bottom, a slightly projecting panel inlaid with a veneered panel edged with banding; a carved floral ornament; a small panel (originally fitted with a brass or composition mount); and a carved scroll. The side units follow the same pattern as the central section, with the omission of the brass inlaid oval in the upper panel and the substitution of a cock-beaded drawer with a central brass backplate and ring pull in the lower section. The motifs of these side units are continued around the curved sides of the case, with the substitution of a bottom panel with a brass inlaid rectangle for the drawer. The vertical elements flanking the center section are repeated on the side of the side units and at the rear of each side of the case. The piano is supported by two massive turned and reeded pedestals, with front and rear concave legs carved with pointed leaves and terminating in brass hairy-paw feet and casters. The pillars are joined to the pedal post with turned and reeded stretchers, and the outside face of each pedestal is carved with a floral motif. The pedal post is lyre-shaped with brass strings backed with a mirror and has gilt floral carving at the top and gilt scrolls at its base. The support for the lyre has horizontal reeding contained within a rectangle of brass stringing and has a molded base. The left side and center section of the front facade are hinged to the corresponding portion of the lid; the appropriate front portion of the lid is then hinged, at the depth of the keyboard, to the corresponding rear portion of the lid. Both of these parts are lifted to reveal the keyboard; the hinged portion of the front facade stands in a vertical position to form a music rack, in conjunction with a small strip screwed to the hinged portion of the front of the lid. The right sides of the front facade and lid are hinged similarly. The entire lid also is hinged to the back of the case and when lifted is supported by braces screwed to the sides of the case. A secondary lid within the case is painted a light green with a border of red and white flowers. It is hinged to the back of the case and lifts to reveal the works and action. The nameboard and the panels on each side of the keyboard are decorated with an upper course of patterned inlay and a broad horizontal panel of figured light inlay edged with patterned inlay. The center of the nameboard contains a black oval with the name of the instrument maker in gold; the oval is flanked by gold scrolls and leafage. Each side of the nameboard contains a panel of pierced carved tracery outlined against a bright silvery metal background. The nameboard lifts out and has an adjustable folding music rack screwed to its back. The piano is screwed and bolted to a sturdy frame. The pedestals are double through-tenoned to longitudinal boards that are in turn screwed to transverse supports dovetailed to the rear of the frame. The curved end rails of the case are built up of horizontal laminations. The sides of each drawer are dovetailed to the front and back; the bottoms are beveled on their front and side edges, let into grooves in the front and sides, and nailed to the underside of the back. The right drawer is deeper than the left drawer.

Pianos and Radio

Inscriptions: The nameboard is inscribed "Patent, / John Geib Jr / NEW YORK." Stamped on the interior to the left of the keyboard is "5607." "A Gilt Centre Nº 1" is written in pencil on the back of the nameboard, and "Ornament N 1" is written in pencil on the bottom of the sounding board. "Thomson" and "Jeffrey Johnson" are scratched on the underside of the base, behind the lyre. The keys are numbered in pencil, and the casters are stamped "371" on the base. The modern "Tredway Brothers / Ticonderoga NY" is written in large black letters on the outside of the back. There is writing in pencil, probably modern, on the underside of the bottom of the left drawer.

Condition: The left front and right rear casters and feet have been strengthened with iron braces. Brass or composition mounts, perhaps lyres or lion masks, were originally located in the panels flanking the drawers, as indicated by the presence of filled nail holes. The pedal action is missing, and there has been minor damage to the mirror of the lyre. The catch to hold up the sounding board is broken, and the sounding board has been damaged. Small interior lids to the left and right of the keyboard are missing, and the pierced tracery on the nameboard has suffered losses. There have been many minor repairs to the inlays and veneer. The piano was cleaned, refinished, and repaired by Emile Mazzola in 1962.

Woods: Case, mahogany veneer on eastern white pine; pedestals, base, mahogany; drawer sides, backs, bottoms, yellow poplar; brace above left pedestal support, other elements, American black cherry; keys, basswood with ebony and ivory facings; soundboard, spruce; other piano elements, soft maple and eastern white pine; inlays, light and dark woods; figured panel on nameboard, probably maple rather than satinwood.

Dimensions: H 89.2; W 175.6; D 63.0.

Bibliography: Charles O. Cornelius, "The Distinctiveness of Duncan Phyfe," *Antiques* 2, no. 5 (November 1922): 208 fig. 7; Charles Over Cornelius, *Furniture Masterpieces of Duncan Phyfe* (Garden City, N. Y.: Doubleday, Page for the Metropolitan Museum of Art, 1922), pl. 52; Charles Messer Stow, "The Theme of Luxury in the Garvan Collection," *Antiquarian* 15, no. 3 (September 1930): 36; William Farquhar Payson, ed., *Mahogany: Antique and Modern* (New York: E. P. Dutton, 1926), between pp. 76–77; *Handbook*, p. 60; "Outstanding Examples from the Mabel Brady Garvan Collections," *YUAG Bulletin* 8, no. 2 (February 1938): 44; McClelland, pl. 84; Nancy A. Smith, "The Case of the Nineteenth-Century Piano: Grand, Square, and Upright," *Valuation* 29, no. 2 (June 1984): 16–17.

Provenance: R. T. Haines Halsey, New York, N. Y.; purchased by Francis P. Garvan, New York, N. Y.

WITH many details characteristic of furniture made in New York City in the early nineteenth century, the case and trestle base of this elaborate square piano have long been attributed to the workshop of Duncan Phyfe (1768–1854). Although this attribution has yet to be confirmed, one would not be surprised to learn that a piano of this quality was made by the leading furniture maker of his time and place. The maker of the works, John Geib, Jr., was active independently from 1815 until 1819, or perhaps 1822, thus providing a narrow date range for this object.[1] Recent research has not confirmed a long-standing tradition that Geib advertised that he worked out of Phyfe's shop.[2] The names "Thomson" and "Jeffrey Johnson" written on the case may be those of as yet unidentified craftsmen. Similar pianos with works by Geib are in the collection of Winterthur Museum (57.726) and the Museum of the City of New York.[3] A group of related pianos with works by the firm of Thomas Gibson and Morgan Davis (working 1801–1820) have cases that also have been attributed to Phyfe's shop by some writers.[4]

The Mabel Brady Garvan Collection 1930.2775

231a

1. Montgomery, p. 480. The number stamped on this piano, 5607, would indicate a date between 1815 and 1820, according to N. E. Michel, *Michel's Piano Atlas* (Rivera, Calif.: N. E. Michel, 1957).
2. Michael Kevin Brown, "Duncan Phyfe" (M.A. thesis, University of Delaware, 1978), pp. 55–56.
3. Montgomery, no. 450; *Antiques* 80, no. 4 (October 1961): 358.
4. Warren, *Bayou Bend*, no. 199; *Girl Scouts Exhibition*, no. 782; Celia Jackson Otto, *American Furniture of the Nineteenth Century* (New York: Viking Press, 1965), no. 44 (Henry Ford Museum); and McClelland, pl. 86.

232

232

232

Piano
Adam and William Geib (working ca. 1821–ca. 1828)
New York, New York, 1824

Description: The rectangular top of this piano is rounded at the front corners. It is bordered on all four sides by an inner rectangle of brass stringing, a band of rosewood veneer, a second rectangle of brass stringing, in this instance curved at its front corners to conform to the case, and a second, smaller band of rosewood veneer. The top is edged on the front and sides with applied half-round molding of rosewood. The front and sides of the case are divided into upper and lower sections by an applied cast brass ornamental band. Above this band, the upper section is decorated at the front, the front corners, and the sides with panels formed by double rectangles of brass stringing. Below this band, the lower section holds three drawers in line, with the center drawer concave and of greater width. The side drawers are fitted with one and the center drawer with two circular stamped brass pulls, and each drawer contains a rectangle of brass stringing. The drawers are flanked and separated by an applied stamped brass ornament that is repeated at the rear of each side. The sides of this lower section contain rectangles of brass stringing. Above each leg there is a wooden plaque with a center line of brass stringing. The piano is supported by six turned and carved legs in the form of a baluster, each with a double brass ring at the top and each fitted with ornamental brass cup casters. The pedal posts at the rear, to the left of center, are shaped in conformity with the legs. The section of the front facade covering the keyboard is hinged to the corresponding portion of the front of the lid, and the entire front section of the lid is hinged to the rear of the lid at the depth of the keyboard. When in the open position, the vertical portion of the front is supported by a brass rod to form a music stand, again in conjunction with a strip screwed to the underside of the lid. The entire lid also is hinged to the back of the case and is supported in the open position by braces screwed to each side of the case. The nameboard here is a single curved board fitted to the case. It bears near its top a line of brass stringing, and the instrument maker's name is written in black in a gilt rectangle located in the center and flanked by gilt leafage. The inscription is in turn flanked by a pierced trelliswork design, with flowers at the intersection of the diagonals embellished with a brass

232a

Pianos and Radio 451

inlaid dot at their center, backed by red and silver fabric, and by gold depictions of musical instruments surrounded by leafage. A folding music rack is applied to the back of the nameboard. The piano is again screwed and, in this instance, pegged to a sturdy frame. Here, the six legs are housed in thick transverse framing members, while the rails beneath the drawers are quite light and dovetailed to these framing members. On each drawer, the sides are dovetailed to the front and back; the bottoms are beveled on their front and side edges, let into grooves in the front and side, and nailed to the underside of the back. Little triangular blocks are glued to the case as stops.

232b

Inscriptions: A rectangular panel in the center of the nameboard bears "New patent / A. & W. Geib, / 23, Maiden lane, / New-York." Stamped on the interior to the left of the keyboard is "6095." "Geib 240 with Cornice Febry 24th 1824 / Soon as possible" is written in pencil on the back of the nameboard, underneath the applied base of the music rack. Each end of the nameboard is stamped "240," and the same number is stamped on a small block to the left of the nameboard; "240" is also written in white chalk on the underside of the drawer bottoms. The keys are numbered in pencil.

Condition: A crack in the lid was reinforced with a butterfly cleat, and repairs made to the veneer and brass stringing in 1965. Pieces of plywood have been used to back the textiles on the nameboard. Small interior lids and the large lids covering the works and action are missing.

Woods: Rosewood veneer, mahogany veneer, mahogany; frame, eastern white pine; drawer linings, yellow poplar; keys, basswood with ebony and ivory facings; soundboard, spruce; other piano woods, possibly a maple and other unidentified woods.

Dimensions: H 86.9; W 172.1; D 64.8.

Provenance: Mrs. Carll Tucker, New York, N. Y.

THIS slightly later example, its date betrayed by its incipient piano legs, is by John Geib, Jr.'s brother Adam and his nephew William, who operated a piano and music store together at 23 Maiden Lane from about 1821 to 1828. A closely related piano by A. and W. Geib is in the Valentine Museum, and an example with a pedestal base is in the Brooklyn Museum.[1] Other square pianos made in New York in the 1820s by William Wale, Nunns and Clark, and others share the heavy turned legs of this example.[2] An example by Alpheous Babcock of Boston, fashioned in a similar style, is now part of the extensive Yale collection of musical instruments, which includes more than a hundred American objects.[3]

Gift of Mrs. Carll Tucker 1965.58

1. Helen Scott Townsend Reed, "Decorative Arts in the Valentine Museum," *Antiques* 103, no. 1 (January 1973): 173; Kevin L. Stayton, Shelley Mills, and Larry Weinberg, "The Harrison House Rooms at the Brooklyn Museum," *Antiques* 126, no. 4 (October 1984): 885. See also *Antiques* 126, no. 4 (October 1984): 760; and Fitzgerald, fig. VI–25, for related pianos described as by "H. and W. Geib."
2. *Antiques* 107, no. 5 (May 1975): 827; *Antiques* 91, no. 6 (June 1967): 769.
3. Nicholas Renouf, "Selections from the Yale University Collection of Musical Instruments," *Antiques* 117, no. 6 (June 1980): 1133–1135, pl.II. See also Sibyl Marcuse, *Musical Instruments at Yale: A Selection of Western Instruments from the 15th to the 20th Centuries* (New Haven: Yale University Art Gallery, 1960). The Yale Collection of Musical Instruments is housed at 15 Hillhouse Avenue, New Haven.

233

Cabinet radio
Philco Radio & Television Corporation
Philadelphia, Pennsylvania, ca. 1935

Description: The top has two transverse lines of black inlay, dividing the top into three panels, with the veneer laid longitudinally on the end panels and in a transverse direction on the center panel. The top is molded at the front and sides and is recessed in the center. The front corners of the case are rounded, and there are vertical lines at the joint between the straight sides and the curved portions. The upper section of the case is decorated with multiple projecting moldings which carry around the curved sides of the case and flank the recessed center section. Below these moldings, on each side, is a line of black inlay, which meets and continues down the

inside of an applied vertical strip that also flanks the center section and that has a shaped lower end. The upper part of the center of the case slopes backward and is decorated with highly figured veneer, with vertical lines of black inlay at each side which are aligned with those on the top. At the top of the center is a black plastic dial, lit from behind, with the company name in gold letters below. Below the station dial is the station-selector knob, also in black plastic, and below it are three smaller dials in line, being, from left to right, the on/off switch and volume control, the wave-band switch, and the tone control. A strip of horizontal molding separates the control section from the speaker section below. There are three vertical strips over the speaker section, each "creased" at the center and separated by V-shaped strips at the base. The speaker section is outlined by an applied strip at the sides and base; its edges are molded. The radio is supported by a slightly recessed base shaped in conformity with the case. There is another on/off switch on the upper right side of the case. The top of the case is screwed and glue blocked to the upper framework. The stepped moldings are run on a transverse block at the sides and a longitudinal block at the front, which are joined and braced with a triangular corner block. The works of the radio are screwed to a platform housed in the sides. The control panel and speaker panel are sloping plywood boards. There is a longitudinal brace below the speaker. The sides of the case are tenoned to an upper and a base framework, and multiple blocks are screwed and glued throughout the case. There is no bottom to the case.

Inscriptions: "PHILCO" appears in gold letters beneath the dial. A rectangular label with rounded edges, printed in white letters on a blue ground, is pasted to the back of the works and reads: "PHILCO RADIO / CHASSIS TYPE 16 CODE 126 / A.C. VOLTS / 115 / CYCLES / 50–60 / WATTS / 130 / PATENTED AND PATENTS PENDING / For License Notice— See License Label / PHILCO RADIO & TELEVISION CORP. / PHILADELPHIA, PA. MADE IN U.S.A." A paper label pasted to the inside of the left side of the case reads: "PART NO. 10114-B / CHASSIS 16-X." A fragment of a paper label pasted to the inside of the right side of the case is headed "PHILCO MODEL 16 (Code 125–126)" and is printed with a diagram of the radio, identifying the controls and numbering the components. "PHILCO / PLANT / 25 / FURNITURE" is stamped on the outside of the base at the rear. There are numerous shop marks and numbers.

Condition: The radio is not in working condition. The sound baffle behind the speaker was damaged by water in 1980 and has been removed; the cloth strips in front of the speaker were also water stained. The base has been refinished, and new glue blocks added at the rear.

Woods: Exterior, probably walnut veneer, with inlaid black stringing; vertical strips over speaker, red gum; other elements, red gum, yellow poplar, Douglas fir plywood.

Dimensions: H 103.1; W 66.5; D 33.4.

Provenance: Purchased in the 1930s by Miss C. Rachel Trowbridge (d. 1982), New Haven, Conn.

The new 1935 Philco model 16–X with its patented "Inclined Sounding Board" cost $175 when it was introduced to the market in summer 1934. It was only one of many types of radios offered by Philco, ranging in price from $75 to $600, for a special remote control model. Although the Philco com-

pany traces its origins to 1892, it had been producing radios only since 1928. At that time, the AC vacuum tube was invented, eliminating the need for cumbersome and messy wet storage batteries. Radios could then be operated on regular house current, and they quickly became more accessible and desirable. Adopting the mass-production methods of the automobile industry, Philco began producing and selling radios in vast quantities, quickly becoming a leader in the field.[3] Throughout the Great Depression, according to a president of Philco, "people bought a radio in preference to an automobile or even furniture" because of radio's great value as a source of entertainment and information, and the company was able to prosper. The 1930s also witnessed the rise of radio as an important political tool. Many companies, including Atwater Kent, Stromberg-Carlson, Magnavox, RCA, and Zenith, as well as Philco, made cabinet radios in a wide variety of styles, many of them revivalistic in nature. The Sears Silvertone, however, is a good example of another impressive cabinet radio in the art deco mode of the Philco 16–X.[4]

Gift of Miss C. Rachel Trowbridge 1971.43

1. Advertisement, *Saturday Evening Post* (16 June 1934), p. 3.
2. A brief history of the company is given in William Balderston, *"Philco": Autobiography of Progress* (New York: Newcomen Society in North America, 1954).
3. Two illustrations of the Philco factory in 1937, indicating the "sexual division of labor" in the production line, with women "doing the delicate work, while the men do the physical assembly and checking," are included in Fedric M. Miller, Morris J. Vogel, and Allen F. Davis, *Still Philadelphia: A Photographic History, 1890–1940* (Philadelphia: Temple University Press, 1983), pp. 263–264.
4. Ralph Muchow, "Radios: Tuning in to Yesterday," in *The Encyclopedia of Collectibles: Radios to Signs* (Alexandria, Va.: Time-Life Books, 1980), pp. 6–19; the Silvertone is illustrated on p. 14.

Appendix

This appendix includes a photograph of and brief note about twenty-eight objects that have been excluded from the main catalogue because of their condition. In some cases, however, these objects will have considerable interest for students of a particular regional form or characteristic.

Originally, it was planned that these objects would be treated in depth in volume four of this series; the abbreviated entries given here, due to a lack of space, merely alert the reader to the presence of these objects in the Yale Study Collection. Only selected bibliographical references are given, and the woods have been identified, in most instances, by eye. Overall height, width, and depth are given for each object. More information on each example is provided in the Art Gallery object files.

1 Box

Connecticut Valley, ca. 1700, with modern alterations
Pine, oak, maple
H 21.7; W 68.6; D 40.7

In the style of a Connecticut Valley, Hadley-type box, carved with the initials PC, this box has been heavily re-worked. The top and hinges are old but not original to the box, and both the backboard and the bottom show signs of having been used originally for another purpose. The carved Hadley motifs on the front are unusually shallow and tight, perhaps because the front is made of maple. The sans-serif initials are unusual, but not unknown in Hadley-type furniture.

REFERENCES: Rogers, "Garvan Furn. (1960)," fig. 1; Rogers, "Garvan Coll. (1962)," p. 6; *Forgeries and Restorations*, no. 17.

The Mabel Brady Garvan Collection 1930.2236

App. 1

2 Box

Modern; in the style of Essex County, Massachusetts, ca. 1700
Pine, oak, yellow poplar
H 24.8; W 68.6; D 45.7

The numerous nail holes in unexpected places in this box suggest that it is constructed out of old wood originally used for another purpose. The carved palmettes, of the type associated with the William Searle–Thomas Dennis school of Essex County, are atypically carved on yellow poplar, a wood not generally associated with seventeenth-century boxes of this type.

REFERENCES: Irving P. Lyon, "The Oak Furniture of Ipswich, Massachusetts, Part III," *Antiques* 33, no. 2 (February 1938): 74; "Living with Antiques," *Antiques* 45, no. 4 (April 1940): 191; Helen Park, "Thomas Dennis, Ipswich Joiner: A Re-Examination," *Antiques* 78, no. 1 (July 1960): 42; *Antiques* 86, no. 4 (October 1964): 458; *Forgeries and Restorations*, no. 15; Kirk, *Am. Furn. & Brit. Trad.*, fig. 407.

Gift of C. Sanford Bull 1950.69

App. 2

3 **Miniature chest with drawers**
 New England, ca. 1700, with modern alterations
 Oak
 H 49.5; W 64.5; D 38.1

This object, originally a chest with one drawer, has been altered to its present form of a paneled chest with three drawers. The turned feet have been added as well, creating an even more desirable form.

REFERENCE: Nutting, *Treasury*, no. 49.

The Mabel Brady Garvan Collection 1930.2133

App. 3

4 **Chest with drawer**
 Wethersfield, Connecticut, ca. 1700, with modern alterations
 Oak
 H 78.7; W 118.4; D 52.1

On loan for many years to the Webb-Deane-Stevens Museum in Wethersfield, this chest has a history in the Webb family and is in the style of furniture generally attributed to Peter Blin of Wethersfield (see cats. 26–27). Unfortunately, it has been so heavily restored as to be virtually a modern object. The top is new, all of the applied ornament is new, the carved panels are probably not old, and the moldings have been replaced.

REFERENCES: *Antiques* 86, no. 4 (October 1964): 458; Kirk, *Impecunious Collector's Guide*, fig. 127.

Gift of J. Watson Webb 1946.35

App. 4

5 **Chest**
 Possibly Continental, ca. 1860, with modern alterations
 White oak, ash, beech
 H 82.6; W 141.0; D 63.5

This large chest, carved with an eagle and flower basket roughly in the style of Samuel McIntire, was acquired as a Massachusetts example of the federal period. However, the ark form, the wedged dovetails, the pegged construction, and the wheel apparatus strongly suggest that the object is of European origin, although it may have been made by a Continental-trained craftsman working in Pennsylvania,

App. 5

Appendix

Texas, Canada, or elsewhere in North America. Kirk has pointed out that the carved decoration, which does not correlate properly with the shrinkage of the chest, is a later addition. A painted inscription on the back includes the date 1860, suggesting a date for the chest's manufacture. Another large, domed chest with a carved eagle and basket, and with a carved view of Mount Vernon, has been published; see *American Collector* 17, no. 11 (December 1948): 4.

REFERENCE: Kirk, *Early Am. Furn.*, fig. 179.

Gift of Miss Maud A. K. Wetmore 1950.144

6 **Chest of drawers**
Massachusetts, 1700–1720, with modern alterations
Maple, burl veneer, walnut, eastern white pine
H 94.0; W 91.8; D 51.4

In the style of a chest of drawers of ca. 1710, this object is the upper case of a high chest of drawers to which a base with bracket feet has been added. The original high chest was probably of the turned-leg variety (cat. 122), although Myrna Kaye recently has raised the possibility that it was a later type with cabriole legs because of the lipped drawer fronts and other details (letter, Art Gallery object files).

REFERENCES: Kirk, *Early Am. Furn.*, fig. 183; Kirk, *Am. Furn. & Brit. Trad.*, fig. 477; Harold Sack, "Authenticating American Eighteenth-Century Furniture," *Antiques* 127, no. 5 (May 1985): 1126.

The Mabel Brady Garvan Collection 1930.2230

7 **Chest of drawers**
Probably English, ca. 1800, with modern alterations
Mahogany, mahogany veneer, southern yellow pine, yellow poplar
H 106.7; W 109.3; D 55.9

Acquired by Francis P. Garvan as a Virginia example, this bow-front chest of drawers is a problematic object. Its fitted upper drawer is more typical of English than American furniture, and the interior has been heavily restored. New fastening hardware has been used to secure the drawer linings, back, and other interior elements, and the secondary woods used in the interior construction are in pristine condition.

REFERENCES: Ormsbee, *Story Am. Furn.*, p. 75; *Forgeries and Restorations*, no. 26.

The Mabel Brady Garvan Collection 1930.2123

App. 6

App. 7

replaced. The finials and brasses are replacements, the base is new, there have been many minor repairs, and the object has been heavily refinished.

REFERENCE: *The American Heritage Society Auction of Americana*, 6–8 November 1975 (New York: Sotheby Parke Bernet, 1975), no. 1208.

Gift of Thomas S. Green, Maud Green Park, Priscilla P. Green, and James Wilder Green 1982.105

9 **Dressing table**
 American, 1690–1720, with modern alterations
 Walnut, yellow poplar, pine
 H 72.1; W 74.9; D 49.2

Although related to other single-drawer examples from the 1690–1720 period (see cat. 98), this small dressing table is largely a twentieth-century creation. About one-quarter of the top is a replacement, the case sides have unexplained plugged holes, the turned stretchers are atypical, and the molding under the drawer and on the case sides is an addition. The table has been heavily refinished.

REFERENCES: *Fine Early American Furniture Gathered by Jacob Margolis, Cabinet Maker of New York City*, 9–10 Decem-

App. 8

8 **Chest-on-chest**
 Massachusetts, ca. 1760, with modern additions
 Mahogany, eastern white pine, maple
 H 264.0; W 132; D 53.6

Although heavily restored, and thus placed here rather than in the main catalogue, this chest-on-chest was acquired for the Study Collection as an important example of early eighteenth-century Massachusetts furniture. It is one of four examples of the form known (see cat. 78), and descended in the Massachusetts family of the donors. With the exception of the small pediment drawer (which is original and retains a lining of marbled paper), the drawer linings have been

App. 9

Appendix 459

ber 1927 (New York: Anderson Galleries, 1927), no. 168; Miller, 1:698–699, no. 1284; *Forgeries and Restorations*, no. 22.

The Mabel Brady Garvan Collection 1930.2612

10 **Dressing table**
Modern; in the style of Pennsylvania, ca. 1700
Walnut, yellow poplar
H 68.9; W 70.5; D 45.1

Acquired by Francis P. Garvan as a Pennsylvania or Maryland dressing table of ca. 1700, this object gives every appearance of being a modern reproduction, although it is now at least more than sixty-five years old. It shows no evidence of period construction or of wear commensurate with its purported age.

REFERENCES: *Illustrated Catalogue of the Rare and Extremely Choice Collection of Early American and English Furniture Formed . . . by . . . Mr. Louis Guerineau Myers*, 24–26 February 1921 (New York: American Art Association, 1921), no. 518; Nutting, *Treasury*, no. 396.

The Mabel Brady Garvan Collection 1930.2134

App. 10

11 **Dressing table**
Massachusetts, 1730–1760, with modern alterations
Walnut, walnut veneer, eastern white pine
H 77.8; W 85.1; D 54.9

Extensive repairs and alterations suggest that this dressing table should be considered as a part of the Study Collection. The top, although made of old wood, is not original to the dressing table; it has been pieced in each corner, and shows considerable signs of inexplicable wear and nailholes on its underside. The thinly cut veneer on the front of the case and on the top is a modern replacement, and the cock beading and drops are new. The decorative shell in the center drawer is not original; the applied decoration covers an old hole for a pull located about two inches above the current brass pull. The top four inches of the right rear leg is a replacement, a repair suggesting that the table was disassembled at some time.

The Mabel Brady Garvan Collection 1931.1241

App. 11

460 *American Case Furniture*

12 **Bureau table**
　　Modern; in the style of Newport, Rhode Island, 1770–1795
　　Mahogany, eastern white pine
　　H 84.1; W 93.0; D 49.6

This object represents an instance where old materials have been used to create a form that collectors highly desire (see cat. 109). In numerous places, the wood used to fabricate this Newport-style dressing table shows evidence of having been used originally for another purpose. The carved shells, when compared to those on authentic Newport examples, seem poorly drawn and compressed. The object was acquired for the Study Collection in 1976.

REFERENCES: *Antiques* 102, no. 3 (September 1972): 305; Ward, *Eye of the Beholder*, cat. 2; Harold Sack, "Authenticating American Eighteenth-Century Furniture," *Antiques* 127, no. 5 (May 1985): 1128.

Leonard C. Hanna, Jr., B.A. 1913, Fund　1976.108

App. 12

13 **Dressing table**
　　Modern; in the style of Connecticut, 1770–1790
　　Cherry, yellow poplar, oak, pine
　　H 75.1; W 90.2; D 53.5

In the style of dressing tables now associated with the Newtown-Woodbury area of Connecticut (see cat. 104), this example is probably a modern fabrication made of old and new wood. It was a gift to the Study Collection in 1975.

REFERENCE: *Antiques* 101, no. 5 (May 1972): 757 (illustrated with a matching high chest).

Gift of Marshall Field　1975.124.1

14 **High chest of drawers**
　　American, ca. 1700, with modern alterations
　　Pine, maple
　　H 150.9; W 99.1; D 50.8

Although the legs of this object may be old, the upper case is fabricated from old wood which has been assembled and coated with new paint to cover the freshly cut edges.

App. 13

App. 14

REFERENCE: Kirk, *Early Am. Furn.*, fig. 184.

The Mabel Brady Garvan Collection 1930.2575

15 High chest of drawers
Philadelphia, 1755–1795, with modern alterations
Walnut, yellow poplar, cedar, pine
H 241.3; W 114.9; D 59.1

This heavily refinished high chest has been upgraded with added carving to create a high-style Philadelphia example (see cat. 147, for example). The rococo style carving on the small center drawers in both the upper and lower cases is new, and thus completely alters the visual statement made by the object. The central carved cartouche and finials are also modern additions.

REFERENCE: *Notable American & English Furniture & Decorations*, 13–15 March 1947 (New York: Parke-Bernet Galleries, 1947), no. 635.

The Mabel Brady Garvan Collection 1930.2596

App. 15

462 American Case Furniture

App. 16

App. 17

16 **Chest-on-frame**
Pennsylvania, 1755–1795, with modern alterations
Walnut, pine
H 165.7; W 102.6; D 58.4

This object represents a marriage, a common type of altered object in which the upper and lower case were not originally made for each other. Here, the frame has been altered to accomodate a chest with six drawers. The brasses are replacements.

The Mabel Brady Garvan Collection 1930.2393

17 **Base of high chest**
Connecticut, 1730–1760, with modern alterations
Maple, yellow poplar, pine
H 81.3; W 90.8; D 47.9

Acquired at auction as a Connecticut dressing table in the Queen Anne style, this object is the base of a high chest to which a new top has been added, an alteration identical to that made to a Philadelphia high chest in the collection (cat. 148). Here, however, the alteration was clearly made with the intent to deceive, and the newly created dressing table was auctioned as such in 1930.

REFERENCE: *Flayderman Coll.*, no. 156.

The Mabel Brady Garvan Collection 1930.2386

18 **High chest of drawers**
New Hampshire, 1770–1790, with modern alterations
Maple, eastern white pine
H 208.3; W 103.9; D 51.8

Another example of a married object, this high chest does not exhibit the consistency of craftsmanship one expects to find in eighteenth-century furniture. Here, the drawers in the upper case have been reworked to match those in the lower case, although the dovetails exhibit substantial differences. The Dunlap-style carving (see cats. 64–65, 88, 162) is an added embellishment. The lower case has been modified in depth to accommodate the upper case.

REFERENCES: *Notable American & English Furniture & Decorations*, 13–15 March 1947 (New York: Parke-Bernet Galler-

Appendix 463

App. 18

App. 19

App. 20

ies, 1947), no. 625; Rogers, "Garvan Coll. (1962)," p. 11; Louis B. Wright et al., *The Arts in America: The Colonial Period* (1966; reprint, New York: Schocken Books, 1975), fig. 234; *Forgeries and Restorations*, no. 25; Nancy A. Smith, *Old Furniture: Understanding the Craftsman's Art* (Boston: Little, Brown and Company, 1975), figs. 193–194; Harold Sack, "Authenticating American Eighteenth-Century Furniture," *Antiques* 127 no. 5 (May 1985): 1121.

The Mabel Brady Garvan Collection 1950.697

19 Desk
Massachusetts, 1690–1730, with modern alterations
Maple, cherry, walnut veneer, yellow poplar
H 107.6; W 91.4; D 51.1

Although this is at first glance an impressive example of a richly veneered desk of the 1690–1730 period, its pristine condition suggests that it has been heavily reworked or perhaps fabricated in modern times. The maple sides of the case are stained and bear worm holes, suggesting that they were originally painted. The presence of yellow poplar as a secondary wood is unusual in what purports to be a Massachusetts example. The hinges, moldings, and feet are replacements.

REFERENCES: *Handbook*, p. 58; Walter A. Dyer, "The American Scrutoire-Desk: Primitive—Queen Anne," *Fine Arts* 18, no. 5 (April 1932): 31; Ormsbee, *Story Am. Furn.*, p. 131; Symonds and Ormsbee, *Antique Furn.*, p. 122; Nagel, pl. 5b; *Forgeries and Restorations*, no. 24.

The Mabel Brady Garvan Collection 1930.2119

20 Desk
New England, 1700–1735, with modern alterations
Cherry, maple, yellow poplar
H 100.6; W 82.9; D 49.8

Although acquired in the nineteenth century by the early collector and author Irving W. Lyon, this small desk has undergone considerable restoration. The desk interior is a complete replacement, the back of the case is new, the moldings have been renewed, and the case drawers have undergone considerable repairs.

REFERENCE: Lyon, fig. 48.

The Mabel Brady Garvan Collection 1930.2573

21 Child's desk
New England, 1760–1770, with modern alterations
Maple, eastern white pine
H 73.0; W 61.3; D 34.3

This small desk has been thoroughly re-built, as is clearly visible even in a photograph. The upper edges of the two lower case drawers have been pieced, the base molding and

App. 21

feet are new, the brasses and hinges are replacements, and the desk interior has been completely re-worked. On the outside of the back is a painted inscription that gives the date 1823 and what appears to be "Sutland, Mass."

The Mabel Brady Garvan Collection 1930.2074

22 Desk
Modern; in the style of Chester County, Pennsylvania, 1760–1780
American black walnut, southern yellow pine, yellow poplar
H 111.8; W 102.9; D 54.6

Although purchased from Francis D. Brinton by Francis P. Garvan as a rural Pennsylvania desk of the third quarter of the eighteenth century, this object has either been thoroughly rebuilt in the twentieth century or totally fabricated as a fake. The desk interior is completely rebuilt, and is unusual in that the platform under the drawers lacks a molding. The color of the backboards lacks age; the feet

Appendix 465

App. 22

are new; the drawers have been taken apart and put back together, if they are old; the brasses are new, and so forth. There are several pencil inscriptions on the desk that give the name and address of the Margolis shop in New York City, and the name and address of, possibly, "A. Kutler." One of the inscriptions seems to include the words "made by" in a phonetic spelling, and the inescapable conclusion is that this desk was either restored in the Margolis shop to a point unacceptable to modern standards, or it was fabricated there and passed off as genuine.

The Mabel Brady Garvan Collection 1930.2186

23 **Desk**
Annapolis, Maryland, 1790–1815, with modern alterations
Mahogany, light- and dark-wood inlays, pine, oak, yellow poplar
H 104.8; W 103.5; D 52.7

Traditionally attributed to John Shaw (1745–1829) of Annapolis and acquired by R. T. Haines Halsey for Francis P. Garvan, this desk has been so heavily restored that a modern attribution is problematic. The feet have obviously been cut, and the brasses are new. The interior of the desk has been thoroughly reworked, the lid and drawer dividers have been pieced, the desk has been refinished, and there have been many other repairs and restorations. A clue to these restorations is given in an inscription on the bottom of the dustboard above the second case drawer: "Repaired by / John D. [Duil?]son's / Nov. 30 1922 / Annapolis / Md." Although the desk may well have originated in the Annapolis area, recent scholarship has not accepted the attribution to John Shaw.

REFERENCE: "Annapolis Windows," *Antiques* 17, no. 5 (May 1930): 430.

The Mabel Brady Garvan Collection 1930.2715

24 **Desk and bookcase**
Massachusetts and Pennsylvania, 1755–1795, with modern alterations
Walnut, yellow poplar (bookcase); mahogany, eastern white pine (desk)
H 271.8; W 109.5; D 58.4

This married object consists of a Pennsylvania bookcase mounted on a Massachusetts desk; each section has been refinished to mask this alteration. The prospect door of the desk interior has been carved with a Pennsylvania-style

App. 23

466 *American Case Furniture*

25 Secretary

New England, 1790–1820, with modern alterations
Mahogany, pine
H 253.0; W 120.7; D 57.5

When owned by Francis P. Garvan and illustrated by Nutting, this secretary was fitted with a scroll-topped pediment that was a later addition; the original pediment has been lost. At the other end of the object, the feet have been replaced. These alterations may have come about because the object was too large for a twentieth-century interior; another secretary so truncated is illustrated in *Antiques* 5, no. 5 (May 1924): 238. The brasses are also replacements.

REFERENCE: Nutting, *Treasury*, no. 723.

The Mabel Brady Garvan Collection 1930.2578

App. 24

shell, similar to the one in the bookcase tympanum, to further confuse the issue.

REFERENCES: Miller, 1: no. 847; *Notable American & English Furniture & Decorations*, 13–15 March 1947 (New York: Parke-Bernet Galleries, 1947), no. 636; Kirk, *Early Am. Furn.*, fig. 181; Ward, *Eye of the Beholder*, cat. 45; Fitzgerald, p. 278; Harold Sack, "Authenticating American Eighteenth-Century Furniture," *Antiques* 127, no. 5 (May 1985): 1125.

The Mabel Brady Garvan Collection 1950.699

App. 25

Appendix 467

App. 26

26 Cupboard
Essex County, Massachusetts, ca. 1680, with nineteenth-century alterations
Oak, pine, maple
H 160.3; W 118.6; D 60.0

This cupboard was once in the collection of the noted Salem antiquarian Henry F. Waters (1800–1900), but, as John T. Kirk has noted, it now exists "as a serious mistake by a well-intentioned collector" who tried "to make pieces look as they did originally." Irving Lyon visited Waters in 1883 and jotted notes on the Waters collection in his journal: "a cupboard [probably this example] had been spoiled in doing over—scooped or planed down so as to look fresh as new oak—& I think other liberties had been taken with feet and possibly mouldings" (quoted in Elizabeth Stillinger, *The Antiquers* [New York: Alfred A. Knopf, 1980], p. 72). The cupboard has been so thoroughly restored, with its applied ornaments and moldings renewed, that it is no longer of primary value as a document of seventeenth-century Essex County joinery.

REFERENCES: Newton W. Elwell, *Colonial Furniture and Interiors* (Boston, 1896), pl. 48; Singleton, p. 169; Frances Clary Morse, *Furniture of the Olden Time* (1902; reprint, New York: Macmillan Company, 1908), p. 82; *Fifth Sale of Fine Early American Furniture Gathered by Jacob Margolis, Cabinet Maker of New York City* (New York: Anderson Galleries, 1924), no. 562; Herbert Cescinsky and George Leland Hunter, *English and American Furniture* (Garden City, N.Y.: Garden City Publishing Co., 1929), p. 47; Irving P. Lyon, "The Oak Furniture of Ipswich, Massachusetts, Part V: Small-Panel Type Affiliates," *Antiques* 33, no. 6 (June 1938): 322; Kirk, *Early Am. Furn.*, fig. 189; Richard H. Saunders, "Collecting American Decorative Arts in New England: Part I, 1793–1876," *Antiques* 109, no. 5 (May 1976): 997, 1001; Ward, *Eye of the Beholder*, cat. 33; Barbara McLean Ward and Gerald W.R. Ward, eds., *Silver in American Life: Selections from the Mabel Brady Garvan and Other Collections at Yale University* (New York: The American Federation of Arts; Boston: David R. Godine, 1979), cat. 77.

The Mabel Brady Garvan Collection 1930.2778

App. 27

27 Cupboard
Possibly English, ca. 1670–1690, with modern alterations
Oak, cedar, maple
H 154.3; W 116.5; D 57.5

The lower case of this seventeenth-century cupboard has been reworked; the doors, partitions, and sides are all new, thus creating some confusion as to the original appearance of the object. It may well have presented a more elaborate facade than its present, simple appearance would suggest. The bottom of the dovetailed drawer is a replacement, and the moldings on the drawer front and on the center section of the upper cupboard have been lost. The turned columns of oak suggest that the cupboard may be English; however, the age of these columns has been questioned. Although its early history is unknown, the cupboard was in all likelihood acquired as an American example by the pioneering collector C. Wyllys Betts, who bequeathed it to Yale in the late nineteenth century.

Bequest of C. Wyllys Betts, B.A. 1867 1887.8

28 Cellarette
Modern; in the style of Massachusetts, 1790–1815
Mahogany, mahogany veneer, light- and dark-wood inlays, eastern white pine, spruce
H 71.8; D 54.6; D 34.3

This is a modern fake of a relatively rare form in American furniture. The legs, probably cut down from a larger object, are doweled into the shaped skirt (which itself is modern). Banding and stringing have been added to mask this modern form of construction.

The Mabel Brady Garvan Collection 1930.2065

App. 28

Appendix

CONCORDANCE

1800.3	172	1930.2111	216	1930.2204	217	1930.2262	20
1800.4	26	1930.2112	25	1930.2205	130	1930.2264	124
1887.5	22	1930.2121	16	1930.2206	101	1930.2265	21
1887.6	197	1930.2124	146	1930.2207	113	1930.2271	194
1887.7	195	1930.2125	108	1930.2208	94	1930.2272	162
1926.114	205	1930.2132	24	1930.2211	88	1930.2275	111
1930.2000	147	1930.2145	1	1930.2212	84	1930.2276	178
1930.2001	116	1930.2146	93	1930.2214	56	1930.2277	160
1930.2003	82	1930.2147	90	1930.2215	53	1930.2278	202
1930.2016	184	1930.2148	126	1930.2216	39	1930.2308	222
1930.2017	67	1930.2149	61	1930.2218	35	1930.2309	135
1930.2023	188	1930.2152	64	1930.2219	33	1930.2310	141
1930.2034	92	1930.2154	63	1930.2222	48	1930.2311	128
1930.2036	157	1930.2158	159	1930.2228	145	1930.2312	127
1930.2037	118	1930.2159	96	1930.2229	55	1930.2313	133
1930.2054	38	1930.2162	83	1930.2231	11	1930.2315	183
1930.2055	143	1930.2171	215	1930.2232	200	1930.2316	119
1930.2056	97	1930.2172	214	1930.2234	6	1930.2317	165
1930.2061	167	1930.2174	163	1930.2235	10	1930.2319	70
1930.2062	117	1930.2189	199	1930.2237	8	1930.2321	37
1930.2072	81	1930.2190	28	1930.2239	7	1930.2322	191
1930.2075	104	1930.2191	27	1930.2240	34	1930.2323	152
1930.2079	80	1930.2192	198	1930.2241	174	1930.2346	187
1930.2083	166	1930.2193	148	1930.2245	45	1930.2347	204
1930.2088	114	1930.2195	79	1930.2250	107	1930.2384	100
1930.2093	186	1930.2196	31	1930.2254	42	1930.2385	102
1930.2109	51	1930.2197	122	1930.2260	2	1930.2387	120

1930.2388	164	1930.2627	115	1931.1236	211	1960.54.2	36
1930.2389	150	1930.2632	149	1931.1271	170	1964.46	132
1930.2391	54	1930.2634	153	1931.1310	209	1965.58	232
1930.2392	65	1930.2653	30	1931.1311	208	1966.63	134
1930.2397	156	1930.2655	15	1936.312	18	1966.126	229
1930.2398	151	1930.2660	203	1940.54	169	1968.9	131
1930.2438	230	1930.2664	99	1940.320	177	1970.55	224
1930.2439	12	1930.2677	103	1942.252	52	1970.98.4	185
1930.2443	144	1930.2678	142	1942.255	196	1971.43	233
1930.2444	136	1930.2682	58	1946.4	182	1971.45	3
1930.2445	106	1930.2721	210	1949.243	179	1971.51	201
1930.2462	17	1930.2726	78	1949.244	137	1971.70	190
1930.2464	13	1930.2728	72	1950.65	219	1971.115	223
1930.2465	14	1930.2731	40	1950.67	29	1972.89	43
1930.2474	68	1930.2733	47	1950.68	23	1976.99.1	189
1930.2480	59	1930.2736	206	1950.70	5	1977.40.7	227
1930.2483	129	1930.2764	212	1950.77	139	1977.40.8	193
1930.2485	46	1930.2765	32	1950.78	105	1977.40.17	75
1930.2486	49	1930.2775	231	1950.698	91	1977.40.18	76
1930.2487	176	1930.2993	95	1950.725	4	1979.27	225
1930.2492	220	1930.2994	121	1950.784	181	1979.79.1,.2	192
1930.2493	62	1930.2995	50	1951.56.1	161	1981.53.8	226
1930.2503	66	1930.2996	213	1951.56.2	98	1984.14.2	228
1930.2505	89	1930.2999	218	1952.50.3	69	1984.14.12	77
1930.2506	158	1930.5051	19	1952.50.4	60	1984.23.2	171
1930.2508	112	1931.117	73	1953.50.1	155	1984.32.29	175
1930.2524	57	1931.314	110	1953.50.3	71	1984.32.36	140
1930.2533	86	1931.1208	74	1954.37.24	168	1984.32.40	85
1930.2546	154	1931.1214	41	1954.37.28	138	1984.56	9
1930.2570	87	1931.1227	123	1955.50.1	180		
1930.2606	221	1931.1232	207	1957.37	109		
1930.2614	125	1931.1233	173	1960.54.1	44		

INDEX

Abrams, Michael A., owner, 166
Adams, Nehemiah, cabinetmaker, 357
Addison Gallery, Phillips Academy, Andover, Mass., 205
Adler, Mrs. F. C., owner, 421
Affleck, Thomas, cabinetmaker, 189, 283
Ahern, W. S., owner, 445
Alamance County, N.C., cellarette, 444–445
Albree, Mrs. Chester B., owner, 240, 241
Albright Art Gallery, Buffalo, N.Y., 439
Alder, 443
Allen, Clarence, owner, 201
Allen, William C. [or H.], name on desk and bookcase, 334
Allston, Elizabeth D., owner, 365, 430
Alston, William, owner, 365, 430
America, furniture attributed to: chest of drawers, 154–155; library bookcases, 366–367, 372–373; living room case, 438; miniature sideboard or chest of drawers, 76; sideboard, 418–420
American and New England Studies Program, Boston University, 344
American Express Co., 254
American Museum in Britain, Bath, England, related example in, 118
American Railway Express Co., 134, 184, 186, 243, 411
American Union, 134
Andrew family, owners, 378
Annapolis, Md., dressing table, 232–233
Antiquarian and Landmarks Society, Hartford, Conn., 111
Apperson, Mrs. A. H., owner, 419
Apperson family, owners, 419
Appleton, inscription, 180

Arnold, Charles W., owner, 388
Arons, Harry, dealer, 139, 140, 255, 260
Art Institute of Chicago, related examples in, 149, 239, 248, 308
Ash, white and black, as secondary wood, 110, 325, 421, 424, 432, 442, 445
Aspen, as secondary wood, 68, 107, 197, 207, 238, 245, 251, 260, 330
Atwater Kent radios, 454
Atwood, Thomas, owner, 383
Ayer, Fred Wellington, collector, 140, 318

B. Altman & Co., New York, 178
Babcock, Alpheous, pianomaker, 452
Badlam, Stephen, chest-on-chest, 171–177
Baker, Benjamin, cabinetmaker, 272
Bald cypress, 365
Baldwin, Emily (Perkins), owner, 252
Baldwin, Roger Sherman, owner, 252
Baldwin, Simeon E., owner, 252
Baltimore, Md.: buffet, 410–411; library bookcases, 372–373; sideboards, 425–427, 427–428
Baltimore Museum of Art, Baltimore, Md., related example in, 84
Barbour, inscription, 286
Barbour collection, Connecticut Historical Society, related example in, 184
Barnes, H. G., inscription, 226
Barnstable, Mass., 198
Bartram, James, cabinetmaker, 76
Bartram, James Howell, 75–76
Bartram, John, 76
Bartram's Garden, Philadelphia, related example in, 65

Basswood: as piano keys, 452; as primary wood, 69, 113; as secondary wood, 156, 367, 450
Bayou Bend Collection, Houston, Tex., related examples in, 197, 217, 343
Beard, J. K., dealer, 395
Beatty, Mary, owner, 227
Beatty, Reading, owner, 227
Beech, as secondary wood, 69, 70, 90, 132, 135, 242
Beinecke Rare Book and Manuscript Library, Yale University, 160
Bentl, John, inscription, 445
Bentley family, owners, 180
Berkey and Gay, furniture makers, 442
Berkley, Henry J., 232–233
Berks County, Pa., chests with drawers, 115–118
Berlin, Conn., 214
Berliss, Mr. and Mrs. Arthur D., Sr., donors, 325
Bernard, J. F., owner, 127
Berne, Ind.: cabinet, 440–442; long chest, 160
Betts, Charles Wyllys, bequest of, 86, 381, 382, 385, 469
Beverly, Mass., 168
Beverly Historical Society, Beverly, Mass., related example in, 177
Bigelow, Francis Hill, collector, 304
Bingham Fund, Millicent Todd, 62
Birch, as secondary wood, 198, 201, 252, 265, 274, 292, 373, 437. *See also* Birch veneer
Birch veneer, 149. *See also* Birch
Birmingham, England, brassfounders, 148, 426, 430

Index 473

Bissell family, joiners, 104
Blackie and Son, London furniture makers, 433
Blake, Katherine Devereaux, owner, 141
Blake, Theodore E., donor, 424, 425
Blin, Peter, joiner: chests, 90–94; cupboards, 379–383
Blondel, Jacques-François, *De la distribution des maisons . . .* , 443
Board cupboards, 389
Bohin, Margreda, owner, 116, 117
Booker, Florence, owner, 409
Bossert, George, owner, 116
Boston, Mass.: chest-on-chest, 171; chests of drawers, 125, 129, 134, 140–141; chest with drawers, 87; clothespress, 165; desks, 301–306; desk and bookcases, 333–339; dressing tables, 197, 205; high chests of drawers, 237–239, 244–245, 249–250
Boston Olive Branch, 134
Bowdoin College Museum of Art, Brunswick, Maine, related example in, 436
Bowen, Mary, owner, 213, 214
Bowen, Nathan, cabinetmaker, 168
Bower, John, engraver, 77, 78
Bowne family, owners, 239
Boxes, joined, 59
Boxford, Mass., 169–171
Bradstreet, David, owner, 306
Brainstorm Farm Antiques, Randolph, Vt., 113
Brightenstein, Providence, R.I., packers, 343
Brinton, Francis D., collector, 193, 231, 465
Brixey, Doris M., donor, 148, 182, 267, 268, 336, 337
Brixey, Richard DeWolfe, collector, 182, 267, 336
Bryant, Ira, owner, 292
Bronson, Bertrand H., owner, 367
Bronson, Thomas Bertrand, owner, 367
Bronxville, N.Y., 158, 159
Brooklyn Museum, Brooklyn, N.Y., related examples in, 60, 135, 310, 452
Brooks Reed Gallery, dealers, 270, 277
Brown, A., 277
Brown, Asher, woodworker, 277
Brown, John, owner, 342–344
Brown, Joseph, 343
Brown, Moses, 177, 343

Brown, Nicholas, 343
Brown, Samuel, dealer, 240, 241
Brown & Ives, 343
Buck, Henry Robinson, donor, 323
Buck, Susan, owner, 323
Buckley, Charles, author, 149
Buckley, Ruth (Fry), owner, 230
Bucks County, Pa., 227
Buel, Samuel, joiner, 62
Buel, William, box, 60–62
Bulkeley, Houghton, owner/author, 62, 93
Bulkeley, Mr. and Mrs. Morgan G., owners, 62
Bull, C. Sanford, collector, 64, 84, 87, 93, 95, 97, 98, 140, 151, 153, 204, 262, 300, 310, 348, 456
Burdon-Miller, Rowland, donor, 212
Burnham, Benjamin, cabinetmaker, 308
Butler, William, owner, 302
Butternut, as secondary wood, 155, 180, 299, 310, 351

C. M. Traver Company, 334
Camp, Gertrude H., dealer, 147, 148, 190, 201, 225, 248, 306
Canaan, Conn., 143
Canada, furniture in, 156, 321
Canfield, Miss, inscription, 213, 261
Cannon, Mrs. Beekman C., inscription, 211, 212, 265
Captain's desk, 320
Career Group, Dunbar Furniture, 161, 442
Carey, Frances Wolfe, dealer, 224, 313
Carnegie Institute, Pittsburgh, Pa., related example in, 189
Carpenter family, owners, 308
Carroll, Charles, owner, 232
Carroll, Madame, owner, 372
Centre County, Pa., chest, 118–119
Cedar, as secondary wood, 92, 94, 127, 382, 390. *See also* Cedar, Atlantic white; Cedar, eastern red; Cedar, northern white; Cedar, southern red
Cedar, Atlantic white, as secondary wood, 71, 73, 75, 90, 132, 141, 147, 203, 218, 221, 224, 225, 226, 228, 230, 231, 248, 252, 254, 282, 284, 286, 313, 317, 385, 405. *See also* Cedar; Cedar, eastern

red; Cedar, northern white; Cedar, southern red
Cedar, eastern red: as primary wood, 203; as secondary wood, 131, 137, 153, 203, 332, 378, 381, 386. *See also* Cedar; Cedar, Atlantic white; Cedar, northern white; Cedar, southern red
Cedar, northern white, as secondary wood, 132, 254. *See also* Cedar; Cedar, Atlantic white; Cedar, eastern red; Cedar, southern red
Cedar, southern red, as secondary wood, 365, 430. *See also* Cedar; Cedar, Atlantic white; Cedar, eastern red; Cedar, northern white
Cedrela (Spanish cedar), 127, 159, 349
Ceylon satinwood. *See* Satinwood
Chapin, Aaron, cabinetmaker, 183, 215–216, 420
Chapin, Eliphalet, 185; desk-on-frame, 298–300; dressing table, 214–216; high chest of drawers, 278–280
Charleston, S.C.: chest of drawers, 152–153; library bookcase, 363–366; sideboard, 428–431
Charlestown, Mass., 168, 169
Cheney, Silas E., cabinetmaker, 420
Cherry, American black: as primary wood, 143, 151, 181, 183, 185, 211, 212, 213, 214, 215, 229, 246, 260, 261, 265, 274, 276, 277, 279, 286, 298, 299, 308, 314, 321, 332, 346, 348, 351; as secondary wood, 73, 78, 127, 241, 304, 313, 322, 341, 349, 358, 415, 424, 435, 450
Chesebrough, Caroline L. H., owner, 343
Chester County, Pa., 71, 75, 218, 231; clothespress, 390–392
Chester County Historical Society, West Chester, Pa., related examples in, 75, 248
Chestnut, as secondary wood, 73, 86, 87, 90, 108, 127, 132, 151, 157, 159, 173, 178, 217, 238, 246, 252, 254, 256, 267, 269, 271, 274, 292, 325, 341, 349, 378, 386, 393, 423, 435, 437
Child's desks, 293–294, 300–301
Chippendale, Thomas, *Gentleman and Cabinet-Maker's Director*, 166, 193, 230, 366
Chipstone collection, related example in, 135. *See also* Stone, Stanley, collection
Chisholm, Archibald, dressing table, 232–233

474 *American Case Furniture*

Christ Church, Philadelphia, 148
Clafton, D., inscription, 107
Clap, John, cabinetmaker, 323
Clap, Mary Saltonstall, owner, 252–253
Clap, Thomas, president of Yale and owner, 252–253
Clark, inscription, 347
Clark, Horace, 183
Clark, Joel, owner, 297, 298
Clark, Margaret Tyler, donor, 353
Clark, Samuel, house, 183, 298
Clarke, A. W., agent for Francis P. Garvan, 224, 270, 342
Clayton, D., inscription, 107
Clement, Samuel, cabinetmaker, 238–239
Clifton, house of William Alston, 365–366, 430
Clisby, William, II, owner, 303
Coffer, 77–78
Coffin, John Hill, inscription, 286
Colchester, Conn., 210
Collings and Collings, dealers, 340, 342–343
Colonial Williamsburg, related examples in, 120, 189, 332
Conestoga wagon toolbox, 78–79
Connecticut: boxes, 60, 62; buffet, 402–403; chests and chests with drawers, 83, 100, 103, 110; chests of drawers, 142, 150–151; chest-on-chests, 180, 182; chest-on-chest-on-frame, 184; clothespress, 389–390; cupboard, 377–379; desk, 306–308; desk and bookcase, 331–332, 344–348; desks-on-frames, 297–300, 308–310; doctor's cabinet, 350–351; dressing tables, 206, 208, 211–213; high chests of drawers, 246–247, 250–255, 259–264, 275–277
Connecticut cities, towns, and counties. See Berlin; Canaan; Colchester; Durham; East Granby; East Windsor; Griswold; Guilford; Hartford; Kent; Killingworth; Lebanon; Lisbon; Litchfield; Litchfield County; Madison; Middletown; Milford; New Haven; Newington; New London County; Newtown; North Branford; North Stonington; Norwalk; Norwich; Putnam; Saybrook; South Windsor; Stratford; Suffield; Waterbury; West Granby; Wethersfield; Windsor; Woodbury

Connecticut Historical Society, Hartford, related examples in, 102, 184, 210, 216
Connecticut Valley: boxes, 62–64, 66; chest, 103; chests with drawers, 95, 97–98, 111
Cooke, Edward S., Jr., author, 211, 263
Cooley, Paul, dealer, 443
Cooper, Dan, designer: sideboard, 440–441; wall shelf, 373
Cooper, Wendy A., author, 344
Coopernail, George, owner, 94
Cottonwood, as secondary wood, 267, 371
Craftsman Workshops, sideboard, 436–438
Crosby, Huldah, owner, 303
Crystal Palace, London, 432
Courtenay, Hercules, carver, 283
Cumberland County, N.J., 218
Cupboard with drawers, 383–387
Currier Gallery of Art, Manchester, N.H., related examples in, 145, 433
Curtis, William B., owner, 402
Cushing, Harvey, owner, 372

Dana, Maria Trumbull, donor, 350
Davidson, James, owner, 98
Davis, inscription, 229
Davis, Morgan, pianomaker, 450
Dayton, Mehitable (Stratton), owner, 276
Dedham, Mass., chests, 130
Deerfield, Mass., board chests in, 103, 112
Delaware. See Wilmington
Delaware Valley: buffet, 404–405; desk, 311–313; dressing tables, 204–205, 218–220, 223–224, 228; table chest, 71
Denison, Daniel, II, cabinetmaker, 274
Denny, Daniel, Leicester, Mass., 292
Denny, Mary, inscription, 292
Denny, Samuel, owner, 292
Derby, Anstis, owner, 175
Derby, Elias Hasket, owner, 172, 174–176
Derby, Elizabeth Crowninshield, owner, 174–177
Derby family, owners, 170
Deshler, David, merchant, 189
Deskey, Donald, desk, 324–325
Deskey-Vollmer, desk, 324–325

Devereaux, Sarah Elizabeth Johnson, owner, 141
Dietrich collection, related example in, 197
Dolan, John T., cabinetmaker, 359
Dole, John, inscription, 321
Dominy family, woodworkers, 264
Dorchester Lower Mills, Mass., chest-on-chest, 171–172
Drop-panel furniture, 148–149
Dunbar Furniture Company: long chest, 160–161, cabinet, 440–442
Dunlap, John, 146
Dunlap, Samuel: chest of drawers, 145–146; desk, 310–311
Dunlap, Whitfield, 146
Dunlap family, cabinetmakers: chests of drawers, 144–146; chest-on-chest, 185–187; desk, 310–311
du Pont, Henry Francis, collector, 215
Durham, Conn., cupboard found in, 385
Dyer, Walter A., author, 382

Eagle Lock Co., Terryville, Conn., inscription, 324, 437
East Granby, Conn.: chest-on-chest, 182; desk-on-frame, 297–298
East Windsor, Conn.: chest with drawer, 103–104; desk-on-frame, 298–330; dressing table, 214–215; high chest of drawers, 278–280
Eastern shore, Va., chests, 119–121
Eastman, Elizabeth, owner, 98
Easton, Pa., miniature chest of drawers, 156–157
Eastwood, N.Y., sideboard, 436–438
Ebony, 443, 450, 452. See also Ebony veneer
Ebony veneer, 325. See also Ebony
Edsall, Thomas, turner, 88, 128
Edwards, Jonathan, owner, 212, 330
Eliars, furniture maker, 432
Eliot, Cornelia, owner, 86
Eliot, Jacob, cabinetmaker, 350
Eliot, Joseph, minister, 86
Elizabethan revival style, 369
Ellis, Horace, cabinetmaker, 156
Elm, as secondary wood, 160, 442
Emmons, Mrs., owner, 185
England, carving traditions: Gloucester-

Index 475

shire, 84–85; Huntingdon, 62; Lancashire, 63–64, 97; Leeds area, 379; North Country, 97; Somerset, 84; Suffolk, 60; West Country, 84–85; Westmorland, 63–64; Yorkshire, 63–64, 97
Ernst, Mr. and Mrs. G. G., collectors, 75, 197
Erving, Henry Wood, collector, 93, 220, 379, 382
Essex County, Mass., 137, 167–168, 321; box, 67; chest-on-chests, 169, 170; high chest, 239–241
Essex Institute, Salem, Mass., 176; related example in, 131
Evans, David, cabinetmaker, 317
Evans, Edward, cabinetmaker, 332
Evans, Martha Postrema, owner, 148
Evans, Robert Tower, owner, 148
Evans, Sarah Tower, owner, 148
Evans family, owners, 190
Ewing, Maskell, Jr., owner, 363

Fabian, Monroe, author, 115, 116, 117, 118
Farr, Willoughby, dealer, 141
Faux-livres, on desk, 317
Federhen, Deborah, author, 148
Feike. *See* Feite, Samuel
Feite, Samuel, inscription, 314
Fellowes, Frank Wayland, artist, 92
Field, Marshall, donor, 461
Fitch, Isaac, desk, 348–350
Flayderman, Philip, collector, 85, 150, 171, 256, 336, 355
Forbes, Lydia, owner, 298
Forman, Benno M., author, 128, 238–239, 245
Forst, Abraham, cabinetmaker, 301
Fourdinois, Alexandre Georges, furniture maker, 432
Fraktur, 117, 287
Framingham, Mass., 59
Frankenfield family, owners, 202
Frankl, Paul T., designer, 325
Fraser, Eliza Ferguson Evans and John, owners, 148
French, Richard, dealer, 392
French cabinet, 435
Frothingham, Benjamin, cabinetmaker, 168

Furgarson, Samuel, cabinetmaker, 183

Gardiner, Avis and Rockwell, dealers, 68
Gardner, Joseph, owner, 75
Garvan, Beatrice, author, 78, 363
Garvan, Francis P. *See* Mabel Brady Garvan Collection
Garvan, Mabel Brady. *See* Mabel Brady Garvan Collection
Garvan Collection. *See* Mabel Brady Garvan Collection
Gatehouse, John, cabinetmaker, 332
Geer, John Wheeler, cabinetmaker, 180, 274
Geib, Adam and William, piano, 451–452
Geib, John, Jr., 452; piano, 449–451
Georgia, furniture in, 187, 395, 409
Germantown, Pa., 202
Gibbons, William, joiner, 102
Gibbs, James, *A Book of Architecture* (1728), 176
Gibson, Thomas, pianomaker, 450
Gillam, Charles, craftsman, 101
Gillows papers, 193, 230
Gloucestershire, England, carving traditions, 84–85
Goddard, Daniel, cabinetmaker, 217
Goddard, John, cabinetmaker, 343
Goddard family. *See* Townsend-Goddard families
"Good Design Is Your Business," Albright Art Gallery, Buffalo, N.Y., 439
Goodman, Louis J., dealer, 359
Goodspeed, Mr. and Mrs. Charles, owners, 158
Goodwin, William B., collector, 85, 215
Gostelowe, Jonathan, 190; chest of drawers, 146–148
Gothic revival style, 369–372
Green, Arthur Leslie, dealer, 255
Green, James Wilder, donor, 459
Green, Priscilla P., donor, 459
Green, Thomas S., donor, 459
Green family, owners, 166
Greene, Richard Lawrence, author, 96, 98
Griffin, Clara M., owner, 132
Griswold, Conn., 180
Guilford, Conn., 427; chests, 85–86, 100–101; cupboards, 378, 383–386
Gum, red and black, as secondary wood, 70, 295, 313, 323, 430, 453
Gunston Hall, Lorton, Va., related example in, 228
Gustafsson, Nelson, furniture maker, 436

Hadley, Mass., chests, 95–100, 112; inscriptions: "EE," 98; "IP," 97, 98; "MR," 96; "M" and "D," 99, 100
Hale, Elizabeth (Strong), 111
Hale, Mary, 111
Hale, Nathan, 111
Hall, John, Sr., and Jr., joiners, clothes-press, 390
Hall, Samuel, joiner, 390
Halsey, R. T. Haines, collector, 154, 233, 411, 450
Hambley, John, desk, 370–371
Hampshire County, Mass., chest with drawers, 99
Hammersmith, Saugus, Mass., 88
Hampton, N.H., cupboard, 387–389
Hampton Falls, N.H., 388
Handlebar Antiques, Los Angeles, Calif., 437
Hands, Thomas, English brassfounder, 426, 430
Hanna, Leonard, Jr., Fund, 461
Harden Furniture Company, reproductions, 139, 211, 217, 256, 276, 344
Harewood (figured maple), 157
Hartford, Conn.: desk-on-frame, 308–310; high chest of drawers, 275–276
Hartshorn, Ebenezer, cabinetmaker, 206
Harvey, Mary Steel, owner, 227
Harvey, Samuel D., owner, 227
Hatfield, Mass., chest with drawers, 111–112
Hatfield chests, 99–100
Havens family, owners, 84
Hawks, John, joiner, 112
Heckscher, Morrison H., author, 217
Hemlock, eastern, as secondary wood, 88, 135, 185, 254, 292
Henniker, N.H., chest-on-chest found in, 146
Henry Ford Museum, Dearborn, Mich., related examples in, 60, 408
Henry Whitefield Museum, Guilford,

476 *American Case Furniture*

Conn., related example in, 101
Hepplewhite, George, *Cabinet-Maker and Upholsterer's Guide*, 138, 193, 363, 428
Herreshof, Nat, yacht designer, 343
Hermann Society, owners, 77–78
Hersh, Henry S., craftsman, 79
Herter Brothers, furniture makers, 436
Hewitt, Benjamin A., author, 176
Heyward-Washington House, Charleston, S.C., related example in, 366
Hickory, as secondary wood, 292, 296
High Museum, Atlanta, Ga., related examples in, 425, 437
Hildebrand, Caspar, inscription, 114, 115
Hilliker, H., owner, 214
Hinckley, Thomas, Plymouth Colony governor, 198
Hine, Grace E., Dedham, Mass., 382
Historic Deerfield, Deerfield, Mass., related examples in, 84, 113, 270, 280, 292
Historical Society of Pennsylvania, Philadelphia, related examples in, 219, 221
Hoagland, Samuel, cabinetmaker, 156, 157
Hoffmann, Wolfgang, designer, 159
Hogan, Charles Beecher, donor, 212
Hollister family, owners, 276
Holly, 365, 373
Holmes, Frank J., restorer, 421
Holyoke, Edward, owner, 239
Hopkins, Gerrard, cabinetmaker, 411
Hoppner, John, artist, 323
Hornor, William Macpherson, author, 189, 222, 232, 284, 317
Hosley, William N., Jr., author, 63
Hosmer, Walter, cabinetmaker, 379
Hostetter, Mrs. A. K., owner, 78
Houghton, John, joiner, 60
Housatonic Valley, Conn., 260
How, Bates, chest of drawers, 142–143
How family, Connecticut, 143
Howard, Thomas, Jr., sideboards, 415–417
Howell, William, cabinetmaker, 198
Hoyt, Charles, donor, 212, 265
Hubbard, Elijah K., owner, 369
Hubbard, Faith Wadsworth Silliman, owner, 349, 350
Hubbard, Henry Griswold, owner, 369, 370
Hubbard, Margaret Sill, owner, 369
Hubbard, Oliver Payson, owner, 350

Hudnut, Alexander M., owner, 218
Huntingdon, England, carving traditions, 62
Huntington, Betsy, Litchfield, Conn., 139–140
Huntington, Joshua, Norwich, Conn., 139–140
Huntington collection, American Art Sale, 189
Hurry, Renwick C., dealer, 405

Independence Hall, Philadelphia, 147
Indiana. *See* Berne
Ipswich, Mass., high chest, 239–241
Ipswich Historical Society, 357
Ivory piano keys, 450, 452

Japanese metal pulls, 161
Jenkins, Mary, Nantucket, Mass., 303
Jenkins, William, brassfounder, 426, 430
Jennison, Reuben, auctioneer, 277
Jewitt, J. B., inscription, 135
Johnson, Catherine, owner, 202
Johnson, Edmund, cabinetmaker, 318, 357
Johnson, Jeffrey, inscription, 450
Johnson, Robert Gibbon, house, Salem, N.J., buffet from, 405
Johnson, Samuel, minister, 141
Johnson, William Samuel, owner, 141
Johnson family, owners, 211
Joinery, London-style, 102, 128
Jonathan Edwards College, Yale University, 211–212, 265
Jordan, Wilfred, curator, 147

Kane, Patricia E., author, 84, 86–87, 96, 99–100, 131, 365, 390
Karpen, Samuel R., furniture maker, 325
Kast, or *kas*, 392
Kendall, Sargent, artist, 92
Kennedy, Jacqueline, 363
Kent, Conn., 143
Kentucky, 409

Killingworth, Conn., 62
King, Alexander, owner, 215
Kingwood veneer, 373
Kipper, Katrina, dealer, 261
Kirk, John T., author, 63, 67, 88, 100, 109, 131, 180, 190, 238, 247, 280, 343–344, 348, 381, 426
Kirkham, Hannah Atwood, owner, 383
Kirkham family, owners, 382–383
Kittinger Company, reproduction of high chest, 283
Kleiderschrank, 392
Knittle, Rhea Mansfield, dealer, 409
Kutler, A., inscription, 466

Lancashire, England, carving traditions, 63–64, 97
Lancaster County, Pa., 79; chest, 114–115; dressing table, 222–223
Lancaster Public Library, Lancaster, Mass., cupboard in, 382
Lane, Samuel, craftsman, 389
Lannuier, Charles-Honoré, cabinetmaker, 443
Larned family, owners, 207
Latham family, owners, 210
Lawton, Herbert, collector, 270
Lebanon, Conn., desk and bookcase, 348–350
Lebanon County, Pa., 118
Leeds, England, carving traditions, 379
Leete, Mrs., agent, 386
Lehigh County, Pa., chest with drawers, 116–117
Lehman, Harold M., owner, 382
Leibundguth, Arthur W., author, 92
Leicester, Mass., desk, 291–292
Lemon, Charles, craftsman, 176–177
Lemon, John, craftsman, 176–177
Lemon, William, craftsman, 176–177
Lewis, Isaac, owner, 424
Liebert, Herman W., donor, 367
Lignum vitae, 127
Lindens, Washington, D.C., related example in, 220
Linton, Ralph, collection of African art, 373
Lisbon, Conn., 179
Litchfield, Conn., 151
Litchfield County, Conn., 143

Index 477

Litchfield Historical Society, Litchfield, Conn., 184
Lititz, Pa., 223
Little, Nina Fletcher and Bertram K., collection of, 107
Liverant, Nathan, and Son, dealers, 62
Lloyd, William, cabinetmaker, 419
Lock plates, on boxes, 66
Locke, Mathew, 148
Lockwood, Luke Vincent, author, 378
Logan, Deborah Norris, owner, 219
London, England, joinery traditions, 102, 128
Long chest, 161
Long Island, N.Y., high chest of drawers, 264–265
Loomis, Amasa, owner, 216
Loomis, Nathaniel, joiner, 63, 104
Lord and Taylor, N.Y., department store, 157–158
Louis XVI style, 436
Lyman Allyn Museum, New London, Conn., 136, 218
Lyon, Charles Woolsey, dealer, 70, 73, 84, 103, 143, 176, 180, 205, 206, 250, 270, 274, 383, 386, 406, 421
Lyon, Irving P., owner, 84, 240
Lyon, Irving W., author and collector, 84, 92, 215, 240–242, 263, 275–276, 379, 383, 386
Luther, Clair Franklin, author, 96, 97, 98

Mabel Brady Garvan Collection, 59–60, 62, 66–67, 70–74, 76–79, 84–85, 89–90, 95, 97–98, 100–104, 106–110, 112, 115–121, 128, 130–131, 133–135, 137–139, 141–143, 145, 149–150, 152, 154, 157, 166, 168, 170–171, 177, 179–180, 184–185, 187, 189, 191–193, 198–201, 203, 205–208, 210–211, 213–214, 216–217, 219–220, 222–225, 227–230, 232–233, 239, 241–242, 244, 247–248, 250–251, 255–256, 259–261, 270, 272, 274, 276, 277, 280, 283–284, 287, 293–296, 298, 301, 303–306, 308, 311, 313, 315, 317–318, 320, 323, 332, 335, 339, 344, 346, 351, 355, 357, 361, 363, 366, 370–371, 379, 383, 386–387, 389, 390, 392–393, 395, 400, 403–405, 407–411, 416–417, 420, 422–423, 426, 428, 430, 436, 444–445, 450, 456–458, 460, 462–469

Macassar ebony, 325
MacCarthy, Frank W., dealer, 66, 96, 112, 404
McDonough, Charlotte Rosella, owner, 370
McIlwaine, Mrs. Clark, donor, 353
McIntire, Samuel, architect, 176
McKnight, Dr., owner, 206
McLaughlin, Mrs. M. D. F., 359
McManus, J. Carey, inscription, 401
McStevens, Dr., owner, 220, 428
Madison, Conn., cupboard found in, 386
Magnavox radios, 454
Mahogany: as primary wood, 75, 78, 137, 140, 141, 142, 147, 148, 153, 154, 155, 166, 168, 169, 170, 173, 178, 188, 210, 217, 221, 230, 232, 267, 269, 271, 284, 295, 302, 304, 306, 310, 317, 318, 320, 321, 322, 334, 336, 338, 341, 349, 353, 355, 357, 358, 360, 363, 365, 367, 411, 415, 417, 419, 421, 423, 424, 426, 428, 430, 450, 452; as secondary wood, 157, 160, 317, 325, 358, 363, 367, 369, 442. See also Mahogany veneer
Mahogany veneer, 148, 153, 154, 155, 156, 173, 221, 317, 318, 320, 321, 322, 353, 355, 357, 358, 360, 363, 365, 367, 411, 415, 417, 419, 421, 423, 424, 426, 428, 430, 443, 450, 452
Maine, furniture in, 297, 321. See also Mount Desert
Maple: as primary wood, 139, 254, 435, 443; as secondary wood, 78, 88, 90, 92, 94, 102, 127, 160, 169, 198, 206, 296, 382, 440, 452. See also Maple, hard; Maple, soft; Maple veneer
Maple, hard: as primary wood, 73; as secondary wood, 254, 423, 442. See also Maple; Maple, soft; Maple veneer
Maple, soft: as primary wood, 99, 108, 133, 135, 144, 146, 150, 180, 186, 201, 208, 240, 256, 258, 264, 292, 294, 311; as secondary wood, 106, 112, 127, 129, 132, 180, 207, 210, 238, 242, 244, 246, 251, 252, 254, 269, 274, 306, 323, 330, 378, 381, 423, 450. See also Maple; Maple, hard; Maple veneer
Maple veneer, 78, 157, 159, 254, 296, 323, 353, 435, 443. See also Maple; Maple, hard; Maple, soft
Marblehead, Mass., 168–169
Marcotte, Léon, furniture maker, 436
Margaret Woodbury Strong Museum, Rochester, N.Y., related example in, 433
Margolis, Jacob, dealer, 66, 67, 109, 135, 136, 139, 142, 189, 192, 245, 292, 295, 301, 303, 314, 320, 338, 466
Margolis Antique Shop, New York, 134
Marlborough legs, 231
Marsh, Joanna (Porter), owner, 97
Marshall Field Department Store, 442
Martha's Vineyard, Mass., 303
Martin, Ebenezer, cabinetmaker, 168
Maryland, 220; buffet, 410–411; chest of drawers, 154; dressing table, 227
Maryland cities. See Annapolis; Baltimore
Mason, Ralph, joiner, 128
Mason-Messenger shops, 130, 133
Massachusetts: boxes, 60, 64, 67; chests of drawers, 132, 138–139, 148, 150; chest-on-chest, 167; chests with drawers, 87, 105–106; desks, 291–292, 320–321; desk-on-stand, 319–320; dressing table, 199; high chest of drawers, 241–242; secretary, 352–355
Massachusetts cities, towns, and counties. See Barnstable; Beverly; Boston; Boxford; Charlestown; Dedham; Deerfield; Dorchester Lower Mills; Essex County; Framingham; Hadley; Hampshire County; Hatfield; Ipswich; Leicester; Marblehead; Martha's Vineyard; Nantucket; Newbury; Newburyport; New Marlborough; Plymouth; Rowley; Roxbury; Salem; Saugus; Springfield; Stockbridge; Taunton; Worcester
Massachusetts Historical Society, Boston, related example in, 131
Matteson, Thomas, painted furniture, 113
Mayhew, Edgar DeN., author, 274, 350
Meeks, Dean, 92
Meeks, John and Joseph, desk and bookcase, 368–370
Merwin, Miss, owner, 97
Messenger, Henry, joiner, 128
Metropolitan Museum of Art, New York, related examples in, 62, 84, 88–89, 131, 135, 149, 177, 217, 230, 239, 245, 284, 308, 343, 363, 369, 378, 436
Michie, Thomas S., author, 444
Middle Atlantic states, portable writing desk, 323–324

Middletown, Conn.: chest, 378; clothespress, 389–390
Middletown Savings Bank, Middletown, Conn., owner, 390
Milford, Conn., 378
Miller, Aaron, clockmaker, 212
Millicent Todd Bingham Fund, 113
Milton, John, carved bust of, 177
Milwaukee Art Center, Milwaukee, Wis., related example in, 133
Miniature furniture: chest of drawers, 156–157; chest of drawers or sideboard, 76
Minneapolis Institute of Arts, Minneapolis, Minn., related example in, 284
Mislovits, Anton, cabinetmaker, 92–93
Monroe, Nehemiah, cabinetmaker, 323
Montgomery County, Pa., chest with drawers, 115–116
Montgomery, Charles F., author, 318, 360, 422, 426
Moore, Jerrold N., owner, 369
Moore, Oliver, cabinetmaker, 183
Morson, Charles R., dealer, 99, 144, 270, 287, 426
Moses, Michael, author, 138, 217, 267
Moulton, Benjamin, 388
Moulton, James T., dealer, 240, 241
Mount Desert, Maine, 306
Mueller, Burton, donor, 211, 265
Munn, Stephen Ball, owner, 443
Murray, Robert F., cabinetmaker, 77
Museum of Art, Rhode Island School of Design, Providence, 254–255; related examples in, 142, 343, 436
Museum of Early Southern Decorative Arts, Winston-Salem, N.C., related examples in, 76, 153
Museum of Fine Arts, Boston: cupboard on loan to, 388; related examples in, 86, 128, 131, 176, 197, 227, 250, 343, 378, 382
Museum of Fine Arts, Houston, related examples in, 433, 437
Museum of Modern Art, New York, 439
Museum of the City of New York, related example in, 450
Myers, Louis Guerineau, collector, 77, 284, 363
Myers, Minor, Jr., author, 274, 350

Nagel, Charles, author, 137, 329–330
Nantucket, Mass., 302–303
Nathan Hale Homestead, Coventry, Conn., 111
Needham, Jesse, cabinetmaker, 409
Needles, John, cabinetmaker, 76, 154
Nettlefold, patent lock, 369–370
New England: boxes, 59, 64; buffet, 403–404; chests of drawers, 133, 135, 138–139; child's desks, 293–294, 300–301; chest-on-chest-on-frame, 184; chests with drawers, 89, 106–109; desk, 295–297; desk with later bookcase, 329–331; dressing tables, 200, 209; high chest, 243–244; miniature chest, 69; pipe box, 73; portable writing desks, 322–324
New Hampshire: chests of drawers, 144–145, 148, 150; chest-on-chest-on-frame, 185; cupboard, 387–389; desk, 320–321; painted furniture, 69
New Hampshire cities and towns. See Hampton; Hampton Falls; Henniker; New Market; Newport; Portsmouth; Salisbury; South Hampton
New Haven, Conn., 211; chests, 83–84, 101–102; cupboard, 377–379; high chest of drawers, 251–253
New Haven Antiques Show, 437
New Haven Colony Historical Society, New Haven, Conn., related examples in, 84, 382
New Jersey, dressing tables, 218–220, 223. See also Delaware Valley
New Jersey cities and counties. See Cumberland County; Salem; Salem County
New London County, Conn., 179–180, 182; desk and bookcase, 344–348; doctor's cabinet, 351
New Market, N.H., 168
New Marlborough, Mass., 143
New York cities and towns. See Bronxville; Eastwood; Long Island; New York City; Syracuse. See also New York State
New York City, 155, 158; cabinet, 434–436; cellarette, 442–444; chest of drawers, 157; desk, 324–325; desk and bookcases, 331–332, 368–370; high chest, 237–239; library bookcases, 359–361, 366–367; pianos, 449–452; sideboards, 420–425, 431–433, 440–441; wall shelf, 373; writing table and bookcase, 357–359
New York State: chest of drawers, 155; high chest of drawers, 264–265
Newbury, Mass., 300
Newburyport, Mass., 300, 321
Newington, Conn., 383
Newman, Dr. and Mrs. Matthew, donors, 437
Newport, N.H., 156
Newport, R.I.: bureau table, 216; chest of drawers, 137; chest-on-chest, 177; chest-on-frame, 255–256; desk and bookcase, 339–344; dressing table, 217; high chests of drawers, 265–272
Newton, Mr. and Mrs. Herbert B., collection of, 134
Newtown, Conn., dressing tables, 210–211, 214
Norris, J., 108
North, Martha Fraser, owner, 148
North Branford, Conn., cupboard, 400–402
North Carolina, 407; buffet, 408–409; cellarette, 444–445
North Carolina counties. See Alamance County; Randolph County
North Country, England, carving traditions, 97
North Stonington, Conn., chest-on-chest, 179–180
Norwalk, Conn.: dressing table, 212–213; high chest, 260–261
Norwich, Conn.: desk, 306–308; doctor's cabinet, 350–351
Nunns and Clark, pianomakers, 452
Nusrala, Mr. and Mrs. Edward J., donors, 68–69
Nutting, Wallace, owner/dealer, 59, 390

Oak, red: as primary wood, 66, 68, 87, 88, 90, 127, 129, 131, 132, 133, 135, 136, 385, 386, 390; as secondary wood, 99, 127, 200, 244, 246, 254, 260, 349, 440. See also Oak, white
Oak, white: as primary wood, 59, 60, 62, 64, 66, 83, 85, 86, 92, 94, 96, 97, 98, 127, 129, 132, 136, 378, 381, 382, 385, 437; as secondary wood, 90, 100, 102, 104, 106, 107, 114, 127, 160, 166, 190, 203, 211, 230, 231, 246, 271, 296, 419. See also Oak, red

Index 479

Old Sturbridge Village, Sturbridge, Mass., related example in, 390
Oneida Historical Society, Utica, N.Y., related example in, 62
"Organic Design," Museum of Modern Art, 439
Osborn, Mr. and Mrs. James Marshall, owners, 158, 159, 160, 373, 441
Osborn Collection, Beinecke Rare Book and Manuscript Library, Yale University, 160

Pabst, Daniel, cabinetmaker, 433
Packard, Alpheus S., owner, 175
Packard, Elizabeth, owner, 175
Packard, Elizabeth Derby Walcott, owner, 175
Packard, Martha W., owner, 175–176
Park, Maud Green, donor, 459
Papp, Florian, dealer, 371
Parkman, William, cabinetmaker, 206
Parmley family, owners, 97
Parsons, Charles, author, 145
Pawtuxet, R.I., 416
Peale, Rembrandt, portrait of Henry Wynkoop, 227
Pearson, Mrs. John W., owner, 180
Pease, Matthew and Mary (Butler), 303
Penfield, Charlotte Gilman, donor, 252
Penn, William, 317
Penney, Mrs. John P., owner, 242
Penn's Works, 316
Pennsylvania: buffets, 405–408; chest of drawers, 151; chest-on-chests, 189–192; clothespresses, 390–394; Conestoga wagon toolbox, 78; desks, 294–295, 315–317; desk-on-frame, 313–315; dressing tables, 203–204, 222, 227, 231; high chests of drawers, 284–287; medicine chest, 74–75; table chests, 70–72
Pennsylvania cities, towns, and counties. *See* Berks County; Bucks County; Centre County; Chester County; Delaware Valley; Easton; Germantown; Lancaster County; Lebanon County; Lehigh County; Lititz; Montgomery County; Philadelphia; Richboro; Schulykill County
Pennsylvania Farm Museum, Landis Valley, related example in, 79

Pennypacker, A. J., owner, 118, 119, 152, 223
Pennypacker, Charles, buyer, 223
Pennypacker, Samuel Whitacker, owner, 314
Perkins, Anna (Pitkin), owner, 252
Perry, J. Marsden, owner, 343
Pfisterer, Peter, designer, 439
Philadelphia, Pa., 218; bureau table, 229; cabinet radio, 452–454; chest of drawers, 146; chest-on-chest, 187; coffer, 77; dressing tables, 201, 220–221, 226–227; high chests of drawers, 247–248, 280–284; library bookcase, 361–363
Philadelphia Museum of Art, related examples in, 115, 248, 363, 433
Philco Radio and Television Corporation radio, 452–454
Phillips, Mr. and Mrs. Gifford, donors, 160, 442
Phyfe, Duncan, cabinetmaker, 359, 443, 450
Pickman, Anstis Derby, owner, 175
Pickman, Benjamin, Jr., owner, 175–176
Pine, eastern white: as primary wood, 67, 106, 107, 109, 110, 114, 301, 371, 372, 399, 401, 403, 404; as secondary wood, 66, 68, 69, 73, 77, 83, 88, 90, 98, 108, 117, 118, 119, 127, 129, 131, 132, 133, 135, 136, 137, 139, 140, 141, 142, 143, 144, 146, 149, 150, 151, 152, 153, 154, 155, 156, 166, 168, 169, 170, 173, 178, 180, 181, 183, 185, 186, 197, 198, 200, 201, 206, 207, 208, 210, 211, 213, 214, 215, 217, 238, 241, 244, 245, 250, 251, 252, 254, 258, 260, 261, 264, 265, 267, 269, 271, 274, 276, 277, 279, 292, 294, 295, 296, 298, 299, 302, 304, 306, 308, 310, 311, 317, 318, 320, 321, 322, 323, 330, 334, 336, 338, 341, 346, 348, 349, 351, 353, 355, 357, 358, 360, 363, 365, 367, 369, 415, 417, 421, 423, 424, 426, 428, 430, 443, 445, 450, 452. *See also* Pine, red or Scotch; Pine, southern yellow
Pine, red or Scotch, as secondary wood, 132, 173. *See also* Pine, eastern white; Pine, southern yellow
Pine, southern yellow: as primary wood, 103, 104, 112, 120, 121, 394, 407, 410, 445; as secondary wood, 60, 62, 64, 66, 73, 88, 92, 94, 96, 97, 98, 99, 100, 114, 139, 147, 188, 192, 198, 201, 202, 203,

205, 207, 218, 220, 221, 224, 228, 229, 242, 248, 251, 254, 276, 277, 282, 284, 286, 313, 314, 381, 382, 403, 405, 406, 409, 419, 423, 430. *See also* Pine, eastern white; Pine, red or Scotch
Pipe box, 73–74
Pitkin, Mrs. Albert Hastings, owner, 399–400
Pitkin, Temperance (Clap), owner, 252
Pitkin, Timothy, owner, 252
Pittenger, Daniel, cabinetmaker, 156–157
Plantation desks, 359
Platt, Philip, dealer, 392
Plummer, Luella, owner, 155
Plymouth, Mass., 85, 250
Plymouth Colony, chest with drawers, 89–90
Plywood, 157, 159, 160, 325, 373, 435, 437, 439, 440–442, 453
Portland, Maine, 59
Portsmouth, N.H., 149, 168
Portsmouth, R.I., desk with later bookcase, 370–371
Pratt, Enoch, house, 372
Preston, Conn., 180; high chest of drawers, 272–274
Price books, 323, 360–361, 422
Protat, Hugues, designer, 432
Providence, R.I.: chest of drawers, 137; sideboards, 415–417
Purefoy, H., buyer, 305
Putnam, Conn.: dressing table, 206–207, high chest, 250–251

Queen Anne Cottage Antiques, Accord, Mass., 261

Radeke, Mrs. Eliza Greene Metcalf, owner, 255
Radio City Music Hall, New York, 325
Raised-panel furniture, eastern shore of Virginia, 120–121
Randall, Richard H., Jr., author, 443
Randolph County, N.C., 409
Rankin, Cornelia W., owner, 139–140
Rankin, Laura M. Wolcott, owner, 139–140
Rawson, Grindall, cabinetmaker, 343

480 *American Case Furniture*

RCA, 454
RCA Building, 441
Reifsnyder, Howard, collector, 71, 202, 228, 407
Renaissance revival style, 433, 436
Renwick, Robert, cabinetmaker, 372
Rhode Island, high chest of drawers, 253–255
Rhode Island cities and towns. *See* Newport; Pawtuxet; Portsmouth; Providence; Tiverton
Rhode Island Historical Society, Providence, related examples in, 343–344
Richardson family, owners, 295
Richboro, Pa., 227
Ritchie, Andrew C., museum director, 439
Ritchie, Jane, donor, 439
Robbins, Philomen F., restorer, 379
Robbins, Thomas, diary of, 330
Robbins Brothers, Hartford, Conn., 242
Rochefort & Skarren, furniture makers, 432
Rockefeller Plaza, New York, 441
Root, Mary (Russell), owner, 96
Rose family, owners, 402
Rose house, North Branford, Conn., buffet from, 400–403
Rosewood, rosewood veneer, 127, 323, 353, 369, 435, 443, 452
Roux, Alexander, 432; cabinet, 434–436
Rowell, Sarah, cupboard decoration, 69, 388
Rowlandson, Joseph and Mary, owners, 382
Rowley, Mass., high chest found in, 258
Roxbury, Mass., 323
Russell, Margaret Hubbard, 369
Russell, Mr. and Mrs. T. M., Sr., 369
Russell, T. M., Jr., 369
Russell, William, joiner, 102
Russell-Gibbons shops, attributions to, 102, 378–379
Russell Manufacturing Company, Middletown, Conn., 369–370

S. Karpen & Bros., furniture manufacturer, 325
Sabotnik, inscription, 254
Sack, Israel, dealer, 60, 106, 138, 149, 182, 199, 238, 255, 258, 277, 308, 405, 416–417, 443
St. George, Robert Blair, author, 90
St. Louis Art Museum, St. Louis, Mo., related example in, 437
Salem, Mass., 65–66, 168–169, 172; chest of drawers, 130; desk and bookcases, 333–335, 337–339; gentleman's secretary, 355–357; high chest of drawers, 257–259; tambour desk, 317–318
Salem, N.J., buffet, 404–405
Salem County, N.J., 218
Salem Gazette, 64
Salisbury, N.H.: desk, 310–311; chest of drawers, 145
Salmon, William, *Palladio Londinensis* (1734), 120, 274
Sands, Gordon Eliot, author, 158, 159
Satinwood, 149, 321, 369, 430
Saturday Evening Post, 134
Saugus, Mass., 88
Savery, William, cabinetmaker, 147, 228, 283
Saybrook, Conn., 247; chest with drawers, 100–101
Schmieg, Hungate, and Kotzian, cabinetwork, 324–325
Schrank, 392
Schuylkill County, Pa., 71
Schwartz, Morris, 189
Sears Silvertone radio, 454
Secord, William R., dealer, 215
Seegee, Anne, owner, 230
Seem, Henry, miniature chest of drawers, 156–157
Sergeant, John, owner, 330
Seymour, George Dudley, antiquarian, 92
Seymour, Thomas, cabinetmaker, 177
Shaw, John, dressing table, 232–233
Shearer, Thomas, designer, 323
Sheffield, Joseph Earl, owner, 432, 433
Sheffield Scientific School, Yale University, 432
Sheraton, Thomas: *Cabinet Dictionary*, 200, 292, 357, 426, 430; *Cabinet-Maker and Upholsterer's Drawing Book*, 154, 366, 430
Silliman, Harriet and Benjamin, owners, 350
Silliman College, Yale University, 358
Simons, E., inscription, 275
Simons, Edwin, cabinetmaker, 379
Sizer, Theodore, educator, 92–93
Skillin, John, carver, 171, 176
Skillin, Simeon, Jr., carver, 171, 176
Skillin, Simeon, Sr., carver, 177
Slider, on chest of drawers, 138
Smith, George, *A Collection of Designs for Household Furniture* (1808), 189, 370
Smith, Miss, Exeter, N.H., owner, 388
Snakewood, 95, 127, 128
Snohr, Harry Eduard, cabinetwork, 157–160
Society for the Preservation of New England Antiquities, Boston, related example in, 128
Somerset, England, carving traditions, 84
South Carolina. *See* Charleston
South Hampton, N.H., 388
South Shaftsbury, Vt., chest with drawers, 112–113
South Windsor, Conn., 215
Southmayd, Samuel, owner, 390
Southmayd family, owners, 390
Spanish cedar. *See* Cedrela
Springfield, Mass., board chests in, 103
Spruce, in pianos, 450, 452
Staghorn sumac, veneer, 254
Starr, Burgis P., owner, 378
Starr, Comfort, owner, 378
Starr, Edward Comfort, owner, 378
Starr, Henry B., owner, 378
Starr, Mabel E., owner, 378
Starr, William, owner, 378
Starr family, owners, 102; cupboard, 378
Steckler, dealer, 113
Steel, Mary, owner, 227
Steel, Robert, owner, 227
Steinberg, L., inscription, 411
Steps, for high chest of drawers, 262–263
Sterling, Betty, dealer, 113
Stetson, Charles, dealer, 264, 321
Stickley, Gustav, sideboard, 436–438
Stockbridge, Mass., 330
Stohlern, Maria, 117
Stone, Nathaniel, woodworker, 385
Stone, Stanley, collection, related example in, 239. *See also* Chipstone collection
Stone family, owners, 385–386
Stonorov, Oscar G., designer, 438–439
Stoughton, Thomas, owner, 104
Stoughton family, owners, 104
Stratford, Conn., 208
Stratton family, owners, 276

Index 481

Stromberg-Carlson radio, 454
Stuart revival style, 369
Study Collection, Yale University: boxes, 456; bureau table, 461; cellarette, 469; chests, 457; chests of drawers, 458; chest-on-chest, 459; cupboards, 468–469; desks, 464–466; desk and bookcase, 467; dressing tables, 459–461; high chests of drawers, 461–464; secretary, 467
Suffield, Conn., 247
Suffolk, England, carving traditions, 60
Sulfur inlay, 72
Sussell, Arthur J., collection of, 118
Swan, Mabel Munson, author, 176
Sycamore: as primary wood, 252; as secondary wood, 99, 129, 252, 254
Symonds family, joiners, 131
Syracuse, N.Y., 99

Tabele, James, sideboard, 420–422
Tarbox, Increase N., editor, 330
Taunton, Mass., 107
Taylor, Henry Hammond, dealer, 146, 207, 211, 214, 230, 253, 260, 378, 388, 390
Taylor, Samuel, of Philadelphia, 221
Temple Newsam House, Leeds, England, furniture in, 339
Ten Eyck family, owners, 239
Thomson, inscription, 450
Thurston, John, joiner, 60
Tishman, Richard, collector, 255
Titcomb, Edmund, cabinetmaker, 245
Tiverton, R.I., Hambley family in, 371
Towers, Elizabeth, owner, 147
Townsend, Christopher, cabinetmaker, 270
Townsend, Edmund, cabinetmaker, 217
Townsend, Georgia Pollak Devereaux, owner, 141
Townsend, John, 272; bureau table, 216–217; high chest of drawers, 265–268
Townsend-Goddard families, 178, 272; desk and bookcase, 339–344
Travers sale, 334
Treadwell, Flora G., owner, 168
Treadwell family, owners, 168
Treadwell, inscription, 167
Treadwell, Nathaniel, cabinetmaker, 168
Treat, Henry, joiner, 104
Treat family, owners, 378

Tredway Brothers, Ticonderoga, N.Y., inscription, 450
Trent, Robert F., author, 88, 100, 102, 128
Trowbridge, Mrs. C. Rachel, donor, 453, 454
Trowbridge, Cornelia B., owner, 207
True, Joseph, carver, 176
Trumbull, Eunice Backus, owner, 350
Trumbull, Jonathan, Jr., owner, 350
Tucker, Mrs. Carll, donor, 452
Tucker, Reuben, owner, 87
Tufft, Thomas, cabinetmaker, 219
Tyler collection, cupboard in, 382
Tynan, John, owner, 111
Tynan, William, owner, 346

Valentine Museum, Richmond, Va., related example in, 452
Vermont, furniture in, 168
Vermont. See South Shaftsbury
Virginia: buffets, 408–410; chests from eastern shore, 119–121; clothespress, 394–395
Virginia Museum of Fine Arts, Richmond, related examples in, 378, 433, 436–437
Vollmer, Phillip, designer, 325
von Moltke, Willo, designer, 438–439

W. & J. Sloane, New York, dealers, 360
Wadsworth Atheneum, Hartford, Conn., related examples in, 102, 104, 130–131, 332, 382
Walcott, Samuel Baker and Martha Pickman, owners, 175
Wale, William, pianomaker, 452
Walker, Robert, cabinetmaker, 366
Wallpaper, drawer linings, 139
Walnut, American black: as primary wood, 70, 71, 72, 73, 77, 152, 156, 190, 192, 193, 197, 198, 200, 202, 205, 206, 207, 218, 220, 222, 224, 225, 226, 228, 231, 238, 245, 248, 250, 251, 282, 296, 313, 330, 369, 378, 392, 405, 406, 409, 432, 440; as secondary wood, 114, 127, 129, 131, 132, 156, 160, 254, 296, 410, 432, 439. See also Walnut veneer
Walnut veneer, 77, 131, 160, 197, 198, 200, 202, 206, 207, 238, 245, 250, 251,
369, 432, 439, 440, 441, 453. See also Walnut, American black
Warren Telechron Co., 325
Wasgatt family, owners, 306
Waterbury, Conn., high chest from, 261–263
Waters, Henry, collector, 383
Watson, Abraham, cabinetmaker, 168
Watson, C., owner, 426
Watson, M. L., owner, 120, 121
Webb, J. Watson, donor, 457
Webb, Joseph, Sr., house, Wethersfield, Conn., 245, 400
Webb-Deane-Stevens Museum, Wethersfield, Conn., 457
Webster, Daniel, library, 372
Weil, Henry V., dealer, 69, 72, 88, 90, 110, 128, 129, 131, 132, 169, 186, 200, 208, 221, 227, 243, 244, 272, 332
Weir, John Ferguson, artist, 92
Wenham, Edward, author, 137
West, Herbert, 273
West Country, England, carving traditions, 84–85
West Granby, Conn., 183
Westmorland, England, carving traditions, 63–64
Wethersfield, Conn., 93–95, 104, 214; buffet, 399–400; chest with drawers, 90; cupboards, 379–383; dressing table, 213; high chest of drawers, 263–264
Wetmore, Maud A. K., donor, 458
White, Gideon, owner, 250
White House, Washington, D.C., library bookcase, 363
Whitehead, William, cabinetmaker, 425
Whitelock, George, cabinetmaker, 428
Whitlock, C. E. H., owner, 87
Wilcox, Mark, cabinetmaker, 183
Williams, Elisha, minister, 322–323
Williams, Elisha, house, 400
Williams, Sheriff Ezekiel, owner, 399–400
Williams College Museum of Art, Williamstown, Mass., related example in, 112
Willing, Thomas, owner, 363
Willing family, owners, 363
Wilmington, Del., 204, 428
Windsor, Conn., 84; box, 60
Wineck, Sam, dealer, 390
Winick and Sherman, dealers, 225
Winship, Joseph, restorer, 379

Winterthur Museum, Winterthur, Del., related examples in, 88, 106, 115, 137, 139, 145, 150, 153, 217, 219, 227, 230, 239, 245, 247, 250, 283, 295, 314, 343, 360–361, 422, 450
Winthrop family, owners, 304
Wistar, Caspar, 202
Wolcott, Frederick, Litchfield, Conn., 139–140
Wolcott, Betsy (Huntington), Litchfield, Conn., 139–140
Wolcott, Laura M. (Rankin), owner, 139–140
Woodbury, Conn., high chest, 261–63
Woodward, Abishai, cabinetmaker, 274
Worcester, Mass., 166
Wormley, Edward, designer, 160–161, 440–442
Wyer, William C., owner, 303
Wynkoop, Christina, owner, 227
Wynkoop, Henry, owner, 227, 283
Wynkoop, Susanna Wanshaer, owner, 227

Yale Collection of Musical Instruments, 452
Yale Corporation, 363
Yale Divinity School, 329–330
Yale Medical School Library, 372–373
Yale School of Forestry and Environmental Studies, 430
Yale School of the Fine Arts, 92
Yellow poplar: as primary wood, 79, 100, 102, 111, 116, 117, 118, 242, 244, 262, 393; as secondary wood, 72, 78, 137, 140, 141, 147, 152, 154, 155, 156, 160, 188, 190, 192, 193, 207, 212, 213, 217, 221, 222, 224, 225, 226, 230, 231, 232, 246, 251, 252, 261, 265, 269, 274, 282, 284, 295, 310, 313, 317, 323, 325, 332, 348, 358, 360, 369, 372, 373, 381, 385, 392, 401, 405, 407, 409, 410, 411, 419, 421, 423, 424, 426, 428, 430, 432, 435, 442, 450, 452, 453
Yorkshire, England, carving traditions, 63–64, 97

Zebrawood, 308, 426
Zenith radios, 454

Index **483**

PHOTOGRAPH CREDITS

UNLESS OTHERWISE NOTED BELOW, ALL PHOTOGRAPHS ARE BY CHARLES UHT.

E. IRVING BLOMSTRANN Cats. 15, 18, 18a, 60, 61, 82, 91, 106, 131, 131a, 136, 137, 147, 172, 172a, 188, 191, 195, 197a, 199, 210, 214, 214a, 214b, 215, 215a, 215b, 217, 217a, 217b, 217c, 218, 221, 225; plates 7, 8, 14, 17, 23, 25; app. 20, 23.

FREDERICK BUSH Cat. 205a

E. DECUSATI App. 15

PATRICIA E. KANE Cat. 177c

MUSEUM OF MODERN ART Fig. 4

SOCIETY FOR THE PRESERVATION OF NEW ENGLAND ANTIQUITIES Fig. 2

GEORGE DUDLEY SEYMOUR Fig. 3

JOSEPH SZASZFAI Cats. 224, 229; app. 7, 8

UNKNOWN Cats. 26c, 66a, 160b, 231a; fig. 1; app. 3, 4, 14, 17, 24, 26

EDITED BY PATRICIA R. LISK
DRAWINGS BY WILLIAM J. MACINTIRE

This book was composed on the Monotype machine in Dante types by Michael & Winifred Bixler. The typeface known as Dante was designed 1946–52 by the late scholar-printer Dr. Giovanni Mardersteig for use at his distinguished private press, the Officina Bodoni of Verona, Italy. The present version of this type was adapted for mechanical composition from original punches cut by hand in Paris by Charles Malin.

PRINTED BY MERIDEN-STINEHOUR PRESS
BOUND BY A. HOROWITZ & SONS · BOOKBINDERS
DESIGN & TYPOGRAPHY BY HOWARD I. GRALLA

icon design

icon design

STEVE CAPLIN

SERIES CONSULTANT
ALASTAIR CAMPBELL

CASSELL&CO

First published in the United Kingdom in 2001 by Cassell & Co

Copyright © 2001 The Ivy Press Limited and Alastair Campbell

All rights reserved. No part of this publication may be reproduced in any material form (including photocopying or storing it in any medium by electronic means and whether or not transiently or incidentally to some other use of this publication) without the written permission of the copyright owner, except in accordance with the provisions of the Copyright, Designs and Patents Act 1988 or under the terms of a licence issued by the Copyright Licensing Agency, 90 Tottenham Court Road, London W1P 9HE. Applications for the copyright owner's written permission to reproduce any part of this publication should be addressed to the publisher.

Trademarks and trademark names are used throughout this book to describe and inform you about various proprietary products. Such mention is intended to benefit the owner of the trademark and is not intended to infringe copyright nor to imply any claim to the mark other than that made by its owner.

The information contained in this book is given without warranty and, while every precaution has been taken in compiling the book, neither the author nor publisher assume any responsibility or liability whatsoever to any person or entity with respect to any errors which may exist in the book, nor for any loss of data which may occur as the result of such errors or for the efficacy or performance of any product or process described in the book.

The author would like to thank all the professional and shareware designers whose work is featured in this book – both those who have given their permission and those who I've been unable to contact. My particular gratitude goes to Susan Kare, without whose pioneering designs the computing experience would be far poorer.

A CIP catalogue record for this book is available from the British Library
ISBN 0-304-35420-1

This book was conceived, designed and produced by Alastair Campbell and The Ivy Press Limited
The Old Candlemakers
West Street, Lewes
East Sussex BN7 2NZ

Editorial Director:
Sophie Collins
Art Director:
Peter Bridgewater
Managing Editor:
April McCroskie
Editor:
Joanna Smith
Designers:
Steve Caplin and
Alastair Campbell

Originated and printed by Hong Kong Graphic, Hong Kong

Cassell & Co
Wellington House
125 Strand
London WC2R 0BB

CONTENTS

1. ICONIC HISTORY — 10

2. CONTEMPORARY ICONS — 34

3. PICK & MIX — 84

4. INTERNET ICONS — 104

5. CASE STUDIES — 118

6. DESIGNING ICONS — 132

7. REFERENCE — 178

INTRODUCTION
THE NEED FOR A GRAPHICAL USER INTERFACE

```
C:\>

C:\>autoexec.bat

C:\>c:\TSRfix.exe

C:\>mode con codepage prepare=((850) C:\WINDOWS\COMMAND\ega.cpi)

MODE prepare code page function completed

C:\>mode con codepage select=850

MODE select code page function completed

C:\>keyb uk,,C:\WINDOWS\COMMAND\keyboard.sys
Loading NAVDX, please wait...
Norton AntiVirus startup scan...

Using options from C:\PROGRA~1\NORTON~1

Scanning Memory... OK
Scanning Master Boot Records... OK
Scanning Boot Record... OK
Scanning files... DONE

C:\>
C:\>
```

When the pioneers of personal computing switched on the first IBM PCs back in 1981, this was the kind of start-up screen that greeted them. The Microsoft Disk Operating System, MS-DOS, was licensed to IBM by Bill Gates. DOS was Gates' reworking of the earlier QDOS (the acronym for Quick and Dirty Operating System), and was to provide the foundation for the Microsoft empire.

DOS was universal, reasonably stable, and, to the uninitiated, almost impenetrable. The reams of verbiage that poured onto the screen existed to provide feedback on every aspect of the host computer's start-up processes, rolling out line by line as the PC crunched through its tasks. For those new to computing, this dense command-line interface was off-putting in the extreme: computers at that time were far from being the accessible home appliances of today.

The smiling face shown below is all that appeared on the screens of Apple Macintosh computers when they launched in 1984. This single image replaced the dense lines of code fired at DOS users: but it served precisely the same function.

Both the DOS screens and the 'Smiley Mac', as it came to be known, existed to reassure the user that all was well. DOS spelled out every test, every software audit and every internal process; a checklist of

possible error-inducing situations that were passed or failed one step at a time. Even today, PCs run through an almost identical routine before the Windows environment takes over.

Apple takes the opposite approach. They recognize that people can legitimately use computers without understanding or caring how they work, just as motorists can drive powerful cars while knowing nothing about the mechanics involved. As long as everything is operating smoothly, there's no need to tell the users about it. If there is a problem, then they would be alerted with a message.

This, in a nutshell, is the essence of the computer icon. It is a visual simplification of a complex process. The ancient adage that a picture tells a thousand words is singularly appropriate. This need-to-know approach fuelled the development of the graphical user interface (GUI), concealing from the user all but the most essential information.

As far as icons are concerned, the start-up process is, literally, just the beginning. To open a document using DOS, the user would have to type in a complex string of commands that precisely defined the path to the chosen object – starting with the name of the disk, and laboriously listing each directory and subdirectory until the destination file was pinpointed. A single typing error meant that the command would be invalid. Under the GUI system, the user simply located the icon (which could be placed wherever it was most convenient) and double-clicked it to launch the file or application.

Today, icons exist for every aspect of the computer experience. There are icons for applications, for documents and for folders. There are icons for control panels, settings files, printer drivers and hard disks. All these are executable items: you double-click them to activate them. But there are also icons for processes, alerts, tools and tasks. Animations may show a document being printed, or a file being downloaded from the Internet, or even the computer executing a complex operation. Despite the fact that this visual language is less than two decades old, it has evolved a rich and complex vocabulary, with an identifiable grammar. Graphical concepts that went out on a limb when they were first introduced have now become part of the mainstream language: as users become more and more used to the iconography, so the system becomes more refined and more subtle.

The grammar of icons is based largely on the original Apple model. So any vertical rectangular shape with a turned-down corner represents a document; the presence of 'radio buttons' indicates a settings file, and so on. In recent years the internet has come to be represented by a globe, which may be attached to many kinds of icons – such as letters or envelopes to indicate an email application, or a newspaper to identify a newsgroup application.

In the main, computer icons are of a uniform size: 32 pixels across, 32 pixels down. Yet within this area of just 1024 tiny dots there exists 2 to the power of 1024 possibilities – which is many more than the number of stars in the known universe. Add the colour element, and that number is multiplied beyond imaginable bounds. And yet this data is displayed within an area of around 1cm ($\frac{1}{2}$ inch) square.

Within those tiny confines the icon designer has to define the type of object to which it refers, portray the use to which the application can be put, and make the image distinctive and different to the icons of competing applications. And all this while frequently having the additional burden of making the icon harmonize with other software produced by the same developer, matching colour, shape or house style.

Yet in spite of all these restrictions, icons can be images of great subtlety and artistry. They can effectively

INTRODUCTION

communicate the most complex of ideas in a simple, elegant manner that transcends the boundaries of language and culture. The balance is a fine one: leave out essential information and an icon can be misleading; try to cram in too much data and it can simply be confusing. The icon designer's task is to reduce visual elements to their barest essentials, searching for the leanest, most concise way of representing an idea.

Icon designers use all sorts of tricks to get their message across. Metaphors, allegory and visual puns are all ways of retrieving correspondences from deep in the user's subconscious. Some icons accurately depict objects in the real world: printer drivers, for example, will frequently aim to be exact reproductions, in miniature, of the hardware they control. Others can be startlingly abstract, representing ideals that are often patently unattainable by the software to which they are attached.

Computer icons may be relatively new, but the origins of the iconic form can be traced back thousands of years. Hieroglyphics were the first recorded instances of abstract concepts reduced to tiny, simplified images. In Chapter One, we'll look at the history of icons as it progressed through petroglyphs, hallmarks and naval flags to the internationally recognized symbols on video and audio equipment. We will then trace the history of the computer icon from the earliest days, and discuss the recognizability theory of icons: what makes an icon work? How descriptive must an icon be in order to function? How abstract can the design become? Special attention will be paid to the early MacPaint icons: the first of their kind, but still used in today's graphics applications.

In Chapter Two we will look more closely at toolbar icons, which are used to represent the everyday tools used in graphics, word processing and page layout applications. Many of these are based on the earliest Macintosh designs; some, particularly in the arena of 3-D modelling applications, take the form to a new level of sophistication. We then go on to look at the development from Apple through Windows to the 128-pixel icons of Macintosh OS X. We will also examine the miniature world of pointer icons, that often overlooked, but most vital of fields. These are the different forms taken by the cursor as it operates different tools in a variety of applications, subtly

Above A typical DOS screen showing a file directory.

indicating both the tool and its current mode of operation. The most common type of icon is the application icon, which describes and identifies the application to which it is attached. But application icons consist of more than just a single design: in many cases each file type saved by the application, each preference and settings file, each dictionary and colour model has its own matching icon. It's the extended icon set that makes up the unique suite for each application, and

Above The same data displayed in Windows. The advantage of the graphical user interface is clear: rather than wading through screens of incomprehensible text, the icons at least give a clue to the purpose of the files to which they are attached.

Chapter Three looks at some of the best and most used examples of the form. As well as those icons created for specific software applications, there's a huge range painstakingly drawn by enthusiasts and made freely available over the Internet. Here we will also dip into the vast array of free icons that you can use to enhance your desktop.

The Internet itself offers icons with the one ingredient missing from the standard desktop: animation. Chapter Four looks at a selection of the best animated icons used to decorate websites.

Several case studies in Chapter Five provide an insight into the world of the professional icon designer, from a variety of different standpoints. For example, Susan Kare, who designed the original Macintosh interface, is the designer who brought the GUI interface to reality. At the other end of the business is Katja Rimmi, Head of Interface Design at Adobe Systems, who is responsible for generating and maintaining a complex set of icons across multiple applications.

Finally, Chapter Six will look at the design process itself, examining the constraints imposed by the 32-pixel size. We'll dissect the creative development of a typical suite of icons to show what's possible, what's desirable and what's the most effective way of communicating using this most concise of visual forms.

Steve Caplin
London 2001

10

THE INVENTION OF THE STYLIZED IMAGE • 12

THE NEXT STEP ICONS FOR ESOTERIC USE • 14

UNIVERSAL RECOGNITION • 16

CROSSING THE LANGUAGE BARRIER • 18

THE FIRST COMPUTER ICONS • 20

TOOLBARS THE MACPAINT PARADIGM • 22

RECOGNIZABILITY THE THEORY OF ICON DESIGN • 26

MEANING IS USE – SOMETIMES • 30

PICK A LETTER – OR A NUMBER... • 32

ICONIC HISTORY

11

ICONIC HISTORY
THE INVENTION OF THE STYLIZED IMAGE

Long before the invention of the written word, people committed their thoughts and deeds to posterity by painting. Early cave paintings, such as those in the Chauvet Cave in the Ardèche region of France, date back over 30,000 years, and may even predate the spoken word.

These cave paintings were strongly naturalistic, providing as much detail as possible in order to reproduce accurately the animals and events depicted. But as the needs of communication changed from mere depiction to accounting and history, the images became more and more stylized until they no longer depicted but represented the objects concerned.

Pictograms – pictures that showed individual objects – were soon supplemented by ideograms, which represented not the object but a sensation or idea suggested by it

1 | 2
Egyptian hieroglyphics (*above*) show the degree of simplicity icons achieved: complex ideas became stylized drawings.
Aleph (*right*) and Bet (*far right*), the first two characters of the Hebrew alphabet, originally represented an ox (you can make out its horns) and a house (it's clearly an enclosing structure).

3
Hawaiian petroglyphs a continent away used a similar iconic system for recording information.

THE INVENTION OF THE STYLIZED IMAGE

(the use of the sun, for instance, to represent heat). These images share much in common with today's computer icons. Of largely uniform size, these simplified drawings were instantly recognizable in their day – with the advantage that picture-writing transcended language barriers (although, in the case of Egyptian hieroglyphics, the images had become so stylized that their meaning was entirely lost until the translation of the Rosetta Stone in 1822).

Hieroglyphics appeared in Mesopotamia, Romania, Iran, the Americas and Egypt in about 3000BC. While the characters soon came to represent individual phonetic sounds as well as objects (so that names, for instance, could be written), the Mayan and Aztec ideograms continued to use separate pictures for each concept until well into the 16th century. Chinese and Japanese characters, even today, are based on ancient scripts that were purely representational. In many languages, icons represented both objects and letters: so the first two letters of the Hebrew alphabet, Aleph and Bet (from which we ultimately, via Greek, derive our word 'alphabet') also mean, respectively, 'ox' and 'house' – which, with a pinch of imagination, they can be seen to resemble.

4
Japanese characters have become so far removed from the objects they originally denoted that no amount of scrutiny could reveal what these packages contain.

5
The so-called 'Newspaper Rock' in Utah is a huge area of intricate icon 'text' carved into a cliff wall. The carvings were carried out by a variety of peoples over generations, beginning about 1,500 years ago.

ICONIC HISTORY

THE NEXT STEP: ICONS FOR ESOTERIC USE

Even long after the written word became the universal means of communication, iconic images continued to be used for specialized purposes. The Royal Navy developed its pictorial code of flags, in which each flag represented both a letter and a declaration, during the Napoleonic Wars: these icons had to be learnt rather than intuited, but as there were so few of them this posed little problem.

Trade organizations developed their own icons that were often deliberately obscure, so that their meaning was apparent only to the initiated. The use of hallmarks on gold and silver, started by Edward I in 1300, serves to show both the purity and the date of manufacture of an item. Since 1478, a single letter has been used to show the creation date, using different letter styles within differently shaped shields each 26 years as the end of the alphabet is reached.

Almost every trade and profession has its own set of icons. Alchemists used icons to represent the various elements; astronomers still use icons to depict the planets and stars. Recognizability and compactness of form are paramount: a circle with a dot in it, representing the sun, is far quicker to find on a crowded map of the heavens than the word it replaces.

The iconography of heraldry, still jealously protected in England by the Royal College of Arms, is a precise art

1
Alchemical symbols were designed to be esoteric, mystic devices understood only by the select few: worse still, the designs varied considerably from country to country.

2 | 3 | 4 | 5
Naval flags indicate both a letter of the alphabet and a common phrase. Clockwise from top left: F (I am disabled; communicate with me); L (you should stop your vessel immediately); G (I require a pilot or I am hauling nets); Y (I am dragging my anchor).

6
The arms of William Shakespeare, granted to him in 1606, and originally conferred on his father in 1596. As with many devices in heraldry, this plays on the pun on his name – the spear motif originated in tournaments.

THE NEXT STEP: ICONS FOR ESOTERIC USE

whereby each emblem, colour and motif within a coat of arms relates to a specific deed or action. A diagonal band from top left to bottom right (the 'bar sinister') signifies bastardy; arms displayed on a lozenge rather than a shield signify those of a widow. To make matters worse, no two men can hold the same coat of arms at one time – the arms of a son have to be different to those of his father during his lifetime.

One of the most successful and long-lasting uses of icons has been in musical notation. Essentially a graph of time (x-axis) against pitch (y-axis), music has been written down since the seventh century, when plainsong was shown by dots above the text. Modern musical notation, using different symbols for different note lengths, was invented by the Benedictine monk Guido d'Arrezzo in the 11th century. It was he, incidentally, who also came up with the Do Re Mi system to help singers learn new tunes. Originally Ut Re Mi Fa Sol La, the names were based on the first lines of a ninth-century hymn: UT queant laxis REsonare fibris MIra gestorum FAmuli tuorum, SOLve polluti LAbii reatum (the Ut was later changed to Do for Dominus). Musical notation continued to be refined over the centuries, by such innovators as Mozart's father Leopold, who contributed the double dot.

7
The opening bars of Beethoven's Fifth Symphony, shown both in standard musical notation and as a simple graph of the same data. The top version is clearly far easier to take in when sightreading.

8
Hallmarks on gold and silver serve to indicate the date and place of manufacture.

ICONIC HISTORY
UNIVERSAL RECOGNITION

Some icons have become so ingrained in the public consciousness that we recognize them almost as if they were part of the language. Take the symbols on playing cards, for instance: the heart and diamond may be seen as truly representative (although even the heart shape is an iconic device that bears little resemblance to the original blood-pumping organ), but what of the spade? Has there ever been a digging implement with that bizarre shape? And does that club have anything in common with the weapon of the same name? These symbols are now too well known to warrant a second glance, and yet there must have been a time when their meaning needed to be explained. Strange though they may be, playing cards appear in many cultures: while the letters indicating the royal cards may change, the hearts, spades, diamonds and clubs are universal.

Icons can be specific, esoteric, arcane and even obtuse. But arguably none carries so much weight as the icon of a country – its flag. Certainly, none is so furiously argued over. And yet the flags of major countries today have evolved over time to reach their current form: the United States flag, to take the best-known example, has added a star (and therefore had to change the geometric layout of stars it contains) each time a new state was added to the union.

The Union Flag, often referred to as the Union Jack, itself underwent a series of changes. The white saltire on a blue background, the flag of the patron saint of Scotland, St Andrew, was added to the simple cross of St George (the flag of England) in 1606, with the accession of James I (James VI of Scotland) to symbolize the new unity between the two countries. And it was not until

1
The icons on playing cards are familiar to people of all cultures from childhood.

2 | 3
The flag of Great Britain as it appeared before 1801 (2), and the version in use today (3).

1801, after the union of Great Britain and Ireland, that the cross of St Patrick was included in the design.

In a time when illiteracy was prevalent, trade icons were important to give passers-by an indication of the business being conducted within. Many were strictly representational – a hanging key for a locksmith, a pair of spectacles for an optician. Others, such as the three golden balls for a pawnbroker (deriving, apparently, from the coat of arms of the Medici family) are not so intuitive. For most people, the icon of note was the local pub sign, which provided both a visual reference for those unable to read the name and a unique identifier for the pub. The more outrageous the pub's name, the easier it was to remember: and so we get the Frog and Nightgown, the Queen's Head and Artichoke, and a host of other implausible pairings.

In some specialized situations, the need for speed of recognition is more important than ease of comprehension. Road signs typify this requirement. A directive must be taken in and understood while the viewer is driving past it at great speed, and there simply isn't time to read words or decipher complex images.

In extreme cases, such as the No Entry sign pictured below, the original sign, complete with written instruction 'No Entry', was eventually altered to have the wording removed. The new sign may have to be learnt, but if the viewer is going at any speed the text would simply be too distracting; and it's almost impossible to see text without reading it.

The detail of road signage may vary from country to country, but the essential designs are universal – a fact we'll examine in the next chapter.

6
Public house signs served to identify the inn for an illiterate population, while providing an image that would stick in the mind.

4 | 5
The original (4) and the 'iconized' (5) versions of the same sign. Dropping the wording increases speed of recognition.

ICONIC HISTORY
CROSSING THE LANGUAGE BARRIER

Quantum leaps in transportation and communications technology in the late 20th century have enabled large corporations to virtually ignore international boundaries. Such was the boom in manufacturing that the demands of vast global concerns made it financially impractical to localize products for specific countries. Once it was no longer viable to print words in a variety of languages on products, another solution had to be found: and so the icon, as a means of mass communication, was reborn.

The icons used on video recorders, tape recorders and CD players are prime examples of the type. Some of the images are intuitive – Play, Fast Forward and Rewind all depict their purpose. But those for Stop (a square), Record (a circle) and Pause (two vertical bars) are far from clear: their meaning must be learnt. But despite their initially impenetrable appearance, these icons have, in the space of a couple of decades, become some of the most highly recognized symbols in the world. Even though the icons usually still have their function printed above them in English (the largest single market for such technology), the symbols are intelligible in any language.

Today, icons abound: on mobile phones, washing machines, microwave ovens, packets of frozen food, electrical appliances (I and O having replaced the words On and Off) – the list grows almost daily.

Corporate logos, such as those for Nike, McDonalds and Apple, have become so widely recognized that the company name now rarely appears with it in advertising

1
The icons on video recorders, CD players and tape decks are universally recognizable.

2
Applications such as Adobe After Effects mimic these icons and appearance for ease of recognition.

material – a sure test of the icon's strength. Achieving this degree of market penetration depends upon a huge marketing budget, but also requires a logo that is both simple and unique.

Some corporations manage to take mere recognition of their logo as the starting point for something altogether more pervasive: the perception of the logo as a desirable entity in itself.

Arguably none has achieved this somewhat dubious goal as effectively as sports equipment manufacturer Nike, for whom heavy investment in advertising has paid off in the most spectacular way: eager to show their brand loyalty, boys worldwide shave the company's logo into the backs of their heads.

Just how cool can a logo get?

3
Apple's software DVD player is an almost exact copy of the control panel from a video recorder.

4
The Nike logo is universally recognized due to extensive advertising. The logo itself has become an entity in its own right.

5
The Nike logo is so well known that this outlet in Japan has no need to spell out the word in letters.

ICONIC HISTORY

THE FIRST COMPUTER ICONS

The smiling face is the icon that greeted proud owners of their new Apple Macintosh 128K computers in 1984. From the start, it was clear this was a completely new direction in the computing experience. Gone was the clumsy, text-driven command line interface: in its place a cheerful, grinning icon.

This icon appeared as soon as the computer was switched on and the floppy system disk inserted (hard drives were too costly to build into the machines).

As well as providing a cute icon to look at while the computer started up, it performed another function: to reassure the user that the system disk had indeed been found, that the software was loading correctly – in short, that all was well.

The fact that the simple icon was also an exact representation of the computer on which it appeared was another clever branding exercise. Up until this point the majority of computers – including the so-called IBM compatibles – had been modular items, with trailing cables linking the CPU, monitor and floppy disk drive. Here at last was an all-in-one solution in a user-friendly case.

Building the entire machine into a single box made the idea of using computers non-threatening for the first time ever. It's a formula that has won Apple users ever since: the best-selling iMac, which single-handedly revived Apple's fortunes on its release in 1998, was another all-in-one machine. And yet the iMac, like all Apple computers, still starts up with the icon shown here (right) as a homage to the origins of the company.

A screen from the Apple Lisa computer, the immediate predecessor of the Macintosh, showing the beginnings of the graphical user interface.

And yet, in truth, the Macintosh was not the first computer to use a graphical user interface – nor even the first Apple computer to do so.

The GUI was first dreamed up in the 1950s, and was developed in the 1970s at Xerox Palo Alto Research Center (PARC). The Alto, the first prototype computer to use a graphical interface, was the size of a piano and Xerox believed it to be unmarketable. Steve Jobs, co-founder of Apple, saw the Alto on a visit to PARC in 1979, and he liked what he saw.

In January 1993 Apple launched the Lisa computer, with its ground-breaking (if by today's standards rudimentary) interface. The screen shot (left) shows the Draw application open, with the desktop in the background. Already, the fundamentals of the GUI system are in place: the WasteBasket (later renamed Trash in the US) for throwing away documents, piles of paper to represent files, a 'clipboard' to store copied items, and a 'desktop' behind it all. It was a near-perfect metaphor for the conventional office layout, designed as far as possible to represent the user's desk.

This concept was not only innovative, it was a stroke of genius. Making the files, programs, controls and even the 'delete file' command into everyday objects demystified computers at a stroke. As coherent metaphors go, this one was hard to beat: so utterly appropriate was it that it formed the basis for the model still used by computers worldwide today – not just by Apple, but in the operating system owned by its far larger and more powerful adversary, Microsoft.

THE FIRST COMPUTER ICONS

1
The 'Smiley Mac' icon that welcomes users when they switch on their Macintosh computers.

2 | 3 | 4
Applications (*2*) created documents (*3*) which were stored in folders (*4*). Although this now seems the obvious way to do things, it's a far cry from the DOS system of programs, files and directories accessed by laboriously typed keyboard commands.

5 | 6
Fonts were 'carried' from place to place in suitcases (*5*). To move a suitcase from one place to another, the Font/DA Mover was used – in the shape of a truck (*6*). Why? Because when you move house, you transport your suitcases in a removals lorry.

ICONIC HISTORY

TOOLBARS: THE MACPAINT PARADIGM

MacPaint was the graphics program shipped with early Macintosh computers. As a 'bitmap' editor, it allowed users to draw on screen by turning pixels on or off – that is, by changing their colour from white to black. (As a matter of interest, MacPaint still works on Macintosh computers today – despite the fact that it takes up just 64K on disk.)

What interests us, of course, are the icons. A lasso? A marquee? A tipping paint can? These symbols must have seemed bizarre at the time, but they are all, with some minor adjustments, precisely the icons that remain in use today in the state-of-the-art graphics programs – such as Adobe Photoshop, MetaCreations Painter and CorelDraw – that take MacPaint as their starting point.

The original MacPaint interface, shown at actual size. Macintoshes then had 9-inch black and white screens.

Marquee

The Marquee tool is used for making rectangular selections, drawn from corner to corner. The selected area is indicated on the drawing by an enlarged version of the tool icon, with one main difference: it's now animated. The array of dashes and spaces, known as 'marching ants', chase each other around the perimeter, which helps to indicate that this is a selection, rather than part of the drawing.

What of the name 'marquee'? This marquee is not the large tent hired for weddings, but is named after the arrays of lightbulbs that appear around the titles and stars outside theatres. When set to flash on and off, these lights appear to chase each other around the rectangle they enclose – just like the marching ants of the MacPaint tool.

Lasso

The Lasso is a tool for creating irregular, freeform selections drawn with the mouse. Like the Marquee, its selection boundary is shown in animated form, using the same marching ants.

Again, though, what of the name? The answer, once again: consider the function. A lasso is a length of rope used primarily by cowboys for 'selecting' cattle in a field. Being rope, it can take any shape, and it's part of the peculiar nature of a lasso that, thanks to an ingenious slip-knot device, its length can be varied according to requirements. Unlike any other length of rope, a lasso always forms a complete enclosure – just as the tool does in MacPaint. Trace with the Lasso tool and a selection line is drawn: but let go of the mouse button and the beginning and end are joined to form a loop. Once again, both the name and the icon for the tool prove to be apt metaphors for the tool's operation.

'Grabber' hand

MacPaint had no scrollbars with which to move the area viewed on screen. This caused a significant problem: users were commonly printing to either A4- or US Letter-sized paper, but viewing the document within a portion of a tiny 9-inch monitor. How would the user then access the remainder of the printable area?

Think of the window as just that – a window, through which the paper is seen. What could be more natural than to raise your hand to grab the paper and move it around?

A good enhancement of the grabber hand (in some applications) was a feature that made the fingers clench as the mouse button was held down, to show the hand actually grabbing the paper.

This icon has proved so viable that its use has spread far beyond drawing and painting programs. Even QuarkXPress, despite its refusal to follow convention, uses this identical grabber hand for exactly the same purpose.

ICONIC HISTORY

Text tool

To use a letter of the alphabet to indicate the text-entry tool is an obvious choice: but which letter, and which typeface?

The choice of typeface, loosely Times Bold, is a deliberate decision to not use an obvious 'computer' face. By not making the icon appear futuristic but settling for an old-fashioned, cosy alternative, the icon bears out one of the primary rules of icon design: choose the familiar over the innovative wherever possible.

Times is still the font used to portray equivalent icons in most applications today, although the choice of letter varies between A (the natural choice, being the first letter in the alphabet) and T (standing for Text). Adobe applications prefer T; others, such as QuarkXPress, have stuck to A.

Right The MacPaint application icon, clearly showing the program's function while conforming to the standard application icon design.

Paint bucket

The Bucket tool fills bounded areas with the currently selected colour or pattern. 'Bounded' in this instance means any area entirely surrounded by black pixels: a white gap of even one pixel's width would cause the paint bucket tool to 'leak' into the surrounding area, usually flooding the illustration with the pattern. But hey, after all, that's what the Undo key is for.

It's the 'flooding' metaphor that gives the bucket its resonance. Unlike a brush, used laboriously to paint an area bit by bit, paint tipped from a bucket will fill a space almost instantly. And if that space is bounded, say by a casually discarded lasso, then the bucket will operate only within that area.

Spray can

The Spray Can paints an irregular array of dots within a confined and roughly circular area, and is used to add texture to drawings.

It is partly the roughness of the end result that produced this icon for the tool, and partly an in-built anarchy that was prevalent at Apple at the time: the spray can, after all, is more familiarly used by graffiti artists than car body sprayers.

Technological improvements including colour monitors, pressure-sensitive graphics tablets and an increase in the speed of screen redraw have meant that the equivalent tool's function in contemporary applications has become far smoother. So the icon, inevitably, had to change, making it one of the few MacPaint icons that failed to survive – it is now more generally represented as an artist's airbrush. The airbrush – a difficult tool to render within a tiny graphic grid – is familiar only to those who have seen one, thus excluding most new computer users.

There again, maybe the new icon merely highlights the difference in ethos between anarchic Apple and corporate Adobe.

TOOLBARS: THE MACPAINT PARADIGM

Paintbrush

The Paintbrush is the everyday tool for splashing colour about: a paintbrush is the obvious icon to choose.

But why this large, clumsy decorator's brush, rather than the precise artist's tool? Was it a snide reference to the comparative clumsiness of the tool's function, or yet another instance of Apple's irrepressible sense of humour?

Not a bit of it. For the paintbrush could daub not only black and white, but any of the patterns or simulated shades of grey picked from the pattern palette. This icon serves a dual purpose: it represents both a paintbrush and a wallpaper paste brush – the only way of applying a pattern to a blank wall.

This icon, too, has fallen by the wayside: modern applications uniformly reject it in favour of a true artist's brush. But then the pattern function is taken care of by other means, and the brush has only the single use.

Pencil

The Pencil tool has the curious function of drawing in black when the first pixel drawn upon is white, and drawing in white when the first pixel is black. A tool for precise editing, it serves both to draw and to erase, without the need to switch tool to perform the opposite function.

So why a pencil? Because of the eraser built into the other end, of course. Flip a pencil over and you can rub out the line you've just drawn.

In Photoshop, the ultimate descendent of MacPaint, the pencil tool draws a hard-edged, pixellated line, reflecting the way it performed in MacPaint. It no longer has the erase function, however.

Right It's perhaps surprising that such a simple icon – essentially an extended box – can so accurately depict an eraser, rather than, say, a harmonica, or a bar of chocolate, or a step. But within the context of a drawing application, there's little else in an artist's toolbox that has precisely this shape and form; it may be simple, but it is effective and has lasted to this day.

Straight line

The Line tool draws a straight line between the position of the tool when the mouse button is depressed and the position when the button is released.

The temptation to make the icon either exactly horizontal or exactly vertical must have been immense: after all, it would appear much smoother that way, without the ugly stepping effect brought about by the angle. But an orthogonal (right-angled) design could easily have been confused with a spacer or other graphic device so mere aesthetics had to give way to heightened recognizability.

25

ICONIC HISTORY

RECOGNIZABILITY: THE THEORY OF ICON DESIGN

The icons below are all clearly recognizable as magnifying glasses. They all indicate tools with the same purpose: to zoom in on the artwork in view. More subtly, they're all magnifying glasses as held over the page by right-handed users.

Once an icon has become a paradigm it is virtually unshakeable: individual software developers may tweak the design and customize it to suit their own interface, but it's almost impossible to change it without risking incomprehension on the part of the user. The dialect may vary, but the language remains the same.

There are two schools of thought in the field of icon design – whether on computer screens or on washing machines, on mobile phones or on photocopiers. Either an icon should be immediately recognizable, so that the tool's purpose is self-evident, or the user should have to learn the icon's meaning and then trust that all similar devices will conform to the same graphic language.

Where icons are designed from scratch, users can expect a uniformity of purpose that makes them belong together as a set, as well as giving an easily understood indication of their meaning. Such is usually the case with computer icons; in the real world of telecommunication and household appliances, however, this uniformity is rarely attained and users are often left struggling to decipher a string of incomprehensible designs.

The top row of washing machine icons, right, are clear enough: they indicate the temperatures at which clothes should be washed. The only learned element here is the fact that a single bar beneath the washing bowl stands for synthetics, and a double-dashed bar stands for woollens.

The second row denotes the temperature at which clothes may be ironed. Once again, the meaning is clear: three dots for high temperature, two for medium, and one for low. Once explained, these three icons cannot

1

2

3

4

5

6

7

8

easily be forgotten, and for most users it can safely be assumed that the meaning of the icons would be immediately apparent.

But what of the bottom row? These four icons give no indication whatsoever of their meaning – despite the fact that these are probably the most important of all, from the point of view of caring for your clothes. The letter P in a circle may mean Dry Clean to a dry cleaning operator, but to the end user it's a mystery that must be learned. Worse still are the three crossed out symbols, which denote (from left to right) Do Not Dry Clean, Do Not Bleach and Do Not Tumble Dry. The oversimplification of the symbols has led to complete incomprehensibility: even when learned once, there's nothing about these icons that serves to jog the memory or to confirm one's guess about their purpose.

To the sophisticated computer user, the cleaning symbols shown here are downright laughable. But was MacPaint's Lasso icon any less opaque back in 1984? At least in the field of computer applications, the consequences of misreading an icon are generally more immediately apparent, and certainly involve fewer shrunken pullovers.

Because computers are strange, unknown quantities – at least to novice users – the emphasis must be on familiarity wherever possible. In most cases, this means linking the complex function of a new tool (such as a painting tool which fills bounded areas) with a familiar, everyday object (in this case, a paint pot). To create an icon that is immediately recognizable is one thing: to represent an object with which the user is already comfortable takes the process a significant stage further.

And so the tendency is towards icons depicting deliberately low-tech, often old-fashioned implements as a way of reassuring possibly technophobic users that the new technology is within their grasp. It's hard to be

Left Magnifying glasses from popular applications
1 Painter
2 Photoshop
3 QuarkXPress
4 Macromedia FreeHand
5 CorelDraw
6 Macromedia Flash
7 auto•des•sys form•z
8 MetaCreations Bryce

Right The symbols used on clothes to indicate cleaning requirements are a mixture of the obvious and the downright incomprehensible.

ICONIC HISTORY

frightened of a paint can, or a pencil, or a suitcase: in the Macintosh Font/DA Mover example (see page 21), a removals truck with a cheerful letter A emblazoned on the side makes the otherwise complex process of loading fonts into the system far less daunting.

The Bézier curve, the fundamental drawing tool used by high-end drawing applications, is a sophisticated tool operated by means of anchor points, tangents and direction handles. But from the start this tool was represented in icon form by an old-fashioned ink pen. This need to demystify complex technologies pervades every walk of life. The police speed cameras in use on highways are represented by an archaic box camera of the sort not seen in common use for fifty years. Mobile phones, technologically at the cutting edge of modern telecommunications, represent 'dial' and 'hang up' buttons with the icon of a telephone receiver – but this receiver clearly does not belong to the kind of phone on

1 – 6
Out with the new, in with the old: an archaic icon for the Bézier curve tool (1), together with non-computer icons for a speed camera (2), an electronic camera indicator (3), mobile phone controls (4, 5), and a car horn (6).

which the symbol appears; it is an old-fashioned phone. Even the phrase 'hang up' harks back to the days of the candlestick telephone, when the earpiece was literally hung back on the hook to end the call.

Modern cameras, which use a complex loading mechanism to enable the user to simply drop a new film into place, indicate the presence of a film by an icon showing two linked reels – despite the fact that the user now never sees this process. Car horns, in reality small electrical buzzers, are indicated on the steering wheel by a traditional bugle.

Yet nowhere is the need to demystify more pressing than in the computer environment. Keyboard instructions still talk in terms of 'carriage returns'; email is copied to multiple users using the 'cc' function – an abbreviation for carbon copy; pages of text are scrolled up and down using 'thumbwheels'. The more sophisticated technology becomes, the greater is the need to express it in everyday terms in order to reassure the user. The Wait cursor used in Microsoft Windows is not a high-tech digital clock, nor even its familiar analogue equivalent, but an hourglass; the Macintosh equivalent is an analogue wristwatch.

Apple Remote Access, the powerful networking software developed by Apple to enable both computer-to-computer and Internet connections, is represented by the image of a globe (in common with most Internet applications) adjacent to a telegraph pole, that most old-fashioned of telecommunication devices.

Photoshop's Cloning tool, which smoothly copies one section of an image on top of another, is represented not by a reference to cloning technology but by a rubber stamp of the kind barely seen in the computer age.

Sometimes software developers are so stumped for an idea for an icon that they take a wild leap in the dark. When bitmap programmers first came up with a tool that would automatically select areas of a similar tonal range, they were so impressed with themselves that they called it a Magic Wand, and gave it an icon to match. Everyday objects need not be literally the things we see every day.

Left The icons for Apple Remote Access (7); the Windows Wait icon (8); and Photoshop's Cloning (9) and Magic Wand (10) tools. High-tech they aren't.

ICONIC HISTORY

MEANING IS USE – SOMETIMES

Theories vary as to the purpose of application icons. Some see them as graphic images that will simply serve to identify the product once its icon is learnt; for others, the icon must give a fair indication of the function of the product.

The dozen icons for 3-D modelling applications shown on this page fit into the latter category. The top row shows the icons for traditional, mid-range and heavyweight programs: from left to right, Maxon Cinema4D, auto•des•sys form•z, MetaCreations Infini-D and RayDream Studio. They clearly display three-dimensional objects; indeed, in the case of form•z, it shows nothing else, whereas at least Cinema4D implies its movie-generating capability. The Infini-D icon shows 3-D modelling as an art form (it's on a pedestal) as well as the movie making (the hint of a film strip down the side). The RayDream icon is more tongue-in-cheek, creating its initials from 3-D primitives.

The middle row shows icons for Byte by Byte Sculpt3D, Play Amorphium, VALIS PixelPutty and Jarfish Design's Clayscape. These programs set themselves apart from the standard modelling environment, offering a more naturalistic approach. In the case of Amorphium, the modelling is clearly hands-on.

The 3-D programs shown in the bottom row are for programs that take 3-D model creation in different directions from the norm. The first two, Virtual Reality Laboratories' VistaPro and Bryce, are specialist landscape generators, and their icons indicate this perfectly. The third, Poser, is a figure modelling tool – again, the icon represents the function. The final icon in the set is Carrara, a recent modeller from MetaCreations aimed at making 3-D more acceptable to a wider audience. In reality, Carrara is a rehash of RayDream with a revised interface and some new functionality but the designers have chosen to represent it by using an aspirational

Left Icons from:
1 Cinema4D
2 form•z
3 Infini-D
4 RayDream Studio
5 Sculpt3D
6 Amorphium
7 PixelPutty
8 Clayscape
9 VistaPro
10 Bryce
11 Poser
12 Carrara

Right More descriptive icons:
13 Caere Omnipage
14 Maxis SimCity
15 Macintosh Disk First Aid

MEANING IS USE – SOMETIMES

Left The need to represent an application's function can sometimes overwhelm the icon designer.

image of the kind of complex yet clearly artistic model users might like to build with it. The implication is that Carrara is a tool of the artist rather than the technician.

Many other kinds of application follow this 'meaning is use' approach. Three examples chosen almost at random, and shown opposite, are optical character reader (OCR) package Omnipage, city-building game SimCity, and Apple's disk-recovery program Disk First Aid. In all three cases, the function of the program can be intuited from its icon.

Sometimes, the function of an application is so complex that the icon designer struggles to encapsulate its many features within a single 32-pixel image. At the top of this page are four instances of icons that are so complex their meanings are hard to read. Phonebook Converter, part of the ISDN data transfer application of Hermstedt's Grand Central, links four separate icons together with a bent arrow device. DropStuff, part of Aladdin's Stuffit compression set, shows both a file and a folder dropping into a hand-cranked mill that will produce a Stuffit file – and a portion of the Stuffit icon, a vice compressing a file, is shown dropping out of the bottom. The Preferences file for PG Music's music program Band-in-a-Box reduces the splash screen from the program to a tiny monochromatic rendering that tries to encompass most of an orchestra (at which it fails).

More interesting is the Extensis Portfolio icon. This program allows users to store picture, sound and movie thumbnails within a searchable database, and the icon represents an artist's portfolio containing an example of each – a film spool, a CD and a photograph. By rights, this icon ought not to work, as it is clearly far too complex but somehow the elements do gel, producing a result that, surprisingly, does the job.

Some software developers have turned their backs on the representational scheme altogether, as is shown most notably by the four icons from Macromedia applications shown at the foot of this page. These represent a striking departure from the norm: created by the innovative designer Neville Brody, they're clearly all part of the same set, but go no way towards explaining the function of the programs to which they are attached.

Left A refreshingly different approach: four icons from the Macromedia stable, designed by Neville Brody.

ICONIC HISTORY
PICK A LETTER – OR A NUMBER…

For some icon designers, the easy solution is to build an icon based around the initial letter of the application to which it is appended.

Font developers have followed this route since the earliest days, partly for reasons of convention (that's how font icons ought to look) and partly because the best way a font manufacturer can indicate the purpose of their product is to show a type letter.

Adobe, Bitstream, Monotype and Linotype were the first to produce computer-based fonts commercially. Monotype's original PostScript font icon is one of the more hideous designs to have graced our screens: the TrueType version is somewhat more attractive.

Other, smaller font developers have followed suit – even if the Ampersand Digital Foundry's icon turns the initials into a background design.

For other software developers, it's largely a matter of who got there first. Once Microsoft had staked its claim on the letter W for its word processing application Word, it would be unthinkable for others to copy the form. Similarly, Apple all but cornered the Q market with QuickTime and QuickDraw 3D, although that didn't stop CE Software using a different version of the letter Q for its macro program QuicKeys.

Adobe's A (first used for its fonts) returned in lower case italic form for Adobe Type Manager, appeared briefly in the file icons for its drawing program Illustrator, and eventually turned into the company's corporate logo in a greatly stylized form.

A few designers choose to brand each new release with a unique number. The problem is clearly shown in the case of the Adobe After Effects icons, opposite. With each upgrade, the entire suite of icons must be redesigned to ensure that every component includes the new number: it's a time-consuming process which adds little to the user experience.

Left Icons for fonts published by:
1 Adobe
2 Bitstream
3 Monotype (PostScript version)
4 Monotype (TrueType version)
5 Linotype
6 FontDaFont
7 FontShop
8 Fontek
9 FontBureau
10 Ampersand Digital Foundry

Left Other alphabetical icons:
11 QuicKeys
12 QuickTime
13 QuickDraw3D
14 Action Utilities
15 Adobe Type Manager
16 Microsoft Word
17 Microsoft Internet Explorer
18 Avid Elastic Reality
19 MetaCreations LogoMotion
20 Strider Typestyler

PICK A LETTER – OR A NUMBER...

Above and **below**
The suites of icons for versions 3 and 4 of Adobe After Effects. All the component icons have to be redrawn for each new release.

33

PAINT APPLICATION TOOLS • 36
DRAW APPLICATION TOOLS • 38
WORD-PROCESSING & PAGE-LAYOUT TOOLS • 40
3-D APPLICATION TOOLS • 42
3-D THE METACREATIONS SOLUTION • 44
ANIMATED TOOL ICONS • 46
WINDOWS V MACINTOSH • 48
MACINTOSH SYSTEM ICONS • 52
THE NEXT MAC OS • 54
POINTER ICONS • 56
POINTER ICONS – WORTH THE WAIT • 60
CURSOR ICONS & TOOL VARIANTS • 62
POINTER ICONS THE NEXT STEP • 64
APPLICATION ICONS FAMILY RESEMBLANCES • 66
APPLICATION ICONS THE EXTENDED SET • 68
ADOBE ILLUSTRATOR • 70
MACROMEDIA FREEHAND • 72
COREL DRAW/PAINT • 74
QUARKXPRESS • 76
METACREATIONS • 78
NETSCAPE NAVIGATOR & INTERNET EXPLORER • 80
WORD-PROCESSOR APPLICATIONS • 82

CONTEMPORARY ICONS

35

CONTEMPORARY ICONS
PAINT APPLICATION TOOLS

As has been stated earlier, all graphics applications ultimately owe their design and, in particular, their icon set, to MacPaint. Nowhere is this more true than in painting programs, the natural descendants of that early bitmap editor.

Many of the common tools can be traced directly back to MacPaint, and not just the obvious ones: the lasso, the grabber hand and the tipping paint bucket are all icons that make sense only if you've already learnt the vocabulary.

Other icons have emerged over the years and have become standardized through general acceptance. The Pen (see following pages) is not the only new icon to have achieved widespread usage. The Crop icon is now widely used, and has become easily understood. Represented by two intersecting corners with a diagonal line drawn through them, it's one of the few icons that has no link to any object in the physical world. The Magic Wand, a tool that finds adjacent pixels of similar colour, may have seemed magical when it first appeared; today its function is mundane. The Eyedropper icon, too, has become ubiquitous, despite the image's link to the tool's purpose being particularly tenuous. The tool samples the colour of the pixel directly beneath its 'hot spot', and the icon uses the metaphor of the eyedropper sucking up the colour from the page.

As the examples here show, the key icons for common tools have a striking degree of uniformity.

2 | 3
The toolbox from Painter 6. Beneath it is shown the Brushes palette from the same program, which uses a far more illustrative technique to enhance the 'real life' feel of Painter's tools.

1
The widely accepted and used icon for the Crop tool.

PAINT APPLICATION TOOLS

4
The toolbar icons in Photoshop all have variants that change the tool's function. Shown here is the full set of tool icons expanded next to the main toolbar.

5 | 6 | 7
The toolbar icons from Jasc Paint Shop Pro (5), Windows Paint (6) and CorelPaint (7). Both Paint Shop and Paint retain the spray can icon for the Airbrush tool, as originally used in MacPaint.

4

5

6

7

CONTEMPORARY ICONS
DRAW APPLICATION TOOLS

Draw tools, like paint tools, have formed their own set of conventions for icon depiction. Some are designed to be intuitive, and vary slightly between applications: you need only compare the transformation tools in Illustrator and FreeHand, for instance, to see that while they are clearly based on the same concepts, they are variations rather than identical copies of each other. Both use a circle with an anticlockwise-pointing arrowhead for the Rotate tool; both use a triangle reflected across a vertical line for the Reflect tool; both show rectangles of differing sizes for the Scale tool, and so on. Users of one program would have no difficulty getting to grips with the other, which is precisely the point: the need to tempt users from another application is paramount.

The basis of modern drawing applications is the Pen tool, used for drawing Bézier paths. This tool (and its icon) originated in Adobe Illustrator in 1987. Back then, it seemed a curious choice of image: Bézier curves are editable, flexible shapes that can be changed after they have been drawn. So why use a deliberately old-fashioned nib pen? One answer may be that the Bézier curve belongs properly to 'draw' (object-oriented) programs as opposed to 'paint' (bitmap) programs, previously indicated by such iconic devices as a pair of compasses and set squares. This pen is clearly not a technical drawing instrument (such as a Rotring pen) confined to drawing straight lines and ellipses: seen as a dip pen, rather than a fountain pen, it represents an artist's rather than a draughtsman's tool. As the examples above show, the designs for this icon used by major illustration applications vary only in the finest detail: while no two Pen icons are precisely identical, there's little to differentiate them.

7 | 8
Toolbar icons from CorelDraw (7) and FreeHand (8).

1 – 6
Variations on the icon for the Pen tool, the staple of drawing applications:
1 Adobe Illustrator
2 QuarkXPress
3 MetaCreations Painter
4 Macromedia FreeHand
5 CorelPaint
6 Deneba Canvas

DRAW APPLICATION TOOLS

9 | 10
Toolbars in both Illustrator (9) and Canvas (10) have been made in 'tear-off' form – that is, by clicking on the arrow next to an icon you can not only select a variant of the tool from a pop-up display, but also drag it into a separate floating palette. If you don't mind screen clutter, this is a useful way to give instant access to the precise tools you need.

39

9

10

CONTEMPORARY ICONS

WORD-PROCESSING & PAGE-LAYOUT TOOLS

Word-processing applications differ from many others in that they have relatively few icons built in. After all, the programs are designed for writing text, and additional tools are few. The icons on this page are from Microsoft Word, showing the main toolbar (with its icons for creating graphs, tables, inserted drawings and so on) as well as the standard icons for left-aligned, centred, right-aligned and justified text.

The two dialogue boxes here show the variations for shadows (applied to text or graphics) and 3-D views of objects. All these settings can be customized by the user, but the simple range of icons serves to provide a useful starting point: they all give an easily understandable indication of the type of effect that will result.

Page-layout applications vary more in their approach. The Adobe PageMaker toolbox opposite (6) clearly lends much of its feel to the expanded toolbox for Adobe's new high-end page-layout program, InDesign (5). This has been launched as a direct competitor to the market leader, QuarkXPress (4), but a glance is enough to show that the two applications share hardly any icons in common.

Adobe has always been keen to provide a consistency of feel for users of its other products, and this aim has been paramount here: where they will suffer is in winning over XPress users, who will find it difficult to adapt to a working method that seems so radically different.

1 | 2
Two dialogues from Microsoft Word, showing an iconic representation of 3-D and shadow settings.

3
Word's main toolbar.

WORD-PROCESSING & PAGE-LAYOUT TOOLS

4 | 5
The extended toolbar icon set from QuarkXPress (4) and the toolbar used in Adobe InDesign (5), the latter copying the Adobe look and feel. These two applications take a very different approach, with XPress having a distinctly 'old-fashioned' appearance – that is, flat but functional – due largely to Quark having developed XPress in almost complete isolation during its many years of market dominance.

6
The limited toolbar icons in Adobe PageMaker – the original 'desktop publishing' application. This, too, sustains Adobe's house style.

CONTEMPORARY ICONS
3-D APPLICATION TOOLS

3-D modelling applications have their own unique interface problems, arising from the sheer impossibility of accurately manipulating a three-dimensional object on a two-dimensional screen.

Whereas the icon sets in most types of application have more or less settled down to a generally accepted visual vocabulary, there's no such consistency in the 3-D world, in which each application creates its icons from scratch, with little or no reference to the routes others have taken.

Even worse, many of the 'high-end' modelling applications such as NewTek LightWave refuse to use icons at all, instead cluttering their screens with rows of identical buttons containing mere text. Others, such as Cinema4D (below), use a wide and baffling array of icons.

The greatest disagreement seems to be over how to indicate tools for moving, scaling and rotating objects in the 3-D environment. The toolbars from form•z (below right), are fairly typical of the genre – fiddly and somewhat confusing.

The approach taken by MetaCreations' landscape modeller Bryce (right), is by contrast both revolutionary and intuitive.

Based around a terracotta cube (to represent the object), the three basic transformations are indicated by Bryce in simple terms on the tool's icon. So the Rotation tool has three rings around the cube, the Scale tool has a tiny cube on the end of each of its six vertices, and the Translation (moving) tool works in the same way except with an arrow to indicate movement. As each ring or point is selected, the icon changes to show the type of transformation taking place: once it has been learned, this clever metaphor can never be forgotten.

3-D APPLICATION TOOLS

2 | 3
Different approaches to the problem of manipulating objects in three dimensions. Whereas the toolbar from form•z (3) is typical, the Bryce solution (2) is more intuitive. The top row shows the rotation tool, with rings that highlight for rotation in the x, y and z planes: the appropriate ring highlights as the cursor is dragged over it. The next three rows show the icons for scaling in the x, y and z axes (unidirectionally as well as bidirectionally), and the bottom two rows show the tool used for moving an object along the same axes.

1
The icon set from high-end 3-D modelling program Cinema4D. While some of these icons are self-explanatory, many others require an excursion to the reference manual to find out what the tools do.

CONTEMPORARY ICONS

3-D: THE METACREATIONS SOLUTION

The MetaCreations Bryce interface, with its 'touchy-feely' approach, was the first to bring a 3-D feel to a 3-D modelling program. This look and feel has been used in MetaCreations' other new 3-D applications – such as figure modeller Poser, and Carrara, the successor to RayDream – for good reason: these large, bold icons show exactly how the tools work at a glance. But rather than being copied wholesale, the interface has been tweaked for each application.

Shown below are three different versions of the tool icons for changing the camera view. The first, as used in Bryce (*1*), uses a large ball to rotate the scene in three dimensions. Above that are shown the icons for translation in the x, y and z axes, indicated by 3-D cross arrows rendered in the appropriate planes.

The Carrara interface (*2*) copies that of Bryce directly, with the tools changed from dull terracotta to gleaming bronze (in keeping with the feel of the remainder of the application).

The device is further modified in Poser (*3*), which keeps the rotating ball but replaces the arrows with pointing hands in the x plane. The movement icons for the y and z planes show hands with the palm front and sideways: if your hand were placed on the plane, this is how it would appear when you moved the plane around. This approach is about as intuitive as you can possibly get.

1 | 2 | 3
Three versions of the MetaCreations 3D interface, taken from Bryce (*1*), Carrara (*2*) and Poser (*3*).

3-D: THE METACREATIONS SOLUTION

The 3-D approach continues throughout these applications. In Bryce, for example, the tools for creating water, cloudscapes and terrains, as well as primitive 3-D objects (sphere, cube, torus and so on), are shown not as line illustrations in button boxes, but as true objects arranged on a three-dimensional shelf (below). As a step towards demystifing the 3-D modelling environment, this approach is to be commended.

Other developers have been quick to jump on the bandwagon. The camera tools used in the clay modelling program Amorphium (right), for instance, are clearly inspired by the MetaCreations solution. Those gleaming gold jewels (far right) are not primitive objects but brush shapes, used for imprinting the virtual clay that is at the centre of this modeller.

An interface like this is aimed squarely at the user who is new to 3-D modelling, and who has in the past been put off by talk of nurbs, B-splines and the other esoteric jargon of the 3-D environment. Such potential users form a large part of the untapped market for 3-D applications – one which developers are keen to exploit. If a working environment such as this can appear welcoming, it goes a long way towards winning over potential users.

The MetaCreations interface was designed in large part by visionary interface designer Kai Krause, whose lack of financial acumen caused him to leave the company he had created and built up. Artists and businessmen, as ever, are two different species.

4 | 5
If imitation is flattery, then the MetaCreations design team should consider themselves highly complimented by the interface used in Amorphium.

6
3-D object selection in 3-D form: all the items on this shelf in Bryce can be dragged into the scene to build up the modelling environment.

CONTEMPORARY ICONS
ANIMATED TOOL ICONS

Animations are rarely used within application icons as they tend to distract the user from the task in hand. If you're going to animate your icons, you need a compelling reason to do so.

One application that meets the criteria for animation is Adobe's video-editing program, Premiere. It contains dozens of filters for merging one piece of video footage into another, and while they all have names – Barn Door, Centre Peel, Cross Dissolve and so on – the addition of icons to represent each one means that the user can choose a transition without having to refer to the manual to see what each one does.

Since the application is dedicated to creating moving images, it's essential that if the icons are to do their job (that of informing the user as to the tool's purpose) then they need animation to get the point across.

The examples shown here, frame by frame, are just half of each animation: they cycle from A to B and back again. And while in many cases it's simply a matter of running the animation backwards, in others the process is not symmetrical.

Few applications use this kind of running animation: but in this case, it's essential.

A selection of animations from Adobe Premiere, showing graphically the transition effects produced by each one. By sticking to a simple A and B motif (rather than a photographic image) the effect is shown much more clearly.

ANIMATED TOOL ICONS

CONTEMPORARY ICONS

WINDOWS V MACINTOSH (1)

Apple may have been the first to devise and promote the use of icons on computers, but others were quick to exploit the new technology. The most obvious culprit, of course, is Microsoft Windows.

Bill Gates launched the Microsoft empire with DOS, the command-line interface that was entirely text driven, and which achieved supremacy through its adoption by IBM as the standard for their personal computers (and therefore for later 'IBM-compatible' computers).

Windows, the icon-led interface that was to replace DOS, copied a great part of the Macintosh look and feel, using scroll-bar windows, cursor icons and, of course, icons. Shown here is a selection of 'control panel' icons common to both the Macintosh and the Windows platforms. It's clear even at first glance that many of these icons share a common heritage.

The icon for the system itself – the nerve centre of the computer – depicts a desktop computer in Windows, and a folder badged with the MacOS logo in the Macintosh system. Interestingly, the Macintosh used to employ an image of its all-in-one Macintosh computer as the system icon, but this was later changed to a folder for reasons of greater clarity. The System file became a holder into which component items could be dropped.

Other system icons developed in tandem, perhaps without direct reference to each other's operating systems, because the icon chosen by each camp was demonstrably the best image for the job.

In order to distinguish between application and document icons (often third-party software with its own design ethics), Apple made the decision to brand control panels with a uniform frame, in the form of a bevelled grey square featuring a slider bar. This slider implied the user control within the item, while the uniformity made it clear to the user that these items were all control panels and not other kinds of documents.

Windows	Macintosh	
		System
		Keyboard
		Internet
		Mouse
		Network
		Date and Time
		Modem
		Sound and Monitor
		Fonts

Some Windows icons take as their inspiration the distinctive styling of Apple icons. The standard document icon on the Mac, for instance, shows a blank page with the top right-hand corner turned down. When this document belongs to a particular application (generally the application that created it) then that application's own icon is shown within it; when the creator of the document is unknown, the content of the icon is left empty. The Windows icon for an unknown document is identical, except for the addition of the Windows flag in the centre.

Right from the start, Apple used the concept of 'folders' as containers for documents and applications, while these were referred to in DOS as 'directories'. Apple folders were initially represented as slightly shaded, single-colour rectangular icons with a tab in the top left corner. When Windows copied this design to the last pixel, Apple switched to a skewed, more three-dimensional isometric view, with an added shadow for extra depth.

Early Macs showed hard disks as the image of the computer itself, following the all-in-one theme; but as system configurations became more modular, they changed to an uninspiring image of a grey box to represent all kinds of hard disk. The perspective viewpoints may vary, but it's otherwise almost identical to the icon currently used for Windows hard disks.

Right Windows and Macintosh icons for documents, folders and hard disks.

CONTEMPORARY ICONS
WINDOWS V MACINTOSH (2)

One of the many significant innovations in the design of the Macintosh graphical interface was the notion of the Trash (or WasteBasket, depending on your country of residence). Items thrown away are stored here for eventual permanent deletion, offering the opportunity to recover the files later if it turns out they have been trashed accidentally. To indicate that files had been dumped in the Trash, the icon transformed – in earlier versions of MacOS – into a bulging trash can; with later system releases however, this odd image (metal tins don't bulge, after all) was modified to represent an obviously full trash can with the lid removed so you can see the contents.

The Windows take on this is the more environmentally friendly 'Recycle' bin, which is both a sop to trendy liberal thinking and a logical step forwards: on emptying the container the bytes of hard disk space used for these files will not actually be destroyed, but reused.

Copying icons from another operating system often means making changes simply to demonstrate that a change has been made. The MacOS Calculator icon, for example, shows a vertical design representing a traditional desk calculator, which at first sight differs from the Windows version only in its orientation: calculators, after all, can be bought in both portrait (vertical) and landscape (horizontal) designs. The Mac icon, however, fits the bill more closely, for in this version the layout of the calculator precisely matches the layout of the numerical keys on an extended keyboard.

Designers will often seize upon one property of a real-world object as its defining characteristic. In the case of the Notepad, this property is not the paper itself but the spiral binding. The Notepad differs from a word-processing application in that it is designed for short, quick note taking rather than extensive text entry.

1 | 2 | 3
Windows and MacOS icons: the Calculator (1), Notepad (2) and QuickTime movie files (3).

4 | 5
Windows and Macintosh icons for the Recycle bin (4) and the Trash can (5), shown both empty and full.

6 | 7
The generic Windows printer icon (6), and the MacOS icons for their recent range of printers (7).

8 | 9
The MacOS LaserWriter II icon (8) next to a photograph of the classic Apple printer it represents (9).

By employing the spiral device it's clear that these are individual notes which can be 'torn off' and discarded after use: it also carries the metaphor of the press reporter who needs to jot down facts in a hurry. In real life, few of us still use this type of spiral-bound notebook, but then icon design is often about metaphor rather than a strict adherence to reality – except in such cases where accurate representation is a significant aid to comprehension.

The printer icons are just such a case in point. Microsoft is purely a software company, and so the icon for printers is a single, generic printer. Apple, on the other hand, have always made their own hardware, and (in the early days at least) it was a safe bet that anyone buying an Apple computer would also be buying an Apple printer to go with it. So the Apple printer icons are near-perfect representations of the printers to which they refer, which means that a separate icon is required for each printer driver. More than a mere conceit, this approach is central to making the user feel at ease with the complete system: it's easy to see at a glance which printer driver to choose if it looks just like the printer on your desk.

An example of this close matching of icon and reality is the LaserWriter II icon, next to the actual LaserWriter to which it refers. The icon has had to be compressed horizontally to fit within the standard icon shape, but otherwise it's clearly the same machine.

CONTEMPORARY ICONS

MACINTOSH SYSTEM ICONS

Apple pioneered the use of icons in the computer interface, and it has been obsessed with them ever since. Every component of the operating system has its own icon and a small selection of them is shown here.

System files are divided into two categories: Extensions, which add functionality to the system, and Control Panels, which allow the user to control related extensions.

The newest versions of the Macintosh Operating System use 16-bit rather than 8-bit icons – providing 4,096 colours as opposed to the 256-colour limit imposed by Windows. This results in smoother, cleaner icons than would otherwise be possible; the photorealistic image quality speaks for itself.

In the MacOS, Extension icons are generally based on the jigsaw concept. Four different jigsaw frames are used (pointing up, down, left and right) within which the images represent the files used. The bottom row (right) shows the icon set for QuickTime extensions: despite their size, there's room to include both an electronic keyboard and a guitar in the QuickTime Musical Instruments icon (bottom row, centre).

Control Panel icons incorporate a slider to indicate that user-definable controls are available to modify the related Extension.

MACINTOSH SYSTEM ICONS

1
A selection of icons used for Extension files in the MacOS.

2
A selection of icons used for Control Panel files in the MacOS. The bottom two rows of icons are third-party control panels made by developers other than Apple, but they still follow the standard format perfectly.

53

CONTEMPORARY ICONS
THE NEXT MAC OS

At the time of writing this book, Apple was in the process of developing its new operating system, OS X. As well as the extra functionality and stability promised by the new system, Apple unveiled a glimpse of the interface of the future – including a radical departure for icons.

Since the earliest days, designers had been limited to icons that would fit within a grid of 32x32 pixels, apart from a single foray into larger sizes by the NeXT computer platform (then owned, incidentally, by Apple founder and current CEO Steve Jobs). Apple's new icons will break that 32-pixel restriction for an icon 16 times the size: up to 128x128 pixels is the new limit.

Of course, users cannot be expected to rush out and buy computer monitors of a bigger size simply to be able to contain all these vast icons. Which is where the second new and revolutionary technology comes in: scalable icons.

The idea of scalable icons is that icons will remain at the standard 32-pixel size until the cursor is moved over them, at which point they will gradually expand to maximum size for greater readability – rather like a 'Mexican Wave', as shown below. Scalable icon technology is something totally new, although it does currently exist for fonts. By the time you read this it will be operational – who know what the future holds?

1 | 2 | 3
Three 128-pixel icons from Apple's forthcoming operating system.

THE NEXT MAC OS

4
A screen shot of Apple's new system interface, showing the icons in place.

5
The icons are set to grow and shrink dynamically as the cursor moves across them.

CONTEMPORARY ICONS

POINTER ICONS (1)

The original acronym for the graphical user interface we now take for granted was WIMP – Windows, Icons, Menus, Pointer. None of these would work without the pointer.

The basic pointer is the left-pointing arrow, shown (below) in its Windows and Macintosh versions. The two designs are strikingly similar: the Windows version is simply an outline form of the Macintosh original.

When you examine an enlarged view, however, you can see how this design came about. The pointer needed to be clear but unobtrusive, and had to have a definite 'hot spot' (the active end). An arrow was the obvious choice, the tail serving as an indication of where it was pointing from. For the pointer to indicate left makes sense for right-handed users: this is an iconic representation of how your hand would look if you were pointing at the screen. (A more literal version of this metaphor appears in the web pointer, shown bottom right.)

Computer screens, constrained by their ability to display only a rectangular grid of square pixels, are particularly poor at representing angled lines, so these need to be kept to a minimum: 90° angles (pure vertical and horizontal) are clearly the best, followed by 45° and then 30° increments. In both the standard Mac and Windows pointers, the left edge is a true vertical, and the right is exactly 45°, these angles matching the 'return' sections beneath the head. Only the tail uses an awkward angle (22.5°) but this is small enough not to look too jagged.

It's common practice for the pointer icon to change within an application to indicate which tool is currently selected, and all computer users are familiar with the basic set of pointer icons used in their favourite applications. What is perhaps not appreciated is the sheer quantity of different icons that this approach entails: Photoshop, to take just one example, uses no fewer than 149 separate pointer icons to show each state of each tool – a formidable design challenge by any standards. All these icons (opposite) are constrained by the need to be monochromatic and to fit within a 16x16-pixel grid; and yet each must be immediately identifiable. Pointers must show which family group they belong to while being distinctive themselves. Furthermore, they must also give the user a good indication of their purpose.

1 | 2 | 3
Pointers from the Windows (1) and Macintosh (2) interfaces, plus the pointer from a web browser (3).

POINTER ICONS (1)

4
All these images are pointer icons from a single program: Adobe Photoshop. This is an indication of just how many pointer icons are required to show which tool is in use, and its precise mode of operation at the time.

CONTEMPORARY ICONS
POINTER ICONS (2)

QuarkXPress, the page-layout application that has dominated the professional publishing market for a decade, uses a relatively small set of pointer icons. This is largely because the application's interface is little changed since version one: new features have been added over the years, but there has never been a complete overhaul of the appearance of the program.

When you compare the XPress icons (below) with the much larger set of pointer icons used in its newest rival, Adobe InDesign, it is clear that the InDesign solution offers far more clues as to what each tool is doing at each moment.

InDesign was launched in 1999 as a successor to Adobe's own page-layout program, PageMaker, which had steadily lost ground to XPress despite having been the world's first desktop publishing application.

Hailed by the computer industry as the much awaited 'Quark Killer', the aim of Adobe InDesign was to replicate the functionality of QuarkXPress while adding significant improvements to it, most notably in the area of the drawing tools. The InDesign interface was designed to complement that of Adobe's other leading graphics applications, Illustrator and Photoshop, and thereby to be instantly familiar to users of both of these programs.

Metaphors such as the Pen tool, the Brush and the Crop tool were carried through to the new application, subtly altered to show their slight difference in operation. For while presenting users with a familiar interface is certainly a good thing, it would be a mistake to confuse them by implying that a tool's function in one program was identical to that in another.

Adobe's need to woo Quark customers meant that several cursor icons were made identical to those found in XPress – the Padlock (to indicate a locked item), the Magnifying Glass (used for zooming into and out of the page), and the ubiquitous 'grabber hand'. This is not to say that Quark initiated the use of these icons: many,

Left The pointer icon set from QuarkXPress.

Opposite The pointer icon set from Adobe InDesign, which borrows metaphors from other Adobe applications.

POINTER ICONS (2)

such as the grabber hand, came originally from MacPaint. Whereas the grabber hand in QuarkXPress is still a static item, as it was in MacPaint all those years ago, the InDesign version follows the newer convention of changing from an outstretched hand to a clasping hand when the mouse button is depressed. This would be at the moment when the hand, if it were a real one, would actually be grabbing an item.

CONTEMPORARY ICONS

POINTER ICONS – WORTH THE WAIT

However fast and up-to-date your computer, there will always be times when you're sitting there waiting for something to happen – tasks to process, web pages to load, and so on. The Windows solution is to show the hourglass image (left) as a static icon.

The Macintosh solution, however, is to display an animated pointer that demonstrates that your computer is still processing: if the cursor doesn't move, then you know it's frozen.

The initially static 'watch' icon was changed to the animated version, with its hands spinning round, early on in the Mac system development cycle. Some applications then began to use the simple device of a quartered black-and-white circle, which had the great advantage that by using only two different designs it could appear to spin round.

It wasn't long before applications began to use their own animated pointers instead, a selection of which are shown here. The email application Qualcomm Eudora opted for the swinging pendulum while file transfer takes place, a cycle of four repeating designs. The file transfer protocol (ftp) application Dartmouth College Fetch uses a running dog, one of the very few bidirectional pointers around. The direction in which the dog is running indicates whether files are being uploaded or downloaded.

Internet Explorer's approach to waiting is to show a page gradually filling up with text as the web page loads, a complex device that uses no fewer than 14 icons to achieve its purpose.

The animation program Adobe After Effects keeps the standard cursor, but fills it with bands of white and black that appear to travel through the cursor as time goes on; and the graphic file translation application Equilibrium DeBabelizer reduces the clock hands to a circular wipe motion within a circle, a concept which Incwell's SuperCard (and others) take one step further by portraying a rotating globe.

A novel approach is taken by the ISDN transfer program Grand Central, which shows a telephone keypad being 'dialled' – buttons are blacked out in an apparently random sequence as if the keys were being pressed in turn.

There are many more instances of animated wait pointers, but they all share the common feature of reassuring the user that the computer is still running, and that it is still processing data.

POINTER ICONS – WORTH THE WAIT

Wait icons

Standard Macintosh

Alternative Macintosh

Eudora

Fetch

Internet Explorer

After Effects

DeBabelizer

SuperCard

Grand Central

CONTEMPORARY ICONS
CURSOR ICONS & TOOL VARIANTS

The cursor icon, also known as an I-beam, is used in word-processing applications to show the point at which text typed on the keyboard will be entered on the page. In other applications, such as those for illustration or page layout, the cursor is used to distinguish between a tool used for text entry within a text box and a tool used for moving or reshaping the text box itself. Because many applications do not require a different tool to be selected for editing text, the change in icon is needed to indicate the change in the tool's function.

As a piece of design, its apparent simplicity belies its ingenuity. The main thrust of the icon, the strong vertical line, is a mere one pixel in width to allow precise positioning between text characters. When editing text in a page-layout application the type can appear almost unreadably tiny on screen, particularly when working on a page at a greatly reduced view: the cursor must be clear even when positioned between two characters which may themselves be only two or three pixels wide. A mere vertical line would be too hard to distinguish, and so the tails at top and bottom were added to give apparent bulk to this slimmest of icons.

And yet the cursor itself is not a static icon. Once layout and illustration programs allowed text to be entered along curved paths and within shaped and angled text boxes, it was clear that a single vertical cursor would be insufficient to indicate the active position within a block of text.

The further enhancement of vertically oriented text (used primarily for setting Japanese characters) requires a horizontal cursor as well.

XPress uses four text cursors – one horizontal, one vertical, and two at 45° angles – used to enter text in rotated text boxes. That way, the cursor can never be more than 22.5° out of true with the text, which makes a good enough approximation.

Illustrator uses only a vertical cursor for regular text entry (the horizontal versions are for vertical text only), which makes it much harder to edit text on a curved path; but it has separate icons for text within rectangular and irregular text boxes. Macromedia FreeHand follows the QuarkXPress model more closely, with the addition of a tiny baseline indicator that necessitates an extra set of icons for upside-down text.

Pointer icons can show not just which tool is currently active, but in which mode that tool will

Above Text viewed at a tiny size (the screen grab here is enlarged to 180%) still shows the text cursor clearly: it's perfectly apparent to the user that the current text entry point is between the letters p and r of the word 'precise'.

CURSOR ICONS AND TOOL VARIANTS

QuarkXPress

Adobe Illustrator

Macromedia FreeHand

Left Cursor variations used in XPress, Illustrator and FreeHand.

Right The 14 variant pointer icons for Photoshop's Lasso tool, and the 16 variant pointer icons for the Pen tool.

Adobe Photoshop

operate. The examples here (above right) show two of the tools used in Photoshop – the Pen and the Lasso – with their variants.

The Lasso tool has 14 different states, showing the result of holding down different modifier keys: holding the Shift key with the basic Lasso adds to the selection, holding the Option/Alt key subtracts from it, and holding both keys together intersects a new selection with an existing one. The two Lasso tool variants provide the additional ten icon designs.

The Pen tool, with its Magnetic and Freehand variations, adds no fewer than 16 different icons to the Photoshop set, all based upon the same basic design but differing enough to show the user exactly what the tool is going to do.

Photoshop's Free Transform tool allows the user to rotate selections or layers. When the cursor is moved outside the selection area the icon changes to indicate a rotation (rather than a scale or distortion). Because there are eight anchor points on the Free Transform box (one at each corner and one on each side), eight pointer icons are needed to show the type of rotation that will take place when the pointer is moved outside each of the anchor points. This may seem like excessive attention to detail, but it's another contributory factor in heightening the user experience and making an otherwise complex application that much easier to understand.

Pointer icons are often overlooked in the rush to market, and Photoshop is one of the few applications to use them extensively; their value is never in doubt.

CONTEMPORARY ICONS

POINTER ICONS: THE NEXT STEP

MetaCreations, under the guiding hand of designer Kai Krause, has always pushed the boundaries of interface design. First, Kai's Power Tools presented the user with a dialogue window quite unlike that seen in any standard operating system; with later software, the interface changes went further still.

Shown here are the icons from two of Kai Krause's products – Kai's Power Tools 6, a plug-in set designed for Adobe Photoshop, and the easy-to-use photographic retouching and enhancement application, Soap (which is now published by Scansoft, and no longer part of the MetaCreations stable).

The icons shown here are not merely toolbar icons, or even application icons, but pointers. When users pick up a paintbrush or an eraser, they're actually painting with a three-dimensional, lifelike representation of the 'real world' tool. Each tool casts its shadow, which falls translucently over the image beneath. This is no mere

Left Pointer icons from Photoshop plug-in suite KPT6, used to smudge, erase, distort, twirl and pinch the artwork. The bottom row shows the icons from the Gel component, which is used to paint a translucent and refractive medium over the image.

POINTER ICONS: THE NEXT STEP

fancy on the part of the designers: the shadow, together with the object to which it belongs, serves to indicate which part of the tool is in contact with the paper – and therefore where the active tip of the tool lies. Without the shadow underneath, the eraser could rub out from either end; with the shadow in place, there's no question of the hot-spot location. This is a far cry from the simple, tiny, black-and-white pointers that are used in other applications, and this represents one indication of the possible future direction of operating systems: the user-friendliness of the system is beyond doubt.

Above When users of low-end photo retouching program Soap click the tab to open the painting tools, this drawer pops open displaying the tools available. Once dragged out of the drawer onto the desktop, the tools become available for use.

Right The tools can be arranged on the desktop in any way the user chooses, just like real tools. When applied to the image, they become huge three-dimensional cursors, with variants not just for tool type, but for size of brush, pencil and eraser as well.

CONTEMPORARY ICONS

APPLICATION ICONS: FAMILY RESEMBLANCES

Every application has its own icon: this much is obvious. But most applications also have a range of icons for associated files – either documents output by the application, or settings files used by it.

Photoshop, once again, is our prime example of the wide range of file icons used by such applications.

The main application icon is a single eye which gazes out of its maroon-bordered square box (right). This is taken as the basis for the huge range of additional designs needed for associated files, and also forms the focal point for the splash screen which appears when the application is opened.

The icons opposite show the full range of files used by Photoshop. The top row (1) shows the application icon at actual size, together with the icon for plug-in tools – proprietary or third-party filters which add features to the main program. The plug-in icon is an image of an impossible object which can be represented as an image, but which cannot exist in the real world. It's an ideal metaphor for an application dedicated to distorting reality. When shown in list views, this impossible object is represented without the square background.

The next two rows (2) show icons for various file formats output by Photoshop – TIFF, EPS, JPEG, and so on. Here, the eye motif is incorporated into the generic document icon of a sheet of paper with the corner turned down. This indicates that they are documents as opposed to any other type of file. The consistent use of maroon within the icon further links it to Photoshop. It's particularly ironic, then, that most users set Photoshop to create documents with miniature versions of the file itself as the icon, so these designs are rarely seen.

The following four rows (3) show icons for the various preferences and settings files needed by the host application. Photoshop has an unusually large number of these, yet the icon for each is distinguished both by an image that represents the file's purpose, and by the name of the file type. This label is particularly useful since users can give settings files any name they choose: so even if a colour swatch file is called, say 'Web Safe House Style', both the image and the label will identify its purpose.

The eye motif has in the main given way to individually designed illustrations for each settings file, but the link to Photoshop is maintained by the consistent use of this unusual colour scheme. The icons showing graphs reproduce the graphs used for custom settings within the application; the brushes, gradients and CLUT (colour look-up table) icons are self-explanatory.

As ever, the design of the icons is painstaking in the extreme. The Profile graph shows cyan, magenta, yellow and black curves, drawn in such a way that the curves look truly curved (too steep a slope and the jaggedness would be apparent). The Gradient icon uses patterns of alternating pixels between the bands of grey: when viewed at 72 pixels per inch, these give the impression of a smooth gradient.

Unusually, there are even icons for the different folders in which Photoshop items are stored, as a further aid to recognition (4). These can hold colour palettes, plug-ins, brush libraries and colour libraries, as well as the main folder for the application and all its subfolders.

Even temporary files (erased when the application quits) have their own icon (5): in normal use, barring system crashes, no one should ever see these icons.

APPLICATION ICONS: FAMILY RESEMBLANCES

1 | 2 | 3 | 4 | 5
The complete suite of Photoshop icons
1 Application and plug-in icons
2 File format icons
3 Preferences and settings icons
4 Folder icons
5 Temporary file icons

6 | 7
Enlarged views of the Profile (6) and Gradient (7) icons from Photoshop.

CONTEMPORARY ICONS

APPLICATION ICONS: THE EXTENDED SET

Designing a separate icon for each file associated with an application may seem like a mammoth task in itself. But the design process doesn't stop there.

All icons are for the standard 8-bit (256-colour) environment of all modern computers. Later versions of the Macintosh Operating System are able to display icons generated with a larger number of colours, resulting in a smoother on-screen appearance; but because software developers can never be sure what system their applications are destined to run on, all play safe and stick to the 256-colour standard used by both Macintosh and Windows systems.

But as well as designing these 8-bit icons, the whole set must be replicated both in 2-bit (black and white) and 4-bit (16 colours). This last requirement is to ensure compatibility with much older operating systems, although it's hard to imagine any user getting to grips with a program like Photoshop on a computer capable of displaying only 16 colours. The 2-bit icons shown here (right) use a chequerboard pattern to simulate mid grey: the Gradient icon is pure black and white with a small band of grey in the centre, rather than an ugly dithered attempt to reproduce the smooth gradient using black-and-white patterns alone.

Above The 2-bit (black-and-white) versions of the standard Photoshop icons.

Left The 'list view' version of some of the icons at 16x16 pixels.

APPLICATION ICONS: THE EXTENDED SET

The standard size for an icon is 32x32 pixels. When folders are displayed using list rather than icon views, a further set of icons is needed to sit next to the file's name so yet another set of icons must be created – this time at a quarter of the original size, or 16x16 pixels. Once again, these icons must also have versions in 2-bit and 4-bit colour for all purposes.

Some developers take little care over these tiny images, choosing merely to reduce the size of the original icons and hope for the best. The best results come from custom development of these list icons, as is seen here: by enlarging pairs of 32-pixel and 16-pixel icons to the same size, it becomes clear that while the smaller set relates to the larger, they are not merely shrunken copies.

The three sets shown here (right) illustrate the point. Both sets of icons have been enlarged to the same size to show the difference – the 32x32 icons to 350% of their original size, the 16x16 icons to 700%.

The full-size Kernel icon (top) uses a 3x3 grid of numbers; the small icon reduces this to a 3x2 grid. Similarly, the 4x3 grid of the Swatch icon is cut down to 3x3 for the smaller size. The Inks icon cannot be approached in the same way, since four printing inks are commonly used irrespective of how a folder may be viewed. Cyan, magenta, yellow and black must be shown for the icon to work, so the overall design has been simplified, while retaining the four-colour theme.

The type at the bottom of the 32-pixel icons is just five pixels high, the bare minimum needed to render characters such as 'S' and 'E'. Clearly there was no possibility of reproducing this on the 16-pixel icons, and so the lettering has been omitted altogether..

1 | 2 | 3
A comparison of three pairs of standard 32-pixel and their corresponding 16-pixel (list view) icons used in Photoshop, enlarged to the same size for comparison: icons for Kernel (1), Swatch (2) and Inks (3) settings.

CONTEMPORARY ICONS
ADOBE ILLUSTRATOR

The identity for Adobe Illustrator, the first PostScript drawing application, has for years been based on a detail from Sandro Botticelli's painting *The Birth of Venus*. It's a curious choice of image: after all, this painting is almost the epitome of the kind of artwork that cannot be generated with a PostScript program, which uses clean lines and fills rather than textural fills.

The image has long been used on the packaging, instruction manuals and startup screen of the application, the emphasis being upon the long flowing hair of Venus. This could give some clue as to its raison d'être: it's the flowing curves that makes a PostScript tool stand out. Illustrator appeared long before Photoshop, at a time when the only alternative was the clunky graphics of MacPaint and MacDraw; these curves were what set the new program apart.

The original application icon for Illustrator was a large italic letter A, which now survives only as the icon for files saved in Illustrator 3 format – an earlier format which does not support all the features of the current version, but still offers greater compatibility with other graphics applications.

As with Photoshop, another application from the same stable, the Illustrator icons use a consistent colour scheme to identify and unite the set. Again, as with Photoshop, the icons incorporate the type of the filter in words as a further clue to their function. The document icons

ADOBE ILLUSTRATOR

(a different one for each type of file exported by the application) once more feature a subdued, knocked-back version of the main icon as a background. Again, the icons for the settings and preferences files feature both a written description and an illustrative image.

There are far fewer icons in the Illustrator set than there are for Photoshop, since there are fewer settings files associated with it.

Left The icon used by earlier versions of Illustrator, now found exclusively in files saved in the earlier format.

Below The complete icon set for Adobe Illustrator (version 8).

CONTEMPORARY ICONS
MACROMEDIA FREEHAND

Above The main application icon for FreeHand.

Below The full set of FreeHand icons.

FreeHand is Illustrator's direct competitor. Its identity was originally based around the stylo pen, the precise graphics tool used by technical artists before the advent of desktop publishing technology (and which the new applications were intended to replace).

Using this pen as the application's icon (as well as in promotional material, wielded by a stylized superhero figure) gave novice users a visible sign that while they were about to learn a whole new way of working, they'd be using tools which would give similar results to those they'd achieved previously using traditional tools.

This icon lasted up until version 7 of FreeHand, launched in 1996, after which it presumably became clear that the new breed of graphic artists had learned their trade using computer technology. Few, if any, had ever used a stylo pen, and it is likely that many of them had no idea what this icon represented. This pen icon is now reserved for files saved in an earlier-version format of Macromedia FreeHand.

The new FreeHand icon, designed by Neville Brody along with the rest of the Macromedia suite, is strictly non-representational: the icon itself gives no clue as to the function of the application to which

MACROMEDIA FREEHAND

it refers. This is an entirely new approach to icon design, and one we will be examining more closely in Chapter 3.

Like the Adobe applications, FreeHand follows the convention of incorporating the name of the file export type (EPS, GIF, JPG and so on) in the document icon. Unlike Adobe, however, Macromedia has not seen the need to design an icon for each preset and file associated with the application.

The mono (2-bit) icons for FreeHand follow their full colour counterparts closely, albeit in a necessarily simplified form. The main application icon is reproduced in black, white and 'grey' (formed, as usual, by using a chequerboard pattern of black-and-white pixels). Subsidiary icons, however, stick to pure black and white, as can be seen in the comparison (right) of the colour and mono versions of the Application icon and the Xtras (plug-ins) icons.

Interestingly, although this Xtras icon is the one built into the program itself, the Xtras themselves are represented by the four-piece jigsaw puzzle icon shown on the facing page at bottom right.

1 | 2
The old icon for FreeHand, used until version 7, with the stylo pen motif (*1*). Shown beside it is an example of the pen wielded by a stylized superhero (*2*), which appeared in all the promotional material for the application.

3 | 4 | 5 | 6
A comparison of the colour and mono versions of Application (*3*, *4*) and Xtras (*5*, *6*) icons, showing the different treatments used in the two versions.

CONTEMPORARY ICONS
COREL DRAW/PAINT

CorelDraw dominates the mid-range drawing market. Despite providing a range of tools and environments now available with the combination of both CorelDraw and its bitmap component, CorelPaint, it has never achieved the supremacy among graphics professionals that is enjoyed by Photoshop, Illustrator and FreeHand, but its early presence on the Windows platform gave it a head start in the PC market.

The CorelDraw icon is a butterfly, an image surprisingly copied by Adobe for InDesign, their page layout application. Once again using the generic document motif as the basis for exported files (a vertical page with the corner turned down), CorelDraw offers few surprises in its complete icon suite – although it is still clear what the icons refer to. Targeting Photoshop directly, CorelPaint uses a camera and picture frame as

COREL DRAW/PAINT

its main icon to suggest its capability for photo manipulation. This image is not carried through to the other icons in the set: instead, a paintbrush hovering over a standard document icon is used both for exported file types (TIFF, EPS and so on) and for preferences and some settings files. The only link with the main application icon is the tiny camera incorporated into the exported file icons design.

Like Photoshop, the image of a curve on a graph is used for colour management files, although in CorelDraw these look hasty and inconsistent.

Opposite The complete icon set for CorelDraw.

Below The icon set for CorelPaint, the bitmap editing component of CorelDraw.

CONTEMPORARY ICONS

QUARKXPRESS

Although Aldus PageMaker was the first desktop publishing (page-layout) application on any platform, QuarkXPress quickly achieved supremacy among graphics professionals due to its greater precision, flexibility and enhanced ability to handle and output imported graphics files.

Unusually, Quark have kept the same icon set virtually intact since the program's inception. This makes the main Application icon (left) look particularly outdated. It is one of the few remaining application icons still to be based upon the original template that was designed by Susan Kare for the original Macintosh Operating System. The original icon showed a pen-wielding hand poised over a 45° rotated square (shown below).

Given the constraints this format imposed, the icon still manages to show the use and purpose of the application perfectly: the tiny square space shows a page layout complete with banner headline, text, and graphic images. The major difference is the addition of a round-cornered purple box behind the logo. This colour background would serve to unite the icons in the set (although some of them still follow the earlier orange theme).

The imperative for XPress icons is strictly representational. It's here that the skill of the icon designer can be seen clearly. The Dictionary icon uses a drop capital A to show the first letter of the dictionary, followed by a representation of the words on the page. Some of these 'words' are depicted by a single black pixel, others by rows of three pixels: the overall effect is of a string of words of different lengths.

The Library icon is similarly pictorial. The Library is an XPress file that holds items frequently used in a document; true to its name, the icon shows a row of books. Rather than making all the books the same size (which could look like a multicoloured box), the books vary both in height and in width to give a good indication of the variety of elements that can be incorporated into a library file.

1 | 2
The main Application icon for QuarkXpress (1), and the original application icon for the MacOS (2), on which it is based.

The Document icon is clearly based on the main application icon, using a similar mixture of elements representing both text and graphics within a standard document frame. The yellow square and green rectangle mimic the application icon directly, but other elements have been changed to show the versatility of the program: the orange rectangle that represented a banner headline is now a circular graphic with a caption beneath it. In addition, the yellow square now has a cross drawn through it, imitating the style of an empty picture box when first drawn in XPress.

Again, following convention, the Template icon (fourth from left on the top row, below) is a 'ghosted' version of the full QuarkXPress document icon.

3 | 4 | 5
XPress icons for Dictionary (3), Library (4) and Document (5) files.

6
The range of icons that make up the XPress set.

CONTEMPORARY ICONS
METACREATIONS

While most software developers go to extreme lengths to emphasize the fact that all their applications belong to the same family, MetaCreations takes the opposite approach. Each application is seen as an entirely distinct entity which just happens to be made by the same company. This is in part due to the fact that MetaCreations is itself the result of the amalgamation of several graphics developers – HSC software, Fractal Design, Specular and others. This disparity has reasserted itself: MetaCreations has sold off its graphics arm, and the applications shown here are once again owned by different publishers.

The icons for Bryce (*1*) show the use of the application: to design and generate realistic 3-D landscapes. The model itself is shown in the application icon; the file icon shows a head-on view of the same model. The PICT icon, representing an image file output by the application, shows the kind of flat (two-dimensional) view that can be generated by the program.

This moody, artistic and clearly 3-D-rendered set of icons shows a marked contrast to the icons for the natural-media illustration program Painter (*2*). Here, the icons are highly graphic interpretations of the tools used in painting – with the pot of pens, pencils and brushes making

1 | 2
The icons for MetaCreations' landscape modelling program Bryce (*1*) and for the bitmap painting program Painter (*2*).

the icon for the application itself. There's a strong sense of humour here in the design, too: note the paintbrush used as a microphone for the recorded actions file, and the quirky table lamp used to represent the lighting file.

Poser (*3*) is another 3-D modelling application, this time one that permits the user to pose and distort human figures. Its icon is that of the wooden mannequin used by artists to help them draw posed figures. Originally, this application was seen as little more than an artist's helper, although continued upgrades have made it into a sophisticated modelling tool.

Goo (*4*) is a consumer application that allows users to distort images by smudging them with a virtual paintbrush. Although used mainly for distorting facial expressions, the icon merely shows a blob of paint that has already been smudged. The settings files (bottom two rows) are based on the appearance of buttons and controls within the program itself.

The disparity of imagery shown here goes well beyond the icon level: as a graphics company, MetaCreations suffered from a lack of focus. The crisis of identity was a real one, shown by MetaCreations' decision to sell off its graphics arm to concentrate on 3-D web delivery.

3 | 4
The icons for figure modelling application Poser (*3*) and for the freeform paint distortion program Goo (*4*).

CONTEMPORARY ICONS

NETSCAPE NAVIGATOR & INTERNET EXPLORER

Netscape Navigator and Microsoft Internet Explorer are the two giants of the web browser field, slugging it out in an ongoing battle for supremacy. Netscape came first; but, as is so often the case, Microsoft's muscle and financial strength soon ensured that Explorer gained the lion's share of the market.

The icons for Netscape are unusual in that they are used not just for the application and its associated files, but as placeholders for the images, movies, java elements and other components that make up the complex world of web design.

If everything's working correctly, the user should in theory seldom or never see these icons; instead, they should be presented with the images and movies to which they refer.

1 | 2
The icons for Netscape Navigator, both for files (*1*) and for image file representations in the browser windows (*2*).

NETSCAPE NAVIGATOR & INTERNET EXPLORER

But the Internet being what it is, pictures are not always found and movies do not always load. In these cases, an icon appears on the web page in their place to show the user that something should have appeared but didn't. Netscape goes one step further, by using both broken and question-mark icons to indicate that a required page file couldn't be found or failed to load.

The Explorer icons shown here are file icons only, representing files downloaded and settings files.

One novelty is the icon for downloads in progress, which uses a sequence of ten icons showing a thermometer rising progressively to indicate the file's arrival. While Explorer's Download Manager window performs a similar task, the icons are a useful addition if you happen to be downloading files in the background.

3
The file icons used by Internet Explorer, including the 10-frame download icon.

CONTEMPORARY ICONS
WORD-PROCESSOR APPLICATIONS

Love it or hate it, Microsoft Word is the world's leading word processing application. Continually upgraded since its first appearance, Word now has more tools, gadgets, helpers and wizards than are strictly necessary in such a program, but its position appears unshakeable.

Both the name and the icon indicate its pre-eminence. Microsoft nabbed the single syllable Word early on, leaving the competitors to struggle with such nomenclatures as WordPerfect, WriteNow, FullWrite, SimpleText and even YeahWrite (a name that only works when spoken aloud). Microsoft also got there first with the icon: once they'd used the letter W, no-one else could touch it without looking foolish.

The main settings files are based on the application logo, but the book device (with variations) is used for such elements as global spelling and hyphenation dictionaries, their regional equivalents, and the thesaurus module.

Icons have been added to Word piecemeal over the years as new elements have been bolted on to the program, and little or no attempt has been made to make them all appear part of the same generic set; but the dictionary and thesaurus icons, representing spiral-bound books, speak for themselves.

If Word's icon set is somewhat disparate, then that makes the icon set of competitor WordPerfect almost schizophrenic. Corel's rival word processor uses an elegantly drawn fountain pen motif as its application

1
The mixed icon suite from Microsoft Word.

2
The disparate range of icons used by WordPerfect.

icon, which is carried through to the character map icon. The purple swash background appears in three further icons, but after that the coherence breaks down.

These icons have clearly not only been designed by different people at different times, but by designers who have paid little or no attention to the existing set.

WordPerfect ships with other bundled production applications, such as a painting program (indicated by the somewhat bizarre combination of household paint tin and ornate picture frame). Even here, the dull brown of the frame bears little resemblance to the gleaming gold of the fountain pen's nib. Only the Dictionary icon, curiously badged with a yellow question mark (as if it isn't sure of its provenance) ties into the main set by sharing a common colour base.

Ultimately, the user experience of the application is hardly diminished by the vagaries of the icon suite. But when other developers put so much effort into unifying the appearance, the odd rogue application stands out.

CHOOSE YOUR OWN ICONS •	86
REINVENTING THE FOLDER •	88
REINVENTING THE FOLDER ONE STEP FURTHER •	90
CUSTOM DISK ICONS •	92
FADS & FOIBLES •	94
ESOTERICA & MINORITY INTERESTS •	96
WHERE THERE'S A CULT, THERE'S AN ICON •	98
BREAKING THE BOUNDARIES •	100

PICK & MIX

PICK AND MIX
CHOOSE YOUR OWN ICONS

Icons are key elements in the way we interact with our computers. And just as the way we organize our computers is a highly personal matter – which applications and utilities we use, the organization of our filing systems, and so on – so the very look of the computer becomes a reflection of our personality.

Many people are satisfied with the image of a dull grey box as the icon for their computer. But it could just as easily be the *Starship Enterprise*, or a hamburger, or Bart Simpson: and there is no shortage of budding designers willing to spend many hours toiling away rendering their favourite objects and cartoon characters into a 32-pixel grid for others to enjoy.

For some years Macintosh users have had the ability to change any icon on their computer simply by opening the Get Info dialogue for any file or folder and pasting in the icon of their choice, and it's on this platform that the icon designer has had his start.

In Windows, icons work rather differently. The icon for a file is linked to the suffix that determines the kind of file it is. So a .txt file will always have a text file icon, and so on. It's a relatively easy process to patch the system so that all .txt files are represented by Darth Vader rather than by the image of a page of text with the corner turned down; but this is a system-wide process, and only 'shortcuts' (aliases) are allowed to have custom icons displayed for each instance.

The icons shown in this chapter are just a tiny selection from the many thousands of icon designs, some of which are freely available on Internet sites, and some are from shareware CD-ROM collections. They are nearly all designed by amateurs – in the sense of those who love the work that they do. However, there is no doubting the professionalism and talent of many of these designers.

Of course, anyone can knock up an icon or two and distribute them via the Internet, and websites are full of poor quality work. But the real gems are there, if you take the trouble to look for them.

CHOOSE YOUR OWN ICONS

Designing a one-off icon is hard enough; creating an icon set that is both cohesive and attractive is harder still. On these pages we'll look at some of the best sets of icons around today.

1
To replace an icon with a custom design on a Mac, simply copy and paste in the Get Info dialogue.

2
Windows users can replace whole themes at a stroke.

3
Customizing icons in Windows means replacing every instance of a file type.

PICK AND MIX
REINVENTING THE FOLDER

The desire to personalize one's computer is all-pervasive, and icon designers often expend tremendous effort creating an alternative to the drab, everyday images built into the operating system itself.

The icons on this page were designed by Gedeon Maheux in 1998 as replacements for standard items in the Macintosh system. The top two rows are simply folders, colour-coded for ease of recognition; the next two rows show file icons that can be attached to any document. At the bottom are specific folder and system icons designed to replace those shipped with the computer. Sometimes, the subtlety goes a little too far. For example, the difference between the empty and full trash cans (the last two icons) is barely apparent.

On the facing page are two sets of folder icons designed by Jason Wohlstadter. These may be attached to any folders, and clearly follow the basic folder outline to ease recognition. The 'Testarossa' series, at the top, is intended to appeal to all Ferrari fans; the lower set has the grimy sci-fi appeal popularized in the film *Blade Runner*.

Above Designer Gedeon Maheux's replacement folder and system icons are available from www.iconfactory.com.

REINVENTING THE FOLDER

1 | 2
Two sets of folder icons: the 'Testarossa' series (1) and a grimy sci-fi style set (2), designed by Jason Wohlstadter, from www.epochicons.com.

PICK AND MIX
REINVENTING THE FOLDER: ONE STEP FURTHER

Folder icons need not, of course, look like folders. The reasoning followed by Lars Wiegman, who designed the innovative system and folder icons on this page, is that the consistency of the icon set makes up for the initial novelty of the form. It's an attractive and intriguing collection, with the clever device of using faded icons (centre row) to represent folders that hold disabled items.

These folder icons show a design sense and a restraint that's wholly professional in nature, even if the meaning of some of the images isn't immediately apparent.

Of course, folders are no more than containers, which explains the different approach taken by the three artists featured on the facing page. The top two rows are luggage icons by Ken Mastri; the next two show a variety of boxes and other containers designed by Kim Ji-Hyun.

The bottom three rows on the facing page enable you to turn your desktop into a virtual town (as long as you can remember which buildings your files live in). They are designed by Swedish artist Carl Johan Rehbinder, whose personal website at www.multiart.nu/cci includes a huge range of icon designs – including one set of 70 Swedish road signs.

Above What seems strange in the individual instance makes perfect sense as part of a group.

This carefully designed icon set entitled Florence is by Lars Wiegman.

REINVENTING THE FOLDER: ONE STEP FURTHER

Left Why keep it in a folder when you can keep it in a suitcase: original designs by Ken Mastri, from www.members.zoom.com/electricon.

91

Left Why keep it in a suitcase when you can keep it in a box: containers by Kim Ji-Hyun.

Left Village people by Carl Johan Rehbinder.

PICK AND MIX
CUSTOM DISK ICONS

Custom icons can be attached to virtually any object – not just folders and documents. Removable media is another area ripe for personalization.

The icons on this page are designed to be attached to Zip disks. Created by Bill Kesler in 1997, this is just a sample from the vast range of icons created. Some are generic disk icons that can be attached to any disks, such as the numbered icons in the top two rows or the coloured icons below them. The remainder are icons for disks with a specific type of content – Fonts, Photoshop files, images, sounds, and so on.

Matt Slot's 1996 range of floppy disk icons (facing page) do not relate to specific types of item, although he also created a selection of icons that did. Instead, they go to some lengths to depict exactly the floppy disk that was inserted: not only do they come in black, blue and grey, just like the real thing, they're also supplied with labels in exactly the same colours as their real-world counterparts.

But if there's one thing computer users love, it's computers; and the Apple collection by Carl Johan Rehbinder represents the current range to perfection.

Right Zip disk icons by Bill Kesler.

CUSTOM DISK ICONS

1
Part of a large collection of floppy disk icons designed by Matt Slot.

2
Icons depicting a recent range of Apple computers, including the 'fruit flavoured' iMacs, by Carl Johan Rehbinder, from www.multiart.nu/cci.

PICK AND MIX
FADS & FOIBLES

Once you have accepted the fact that a folder need not look like a folder and a file need not look like a file, the capacity for freedom of artistic expression becomes truly unleashed.

The Diner icons by George Agpoon, available from his website at www.spoondesign.com, are beautiful examples of the artform, inspired by George's own love of traditional diners (note the regular and decaf coffee, with and without cream in the cups, and the empty pie plate). His belief in the need for custom icons is simple: 'Good computer icons can humanize the computing experience, which is really important because technology can be so dehumanizing. They remind us of the things that exist beyond our screens, and that maybe we should get out sometimes.'

An interesting feature of these icons is that the List view version, usually ignored by amateur designers, features not a miniature version of the icon but the letter D (for Diner) as a logo. Each time a folder using these icons is opened, the logo appears at the top: a neat way of marking your presence.

The chocolate range (white, milk and nut shown here) is a true chocoholic's delight – designed by Carl Johan Rehbinder, a self-confessed chocolate freak.

FADS & FOIBLES

The Paurian collection of autumn icons are gentle but lovingly rendered leaf designs; and Jeremy Harrison's hominid skulls are as accurate as they are entertaining.

There are many Volkswagen fans out there, but it takes a true devotee to love the van as well. These are unusual in being photographic reductions of the original vehicles – unusual because photographic icons rarely have the sharpness and conciseness of line of their hand-drawn counterparts.

1 | 2 | 3 | 4 | 5 A range of custom icons: Diner set (1) by George Agpoon; the chocolate range designed by Carl Johan Rehbinder (2); Paurian autumn icons (3); Volkswagen icons (4); and anatomically-correct hominid skulls by Jeremy Harrison (5).

PICK AND MIX
ESOTERICA & MINORITY INTERESTS

On the previous pages we looked at icons created out of a private passion on the part of the artist. Here, that passion is taken several steps further with a quality and accuracy that beggars belief.

Reby Lee's Solar System collection (available from www.hk.super.net/~rebylee) features planets, moons and asteroids created with a high degree of skill. He's obviously seriously into astronomy, and it's a safe bet that his desktop is arranged with astronomical accuracy.

But the spendour of these planetary bodies pales in comparison with Reby's other tremendous collection, the 32-bit Trilobyte set. Based on original photographs at the Extinctions fossil company (www.extinctions.com), these accurate and beautiful renderings of fossils are a truly astonishing piece of work.

1 | 2
Reby Lee's Solar System collection (1) and Trilobyte set (2).

ESOTERICA AND MINORITY INTERESTS

2

PICK AND MIX
WHERE THERE'S A CULT, THERE'S AN ICON

Cult followers have always sought images of their passions. The Internet has provided a unique and easy way for devotees of a particular art form to exchange ideas, and the promulgation of icons is no exception.

Shown here are The Beatles, Beavis and Butthead, *The Simpsons*, Winnie the Pooh and a Disney collection. There's also a particularly fine set of *Star Wars Episode One* icons, complete with leading characters and spaceships.

The actual list is almost limitless, taking in virtually every imaginable fan-club theme. Some, naturally, are more successful than others; icons based on cartoons are particularly easy to render in a 32-pixel grid, whereas those of real people tend to be much harder to get across. This much is clear in the comparison between the meticulously rendered *Star Wars* figures and the slightly dodgy Beatles' faces.

1 The Fab Four, after a fashion.

2 Get your own *Beavis and Butthead* collection from www.geocities.com/Baja/8696/.

3 Matt Slot's homage to *The Simpsons*.

4 Even Winnie the Pooh is online – Topher's Castle is at www.geocities.com/enchantedforest/3278.

WHERE THERE'S A CULT, THERE'S AN ICON

5
Tremendous *Star Wars* work by Talos Tsui, available at www.iconfactory.com.

6
Matt Slot takes on Disney.

PICK AND MIX
BREAKING THE BOUNDARIES (1)

A common trick used by software developers is to fill the main windows of their installer CDs with what appears to be a single, large image – such as the installer disk for Eidos' popular game Tomb Raider (below). Of course, this is impossible. So here's how it's done.

What appears to be one image is in fact made up of several individual icons, attached to empty folders without names. These folders are butted up against each other so that the joins are seamless. The blown-apart Tomb Raider on the right hand page shows how the process works.

The icons are not fixed in place, so the user can move them around and so spoil the effect; but because CD-ROMs are read-only, the new positions are not stored and each time the CD is reopened the icons appear in place again, and the illusion is once more complete.

BREAKING THE BOUNDARIES (1)

Once a time-consuming manual task, there are now shareware applications that automate the creation of impressive splash screen images. We'll look in more detail at one of these shareware programs in Chapter 6, showing how easy it is to create a splash screen of this type.

1
The main window of the Tomb Raider CD, with its image of Lara Croft made up from an array of icons that are attached to empty folders.

2
The individual icons that make up the Lara Croft image.

3
The CD splash screen from MetaCreations' figure-modelling program, Poser.

PICK AND MIX
BREAKING THE BOUNDARIES (2)

Icon designers are always innovators. If they weren't, they'd be satisfied with the icons that already exist. But sometimes, an idea comes along that is little short of revolutionary.

Michael Smith's UltraDrop folder set was designed back in 1994, when many users were struggling with 13- or 14-inch monitors. On these small screens, desktop space was at a premium. Using the Snap to Grid feature meant that icons would automatically jump to the nearest alignment point, enabling icons to be precisely aligned next to each other – or even on top of each other. Smith's ingenious approach was to fit multiple icons within the same 32-pixel space.

The top row shows two, four, and two sets of five icons occupying the same physical space; below that are four- and eight-drawer filing cabinets, available in both metal and wood, and holding respectively four and eight icons. As the eight-drawer wooden cabinet example shows, each drawer is a separate icon in its own right that can be attached to any folder you choose: so up to eight folders can be fitted in the space of just one.

Of course, you can't tell at a glance which drawer to open to locate the folder you're looking for; but there are several ways around this problem. For one thing, the name of the folder will highlight (come to the front) when each drawer is clicked on; and using the Labels system built into the Macintosh Operating System, you can specify a different label (and therefore a different colour) for each of the drawers as a further aid to the memory. This is an icon device that plays little part in today's world of large screens and high resolutions, but at the time it was designed, it was a near-perfect solution to a perhaps otherwise impossible problem.

1
UltraDrop Folders squeeze up to eight folders into the space of one, each being assigned its own area or drawer – as long as you remember which is which.

2
Sample icons from Kineticon, which places animated icons on the Mac desktop.

3
The Editor window from Kineticon.

Sherman Uitzetter's shareware Kineticon is also innovative in a different way (Mac only, www.kineticcreations.com). The extension patches the system so that it can display animated icons instead of the traditional static images. Standard icons bundled with it include a Trash can with eyes inside, a spinning floppy disk and replacement SimpleText (text editor) icon, which creates the standard icon as you watch. The application also ships with an editor so that you can build your own designs – such as the glowing spot orbiting a ball, shown above. Users can control the looping mode (back and forth, continuous and so on) as well as the speed in frames-per-second. It's even possible to set the icon to animate once every seven seconds (or whatever time span you like), waiting at rest in the meantime.

104

IT'S BIGGER – AND IT MOVES • 106

CARTOON ANIMATIONS • 108

PHOTOGRAPHIC & HAND-DRAWN ICONS • 110

3-D MODELLING • 112

COPYCATS: THE OPERATING SYSTEM • 116

INTERNET ICONS

105

THE INTERNET
IT'S BIGGER – AND IT MOVES

For the icon designer, the Internet offers two further capabilities over application and operating system design: icons can be any size you like, and they can move.

The Netscape icon, which runs in the top right-hand corner of the browser window, was perhaps the world's first fully animated application icon. When the Internet started, animated GIF images were unheard of; the complex series of images shown here was built into the browser program itself, showing a celestial scene with shooting stars and planets swirling around the letter 'N' for Netscape.

When Microsoft brought out Internet Explorer in direct competition with Netscape, they copied the look and feel of the original program down to the last detail – including placing their own animated icon in exactly the same position as that of Netscape. The facing page shows all of the 42 individual images that make up the Explorer icon, showing the letter 'E' (for Explorer) gradually being eclipsed by a globe and then very slowly being revealed again.

Both are supreme pieces of design, tweaked to the last detail and animated to perfection. Even if the page in view is static, the smooth motion of the icon hints at the vastly greater capabilities that the web has to offer. Whereas the Netscape icon is clearly hand-drawn (in the sense of each frame being individually composited), the Explorer icon has 3-D modelling application written all over it.

The Explorer icon also appears larger on the screen, and is drawn at a higher resolution, and whereas the Netscape icon is the standard 32x32 pixels, the Explorer version is a full 48x48 pixels.

1 | 2
Animated application interface icons for Netscape Navigator (1) and Internet Explorer (2), reproduced here in proportion to each other, the Netscape icon being 32x32 pixels while the Explorer icon is 48x48 pixels.

IT'S BIGGER – AND IT MOVES

107

2

THE INTERNET
CARTOON ANIMATIONS

As we saw in the previous chapter, cartoon images are particularly convincing when rendered on computer screens using limited colours and small file sizes. The use of flat colour reduces the file size of the image, and even more so when that image is animated.

'Real' animated cartoons simulate motion by using far fewer frames than traditional film, and the technique works just as well for animated GIF files.

The walking cartoon character, below, uses just six frames on a repeated cycle to make the figure look like he's walking. Because this character originated in a computer game, it's likely that the author of this GIF file simply pulled images out of the original program in order to create this convincing animation.

But animations don't always need to employ full character movement in order to get their point across.

Because icon designers for the Internet are no longer limited to the 32-pixel size demanded of standard system icons, they can use as much space as they like to get their point across. A good example is the Bart Simpson animation on the facing page, which uses 16 frames built around a grid of 137x116 pixels in size.

This raises the question at what point does an icon become a movie, or an illustration, or a work of art? As with so many things on the Internet, the distinction has become blurred.

All the icons featured in this chapter (with the exception of those from Netscape and Explorer, of course) are freely available for users to incorporate on their websites. There are many sources of animated icons on the web, the best being www.gifs.net which includes over 1200 animations on its indexed website.

Homer Simpson, below, is essentially made up of the same head which rises and falls above the 'wall' defined by the thin yellow line seen in the first frame. The up and down motion of the head is enough in itself to give the impression of movement: but the designer has added several tweaks to make the animation more enjoyable.

The position of Homer's hands varies as his head appears and disappears, and the centre two frames have an added sparkle that flashes between his eyes and his teeth. In addition, the subtle alteration of the shape of one eye in the following frame makes the whole figure appear to lean forward slightly.

1 | 2 | 3
On the Internet, file size is everything. The more complex an animation is, the larger the resulting file; and the larger a file, the longer it takes to download.

The Sonic the Hedgehog icon (1) is just 12K in size, as is Homer Simpson (2). Bart (3), weighs in at 48K, due to its larger size and complex construction.

CARTOON ANIMATIONS

109

3

2

THE INTERNET
PHOTOGRAPHIC AND HAND-DRAWN ICONS

Many animated icons are 'hand-drawn' – that is, created individually frame by frame, using a paint program such as Adobe Photoshop. While some use photographs as their starting point, many are drawn from scratch.

The punching hand (above) is a surprisingly effective image when animated, appearing to punch out of the page (note the tear marks) before pointing aggressively at the viewer. The apparently sudden jumps between the frames of the fist and the opening hand are entirely lost in the animation, which gives the illusion of smooth but rapid movement, and the photographic nature of the original images adds to its realism.

Some hand-drawn images, such as those eight that make up the running cheetah (below), are painstaking works of art. Again, the animated version is far more convincing than a series of stills can ever achieve. The animation may well have been based on real photographic film footage, but that doesn't detract from its effectiveness.

Many websites use counters to indicate the number of visitors to the site, and the rolling counter animation (left) is a clever parody of the standard format. It animates quickly, so that the numbers appear to be changing at a terrific rate. This sense of speed is accentuated by the fact that the further to the right the numbers are (in reality, each would move ten times as fast as its left-hand neighbour), the more vertically blurred they become – giving the impression that they're whizzing past at tremendous speed.

The planet with its orbiting moons, on the facing page, has been cleverly drawn so that the moons appear to be going round the planet, although in fact their size remains constant. It's the speed of motion that deceives the eye, and distractions such as the shooting star that whizzes past in the background add visual interest.

PHOTOGRAPHIC AND HAND-DRAWN ICONS

1 | 2 | 3 | 4

The simplicity of the running jaguar (4) means that this icon takes up just 12K on disk – the same size taken up by the punching hand (1). The spinning counter (2) doubles that size to 24K, whereas the much larger planet and moons animation (3) takes up a full 80K of disk space.

3

4

THE INTERNET
3-D MODELLING (1)

3-D modelling programs provide one of the easiest and quickest ways to create multi-frame animations. Once an object has been modelled, it can be viewed from any angle; individual frames can then be exported and tweaked as necessary, or the animation can be exported as an animated GIF file.

The spinning 7Up can (right) is a good example of how even a tiny icon can be given tremendous visual interest by adding basic animation to it. Modelling the can is not a difficult task; but it is likely the creator had access to the original flat artwork for the product in order to wrap the image around the can.

Objects can be created from the imagination as well as copying things found in the real world. The spiky ball at the foot of the facing page spins on its vertical axis. The ball may only be a tiny object, but the 40 images required to make the animation move smoothly still bring in the file size at around 40K.

A particularly pleasing animation is the spinning spaceship (opposite). This simple 3-D model is of the sort that could be created in half an hour by any competent modeller, but the effect of the animation (partly due to the large size of the image, at 144x52 pixels) is impressive.

The overriding temptation, when using 3-D programs, is to make the animated GIF look as good as the preview in the program – which means dozens of frames for the smoothest animation. But when designing for the Internet, size is everything and very large GIF downloads will prevent visitors returning to your site.

3-D MODELLING (1)

1 | 2 | 3
The more complex the image used in an animation, the larger the file size. The spinning 7Up can (1) is a 40K file, whereas the simpler spiked ball (3) is just 20K. The large spaceships (2) result in a file size of 46K.

THE INTERNET
3-D MODELLING (2)

Artwork created using 3-D modelling programs doesn't have to be complex – and it doesn't need to be futuristic, despite the overwhelming temptation to build fantasy spaceships and asteroids.

The spinning floppy disk icon, right, simply indicates a file that can be downloaded to disk. The icon is so self-explanatory that there's barely any need for text instructions: the downwards-pointing arrow (down for downloading, up for uploading) and the disk itself are enough to explain the purpose to the user. But it's the kind of image that could only have been created with a 3-D modeller: details such as the light flare on the metal sliding disk cover would be almost impossible to create effectively by any other means. The drop shadow, placed far enough away to allow the disk room to spin above the page, is another entertaining feature.

However, remember that all of these features take their toll on the file size, which is impractically large at 56K.

Altogether more complex is the rippling Canadian flag icon, which uses just ten images to get its message across. When viewed as an

1 | 2 | 3
The Canadian flag (1) takes up just 20K on disk compared with a relatively large 56K for the complex floppy-disk animation (2). At just 60K, the large spinning compass (3) seems like much better value.

animation, this flag really does appear to wave convincingly in the breeze. The ripples move smoothly from left to right, the final frame linking back into the first to create an endlessly-repeating animation. This is one example of a computer-generated image that looks truly photographic when in motion.

The spinning compass, right, requires no fewer than 40 frames to enable its smooth animation. As the pointer passes each of the corners and the north point, the indicator at that position lights up with a smooth glow that takes five frames to come to full brightness and to fade away again.

At the bottom right corner of the compass is an array of four tiny lights: these illuminate in turn as the pointer moves over them.

3

THE INTERNET
COPYCATS: THE OPERATING SYSTEM...

A favourite trick among website designers is to copy the operating system, so that their site looks like a typical user's desktop.

The download area of the Psion website takes the animation technique used by Windows and applies it to the header of the area. On Windows, the icons for copying and printing files demonstrate the process by showing a piece of paper flying between two static icons – a computer and a printer, or a computer and an external disk. Here, the paper flies between a standard folder (representing the storage area of the website) and the user's Psion device, in this case a Series 5 palmtop machine.

Each frame of the animation is drawn separately, showing the paper flying and twisting through the air as it completes its path. As a little extra joke the paper does a pirouette in mid-air before continuing its journey to the Psion.

While the animation may be pretty to watch, it is, in this instance, a little confusing. The animation shows the copying in progress – but runs whether or not a file is being downloaded. Users might spend some time watching the animation and waiting for their download to complete, without realizing it hasn't started yet.

Above Linking two icons with an animation was originally a Windows trick, here copied on the Psion website.

COPYCATS: THE OPERATING SYSTEM

...AND THE AWARDS

Right Internet sites, like any media industry, love showering each other with awards – and many sites proudly display their badges of excellence on their home page.
The Corporation (www.thecorporation.com) provides a wide selection of humorous fake awards, a few of which are shown here. These are freely available to download from its website.

the corporation
THIS SITE BITES

the **99¢** AWARD

A **Linus McAllister** Memorial Web Page

I LOST ALL OF MY MONEY TRADING ON THE **WEB**

THE LOW COUNTER AWARD
0001
FOR MEDIOCRE WEBSITES

This site has been proofed for accuracy on the
VISTAWEB-3000

<joke>
<This site is made with certified
VIRUS FREE
HTML>
</joke>

HYPOCRITICAL ANARCHIST'S
Patriot AWARD

TONY'S
4 SLICE SITE

the **genX** AWARD for User Profile & Target Market EXCELLENCE

CARPAL TUNNEL Site of the Week

THE OFFICIAL **AOL** Trial Disk COLLECTION AWARD

My First **CIGARETTES**

This site is **BRAILLE CAPTIONED** for the **VISION IMPAIRED**

I'd rather be watching **TV**

STARGAZER **LOST SATELITE AWARD**

SELL OUT SITE OF THE MONTH

The **OFFLINE PRESS** ANALOG AWARD

If this were your page, you'd be **HOME** by now.

This site is best viewed with **VistaView 3D NavGoggles**

TOP 95% of the **WEB AWARD**

TITANIC NAVIGATION AWARD

IAMBIC PENTAMETER MAN **SUPER SITE**

STOP KITTY PORN FELINE EXPLOITATION

Eternally **UNDER CONSTRUCTION**

117

THE INNOVATORS • 120

SUSAN KARE • 122

KATJA RIMMI • 126

CASE STUDIES

119

CASE STUDIES
THE INNOVATORS

Today's icon designer has a wealth of reference material to draw upon. For every type of file, folder, application, control panel, hardware driver and storage medium there is an established language, a ready-made catalogue of symbols and cultural references reduced to iconic form. For every new application, the designer has only to study a quarter of a century of innovation and evolution to see which metaphors work and which fall on stony ground. The challenge now is to come up with something new, but within the established framework of the graphical tradition.

Back in the early 1980s, the computer icon had yet to be invented. At the sharp end of the process was Susan Kare, whose contribution to the world of icon design cannot be overstated. It was she who designed the original Apple icons, and who, to a large extent, shaped the graphical user interface we use today. Designing those first icons meant not only creating the physical instance of the drawings, but devising the entire metaphor from scratch. Yet where we might have expected those early icons to be tentative, awkward first steps, we find instead bold and enduring statements.

THE INNOVATORS

Creating an environment from scratch is one skill; maintaining a complex network of interlocking, related icons is another speciality entirely. Katja Rimmi, User Interface Manager at Adobe Systems, is responsible for maintaining the consistent look and feel that is pivotal to Adobe's vision of a coherent graphics market.

Where some software publishers choose to celebrate the diversity of their products, Adobe chooses the route of pure consistency. Its argument is that if users are used to one Adobe product, then when it comes to buying new software they'll feel more at home in an environment that's both familiar and comfortable. This extends throughout the application design process: not only the icons but above all the toolbars, cursors and palettes must be as similar as possible across core graphics applications. At Adobe, it's Katja Rimmi's job to ensure that the consistency is maintained.

The work of these two designers represent very different aspects of the icon design process, yet both are integral to the experience of using contemporary software. Over the next few pages we'll look in more detail at their careers and output.

121

Tool palettes:
1 Illustrator 8.0
2 Illustrator 9.0
3 Photoshop 4.0
4 Photoshop 5.0
5 Photoshop 6.0
6 ImageReady
7 InDesign

CASE STUDIES
SUSAN KARE

Few designers can have had as much impact on the day-to-day lives of computer users as Susan Kare. A fine arts graduate (with an MA and a PhD to her name), Susan left her job as Assistant Curator at the Fine Arts Museum in San Francisco to become a freelance graphic designer. Then she got a call from Andy Hertzfeld, one of the original Macintosh programmers (and an old high school friend). Apple was developing its graphical user interface, and needed a designer to work on proportional fonts and icons. And so, in 1982, Susan Kare joined Apple Computer as its Creative Director.

Susan was responsible for the icons that have now become part of the graphic language. From the original MacPaint interface, to the system, file and application icons, Susan's icons have formed the basis for the icon set still in use today.

'I feel happy that a number of these have, at least briefly, weathered the test of time,' she says modestly.

The Macintosh icon set, the first of its kind, was a step in the dark for the developing team. 'I had a lot of freedom to come up with ideas, and got comments and suggestions from many people in the Macintosh group. The icon set evolved over time as we tried and replaced images and fonts. The first thing I did was the Chicago font, originally called Elephant.'

That Chicago font was just one of the set of bitmap fonts that shipped with early Macs. In the days before scalable PostScript, each font had to be custom drawn for each screen size at which it was going to be used. At a time when font displays on computers were ugly, rudimentary arrays of pixels, a proportional, serif typeface like New York made documents look, for the first time, as if they weren't created on a computer.

One of the more extraordinary font designs was '5 dots' – so called because it managed to render an entire alphabet in a height of just five pixels. Squeezing text into such a tiny space is still relevant, even in today's world of 1440dpi inkjet printers: look at any contemporary application icon that includes text, and it will be based on Susan's original 5 dots design.

1
The toolbox from MacPaint, designed in the early 1980s. Most of these icons are still used in graphics programs today.

2 – 9
An assortment of icons designed for the original Macintosh interface:
2 Folder icon
3 Printer icon
4 Alert icon
5 Startup icon
6 Application icon
7 System icon
8 Watch cursor icon
9 Document icon

SUSAN KARE

Chicago ABCDEFGHIJKLMNOPQRSTUVWXYZ
abcdefghijklmnopqrstuvwxyz 0123456789 10

New York ABCDEFGHIJKLMNOPQRSTUVWXYZ
abcdefghijklmnopqrstuvwxyz 0123456789 11

Geneva ABCDEFGHIJKLMNOPQRSTUVWXYZ
abcdefghijklmnopqrstuvwxyz 0123456789 12

5 dots ABCDEFGHIJKLMNOPQRSTUVWXYZ abcdefghijklmnopqrstuvwxyz 0123456789 13

Cairo 14

Los Angeles ABCDEFGHIJKLMNOPQRSTUVWXYZ
abcdefghijklmnopqrstuvwxyz 0123456789 15

Athens ABCDEFGHIJKLMNOPQRSTUVWXYZ
abcdefghijklmnopqrstuvwxyz 01234567890 16

San Francisco ABCDEFGHIJKLMNOPQRSTUVWXYZ abcdefghijklmnopqrstuvwxyz 0123456789 17

ABCDEFGHIJK 18

10 – 18
A range of bitmapped fonts designed for the first Macintosh computers. The tiniest screen font ever, '5 dots' (*13*), was just five pixels high: shown here (*18*) at 1000% of its original size.

123

CASE STUDIES

When Steve Jobs left Apple to found NeXT computers in 1986, Susan joined him in the project, managing the fledgling company's graphic identity. Two years later, she joined the opposition: the days of DOS were at an end, and Susan was hired to design the icons, buttons and screen appearance for Microsoft's Windows 3.0 operating system. One particular challenge was to design the cards for the Solitaire game included as part of the Windows package. 'I really enjoyed working on the cards: the challenge was making them seem like real playing cards, and making something as rich as possible with the 16-colour VGA palette.' Susan didn't even have the luxury of a scanner back then: 'These were done pre-scanners – we had one very rudimentary black-and-white one. I just drew these cards with the Paint Brush program in Windows.'

With a client list that includes AT&T, Motorola, IBM, Sony Pictures and Sun Microsystems, Susan has transformed the way we work. Her timeless designs may have been modified and adapted over the years, but the principles remain.

Susan is not always happy about the direction some of her icons have taken in the hands of others. 'I'm puzzled by Apple's use of the head in profile used independent of the square that cropped it,' she says of the figure originally designed as the icon for an alert dialogue (see page 122). 'It was a face fragment, not a whole face.'

But the designer who gave us the watch icon, the Trash can and the Lasso tool spends little time looking back. Hired by IBM to liven up IBM's successor to its OS/2 operating system, Susan's talents are as much in demand as ever.

'In general, I believe that icons should work a bit like traffic signs: they should convey information without distracting the user; without competing with the data in an application. Ideally, they should suggest something about the functionality. If it is not completely evident, then the function should be easy to remember if the user is told only once.'

Opposite The interface set for Windows 3.0, designed in 1988.

Above Four of the hand-drawn playing cards from the Windows set.

CASE STUDIES
KATJA RIMMI

Katja Rimmi is the User Interface Manager at Adobe Systems. After gaining her degree in Photography and Graphic Design, she joined multimedia software company mFactory, where she designed the user interface (UI) for its groundbreaking multimedia authoring application mTropolis – later bought (and immediately closed down) by Quark. Katja moved to Adobe in 1997.

'My first product at Adobe was the interface for Photoshop 5. The engineers had been on the product for many years, so they were very experienced; they were a well-oiled machine, which was refreshing after having been at a start-up where everything was kind of chaotic. We didn't want to make any radical changes; we were careful to make as few keyboard shortcut changes as possible. It really wasn't a very dramatic release in terms of interface. The next versions will be more of an attempt to focus on the interface.'

Photoshop 5 followed hot on the heels of version 4, which caused consternation among some users over the changes in its interface design. In many ways, moving from 3 to 4 was like learning a new product. Did this experience limit the range of possibilities introduced in version 5?

'Photoshop is a very old product, and making changes to it is different from making changes to a product that was made from scratch over the last couple of years. This is one of the things we run into most often, that users shouldn't have to be aware of. But it certainly affects our job as UI designers. This is one of our biggest challenges: how to keep the products in sync, and at the same time how to evolve features so that the UI is better.'

Adobe is king of graphic arts software, and many of its users are visually highly literate. Does this pose particular problems for the icon designer, or does it make the process easier?

Brainstorming — Application — Application

Semi-final icons — Application — Project

Final icons — Application — Project

While software developers are reluctant to allow the public release of ideas which didn't make it past the drawing-board stage, the defunct nature of mFactory allows us access to the early concepts for the mTropolis icon suite. The comparison between the initial ideas, the near-misses and the final set gives us a unique insight into the world of corporate icon design. All the icons are based around buildings, in keeping with the metropolis theme. But whereas the 'semi-final' icons used a two-point perspective, the front face of each building was squared up for the final release. The Roman Coliseum icon for the Player lost out to a more contemporary power station, and the colour scheme was unified.

| Player | Library | mToon | Preferences | Mod Resources |

| Player | Library | mToon | Preferences | Mod Resources |

CASE STUDIES

'If your target audience are individuals who are very visual, they're more likely to recognize something obscure. Our challenge lies in the fact that our audience is much more diverse than we often realize. Only about 30 per cent of Photoshop customers are professionals; a large number of them just use it for a couple of limited tasks. It's just something that's in everyone's toolbox.'

Adobe, like many other developers, chooses the archaic over the modern when designing icons: so the Pen tool is represented by an ancient fountain pen, the Clone tool by an outdated rubber stamp, and so on. How are these images chosen?

'The challenge of icon design is to come up with something that will be widely recognized by a great diversity of people, like a paintbrush or a magnifying glass. Whether or not someone actually uses a magnifying glass on a daily basis – and they probably won't, it's kind of an old-fashioned item – is less of a concern than whether or not they'll have some clue as to what it might be. If we were to use a lupe or something more complex, it would be harder to represent and fewer people would recognize it.

'If you think of the typical representation of a telephone as an icon, it's usually the old-fashioned phone, the one with the rotary dial. Certainly few of us uses those today, but we all recognize it as a telephone. You don't see icons of cell phones: we're just using something that's generic enough that a large number of people will recognize it.'

Which is all very well, but a generation is coming to computers which has no knowledge of rotary telephones or fountain pens. Will these icons make any sense to them, or will they simply represent long-dead objects whose meaning is obscure?

'I don't worry so much about cross-generational issues as about cross-cultural ones. We have enormous problems with them. A lot of software developers

1 | 2 | 3 | 4
Toolbars from Photoshop (1), Illustrator (2), InDesign (3), and ImageReady (4). Maintaining a consistent 'look and feel' is essential to Adobe's design philosophy, providing users of new software with a familiar environment.

underestimate the difficulty of making your product suitable for a different market. A lot of developers assume that a straight translation is all that's needed; we're starting to discover that for the Japanese, the product line needs to be different. It's an entirely different world from the one we're accustomed to. Their techniques are different, their tools are different, and they've been putting up with less than adequate products for a long time.'

So at what point in the development process do the icons begin to appear? And which comes first, a tool's icon or its name?

'As marketing, engineering and interface design collaborate on the creation of a new tool, the functionality and the name are often defined at the same time. Partly from necessity, since we need something to refer to in our discussions. The name, icon and behaviour are all things that we are open to changing, based on the user feedback we receive during our design process. We collect feedback from our alpha testers, site visits and from usability testing along the way.'

The 32x32-pixel constraint of icon design can be maddeningly frustrating: some ideas simply can't be translated successfully into this tiny size. Does the limitation ever get too much?

'At times, yes. You're in a world of miniature art, and you go a little crazy after a while. We've tried to create as much of a system as we can, so it's not too maddening. Our most challenging task is taking box art – the actual product – and making that into a 32x32 icon.'

A notable example of this difficulty is the InDesign icon, a fuzzy representation of a butterfly drawn in greyscale. It has little of the sharpness of other icons: it clearly seems a case of the box art not being reproducible at icon size.

CASE STUDIES

Adobe application icons InDesign Illustrator

'All of our product icons are monochromatic with a colour border. In the case of InDesign [above], the border is teal which is perhaps too neutral to be distinguished. We are starting to dabble in full colour and will evolve our icon guidelines over time. We want to tie the packaging artwork into the application and document icons for consistency. However, something that looks great at a large size doesn't always scale well and vice versa. The butterfly symbolizes freedom (the freedom that InDesign gives to designers) and it works very well for packaging. But it was difficult to scale down to such a small size. Here lies the challenge for our designers. We're working on it!'

One of Adobe's best-known applications, Illustrator, uses a section from Botticelli's *The Birth of Venus* as its icon. And yet this masterpiece of oil painting is precisely the kind of artwork that cannot be created with Illustrator. So why was it chosen?

'Illustrator has evolved over the years from a product that focused on templates and tracing to one that can be used to create sophisticated artwork. The packaging has evolved, as well. The first version years ago was very simple line art; the painting as backdrop was added in more recent versions. In either form, I think that the Illustrator packaging is creative, artistic, and also beautiful.'

The biggest shake-up in the interface design world for some years has come in the shape of OS X, Apple's next-generation operating system. OS X uses scalable icons, which zoom up to 128x128 pixels when the user passes the cursor over them in the task bar. What are the implications for the designer?

Photoshop

ImageReady

'OS X is allowing us to go full colour, and at a larger size. If developers want to provide multiple sizes so they will look good at all those sizes, then they can; if they want to provide just one size and have it scaled in both directions, they can. For us, because we want it to be high quality, it will mean having to design multiple icons at different sizes. It'll mean a lot more work for us, but I think it will be of benefit to the customer. It'll be nice to have the opportunity to work on something that's larger than 32x32.'

OS X also introduces coloured lights in its window title bars, a feature which many at the design end of the market have criticized as potentially distracting. What is Adobe's view of this development?

'We've been offering our feedback to Apple from the perspective of our customer base. Certainly, the use of colour and animation are two large concerns right now. For some customers, the use of colour in the UI is fine; but for those focusing on colour correction and colour preservation, it can be frustrating.'

OS X may be the immediate next step, but what of the future? How does Katja see the user interface changing in future system releases?

'The user experience for OS X took us all off guard – none of us really knew what they were up to, and how dramatic the changes were. I'm sort of hoping that things will stay stable for a couple of releases, because I'm still reeling from the changes in this one.'

So is OS X, overall, good or bad?

'I haven't yet spent a lot of time working with it as my daily platform. Only through long-term use can you really tell if a thing's going to drive you crazy.'

THE BASICS • 134
ICON FAMILIES • 140
ICON MASKS • 142
DESIGN TOOLS • 144
THE DESIGN PROCESS • 150
TYPE WITHIN ICONS • 162
ICONS FROM SCANNED IMAGES • 164
ANIMATED ICONS • 168
WINDOW ICON ARRAYS • 176

DESIGNING ICONS

133

DESIGNING ICONS
THE BASICS: LINES & ANGLES

Icons are bitmap images, in which the design is created using an array of pixels arranged (generally) in a 32x32 grid. Unlike PostScript images, in which lines are vector objects defined by mathematical parameters, bitmap images use nothing but squares of colour to create the line.

Icons appear on monitors that usually have a display resolution of 72 dots per inch (although many users opt for a higher resolution, if their graphics card is powerful enough). Bitmap images prepared for printed materials, such as scanned photographs, use a much higher resolution to conceal the pixellation from the reader; in addition, high-resolution images use anti-aliasing techniques (a slight blurring of the pixels) to further distract from the pixel base.

For the icon designer, anti-aliasing is generally not an option within such a tight grid, because of the extra pixels needed for the blurring effect. This imposes severe restraints on the design process: most importantly, the dominant angles chosen for an icon must be those which look smoothest on screen. Some angles work well, others look awful; in this section we look at ways of choosing angles that will make icons look their best.

Without doubt the smoothest angles you can use are orthogonals – that is, lines at 90° increments. To put it another way, verticals and horizontals.

These angles cause the pixels to butt right up against one another, effectively hiding the pixellation altogether. But an icon composed entirely of 90° angles would look rigid and amateurish; it's rare, if ever, that an icon set uses just these angles.

Many icons use 90° angles as their basis. The standard file and folder icons, for example, are essentially rectangles with minor variations – turned down corners for document icons, small tabs for folders.

After 90°, the smoothest angles are those at 45° increments. The reason is clear: the pixels step one vertically and one horizontally all the way along the line in a regular pattern. The resolution of computer screens is just fine enough that the eye is deceived into seeing these stepped arrays as smooth lines.

The early Macintosh application icons were all designed using this rotated square as an outline shape, within which extra elements were added to indicate the function of the program to which the icon belonged.

The next best angles after 45° are 30° increments – that is, 30°, 60°, (90°), 120° and so on. The stepping process here isn't quite as smooth as 45° lines, but again the eye is willing enough to be deceived. This time, the pixels step two up and one along (or two along and one up, as the case may be).

Angles of 30° provide the best compromise between smoothness and flexibility. Architects and draughtsmen use lines at these angles (in combination with verticals and horizontals) to create 'isometric' drawings – three-dimensional views lacking in perspective.

Once you go beyond 90°, 45° and 30° angle combinations, the icons start to look more ragged. One way of minimizing the stepping effect is to ensure the lines follow a regular pattern. The left side of the triangle above, for instance, is a line at 56.3° from the horizontal: it's made up of pixels that step two up and one along, then one up and one along, this pattern repeating along its length.

The other two sides in this figure are composed of alternate steps of two and three pixels, producing a line of 68.2° and 21.8° from the horizontal respectively.

The regularity of the stepping helps the line to work, but it's clearly less satisfying than any of the previous options: you should not make dominant angles in this way.

Lines with no repeating pattern, or with one that's so irregular it is hard to discern, look worst of all. An icon designed in this fashion will look ugly and amateurish; lines like this are to be avoided at all costs, even as minor elements within an icon.

DESIGNING ICONS

THE BASICS: CORNERS & CIRCLES

Once the dominant angles are decided upon, the next step is to choose the outline shape for the icon. Again, the limitations of the bitmap format come into play: a pixel out either way can mean the difference between an amateurish and a professional-looking icon.

The problem is the way the pixels fall at the corners. The top example shows rectangles drawn at 45° angles: in the first (*1*), the bottom and right-hand corners are composed of two pixel blocks rather than single pixels, which gives an uncomfortable feel to the icon. This situation is easily remedied by moving the line which subtends these two corners left and up by a single pixel, as is seen in the second illustration (*3*).

The bottom diagrams on this page show the same problem applied to rectangles drawn at 30° increments (30° and 60°). Here, again, the top and right corners work according to the 2x1 stepping rule; but the bottom and left corners fudge the join, again making the corners appear cut off. Once again, this problem is fixed by moving the line a single pixel up and left.

The need to adjust the position of lines to make corners work is a small matter, but it does affect the overall design of the icon. It's not possible, for instance, to create a diamond-shaped icon (a square rotated 45°) that perfectly fills the 32x32 grid: the need to have a single pixel at each corner means that the total width must always be an odd number of pixels, so the icon must be one pixel short of the grid size.

1 | 2 Corners look blocky when the joins don't follow the rule for drawing the line angles.

3 | 4 The solution is to move the lines by a single pixel so that the corners work smoothly.

While this is not a severe constraint, it's one that must be borne in mind during the design process.

Circles and ellipses can often be the hardest shapes to create convincingly within the confines of a square pixel grid. As the diagram

THE BASICS: CORNERS & CIRCLES

5
Circles will always have flat sides, no matter how carefully they are drawn.

(above) shows, the smaller the circle becomes, the more jagged the end result will be.

Even at the largest size, there are still uncomfortably long stretches of straight lines (here made up of groups of six pixels) at the extreme top, bottom, left and right. As the circles decrease in size, it's the curves between these flat edges that lose resolution, becoming proportionately smaller in relation to the space taken up by the flat sides. This is not merely a question of drawing the circle more accurately; the images shown are the best possible fit within the grid.

Rounded corners on rectangles, however, can be achieved to good effect with only the minimum of effort. In the two examples shown right, the corners of both of the squares have been rounded off. In the first, a single pixel makes the rounding off work: it's a clean and neat solution, which hides all the jaggedness associated with true circles. As the corner radius increases, as in the second example, the effect becomes more jagged and less convincing.

6 | 7
When rounding off the corners of rectangles, less is more: the single pixel rounding is a far cleaner solution than the wider-radius effect.

DESIGNING ICONS

THE BASICS: COLOUR

All modern computers are capable of displaying at least 256 colours, otherwise known as 8-bit colour (2 to the power of 8 is 256).

These 256 colours, a subset of the total possible range of over 16 million colours (24-bit colour) are composed of combinations of red, green and blue, and for the sake of comparison the values of each colour have been shown here in the 24-bit range, which runs between 0 (no colour) and 255 (full-strength colour). The total number of colours available is therefore 256x256x256, or 2 to the power of 8+8+8, which equals 16,777,216 total colour combinations.

While, as has been stated, there are no computers now manufactured that use fewer than 256 colours, this wasn't always the case: the earliest colour systems were capable of displaying only 16 colours (2 to the power of 4). Most Windows icons are still created using just these 16 colours, and the option to display 'maximum colours' is rarely enabled by users.

While Apple Macintosh computers use 256 colours by default, Apple themselves have traditionally restricted the colour set for their icons to a range of 34 colours selected from this total capability in order that all icons on the Mac desktop have a harmony of appearance. As the Apple *Human Interface Guidelines* has it:

This entire set of 34 colors was chosen to be subtle. Subdued colors avoid a 'circus' effect on the screen.

If you use too many of the same types of colors, people can't discern what is important as easily. Ramps of color based on the initial colors chosen were created to provide shading and blending capabilities. Some light colors were included in the set to be used for large areas… the total set of colors provides maximum flexibility in design.

Apple also included the seven colours in the Apple logo (although it has now officially ditched that expensive logo in favour of a single-colour version).

All Apple system icons use this 34-colour set, as do icons for applications, files and folders created by third-party manufacturers who choose to stick to Apple's interface guidelines. Perhaps surprisingly, most do: the result is, as Apple intended, a harmonious appearance to the desktop, keeping bright colours to a minimum.

This 34-colour set is shown on the facing page (far right). It's clearly a more subtle set than that used by Windows (near right), with a wide range of grey shades to enable fully shaded objects to be drawn. Where colours are required that don't fit within the set, Apple recommends (and itself employs) dithered chequerboard patterns of colour to make the new variant.

The Windows colours show a clear arithmetic sequence: with the exception of a single shade of mid-grey, the colours are made from all possible combinations of no colour (0), half strength (127) and

The standard 256-colour palette that makes up the total range of 8-bit colour.

THE BASICS: COLOUR

full strength (255) for each of the red, green and blue channels. As a result, the Windows desktop takes on a brash, toy-like appearance, with primary colours screaming at the user.

Because of the limitations of commercial four-colour printing, the colours shown here on the page appear much duller than their true on-screen counterparts. The true RGB (Red, Green, Blue) values are given for reference.

2
The Windows 16-colour palette, showing the RGB composition of each colour.

3
The preferred Apple colour palette, which uses 34 colours chosen to ensure a harmony of appearance on the desktop.

4
The full range of 16.7 million colours (24-bit) is rarely used for icon design.

RED	GREEN	BLUE
0	0	0
0	0	127
0	127	0
0	127	127
127	0	0
127	0	127
127	127	0
191	191	191
127	127	127
0	0	255
0	255	0
0	255	255
255	0	0
255	0	255
255	255	0
255	255	255

RED	GREEN	BLUE
0	0	0
17	17	17
34	34	34
68	68	68
85	85	85
119	119	119
136	136	136
170	170	170
187	187	187
204	204	204
221	221	221
238	238	238
255	255	255
51	51	102
102	102	224
153	153	255
204	204	255
51	0	153
0	0	221
0	153	255
153	255	255
51	102	102
51	153	102
0	187	0
51	255	253
255	102	51
204	153	102
255	204	153
255	255	204
153	102	153
153	0	102
255	102	204
221	0	0
255	255	0

139

DESIGNING ICONS
ICON FAMILIES

1
256-colour icon for both 32x32-pixel size (*above*) and 16x16-pixel size (*left*).

2
16-colour icon for both 32x32-pixel size (*above*) and 16x16-pixel size (*left*).

Icons in professionally designed applications are never created in isolation. Apart from the need to create file and settings icons that reflect the main application icon, there's also the requirement to create six or eight separate pieces of artwork for each icon. These are known as families and these families ensure that the icon will work as a double-clickable item, and that it will work equally well on all computers.

Shown here is the icon family for Apple's CD Audio player. The main icon for the family is the 8-bit (256-colour) version; a second 4-bit version, in 16 colours, is required for systems incapable of 8-bit display. A further icon, stripping out all the colour, is needed for black and white displays. The final piece of the jigsaw is the icon mask, which defines the icon's limits. For more on masks, see the following section in this chapter.

ICON FAMILIES

3
Two-colour (black-and-white) icon for both 32x32-pixel size (*above*) and 16x16-pixel size (*left*).

4
The icon mask created for both 32x32-pixel size (*above*) and 16x16-pixel size (*left*).

As well as the 32-pixel icons, a quarter-size set at 16x16 pixels is needed for list and small icon views. Usually this is a design based on the original rather than simply a reduction of the original. In the example shown here, the 16-pixel icon is a simplification of the 32-pixel main icon: it clearly relates to the original, but the constraints of this far smaller size mean that much of the detail has to be omitted to make it fit in the space.

The examples shown here are particularly good reductions of the original, keeping the feel while losing most of the detail.

On Windows platforms, the 256-colour icon is usually dispensed with altogether, and only 16-colour versions of the two sizes need to be created.

DESIGNING ICONS
ICON MASKS

Masks are an essential part of icon design. They play two roles: firstly, to define the area clicked by the user to activate the file; and secondly, to enable the icon to appear against a coloured or patterned background – for instance, if the icon is placed by the user on the desktop rather than within a folder.

If an icon's mask is not created by the user, one will be made for it automatically. So, on a Macintosh, any image can be created and placed on a file or folder by simply copying it and pasting it within the file's Get Info dialogue. The system will then calculate where the mask is, based on the assumption that external contiguous white areas are not included within the mask design. Any areas bounded by a dark outline (preferably black) are deemed to be within the icon area; light areas without an outline can cause some confusion.

The simple telephone icon on the facing page looks acceptable when displayed on a white background. But when placed on a coloured background, it's clear that the area between the phone and its cable on the left-hand side, which should appear transparent, is in fact pure white. This is because the mask was not drawn specifically for the icon, but was created automatically.

1 | 2 | 3
When an icon has a correctly defined mask, it appears properly silhouetted when placed against a white, coloured or patterned background.

4 | 5 | 6
The icon's mask defines the clickable area. The first two cursors are selecting the icon, whereas the third misses.

4 Hit

5 Hit

6 Miss

The silhouette below the image shows the actual mask created; the correct mask produces a transparency effect.

The question of the clickable area for the user is more important than might at first appear. If an icon is composed of a number of disparate, fiddly areas with no overall enclosing shape, it can prove difficult for the user to select it: clicking on an area outside the mask (but within the 32x32-pixel grid) can

produce no effect if the area clicked upon by the pointer happens to be a transparent area within the icon's bounding area.

On the Windows platform, masks are standard 1-bit objects – that is, each pixel is either black (on) or white (off). The same was true on the Macintosh until OS 8.5, when 8-bit masks were introduced. For the first time, this gave designers the scope to use semi-transparent areas within an icon design. The darker the shade within the mask, the more opaque the icon is at that point. Transparency enables the icon to fade away on the desktop, as well as within a white-background folder, and is used to create the subtle fading shadows seen on modern Macintosh icons.

If your end user does not have the latest system versions, the masks won't work and the icon will look ugly. For this reason, most icon designers still use 1-bit masks unless they're sure it will be displayed on an appropriate platform – for instance, when creating applications that run only under that operating system. In general, 1-bit masks are used for compatibility.

To create a correct mask a dedicated icon editing program should be used, such as ResEdit, Iconographer, IconEdit or IconForge. These are discussed overleaf.

7 | 8 | 9
Examples of 1-bit (black-and-white) and 8-bit (256 greys) masks, showing the soft edge produced by the latter (8). The last example (9) is an extreme case, using a gradient from black to white to gradually fade away the icon.

10 | 11
Incorrectly drawn masks can result in icons that display badly when placed on coloured backgrounds, as is highlighted by these instances showing the incorrect (10) and correct (11) way to create a mask.

DESIGNING ICONS

DESIGN TOOLS: CUSTOM ICON APPLICATIONS

There are dedicated tools for creating icons and the resources that accompany them, available on both Mac and Windows platforms. While these applications offer only a fraction of the image editing capabilities of a fully-fledged bitmap program such as Photoshop or PaintShop, they have the advantage of creating icon masks easily, as well as restricting the colour set to 16 colours and, for the Mac, the 34 colours recommended by Apple in its manual, *Human Interface Guidelines*.

The standard Mac application is ResEdit, available free from Apple (www.apple.com). ResEdit is a powerful tool for modifying the resources within files and applications. While being a dangerous tool in the hands of experimenting amateurs, when used solely for icon creation it offers an appealing combination of ease of use and extended functionality.

A more powerful, dedicated icon program is the shareware Iconographer (available from

1
The Icon Editor in ResEdit, the resource editor supplied free by Apple.

2 | 3
The Mac application Iconographer adds Photoshop-like editing tools and colour editors, as well as providing support for 8-bit masks and Windows icons.

www.mscape.com) which provides support for Apple's new 8-bit masks, 16-bit icons and for Windows icons. It also provides useful colour and contrast controls.

There is no similar program available from Microsoft, so, as usual, shareware developers have created their own alternatives. Two of the best are IconEdit (available from www.alberts.com) and the powerful IconForge (www.cursorarts.com), which adds animation functions to its range of tools. As with most shareware products, these programs may be used for a trial period before you decide whether or not to purchase them.

There are many benefits to using a dedicated icon application, even if your initial work is done in a high-end paint application. Apart from the mask creation, there's the ability to view and switch between elements of the same icon family (256-colour, 16-colour and mono versions, as well as large and small sizes).

It is also possible to view an enlarged and actual-size version of the work in progress within the same window, which makes it easy to make fine single-pixel adjustments to an icon.

4
IconForge is a powerful editing tool for Windows, offering sophisticated animation controls as well as standard icon creation effects.

5
IconEdit, one of the shareware applications made for the Windows platform. IconEdit provides basic editing tools, but doesn't show the icon on patterned backgrounds.

DESIGNING ICONS

DESIGN TOOLS: PHOTOSHOP

Photoshop is the justified king of the bitmap-editing world. Designed as a photo-retouching program, its application stretches far beyond. Photoshop can be used for virtually any pixel-based design or illustration task.

There are many advantages to using a high-powered program like Photoshop, even for creating the tiny images required for icon design. The most obvious feature is the layer implementation of the program. Each layer in Photoshop can hold a single element, which can be moved, rotated, edited and recoloured independently of the rest of the illustration. It's as if the image on each layer were painted on a sheet of glass, enabling complete transparency in all areas not filled with opaque pixels.

In the example below, a simple Internet icon is constructed from three layers – a globe, a phone and a pencil. Layering allows the icon designer to move the elements around, flipping them as required.

1 | 2
Photoshop's Layers feature (1) allows each element in a composition to be placed on its own layer, which can then be moved, edited or recoloured individually. The Layers functionality makes editing and designing icons far easier, as each item can be treated as a separate object (2).

By dragging each layer up and down within the layers palette, the layers can be reordered. So the phone, initially between the globe and the pencil, could for instance be moved behind the globe layer. It's this flexibility that allows the designer tremendous creative freedom to experiment with all aspects of the design.

Another useful feature is the ability to open more than one view of the same artwork. This is of particular benefit in icon design as it enables you to work on a greatly enlarged view for single-pixel editing, while keeping an actual-size view open in a separate window. Among Photoshop's other features is the ability to replace a colour selectively within a layer: the example below shows the telephone being recoloured from its original purple colour to a strong green, simply by selecting the range of purples and dragging the Hue slider to change every instance of that colour. Note that colours outside the range – such as black and white – are not affected.

3
The Replace Color feature makes it easy to change colours within a layer, without having to manually select the colour first.

DESIGNING ICONS
DESIGN TOOLS: PHOTOSHOP & ANTI-ALIASING

Anti-aliasing is a technique used in digitized images to compensate for the stepped appearance which may result because the images are made up of grids of individual pixels rather than continuous tones.

The term 'aliasing' originates in the technology used to display type on monochrome monitors. Because it wasn't possible to render type at small sizes exactly, due to the pixellation effect of the monitor's grid pattern, pixels were placed as near as possible to their correct location. This resulted in an ugly, jagged effect.

Anti-aliasing, which is only possible on monitors capable of displaying a range of greys or colours, gets around this problem by blurring the edges slightly, creating additional pixels that use an intermediate range of colours to blend the edges into the background.

An example of anti-aliasing in practice can be seen in this circle (right), which has a two-pixel-wide outline. The jagged effect is clearly noticeable, even at small sizes. One solution is to anti-alias the circle: the result is a much smoother shape, the slight fuzziness serving to distract the eye from the jaggies. The enlarged version of the circle clearly shows the extra pixels added to create the smoothing effect.

While anti-aliasing is an excellent technique when used in large images, either for print or web delivery, the tiny size constraints of icon design means that there generally isn't enough space within the 32-pixel grid to contain the extra pixels needed for a convincing blending effect.

Because Photoshop is primarily designed for editing and creating large images, anti-aliasing is turned on as the default setting – not just for the elliptical Marquee tool, but for a host of other tools: the Lasso, the Line tool, the Magic Wand tool and the Paintbrush.

Anti-aliasing is almost always too high-powered for icon creation, and so should be turned off unless you're sure it's an effect you want – and that it's one you can

1 | 2
Anti-aliasing can make circles appear smoother (2), but it's a luxury that icon designers rarely have the space to get away with.

3 | 4
Photoshop's Paintbrush always anti-aliases (3), even when drawing straight lines. For more precise control, you can use the Pencil tool (4).

control within the limitations of the grid size. Even orthogonal lines drawn with the Line tool become fuzzy when anti-aliasing is turned on: a single-pixel-wide line will appear with pale borders on either side of it. The Paintbrush tool always anti-aliases, making it useless for precise editing. The feature can be disabled for most tools by unchecking the box in the tool's Options palette, but you should always use the Pencil rather than the Paintbrush for precise editing of individual pixels. The Eraser tool should also be set to Pencil or Block mode to avoid creating fuzzy erasures.

The problem with anti-aliased icon borders, is that only computers running recent Macintosh operating systems can display icons with fuzzy edges. For wider compatibility, masks must be 1-bit images that are pure black and white, either on or off. While it may in some circumstances be acceptable to use an anti-aliased image within an icon – such as the eyeball shown below – when placed on a coloured background an unpleasant, ragged halo is produced. Placing the anti-aliased element within a crisp border, such as the black circle shown, guarantees that the icon will work on any background.

5 | 6
Straight lines drawn with the Line tool, with anti-aliasing turned on (5) and off (6). When it's on, even horizontal and vertical lines are unacceptably fuzzy.

7
Turning off anti-aliasing is simply a matter of unchecking the relevant box in the tool's Options palette.

8 | 9 | 10 | 11
Anti-aliased edges may look smooth when seen against a white background (8), but if the icon is placed on the desktop the icon mask won't be able to cope with the nuances of transparency required to make the image blend in with the background (10).

DESIGNING ICONS

THE DESIGN PROCESS: INITIAL IDEAS

The first step in designing icons – or designing anything, for that matter – is to turn away from the computer and think about what's involved. Here, we'll look at the process involved in designing a suite of icons for an imaginary technical drawing application.

Preliminary sketches are best done on paper, so that you're not sidetracked by the technicalities and constraints of the process of making the design work.

The decision was taken to represent the application by an icon that would give an indication of its purpose, and so several elements were considered – all of them making use of common tools used in the conventional technical drawing process.

The set square and compasses shown right (*1*) were the first idea, and it had much to recommend it: the set square, easily recognizable as a drawing implement (and, moreover, one associated with precision) has the advantage that it can be drawn using only vertical, horizontal and 45° diagonal lines, which would guarantee the smoothest outlines possible. The set square was tried again (*2*), this time using a small figure to hold up the tool.

The protractor, another common drawing tool, was an obvious contender. But as (*3*) shows, that half circle would cause problems: circles can easily look ragged and unattractive. The x/y graph (*4*) was quickly dismissed, since the icon would be too bitty and would not hold together. Similarly, both the compass on its own (*5*) and the technical ink pen (*6*) went by the wayside, because of the difficulty that users would have in double-clicking an icon of such thin and spindly proportions.

The graph (*7*) was ruled out for the opposite reason: while being easy to select, it's too square and unimaginative.

THE DESIGN PROCESS: INITIAL IDEAS

The drawing board (*8*) seemed like an attractive idea at first, until the realization that the complex angles required to make the perspective work would be impossible to achieve without creating ugly jaggies.

The roll of tape (*9*) was considered too obscure, and the pencil tip (*10*) too chunky (if it had included the whole pencil, it would have been far too thin). The double protractor (*11*) looked too much like the London Transport logo, and the micrometer screw gauge (*12*) was too much of an engineer's tool.

The lighter fuel (*13*), used by every 'traditional' designer to clean up artwork, may be misleading to those whose careers began with the computer. But the opposite approach (*14*) in which elements found in the program itself are used goes too far the other way.

The ink bottle (*15*) and map pin (*16*) failed to fit the bill, and the hand holding the drawing pen (*17*) looked too much like a word-processing application. The tape measure (*18*) showed promise, as did the pot of tools (*19*) – which showed the range of drawing tools available in the program. The scalpel (*20*) might have indicated a cutting-edge tool, or it might merely have suggested that this was a program for surgeons.

21 | 22 | 23 | 24
The ones that got away: none of these potential icons is really strong enough – or conveys the correct message – to make it in the final analysis.

A number of ideas was worked up, none of which quite got the point across. The miniature man was too cute, and the compasses suffered from the angle problem: so much anti-aliasing was required to make the angle work without looking jagged that they just became a blur.

The tape measure seemed a good bet until we found it was impossible to combine other elements with it. The set square, however, remained a strong motif: instantly recognizable, bold, dominant and easy to select. This was chosen as the focus of the final design.

DESIGNING ICONS

THE DESIGN PROCESS: THE APPLICATION ICON

The set square, as the main focus for the icon, had to be as convincing as possible. The orange colour was selected to be reminiscent of the orange plastic set squares used both in school and by draughtsmen.

The 45° angle was one of the keys to this device's strength, and meant that subtle shading could be added to show the bevelling on the edges: this would give the impression of light shining through the bevels. Tick marks along the edges give the impression of measurement rules.

After experimentation, the decision was taken to merge the set square with the pot holding the drawing tools.

After creating a new layer, the front side of the pot was drawn in shades of blue to simulate shading. To make the shading more subtle, a chequerboard pattern of alternating pixels was used between differing shades of blue. This pattern is generally more effective than simply drawing bands of very similar blues, as this can easily lead to an unwanted banding effect that would make the pot look as though it was striped.

Once created, the pot could now be sent to the back simply by dragging the layer that contains it behind that of the set square.

Photoshop's layers feature is perhaps the most compelling reason to use the application, rather than a dedicated icon-creation program. The ability to move, reorder and rearrange layers enhances the creative process tremendously: final decisions can be put off until all the elements are in place, freeing the designer from what would otherwise be overriding constraints.

The pot could easily have been hidden directly behind the set square. But by allowing a portion of it to be seen through the hole, the sense of three-dimensionality is enhanced – even though only a few pixels of blue are actually visible.

! IMPORTANT: CHECK YOUR COLOURS

Before you start drawing in Photoshop, make sure you are using colours from the standard Mac or Windows 256-colour palette, rather than Photoshop's default 16 million colours. Otherwise, your icon will be turned automatically into 8-bit colour, and your work will have been wasted.

THE DESIGN PROCESS: THE APPLICATION ICON

The next step was to fill the pot. Again, a separate layer was created for each pen and so on, so that they could be moved and flipped if necessary.

The drawing pen was drawn at a precise 45° angle, in the opposite direction to the dominant angle of the set square to prevent it looking too arranged. It's almost impossible to depict a technical drawing pen accurately with so few pixels, so clues were given which would aid recognizability – the grey band around the top, and the extended tip (in reality, a nib of two pixels rather than one).

The pen was made red, a common colour for the real thing, with a darker band of maroon on the underside to create the shading effect.

Pencils are easy to draw: it's that single black pixel at the tip, representing the lead, that makes the device work within the icon.

A more serious consideration, however, was the angle at which to draw it. 45°, the perfect angle, would have made it exactly parallel to the set square; this would have looked too forced, and destroyed any impression that it had been dropped casually in the pot. So the next best angle, 60°, was chosen instead. With a stepping ratio of two up, one across, this is a necessarily more jagged angle than 45°; but as a small element of a much larger image, the angle would work without drawing too much attention to itself.

153

The compasses, originally drawn for an earlier version of the icon (see previous pages) was resurrected to fill the back of the pot.

Where the pen and pencil had to be upended in the pot in order to see the business end, the compass could easily be depicted by showing just the join at the top.

Being made of reflective metal, the compasses couldn't be drawn in a single colour with shading added on the lower edge. Metal reflects light in unpredictable ways so the shading had to be more random to avoid it looking like plastic. Because of the awkward angles of the arms, the compasses were placed low down in the pot to mask the jaggedness.

DESIGNING ICONS

With all the elements in place, all that was needed to complete the pot itself was the addition of a back (interior) side. Once again, a new layer was created so that this wouldn't interfere with the elements contained within.

Once the pot and all its contents were in place, these layers were grouped together so that they could be moved as a whole, in order to find the best possible location behind the set square.

The plastic of the set square is translucent rather than opaque, so to make the effect more realistic some of the pot needs to show through.

This was drawn in place, pixel by pixel, on yet another new layer. A dull, pale brown was used to simulate the blue pot being seen through an orange medium, and the chequerboard pattern that made up the pot's shading was continued into this brown layer.

Because the bevelled edges would refract rather than allow light to travel straight through, a stronger orange was used instead of choosing another shade of brown. This manages to give the impression that the bevels are on a different plane to the rest of the set square, but slightly darker to allow some of the pot's surface to show through.

The final step in the creation of this icon was to add a shadow (on yet another layer).

If it were certain that the icon would only be displayed on an Apple computer running system 8.5 or greater, the shadow could have been drawn using shades of grey to give a soft, fading edge, since that system supports 8-bit masks. But for greater compatibility, it was drawn using just a single shade.

The shadow of the pot was drawn at 45°; the shadow of the pencil, which sticks out from the pot at an angle, was drawn at the same angle to minimize the jagged effect.

THE DESIGN PROCESS: THE APPLICATION ICON

The screen shot below shows how the workspace was set up in Photoshop to make the creation process as easy as possible. The main image was zoomed in to 1200% so that individual pixels could be edited easily. A second view was opened at 100% and placed to one side, so the image could also be viewed at its final size.

The icon, as is usual, was drawn in a 32x32-pixel grid. But this meant that there was always a thin black border around the image area (a Photoshop default) which conflicted with the view of the icon. To remedy this, the canvas size was increased slightly, and the area outside the 32-pixel grid filled with pale blue. That way, it was possible to see the icon's bounds while still being able to judge how it would look on the desktop.

Note, also, that each element has its own layer. The more layers, the more control you have. And by naming each layer as you go along – it takes a matter of seconds – you can be sure not to draw on the wrong one.

DESIGNING ICONS

THE DESIGN PROCESS: THE FAMILY (1)

For a complete professional solution, each single icon needs to be created in all its states – 256 colour, 16 colour and black and white, with an associated mask – for both large and small views.

Any custom icon tool should be able to assist in the creation process; here, Apple's freely available ResEdit has been used to show how the task can be accomplished.

The icon needs a new resource fork, which is easily created either within the file containing the application to which it is attached, or in a new file. This resource, of the type icl8 (see above), will hold the data for the 8-bit version of the icon.

The simplest way to get the icon in place is to copy and paste it from Photoshop – make sure that Export Clipboard is checked in Photoshop's preferences dialogue first, or the copy won't be made. When pasted into ResEdit, the icon will appear both in the large editing window and at actual size. Also displayed are the icon as it will appear on a chequerboard grey background, as an 'open' file (in use) and as an 'offline' file (located on an ejected disk). At present, the icon mask is a 32-pixel square that does not conform to the icon's outline.

The 2-colour icon (black and white) is most easily created in

THE DESIGN PROCESS: THE FAMILY (1)

1
ResEdit's New Resource Type dialogue.

2 | 3
The 8-bit version, created in Photoshop and pasted into ResEdit (2), together with the 1-bit (black-and-white) version (3).

4 | 5
The icon mask (4), generated from the 1-bit version, with the 4-bit, 16-colour version (5), generated from the 8-bit version.

out well on any background. Then again copy and paste the icon from Photoshop into ResEdit.

The icon mask can easily be created next, by pasting in the black-and-white version and filling all the white spaces within the icon with black to create a solid mask. The effect can be seen instantly: the icons in the panel on the right now appear correctly drawn on their backgrounds.

The 4-bit version can also be created directly from the 8-bit version, using copy and paste. When reduced to 16 colours, the icon will look brash and unsubtle: that authentically plastic orange, for example, is replaced with a dazzling yellow.

Some dithering may appear as ResEdit attempts to simulate the original colour by using a pattern made up of closest matching shades; these will almost always look awful, and should be edited out pixel by pixel using colours from the true 16-colour set.

Photoshop by making a new layer and drawing over the elements of the original. The translucent set square is rendered using a chequerboard pattern of pixels; elsewhere, the decision has to be made whether elements are shown in black or white. Subtle shading is impossible so the right side of the pot is solid black, as is the pencil barrel. It's useful to give the icon a solid black outline, so that it stands

DESIGNING ICONS

THE DESIGN PROCESS: THE FAMILY (2)

Small icons are sometimes generated by reducing the large version, and sometimes created as new pieces of artwork that relate to the original without copying it directly. Here, the former course of action has been followed to show the potential problems.

Since the small versions are half the height and half the width of the large icon, they are composed of one-quarter of the number of pixels. This makes them technically far harder to work with.

The simplest way to begin is to reduce the image size of the original icon, in Photoshop, from 32x32 to 16x16 pixels. Photoshop, however, is designed primarily for working with photographic images and will, by default, treat any resizing as if it were a scanned image. Simply reducing the icon's size will result in the blurry, unsatisfactory result shown in (*1*) above. This is due to bicubic interpolation, a sophisticated technique designed to improve the look of photographic images, which results in anti-aliasing that's inappropriate to an image of this size. When bicubic interpolation is turned off and 'nearest neighbour' selected instead (found in Photoshop's Image Size dialogue box), the result is far crisper, as the next picture (*2*) shows.

Much of the subtlety, however, has been lost by this simple resizing procedure. The small icon then needs to be retouched as shown in (*3*) so that the shading and bevelling can be recovered.

Once the small icon has been edited so that you're happy with the results, it's time to follow the same process as used for the original icon, of copying and pasting into ResEdit, tweaking the 1-bit and 4-bit versions and building the icon mask in exactly the same way. After all these stages, the complete icon family will now have been created. The resource editor will now show a separate resource for all the states for this icon (*4*) within its information window.

THE DESIGN PROCESS: THE FAMILY (2)

159

5
The variant states of the small icons are created in exactly the same way as those of the large icon.

6 – 13
The complete icon family for the application icon:
6 8-bit, 32×32
7 4-bit, 32×32
8 1-bit, 32×32
9 mask, 32×32
10 8-bit, 16×16
11 4-bit, 16×16
12 1-bit, 16×16
13 mask, 16×16

DESIGNING ICONS
THE DESIGN PROCESS: RELATED FILES

Applications rarely exist on their own. Almost all create files of one sort or another; many have additional settings files, including preferences, colour palettes, custom brushes, dictionaries and so on.

For this fictional drawing application, the final stage is to create the associated file icons that make up the set.

The first set of icons, shown on this page, are the document icons attached to files created by the main application. For recognition, all these icons use the standard turned-corner design that defines them as documents. Sticking to common practice in this way makes it easier for the user to navigate a folder full of files.

The first icon is the 'native' file – that is, the icon for a document created by (and intelligible only to) the application. This is a simplification of the main application logo, set behind a different sort of set square: this one uses 30° and 60° angles, rather than the 45° square used for the main application.

The exported documents can be of many different types, and the usual practice is to create a generic icon for them and to vary the lettering beneath. Three export types are shown here.

There may be many kinds of settings files, depending on the type of application they relate to. On the facing page the six settings files are based around the set square, with icons in the corners to differentiate them.

Again, following standard procedure makes it easier for the user. And so the Preferences icon uses 'radio buttons' that typically indicate either/or choices in dialogues; the Colour icon uses swatches of red, green and blue; and the Setup icon represents a standard monitor display. By limiting the icons to standard shapes (document or square) you're also avoiding the problem of having to create a fiddly mask for each icon.

1 | 2 | 3 | 4
The icon for a standard document created by the drawing application (1), together with icons for exported file types (2, 3, 4).

THE DESIGN PROCESS: RELATED FILES

5 | 6
A range of icons for settings files that use words as well as visual clues to identify their purpose (5). The icons at actual size (6).

DESIGNING ICONS
TYPE WITHIN ICONS: ECONOMY OVER STYLE

The alphabet on this page was designed in the early 1980s by Susan Kare as part of her development of the first Macintosh interface. Called '5 dots', it's precisely five pixels high, and is an extremely economical way of conveying readable text in the smallest possible space.

When text is used within icons, however, space is at an incredible premium. So much so, in fact, that even 5 dots is frequently too wide. The limitation of the 32-pixel width means that a word such as 'GRADIENT', used, for example, on one of the Photoshop settings icons, is exactly 29 pixels wide – which means that once a pixel is taken off the square for a drop shadow, there's only one pixel either side to contain the word. If 5 dots had been used, the word wouldn't fit.

Given the design limitations, there isn't that great a choice of typography for use within icon design. The text must be legible and economical with space; and so the letter forms shown on this page tend to be used

TYPE WITHIN ICONS: ECONOMY OVER STYLE

instead when space demands it. The type isn't as clear or as elegant as 5 dots, but it does get the point across in the smallest space. Although many of the characters can be condensed – the letters 'A', 'B', 'C' and 'D', work as well in three-pixel widths as they do in four – some characters refuse to be condensed. 'M' and 'W' always demand five full pixels, and 'N' (rather irritatingly) cannot be displayed in fewer than four pixels: knock out one of the dots of the diagonal and it turns into H.

1
'5 dots', the original tiny font designed for Apple by Susan Kare.

2
A slimmed down version, more suitable for rendering tiny text within icons.

DESIGNING ICONS
CREATING ICONS FROM SCANNED IMAGES (1)

Scanned images are always hard to work with when reduced to icon size, which is why almost all icon designers choose to draw from scratch instead. That said, it's possible to achieve reasonably convincing results with the least amount of effort.

The hardest part of the process is in choosing an image that will work at the size required. The clock (*1*) might appear to be a simple enough device for use as an icon, but when reduced down to 32x32 pixels (*2*) it becomes too fuzzy and indistinct. And it gets worse: simply reducing the file size still produces a 24-bit (millions of colours) image. When reduced to 8-bit colour depth (*3*) even more of the subtlety is lost.

The baby's head (*4*) is far more suitable, as it combines simplicity with instant recognition – faces are always easy to make out. When reduced to icon size (*5*) the features are still clearly visible.

Once again, though, this is a 24-bit rendering of the original image. Changing the mode from RGB to Indexed Colour, which enables you to choose between Mac, Windows and web colour sets, reduces the number of colours to the standard range. Generally, there are three main ways of converting RGB to indexed colour, which aim to keep colour fidelity as much as possible.

A straight, no-dither conversion (*6*) creates solid blocks of the colours that most closely match the original. This is usually an unsatisfactory approach, resulting in a posterized (flat, stepped colour) effect that looks unconvincing. The Pattern Dither solution (*7*) creates a regular pattern of colour that works well for flat colours, but looks too like a chequerboard when used on skin tones. The best results are obtained using Diffusion Dither (*8*), which uses a random pattern to hide the regularity.

Since small features are lost in the reduction process, it's often necessary to put them back in manually, a pixel at a time. With no highlights in the eyes and teeth, this baby looks dead.

The obvious choice (*9*) is to place white pixels in the eyes, with one for each tooth. But this looks phoney and artificial: for a more subtle approach, sample light shades from colours within the image (*10*) to create a more harmonious and less glaring result.

CREATING ICONS FROM SCANNED IMAGES (1)

4 | 5
When this baby's head is reduced to icon size, the image is still strong enough to work despite the loss of detail.

6 – 10
Choosing the correct dithering method when converting the image to 8-bit can make a big difference to the realism of the final image.

165

4

5

6

7

8

9

10

DESIGNING ICONS
CREATING ICONS FROM SCANNED IMAGES (2)

Choosing the right starting image is the key to making scanned images work as icons. This row of books (*1*) is neatly squared up, which avoids the anti-aliasing problem around the edges. When reduced down to icon size (*2*) the leather bindings are still recognizable, but the result is too dull to stand out well. Using the Unsharp Mask filter (*3*) to increase the definition helps a lot, as does adjusting the contrast (*4*) so that the books appear brighter. Once the ragged edges are squared off (*5*) the appearance is much neater; and when converted to 256 colours (*6*) the dithering is virtually lost among the leather bindings. That squared-up base is just a little too regular, and looks as if the image has been cropped: deleting a few pixels to give a rounding effect looks far more convincing.

CREATING ICONS FROM SCANNED IMAGES (2)

Working with squared-up images avoids the problem of anti-aliased masks. The baby icon created on page 165 produces an ugly white halo effect around it when placed on a coloured background (7) which looks clumsy. The standard solution, to incorporate a black outline (8), looks poor enough on this background – but when placed on a white background (9) it looks awful.

Most designers, as has been stated, choose to avoid using scanned images in icons. One exception is Human Software, whose Photoshop plug-in Squizz! (far right) uses scanned icons in its interface – with notably poor results.

The icons for Cancel (cutting scissors), and Apply (an auctioneer's gavel) are visible, although one might question the metaphors employed. Those for Recall (a ringing bell) and Save (a piggy bank) can still be made out. But the icon for Reset is wholly unintelligible at this size. Even the icon for Full Page, showing a hand holding a magnifying glass, can barely be made out.

Photographic icons are perhaps a neat way of getting pictures of your children onto your computer, but are probably best avoided for professional purposes when designing icons.

10 Part of the interface for Photoshop plug-in Squizz! which uses photographic icons at a size that's often impossible to decipher.

DESIGNING ICONS

ANIMATED ICONS: THE 3-D MODELLING APPROACH

Almost any 3-D modelling application can be used to create convincing animated icons. Some are dedicated to working with text, others have more wide-ranging uses. Here, the MetaCreations figure modelling application Poser has been used to generate a moving image sequence.

In order that the sequence should loop convincingly, the first and last frames need to be the same (or, at least, close enough so that a jump between them is not noticeable). In this 20-frame sequence, a light circles the image of a head, which winks and then smiles as the light changes from orange to blue and disappears behind it.

Making the movie is the creative part of the process; what comes next is harder. For icons delivered via the Internet, file size is everything. Simply reducing the physical size of the image is one approach; but the file format in which the sequence is saved can make an enormous difference to the file size, and therefore to the time it takes the user to download the animation onto their computer.

The sequence shown in (*1*) is a medium-quality QuickTime movie, saved in millions of colours (24-bit). The images look their best in this format – but at a cost: this file takes up a massive 84K of disk space,

1
QuickTime movie, medium quality, 24-bit colour.
File size: 84K

2
QuickTime movie, low quality, 16-bit colour.
File size: 32K

ANIMATED ICONS: THE 3-D MODELLING APPROACH

3
GIF file, dithered.
File size: 24K

4
GIF file, no dither.
File size: 12K

which is far too large to justify the delivery time. By reducing the number of colours to 'thousands' (16-bit) and lowering the quality of the QuickTime movie to Low (*2*) the file size is reduced significantly – this time to 32K. The image quality, however, is noticeably poorer.

The other common format for delivering small animations is the GIF file. This has the twin benefit of producing smaller files, while allowing animations to loop endlessly. Sequence 3 uses a dithering technique to reduce the number of colours, using patterns to simulate intermediate shades. At just 24K, this represents a significant saving on the file size.

By turning off the dithering option, which results in flat (and sometimes inappropriate) colours, as seen in (*4*), the file size is further reduced to a tiny 12K.

With web design there is usually a trade-off between image quality and file size, and the result is almost always a compromise. Using strong, flat colours can help to minimize the effects of compression, and restricting the amount of movement between frames also helps keep file sizes down.

DESIGNING ICONS
ANIMATED ICONS: TWEENING

One of the simplest ways of creating an animated icon is to use a custom animation program such as Extensis PhotoAnimator, shown here, which is available for both Windows and Macintosh platforms. PhotoAnimator can output animated GIF files.

With an application of this type, you set specific marker points within the animation, known as keyframes. The application then performs an operation known as 'tweening', whereby it calculates the position of each object between each pair of keyframes. In the simple 12-frame animation shown here, the red ball bounces from top left to bottom centre, then up to the top right and across to top left. Three sets of keyframes are required for this motion.

PhotoAnimator uses a simple interface to determine the position of each element. The Image Repeat dialogue, shown right, shows the second stage in the bounce movement – from bottom centre to top right.

The main interface window of Extensis PhotoAnimator, which was used to create the simple animation shown here.

ANIMATED ICONS: TWEENING

2 The dialogue for setting movement between two keyframes over time.

3 The simple dialogue used to determine transitions.

4 The 12 frames that make up the finished animation.

As well as simply moving objects, the software can perform a variety of transitions. So the word 'ICON' takes six frames to disappear, using a simple fading mask; it then comes back into view from the bottom up, using a barn-door transition to reveal itself gradually.

The main window, on the facing page, shows the four layers that make up this animation: the ball, at the top; the word 'ICON', which remains static, with its mask shown below it; and the background frame, which includes the word 'ICON' in grey. This last version of the word is visible only when the yellow word is transparent.

The size of the finished GIF file depends upon the number of colours used to display it. As a dithered 256-colour file it weighs in at around 10K; when reduced to 16 colours with no dither, this size drops to under 6K.

As ever, there's a trade-off between quality and file size. For Internet delivery, the size of the file is of paramount importance: visitors to a web page may wait once for a host of flashy graphics to load, but they're unlikely to return if they feel their time and call charges have been wasted.

DESIGNING ICONS

ANIMATED ICONS: STEP BY STEP (1)

The other approach to creating animated icons is to build them frame by frame. This is not, of course, to suggest that each frame must be drawn individually: the programs are sophisticated enough to avoid that. This example uses Adobe ImageReady, which ships with Photoshop and provides a good environment for creating basic animations.

In this animation, two apparently distinct icons, a globe and a light gauge, are linked by sparks which fly between them as they interact. On the user's desktop, this kind of process is almost impossible; on the Internet, almost anything can be achieved. By toying with users' expectations, you encourage them to look afresh at familiar objects.

In ImageReady, you create new frames one at a time; each frame is initially identical to the last. By varying the visibility and position of layers in the artwork for each frame, the animation is gradually built up.

While layers and their masks can be moved between frames, they cannot be distorted, rotated or otherwise edited at the pixel level: this kind of 'destructive' change would affect the layer's appearance in every frame.

ANIMATED ICONS: STEP BY STEP (1)

Frames 1 to 11 in this animation show a light gauge rising, one step at a time, and changing colour as it rises. When it reaches the top, a nozzle and glass tube rise between frames 12 and 14: three different sparks cycle between frame 15 and frame 21.

While the sparks run, the globe (until now a static element) spins on its axis. This is simply constructed from two elements: a shaded blue ball, and a flat map of the world. The globe spins between frames 15 and 21, at which point it returns to its original position. The gauge then drops to zero, and the process begins again.

On the following pages is a more complete explanation of how the layers in this animation were created, and how they interact.

When creating an animated GIF, you have the option of determining how long each frame will last before the next appears. Here, each of the frames showing the gauge rising lasts half a second; the frames showing the globe spinning have no delay, so that the globe appears to spin quickly. The final frame, showing the globe stationary and the gauge at zero, lasts for two seconds before the animation begins again. ImageReady has many additional features, including the ability to see both the original RGB image and the web-optimized version side by side, showing both the finished result and the size of the resulting file – in this case, 39.7K – together with the time it will take to download. ImageReady has much of the editing power of Photoshop, and documents can be freely exchanged between the two.

Opposite The main interface of Adobe ImageReady, which allows the simple construction of animations with many useful enhancements.

Above The 24 steps in an animation created frame by frame.

DESIGNING ICONS

ANIMATED ICONS: STEP BY STEP (2)

The key to creating a successful animation lies in preparing the layered artwork correctly. Thanks to the flexibility of the interaction between Photoshop and ImageReady, you don't need to plan every element down to the last detail before you begin: alterations and additions can be made in ImageReady as you go along, or, if more image editing power is needed, you can switch the illustration back into Photoshop and edit it there.

Thirteen separate layers were created to build the animation shown on the previous page. These layers are shown here on a blue background to delineate the icon's boundaries; in reality, of course, the background was white. The layers appear here in order from the bottom up – so layer 1 lies at the bottom of the pile, layer 13 at the top.

Any element erased from a layer will affect that layer in all frames within the animation. But a layer mask can hide parts of the layer selectively, and can be animated independently of the layer to which it is attached; this greatly extends the possibilities of the animation process. This technique has been used to make the gauge rise (see layers 7 and 8 for details).

1
The base layer, holding the backgrounds for both the top and bottom icons.

2
The first part of the nozzles used to 'fire' the sparks. These are turned on first in frame 12.

3
The second part of the nozzles, appearing in frame 13. Splitting them in two makes them appear to grow.

4
The blue 'glass' sleeve, as it appears half way up (and half way down). When fully extended, it contains the sparks.

5
Making this red light appear to flash is a simple matter of turning it on and off alternately for successive frames.

6
This blue light was created by duplicating the red light and changing the hue.

7
The gauge is a series of horizontal bars fading from green through orange to red. Although the layer appears to animate, it's only the mask that moves.

8
This is the mask for the gauge. In this position, the gauge is fully visible: the mask starts at the bottom and rises by 4 pixels on each frame to animate the gauge.

ANIMATED ICONS: STEP BY STEP (2)

9
This simple shaded ball forms the basis for the globe, created by filling a circle with blue and painting light and shade onto it.

10
This flat map of the world is the only layer in the composition that's wider than the finished icon. This is because this layer moves from left to right throughout the animated globe sequence. When grouped with the ball layer, the map is visible only where it intersects the ball; set to Hard Light mode, it allows the shading to show through.

The composite image above shows the countries overlaid on the ball, but not yet grouped with it; the effect of the Hard Light mode can be seen clearly in the shading transferred from the ball to the countries on top.

11–13
Three separate layers hold the three elements of the spark. By cycling through these layers, the spark appears to dance around. Alternating between two layers would look as if it were simply flashing; the third layer deceives the eye into seeing a more random movement.

14
This frame sits above the globe. Fine horizontal white lines (barely visible here) give it a TV-screen appearance.

DESIGNING ICONS

WINDOW ICON ARRAYS

In Chapter 3 we looked at CD-ROM developers who create arrays of icons that appear as single large images in their CD windows. This effect is not hard to achieve and there are several shareware applications that automate the task for you. Here, we've used the Macintosh application Pict-2-Icons (available from http://thomas.cyberdream.net) to build a splash screen for a fictitious software company.

The first step is to create the artwork to the required size in a program such as Photoshop (*1*). By keeping each element on a separate layer it's easy to edit it afterwards. Performing a Select All and then Copy Merged command will place a composite copy of the image on the clipboard, which can then be pasted into Pict-2-Icons.

Pict-2-Icons does a fair job of dividing the image up into 32-pixel squares (*2*), adding extra space where necessary to ensure that the window is composed of icon-sized chunks. The software then attempts to fit the jigsaw pieces of the puzzle together within a folder window designated by the user. It makes a fair stab at it, and the occasional misplacement is easy to correct manually. The result (*3*) is a convincing image that will look imposing when the user opens the CD-ROM on the desktop.

WINDOW ICON ARRAYS

1 | 2
After preparing the artwork in Photoshop (*1*), copy it into Pict-2-Icons to have it automatically divided up into icon-sized chunks (*2*).

3
The finished icon array as it appears in the CD-ROM window.

3

It's worth stressing that this use of icons is really only suitable for CD-ROM distribution. The reason is simple: if any item is selected, that square (the icon in that position) will be highlighted and a blank text box will appear beneath it. If it is moved, or if a 'clean up' command is invoked to tidy the window, the icons will be entirely misplaced and the image will be lost. Piecing the original image back together would be a task suitable only for diehard jigsaw enthusiasts.

When distributed on CD, the original media is locked. This means that changes to the arrangement are not recorded; simply closing and reopening the window will reset the positions of all the constituent icons back to their original positions, and the image will be reconstituted.

GLOSSARY · 180

INDEX · 190

REFERENCE

REFERENCE
GLOSSARY

access path The description of the route taken to access a file, created when the file is opened.

active icon The status of the currently selected icon in a window or on the desktop, indicated by highlighting, usually as a negative of its inactive image.

active window The frontmost desktop or document window. Usually, only the contents of the active window can be modified by the user, although some types of window, such as floating palettes, allow their contents to be modified simultaneously. The active window is usually indicated by a bold title bar and active scroll bars.

airbrush tool A 'tool' used in some application programs to simulate the behaviour and effect of a mechanical airbrush.

airbrush/airbrushing A tool, invented in the USA around 1900, used in illustration and photographic retouching, in which a fine spray of paint or ink is propelled by compressed air.

aliasing The jagged appearance of bitmapped images or fonts occuring either when the resolution is insufficient or when they have been enlarged. Sometimes called jaggies, staircasing or stepping.

alpha channel A place where information regarding the transparency of a pixel is kept. In image files this is a separate channel – additional to the three RGB or four CMYK channels – where 'masks' are stored, simulating the material used in platemaking to shield parts of a plate from light.

alpha test The first testing, usually by the team developing it, of a complete software program in order to discover and eliminate errors ('debugging').

alpha version The first complete version of a newly developed software program, prior to testing and eventual release.

alphanumeric set The complete set of alphabet characters, numbers, punctuation and associated symbols and accents of a font.

anchor The facility, available in many applications, to define a fixed point, such as top left, top right, etc., for an item such as a text or graphic box, pages, or page rulers. Accordingly, values attributed to the item relate to the anchor point. In some applications, graphics or rules can be anchored to text so that they flow with it.

angle of view The angle between opposite faces of a viewing pyramid (the structure created by drawing two lines from the centre of a view to its edges).

animated GIF A 'GIF' (graphics interchange format) file comprised of multiple images, simulating an animation when played back in a web browser.

animation The process of creating a moving image by rapidly moving from one still image to the next. Traditionally, this was achieved through a laborious process of drawing or painting each 'frame' (a single step in the animation) manually on to cellulose acetate sheets ('cels', or 'celles'). However, animations are now more commonly created with specialist software which renders sequences in a variety of formats, typically QuickTime, AVI, Flash and animated GIFs.

animation value The value applied to a keyframe in an animation sequence which represents a change in the object's property and, in turn, determines how the animation of a sequence is interpolated.

anti-alias/anti-aliasing A technique of optically eliminating the jagged effect of bitmapped images or text reproduced on low-resolution devices such as monitors. This is achieved by blending the colour at the edges of the object with its background by averaging the density of the range of pixels involved. Anti-aliasing is also sometimes used to filter texture maps, such as those used in 3-D applications, to prevent moiré patterns.

Apple menu A menu item on a Macintosh computer, identified by the Apple logo, which is generally available in all applications and where, for example, information on memory usage and open applications can be gathered.

Apple Remote Access A Macintosh application which enables one Mac to connect to another via a modem, and then remotely control and access all the files and network services available to it.

application menu A standard menu which lists all opened applications and enables you to switch between them.

application (**support**) **file** A file used by applications for specific operations which are unique to that application, such as checking spelling or providing help.

application/application program A software program enabling the user to create and modify documents for a specific purpose, thus distinguishing it from operating system software and utilities (software which improves the functioning of your computer rather than enabling you to create anything). Typical application groups are for page layout, graphics, word processing and spreadsheets.

arrow pointer *x-ref* POINTER

ASCII (*pron.: asskee*) *acronym: American standard code for information interchange* A code which assigns a number to the 256 letters, numbers and symbols (including carriage returns and tabs) which can be typed on a keyboard. ASCII is the cross-platform, computer industry-standard, text-only file format.

authoring tool/application Software which enables you to create interactive presentations, such as those used in multimedia titles and websites. Authoring programs typically provide text, drawing, painting, animation and audio features, and combine these with a scripting language which determines how each element of page, or screen, behaves, such as an instruction contained within a button to tell the computer to display a different page or perform a specific task.

automatic text box A text box into which text flows when a page is automatically inserted. This is a feature of page-layout and word-processing applications.

axis (*plural: axes*) An imaginary line which defines the centre of the 3-D universe. In turn, the x, y and z axes (width, height, and depth, respectively) define each of the three dimensions of an object. The axis along which an object rotates is the axis of rotation.

banner (**1**) A headline which occupies the full width of a page of a newspaper or magazine.

GLOSSARY

banner (*2*) On a web page, an image used to attract attention, usually an advertisement.

beta test Software which is released – after alpha testing and prior to commercial release – for testing by designated members of the public for the purpose of eliminating errors ('debugging').

beta version The version of a software program prior to commercial release, used for final checks for errors ('beta tests'). Beta versions are also frequently used for review purposes.

Bézier curve In drawing applications, a curved line between two 'control' points. Each point is a tiny database, or 'vector', which stores information about the line, such as its thickness, colour, length and direction. Complex shapes can be applied to the curve by manipulating 'handles' which are dragged out from the control points.

binary file A file in which data is described in binary code rather than text. Binary files typically hold pictures, sounds, or a complete application program.

binary system Numbering system which uses two digits, 0 and 1, as distinct from the decimal system of 0–9.

bit A commonly used acronym for binary digit, the smallest piece of information a computer can use. A bit is expressed as one of two values – a 1 or a 0, on or off, something or nothing, negative or positive, small or large, etc. Each alphabet character requires eight bits (called a 'byte') to store it.

bit density The number of bits occupying a particular area or length.

bit depth The number of bits assigned to each pixel on a monitor, scanner or image file. One-bit, for example, will produce only black and white (the bit is either on or off), whereas 8-bit will generate 256 greys or colours (256 is the maximum number of permutations of a string of eight 1s and 0s), and 24-bit will produce 16.7 million colours (256 × 256 × 256).

bit map/bitmap Strictly speaking, any text character or image comprised of dots. A bit map is a 'map' of 'bits' which describes the complete collection of the bits that represent the location and binary state (on or off) of a corresponding set of items, such as pixels, which are required to form an image, as on a display monitor.

bitmapped font A font in which the characters are made up of dots, or pixels, as distinct from an outline font which is drawn from 'vectors'. Bitmapped fonts generally accompany PostScript 'Type 1' fonts and are used to render the fonts' shape on screen (they are sometimes called 'screen' fonts). To draw the shape accurately on screen, your computer must have a bit map installed for each size (they are also called 'fixed-size' fonts), although this is not necessary if you have ATM installed, as this uses the outline, or 'printer' version of the font (the file that your printer uses in order to print it). TrueType fonts do not require a bitmapped version.

bitmapped graphic An image made up of dots, or pixels, and usually generated by 'paint' or 'image-editing' applications, as distinct from the 'vector' images of 'object-oriented' drawing applications.

browser (*1*) An application enabling you to view or 'browse' web pages on the Internet. The most widely used browsers are Netscape's 'Navigator' and Microsoft's 'Internet Explorer'. Version numbers (sometimes referred to as 'generations') are important, as these indicate the level of HTML that the browser supports.

browser (*2*) An application for cataloguing and viewing image, animation and sound files, so that it is easy to keep track of where they are on your hard disk or archive media.

bundle In the Mac OS, a bundle is a resource which associates files with icons.

byte A single group made up of eight bits (0s and 1s) which is processed as one unit. It is possible to configure eight 0s and 1s in 256 permutations: thus a byte can represent any value between 0 and 255 – the maximum number of ASCII characters – one byte being required for each.

camera angle A general term describing the viewpoint of a camera, but also specifically referring to its angle from the horizontal.

camera moves A feature of 3-D applications which allows you to perform typical film and video camera movements in animated sequences, such as 'pans', 'tilts', 'rolls', 'dolly shots' and 'tracking shots'.

clipping path A Bézier outline that defines which areas of an image should be considered transparent or 'clipped'. This lets you isolate the foreground object and is useful when images are to be placed on top of a tint background in a page layout, for example. Clipping paths are generally created in an image-editing application such as Adobe Photoshop and are embedded into the image file when you save it in EPS format.

clone In image-editing, to duplicate pixels in an image in order to replace defective ones, or to add to an image by duplicating parts of the same, or another, image.

CLUT *acronym: colour look-up table* A preset table of colours (to a maximum of 256) which the operating system uses when in 8-bit mode. CLUTS are also attached to individual images saved in 8-bit 'indexed' mode – that is, when an application converts a 24-bit image (one with millions of colours) to 8-bit, it draws up a table ('index') of up to 256 (the total number of colours depends on where the image will be viewed – Mac, Windows or web, for example) of the most frequently used colours in the image. If a colour in the original image does not appear in the table, the application chooses the closest one or simulates it by 'dithering' available colours in the table.

CMM *x-ref COLOUR MANAGEMENT MODULE*

CMYK *abb.: Cyan, Magenta, Yellow* and *blacK* (black is represented by the letter 'K', for 'key' plate). The four printing process colours based on the subtractive colour model. In colour reproduction, most of the colours are achieved by cyan, magenta and yellow, the theory being that when all three are combined, they produce black. However, this is rarely achievable and would be undesirable since too much ink would be used, causing problems with drying time, etc. For this reason black is used to add density to darker areas, while to compensate, smaller amounts of the other colours are used (this also has

cost benefits since black is cheaper than coloured inks). The degree of colour that is 'removed' is calculated by a technique known as 'undercolour removal' (UCR).

colour library An application support file which contains predefined colours. These may be the application's default colours, colours defined by you, or other predefined colour palettes or tables.

colour management module A profile for managing and matching colours accurately across different platforms and devices. CMMs conform to a colour management system (CMS) such as that defined by the International Color Consortium (ICC). CMMs interpret the ICC profiles which describe the RGB and CMYK colour spaces on your computer. There are usually existing ICC profiles which are installed on to your computer by ICC-compliant applications such as Adobe Photoshop, or you can create your own. The selected profile is then embedded in the image you are working on so that it can later be used as a reference by other devices in the production process.

colour management system The name given to a method devised to provide accuracy and consistency of colour representation across all devices in the colour reproduction chain – scanners, monitors, printers, etc. Typical CMSs are those defined by the International Color Consortium (ICC), Kodak's Digital Science Color Management System, Apple's ColorSync and Microsoft's ICM.

command-line interface A user interface in which instructions are given to the computer by means of a chain, or line, of commands via the keyboard only. For example, the MS-DOS (Microsoft Disk Operating System) interface may prompt you to select one item from a list of options, then another, and so on until you reach your goal. In the worst examples of a command-line interface, you may not be presented with any options at all, but are simply expected to know the command – 'DIR' to display the contents of a directory, for example. The opposite of GUI (graphical user interface).

computer graphics Strictly speaking, any graphic item generated on, or output by, a computer, such as page layouts, typography, illustrations, etc. However, the term is sometimes more specifically used to refer to a particular genre of computer-generated imagery, such as that which looks as though it were generated by computer.

control character A non-printing character generated by the 'control key' (a 'modifier key' – one that is used in conjunction with another) which is used by some applications to perform a particular function.

control panel A small application which enables you to configure system software or to customize various aspects of your computer, such as date, speaker volume, etc.

control point In 'vector'-based (drawing) applications, a little knob, or point, in a 'path' (line) which enables you to adjust its shape or characteristics by means of 'Bézier control handles'.

controlling dimension One of the dimensions – either height or width – of an image, which is used as the basis for its enlargement or reduction in size.

creator code signature In documents generated by applications written for use on Macintosh computers, a four-letter code assigned to identify the application which created the document. Each creator 'signature' is registered with Apple Computer so that each is unique – for example 'QXP3', for example, identifies QuarkXPress, while Adobe Photoshop's creator code is '8BIM'.

cross-platform The term applied to software, multimedia titles, or anything else (such as floppy disks) that will work on more than one computer platform – that is, those which run on different operating systems, such as the Macintosh OS or Microsoft Windows.

crosshair/crossbar pointer The shape the pointer, or cursor, adopts when, in some applications, you select a particular 'tool'.

cursor The name for the blinking marker that indicates the current working position in a document, for example, the point in a line of text at which the next character will appear when you strike a key on the keyboard. The cursor may be represented by a small vertical line or block and is not to be confused with the 'pointer' – the marker indicating the current position of the mouse.

definition The overall quality – or clarity – of an image, determined by the combined subjective effect of graininess (or resolution in a digital image) and sharpness.

desktop (publishing) system A collection of standard desktop hardware devices and off-the-shelf software applications capable of handling the entire desktop publishing process. As distinct from specialist equipment, such as drum scanners, used in high-end prepress systems.

dialogue box A box that appears onscreen requesting information or a decision before you can proceed further, such as the box which appears when you save a file, asking you what to call it and where to save it to.

dimmed command The condition of an item in a menu or dialogue box when it is disabled or unavailable for use. The disabled item is displayed as grey or in a paler colour than its active counterpart, and is thus 'dimmed'. Also known as a 'greyed' command.

dimmed icon The condition of an icon which indicates that a file or folder is open or that a disk is unmounted (not available, as in an ejected disk). Also known as a 'greyed' or 'ghosted' icon.

disabled x-ref DIMMED COMMAND, DIMMED ICON

dither(ing) A technique of 'interpolation' which calculates the average value of adjacent pixels. This technique is used either to add extra pixels to an image – to smooth an edge, for example, as in 'anti-aliasing' – or to reduce the number of colours or greys in an image by replacing them with average values which conform to a predetermined palette of colours. For example, when an image containing millions of colours is converted ('resampled') to a fixed palette ('index') of, say, 256 colours. A colour monitor operating in 8-bit colour mode (256 colours) will automatically create a dithered pattern of pixels. Dithering is also used by some printing devices to simulate colours or tones.

download To transfer data from a remote computer – such as an Internet server – to your own. The opposite of upload.

downloadable font A font that can – or must – be loaded into the memory of your printer, as distinct from one that is already resident in its ROM or hard disk. Since printers usually come with very few preinstalled fonts, this often means that all the fonts you use must be downloadable. This is why, if you are using PostScript Type 1 fonts which come in two parts – screen font and printer font – the latter is frequently described as a 'downloadable font'.

draw(ing) application Drawing applications can be defined as those which are object-oriented (they use 'vectors' to mathematically define lines and shapes), as distinct from painting applications which use pixels to make images ('bitmapped graphics'). Some applications do combine both.

driver/device driver A small piece of software that tells a computer how to handle or operate a piece of hardware, such as a printer, scanner or disk drive. Depending on its function, a driver may be located with the operating system software and therefore loaded at start-up, or it may form a 'plug-in' to an application (as do some scanner drivers, for example).

drop-down menu The menu that appears when you click on a title in the menu bar along the top of your screen. Also called 'pop-down menu' or 'pull-down menu'.

edit menu A standard menu in most applications (in the Mac OS, one of the three standard menus alongside the 'Apple' and 'File' menus), containing commands for such actions as cut, copy and paste.

ellipse/oval tool In graphics applications, particularly those used for painting, drawing and page make-up, a tool which enables you to draw ellipses and circles.

ellipsis (1) A sequence of three dots (…) used within text to indicate a pause, or that part of a phrase or sentence has been left out. An ellipsis can be generated by a single keyboard character.

ellipsis (2) In menus and dialogue boxes, three dots following a command indicating that additional information is required before the command can be carried out.

encapsulated PostScript (EPS) A standard graphics file format used primarily for storing 'object-orientated', or 'vector', graphics files (a vector is a tiny database giving information about both magnitude and direction of a line or shape) generated by 'drawing' applications such as Adobe Illustrator and Macromedia FreeHand. An EPS file usually has two parts: one containing the PostScript code which tells the printer how to print the image, the other an on-screen preview which can be in PICT, TIFF or JPEG formats. Although used mainly for storing vector-based graphics, the EPS format is also widely used to store bitmapped images, particularly those used for desktop colour separation ('DCS'), and these EPS files are encoded as either 'ASCII' – a text-based description of an image – or 'binary', which uses numbers rather than text to store data. Bitmapped EPS files to be printed from a Windows-based system use ASCII encoding, whereas those to be printed on the Mac OS are usually saved with binary encoding, although not all printing software supports binary EPS files.

EPS *acronym: encapsulated PostScript* see ENCAPSULATED POSTSCRIPT

export A feature provided by many applications allowing you to save a file in an appropriate format so that it can be used by another application or in a different operating system. For example, an illustration created in a drawing application may be exported as an EPS file so that it can be used in a page-layout application.

extension A file which adds functions to a computer or application. Operating system extensions include such things as hardware 'drivers' which control devices such as printers and monitors, whereas application extensions (usually called 'plug-ins') can include any kind of enhancement, from mundane file-handling operations (such as importing and exporting documents) to more exciting special effects.

extension/init conflict A problem caused by some extensions being incompatible with other extensions, system files, or applications, and which may cause your computer to crash or behave erratically. Utilities are available which test and resolve extension problems.

external device Any item of hardware that is connected to a computer but resides externally – a disk drive, for example may reside internally or externally.

external reference A resource that resides in a location outside of the application using it.

eyedropper tool In some applications, a tool for gauging the colour of adjacent pixels.

file A collection of data which is stored as an individual item on a disk. A file can be a document, a folder, an application or a resource.

file compression A technique of consolidating data within a file so that it occupies less space on a disk and is faster to transmit over telecommunication lines.

file extension The abbreviated suffix at the end of a filename which describes either its type (such as EPS or JPG) or origin (the application which created it, such as QXP for QuarkXPress files). A file extension usually comprises three letters (although Macintosh and UNIX systems may use more) and is separated from the filename by a full stop.

file format The way a program arranges data so that it can be stored or displayed on a computer. This can range from the file format used uniquely by a particular application, to those that are used by many different software programs. In order to help you work on a job that requires the use of several applications, or to work with other people who may be using different applications to yours, file formats tend to be standardized. Common file formats are TIFF and JPEG for bitmapped image files, EPS for object-oriented image files, and ASCII for text files.

file menu One of three standard menus appearing in the menu bar of most applications, where you invoke commands which allow you to create, open, save, print and close files, and quit applications.

file type In the Mac OS, the four-letter code assigned to every file when it is created which identifies its kind or format, such as 'APPL' for an application, 'TEXT' for text files, and so on. Special software such as ResEdit is generally required to identify the file type.

filename The name given to a file. Macintosh filenames can be up to 31 characters long, whereas Windows filenames can be up to 255 characters, although it is usually safer (especially if the files are to be transferred between computer systems) to use the DOS naming convention of '8.3' (eight characters followed by a three-character suffix – all capitals). Windows filenames cannot contain any of the following characters: / \ | : * ? ' $$$ and when naming Macintosh files it is best to avoid: • : / \ since these can interfere with some program functions.

filter A filter, strictly speaking, can be any component which provides the basic building blocks for processing data. However, the term is more commonly used to describe particular functions within an application, such as importing and exporting data in different file formats or, in image-editing and drawing applications, for applying special effects to images.

floating palette A palette which is available all the time and can be positioned anywhere on your screen by dragging its title bar.

folder The pictorial representation of a directory, being a place provided by computer operating systems where you can organize your documents, applications, and other folders (when one folder is inside another, it is said to be 'nested'). Folders form the basis for the organization of all data on your computer.

font downloading The process by which a font file is downloaded, or sent, to a printer. A font may be available in the printer's built-in ROM chips, on its hard disk, manually downloaded into its RAM, or automatically downloaded by the printer driver when it is needed.

font file The file of a bitmapped or screen font, usually residing in a suitcase.

foreground application When working on a computer, the application that is currently active.

foreign file A document created in a different application or computer system to the one you are using.

format *x-ref* FILE FORMAT

frame (**1**) On the web, a means of displaying more than one page at a time within a single window – the window is divided into separate areas ('frames'), each one displaying a different page. Confusingly, although a window displaying frames may contain several pages, it is nevertheless described as a singular page. A common use of frames is to display a menu which remains static while other parts of the web page – displayed in the same window – contain information which can, for example, be 'scrolled'.

frame (**2**) An individual still image extracted from an animation sequence.

frame grab(**bing**) The capture of a single still frame from a video sequence.

frame-rate The number of individual frames in a film or video sequence displayed in one second. The common frame-rate for sequences used for computer display is 12–15 frames per second (fps), while in film it is 24fps, NTSC video 30fps and PAL video 25fps.

frames per second (**FPS**) The number of individual still images which are required to make each second of an animation or movie sequence.

freeform tool In graphics applications, any tool which allows you to draw shapes 'freehand'.

freehand tool *x-ref* FREEFORM TOOL

ghost icon *x-ref* DIMMED ICON

GIF *abb.: graphic interchange format. x-ref* GRAPHIC INTERCHANGE FORMAT

GIF89a *x-ref* TRANSPARENT GIF

grabber hand/tool In some applications, the tool which enables you to either reposition a picture inside its box, or to move a page around in its window.

graphic (**1**) A type design derived from drawn rather than scripted letter forms.

graphic (**2**) A general term describing any illustration or drawn design.

graphic interchange format (**GIF**) A bitmapped graphics format originally devised by Compuserve, an Internet Service Provider (now part of AOL), and sometimes (although rarely) referred to as 'Compuserve GIF'. There are two specifications: GIF87a and, more recently, GIF89a, the latter providing additional features such as transparent backgrounds. The GIF format uses a 'lossless' compression technique and thus does not squeeze files as much as the JPEG format, which is 'lossy' (some data is discarded). For use in web browsers, JPEG is the format of choice for tone images such as photographs, whereas GIF is more suitable for line images and other graphics, such as text.

graphical user interface (**GUI**) The concept of some computer operating systems which allows you to interact with the computer by means of pointing at graphic symbols (icons) with a mouse rather than by typing coded commands. Also known as 'WIMPs' or 'pointing interface'.

graphics tablet/pad Digitizing tablet

greyed icon Dimmed icon

grid (**1**) A structure used for designing publications with multiple pages, such as books and magazines, to aid consistency throughout the publication. The grid usually shows such things as column widths, picture areas and trim sizes.

grid (**2**) In some applications, a user-definable background pattern of equidistant vertical and horizontal lines to which elements such as guides, rules, type, boxes, etc., can be locked, or 'snapped', thus providing greater positional accuracy.

GUI (*pron.: 'gooey'*) *abb.: graphical user interface.*

guides In many applications, non-printing horizontal and vertical lines which help you position items with greater accuracy.

hierarchical file system (**HFS**) The method used by the Mac OS to organize and store files and folders so that they can be accessed by any program. Files are organized inside folders which may, in turn, be inside other folders, thus creating a hierarchy.

hierarchical menu A menu containing items which, when selected, generate their own menus, called 'submenus'. The presence of a submenu is normally indicated by a triangular symbol to the right of the menu item.

horizontal scaling A feature of some applications to condense or expand type. Horizontal scaling retains the exact attributes of the source font but distorts its appearance. While the feature can sometimes be used advantageously, it can also produce ugly typography, in which cases the specially designed condensed or expanded versions of the font, if available, may look more aesthetic.

HTML *abb.: hypertext markup language* A text-based 'page description language' (PDL) used to format documents published on the World Wide Web, and which can be used with web browsers.

human interface *x-ref* INTERFACE

I-beam pointer The shape of the pointer when it is used to edit or select text. As distinct from the 'insertion point' or 'cursor', which indicates the point at which text will be inserted by the next keystroke. Also called the 'text tool'.

IBM PC *abb.: IBM personal computer* Usually describing a PC made by IBM but also often used as a generic term for any PC which is 'IBM compatible' (actually meaning – usually – one that runs either Microsoft's 'DOS' or 'Windows' operating systems), thus distinguishing them from other computers, such as Apple Computer's 'Macintosh' series.

ICC profile *x-ref* COLOUR MANAGEMENT PROFILE

icon In a computer 'graphical user interface', a graphic representation of an object, such as a disk or file, or of a concept or message.

ideogram A symbol used to indicate a concept or emotion, such as joy, sadness, warmth etc.

image file Any digital file in which a graphic image such as a photograph is stored, as distinct from other data such as in a text file, database file or 3-D file, etc. Image files can be saved in a variety of formats, depending in which application they were created, but typically TIFF, GIF, JPEG, PICT, BMP, EPS, etc. Confusingly, the data format in which some images are stored is actually text, such as in an EPS graphic which is saved in 'ASCII' (text) format – but the file is still an image file. Not to be confused (!) with a 'disk image' which is the contents of a volume stored in a single file.

image-editing application, image editor A computer application for manipulating either scanned or user-generated images. Image-editing applications are pixel-based ('bitmapped' as opposed to 'vector'), and provide features for preparing images for process colour printing (such as colour separations), as well as tools for painting and 'filters' for applying special effects. Also called 'image-manipulation program' or 'paint program'.

image-manipulation program Image-editing application.

import/export filter In some applications, a feature for translating a file from the host format to that of another, and vice-versa.

indexed colour In some applications such as Adobe Photoshop, an image 'mode' of a maximum of 256 colours which is used to reduce the file size of 'RGB' images so that they can be used, for example, in multimedia presentations or web pages. This is achieved by using an indexed table of colours ('a colour look-up table', or 'CLUT') – either an existing table using a known palette of 'safe' colours or one constructed from an image – to which the colours in an image are matched and, if a colour in the image does not appear in the table, the application selects the nearest colour or simulates it by arranging the available colours in a pattern called 'dithering'.

init *abb.: initialization program* A small utility program ('extension') that runs automatically when your computer starts up and which modifies the way in which it operates. Some inits perform transparent tasks such as enabling peripheral devices to work, while others may be 'control panel' programs, which allow you to configure or customize their functions.

inkjet printer A printing device that creates an image by spraying tiny jets of ink onto a paper surface at high speed.

input resolution The degree of definition by which an image is 'captured', or recorded, so determining the final quality of output. Final output quality depends on three aspects of input: scan resolution, the size of the original image as compared with its final size (in which case resolution of the scanning device itself may also be significant), and resolution of the output device. To calculate input resolution, multiply the eventual halftone screen frequency by two and then multiply that answer by the ratio of the final image size to its original dimensions. For example, if the image is to be printed with a halftone screen of 150 lines per inch, multiply 150×2 to get 300. If the image has an original size of 2×3 inches but will be printed at a size of 6×9 inches, it has a ratio of 3 (9 ÷ 3). So, 300×3 = 600 – the input resolution, in dots per inch, for scanning the image.

insertion point The point in a document or dialogue box at which the next character or action typed on the keyboard will appear. It is indicated by a blinking vertical line ('text insertion bar') which can be positioned in the appropriate place by using the I-beam pointer and clicking.

installer A program which enables you to load software on to your hard disk. Installer programs will also put the application support files in their appropriate places, creating folders for them and putting files, if necessary, into your system folder. Installers are also updating programs.

interface The physical relationship between human beings, systems and machines – in other words, the point of interaction or connection. The involvement of humans is called a 'human interface' or 'user interface'.

interlaced GIF A 'GIF89a' format image in which the image reveals increasing detail as it downloads to a web page.

invisible file Any file that is not visible but nonetheless exists, such as directory files and icon files. Files can, for security reasons for example, be made invisible using a suitable utility program, although such files may still appear in directory dialogue boxes. It is common practice to make the support files of multimedia applications invisible.

item tool In some applications, a tool with which you can select, modify or move items.

jaggies/staircasing/stairstepping *x-ref* ALIASING

Java A programming language devised by Sun Microsystems for creating small applications

('applets') which can be downloaded from a web server and used, typically in conjunction with a web browser, to add dynamic effects such as animations.

JPEG, JPG *acronym: joint photographics experts group* An ISO group which defines compression standards for bitmapped colour images. The abbreviated form, pronounced 'jay-peg', gives its name to a 'lossy' (meaning some data may be lost) compressed file format in which the degree of compression from high compression/low-quality to low compression/high-quality can be defined by the user, thus making the format doubly suitable for images which are to be used either for print reproduction or for transmitting across networks such as the Internet – for viewing in web browsers, for example.

key frame A single animation frame in a QuickTime sequence in which information is stored as a reference so that subsequent frames only store changes in the frame ('differences'), rather than storing the whole frame each time, thus making the file smaller. The frames based on changes are called 'delta frames' or 'difference frames'.

lasso The lasso-shaped tool provided by many drawing and painting applications to make a selection.

layer In some applications and web pages, a level to which you can consign an element of the design you are working on. Selected layers may be active (meaning you can work on them) or inactive. Some applications may lay items one on top of another in the order that you created them, and in some cases will allow you to send items to the back or to bring them to the front.

layout A drawing which gives the general appearance of a design, indicating, for example, the position of text and illustrations. The term is more also used in the context of preparing a design for reproduction, where it is called a 'tissues' or 'overlay', the terms deriving from the transparent paper often used for drawing layouts.

library A feature of some applications which provides a facility for storing frequently used items or attributes (such as colours) that you have created so that you can access them immediately from within any document.

line tool In graphics applications, the tool used to draw lines and rules. If the tool can only draw horizontal and vertical rules it is usually called an 'orthogonal' line tool.

locked file A data file which cannot be modified or deleted.

magnify tool, magnifying glass A tool in most computer applications that will enlarge or reduce an area of the screen or part of a document. Also called a 'reduction tool' or 'reduction glass'.

margin guides A feature in some applications in which non-printing guides define areas of text or images.

marquee In some applications, a moving broken line drawn around an object or area in order to 'select' it or, in some cases, an area defined by an application to show that the space within is active or selected. The moving lines are colloquially known as 'marching ants'.

mask Any material used to protect all or part of an image or page in photomechanical reproduction, photography, illustration or layout. Many computer applications provide a masking feature which enables you to apply a mask to all or selected parts of an image. Such masks are stored in an 'alpha channel' and simulate the physical material used in platemaking which is used to shield parts of a plate from light.

masking To block out an area of an image with opaque material to prevent reproduction or to allow for modifications such as adjusting the values of colour and tone.

menu The display on a computer screen showing the list of choices available to a user.

menu bar The horizontal panel across the top of a computer screen containing the titles of available menus.

menu command A command given to your computer from a list of choices available within a menu, as distinct from a command made via the keyboard ('keyboard command').

menu indicator Symbols within a menu that expand the range of options. An ellipsis (…) following an item means that selecting it will display a dialogue box before the command can be executed; a check-mark indicates a command is already active; a right-pointing triangle points to a submenu; and a down-pointing triangle indicates that there's more on the menu.

menu title The title of a menu as displayed in the menu bar.

menu-driven A computer or application interface in which commands are given through a list of choices available from a hierarchy of menus. Synonymous with a 'command-line interface'.

modal dialogue box A dialogue box that, until it is closed, will not allow any activity to take place onscreen other than that within its box.

monogram A design comprised of interwoven characters, usually two or more.

monospaced (**font**) A font in which the type characters all occupy the same width space (as on a typewriter), as distinct from proportionally spaced fonts, which are more common. 'Courier' is a monospaced font. Also called 'fixed-width fonts'.

monotone Reproduction in a single colour, without tonal variation.

mouse The small, handheld, mechanical device which you manipulate to position the pointer on your monitor.

mouse event The action ('event') initiated by pressing the button on your mouse. This can happen at the moment you press the button down ('mouse-down'), or when you release it ('mouse-up').

MPEG *acronym: motion picture experts group* A compression format for squeezing full-screen, VHS-quality digital video files and animations, providing huge compression ratios of up to 200:1.

multimedia A generic term for any combination of various digital media, such as sound, video, animation, graphics and text, incorporated into a software product or presentation.

native file format A file format for exclusive use by the application in which the files were

created, although some applications may be able to read files created in another's native format.

nested folder In GUIs, a folder that is placed inside another folder.

operating system The software (and in some cases 'firmware') that provides the environment within which all other software and its user operates. The major operating systems are Microsoft's 'DOS' and 'Windows', Apple's 'Mac OS' and AT&T's 'UNIX', the latter three of which all use 'GUIs' (graphical user interfaces).

orthogonal line tool x-ref LINE TOOL

orthographic (**projection**) An illustration technique in which there is no perspective (or the perspective is infinite), thus giving parallel projection lines.

output resolution The resolution of a printer, monitor, imagesetter or similar device, usually measured in dpi (dots per inch). The relationship between output resolution and halftone screen ruling determines the tonal range that can be printed. The following formula should be used to calculate the optimum number of greys that can be achieved (remembering that 256 is the PostScript maximum): (output resolution ÷ screen ruling)2 + 1 = shades of grey. So, an image output at 1200dpi and printed with a screen ruling of 90lpi will produce 178 shades of grey. Increasing the screen ruling creates smaller halftone dots and adds detail to an image, but it also reduces the number of greys, so the same image output at 1200dpi and printed with a screen ruling of 175lpi will produce only 48 shades of grey. The screen ruling in four-colour process work is usually 150lpi, so for an image to print with the maximum number of 256 greys it will need to be output with an imagesetter resolution of 2400dpi. A typical resolution for a monitor is 72–90dpi, for a laser printer 600dpi, and for an imagesetter anything upward of 1000dpi.

oval tool x-ref ELLIPSE TOOL

page guides In some applications, non-printing guides that you can set to show the width of margins, position of columns, etc.

page-layout/make-up application Any application that enables you to carry out all of the functions normally associated with page design, layout and make-up.

paint(ing) application Applications which use bitmaps of pixels to create images rather than the 'vectors' that describe lines in drawing applications (called 'object-oriented'), although some applications combine both.

palette A window, often 'floating' (movable), that contains features such as tools, measurements, or other functions.

path A line drawn in an object-oriented application.

PICS animation A Macintosh animation format that uses PICT images to create a sequence.

PICT abb.: picture A standard file format for storing bitmapped and object-oriented images on Macintosh computers. Originally, the PICT format supported only eight colours, but a newer version, PICT2, supports 32-bit colour.

pictogram/pictograph A simplified, pictorial symbol distilled to its salient features to represent an object or concept.

picture box A box which holds a picture, as distinct from a text box.

picture skew The distortion of an image by slanting the two opposite sides of a rectangle away from the horizontal or vertical.

pixel acronym: picture element The smallest component of a digitally generated image, such as a single dot of light on a computer monitor. In its simplest form, one pixel corresponds to a single bit: 0 = off, or white, and 1 = on, or black. In colour or greyscale images or monitors, one pixel may correspond to several bits: an 8-bit pixel, for example, can be displayed in any of 256 colours (the total number of different configurations that can be achieved by eight 0s and 1s).

pixel depth The number of shades that a single pixel can display, determined by the number of bits used to display the pixel. One bit equals a single colour (black), four bits (any permutation of four 1s and 0s, such as 0011 or 1001) produces 16 shades, and so on, up to 32 bits (although actually only 24 – the other eight are reserved for functions such as masking), which produces 16.7 million colours.

pixellation/pixellization An image that has been broken up into square blocks resembling pixels, giving it a 'digitized' look.

plug-in Software, usually developed by a third party, which extends the capabilities of a particular program. Plug-ins are common in image-editing and page-layout applications for such things as special effect filters. Plug-ins are also common in web browsers for such things as playing movies and audio, although these often come as complete applications ('helper applications') which can be used with a number of browsers rather than any specific one.

PNG acronym: portable network graphics A file format for images used on the web which provides 10–30% 'lossless' compression, and supports variable transparency through 'alpha channels' cross-platform control of image brightness, and interlacing.

pointer A general term that refers to any of the many shapes on a monitor that indicate the location and operating mode of the 'mouse'. Typical pointer shapes are the arrow pointer, vertical bar, I-beam, crossbar or crosshair, and wristwatch. Sometimes confused with the 'cursor' (the typing location within a field or piece of text).

polygon tool A tool in some applications with which you can create irregular–shaped boxes, in which text, pictures or fills can be placed.

pop-down menu x-ref DROP-DOWN MENU

pop-up menu A menu in a dialogue box or palette that 'pops up' when you click on it. Pop-up menus usually appear as a rectangle with a drop shadow and a downward or side-pointing arrow.

PostScript Adobe Systems Inc.'s proprietary 'page description language' (PDL) for image output to laser printers and high-resolution imagesetters.

GLOSSARY

PostScript font *x-ref* TYPE 1 FONT

preferences A facility provided by most applications for modifying the default program settings (such as the unit of measurement). Modifications can often be applied to a single document or, sometimes, all documents.

prefs file An application file that records your preference settings so that when you reopen the application you don't need to reset them.

progressive JPEG A digital image format used for displaying JPEG images on web pages. The image is displayed in progressively increasing resolutions as the data is downloaded to the browser. Also called 'proJPEG'.

pull-down menu *x-ref* DROP-DOWN MENU

QuickTime Apple's software program and system extension which enables computers running either Windows or the Mac OS to play movie and sound files, particularly over the Internet and in multimedia applications, providing cut, copy and paste features for moving images and automatic compression and decompression of image files.

QuickTimeVR *acronym: QuickTime 'virtual reality*' An Apple extension which provides features for the creation and playback of 3-D objects or panoramic scenes.

reflection tool In some applications, a tool for transforming an item into its mirror image, or for making a mirror-image copy of an item.

ResEdit An Apple-supplied application for editing resources (icons, sounds, menus, etc.), used for modifying any Macintosh file or software program – system or otherwise.

resolution The degree of quality, definition, or clarity with which an image is reproduced or displayed, for example in a photograph, or via a scanner, monitor screen, printer or other output device.

RGB *abb.: red, green, blue* The primary colours of the 'additive' colour model.

roll In a 3-D environment, the rotation of an object or camera around the z-axis.

rollover The rapid substitution of one or more images when the mouse pointer is rolled over the original image. Used extensively for navigation buttons on web pages and multimedia presentations.

rotation tool In some graphics applications, a tool which, when selected, enables you to rotate an item around a fixed point.

ruler guide In some applications, a non-printing guide which you position by clicking on the ruler and dragging it to the desired location.

sad Mac icon A picture of an unhappy face that can appear at the beginning of start-up on Macintosh computers indicating that a fault has been diagnosed during the start-up tests performed by the computer. Often accompanied by a sound that differs from the usual harmonious startup chord.

save dialogue box A box appearing onscreen the first time a document is saved, requiring the user to supply its title and location.

scale drawing A drawing such as a map or plan which represents the subject matter in proportion to its actual size and to a specified scale. For example an object drawn to a scale of 1:10 means that one unit of measurement on the drawing is equivalent to 10 of the same units on the object at full size – so one inch on the drawing equals 10 inches at full size.

scale/scaling The process of working out the the degree of enlargement or reduction required to bring an image to its correct reproduction size.

selection marquee/rectangle/box A dotted line which forms a rectangle or box. The line is drawn by means of the pointer or a selection tool, and vanishes immediately the selection is made, or becomes a marquee.

shareware Software which is available through user groups, magazine cover disks, etc., which is usually only paid for by those users who decide to continue using it. Although shareware is not 'copy protected' it is protected by copyright and a fee is normally payable for using it, unlike 'freeware'.

spacer A blank, transparent GIF, one pixel wide, used to space elements on a web page.

spline The digital representation of a curved line that is defined by three or more control points, common in 3-D applications.

square corner tool A feature of most graphics applications, this is a tool used for drawing squares and rectangles. Also called a 'rectangle tool'.

start-up The process of turning on the power to a computer, and the start-up procedure it goes through in which certain checks are made – such as checking the RAM – and the operating system loaded into memory. If there is a fault it will be reported accordingly, or the computer may fail to start altogether. Also called 'booting up'.

start-up document *x-ref* INIT

suitcase file On computers running the Mac OS, a font file (TrueType), screen font file (PostScript 'Type 1'), or collection of sound files, represented by an icon of a suitcase.

symbol A figure, sign or letter that represents an object, process or activity. A computer icon, for example, is a pictorial symbol.

system The complete configuration of software and hardware components necessary to perform electronic processing operations.

system disk A disk containing all the necessary files of an operating system to start up the computer and carry out processing operations.

System Folder On computers running the Mac OS, a folder that contains all the files, including System and Finder files, necessary for running the operating system. Also called the 'blessed folder'.

taper angle The direction in which graduated tones or colours merge into one another.

tear-off menu In some applications, a menu that can be 'torn' away from the menu bar by dragging it on to the desktop, where it can be moved around as you need it.

temp file A temporary file, used by the application that created it.

text box In frame-based applications, a container in which text can be entered and edited.

text editor Any application used to enter and edit text.

text field Any 'field', such as in a dialogue box, into which you enter text.

text file A file containing only ASCII text bits, with no formatting, which can be 'read' on any operating system.

text insertion bar *x-ref* INSERTION POINT

text path An invisible line, either straight, curved or irregular, along which text can be forced to flow.

text string Strictly speaking, any sequence of type characters, but often used to distinguish actual text from that which contains formatting instructions.

text tool *x-ref* I-BEAM POINTER

TIFF, TIF *acronym: tagged image file format* A standard and popular graphics file format originally developed by Aldus (now merged with Adobe) and Microsoft, used for scanned, high-resolution, bitmapped images, and for colour separations. The TIFF format can be used for black-and-white, greyscale and colour images which have been generated on different computer platforms.

tool A feature of most graphics applications, the piece of kit with which you perform specific tasks. A tool is a function represented by an icon which, when selected, is then used to perform the designated task, i.e. you use a box tool for creating boxes.

tool palette/box In those applications that feature tools, the floating window on which they are displayed for selection.

toolbox The part of the Mac OS written into the ROM chip that enables software developers to take advantage of the Mac OS interface, handling such things as dialogue boxes, windows, fonts, keyboard and so on.

transformation tool In some applications, the name given to tools that change the location or appearance of an item, such as 'scale' or 'reflection'.

transition A visual effect which blends two or more frames of an animation, movie or video.

transparent GIF A feature of the 'GIF89a' file format which lets you place a non-rectangular image on the background colour of a web page.

tween A contraction of 'in-between'. An animator's term for the process of creating extra frames to fill in-between keyframes in a 2-D animation.

twenty-four-bit/24-bit colour The allocation of 24 bits of memory to each pixel, giving a possible screen display of 16.7 million colours (a row of 24 bits can be written in 16.7 million different combinations of 0s and 1s). Twenty-four bits are required for CMYK separations – eight bits for each.

Type 1 Font The Adobe PostScript outline font technology contains 'hints' for improved rendering onscreen. Type 1 fonts come as two files: an outline printer file and a bitmapped screen file.

unsharp masking (USM) A traditional film compositing technique used for 'sharpening' an image. This can also be achieved digitally, with image-editing applications which use filters to enhance the details in a scanned image by increasing the contrast of pixels, the exact amount depending on various criteria such as the 'threshold' specified and the radius of the area around each pixel.

upload To send data from your computer to a distant computer such as a server. The opposite of download.

user interface *x-ref* INTERFACE

utility (program) A program that enhances or supports the way you use your computer generally, as distinct from those programs which enable you to do work specifically ('applications'). Typical utilities are programs for backup, font management, file-finding, disk management, file recovery, plug-ins, screen savers, etc.

vertical alignment The placement of items such as images or lines of text in relation to the top and bottom of a page, column or box.

vertical bar pointer *x-ref* I-BEAM POINTER

vertical centring The equidistant positioning of text ('vertical justification') or any other item from the top and bottom of a page, column or box.

web *x-ref* WORLD WIDE WEB

web authoring The process of creating documents (usually in HTML or XML format) for publishing on the World Wide Web.

web browser *x-ref* BROWSER

web page A published HTML document on the World Wide Web.

website The address, location (on a server), and collection of documents and resources for any particular interlinked set of web pages.

WIMPs *acronym: windows, icon, mouse (or menu) and pointer* The constituent parts of a computer graphical user interface.

window Part of the 'graphical user interface' (GUI) of a computer, a window is an area of a computer screen that displays the contents of disk, folder or document. A window can be resized and is scrollable if the contents are too large to fit within it.

Windows The PC operating system devised by Microsoft Corp. which uses a graphical user interface (GUI) in a similar way to the Macintosh OS. Using special software or hardware, Windows can be run on a Macintosh computer, but the Mac OS cannot be used on PCs designed to run Windows.

World Wide Web Consortium (W3C) The organization which is jointly responsible with the IETF (Internet Engineering Task Force) for maintaining and managing standards across the web.

World Wide Web (WWW) The term given to describe the entire collection of web servers all over the world which are connected to the Internet. The term also describes the particular type of Internet access architecture which uses a combination of HTML and various graphic formats, such as GIF and JPEG, to publish formatted text which can be read by web browsers. Also called 'The Web' or 'W3'.

wristwatch/hourglass pointer On your computer, the shape the pointer icon assumes to indicate that a process is underway but not yet complete.

x, y coordinates The point at which data is located on two-dimensional axes: horizontal (x) and vertical (y) – for example, on a graph, monitor, bitmap, etc. Three-dimensional coordinates are known as 'x, y, z coordinates' (or axes).

REFERENCE
INDEX

3-D application tools 42–3
3-D Modelling 112–15, 168–9

A
Adobe 24, 32, 38, 40
 animation 172
 contemporary icons 46, 72, 74
 hand-drawn icons 110
 Illustrator 70-1
 innovation 121, 126, 128, 130–1
 Photoshop 22
 pointer icons 58, 64
 wait icons 60–1
advertising 18–19
After Effects 32, 60–1
Agpoon, G. 94
Aladdin 31
alchemy 14
Aldus 76
aliases see also anti-aliasing 86, 148–9
alphabets 13, 122, 162
Alto 20
Amorphium 30, 45
Ampersand Digital Foundry 32
angles 134–5
animated icons 46–7, 168–75
anti-aliasing 134, 148–9, 166–7
Apple 18, 20, 25, 31–2
 colour 138
 contemporary icons 48–9, 51–2
 custom icons 144, 145
 disk icons 92–3
 families 140, 156–9
 innovation 120, 122, 124–5, 130–1
 operating systems 54
 Remote Access 29
application icons 66–9, 152–5
Apply 167
astronomy 14
AT&T 125
auto.des.sys form.z 30, 43
awards 117

B
Band-in-a-Box 31
Barn Door 46
Beatles 98
Beavis and Butthead 98
Bézier curves 28, 38

bitmap edit 22, 36, 134, 136, 146
Bitstream 32
Block 149
Botticelli, S. 70, 130
Brody, N. 31, 72
Brush 58
Bryce 30, 42, 44–5, 78

C
Calculator 50
cameras 28–9
Cancel 167
car horns 29
Carrara 30–1, 44
cartoon animations 108–9
case studies 120–31
cave paintings 12
CD players 18
CD-ROM distribution 177
CE Software 32
Centre Peel 46
Chauvet cave 12
Chicago font 122
choosing icons 86–9
Cinema4D 30, 42
circles 136–7
Clayscape 30
Cloning 29, 128
clubs 16
colour 138–9, 152, 164
colour look-up table (CLUT) 66
Control Panels 52
copying 116
Corel 82
CorelDraw 22, 74–5
CorelPaint 74–5
corners 136–7
corporate logos 18–19, 32
Crop 36, 58
Cross Dissolve 46
cross-cultural development 128–9
cults 98–9
cursor icons 62–3
custom icons 86–7, 92–3, 144–5

D
Dartmouth College 60
demystification 28, 29
design
 basics 134–9
 families 140–1

masks 142–3
 process 150–61
 theory 26–9
 tools 144–9
diamonds 16
Dictionary 76, 83
Diffusion Dither 164
Diner icons 94
Disk First Aid 31
disk icons 92–3, 114
Disney 98
Document 77
DOS 48, 49, 124
5 dots 122, 162–3
Download Manager 81
draw application tools 38–9
DropStuff 31

E
editing 143
Eidos 100
ellipses 136–7
email 29, 60
English language 18
Equilibrium DeBabelizer 60
esoteric use 14–15
Explorer see Internet Explorer
Export Clipboard 156
Extensions 52
Extensis 31, 170
Extinctions 96
Eyedropper 36

F
families 140–1, 156–9
Fetch 60
first icons 20–1
flags 14, 16, 114–15
folders 88–91
font designs 122–3
form.z 30, 42
fossils 96
Fractal Design 78
frame-by-frame animation 172–5
Free Transform 63
FreeHand 38, 62, 72–3, 74
Full Page 167
FullWrite 82

G
Gates, B. 48

Get Info 86, 142
GIF files 106, 108, 112, 169, 171, 173
Goo 79
Grabber hand 23, 36, 58–9
Gradient 66, 68
Grand Central 31, 60
graphical user interface (GUI) 20

H
hallmarks 14
hand-drawn icons 110–111
Harrison, J. 95
hearts 16
heraldry 14–15
Hermstedt 31
Hertzfeld, A. 122
hieroglyphics 13
Hourglass 60
household appliances 26
HSC 78
Human Software 167

I
I-beam 62
IBM 20, 48, 125
IconEdit 143, 145
IconForge 143, 145
Iconographer 143–4
ideograms 12, 13
Illustrator 38, 58, 62, 70–2, 74, 130
iMac 20
Image Repeat 170
Image Size 158
ImageReady 172–4
Incwell 60
InDesign 40, 58–9, 74, 129–30
Indexed Colour 164
initial ideas 150–1
Inks 69
innovation 120–31
Internet 29, 81, 86, 106
 animation 172
 cartoons 108
 3-D modelling 112
 tweening 170
Internet Explorer 60, 80–1, 106, 108

J
Jarfish Design 30

INDEX

Jobs, S. 20, 54, 124

K
Kare, S. 76, 120, 122–5, 162
Kesler, B. 92
Kernel 69
Kim Ji-Hyun 90
Kineticon 103
Krause, K. 45, 64

L
Labels 102
language barriers 13, 18–19
LaserWriter 51
Lasso 22–3, 26, 63, 125, 148
Lee, R. 96
letters 32–3
Library 76
lines 134–5
Linotype 32
Lisa computer 20

M
McDonalds 18
MacDraw 70
Macintosh 20, 22, 28–9, 48–53
 choosing icons 86
 colour 138
 custom icons 144
 design tools 149
 folders 88
 innovation 122
 masks 142–3
 Operating System 68, 76, 102
 pointer icons 56
 tweening 170
 type 162
 window icon arrays 176
MacPaint 22–6, 36, 59, 70, 122
Macromedia 31, 62, 72–3
Magic Wand 29, 36, 148
Maheux, G. 88
market penetration 19
Marquee 22, 23, 148
masks 142–3, 145, 157–8, 160, 167
Mastri, K. 90
Maxon Cinema4D 30, 42
meaning 30–1
MetaCreations 30, 42, 44–5, 64
 animation 168
 development 78–9

Infini-D 30
 Painter 22
mFactory 126
Microsoft 20, 29, 32, 40
 comparison 48, 51
 custom icons 145
 innovation 124
 Internet Explorer 80, 106
 word processor applications 82
mobile phones 28–9
modelling applications 42
Monotype 32
Motorola 125
mTropolis 126
music notation 15
Musical Instruments 52

N
Napoleonic Wars 14
native files 160
Navigator 80–1
Netscape 80–1, 106, 108
NewTek LightWave 42
NeXT 124
Nike 18–19
Notepad 50
numbers 32–3

O
Omnipage 31
operating systems 54–5, 117
optical character reader (OCR) 31
OS X 54, 130–1

P
page layout tools 40–1, 58
PageMaker 40, 58, 76
paint application tools 36–7
Paintbrush 124, 148–9
Paint bucket 24
Painter 78
PaintShop 144
Palo Alto Research Center (PARC) 20
Pattern Dither 164
Paurian autumn icons 95
Pen 36, 38, 58, 63, 128
Pencil 24, 149
personalized icons see also custom icons 86–93
Phonebook Converter 31

PhotoAnimator 170–1
photographic icons 110–111, 167
Photoshop 25, 29, 58, 63–4
 animation 173–4
 application icons 66, 68, 152, 155
 custom icons 144
 design tools 146–9
 drawing applications 70–1, 74–5
 families 156–8
 hand-drawn icons 110
 innovation 126, 128
 scanned images 167
 type 162
PICT 78
Pict-2-Icons 176
pictograms 12
Play Amorphium 30
playing cards 16
pointer icons 56–61, 62–5
Portfolio 31
Poser 30, 44, 79, 101, 168
PostScript 32, 70, 122, 134
Power Tools 64
Preferences 31
preliminary sketches 150
Premiere 46
printers 51
professions 14
Profile 66
Psion 116
pub signs 17

Q
Qualcomm Eudora 60
QuarkXPress 23–4, 40, 58–9, 62, 76–7
QuickDraw 32
QuicKeys 32
QuickTime 32, 52, 168–9

R
RayDream 30, 44
Recall 167
recognizability 26
Recycle bin 50
Reflect 38
Rehbinder, C.J. 90, 92, 94
related files 160–1
removable media 92
ResEdit 143–4, 156–8
Reset 167

Rimmi, K. 121, 126–31
road signs 17
Rotate 38
Royal Navy 14

S
Save 167
Scale 38
scanned images 164–7
Scansoft 64
Sculpt3D 30
settings files 160
Setup 160
shareware 86, 103, 144–5
shortcuts 86
SimCity 31
SimpleText 82, 103
Simpsons 98, 108–9
Slot, M. 92
Smith, M. 102
Snap to Grid 102
Soap 64
Solar System collection 96
Sony Pictures 125
spades 16
Specular 78
speed cameras 28
Spray can 24
Squizz! 167
Star Wars 98
step-by-step animation 172–5
Straight line 24
Studio 30
Stuffit 31
stylized image 12–13
Sun Microsystems 125
SuperCard 60
Swatch 69
system icons 52–5

T
tape recorders 18
technophobes 27
telecommunications 26
Template 77
Testarossa series 88
Text tool 24
theory of design 26–9
thumbwheels 29
Tomb Raider 100–1
tool variants 62–3

INDEX

toolbars 22–5
trade 14, 17
Translation 42
Trash 20, 50, 103, 125
Trilobyte set 96
TrueType 32
tweening 170–1
type 162–3
Type Manager 32

U
Uitzetter, S. 103
UltraDrop 102
universal recognition 16–17
Unsharp mask filter 166
user interface (UI) 126, 131

V
VALIS PixelPutty 30
variants 62–3
video recorders 18
Virtual Reality Laboratories 30
VistaPro 30
Volkswagen 95

W
Wait icons 29, 60
washing machines 26–7
WasteBasket 20, 50
Watch 60, 125
web browsers 80–1
websites 86, 90, 94, 96, 98–9
 addresses 103, 108, 110, 116–17, 176
 custom icons 144–5
Wiegman, L. 90
WIMP 56
window icon arrays 176–7
Windows 29, 48–51, 52, 74
 application icons 68
 choosing icons 86
 colour 138–9
 copying 116
 custom icons 144
 families 141
 innovation 124
 masks 143
 pointer icons 56
 tweening 170
 wait icons 60
Winnie the Pooh 98

Wohlstadter, J. 88–9
Word 32, 40, 82
word processing tools 40–1, 82–3
WordPerfect 82, 83
WriteNow 82

X
Xerox 20
XPress see QuarkXPress
Xtras 73

Y
YeahWrite 82

Z
Zip disks 92

Copyright Notice
Photographs and illustrations used in this book have been downloaded from publicly accessible file archives and are used in this book for news reportage purposes only to demonstrate the variety of graphics resources available by electronic access. Text and images available over the Internet may be subject to copyright and other rights owned by third parties. Online availability of text and images does not imply that they may be reused without the permission of rights holders, although the Copyright Act does permit certain unauthorized reuse as fair use under 17 USC Section 107.